U0136310

勞榦學術研究叢書1

勞榦先生
學術著作選集（四）

蘭臺出版社

勞榦先生學術著作選集總目

第一冊

前言 4

勞榦學術論文集甲編—自序 6

古代中國的歷史與文化—自序 13

勞榦先生照片 22

勞氏源流 26

一、歷史與政治研究

中國歷史的週期及中國歷史的分期問題 37

戰國七雄及其他小國 52

戰國時代的戰爭 105

戰國時代的戰爭方法 133

論齊國的始封和遷徙及其相關問題 162

秦的統一與其覆亡 172

秦漢九卿考 193

從儒家地位看漢代政治 199

霍光當政時的政治問題 206

對於〈巫蠱之禍的政治意義〉的看法 217

論漢代的內朝與外朝 231

漢代尚書的職任及其與內朝的關係 272

漢代政治組織的特質及其功能 290

禮經制度與漢代宮室 312

漢代的西域都護與戊己校尉 333

漢代的豪彊及其政治上的關係 345

戰國秦漢的土地問題及其對策 368

關於「關東」及「關西」的討論 375

兩漢郡國面積之估計及人口數增減之推測測　378

兩漢戶籍與地理之關係　404

象郡牂柯和夜郎的關係　441

雲南境內的漢代縣治　457

漢晉閩中建置考　469

漢武後元不立年號考　480

論魏孝文之遷都與華化　483

北魏後期的重要都邑與北魏政治的關係　493

北魏州郡志略　534

北魏洛陽城圖的復原　592

第二冊

二、漢簡研究

居延漢簡考釋序目　11

居延漢簡考證　22

居簡考證補正　203

釋漢簡中的烽　217

釋漢代之亭障與烽燧　228

論漢代玉門關的遷徙問題　250

兩關遺址考　263

漢代兵制及漢簡中的兵制　273

「侯」與「射侯」後紀　306

論漢代的衛尉與中尉兼論南北軍制度　309

從漢簡所見之邊郡制度　324

漢代郡制及其對於簡牘的參證　346

漢簡中的河西經濟生活　379

簡牘中所見的布帛　394

秦漢時代的長城　399

三、漢代制度研究

兩漢刺史制度考　402

漢代察舉制度考　424

漢代奴隸制度輯略　475

與嚴歸田教授論秦漢郡吏制度書　486

漢代的雇傭制度　488

漢朝的縣制　499

漢代的亭制　512

再論漢代的亭制　523

漢代的軍用車騎和非軍用車騎　543

關於漢代官俸的幾個推測　555

論「家人言」與「司空城旦書」　567

第三冊

四、思想史研究

《鹽鐵論》所表現的儒家及法家思想之一班　11

釋《莊子・天下篇》惠施及辯者之言　23

記張君勱先生並述科學與人生觀論戰的影響　32

論儒道兩家對於科學發展的關係　36

評余英時《論戴震與章學誠》　45

論佛教對於將來世界的適應問題　53

五、地理與邊疆史研究

從歷史和地理看過去的新疆　61

秦郡的建置及其與漢郡之比較　70

中國歷史地理——戰國篇　79

論北朝的都邑　87

中韓關係論略　96

六、歷法研究

金文月相辨釋　101

商周年代的新估計　144

論周初年代和〈召誥〉〈洛誥〉的新證明　174

周初年代問題與月相問題的新看法　193

修正殷歷譜的根據及其修訂　219

上巳考　268

七、古文字、古文獻及文學研究

中國文字之特質及其發展　289

古文字試釋　309

釋「築」　324

釋武王征商簋與大豐簋　330

評唐蘭古文字學導論　336

六書條例中的幾個問題　343

漢代的「史書」與「尺牘」　358

史記項羽本紀中「學書」和「學劍」的解釋　366

鹽鐵論校記　378

論西京雜記之作者及成書時代　418

春秋大事表列國爵姓及存滅表譔異中篇跋　434

北宋刊南宋補刊十行本史記集解後跋　440

大學出於孟學說　446

古詩十九首與其對於文學史的關係　454

說拗體詩　465

崑崙山的傳說　478

八、碑刻研究

粘蟬神祠碑的研究　489

孔廟百石卒史碑考　492

論魯西畫像刻石三種一朱鮪石室 , 孝堂山 , 武氏祠　509

敦煌長史武斑碑校釋　544

跋高句麗大兄冉牟墓誌兼論高句麗都城之位置　549

第四冊

九、秦漢文化研究

秦漢時期的中國文化　11

漢代文化概述　24

中國古代的民間信仰　46

漢代社祀的源流　69

玉佩與剛卯　81

六博及博局的演變　95

十、其他

論漢代的游俠　116

論漢代陸運與水運　132

漢代黃金及銅錢的使用問題　155

漢代常服述略　204

漢晉時期的帷帳　211

論中國造紙術之原始　225

中國丹砂之應用及其推演　237

黃土與中國農業的起源跋　250

關東與關西的李姓和趙姓　261

古書重印問題　275

《中國古代書史》後序　277

出版品概況與集刊的編印　283

十一、英文論著

Six-Tusked Elephants on A Han Bas-relief　300

City Life and The Chinese Civilization　305

On the Inscription of Che Ling Tsun(矢令尊)　312

From Wooden Slip to Paper　318

The Division of Time in the Han Dynasty as Seen in The Wooden Slips　333

Frescoes of Tunhuang　353

The nineteen old poems of the Han Dynasty and some of Their Social Implications 397

A Review of Joseph Needham's "Science and Civilization in China"Vol. 4, Part 3.　423

The Early Use of Tally in China　428

The Corruption under the Bureaucratic Administration in Han Times　438

The Capital of Loyang; a Historical Survey　446

The Periodical Circles in the Chinese History　453

A View of History and Culture of China　474

On the Chinese Ancient Characters　497

勞榦先生著作目錄　542

後記　562

第四冊

秦漢文化研究

其它

英文論著

秦漢時期的中國文化

一、漢代文化的背景

現在要說的中國文化，主要的是秦漢時代。秦漢雖然是兩個朝代，但就制度上說，是一貫的。中國過去的光榮時代，一般說來是漢和唐，尤其唐代最為著名。但是唐代的最為著名，是因為當時全世界更無一個強有力的國家和唐朝具有同等地位。因此唐代成為當時的唯一大帝國。漢代卻是東面是漢朝，西面是羅馬，東西輝映著。相形之下，漢代在世界上的地位就不及唐代的特殊。

就特殊的世界地位來看，是漢不及唐，但就民族本身的成就來看，卻又是唐不及漢。漢代不論在政治上、在軍事上、在文化上，都是純中國民族做成的，並未曾假借外力。所以不論在那一方面來比較，漢代的成就，自有其特殊的意義。

漢代文化特殊的意義還不只有這一點。中國文化從夏商以來，在春秋戰國時代薈萃集結，成為一個最發揚光大的時期。所以漢代以前華夏民族的努力，也就是使漢代的國力更將充實的大原因。

中國的文化是曾經長期發展的。就我們比較明白的來說要屬於青銅器時代。青銅器時代的文化，是漢代文化的重要背景。中國青銅器時代從那一個世紀開始，中國青銅器的發展，究竟是本地進化而成的，還是從外面傳播而成的，現在都是一些謎。不過到了殷墟文化時代中，銅器的製造技術已經到了相當的高度了。因為中國銅器時代的進展，似乎比埃及和兩河流域晚些，因此中國銅器的發展，有從西方傳來的可能，但是在沒有確實證據之前，應當避免作任何的揣測。

　　這種銅器在殷代或其後的周代，都是非常寶貴的，所以也稱爲重器，除用作兵器之外，大都是屬於重器的範圍。精製的銅器，是當時藝術的一個重要的代表，它們大都屬於王家和貴族，很少有平民鑄造的重器。重器大都和禮節有關，現在尚存的重器，有許多部分還可以和周代禮經中的內容來相印證。從這一點來說，我們可以看出銅器的價值，也可以看出三禮和它們注疏的價值。

　　在殷商時代、西周時代、東周初期及春秋時代，以及戰國時代，一個時代有一個時代的特殊作風，我們可以從銅器的類別、形狀、圖案、文字各方面來歸納，定出相當可靠的標準來作爲鑑別方法，斷定屬於某一個時期，並且從這種斷代的方法，更明瞭了銅器的用途、銅器器形的演變、銅器的眞僞，而從來的幾個錯誤觀念也可以糾正了。

　　春秋戰國之際是中國文化史上的一個大變革時代，在政治方面，舊時的封建貴族已經漸次崩潰，變成了幾個新的君權國家，至於世官、井田等等社會上和經濟上的重要成分，也隨同改革。好幾個國家，因爲他們的君主開疆闢土，和邊境的各民族更增加了和平與戰爭的新接觸，因此在文化上也受了新的影響。倘若將《漢書》中所表現的社會，和《春秋》、《左傳》所表現的社會來相比，那就很可看見春秋時代和漢代，其差異的程度也許比漢代和唐代的差異程度還要大些。所以戰國時代，眞是中國歷史上的偉大時代。不過戰國的史官紀錄，可能和《左傳》和《史記》一樣詳細的，都被秦始皇燒掉了。因此我們對於戰國時代的歷史事實，除去看司馬遷根據《秦紀》所作的簡單表格，和根據傳聞和策士誇張的記錄，作成了拼湊式的世家和列傳之外，他已經發現非常困難，沒有多少可靠的材料，作爲根據。但因爲新史料的陸續發見，使得我們對這一個時代的重要性，逐漸明瞭起來。

　　中國北方不是一個產銅的地區，幾個重要的銅礦都在江南和巴蜀，在江南的如丹陽和豫章的銅山，在巴蜀的如嚴道和朱提的銅山。在殷周時代，雖然這些地方不是和中原沒有交通，但彼此的關係，到戰國時代更爲重要。西周時代，賜金還是一個特殊的榮譽。春秋時代，楚王贈給鄭伯的銅，也和他加上一個「無以鑄兵」的盟約。因爲銅的貴重，所以商代器物格外加工，除此以外也只有兵器，至於靑銅的農器，到現在還未發現過。經過了西周，經過了春秋，到了戰國，銅產隨著南方的開發而增加起來，銅器的應用從國家大事中的「祀」與「戎」之外，推到一般人的日用上去。原來的貴重性質變成了平凡，再加上技巧的進步，厚的銅變成爲薄的銅，雖然花紋和器形受了可能的外來刺激變爲複雜，但是精工的程度總會漸漸的差了。所以到了漢朝成爲銅器美術上的衰頹時期。

斯克泰藝術的輸入，的確是戰國時代銅器藝術的一個新生命，斯克泰藝術的發源地，現在尚不能完全明瞭，不過就現有材料而論，大致東起西伯利亞，西至南俄的頓河（Don）和聶伯河（Dnepr）之間，至少在紀元前數世紀到紀元後約一世紀之間，有一種青銅器文化。在這一帶的民族雖然有流動和移轉，但在他們的文化上，仍保存著一種特點。這個以斯克泰人爲中心的文化，和伊蘭文化、巴比侖文化、西部亞洲文化，以及希臘文化，都有相關。他們都是游牧民族，在游牧生活之中，有他們特殊的印象，這就是用動物和植物的形態來做裝飾，尤其鳥類和獸類鬥爭的形態，在表現方面顯示出來動作和力量。中國的圖案，在殷商時代也常用動物，但所表現的是安靜、和諧、平衡和充實，與這種的設計，顯然是不相同的。

在中國和外國，過去曾藏有許多斯克泰型的戰國銅器，例如 Siren: *A History of Early Chinese Art* 和梅原末治的《戰國青銅器研究》中都舉出了不少的器物。而民國以來大批出土的，如河南的新鄭縣，山西渾源縣的李峪，安徽的壽縣，河南洛陽金村古墓所發現的戰國銅器，河南濬縣發現的銅器，都有不少的斯克泰影響。當然，其中不是沒有中國式的成分，但是將中國的固有成分巧妙的與外來成分配合爲一，這卻是戰國作風中的技巧。這種作風是戰國時代一個傳播相當廣的作風，從前有人稱爲秦式或淮式，都不能夠正確的指示，日本梅原末治戰國式青銅器的研究，定了「戰國式銅器」的名稱，可以說比較是對的。

春秋戰國之際鐵器發展了，但所代替的不是銅器。有些地區是鐵器接上石器，鐵的應用處，主要還是在耕種方面。戰國時代雖然可能已有鐵劍，但主要的還是應用青銅，一直到漢代，還有前面鑲青銅的鐵箭頭，至於鐵刀鐵劍的廣泛應用，應當還是漢代以後的事。尋常日用的美術器，是拿漆器代替銅器的，在長沙發現的楚國漆器，在平壤發現的漢代漆器，都是美術上的精品，而代替了銅器成爲殉葬物品的主體。

漢代銅器的藝術，被漆器的藝術所替代。但銅器藝術殘餘的，還在鏡鑑方面。漢代的鏡鑑經過魏晉南北朝長期的發展，直到唐代，直到日本，還成爲精美的藝術器，到宋以後又漸漸的衰微，到近世才爲玻璃鏡替代。宋代是鏡鑑藝術的衰微時期，卻是瓷器的發展時期，此時除去瓷器有了一個發展的新趨勢而外，漆器也翻新了許多式樣，並且在佛教的藝術上面，也開闢了新的地盤，因此中國的特有藝術，便分配到瓷器、絲繡和漆器上面去。

二、從木簡來看漢代文化

我們現在拿一片漢代的木簡來看，表面上雖然簡單，從大樹變成木簡，便牽涉了不少漢代的文化現象在內。先把大樹鋸下來，需要大鋸子，再將木樁用大鋸子解成木版，然後再用小鋸子將木版子解開，再用削刀將版子削平(鉋字始見於《正字通》，故古代應當沒有鉋子)。這種鋸子和削刀，就代表漢代的工具。這些工具是鐵做成的，因此就牽連到鐵的問題：漢代鐵礦的分布，鐵礦的開採方法，鍊鐵的方法，鍊鐵的燃料，礦山和礦廠的組織和管理，礦山和礦廠工人的性質，礦山和礦廠工人的待遇。再就將生鐵做成工具，又牽涉到城市中的鐵匠，包括鐵匠的行業，鐵匠的訓練，鍊鋼的技巧，鐵匠鋪的布置，打鐵的工具和方法，鐵的成品的售賣(在本店與市場)，售賣時所用的貨幣，以及市場的範圍。此外還牽涉到燃料的運輸問題，生鐵的運輸問題，車的形製，有牛車和馬車，道路的形式，道路的管理。但是以上的種種，有的是可以知道的，有的卻因爲史料不完全，不能斷定了。

就以上所舉的來分析，我們就大致知道的來說，至少有以下的三部門：

第一，關於鐵的方面。漢代對於鐵是非常注意的。漢武帝時的公賣物資，便是鹽、鐵和酒。在《漢書·地理志》中，記有鐵官的有四十一個，照〈食貨志〉說：「郡不出鐵者，置小鐵官」，注稱「鑄舊鐵」，也就是說一百多郡國之中除四十一個鐵官以外，還有六十個小鐵官。這些鐵官管理著來鑄農器給農民，農器之中主要的是犁和鐮。

　　農耕的器具，最早爲耒耜，再進步爲鋤和犁，而犁比鋤還要進步些。在古埃及圖畫之中發現了犁是由鋤進步而來。尤其顯著的，是犁和家畜的使用多有密切的關係。牛耕一件事，是最早起於埃及，再次爲巴比侖、印度、中國，再次爲歐洲，美洲的印第安人卻一直沒有牛耕的事實，連秘魯的印加帝國也算在內。中國對於牛的使用，據說商朝的祖先相土開始，但到了春秋戰國之間，因爲一些不知道的原因，使得牛耕、鐵器、犁的使用，都同時在中國被發明了(騎馬的騎術也是同時)。這些事實，促成了中國農業的進步，促成了糧食的增產，促成了人口的增加，促成了君權國家的形成，也促成了戰爭規模的擴大。這些條件的累積，又是秦漢大帝國能夠形成的主要原因。

　　第二，關於人力方面。中國的地理狀況和人口分布狀況，決定了人力使用的性質。就春秋以來的發展來說，開發地區大致都在黃河流域一帶，這裡緯度大致相同，物產也相類似。地區相當的大，而水路的交通卻不發達。這一個大的區域，形成了同一的農業文化。商業雖然有，但因爲地域分工不過分顯著，所以不能占社會經濟的最重要地位，而商人階級對於社會和國家的貢獻，也並不爲當時學者所重視。此外，經過了夏商周三代，將近兩千年的長期統治(差不多等於東漢到現在的時間)，其中包括許多平衡而安定的時期，平民的人數增加，奴隸的來源缺乏。從〈豳風〉的時代開始，我們看見的農業，便是以平民身分勞動的農民，他們的自由，可能比佃農的限制多些，但似乎還不及歐洲中古農奴那樣多的限制。所以在這種情形之下，是以自由人的勞動爲主，雖然不是沒有奴隸，但奴隸只應當占全部人數中的少數。只有到秦代，利用大量的俘虜和罪人，作爲奴隸來使用。這是殷周以來歷史上的特例，到漢代減輕刑法，官家奴隸便只有不太驚人的數目了。

　　漢代初年工商的生產曾使用過奴隸，《漢書・食貨志》所舉出來的，便是顯明的證據。到漢武帝抑制商人，使商人在社會的領導地位減低，並且將私奴隸沒入官家，於是漢代的鐵官所屬，多爲官奴隸，《漢書・成帝紀》且曾說到鐵官徒的叛變。不過漢代採鐵是一回事，鑄鐵是一回事，鍊鐵和作器又是一回事。從漢代已經使用木炭，並且從《鹽鐵論》「割草不痛」一語，知道漢代已用鋼，鍊鋼是一種技巧上的事，那就除去奴隸以外也用得著冶工了。

　　第三，交通和運輸的問題。關於這一類的問題，對漢代的關係，甚為重要。漢代是一個大陸國家，要維持一個有效的統治，非有一個有效的交通系統不可。美洲的印加及馬雅帝國，西班牙人一到，立即歸於毀滅，其結果都不如埃及和印度，和他們不能充分利用獸力的交通，他們甚至連輪子也沒有，關係很大。漢代便是利用有效的交通系統來克服他的困難的。

　　漢代的陸路交通，普遍涉及全國的各處。平原的運輸是從舊日的阡陌改變而成的。這種道路至少在周代時的「周道」已經是寬直而平坦了。在路的兩旁也有蔭樹，不過這種道路只是利用原有的黃土築成的，並未曾修上碎石或石灰一類的材料，因此一遇大雨便有不便通行的苦惱。在山中的道路，是用人力來開山的，並且還利用木料作成棧道。因為當時火藥還未發明，雖然開路相當困難，但是到了漢代，鐵器已經普遍使用，所以開山究竟比從前要容易些了。尤其到了東漢，更有許多開山修道的記載，我們知道當時不論長江流域和粵江流域都已經開了大道，不論東面到現在的浙江，西面到現在的四川，南面到現在的廣東都可以行車，因此漢人的文化，也就成了車的文化，漢人所到也就是車的所到。

　　古代的政策，最注意是民生的安定，而不是貿易的發達。所以關於交通的處理，是政治上的理由遠遠的超過了商業的理由。縱有若干情況是屬於經濟上的，但經濟上的理由，也是為的是國家的財政和軍事，而不是為了商人的便利。假如為商業上的理由，那中國的西北區域遠不如東方區域的重要。但事實卻不然，全國道路的中心，是在長安和洛陽。而這兩個地方都是政治的意義重於經濟的意義。因此除去純屬於政治上如官吏的巡行和調動，軍隊的遣派和調防等等事項以外，軍事上後勤的輸運，以及各處稅收向中央的提解，和中央對於貧乏地區的資助，也是政治上的理由較為重要。從這一點來看，也就可以看出漢代的社會，商人在中產階級中，並不是一個主要組織成分，而組織中的重要成分，是屬於和政治關係較為密切的知識分子。

　　漢代的政治中心，被限制在黃河流域，而黃河流域的水運很難利用，這就限制了漢代商業的發展。中國沿海的交通，開展已經很久，我們看一看沿海的國家，例如吳越和齊，都有海上交通的事實，但臺灣海峽以北，海上貿易的範圍不大，只能說是地方的而不是全國的。臺灣海峽以南，因爲海流及颱風的關係，又使海上貿易受了很大的限制。但是海道的險惡也擋不住貿易的開展，在西漢晚期，番禺已經成爲重要的都會；到了東漢，到了南北朝，番禺的財富，還是靠著海上的貿易。到了唐宋仍然爲市舶使駐在的重要地方。

　　長江流域貿易的情況，就遠比黃河流域重要。黃河流域的城市，是由政治上的原因創建的，多爲正方形，而長江流域的城市，卻由自然發展而成，都市的形成，多半爲沿河的不規則形，並且往往有一道河街，爲最繁盛的區域，這一點從《水經注》所記載的已經是這樣了。然而中國都城究竟在北方，而國防的重要和商業的利益也是衝突著，南方都市還是遲緩的發展下去。

三、秦漢兩代的思想和政治

　　秦漢兩代是代表著中國大一統的成功。但中國大一統的趨勢，卻不始於秦漢兩代。很古以前雖然不能完全知道，但至少在商代的後期，帝國的規模已經顯然的漸次衍進。到了周初，周公當政，又向各方繼續開展，成爲周代帝國的形式。西周晚年，《詩經 · 北山》所言的「普天之下，莫非王土；率土之濱，莫非王臣。」成了後來一個廣泛傳播的名句。（到戰國時如《孟子 · 萬章篇》，《戰國 · 周策》，《荀子 · 君子篇》，《韓非子 · 說林》，《呂覽 · 慎人篇》都引用過。）西周之亡對於大一統的趨勢是一個逆流，但卻擋不住自然形勢的開展。不論齊桓晉文，是一種變相統一的先導，而《春秋》中的「春王正月」更顯然具有深厚的大一統意義。此外，〈堯典〉和《周禮》不論是甚麼時候寫定的，但其中顯然含有從漢以前便已經亡失的材料，是漢朝人做夢也寫不出來的，其中便也顯著的是基於大一統的觀念來寫定。

　　春秋時代的晉國，挾天子以令諸侯，對於周天子的關係，可以說類似日本幕府時代大將軍與天皇的關係。晉國的成就是對外肅清了狄人雜居華夏的住地，對內確立了集中的君權。憑著晉國的適當的環境，樹立了法律的觀念（例如昭二十九年，趙鞅鑄的刑鼎）。等到三家分晉之後，魏侯承繼了舊晉國的本部，儼然爲晉國正統之所在，尤其是魏文侯時代爲當時的霸主，而李克、吳起都是舊時主要的主張農戰的人。這種主張，後來就成爲商君政策的背景。

秦國一般認爲全是西戎之俗，這是不確實的。不錯，秦國含有很濃厚的西戎氣息，而住於草原文化及華夏文化交匯之處，但卻不這樣簡單。秦的公族是和徐、趙一樣的東方分子，秦的中等分子又含著很顯著的西周遺民，再因爲和晉國世爲婚姻，又受到晉國文化重大的影響。譬如秦的文字，便和西周一脈相承(見王國維〈秦用籀文六國用古文說〉)，而秦的文學又和晉國的文學非常相像(如秦的〈詛楚文〉便和《左傳》所載晉人呂相的〈絕秦文〉同類)。這個東西交錯的新國家，雖然它的文化因素我們還不能做一個精確而詳盡的分析，但它所代表的時代意義決不是偶然的。

秦國在魏國盛極一時的時期，雖然一時潛伏著。但是到了韓國滅鄭的第二年，亦卽西元前 374 年，秦獻公從雍(鳳翔)徙都櫟陽(高陵東)，到了西元前 364 年，便大破三晉之師，這就表示著，秦國的勢力已經開展了。等到秦孝公任用商鞅，更使得日漸強大的秦國，得著更進一步的發展。所以秦的變法只是促進強大，而不是轉弱小爲強大。換言之，秦的變法，是由於秦的發展在客觀條件之下來促成的。

秦國的發展，使得他的政治條件成熟了。商君把三晉的法家的觀念輸入到秦國來，恰合秦國當前的需要。他的政治原則，是強公室而杜私門；他的經濟原則，是不重分配而重生產；再將人民在國家領導之下組織起來，在農和戰兩個原則之下，向國家效忠，然後定出來客觀的法律來支持他的政策。這許多條件，使得秦國成爲一個有組織、有效率的國家，使秦無敵於天下。

從魏惠王之敗到齊湣王之死，將近六十年之間，東方發生了許多變化，結果只落得實力消耗了而各不相下。這是一個關鍵的時代，只有秦惠王滅蜀，獲得了經濟上的重要資源地帶。此後秦更利用蜀地的上游形勢和長江運輸，奪獲了楚國的南郡(湖北省)，再利用他的騎兵和荊益的經濟條件，一步一步的東進。到了始皇卽位之前，秦國已經占有南郡、南陽、河內、上黨，以至於太原。也就是從太行山以西，向南大致沿現在平漢鐵路以西(除去洛陽附近以外)，大致在西元前 260 年左右，都成了秦的領土了。

大一統的思想既然早已經完成，秦的統一天下趨勢已經決定。一統政治的實現，已經只是時間問題了。所成問題的，只是法家的思想，對於秦國的前途，應當如何處分和利用了。在國與國戰爭的時候，法家誠然是一個有效的思想；但治理一個統一的帝國，使他得到太平，是不是一個最適當的思想，究竟還有問題。因此在西元前 249 年，呂不韋作了秦的相國，就深切考慮到這個事實。他召集了天下的賢才，兼儒法，合名墨，而歸本於道家。在他取魏二十城置東郡的第四年，也就是大敗東方各國（除去齊以外）的聯軍第三年，當秦始皇即位第八年的時候（西元前 239 年），他和賓客們完成了他的巨著《呂氏春秋》。這部書的偉大貢獻是將老子的小國寡民主張，莊子的遁世絕俗主張，衍變成了使得一個大一統的具有文化的帝國，可以做到無為而治。但非常不幸的，他的不朽巨著完成了，他的政治生命也就終止了。到了秦始皇九年和十年之間，秦國發生了政變，呂不韋被廢，再被遷到蜀中自殺。

　秦始皇的勝利，呂不韋的失敗，自然政治上非轉變不可，不論將來用那一種主張，至少呂不韋的主張不會再用了。秦的傳統，是一個商君政治下的法家傳統，但秦始皇親政以後的設施，似乎並不全是這樣。秦國的七十博士，實際是仿孔子七十弟子。而秦始皇二十六年的琅琊臺刻石，也還是一個〈堯典〉《大學》和《中庸》的結合品。所以從秦始皇二十六年統一天下到三十四年焚詩書百家語，這九年之中（加上呂不韋死後，秦國統一之前，還有十五年），走的是漢武帝式的儒法兼用的「雜霸」路線。直到三十四年焚書，三十五年坑儒並遣出太子扶蘇，才完全是一個日暮途窮，倒行逆施的現象。於是在一個絕對專制局面之下，完全採用韓非的遺說，國內「無書簡之文，以法為教；無先王之語，以吏為師」，君王成為神秘不可捉摸的怪物，而秦帝國再過六年也就崩潰了。

　道家和法家的基本區別是道家把君主當作一個平凡的人，而法家把君主當成超人。道家憑著人生的經驗而法家憑著分析的頭腦，所以道家世故深而法家理論密。韓非是講法和術的，他對於法術的定義是：「術者因任而授官，循名而責實，操生殺之柄，課群臣之能者，此人主所執也。法者憲令著於官府，刑罰必於民心，賞存乎慎法，而罰加乎姦令者也，此人臣之所師也。」（〈定法〉）但《呂氏春秋》卻主張：「大聖無為而千官盡能。」（〈君守〉）「古之王者，其所為少，其所因多；因者君術也，為者臣道也。」（〈任數〉）「有道之君，因而不為，責而不詔；去想去意，靜虛以待。」（〈知度〉）「人主所惑者，以其智強，智以其能強，能以其為強,為此處人臣之職,而欲無壅塞,雖舜不能為。《分職》秦的實驗失敗了,漢初又回到道家去。道家的主張下,君主的運用技術,較法家的技術還要困難,但漢朝初年,尤其是在漢文帝時,實行成功了。

漢初政治的成功,當然和漢文帝有關,他不僅能無為,而且能守法。他把握住無為而守法的中央,使得一切政治順利推行下去。但是秦國自商鞅以來,立下的強固的政治組織,有效的工作效率,當然也是他能夠實行「無為」的基礎。秦漢政治組織是中國政治史上一個偉大的藝術品。它的特點是制度簡,員額少,任務專,權限明,應付工作的機會多,應付人事的機會少,因此也就可以達到較高的工作效率。秦漢政治的中心雖然集中中央,但各郡的權責卻非常大。太守雖然限於外郡人,作為中央的代表,但他在一郡之中,可以全權處置不受任何阻礙。郡對於縣,也是分層負責,權職分明。就現有的史料來看,漢代郡制之中造成了不少卓越的循吏,而中央政府也就樹立在這個鞏固的基礎上。

漢代對於域外的武功,也是樹立在內政的基礎上。漢代對於最大的敵人匈奴,在主力上並未曾假借外力或外國人的軍隊,而是用著自己的力量來和匈奴作一個生死的搏鬥。這個搏鬥的成功,可以說:第一,秦漢時代,是有計畫而沒有例外的徵兵制(唐代的府兵,只是特殊區域兵,不要誤會為徵兵);第二,秦漢時代,是有一個嚴密的運輸系統(包括道路、車輛、倉庫、通信系統及管理系統),從這一個運輸系統出發,使得可以對敵人作有效的經濟戰。但尤其重要的,還是秦漢時代簡單而有效的中央及地方組織,是一個最適於全體動員的組織,遇見戰事,可以很容易將全部的國家力量用上去。

東漢雖然仍在實行徵兵制度,但廢除了大部分的外郡常備兵,武力要差了一些,不過政治效率仍然很強。只是東漢時代中央不如從前的安定。到了東漢晚期,外戚和宦官、丞相秉政,清明的士大夫階級終於一籌莫展,直到董卓入洛,中樞覆敗為止。這是無可如何的事,這也是中國傳統政治的絕症,因為中國傳統政治,不論好壞,都是一切官吏最後向君主負責。君主一定有智有愚,有賢有不肖,不走向民主之路,絕對無法得到長治久安的。

漢代自從武帝以後,儒家的思想格外抬頭。有人以為便於統治,這是不對的。周秦諸子,不論那一家,不論是道,是法,是墨,都是尊君抑臣,為君王設想，豈僅儒家一家？而況講堯舜，說湯武，也不是儒家以外各家所常道，這對於絕對君權並無好處。當時儒家所以被尊崇，實在是由於理論完整，內容豐富，迴非其他各家可比。因此為太子師傅的往往都是儒家，這就注定了儒家一定成為學術的正統。到了西漢晚年，許多新材料發現了，使儒家內容更為豐富，於是到了光武以後，古文學更成了儒家的正統。

漢代還可注意的一件事，便是自然科學已經開始在萌芽。尤其數學的發展，已經直追希臘而超過印度。此外如「淮南萬畢術」，雖然是一個方士的實驗，但西方化學也是從方士產生的。在應用科學上，如弩機的使用，合金的配製，造紙術的發明，都是很有價值的事。中國文化對於科學是接近的。至於為甚麼後來進展不快，可能還是實際問題和環境問題。中國的士大夫對於科學只認為是副業，而寺院之中又缺乏研究科學的傳統。

在這一點要附帶說明的，便是至少從上古兩漢的中國文化看來，中國文化的本質並未排斥民主和科學，而民主和科學在中國進展不夠成熟的原因，是由於環境上、技術上，及其他本質以外的因素。

四、漢代的藝術及文學

漢代是一個藝術非常發展的時代，因為本身的進展，以及外來的影響，使得漢代的藝術更為成熟。就現存所能知道的來說，可分為陶器、漆器、壁畫、鏡鑑、織繡、石刻各類。在陶器方面來說，大部分屬於殉葬的明器或墓甎。明器方面的代表有人物俑和房屋。在房屋方面，就現在所知道的有住宅、樓閣、門闕、牛車、倉、竈、羊舍及豕圈、田地等；在墓甎上刻畫的有人物、房屋、車馬、龍、鳳、虎，以及桑樹、鹽井等。漆器是漢代藝術的代表，在樂浪、長沙，以及外蒙古都曾經發現過，主要的是奩匣、盤、耳杯及盌。以黑器朱花紋及朱器黑花紋為最多，但也夾著淡黃、棕色和淡綠的花紋。花紋有人物、飛鳥、雲龍及圖案花紋，畫的線條都非常生動。尤其是朝鮮王旴墓及彩篋塚發見的最為著名，這些漆器大都是從蜀郡造成的。壁畫有營城子和陽高縣墓中的壁畫，和漆器屬於同一的風格，並且漆器又和壽縣楚王墓中發現的棺片和所謂「淮式鏡」的風格，有相互的關係。

　　漢代的石刻，以山東、河南及四川爲最多。山東有嘉祥縣的武氏祠、肥城縣的孝堂山、金鄉縣的朱鮪祠，及滕縣的曹王墓等。就中朱鮪祠當爲後漢明帝時代，滕縣石刻爲後漢章帝時代，武氏祠及孝堂山就屬於桓帝及靈帝時代了。河南的石刻有嵩嶽太室石闕及南陽畫像。山東和河南的畫像代表著漢代重要的藝術和史料，這些畫像風格是各不相同的，不過由於刻法的關係大，由於畫法的關係小。四川的石刻尤其以石闕爲多，遍於四川各處。其中最著名的，如馮煥石闕、高頤石闕、王稚子石闕等，每一個石闕都代表建築和繪畫的雙重意義，而兩間孝堂山石室，更是現存的唯一漢代房屋建築。至於石刻的人和獸，最著名的是昆明池的石鯨，但現已不存；渭橋的牛郎織女，已經風化得僅餘痕跡。只餘霍去病墓前的石馬，魯王墓前的石人，南陽宗資墓前的天祿辟邪石獸，武氏祠前的石獅子以及四川高頤墓前的石獅子，尚可看出漢代立體的石刻。其中尤其以石獅子最有力量，而天祿和辟邪也是一種有翼的石獅子。據說一角的爲天祿，二角的爲辟邪，無角的爲獅子，這也只是個勉強的分類罷了(其實天祿和辟邪，也只是造作的人給予當時新作石獅子的命名，並無別的根據)。

　　漢代的銅器，大都以實用爲主，除去奩匣尚有精工雕錯的以外，有藝術意義的，大都屬鏡鑑一類。漢代的鏡，因爲需要作爲照鑑之用，所以銅質比較精細，鏡面也極爲平滑。可以作爲代表的，大半爲花紋流利的淮式鏡，和花紋整齊的 T, L, V 式鏡(大致是摹仿日晷的花紋，作爲辟邪之用的)。大部分爲圓形，有時還有銘文和年號。

　　絲織品是中國對外貿易的重要出品，尤其重要的是織錦和刺繡。斯坦因在樓蘭遺址上曾獲得精美的織錦，其上有雲龍、獅子、麒麟，以及吉祥文字。科茲洛夫在外蒙古庫倫以北的墓葬中，亦曾發現漢代的織錦及刺繡，其上有有翼的獸類及騎馬的仙人，上有「廣成新神，靈壽萬年」等字樣。各種繡風亦兼含有中國作風及希臘作風。這裡所要注意的，是中國除去絲業之外，還有複雜的提花業，及精美的染工。

　　現在所能夠根據的實物，比起當年漢代的藝術品，其比例可稱極少。但在各方面看來，已經有長足的進展。再從這些實物來比較一切的記載，更可以相信這些記載的眞實性。

　　漢代的文學除去散文以外，韻文更值得我們注意。漢代的賦是不合樂而朗誦的，專以鋪陳事實為主，也可說是一種史詩性質的朗誦詩。自然朗誦的對象是貴族而不是平民，所以內容和作法也以貴族為主。不過漸次演變，到了唐代就成了顯著的極端兩支：一為考試所用的律賦，一支就成為民間文學的〈晏子賦〉、〈韓朋賦〉了。五七言詩也是漢代開始的，一個來源是外國音樂的輸入，另一個來源是民間歌謠的轉變。當武帝前後，民間歌謠還是類似《楚辭》的格調，和類似《詩經》轉變出來的格調，但五言詩卻漸漸的發生了。最早的五言詩，似乎是《漢書‧五行志》記述的漢武帝時的童謠，此後五言詩便漸漸的多了。七言詩更應當比較後些。不過五言詩和七言詩的成熟，似乎還在東漢末年到三國之際。

　　中國詩的體裁，兩漢是開一個新的局面之時，後來的不論所謂近體或古體，五言或七言，都是在漢代發源。不過要注意的，便是漢代是一個新的音樂完成的時候，新的詩體的完成也是由於新的音樂的完成。後來的詞和曲，也是同一的軌道，所以今後新的詩體的發展和完成，似乎也應當和新的音樂有多少直接間接的關係。

　　總之，秦漢時代是中國文化發展史上的一個非常重要的時代，今天作一個簡單敍述，許多地方都說不到。但是我推想到，中華民族是一個具有堅韌性的民族，古代的幾盛幾衰，仍然停止不了中華民族的繼續創造。中華民族也是一個富於吸收性的民族，無論那一個新的文化到來都不至於深拒固絕，經過一個相當時間，一定可以融會貫通而造出一個新面目的文化來。所以前途一定是光明的，但責任也是繁重的。

漢代文化概述

壹、漢代的生產狀況與漢代交通狀況

漢代的政治社會，是承繼秦代的政治和社會，又可溯源於三晉的政治和社會。三晉的發展，顯然的，和晉獻公與晉文公的政策有關。從晉獻公盡去桓、莊之族以後，晉再無公族，成爲官僚政治的開始。其次是晉獻公滅耿、滅霍、滅魏、滅虢、滅虞。使晉國的疆土突增數倍，成爲一個軍事侵略的國家。到了晉文公，一方面仿效齊桓公用盟誓的力量來領導諸侯，另一方面却用謀略和戰術取到軍事上的勝利。這些事實都是領導晉國走向戰國的路。因爲晉國以軍事立國，所以晉國的政治也明顯的含著法家的趨向。後來晉國雖然因爲三分而把力量分散，但法家的理論，仍然是從三晉產生的。秦國較爲偏僻，受到三晉的影響極大，所以秦國的一切政策，都是三晉文化的延伸。[1]

爲著國與國之間競爭激烈，諸侯就不得不重用政治和軍事方面的人才，來代替舊日的封建領主，執掌國政。這就形成了官僚制度逐漸代替了封建制度，在官僚制度之下，諸侯可以授給田地以及采邑與高級的官僚。但是演變的結果，田地往往和爵位分開，因此官僚的子孫就可能不是貴族而只是地主。再加上商業資本發展的結果，以及國家爲著增加生產，土地可以買賣，農人的實際身分也隨著改變。在封建制度之下，一般的不管農人的生活怎樣，是好是壞，是優裕或者是貧乏，只要農人和土地是不可分離的，就沒有居住的自由，也就是屬於部曲農這個範疇之內[2]。等到

---

[1] 秦國本甚偏僻，除去繼承些周代的殘餘文化以外，主要的是秦晉來往密切，互通婚姻。因而秦國文化的來源，多半是晉國的。到了戰國初期，晉國三分，晉國的法家思想也爲秦國所襲取。商君之法，實際上是抄襲魏國的，魏國李悝的法經也爲秦法全部吸收，後來爲蕭何九章法的藍本。

[2] 封建制度主要一點是世襲，所謂『工之子恆力工，農之子恆爲農』，就是說職業是不能自由選擇的。井田制度的詳細情形及實行程度，雖然尚有爭論。不論『井田』一辭之下，包含了若干的土地分配形成，但『人』和『地』不容分開，却是一個最大原則。歐洲中古封建時代，農民和土地也是不容分離的，這也就是『serf』制度，這個字在中文中一直譯的『農奴』的，不過爲著和奴隸分別在這裏借用南北朝時的『部曲』二字。

土地領有的性質變了，地主和貴族成爲兩種不同的身分，部曲農（或叫做農奴）也轉化爲佃戶或自耕農。 使土地更有效的開闢，生產也迅速增加。再加上這個時候生產工具和農業技術有一個畫時代的轉變，更影響到當時的經濟和社會。

法家思想，官僚制度和對外的軍事行動是有彼此相互影響的關係的。 戰國時期的秦在這三點得到了最大的成功，秦就憑藉了這些方面的成功來統一中國。 秦的失敗固然是因爲在極端法家思想主持國策之下，過分把政權集中，使得奸臣乘機來篡竊。但秦代制度的綱架，還是爲後來繼承秦代的漢代所接受。 只是漢代在執行方面參酌道家和儒家的原則，使得較爲緩和，因而得到了成功。 至於漢代的經濟和社會方面，那就顯然的是戰國及秦代的延長，這是沒有甚麼問題的。

漢代的生產事項，最重要的還是農業。 中國古代的農業中心地帶，本來要算三河地區（河內、河南、河東[3]） 再從三河地區四面伸張；尤其是齊魯平原和關中平原。依照記載，戰國時期的水利設施正從三河地區開始[4] 水利發展的結果，減少了旱災的威脅，也就是加速人口的增殖，使得中原的人口澎脹，向長江一帶去發展。從漢書所記的西漢人口，和續漢書所記的東漢人口，很清楚的表現從黃河流域南移長江流域的趨勢[5]。 依照地形來說，長江下游（從宜昌到長江口）的沿岸本都是沼澤和森林地帶，所謂『卑溼』和『瘴癘』的地方。 但因爲氣候和雨量適宜於農產的關係，在兩漢時期，對於南方的加緊開發，成爲吳、東晉、南朝立國的基礎。到了唐宋以後，南方的經濟地位，更超過了北方，成爲中央政府的重要財源地帶。

中國古代的穀類，是以黍稷爲主的，豆麥的用途是對於黍稷的補助。 在這幾種以外，也需要到大麻子[6]。 大麥和小麥兩種中，小麥可能還不如大麥的用途普遍。

---

[3] 漢代最重要的地區，是三輔（京兆，馮翊，扶風），和三河（河南，河內，河東），而在三輔及三河間的宏農，附入其內。三輔都在今陝西的涇渭平原，三河是河南及河內在今河南，而河東在今山西。

[4] 戰國時魏文侯使西門豹治鄴開鑿溝渠，通水利，見漢書溝洫志，（及史記河渠書），而戰國策亦記，『東周欲爲稻，西周不下水』的故事，這是未開溝渠以前所未有的。

[5] 見中央研究院安語集刊第五本，勞榦：『兩漢戶口與地理之關係』。

[6] 麻，有人主張爲的假廲借字，不過廲只是赤黃色的黍類，現已有黍，不必把黍的支屬再放進去。照禮記月會的鄭玄注說：『麻實有文理屬金。』此言有文理，就不是赤黃色的廲，只有大麻時黑白相間的，所以可稱爲『有文理』。大麻子是可食的。在中國的西北部經常用的食用油就是大麻子榨出的『麻油』。胡麻（即芝麻）所以稱爲麻，並非其莖可以績麻，乃因爲其種子可以榨油的原故。至於麥，古代一般稱麥大都是指大麥而言。是用麥作飯而非用麥作餅。左傳成公十年『晉侯候欲麥，使甸人獻

　　至於稻這種糧食，在春秋戰國時期仍然是貴重精緻的食品。到漢代江南開發以後，方才漸漸變成了普通的糧類。所以在月令所記穀類是麥(春)，菽(卽大豆，夏)，稷(四季月)，麻(秋)，黍(多)。周禮天官疾醫節，鄭玄注，和大戴禮記曾子問鄭玄注，都指五穀爲『麻、黍、稷、麥、菽(或豆)』，正是戰國時的說法，到了孟子滕文公篇『樹藝五穀』下的趙岐注，就指爲『稻、黍、稷、麥、菽』。改麻爲稻，這就是漢代農產狀況了。

　　漢代的農業雖然比周代初期進步的很多，但嚴格說來比較近古時代，還是粗放的。漢代在漢武帝時期，最著名的『代田』法，也還是休耕制和深耕制的結合體。這和近古以來，中國的田莊差不多是用園藝的辦法來處理還是簡單的多了。

　　自從戰國時期以來，中國的都市已在那裏發展。長安是漢代京師，當然是一個大都市。其他的都市，如同洛陽、邯鄲、臨淄、陽翟、宛、薊，以及巴蜀的成都和江州(重慶)，江南的長沙和吳。嶺南的番禺，這些都市的遺址已經有幾處被發掘過，知道當時的都市設計，規模都相當的龐大。

　　至於都市之間，運輸一項也是非常重要的。以洛陽爲中心做出放射形的道路，在周代已開始建造。戰國時期的幾個强國，爲著軍事和經濟的需要，道路當然被重視的。秦代統一中國，便利用一部分的道路，做成爲天子巡幸的『馳道』。馳道的命意當然是『專爲天下巡幸的快道』。不過天子巡幸的時期究竟有限，周徧天下的馳道，究竟是臨時性的馳道，和長安城內專用的馳道，或永久性的馳道不同。長安城內的馳道是封閉的，等待天子隨時使用。分布天下的馳道，雖然寬度有一定的標準，但其封閉時期應以天子通過時期爲限，平時不可能禁止使用的。所以秦代巡幸的馳道，也就是通達天下的國道。漢代的驛站以及烽臺，也是隨著這些主要的道路去分布的[7]。這種通行的大道，在全國任何地方，都可以通行車輛。從長安直到巴

　　麥，隤人爲之』中間不需研磨，自屬大麥。不過周代似乎早有小麥，詩經周頌思文：『貽我來牟，帝命率育』廣雅『大麥麰也，小麥麷也』，所以麥是大麥和小麥的共名。居延漢簡七十七根簡，官兵釜磑月言簿，其中所說的『磑』是磨麵用的，顯然是指小麥。和居延簡大約同時的鹽鐵論記錄，其中散不篇的『羊淹雞寒』，寒指『寒具』即炸油條，這一定要用小麥去做。御覽八三八引東觀漢記：『董宣爲洛陽令，卒官唯有大麥數斛』，這已用大麥之名以別於小麥，漢書王莽傳中：『王盛者賣餅』，鍾繇稱公羊的賣餅家，何曾蒸餅上不坼作十字不食，也都在居延簡之後了。至於稻，在中國古代是貴重食品，論語陽貨篇：『食夫稻，衣夫錦』，稻和錦都是奢侈的。

[7]　漢代的烽火臺(亭隧)大致是十里左右一座，其排列方式有兩種，一種沿長城橫列，爲的烽火在前線彼此聯絡，一種是沿主要道路自遠而近的縱列，爲的是消息從國都和前方聯絡。

蜀，要算一個艱險的道路。但是在難以跨越之處，還是用緣山架橋的辦法，做成了棧道。[8]　這就使得全國的驛道可以通行無阻了。

中國的河川長度比較長，因此河川的水運也是相當重要的。周代原有的江淮河濟，以及其若干可航的支流，都是可利用航運的。至於長江黃河之間的運河（邗溝）在春秋晚期已經開鑿，到漢代當然廣泛的得到利用。其湘江（長江支流）和桂江（粵江支流）的運河，在秦時也已經鑿通，不過運輸上意義却不如長江以北的運河重要。又成都以北的沱江（也是運河）似乎和秦李冰開鑿灌縣的『都江堰』有關。但據禹貢所說『岷山導江，東別爲沱』。那就這條運河可以推到禹貢這篇的纂述以前。如其禹貢是戰國中期成篇，那就沱江這條運河就在戰國中期以前修成，而在漢代就廣泛的發生用途。

至於這些大河及其支流，因爲流量的關係對於經濟上的貢獻是不一致的，其中長江及其支流當然貢獻最大，其次是粵江（漢代的舟船模型就在粵江流域發現），黃河水運因爲泥沙多流量小，要差一些。但因爲漢代建都長安，黃河和渭水正是運輸上的重要航線，因而對於京城經濟上關係，就成爲十分重要的事實。海運方面，在漢代也是相當重要的。從北方的臨淄算起，經過琅邪、廣陵（揚州）會稽、東冶、番禺、合浦，至於交阯的龍編，再相連九眞和日南。至於國外的航線，那就是從臨淄和掖縣，向東或從會稽和東冶向東可以到達日本及三韓。從番禺和龍編向南，可以到達南洋羣島，不過在西漢時期，中國的商船不曾越過馬刺加海峽，對於印度和中東，只有間接的交通[9]。　中國商船越過新加坡，可能要在東漢以後。

從另外一方面說，陸路對於中央亞細亞以至中東，也是相當重要的，從長安西去，經過隴西金城，通過了河西走廊，然後通過天山北路，或天山南路，都可以達到波斯及亞剌伯。這也就是著名的『絲路』。這條陸路因爲從長安開始，就政治的意義上來說，陸路超過了海路，就經濟意義來說，海路却超過陸路。因爲陸路只靠車及駝馬，其運輸量及運輸費用是無法和海運相比擬的。

中國對外貿易，就後代來說，是絲和茶，不過就漢代來說茶才開始飲用，在中

---

[8]　棧道就是緣山所搭的橋，這只是在一條大道中，最險的各段，無法開出路來，只好緣山搭橋通過。等到火藥發明，就可以炸出道路或山徑，不必用棧道的方法。在現在陝西褒城縣北面，還可以看的很清楚舊時棧道的遺跡。

[9]　見漢書地理志，其解釋見中央研究院史語季刊十六本，勞榦『論漢代之陸運與水運』。

國國內還不曾普遍，對於國外貿易，是不占什麼地位的。　所以漢代對外貿易，還是以各種絲織品爲主，也許夾雜著若干陶瓷用具，當然這時中國陶瓷還在萌芽時期，仍不如五代宋以後的精美[10]。　因爲絲織品只供國內之用也供外銷，從而臨淄和成都也就成爲工業的都市。從外蒙古及西比利亞發現的漢代的織錦看來，漢代織錦精美的程度，的確相當的高。因此這就成爲海上貿易中的主要商品，來換取印度洋沿岸所生的犀角、象牙、香料以及珍珠等貨物[11]。

　　漢代的貨幣承戰國及秦代制度，以黃金和銅錢並爲主幣[12]。　黃金鑄成一定的形狀，作爲貨幣，在戰國時已經做過[13]。　銅錢在春秋戰國時期已有種種不同的形狀，如同鑱形錢、刀形錢以及圓錢等等。到了秦代統一天下，只用圓錢，並且採用了『天圓地方』的說法，把圓錢之中開方孔。圓錢的重量是半兩[14]，　所以圓錢上的文字也用『半兩』二字。每一萬錢只換一塊黃金，秦代叫做一鎰，漢代叫做一斤。秦代貨幣還算穩定，可是到了秦漢之際，天下紛擾，到處有私鑄的貨幣。因此錢的形製便縮小到楡錢那樣大小。雖然錢文仍是『半兩』，可是重量就不是半兩了。這就影響到金融的安定。經過了高帝、高后、文、景四代，一直對於貨幣問題不能解決。直到武帝元狩五年（西元前一一八年），才從屢次失敗之後，得到教訓。由官鑄五銖錢。五銖錢的重量是半兩錢的十二分之五，但因爲鑄造精工，不易仿製，於是得到穩定貨幣的效用。以後各朝代，直至清末，都仍是五銖錢的繼承者。（日本最流行的『寬永通寶』也依照五銖錢的遺制。）至於黃金，因爲產量不足，再加對外貿易流出黃金不少，所以在西漢時代，往往號稱用金若干兩[15]，　實際上却是用錢來折

---

[10] 中國陶釉在商代已經出現。但漢代陶瓷還未能採用高溫，這要等唐代以後才有端倪。到五代的瓷器已進步到和宋差不多了。

[11] 見漢書地理志。

[12] 見中央研究院史語集刊四十二本勞榦：『漢代黃金及銅錢的使用問題』。又參看加藤繁：『唐宋時代に於ける金銀の研究』。

[13] 戰國時代用黃金所鑄的金錠，在中國大陸屢有發現。其重量每錠是一致的，顯然是作爲貨幣之用。

[14] 最早的銅錢可能是兩種情況發展而來。第一，是戰國的貝形錢，那是仿造子安貝而成的，第二，是戰國時代的鑱形錢，以及刀形錢，建是從鑱及刀等工具，用作貨幣式的交換，再進一步鑄成小型的鑱或刀，專作貨幣來行使。至於圓錢的鑄作，以現有的證據來看，顯然較後，尤其以地區來看，可能是從鑱形錢簡化而成的。因爲刀形錢是通行於齊國，而鑱形錢却是以三晉區爲中心。半兩錢是秦國的標準貨幣，但戰國圓錢却也有鑄國名，如東周或西周的錢。

[15] 漢代從西漢晚期起，似已很少再使用黃金，作爲國內的通貨。但漢律上却一直以黃金爲本位，顯然是用一斤黃金以萬錢折合，如同現今法律每一元銀元折合新臺幣三元，是一種類似情形。

合。

古代商人市肆中的房屋，是從村鎮中定期的攤位發展而成的，所以『市』和『里』是不相混的。管仲的四民不雜處，也只是嚴格執行商人的管理罷了[16]。 漢代的長安、洛陽、 成都等城『市』顯然是被分畫到一些特別的區域。商人是指定居住在專供貿易的『市』中，因而商人就被列入『市籍』，商人因此就少了一些特權（如同穿繪錦，坐馬車之類，明著被限制，實際上也限制不住）。至於住在里中的居民，到市較遠，一般荣蔬等食品，應當是從門前叫賣的小販買到的。

貳、漢代的社會

漢代的社會是繼承戰國的社會而來，從戰國時代起舊的封建制度瓦解，成為官僚制度，所謂『布衣卿相』的局面，實際上就是新產生的官僚政治。 但是官僚政治只是從客觀條件下產生出來的，以前並無所因襲。因此官僚的地位，除去不是世襲的以外，其社會地位還是處處比照封建時代的公侯卿大夫，這就形成了新的階級制度。 雖然這一種階級制度比較過去的封建制度對於一些家族是暫時性的特權，但特權不論暫時或長期總算是特權，因此階級的存在還是顯而易見的。

秦統一中國，六國雖然滅亡，六國的貴族變為平民，但是他們的財富顯然未曾因亡國而消失。秦漢兩代雖然把楚昭、屈、景、齊諸田、遷到關中。 也只是使他們離開本上消失他們的號召力量，並且就近容易監視，他們的財富和社會地位，仍舊存在。在漢朝一代，根據法家思想，強宗大族顯然是抑制的對象[17]。 但也只能抑制強宗大族，却不能消滅強宗大族，把強宗大族變成普通的庶民。這個原因當然和秦漢帝國的基本結構有密切的關係。

一個專制帝國的統治，雖然皇帝擁有萬民，但在統治的含義上， 却不僅是皇帝一個人的統治，而是一個家族的統治。 在這一個家族的外圍，還有不少衛星家族，都環拱著帝室這一個主要的家族。 就家族的權勢一點來說，秦漢帝國和商周王朝並無太大的區別。這一個主要家族附帶著若干衛星家族，當然都是豪族中的豪族。豪

---

[16] 秦代在法家原則之下賤視商人。商人都有市籍，和一般人民的籍不同，權利義務都不一樣。

[17] 後漢書百官志，刺史下，劉注引蔡質漢儀，刺史以六條問事，第一條即係檢舉『強宗豪右』，所以政府的國策，是要抑制豪民的發展的。再看一看兩漢書酷吏傳及漢書中的趙尹韓張傳中所記，豪民也是一個主要需要對付的對象。

族與家族，其利益是有許多共同之處。國家的政權旣然在家族之手，那就在王法上不能不相當的保護豪族，而不可能做成一個平民政權。貴戚豪家在法家原則上是應當治，而事實上是不可治，這就構成了法家思想上一個基本的矛盾[18]。

　　從漢武帝起，西漢設『部刺史』來監督『郡太守』，其中監督的標準，計有六條。其中第一條就是關於豪族的，條文是：

　　強宗、豪右，田宅踰制，以強凌弱，以衆暴寡。

其中另外五條是關於郡太守（或王國相）的，其最後一條是：

　　二千石違公下比，阿附豪強，通行貨賂，割損政令。

這就表示著西漢豪強的干犯政令，已經是一個嚴重問題。如何在一個需要維持，家族利益政府之下，同時又要抑制豪族的行動，在一定範圍之內，確實是一個困難的課題。漢書中和後漢書所記，從西漢的郅都以下，東漢的董宣以下，一直到三國初年的曹操，都是酷吏對於豪族鬥法的歷史。雖然，對付豪族都是治標而不治本的，所以政府抑制豪族，而豪族的勢力仍然膨脹下去。

　　豪族的形成，大抵不外㈠皇室后族、皇帝外家、公主，以及公卿或宦官之家族，㈡地方上的大地主，㈢當地人口衆多之族。當然，在第一項中更爲重要，而第一項中，尤其以皇帝外家更爲重要，在西漢時期以及東漢前半段，就形成了外戚政治。但是外戚在全國的分布，究竟是有限的，而公卿大官的後裔就分布甚廣。尤其大官之中往往不少儒生世家，對於子弟的教育格外注意。在這些家族之中就容易產生人才。再加上對於當地行政長官加上人事的關係，在歷代推薦『孝廉』制度之下，儒生世族也就格外占著方便。所以東漢以後幾個世家大族，例如宏農楊氏，汝南袁氏等等就成爲屢代卿相的家庭[19]。這一種世族把持政治的局面，到了魏晉以後更爲顯著，南朝的王、謝、顧、陸；北朝的崔、盧、鄭、李；都成了盤根錯節的世族，其他的寒門不能比擬，一直影響到唐代的政治。到了五代紛亂，宋朝再統一後，就

---

[18] 後漢書劉隆傳帝見陳留吏牘上有書視之，云：『潁川宏農可問，河南南陽不可問。顯宗爲東海公，年十二，在後言曰『……河南帝城多近臣，南陽帝鄉多近親，田宅踰制不可爲準』這就是政府原則上雖抑制豪強。但政府及員自己就是豪強，這就無法執行透徹了。

[19] 參看後漢袁安、袁紹各傳，及楊震傳。

不再重視舊的世族了[20]。

　　漢代社會中另外一種重要的現象，就是游俠。游俠按照字面的意思來說，是（封建時期的）流動武士。但演變到漢代，與其說游俠是流動的武士，不妨說是地下社會的領袖人物。漢代的地下社會，似乎是以幾個領袖爲中心，而其下領導著一個數目的羣衆。我們不能輕易說漢代的游俠社會和近代中國的秘密社會有關[21]，但從漢代的游俠，兩晉南北朝有組織的流亡團體，再推到唐宋以來的秘密社會，其間的演變大致可以推究。再加上漢以後天師道的推進，以及唐宋摩尼教的轉化，使中國地下社會更富於神秘的成分。但和漢代的游俠團體比較，也許有若干有趣的啓示。

　　民間社會因爲工作的利便，總會有組織的。民間基本的組織是『社』，社是一個地方性質集會的最小單位。普通大致一里（一町）就是一社[22]，社是宗教，社交和娛樂的集中所在[23]。漢代承春秋戰國的風俗，商人以及手工業者都是集中居住的，那商人一定有商人的社，手工業者也有批工業者的社。現在我們可以明瞭，從行

---

[20] 自魏晉以來世族高自位置，卽使改期換代，而世族的基本地位，始終存在。隋唐採用科舉選士，仍不得不顧及世族子弟，決不能全以寒畯子弟領先。試看唐代進士名錄，便知其世族的重要性，經五代之亂，世族地位全中，宋代科舉始用彌封，無法知其爲何人所答，也就是不再考慮到世族的地位了。

[21] 漢代長安的偸兒是有組織，有領袖的，見漢書張敞傳。從小偸都有組織看來，那就『游俠』之雄，不可能是無組織。中國後來的幫會，誠然和宋代以來的事魔食菜（見陳垣先生的『摩尼教流行中國考』）有關。但這一類的地下組織，似乎還可溯及更早的史料。

[22] 這裏牽涉到中國古代田地的分畫問題。也就是牽涉到古代井田有無的問題，以及如其有『井田』，那『井田』是否卽儒家理想中的『井田』問題。最早說到田地的疆界的。也許要算小雅『信南山』的『我疆我理南東其畝』。且曾在左傳成二年所記的齊使賓媚人對晉人答辭所引用。而『信南山』詩中的『中田有廬，疆場有瓜』顯然古代的廬，井，阡陌都是規畫好的。至於是否井田，當然另外一番事（引證見陳奐『詩毛詩傳疏』卷五，商務國基本，葉二十八）。但是每一戶的田，畫分成了一個固定單位，再用阡陌爲界，那是不錯的。這種有計畫的分田，更加強每一戶的所謂部曲農身份（serfdom）。但從另外一點說，把田地的面積單位固定一下，免除了細碎的分割，也當然十分有用，自從戰國初年李悝的『盡地力』，也就不以阡陌爲限，商鞅更進一步在秦推行，從此中國的阡陌就只餘漢書匡衡傳所記的殘跡了。不論土地的單位大小如何規定，或者賦稅的徵取及交納的方法如何因時因地各有不同。但古代對於一個農莊的土地面積曾經有計畫的規定過，並且各單位之間以『阡陌』邊界畫分得清清楚楚，那是一個存在過的事實。卽使古典的田莊制度廢去了，但這種畫分的辦法，還在城市之中存在著，這就是『里』制。這種里制後來也稱爲『坊』制。日本式的『町』也是由中國固有文化傳去的，臺灣過去城市的『町』，當然也屬於中國的國粹。直等我接收臺灣，才因爲『崇洋』的關係，把這種舊制改掉了。——這種小單位農莊和住宅區的『里』，也就自然形式了一個宗教信仰的單位，『里社』。

[23] 參看中央研究院史語集刊十一本，勞榦『漢代社記的原流』。

動上說，游俠有游俠的團體，從居住來說，一般人有一般人的社。商人及手工業者為著工作上的利便，不可能沒有某種形式的組合的。漢代行會事項，現存資料甚少，不過從旁證上來看，是一定會有的。此外商人及手工業者是否有學徒的制度？目前也尚無實證。但顯然的，春秋的孔門已經採用了學徒制度[24]。商人及手工業者都需要技術的訓練，尤其手工業者更為需要。而手工業的發展，決不比儒術發展為後。一直到唐，儒術的傳授不肯稱師，而手工者仍然稱師[25]。則漢代的學徒制度應當是一個必然的事。

漢代不論在生產方面，或者在貴族富人的家中服役方面，奴隸和傭工是同樣的應用的[26]。從民族社會變為城邦政治，奴隸制度是可能被採用的。但是領土擴張，人口增殖，成為一個整塊的大帝國時，因為奴隸的來源問題，奴隸制度未必能維持下去。周代是有奴隸的。但奴隸的數量是否可供全部生產的需要，確實是一大的疑問。在春秋的初期，魯僖公二十五年（周襄王十七年，西元前六三五年），晉文公平周亂，周王給他陽樊、溫、原攢茅之田。陽樊不服，晉侯圍陽樊。陽樊人倉葛呼曰：『德以柔中國，刑以威四夷，宜吾不敢服也。此誰非王之親姻，其俘之也？』乃出其『民』，在這裏看到的，全部陽樊的『民』，都和王家沾了一些親姻的關係。那就陽樊的『民』就不是奴隸[27]，而是自由人或者認為準農奴。至於俘虜以後，就成為奴隸。因而按理不能俘虜『王之親姻』。結果把這些自由人，放還給周王。如其陽樊的『民』都是自由人而不是奴隸，我們就沒有理由臆斷別的地方的『民』都是奴隸。

依照社會和經濟發展的程序來看，周代如其確是一個奴隸社會，而漢代承繼著周代，可能是一個奴隸社會。但是以現有材料來看，周漢兩代都曾經使用奴隸，這是不錯的，却是就奴隸的數目和奴隸生產的重要性來說，從所有的材料來分析，都表示著周漢兩代的客觀條件，不足以構成奴隸社會。這當然是一個非常的變異，但這一個變異却事實上存在著。

---

[24] 從論語中的記載來看，孔子和門弟子是在一起共同生活的。這種傳授學問或技能的基本形式，不會前無所因。而且這個『師』字，也正和『工師』的『師』用同樣的『師』字。論語子傳篇：『百工居肆以成其事，君子學以致其道』，正顯示為學和百工為相似之處。

[25] 見韓愈『師說』。

[26] 見中央研究院史語集刊第五本，勞榦『奴隸制度輯略』。

[27] 百里奚為虞大夫，晉滅虞，俘百里奚，沒為奴隸以媵秦穆姬，事見左傳僖公五年，與此可互證。

殷商應當是一個奴隸社會，但人道主義已經開始萌芽[28]。 周的克商，並不是由於周的力量超過了商，而是在商的方面，因爲不滿於紂王以內政，在內部引起了反抗，然後周才得到機會。武王克商後一個短時期，並未嘗把東方問題解決。直到周公當政，採用了人道主義的新思想，加以刑罰威權，才把東方鎮壓下來，試看尚書中幾篇周公的誥誓，都是申明以『保民』爲重要的政策。這個『民』字正指殷民，和左傳中倉葛說到的『王之親姻』所指的『民』，在意義上並無二致。也就是說，周的克殷，本來可以把殷民俘虜來全部做奴隸，來完成周民族的奴隸社會，但事實上是不可以這樣做的。這個傳統延伸下去，就成了春秋戰國以至於漢，在社會雖然有奴隸，而奴隸的工作究竟不是生產上的主流[29]。

叁、漢代的政治基構

漢代的政治基構是秦代政治基構的延伸，其中的結構原則，多半是後秦代的政治結構演變下來的。無疑的，秦的政治基構又是從三晉的制度因襲而來。也就是說，一部分是從周代的傳統制度逐漸改變而成，另一部分却是爲適應法家的理想，經過改造而成的。

漢代的政治，是屬於專制政體的集權政治。中央政府相當集權，而天子有無上的威權。但是比起唐宋以及明清以來的中國，其集權方面，對於漢代來說，還有超過後代之處。尤其在中央，宰相的職責，在地方太守的專權，都有逐漸減低的趨勢。因而天子的威權大爲增加。 但是實際上西漢初年宰相的職責還是天子所賦與。天子還是保持著最後決定之權。後代的發展，只是把宰相處理的手續變的更複雜一些罷了。其中最極端的例子，是明太祖廢除宰相，只留下六部尚書 （後來各皇帝雖採

---

[28] 參看傅斯年先生『性命在訓聯證』。

[29] 關於周代是否屬於奴隸社會問題，歷來都有爭論。不過所有『奴隸社會』有一個重要條件，即奴隸社會的生產方式是以奴隸的勞力爲社會經濟的主要來源，因而奴隸的人數決不能少於自由人的人數。商代是否合於這個條件，從現有材料來看，不能證明也不能反證其究竟是不是。不過周代却不應該合於這個條件的。從戰國先說起，戰國時代的社會和漢代相差甚少，從戰國策，諸子，以及史記所記，再和西漢初年的社會來比，顯然是屬於同一的形態。再向前推到春秋時代左傳中的敍述是相當詳細的，也非常明顯，當時誠然有奴隸，不過主要的生產者，還是在『部曲農』（serf）的手中，而不靠奴隸，這是『封建社會』而不是奴隸社會，孔子決無再擁護奴隸制度的可能。在所有相傳孔子言論之中，也的確沒有一句是鼓吹使用奴隸的。

用大學士制度，但大學士不只一人，亦無直接處理政事之權）。最後由天子自行處理，但天子實際上也管不了許多，司禮監太監就成了事實上的宰相[30]。成為中國歷史上最壞的局面，清代設軍機處，由天子、親王、大學士合議，因而清代的政治就形成了親貴政治。

漢代在中央是三公九卿制度，地方是郡縣制度。三公是丞相、太尉、御史大夫。丞相輔助天子管理全國的行政，太尉管軍中，御史大夫為副的丞相主持監察，九卿是從秦代九卿制度轉下來的，實際上漢代九卿的數目比較九為多，只是號稱為『九』罷了[31]。計為：太常、光祿勳、衞尉、太僕、廷尉、大鴻臚、宗正、大司農、少府、執金吾、京兆尹、左馮翊、右扶風。到東漢為著湊九卿的數目，才罷執金吾的秩祿改低，河南尹雖然和九卿同秩，但不在正式九卿之列，這已經失去從秦到西漢的原意了。

丞相和太尉是中國古代傳統中的相和將，只有御史大夫的成為重職是後起的，史是掌文書記錄的，御史就是皇帝的史，因為掌文書，接近皇帝，就被派兼管監察和彈劾。御史大夫是御史的主管人員，因而也漸次升等，成為副的丞相了。御史大夫既成為副丞相，監察的事後來就成御史大夫的助手，御史中丞的職務了[32]。從漢初以來，御史改任監察，皇帝文書的事就變成專管筆和竹簡的尚書來負責，因此尚書參與了治令事項[33]。等到漢武帝漢宣以後，尚書的主管人員，尚書令，一天一天

---

[30] 明代的大學士，後來兼尚書，所以品秩也成為一品，一般社會也公認大學士卽是宰相，不過大學士還只有票擬之權，凡有奏摺，都得天子批紅。一般奏摺，除去了天子加意見，或留中以外，如天子不表示意見則大學士尚有權斟酌。不過所有奏摺均要經過『司禮監』宦官之手，宦官卽可從中篡竊權力，所以明代從明太祖以來，一直是宦官政治。

[31] 見大陸雜誌十五卷十一期，勞榦『秦漢九卿考』。

[32] 史的本義原指卜筮之官，後因卜筮接近君主，因此史便成為書記之職。並且史與吏亦為同字，所以吏與史二字到漢代仍然通用。在部屬之中幫助令的史稱為『令史』，幫助丞的史稱為『丞史』，幫助尉的史稱為『尉史』。所以御史原為幫助君主，掌領文書的職務。但御史為接近君主侍從之臣，因而也職司糾察及彈劾。而御史的長官御史大夫也職司承轉制詔。這樣演變下去，御史大夫變為副的丞相，御史由御史中丞率領，離開君主的左右，變成專管糾察彈劾的官了。

[33] 尚書本來是少府所屬的一部分（少府專管宮中的事務），尚書是管皇帝文具（筆和札）的，和管衣服的尚衣，管餐食的尚食，同樣的是管皇帝生活上用具的。自御史的職務改變了，皇帝的書記職務，就轉由尚書負責。等到御史大夫成為副宰相，詔令也實際由尚書承轉。這就使得尚書的重要性大增。在武帝時重用文學侍從之臣，形成了一個內朝，而尚書除去有機會參與內朝事務，並且變成了內朝和外朝聯絡之職，重臣參與大政的，也要加上『平尚書事』，『錄尚書事』一類的名義，才能和尚書聯上關係。到了東漢，光武

的重要起來。到了東漢，丞相改爲司徒，御史大夫改爲司空，司徒和司空分擔丞相的事務，尚書令爲接近皇帝，從光武帝開始，尚書令的實權就事實上在丞相之上。

漢武帝時對於中央政治機構上另一個發展，就是內朝。內朝是在尚書以外，另外還有些文學侍從之臣。這些文學侍從之臣，在皇帝左右，形成了顧問的性質。演變的結果，內朝成爲決策的性質，等到決策以後，然後經尚書，傳達給丞相去執行。丞相雖然參加正式的朝會，却不曾參加非正式的內廷討論，因此就把丞相百官的朝會叫做外朝，而參加內廷討論的，叫做內朝[34]。 侍中、給事中、左右曹等官是屬於內朝的，尚書是內朝外朝都需要參加，外朝中的九卿有時加給事中等名義，就參加內朝，到了西漢晚期及東漢，加上錄有書事的名義也參加內朝了。

內朝在武帝時期以後，漸次形成了制度，不過秦漢以來，實際上也不是沒有內朝的性質。在秦始皇時，蒙毅和趙高常在左右，已影響到決策。 漢高帝在任時期不算長，不過蕭何曹參和他都是老朋友，其時外朝和內朝自不必嚴格去分的。高后時決策的人是諸呂及宦官張釋卿之流。 到文帝時自外藩入繼，代國舊臣如宋昌、張武也實際參與機密的，只是武帝大量用文學侍從之臣形成了一種制度[35]。

到了魏晉以後， 尚書分成尚書和中書[36]，再加上了侍中，都逐漸成爲宰相之職，這就是唐代宰相分爲尚書省，中書省及門下省的開始。 原來丞相一銜不再用，而司徒、司空和太尉等銜，也只是一些榮譽性質的加官，不關於實際上的職任了。

漢代的郡縣制度，也是出於舊日的傳統，不過縣的設立，應當比郡更早。 縣的開始是邑楚國把邑宰叫縣公，秦孝公設三十一縣也不叫邑而叫縣。這是因爲縣的字意是懸掛的懸。每一縣卽是一個懸掛法令之處，所以叫做縣。每一縣有縣令（大縣爲令）或縣表（小縣爲長），縣令或縣長雖然在秦漢只是任命的官吏，並非封建的

帝把丞相分爲司徒，太尉，司空三公，而總其成的，却是尚書令，這就是後定仲長說所謂『雖置三公，政歸臺閣』。以後更進一步，唐代三尚三中尚書令就成爲眞宰相了。

[34] 見中央研究院史語集刊十三本，勞榦『論漢代的內朝與外朝』。

[35] 這是繼承戰國的風氣而來的，戰國時如齊的稷下，呂不韋門客，都招集不少文學學術之士。和武帝稍前及同時的，如梁孝王，河間獻王，淮南王安也都是一樣招攬文學之士的。

[36] 中書本是尚書由宦官擔任時，在尚書上加一中字，稱爲『中尚書』後來簡稱『中書』武帝時曾以司馬遷爲中書令（中尚書令），元帝時曾以弘恭和石顯爲中尚書令。但這只表示尚書令由中官來做並非尚書以外別有中書，東漢時期末葉，宦官當政，但五侯十常侍並不假借中尚書令的名義。到曹魏以後，才在尚書以外，更置中書，尚書屬於外朝，中書居內治事。這就是唐代三省制度的初步發展。

諸侯，但追溯到以前，可以看出由封建貴族轉變成官僚的痕跡[37]。 因此從通報引應劭漢官儀說：『大縣有丞，左右尉，所謂命卿三人；小縣一丞一尉者， 命卿二人』這就是漢代縣管仍沿襲了封建時代諸侯的制度。這種情形一直到清末，縣的官廨仍是一個具體而微的宮殿。所謂大堂的就是相當於『前殿』 （也就等於皇宮的『太和殿』或『太極殿』的地位，也就等於佛寺中『大雄寶殿』的地位。中國佛寺或道觀的結構和印度與希臘的廟宇顯然不同， 就因中國為佛道寺院也是仿照封建時代天子以及諸侯宮殿的）。這種宮殿式的結構，通用於一般官廨。按照明清以來制度，天子的殿是九開間。親王郡王是七開間。一般官廨都是五開間，從縣令長以上，各級的主管官員，在官廨上雖然略有點秩的區別，其結構是大同小異的，漢代郡縣的官廨，也應當是大同小異，其不同處不是結構基的不同，而只是規模的大小上。

在郡縣兩級之中，縣是一個基本的組織，郡是在國家發展以後，為著管理的方便，在縣以上加的組織。 也就是縣是從小國的封建諸侯改換成為官僚形式管理的，郡是從戰國以來的大國，改換成為官僚形式管理的。 所以在郡縣兩級的制度中，都是前有所承的。

在郡縣兩級行政管理以外，另外有一級屬於監察功用的刺史。 刺史的來源可以追溯到秦代的『監郡御史』以及漢代初期用來監郡的『丞相史』。 到漢武帝時才設置刺史，監郡御史和監郡的丞相史究竟幾個郡有一個，現在不知道，不過按照刺史的制度來看，這種監察職務應當是若干郡才有一個，而不可能每一郡就有一個監郡御史或丞相史的[38]。

當漢武帝設立刺史的時候，每刺史的監察區只稱部而不稱州。雖然其中大部分借用經傳上的『州』名，但也有只用郡名不用州名的。例如其中的朔方部和交阯部，就不用州字。這樣看來， 漢武帝借用州名只是漢武帝好古的嗜好，在秦時的御史可能就稱為監郡御史部，漢初也只稱為監郡丞相史部。其各部的名稱就只選部內的一個郡名來用，如『朔方部』『交阯部』因為從前沒有州名，也就採用以前舊辦法，用其中一個郡名來代表了[39]。

---

[37] 左傳閔公元年，晉獻公作三軍，趙夙御戎，畢萬為右，以滅耿，滅霍，滅魏，還，賜趙夙耿，賜畢萬魏，以為大夫。所以春秋若干大夫之邑，實為舊國。此後趙和魏也都世襲了封地。戰國時齊國的縣令，皆稱大夫。當時縣令已為流官，不再世襲，但制度上多少尚沿封建時期的前習。又明史四九，禮志三，城隍的廟制，高廣視官署廳堂，可知廟與官署建築的一致性。

[38] 參看中央研究院史語集刊第十一本，勞榦『漢代刺史制度考』。

[39] 朔方交阯以郡名作州名，見中央研究院史語蔡元培先生六十五歲慶祝專號，顧頡剛先生『漢代州制考』。

　　漢代政治結構中主管的重要性，還是執行方面決定事項，基層工作人員還是十分重要的[40]。　現代通行的俗語所說的『科員政治』，實際上也是無法避免的。漢代屬於科員性質的有兩種，一種是『郎』，只一種是『吏』，在尚書臺方面辦公的人員是『郎』，從丞相府、太尉府、御史大夫府、九卿府、郡太守府、郡都尉縣，以及於縣廷，辦公人員是『吏』。郎的選擇本來是由郎中令（後稱大鴻臚）選擇良家子弟充宮中的宿衛。等到尚書的職責加重，需要辦事的人，就調宿衛的郎作為『尚書郎』來充任這種事務。

　　至於『吏』這種職務，那是傳統下一直繼續下來的。　『吏』和『史』本來是一個字，漢代的吏也時常叫做『史』。『史』本來是卜官，司占卜兼司法卜的記錄[41]。在游牧時代，至多不過『刻符為信』，根本用不着文書的[42]，所以只要占卜的『史』，或者巫師識字已經够了。等到政治和社會演進的結果，需要『史』的地方一天一天的增多，於是史的職務分到各處，史的名稱也分到各處。於是史祝的史（即漢代『太史令』的『史』），守藏史的史，歷史書的史，機關中辦事員吏的史，都是同樣用這一個史字，雖然同源異流，可是這些支流都走的很遠。

　　各機關的吏都是由長官辟署的。相當於科長職務的叫做『掾』，相當於科員職務的叫做『屬』，也叫做『史』。史有各種不同的等級，如『卒史』、『令史』、『尉史』等等，其專司謄錄的稱為『佐史』或『書佐』。各部太守每年年終要『上計』，派一個『上計掾』去到京師去報告，這個上計掾經常被留在京都充任『郎』職，西漢後期由各郡推舉『孝廉』孝廉也照例留充『郎』職。而孝廉也往往由郡史選充的。此外各級的吏也偶然可以有機會漸次升任官職。所以漢代『官』和『吏』是並非隔絕的兩種身分[43]。　等到魏晉南北朝以後，高門子弟不任吏職，吏都是由寒門的人充任。唐宋一直到明清『官』和『吏』就成為兩種不同的身分。直到民國採用『科員』制度把科員也算在任官之內，然後『吏』和『官』的身分，才算溝通下去。

---

[40] 漢代郡縣掾屬的大致組織，見隸釋張納碑，及現存曹全碑。

[41] 史與卜官的關係，參見大陸雜誌十四卷，第二期，勞榦：『史字的結構及史官的原始職務』。

[42] 史記一一〇匈奴傳：『無文書，以言語為約束』。

[43] 兩漢察孝廉內部，而孝廉之選，多由掾屬中推薦，見中央研究院史語集刊十七本，勞榦『兩漢察舉制度考』。

肆、漢 代 的 學 術

中國從殷商以來，已經是用毛筆把煤煙墨寫在木製或竹製的窄條，再用繩綑起來，成爲書冊。這種書冊制度，不僅沿襲到紙的發明，並且沿襲到紙的廣泛應用。當然，木（竹）製的窄條，當時叫做木簡（竹簡）的，只是書寫工具的一種，除去木簡以外，至少在周代已經還寫在木版上，稱爲版，或牘，並且也在一些場合下，寫在絲帛的上面。不論採用簡、牘或帛、毛筆的形式是一樣的，用木材的煙所製的墨，也是從來在質料方面沒有差別。只是從商代開始，除去用墨書寫以外，有時亦間或用朱砂寫字，這種辦法也沿襲到最近的中國。

東漢和帝永興元年（西元一〇五年），蔡倫造紙是漢代文化上的一個非常重要的發明。不過在蔡倫造紙以前已經有粗糙的原始紙應用著，蔡倫是一個對方法上改進的人，使其成功更適宜於書寫紀錄的紙。但是蔡倫發明紙以後，紙的應用仍然不够普遍，要再等一百六七十年，晉代（西元二六五——四一九年）開始以後，對於紙才廣泛用起來。另一方面從紙的形製來看，還有一些因素是從木簡時代沿襲下來的。

中國是一個發明蠶絲的國家，也是一個產絲的國家。漢代和印度已有交通，但因爲習慣上應用絲和麻爲原料來做衣服，對於棉的應用並不普遍。到了多天富人是穿皮裘及新絲綿的綿袍，窮人只好用穿過很久的舊絲綿，洗了再用。自宋代以來，印度棉花在中國，已經到處栽植，不必再用翻洗幾次的陳絲。可是在漢代翻洗舊絲却是時常用到的。本來新的絲棉已經是粘成一張一張的層疊上去，等到舊了，再經歷次的浣洗，『陳絲如爛草』，就更會由短的絲頭結成一張一張的薄片，這對是原始的紙張。

從文獻記載上來分析，原始的紙應當是廢絲做成的，不過從陝西灞橋發現出來的西漢紙片（在蔡倫發明以前的），却是以植物纖維做成的。這就顯示著，蔡倫造紙在主要的一點，還是技術上的進步，而不是材料上的推廣[44]。

不論灞橋漢紙以及居延有字的漢紙都顯示這些初期的漢紙只是零塊的，大小及厚薄都不曾標準化，不適宜正式採用或大量使用。蔡倫所製的紙却是由宮廷的資助

---

[44] 關於漢代造紙問題，見中央研究院史語集刊第十九本，勞榦：『論中國造紙術之原始』。

做來專爲宮廷應用的。這就要一步一步的試驗，一步一步的改進，改進到質地勻稱而幅面一致的形式。還種紙當然是模仿縑帛的形式的。所以一直到唐人的卷子，其尺度形式，以及捲上去的辦法，當可追溯到與縑帛的關係出來。

　　從各種不同的字體來說，甲骨文、全文、石鼓文，以至到秦時刻石和權量的文字，雖然結體不同，但是在寫字時的轉折處，都是圓角的，因此在一般說來，這些字體應當都屬於『篆書』。倘若就現在的考古材料看來，這種字體在戰國時期已經開始轉變，爲求書寫的迅速，不能再規規矩矩的保持整齊的圓角，其筆畫的轉折地方，變成了直角式的銜接，而且每一筆畫也不能一貫的保持勻稱，一筆之中前後粗細可以不同。這些比較草率的字體，也就不能再歸入『篆書』這個範疇之內。這就可以認爲是『隸書』的創始。雖然相傳程邈創爲隸書，但程邈還只是一個整理隸書的人，其實隸書事實上早在戰國時期已經存在了。

　　秦漢時代通行的教科書『倉頡篇』[45]，本來是用小篆書寫的。秦漢的璽印也是用小篆體鎸刻的（這種習慣一直傳到後世），所以小篆應當算做標準的字體。只是習慣上隸書早已用來代替小篆。近許多年新發現的漢代木簡和帛書，除去有些用草書以外，絕大多數還是用隸書。甚至原來應當用篆書的倉頡篇也用隸書去書寫了。漢代通行隸書，所以把隸書叫做『今文』，其他篆書（除去小篆以外）都被叫做『古文』。

　　從地下發現的材料看來，漢文帝時代已經把隸書作爲日常的書寫文字了。當然在漢文帝立經書博士[46]之時，各博士所用的經文，也是用隸書書寫的。從文帝時開始，任申培和韓嬰爲詩經博士，更置書經博士，景帝時置春秋博士，到武帝時再增置禮（儀禮）和易經博士，這樣五經就全有博士了。但是博士的傳授是一個系統，宮廷的藏書，又是一個系統，博士還不能隨時去參考宮廷的藏書的。

　　在宮廷裏面，有天祿閣、石渠閣、延閣、廣內、等等建築來藏書（稱爲中秘）。自蕭何收秦圖籍，藏在石渠閣，以後自文帝、景帝到武帝，對於藏書都有增加。其中有的是民間獻書，有的是沒收諸王的藏書，還有的是設置寫書之吏，抄取宮廷以外的藏書，這些藏書在武帝晚年，司馬遷作中尚書令，在他的『史記』中曾用到

---

[45] 見『說文解字序』。

[46] 見漢書八十八『儒林傳』序。

『中秘』的藏書。但是有系統的整理，把『中秘』的藏書編目校訂，並且就此機會把一部分轉抄給民間，却是在以後的漢成帝時代。

在漢成帝河平三年（前一一六年）命謁者訪求遺書，並命光祿大夫劉向總管校勘書籍（後來劉向死了，由其子劉歆繼續去校），爲著有系統的整理，把全部藏書分成了七個部分編爲七略，卽㈠輯略（全部的通論）；㈡六藝略（儒家的六經）；㈢諸子略）；㈣詩賦略；㈤兵書略；㈥術數略（天文、歷數、陰陽）；㈦方技略（醫方及神仙），這是第一個目錄學的分類。到晉代時期才加以分合，成爲甲乙丙丁四部，這四部的分法後來稱爲經、史、子、集，就形成中國式的傳統編目法[47]。

這些中秘的藏書，有些是漢代抄寫的，也有些是在秦御史府收藏的舊籍，還有的是當秦始皇焚書時，在山巖、屋壁掩藏著的書籍，到了漢代又把它們拿出來，隨後歸入天子的秘府。其來源不從一處出來，因而其中的字體，也決不一律。其中除去漢代通用的隸書而外，可能還有秦代的小篆或秦代的隸書。再就是戰國時代的地方性文字了。漢隸和秦隸應當差不多，甚至小篆也還算法定的文字，在漢代會被稱爲『今文』。至於戰國時代地方性的文字，以及更早的金文，就要算做『古文』了。

司馬遷是一個博學之士，他的史記所參考到的，譬如『秦紀』（其來原只有在蕭何所收的秦圖籍中這一個可能），就應當是秦隸或秦篆寫成的，戰國策從地下發現的戰國策殘本來看，也可能是漢代通行文字，至於他所根據的『古文尚書』[48] 及

---

[47] 見漢書三十，『藝文志』。

[48] 漢書八十八儒林傳：『孔氏有在文尚書（王先謙注，詳見藝文志）孔安國以今文談之，因以起其家。遺書得十餘篇，蓋尚書茲多於是矣。遭巫蠱未立於學官，安國爲諫大夫授都尉朝，而司馬亦遷從安國關故，遷書載堯典，禹貢，洪範微子，金縢諸篇，多古文說。』這是一條重要的記述，但也是引起爭論的記述。古文尚書確有其書，本不足異，至於壁中經在漢初不出來，只等魯恭王孔壁才被發現，那是因爲壁中經本爲孔鮒所密藏，孔鮒與陳勝俱死，因而壁中經不能傳於世，亦自合理。其中爲晚清民初『今文學派』所攻擊的是史記明說孔安國早卒，那就在巫蠱之亂時，孔安國已死，此言遭巫蠱未立於學官，與史記所述矛盾。按巫蠱一事，班固實根據劉歆移太常博士書（漢書三十六楚元王傳附劉歆），原書云：『及魯恭王壞孔子宅，而得古文於壞壁之中，逸禮有三十九篇，書十六篇，天漢之後，孔安獻之，遭巫蠱倉卒之難，未及施行』。此文『天漢之後』四字確有語病，或者『孔安國』三字不確。古文尚書確在中秘，曾在東漢時校正張顥百兩篇之僞作。只是獻出的時間，在此書中可能有所誤會。因爲如其爲孔安國所獻，即當在天漢以前，如其在天漢以後所獻，即只能說是孔安國家，而不能說是孔安國。現在旣然知道確有其書，那就劉歆行文中的語病，只是一般解不達意。此是常見的事，

『左傳』那就是漢代通行文字以外的文字(古文)書寫的了。諸書原來所寫的文字，看來不算一個重要問題，但是到了後來，竟成了一個疑難爭執之點。

這個爭執是在經學的方面，漢代已開始有了一點爭執，但是到了清代後期，就成了經學研究範圍內的一個大風波。現在爭執的時代久了，再加上新材料，這個爭執已漸漸的平淡下去，只是講漢代學術的時候還得談到一下。

西漢一代，五經十四博士所用的資料，都是用『今文』（隸書）寫成的，一直到西漢晚期，還是一樣，大家雖然師承不同，却也都得到了習慣上的承認，認爲是可以傳經的。到了劉向歆父子校書中秘，把中秘的書傳播到外邊，使六經傳注更得了一個充實的機會，在諸博士之間也沒有什麼反應。一直到了劉歆把春秋左氏傳提出，使春秋左氏傳獲有春秋公羊傳及春秋穀梁傳同等的地位，這才激起了博士們的反對。他們的理由是左氏春秋傳只書一部有關春秋事實的參考文獻，而不是一部傳述春秋書法義例的師承著作[49]，這只反對左氏春秋傳一書在書中的性質，却不屬於今文古文學派的爭執問題。

十四博士因爲早已立在官學，師承範圍已定，不便輕易吸取新材料。其在民間傳授，未曾立博士的學派，反而有一個方便去大量的吸取新材料，這就使民間學派容易進步。等到中秘材料公開以後，民間學派都多多少少採用了些新材料，這些材料不少是古文寫的。所以民間學派很容易被稱爲古文學派，而原有的十四博士爲今文學派。其實還是枝節問題，基本上不會有太大的區別的。

自東漢晚年鄭玄編注羣紀，以古文本的五經爲主，在引用上加上今文學派的意見，於是古文經成爲標準經文，傳於後世，而今文經除去春秋公羊本和穀梁本以外，到唐以後都不再能看到，因此就引起了今古文之間究竟有多大的分別，如其分別太大，這就是一個嚴重事項了。試看一下皮錫瑞的『經學歷史』，就知道這是一個

一個稍受邏輯訓練的人自不會因偶然解不達意，就魯莽的牽涉到本身有無其事。至於史記中確用了很多古文尚書的材料，這些材料比較浩繁，應當取自中秘而非出自孔安國家。司馬遷曾從孔安國問故，似乎孔安國早已獻出，司馬遷詢其疑義。至於爲什麼孔安國在時不能立於學官，這也簡單。漢時學官牽涉到利祿之途，孔安國如眞的申請立學官，當然也會和劉歆一樣的遇到阻力，孔安國已仕宦至二千石，也值不得爲此引起風波，只要在私家有傳人也就够了。沈欽韓漢書疏證說：『古文之不顯，實緣世主之不好，而學者所苦難，史云巫蠱事不得施行，遂爲疑案』，也未爲得實，因爲客觀的環境，衆人的利益，比什麼都重要。

[49] 見漢書三十七楚元王傳，劉歆移太常博士書。

經學上一個關鍵問題。

　　屬於今文各經的原文，最重要的參考是熹平石經[50]的殘石，但經過整理的結果，仍然殘缺太甚，不能充分證明和現存古文本的異同。除此以外，例如漢碑所引的經典以及從輯佚得來的今文經典都只是些片段，對於解決整個的問題，還是有不少的爭論，直待武威的漢簡中的儀禮全文發現[51]這才證明了今文的經典和古文的經典，其中異同確不太大。『經學歷史』以來的嚴重問題，目前總算解決了。

　　除去五經以外，諸子比較重要的各家在漢代的發展是，墨家在戰國晚期已經消沈了，只有道家和法家到了漢代還照樣的活動。法家在表面上是不再有師承關係在漢代時期，但法家思想却滲透到漢代統治階層的人物思想裏面。不僅兩漢書酷吏傳的人物都是法家，並且皇帝自己也承認漢家制度是『王霸雜之』也就是漢代所用的治國原則是並用儒家和法家學說[52]。道家在惠帝時代曹參當政時期，已經用來做治國的準則，其後文帝景帝相承，也都採用道家。武帝時代雖然採用董仲舒言，罷斥百家，表章儒術，淮南王劉安的計畫也歸於失敗[53]，但漢朝一代，道家之學研究的人還是很多[54]。到曹魏時代，正始玄風，並非突然起來的，而是從東漢老莊的研究延伸下來的。

　　道家的主要方面是政治方面的無為主義和個人對於社會的肆應方法，雖然偶然之間談到『長生』，可是長生決不是道家的基本精神，並且道家所講的長生，和方士的『內丹』、『外丹』也決不一樣。只因在方士之中，找不出來偶像，而老子的生平也是一個迷離撲朔的人物[56]。所以老子也被神仙化了，東漢晚期皇宮中對昏祭

---

[50] 熹平石經張國淦及屈萬里都整理過，熹平石經原底大都屬於今文，但和今傳世古文本，差異不大。

[51] 根據在臺重印的武威漢簡儀禮。

[52] 見漢書第九卷，元帝紀。

[53] 參看胡適先生：『淮南王書』五十一年商務再版本談劉安想用道家治國的計畫。

[54] 參看中華書局楊樹達：『老子古注』附漢代老學者考。

[55] 外丹指從鉛汞硫黃等物所鍊的『丹』，內丹指用靜坐吐納方法，由心理想像中發生『丹』的感覺。早期方士多鍊取外丹，隋唐以後漸有注重內丹傾向。譬如漢代魏伯陽的『周易參同契』本為鍊外丹的書朱熹注周易參同契，即用內丹的解釋（朱熹以前有隋蘇元朗的青霞子，用內丹說釋參同契。）。又參看中央研究院史語集刊第七本，勞榦『中國丹沙之應用及其推演』。

[56] 史記老莊韓非傳，其中老子為數種不同的傳說參互寫成，司馬遷雖與老子的後人通訊，似乎老子的後人亦不能確學老子的生平，所以司馬遷就不能不採取雜說。那麼這位號稱『老子』的，封於段干的李宗之父，究竟真是莊子書的老聃，或者只是一個老子書的編纂人，就很有問題了。

祀過老子。等到佛教傳入中國，民間也就借用多多少少的佛教宗教形成，參合了錬丹術、符咒和薩滿式的迎神法，再把老子放進去算做教主，於是道教就慢慢的形成了。

佛教傳入中國，是民國文化史上一件非常重要的事。在西漢武帝時，張騫通西域；到宣帝時，漢又在天山南路設置都護。這些地區當時已有佛教存在著，可是史籍上未加記載，也許是中國官吏以爲佛教是外國人的宗教，未嘗十分留意的原故。不過佛教的教義是驚人的精釆的，中國人不可能長時期不受感動。東漢明帝給楚王英的詔書中用了伊蒲塞[57]這個術語，可知漢明帝對於佛教內容，不是完全隔膜的。到了永平八年（西元六五年）遣蔡愔到西域求佛法，於是四十二章經這部『經抄』（『經抄』，是因爲四十二章經只是一個佛經的撮要，和中國『史抄』類似。）首次譯成了中文，如佛經到中國之始。

漢代繼承戰國之後，科學技術的發展是值得稱道的。在數學方面，已經採取了代數的思想，而籌算方面又建立了後代常用的數碼和算盤的基礎。籌算是採用了竹製的籌（略如箸形，上不刻字，所以可以借箸爲籌），和算盤一樣的，從左到右橫行的排列[58]。只是算盤用算珠，而籌算用籌。籌分爲兩部分，上部分直排每籌代替『五』，下部分橫排每籌代替『一』加減和進位的方法和算盤相同的。後來的算盤，只是籌算的轉變罷了。

中國的天文學和占星術都是相當發達的，中國歷法的發展，也當然從天文的觀測發展而來。商代已經知道冬至和夏至爲一年中的兩個定點，這就形成了以太陽年爲節氣的年，而太陰月爲月連的據點。因爲用太陰月來積月，用太陽年來積年，所以就不能不用三年一個閏月的辦法，來補充用太陰月紀月所短缺的日數。只是到了漢代，如太初、三統各歷都未曾把正確的歲實測定[59]。所以計算下來還是不够準確

---

[57] 後漢書四十二楚王英傳：『詔報曰，楚王誦黃老之微言，尚浮屠之仁祠，潔齊三月，與神爲誓。何嫌自疑，當有悔吝。其還贖以助伊蒲塞桑門之盛饌』。此事亦在永平八年，未審在明帝求佛以前或以後，但此時明帝確知伊蒲塞（優婆塞，居士），及桑門（沙門，僧侶）固是事實。

[58] 籌算的排列法，見中央研究院，史語所，錢寶琮『中國數學史』。

[59] 中國自戰國以來相傳的四分歷每年爲三百六十五又四分之一日，即歲實爲365.25太初歷也和這一樣。到劉歆始用三統歷，把比較整的數字，推算成奇零的小龍，其歲實爲365.2501624比較現今歷法所用的365.2422三統歷還不及四分歷更爲接近，（朔策，每天文月平均日數，爲29.530864則四分及三統相同）。此後東漢以迄魏晉數度的歷實際比四分歷差不太多，奇零之數，價值不大。直到劉宋大明四年，祖冲之作大明歷，歲實爲365.248148距現用歷法歲實甚近。其朔策爲29.5305915亦距今用歷法朔策29.530588甚近，當推爲歷法一大進步，但大明四年已到西元四六〇年了。

的。

　　從戰國傳下來，有關天文的說法，計有三家，宣夜、蓋天和渾天，『宣夜說』
認爲天本空虛，日月星辰虛懸於天，其說之詳細部分，到漢已不傳了。『蓋天說』
係認爲地是平的在下，天如穹窿在上。每日天旋一次，故日月亦東出而西下，『渾
天說』係認爲『天如雞卵，地似卵黃』地在中心不動，天每日繞地一周，月、金
星、水星、日、火星、木星、土星依次列在地外。其中著名的『周髀』算法就是依
據蓋天說，但張衡所作的天文儀器『渾天儀』却是用的是渾天說。天上的方位，是
以二十八宿爲基準[60]，東方七宿組成『青龍』是角、亢、氐、房、心、尾、箕，北
方七宿組成『玄武』，是斗、牛、女、虛、危、室、壁。西方七宿組成『白虎』是
奎、婁、胃、昴、畢、觜、參。南方七宿組成『朱雀』，是井、鬼、柳、星、張、
翼、軫。這二十八宿加上北極星和北斗星就成爲航海時定方向的標準[61]。但史記天
官書的北斗，二十八宿，加上日月五星，就當時的實用方面來說，占星術上的意義，
却比航海的意義更大。當然，占星學本來就是促成古代天文學發展的因素，這是用
不著懷疑的。占星術促成了天文學的發展，鍊丹術也促成了化學的發展，甚至也促
成醫學及植物學的發展。從戰國時代燕齊的方士求仙服食，秦漢以來的方士也都是
以鍊丹爲長生的方法。鍊丹是以丹沙（硫化汞）爲主要原料，但除去丹沙以外，如
鉛丹、磁石、曾青、硫黃，等等也都是應用過的礦物，除去這些礦物以外，方士們
也到山崖水涯訪求種種不同的植物[62]。此外，鍊丹的方士還要鑄鼎、鑄劍、鑄鏡，
這些就增進了鍊鋼及銅錫合金的技術。並且方士希圖『點石成金』，雖然這種方法
是不能做出眞的黃金的，但却可以製成『僞黃金』，而這種『僞黃金』却仍帶出許
多化學上的方法[63]。

---

[60]　見淮南子天文篇高誘注。又見思想與時代三十四期，竺可楨，『二十八宿起源之時代與地點』思想與
時代四十三期，錢寶琮，『二十八宿起源考』。

[61]　漢書藝文志天文類爲海中星占驗十二卷，海中五星雜事二十二卷，海中五星順逆二十八卷，海中二十
八宿國分二十八卷，海中二十八宿臣分二十八卷，海中日月彗虹雜占十八卷，皆言海中，因爲天文和
航海是有密切關係的。顧炎武雖以爲海中可能指中國，但若指中國，必需有『域外的日月彗虹雜占』
同時附入，把中國當作海中才有意義。漢代並無這些書。所以顧說不可信據。

[62]　方士各處訪求，見葛辨抱朴子登涉篇。

[63]　漢書三十六楚元王傳附劉向傳：『上儁興神仙方術之事，而淮南有枕中鴻寶秘書書言神仙使鬼神爲金
之術，及鄒衍重道延命方，世人莫見。而更生父德武帝時治淮南獲得其書，更生幼而誦讀，以爲奇，

磁石的本身也是一種鍊丹的原料，雖然從磁石未曾鍊出了丹來，可是磁石的吸鐵性質却被發現了。漢初已知磁石引針的方法，並且武帝時方士也利用磁石來做自動的碁石。到了東漢時代，更把磁石做成杓形（爲的星象北斗），而這種磁石杓就可自動的指南，也就叫做『司南』[64]。漢朝航海還是以星家來定南北，這種『司南』的杓，似乎還曾用到航海方面去，但無疑的，這是應用指南針原理的第一步。

漢代醫學已經相當的發達（醫學包括針灸在內），這當然是根據了過去許多經驗，而加以綜合的結果，這種做綜合工作的人，也一定包括受貴族們支持的方士在內。雖然，依照當時的科學知識，對於一般病理現象多解釋是錯誤的，而方士所求的『長生』也當然不可能達到。但他們的綜合工作却使得醫學上的技術以及用藥經驗都能在一定的範圍中可以達到有效。至於藥學，其成績比醫學似乎更爲顯著。神農本草[65] 雖然號稱『神農』也只是一部漢代的著述（最早不過到戰國），這是唐代的蘇敬（宋人避諱，敬改恭）『訂注本草』，宋代的『政和證類本草』，以及明代李時珍『本草綱目』的前鋒。從這部書強調『延年』一辭看來，原來的目的服食重於醫療。但無可否認的，後來的本草從蘇敬到是李時珍的著作，都是以醫療爲主要目的。這也當然是從方士到科學家的一個路程了。至於漢代的藝術，牽涉太廣，應當另文討論。

言黃金可成。上令典尙方鑄作事，費甚多，方不驗。上乃『更生吏，吏劾吏生鑄黃金繫當死。更生兄陽城侯安民上書入國戶半，贖更生罪，上亦奇其材，踰冬減死論。』後來『點石成金』的傳說，應當卽是方士作『僞黃金』的實驗傳述而成的。

[64] 司南見於王充論術：『司南之杓，置之於地，其柄指南』燕京學報第三期，張蔭麟：『中國歷史上奇器及其作者』爲據此材料，推斷的指南針的最早記載。至中央研究院語所考古學報第三期，王振鐸・『司南指南與羅盤針』，記載作一試驗，用鋼作勺形物，傳以磁性，確可指南，惟王氏未強調張蔭麟之考證價值，故外人記述多不及張氏。

[65] ⑩孫星衍問字堂集，校定神農本草序：『舊說本草之名，僅見漢書平常紀及樓護傳。予按藝文志有神農黃帝食藥七卷，今本譌爲食禁。賈公彥周禮醫師疏引其文正作食藥，宋人不考，遂疑本草非七略中書也。賈公彥引中經薄又有子儀本草經，疑卽此也。』嚴可均全上古文從孫說。姚振宗『漢書藝文志條理』，以爲王應麟漢書藝文志考證，將『本草』一書補列，且曾引周禮賈疏，『蓋以禮疏爲誤，故置不復言也』。今案以『食禁』爲今『本草』，亦自可通，原不必改字。因『本草』中屢言『久服輕身延年』一類方士術語，自與『食禁』有關的。王氏考證及姚氏條理，今並在開明二十五史補編中。

中國古代的民間信仰

　　人類團體性的發展，依照比較落後的社會以及猿類的生活來比較，最先應當以家族(family)血親的團體爲主，然後擴充成氏族(clan)及部落(tribe)。在成爲部落以後因爲婚姻上有內婚外婚的種種差別，而世代上又有父系母系的種種差別，加上部落間和平與戰爭的不同關係，都會影響到部落中組織上及性質上的變化。演變的結果，部落擴大，成員間血親的關係減低。等到發展成爲城邦的時候，城邦內的公民自然不會專以血親爲限。只是城邦的政治若是一個君主政治，那麼在王族之中，還會保留特有的氏族形式。

　　在這個氏族之中最重要的事，當然是祭祀及戰爭(包括狩獵)[1]。本文對於戰爭部分涉及的不多，本文中主要討論的是祭祀，所以在此只把祭祀大略敍述一下。祭祀部分，大致可分爲兩組，第一是對於祖先的祭祀，第二是對於自然神的祭祀，當然這兩組祭祀之分也並非盡然明朗的，因爲祖先也許可以和自然現象相關涉。例如社字本作土，是土神，稷是農神，但商代祖先相土就是社神，而周代的祖先棄，則成爲后稷，也就是農神。其中重疊交錯的情形，也未嘗沒有。所應當注意到的，只是這兩組的祭祀功能上各有不同。對於祖先的祭祀，是和宗廟制度、宗法系統互相聯繫的；對於自然界神祇的祭祀，則不與廟制相關。

1　陳槃先生說：「案成十三年《左傳》：『國之大事，在祀與戎。』是祭祀與兵戎爲早期社會中最重要之事。《左傳》此言，古義之孑遺也。然祭祀、兵戎、狩獵三者，其間亦自有互相連帶之關係。蓋古者國君以狩獵所獲之牲供祭祀之用(襄三十年《左傳》：『豐卷將祭，請田焉。子產弗許，曰：唯君用鮮。眾，給而已。』杜《解》：『眾臣祭，以芻豢爲足。』又昭四年《傳》：『楚子合諸侯……宋大子佐後至。王田於武城，久而弗見。椒舉請辭焉，王使往，曰：屬有宗祧之事於武城……敢謝後見。』國君親田供祭，此其例)，而狩獵同時亦有講習軍事之作用，故《白虎通‧田獵篇》曰：『王者、諸侯所以田獵者何？爲田除害，上以共宗廟，下以簡集士眾也。』又曰：『王者祭宗廟，親自取禽者何？尊重先祖必欲自射，加功力也。』然此言『王者諸侯』，言『簡集士眾』，是爲封建社會說法，而於古義已不無相當距離矣。若在初民社會，則止舉祭祀、戰爭可矣，而狩獵自亦在其中矣。拙著〈古社會田狩與祭祀關係篇〉重定本詳之。」(《中央研究院歷史語言研究所集刊》第36本)

　　祖宗的祭祀，據《禮記・王制篇》和〈禮器篇〉，都說天子七廟，諸侯五廟，大夫三廟，士一廟，庶人祭於寢。這裡所說的廟制，是指一個一個的單獨的建築，天子祭七代，共有七個廟，這七個廟，是太祖一個廟，其他六個廟分屬六個世系，在太祖廟的左及右排列著，左邊的廟叫做昭，右邊的廟叫做穆。因為受到數目上的限制，等到祖宗數目超過了七代的時候，那就太祖次一代的廟要讓出來，以後六代的神主依次推進，更換昭穆。換下來的那一代神主，遷到太祖廟的後殿祭祀，不再立廟。這就叫做「祧廟」之制。

　　這種限定數目的廟制，只是儒生講禮的一種理想，儒生是希望把天子的享受以至於生活一律加以限制，免得過分浪費國家的稅收和人民的財富。許多制度雖然是根據舊有的事實造成，可是和舊有的事實並不完全符合。這種限定數目的廟制，晚周是否實行過，現在雖不能定說，可是和商制不符，和周初之制也不相合。到了漢代，一直到成帝時期，才開始實行，又因為有許多困難之處，終於廢止了。只有一般庶人，對於上一代沒有完全的世系記錄，這才會限制到祭祀少數世代的祖先。

　　的確，立廟太多，這種祭祀的負擔，對於物資的消耗還算有限，對於時間上的浪費，卻是無窮。倘若祭祀太多而必需家主自祭之時，那麼家主固定的主要工作是祭祀，其他的事反而成為次要了。依董作賓《殷歷譜》所安排的商代祭祀系統來看，在商代一年中王所要祭的日子，要占一年中的大部分，倘若真的如此，那就祭祀的廢時失事，要成為國家衰廢的原因之一。周、漢以來，天子自己也許不會這樣只把時間用在祭祀。可是看一看漢代的太常是「一年三百五十九日齋，一日不齋醉如泥」，可見一般祭祀的頻繁，已達到可驚的狀態。當然，漢代的祭祀和商代不同，商代是祖宗祭祀非常頻繁；漢代卻是祭祀自然神祇的特多，祭祖的次數已經減少。不過無論如何，就祭祀的總數而言，仍是失之於太多的。

　　因為古代是階級的社會，帝王、貴族和平民，在一切方面不會平等的，祭祀方面也有不同的等次。依照《禮記・曲禮》上說：天子祭天地，祭四方，祭山川，祭五祀（春祭戶，夏祭竈，季夏祭中霤，秋祭門，冬祭行）；諸侯祭其國所在的方位，祭山川，祭五祀；士祭他的祖先[2]。這裡只說了一個大略，還有不甚充分的地方。其實，五祀和祖先，從天子以至庶人都要祭祀的，並沒有什麼等級，只是祖先的祭祀，貴族有廟，平民無廟。五祀外，還有社的祭祀，天子和庶人都要參加，所不同的，天子和諸侯的社是國社，大夫的社是鄉社，士和庶人就只好附入在大夫領導之下去祭了。至於天地山川，那才不是大夫以下所應當祭祀的。

當然，古代的祭祀是屬於多神崇拜的性質，其所祀的神當不只這一點。照《尚書・堯典》所說，天子要「肆類於上帝，禋於六宗，望於山川，遍於群神。」上帝指天而言，六宗指上下四方共六個方位[3]，山川指天下各處代表的山川，群神包括五祀和其他，這就範圍甚廣了。照《禮記・郊特牲》所說，還有八種蜡祭，即：(1) 先嗇（發明農業之神），(2) 司嗇（先代掌農之官），(3) 農（古代的農人），(4) 郵表畷（郵，郵亭；表，標識；畷，田畔），(5) 貓虎（因爲除田中的害獸），(6) 坊（堤），(7) 水庸（水溝），(8) 昆蟲（田中的害蟲，祭害蟲欲其不害田稼）。再按照《禮記・月令》，天子或后妃還要祀高禖（給商代送子的燕子）、大雩（祈雨）、祈年，以及四季之神，句芒、祝融、后土、蓐收、玄冥等神。其未曾道及的，一定還有不少。所以天子所祭的神是非常多的。不過這些神一定禁止平民私祭，當然也不一定能完全辦到。所以除去郊天封禪等規模宏大的以外，一般平民所祭的神，只要經過男巫或女巫的允許，那就什麼神也可以祭。依照《楚辭》的〈九歌〉，雖然地域是中國的南部，而且時代是在戰國中期，但從其範圍的廣泛來看，也可見平民的祭祀，事實上也無法嚴格的限制。（至於〈九歌〉的性質，當於後面討論。）

就中「社」的祭祀是古代平民祭祀中最重要的一部分，擴大起來就成爲一國之

2　楊聯陞先生認爲中國的祖先崇拜也是一件重要的事，文內還應加強，楊先生說到例如令尹子文「鬼當欲食」，以及後漢「魂歸太山」（按見於《三國志・烏桓傳》及〈管輅傳〉）等都應提及的，此外例如《楚辭》的〈招魂〉、〈大招〉等也說到楚國人對於靈魂的觀念。

3　陳槃先生說：「六宗，僞孔《傳》（王肅同）、歐陽、大小夏侯、孔光、劉歆、賈逵、馬融、鄭玄、張髦、司馬彪等，說各不同（詳《正義》）。《正義》引歐陽、小大夏侯《尚書》說並云：『所祭者六，上不謂天，下不謂地，旁不謂四方，在六者之間，助陰陽變化，實一，而名六宗矣。』（《周禮・大宗伯・疏》據《五經異義》引作：「六宗者，上不及天，下不及地，傍不及四時，居中央，恍惚無有，神助陰陽變化，有益於人，故郊祭之。」）『四時』，《禮記・祭法・疏》引作『四方』。」

社稷。社的性質是比較複雜的，在本文以前已有許多的解說[4]，都是各有其理由和根據，但也不免把事實過分單純化一些，這是要鄭重說明的，中國古代的社，就性質方面概括的說，可稱為「某一個地區的保護神的廟宇或其他代表物」，以下再就這個界說加以解釋。

中國的華夏民族，雖然在《詩》、《書》時代好像已經形成了一個民族，但其形成經過還是非常複雜的，因而中國古代的一切制度和生活，就不可當作一些單純的、一元的事物來看。就社所包含的性質來說，它實在應當代表幾種不同文化的接觸與採取，因而形成了它的複雜性。就中如「社樹」「叢祠」「社壇」「社主」「社石」等等，就名稱上雖然都是社，但實質上是各有異同的，則其來源就不能輕率的認為出於一本。自周漢以來，社祠多依社樹。直到《大唐開元禮》，尚稱「應設饌之家先修理神樹之下」，以及「神社之席設於神樹下」，表示唐代的社依唐時的禮應當有樹。但到了現代，土地祠並不一定非有樹不可，據李玄伯和劉枝萬的調查，臺灣土地廟用樹的並不多[5]；此外陝西西安城內，各家門內都有「當坊土地」的小廟，卻並無樹；四川西部宜賓一帶鄉下，土地廟又往往依大樹而建。所以社和樹有某種程度的相關，卻不是普遍的社一定有樹。這種社不一定有樹的事，決非自近代開始，而是有樹之社和無樹之社是兩種不同的傳統。

甲骨文中社與土為一字，均作 ⌂ 或 ☩，像地上有一個長圓物，或不規則形物，有的還在上面祭酒，這不是樹，因為甲骨中的草木不是這樣的畫法，最大的可能是石塊。依照《淮南子・齊俗篇》說：

有虞氏其社用土，夏后氏其社用松，殷人其社用石，周人其社用栗。[6]

彼此互證，意思都顯出了。依《淮南子》所說，夏代和周代立社的方式都是用樹，而商代卻是另外一個系統，這一點也正和傅斯年先生的〈夷夏東西說〉所

4　見凌純聲，〈中國古代社之源流〉（《中央研究院民族學研究所集刊》第 17 期，1964）所引各家的意見。

5　李玄伯，〈臺灣土地廟的調查研究〉（《大陸雜誌》26 卷 10 期，1961）；劉枝萬，〈城隍廟與土地祠〉（《南投縣風俗志》4 卷 10 期，1961）。

6　世界版《諸子集成》本《淮南子》，頁 176。與《論語》「夏后氏以松，殷人以柏，周人以栗」稍有不同，但《論語》傳寫次數較多，或有誤字，且柏與松相應，石字不相應，故石的可能為大，這只是推測，還不能論斷。有了甲骨的土字作比證，那就差不多了。

稱周、夏是一個系統,而商另外是一個系統相符合[7]。這種在中國東部的文化,又似乎和中國沿海向北和東北走向白令海的巨石文化,在其地區上有若干相關之處。巨石(多爾門 dolmon)的性質和它的功用在現今尚不能完全明瞭,不過已知的都是作為墳墓或祠廟之用。商代的社和祖先的神龕(shrine)應當都是石做的。那就和緣海的巨石文化大致是屬於相關的系統。

這種社祠的「石主」的分配大都是在中國沿海區域。《周禮・春官・小宗伯》「帥有司而立軍社」,鄭《注》「社之主蓋用石為之」,賈公彥《疏》「案許慎云:今山陽俗祠有石主,彼雖施於神祠,要有其主。主類其社。其社既以土為壇,石是土之類,故鄭《注》社主蓋以石為之」。其實依照經籍的明文,周社實是用樹,鄭玄稱社主用石,可能是依照他自己親見的古社而立說,鄭玄是高密人,正是山東沿海地區。至於許慎所說的山陽,亦在山東境內,許慎是汝南人不是山陽人,他舉山陽為例來說明石社主,正表示汝南用的不是石社。

社的用樹和用石作社主,可能是出於不同的來源,也就顯示社的性質是各個區域各個部落(tribe)種種不同的保護神,商、周的政治中心,多少做過畫一的工作[9],但因為牽涉到各民族(nation)中生活和信仰的問題,絕無法有效的徹底去做,所以地方性不同的形式,就在不知不覺中保留下去,一直到了漢代的時期。

國家的社,就是國家的保護神,其中包含的意義是很複雜的,在本篇中不必多為推論。但就民社來說,就文獻記載上去看,也是絕不單純。至少有以下各事[10]和民社有關的:

(1) 土神

(2) 穀神或農神

(3) 獵神

7　事實上可能「夏、周、商」式的排列以外,還有非常複雜的分配方式。不過夏、周和商的文化,總是不同的。

8　藝文版《周禮注疏》,頁293。

9　這就是所說的制禮工作。

10　詳見凌純聲前引書,頁 21-30。

(4) 主晴之神

(5) 主雨之神

(6) 高禖

(7) 以人配的社

以下再就各項加以解釋。土神和農神是相互關涉的，商的相土是土神也是農神，同樣的周的后稷是土神也是農神。至於獵神，因為古代獵是和農田的區域一致的，所以田地的田字也就是田獵的田字。在社裡求晴和求雨，因為和農事有關，因而也列為社的範疇之內。所以董仲舒的《春秋繁露》七十五說「天生五穀以養人，今淫雨太多。五穀不和，敬進肥牲清酒，以請社靈，幸為止雨」。這種情形一直到清代，甚至到民國初年，還在城隍廟求晴求雨，正是一貫的傳統。至於高禖和社的關係，在陳夢家據《禮記·月令》說「中春之月，玄鳥至，至之日，以太牢祠於高禖」，是指社，並且還引據了幾條證據，不過他的論據至多只能說高禖是一種社，卻不能普遍的說社都是高禖。這種以特殊例證來概全體是不可以的[11]，所以這一項仍然可以存而不論。至於以人配的社，那是非常早的事，相土和后稷也是以人配社的例子，漢代燕齊之間為欒布立社，號為「欒公社」，更證明以人配社的事在一般平民中也是有的[12]。

戰國時期的史料因為被秦始皇焚掉，存在的實在不夠。不過戰國時代和漢代政治方面的段落雖然不同，社會方面的變化，卻並不顯著。就社會方面的變化而言，戰國及漢代的區別，實遠比戰國及春秋間的區別為少。所以用漢代的社會生活來證明戰國時代的社會生活，應當是可以的。因此從春秋到漢，凡有關社事的，都應當可以舉出來比較[13]。

11　陳夢家，〈高禖郊社祖廟通考〉(《清華學報》131 卷 3 期，1934)。

12　《漢書》(藝文版)37，頁 981。

13　陳槃先生說：「莊公如齊觀社，《公羊傳》曰：『諸侯越竟觀社，非禮也。』《穀梁傳》曰：『觀，無事之辭也，以是為尸女也。』《集解》：『尸，立也，主為女往爾，以觀社為辭。』又鄭樵曰：『案《墨子》曰：燕之社、齊之社稷、宋之桑林，男女之所聚而觀之也（槃案：見《墨子·明鬼》下。「燕之社」，今本《墨子》「社」作「祖」。「桑林」下有「楚之有雲夢也」六字）。則觀社之義，《公羊》為長。』(《六經奧論》四〈三傳篇〉)竹添光鴻曰：『觀社猶觀蜡，皆因賽神之餘而相聚會以為樂，盡所謂一國之人皆若狂者。其源本於《周禮》，其後沿為民俗。今之廟會社戲，猶其遺意。蜡獨行於冬，社在魯莊公二十三年夏[14]，魯公到齊去觀社，曹劌諫說人君不可隨便行動。這次觀社的性質未曾說明白，杜《注》孔《疏》也未曾詳爲解釋，按理來說，莊公這次旅行的目的是「觀」看熱鬧，並不在禮節之內，所以是「非禮的」《論語》上說「鄉人儺，朝服而立於阼階」[15]。這種儺雖然稱爲逐疫，但實際上和巫術和沙滿相關，所以也應爲社的功能的一種。而這種巫術上的儀式，也正有熱鬧可看。比孔子爲後而在戰國初年作成的《周禮》也有好幾處有關社制的，也很可用爲參考。

《周禮·大司徒》說五家爲比，五比爲閭，四閭爲族，五族爲黨，五黨爲州，五州爲鄉[16]。《荀子》楊倞《注》引《周禮》說「《周禮》二十五家爲社」，所以社和閭是相同的單位[17]。這一點《周禮》未曾說明而是漢代依《荀子》和《周禮》互證。不過其說有據，是不錯的，《周禮·地官·大司徒》下說到「社稷之垎」，而〈大司徒·封人〉下又說到掌「王之社壇」。其他散見於〈夏官〉及〈秋官〉，也說到過社，雖然都是國社而非民社，但有民也就有社，則《荀子》楊《注》的閭社決非信筆而書的。

《禮記·祭法》可能和《周禮》同時或者更後，其中說：

> 王爲群姓立社曰大社，王自立社曰王社，諸侯爲百姓立社曰國社，諸侯自立社曰侯社，大夫以下成群立社曰置社[18]。

這裡鄭玄《注》以爲「「置社」是大夫聯合百家共立的社，其立社的家數又和楊

則兼春秋。……此周正之夏，乃夏正之春，所以有觀社之事。其必如齊觀者，齊富強而俗夸詐，習於田獵、馳騁、鬥雞、走狗、蹋踘，其社大抵稱盛，故得使客觀之以示侈；則所謂軍實者（槃案：襄二十四年《左傳》：「楚子使遠啟彊如齊聘，且請期，齊社蒐軍實，使客觀之」），亦飾軍容為游戲，而非先王之蒐明矣。又《風俗通》社南氏、社北氏，其先出自齊倡；鄭樵《氏族略》云：倡優之人，取媚酒食，居於社南北者，因呼為氏。然則倡優多馮社而居。蓋至唐、宋人小說猶有社火、社首之稱。社久為衰世男女徵逐之場，此又《公羊》以為外淫，而《穀梁》同譏為女往者歟？」（《左氏會箋》莊二十三年條）上引諸說合而玩索之，則于莊公觀社之性質，雖不中不遠矣。」

14　671B.C.，《左傳》（藝文版），頁171。

15　《論語注疏》（藝文版），頁90。

16　藝文版《周禮注疏》，頁159。這是說鄉有一萬二千五百家，漢代一個大縣也不過這樣，當然是理想，不是事實。

17　《荀子·仲尼篇》（世界版）「與之書社三百」下，頁67。

18　《禮記注疏》（藝文版），頁801。

惊所引《周禮》說的數目不同。不過這是不必懷疑的，因為地區的不同，地區內的開發情形又各各不同，各地區的地理形勢也決不相同。社是由百姓們自己出錢建立的，事實上也無法由政府嚴格規定去限制數目，所以從二十五家為一社到一百家為一社，都有存在的可能。這類的置社，到漢代稱為里社，也就是後代的當坊土地祠。誠然里制漢代是有的。社制和里制相當也是可以的。不過漢代一里的戶數，也無法分畫得那麼嚴格。

依照《漢書・食貨志》引戰國初年李悝的論點，當時每石穀值錢三十[19]，社閭、嘗新、春秋之祠，年用錢三百。約合農家全年總收入的 6.67%，這也是一個不算太小的數目。不過這數目包括了宗教娛樂和社交的用項，所以不能說是非必需的。這種春社秋社經過了漢到唐宋，還一直相承不斷，例如唐王駕詩「桑柘影斜春社散，家家扶得醉人歸」，正表示古代的「拜拜」是為著大家的歡聚。而漢簡中「對祠具」的雞和酒，也似乎正為著社祭了[20]。

除社日以外還有「上巳」，也和社有類似的集體聯絡的功用，依《論語》曾點所說「暮春者，春服既成，冠者五六人，童子六七人，浴乎沂，風乎舞雩，詠而歸」，按照《續漢書・禮儀志》則為「三月上巳，宦民皆絜於東流水上，曰洗濯祓除去宿垢疢為大絜」。魏晉以來，往往以上巳為重要的盛會，如著名的〈蘭亭帖〉就是飲酒賦詩的詩序。彷彿是一個男子專有的佳節，但據《太平御覽》引《韓詩注》[21]說：「當此盛流之時，衆士與衆女執蘭拂除邪惡，鄭國之俗，三月上巳之辰……詩人願與所悅者俱往觀之。」而張衡〈南都賦〉也說：

19　《漢書》(藝文版)，頁 514，又按漢代穀價約石百錢。

20　〈漢代社祀的源流〉(《中央研究院歷史語言研究所集刊》第 11 本，頁 61)。又陳槃先生說：「案上巳是夏曆三月之第一個巳日。〈南都賦〉作『元巳』，亦是也。厥後則或以三日、或以上巳。洪亮吉考曰：『按沈約云，自魏以後，但用三日，不用上巳 (案出《宋書・禮志》)。今考魏以前亦有用三日者，束晢云「秦昭王三日置酒河曲」，是也。魏以後亦有用上巳者。《元和郡縣志》潤州上元縣鍾山：江表，上巳常遊於此；又《張華集》有〈上巳〉篇；潘尼〈上巳日帝會天淵池作詩〉；阮瞻〈上巳日作賦〉等是也。』(《洪北江全集・卷施閣文甲集》二〈釋歲・三月巳日〉條) 案洪氏又引《太平御覽》稱：『崔寔《四民月令》，三月三日及上除采艾及柳悟。』(同上篇)『上除』即上巳 (《山堂肆考》)。崔寔生當東漢末，是東漢時祓禊，亦三日、上巳並行不悖矣。至於少陵詩言『三月三日』者，其俗固淵原有自，其節物之意義亦與所謂『上巳』『元巳』者無殊，而日期則已有別矣。」

21　《太平御覽》(新興影宋版)30，頁 264。

於是暮春之禊，元巳之辰，方軌齊軫，被於陽瀕。朱帷連網，曜野映雲。男女姣服，駱驛繽紛。[22]

那就「三月三日天氣清，長安水濱多麗人」[23]，決不僅僅是唐代才是那樣了。

以上所說的是百姓們的團體活動。就家庭而言，其中的祭祀還是以「五祀」為最重要，五祀是中霤、門、戶、竈和行，已見前。其中以中霤為最尊。《論語》[24]王孫賈（衛君近臣）向孔子暗示說「與其媚於奧，寧媚於竈」，孔子拒絕了他的意思，說：「獲罪於天，無所禱也。」奧就是指中霤，是一家最尊的地方，竈卻是一家之中工作最多的地方。這裡奧指衛君，竈指近臣。孔子卻提出了更尊的天，可能指天子，這就出於當時一般凡俗之士的意外了。

中霤據《禮記 · 郊特牲》所說的「家主中霤而國主社」[25]，看出是最重要的神。孔穎達《疏》說就是土神。這是表示著土神就一方來說，是以社為主，而就一家來說，卻是以中霤為主。中霤是全建築的中心。依照殷墟遺址的情形來看，王宮是長方形的木構建築，而百姓房子卻是圓形的坑穴。這種坑穴，上面一定有一個圓頂，和「蒙古包」類似，因而正和蒙古包可以比較。蒙古包的中央是有一個煙囪的，日光也可以射下來。正和中霤的地位相符。後代不再祀中霤，是因為中霤形式在後代建築中已不存在[26]，就被土神廟以及佛道的神像代替了。

以上所說的是關於正統的中國，亦卽是北中國的情況，南部中國卽楚國境內的地區，其信仰又不相同。依照《楚辭》中的〈九歌〉[27]，它原屬於民間信仰，是歷來公認的，而這一套信仰，就顯然形成另外一種方式。

〈九歌〉的次序為（一）東皇太一（二）雲中君（三）湘君（四）湘夫人（五）

22　《文選》（藝文影胡刻），頁49。

23　杜甫〈麗人行〉（世界版錢注《杜詩》，頁17)。《御覽》30引《風俗通》說：「禊者絜也，故於水上盥潔之也。」又引晉成公綏游禊賦「妖童媛女，嬉遊河曲，或濯纖手，或濯素足。」所以上巳的原意或為洗濯的節令，而嬉遊當在其次。

24　《論語注疏》（藝文版），頁28。

25　《禮記注疏》（藝文版），頁489。

26　這是就最大部分建築而言，在甘肅西部建築中，平頂房中部仍然有開一個露天的洞，不過此只是特殊的例子。

27　據《楚辭》（世界版，王逸注），頁33。

大司命（六）少司命（七）東君（八）河伯（九）山鬼（十）國殤（十一）禮魂。但〈九歌〉的章數是十一章。無論怎樣分合，無法把它做成適當的九章。自然依照汪中〈釋三九〉原則，也可以指九爲虛指之數，古人稱九有時原不限於九。不過就《楚辭》各章本證，凡言九的都是限於九，而且還有一個〈七歎〉是明確的七章而不是九。那就不可以用偷懶的辦法來解釋了。

比較合理的懸擬，應當先明白《楚辭》是漢代的輯本，其中除去屈原和宋玉舊作而外，還有漢人的作品混入其中。在當時也許行格寫法不同，經過多次的抄寫，就可能不能分辨了。在〈九歌〉之中最可疑的，是〈河伯〉一章，不像楚人的作品。

就文章風格來看，是不容易分出來的。因爲漢代去楚未去，仿製不難。但〈河伯〉一章卻自有其漏洞。（一）江、漢、沮、漳是楚邦之望。湘爲江水支流，湘水洞庭爲楚人所稱道是應當的。河的源流卻不在楚境。楚人無祠河之理。〈天問〉中雖有河伯，那是在那裡講故事，並不是他們日常崇拜的神明，至於漢代的人建都長安，涇渭爲河的支流，情形就不同了。（二）〈河伯〉章說「登崑崙兮四望，心飛揚兮浩蕩」。在戰國時代所作的〈禹貢〉是說「導河積石」的，並無崑崙之說。至漢武帝始依古圖書名河所出曰崑崙[28]。以前學者是不採用崑崙爲河源之說的。雖〈離騷〉有「遭吾道夫崑崙兮，路脩遠以周流；揚雲霓之晻靄兮，鳴玉鸞之啾啾。」也只說崑崙爲遠地，不屬於河。（三）〈九歌〉各章都各有各的特點，並不互相抄襲。只有〈河伯〉一章，一開首「與女遊兮九河，衝風起兮橫波」，和〈少司命〉「與女遊兮九河，衝風至兮水揚波」相類似。可是〈少司命〉章是中間的句子，而〈河伯〉章是在起首，是最重要的句子，這是表示〈河伯〉章的作者並非〈少司命〉章的作者，爲詞彙所限，只好借用〈少司命〉章現成的兩句，才容易寫下去。不過〈少司命〉章的九河是表示少司命的遠游，而〈河伯〉章卻眞指就在九河。況「水揚波」比「橫波」爲生動。這種仿古人的舊作或者好些或者壞些，是自漢到六朝的常習，本不足怪。（四）〈九歌〉中設想的區域，都在湘楚一隅，而〈河伯〉章卻

---

28 見《史記》123〈大宛列傳〉，又傳後太史公贊稱出於《禹本紀》，今《山海經》及《爾雅》均言及河出崑崙，大約是漢武帝以後據《禹本紀》加上去的，武帝以前神話上雖有崑崙，可能和河源是兩回事。又《山海經・海內東經》（藝文版，371-372）崑崙和大夏月支同在一節，又言崑崙山在西胡西北，可能這也是漢時竄入的。

說「子交手兮東行，送美人兮南浦」。南浦在主要地方之東，那麼作歌地方就不會在江湘之浦，而是在長安一帶，也就不是戰國時的楚人歌誦了。

如其〈河伯〉章能證明爲漢人仿作，那〈九歌〉問題就比較可以簡化了。卽最後一章禮魂不在〈九歌〉之內，它是一個總的頌辭，其他「九歌」是以〈東皇太一〉爲主，而作以下的排列，卽：

東君	湘君	大司命	山鬼
(日神)	(水神)	(命運之神)	(山神)

東皇太一
(上帝)

雲中君	湘夫人	少司命	國殤
(雨神)	(水神)	(命運之神)	(忠烈)

其中湘君和湘君夫人均是水神，而且〈湘君〉章說「令沅湘兮無波，使江水兮安流」，所以湘君是一切水的總水神，湘夫人只說「洞庭波兮木葉下」，應當只是湘水之神，所以〈九歌〉中水神已占了兩個，不應當再有別的水神(如河伯)了。

這種民間信仰和黃河流域的華夏有很大的不同。華夏民間的信仰以社爲中心，而楚國的信仰卻似以神巫(Shaman 沙滿)爲中心，另外的是齊國的八神，見《漢書 · 郊祀志》[29]，祀天主、地主、兵主、陰主、陽主、月主、日主、四時主，那就可能是貴族崇奉的，不一定是平民所祀的了。

中國古代的神話

中國民族的神話不能說是貧乏的，就現有殘存的大綱看來，卻也相當的豐富，問題是在不夠詳贍。任何一種神話，都是找到幾句話，非常簡單的概略，再也不能向前追究，因而古代的神話就成了若有若無之間的情況。這種情形之下，我們決不能說古代中國人思想不豐富，因爲在中國四周的民族，如古代日本、西藏、雲南的麼些、台灣的高山族，都曾有十分詳盡的神話被記下來，但漢人自己

29　《漢書》(藝文版)，頁 540。

卻沒有。這並非漢人未曾有過，而是漢人各代有了更豐富的小說和故事，因而取代了原始神話。原始神話既然不再活在人的口頭上，就只剩下被書的注解所引據的幾段短短的概略了。

　　人類在社會中本來是喜歡說故事聽故事的，而講述的英雄故事，和聽話人的社會狀況也不會相差太遠，否則就不能了解，而必需加一番修飾了。就中國的小說而論，《三國演義》大略是從陳壽的《三國志》，再加裴松之《注》演繹而成，可是成書是明人依據宋人的平話，所以許多社會背景卻是宋代或明代的，與三國不同。《封神榜》是明人依據小說《武王伐紂書》的傳統演繹的，其中明代社會、明代思想及明代信仰的成分更多，幾乎和周初情況全不相干。尤其在民國初期鍾毓龍做了一本《中國神話演義》，他的確在下筆時還搜集了不少古代神話的資料，無奈他是一個熟讀章回小說的人，不僅對於文化人類學不曾理會過，就是對於希臘史詩、印度詩以及日本《古事記》也未曾下過一點工夫，所以寫出來的還是《西遊記》、《封神榜》式的近代背景，可見神話保存原來形式實在並非容易。再加上中國是一個歷史記載最完備的國家，歷史故事保存既多，就非常容易供給說故事的人需要，因而詳贍的神話也就難於保存下去了。

　　此外神話本來是非歷史的，如其以文學的眼光及人類學的眼光去欣賞，那就到處珠璣，如其以歷史的方法去批判，那就可能全盤荒謬。〈玄鳥〉、〈生民〉兩章故事，淵源甚早，原始性質甚為濃厚，但不可用考史眼光核實《禮記・月令》「仲春之月玄鳥至，以太牢祀高禖」，宋陳澔《集說》云：

> 《詩》天命玄鳥，降而生商，但謂簡狄以玄鳥至之時，祈於郊禖而生契。故本其為天所命，若自天而降下耳。鄭《注》乃有墮卵吞孕之事與〈生民〉注所言姜嫄履巨跡而生契棄之事，皆怪妄不經，削之可也。[30]

　　這些「怪妄不經」之處，正是其保存古說之處。陳澔的態度，正表示一般經學家或一般歷史學家的態度。這種態度到了極端，就成了對於古代的材料也用現實的眼光來衡量，許多寶貴的材料就不免被湮沒了。當然這種勉強做成的，以及曲解而成的古史是逐漸形成的，不自近古開始。《尚書》〈堯典〉、〈禹貢〉都

30　《五經讀本》（啟明版），第三冊，頁85。

是把神話處置以後留下來的影子。《左傳》世稱爲好談神怪，其實就古代的標準來說，神怪的材料已經被《左傳》作者刪減，其中神怪故事都是刪賸下的，卽令有幾處新添的也是跟隨當時「講史」的風氣，而非其人特別好怪的。無論如何，《左傳》這樣的歷史，對於神話保存上，也是害多利少，因爲他講了許多有趣故事，把神話代替了，較早而非常帶原始氣氛的神話就難以受人注意了。

中國原來是很多部族分占的，他們又各有各的語言和風俗，因而中國的神話也會因來源不同而形成許多不同的支系，戰國以後，再把不同傳說混合起來，表面上大致統一了，但其中不可挽救的矛盾，是仍舊存在的。爲了以後說明神話的系統，現在先將民族的系統大致表解一下。自然實際的情形只會比這個表解所舉的民族更多，情形更複雜，因爲資料不夠，只能加以簡化了。此外，此處只爲解說神話，所以分畫的理由，也不能詳細的解釋。

現就大致的方位，把各民族表解如下：

(1) 北狄系統

(3) 南蠻系統

(4) 東夷系統

(5) 吳越系統

華夏民族的一個特點，是他們的語言應當和漢、藏語系有關，因而他們的神話也就是用漢、藏語系的語言所說出來的神話。當然在這一系語言之中，當時彼此已經是語言的分別而非方言的分別了。至於北狄、東夷、南蠻和吳越在

---

31 楚仍算到廣義的華夏系統，因為在公族方面，楚仍相傳和夏商為同系，較徐嬴為近。並且楚的南遷，似乎是一個民族的移轉，和吳越只是公族相傳為華夏，而其民眾並非華夏的，又不相同。其中問題甚為複雜，應參考殷墟發現、江淮及長沙文物，非本篇所能討論，今發現大凡如此。(對於各族依地區的分法，略參取傅斯年先生及徐炳昶先生、王獻唐先生的意見，不過實際上只有比這種分法更複雜的。)

本篇中的假定，是認為不屬於漢、藏語系。至於應屬於那些語言，現在卻還不能決定。

以下就神話的種類，擬就各項來敘述：

（一）天地開闢的神話

這是較為晚出的，即所謂盤古開天闢地的神話，因為到漢代才見於記述，就有人疑為是借自南蠻，這是不對的。關於天地開闢的問題，在各民族的神話中甚為常見。夏自己不會沒有，決不可以在未有充分證據以前就輕易斷定是外來的，而非中原各民族所原有。故事是這樣的，據說天地未開闢以前，天地是沌混的，後來天地分裂，盤古在其中誕生了。以後天一天高一丈，地一天厚一丈，盤古一天長一丈。從此天極高，地極厚，盤古極長。盤古既死，氣成風雲，聲為雷霆，兩眼為日月，四肢五體為四極五嶽，血為江河，筋為地理，髮為星辰，皮毛為草木，……身之諸蟲化為人類[32]。這當然是非常不經的，所以經史諸籍都未曾徵引。但這種想法卻比較原始，決非漢代人所能偽造。無論如何，即令不是十分普遍，也應當是中原區域之內，有些民族中固有的神話。

盤古傳說是盤古身上的蟲變成人類，但另一傳說，而可能更為重要的傳說，是女媧摶土為人的傳說[33]，這正和《楚辭‧天問》[34]「女媧有體孰制匠之」相符。這是說女媧製造人，誰製造女媧？此外據《山海經‧大荒西經》[35]「有神人十人，號為女媧之腸化為神，處栗廣之野」。這表示女媧的身體也和盤古類似，化為其他神人。雖然傳說殘缺已甚，但可見古代傳說中的女媧是衍生世界和人類的，並且她本身也變為人和萬物[36]。所以在中國的「創世紀」中，女媧和盤古一樣，正是宇宙本身的代表，甚至於可以說盤古傳說正是女媧傳說的分支，只是名字不同罷了。

32　見《繹史》引《三五歷記》及《五運歷年記》。

33　見應劭《風俗通義》（《太平御覽》〔新興版〕78引《風俗通》佚文），頁472。

34　《楚辭》（世界版），頁60。

35　《山海經》（藝文版），頁422。

36　《楚辭‧天問篇》王逸《注》言「一日七十化」，就是化為萬物。（又女媧還有蛇身的傳說，這可能是由於敘述神話的那個部落，他們的族徽是蛇，因而轉變成的。）

　　凡是未經整理過，寫到書上的故事，一定會有變化，女媧創世紀的故事也是一樣的。例如《淮南子·覽冥篇》所說的，就多少有點不同：

> 往古之時，四極廢，九州裂，天不兼覆，地不周載，火爁炎而不滅，水浩洋而不息，猛獸食顓民，鷙鳥攫老弱。於是女媧鍊五色石以補蒼天，斷鼇足以立四極，積蘆灰以止淫水。蒼天補，四極正，淫水涸，冀州平，狡蟲死。顓民生，背方州，抱圓天。[37]

這分明是從衍生天地和人類的故事演變出來的。原來是衍生，到此變成為「補」了。但是在這段故事，又顯示了若干其他重要故事的影子，尤其重要的是洪水神話。連帶著息壤的神話以及馴伏鳥獸的神話。這都是其他英雄神話中重要的節目。

　　洪水神話是創造天地，造人造萬物以外的另一種重要神話，是一個普遍及於全世界的神話。它的背景目前尚不能知道，不過非常可能的是在蒙古、高加索，及玻利尼西亞等種族尚是一個人種的時候，這個傳說已經開始了。所以洪水故事即令有真的背景，也在幾萬年或一二十萬年以前，不會像傳說中的歷史，把它擺在西元前三千年左右那樣的晚近[38]。

　　但是因為夏代是華夏民族一個重要的朝代，夏代神話式的祖先，禹在華夏一支傳說中是治水的英雄[39]。所以夏禹治水成了一個正統的傳說。但從各支神話的殘餘看來，大禹治水的故事也不過是各支神話中的一支罷了。

（二）神的世系及英雄神話

　　現在古史最重要的材料〈堯典〉是將各族不同時代的英雄「全神堂」化，並且將純神話的人物也賦予人性和人格。《國語》中也有一些記載，也是走的和〈堯典〉差不多的路。他的作成時代，大致比〈堯典〉晚些，到了《史記》再擴大而整理起來，

37　《淮南子》(世界版，《諸子集成》本)，頁95。

38　這是指中國歷史把它放在堯舜時候。

39　卻又不是創世的神，這和女媧鍊石補天的故事範圍又不相同。此外在《淮南·天文篇》還有一個共工觸不周山的故事。一般人是把〈覽冥篇〉故事放在一起的，魯迅小說《不周山》即據此兩篇，他的文辭能脫離舊小說窠臼，進入了原始的興味，只可惜還把女禍故事放得後了。

就成功爲相傳的歷史的第一段。在《古史辨》時期，歷史的「層纍造成」說非常流行。他們當時的意思是中國古史上被認爲的時代愈前，其實際上造成的時代愈後。其說有一點根據，卻不能作爲通則。因爲這些傳說也不是無中生有被人託古改制加以僞造的，最大部分還是根據舊有的傳說，只是原來不出自一源，不出自一族，後來拼湊起來總會有拼湊的痕跡。

這般半人半神的英雄是否眞有其人，目前是無法答覆的。猶之脫雷故址雖然證實了它的存在，但是海倫、巴黎士、阿契里斯、優里賽斯等仍然沒有辦法加入正式的歷史上面一樣。中國上古史除了商、周時代確實可信的記載以外，以前我們只敢用發掘到的文化遺產。其他傳說在歷史學的觀點，還是既不足信，也無從疑，只有在神話故事上，卻是有價值的材料。

〈堯典〉無論如何應當比較一般戰國的材料稍早一些，其中不見後來神話中重要英雄黃帝的痕跡，所以黃帝就可能爲堯舜傳說的別支，卽是黃帝可能爲堯或舜的異稱。依照陳侯因資敦所說，自稱爲黃帝之後，而陳又爲舜後，所以黃帝是舜的別名可能性爲較大，黃帝的事業和舜是有不少相同的地方，所不同的是黃帝是華夏各族世系的中心。縱然除去東夷的風、嬴各系不算，華夏中的姜姓也不算，但把唐、虞、夏、商、周五代其他許多小國算做同祖，仍然是一個不可想像的事。

所以堯、舜、禹、伏羲、女媧、盤古等還是就傳說採集而成，黃帝是否根據傳說，還是由於史官筆下的創造，確是一個問題。並且因爲：（一）黃帝姬姓，在周以前姬姓不是一個重要的姓，據〈生民〉詩，周的始祖是后稷而不是黃帝。但到了《國語》的作者，許多族姓都是黃帝子孫，而且黃帝自己卻是姬姓，顯然是爲周室做成的擴大宣傳。（二）黃帝從名稱的意義上來說，爲青黃赤白黑五帝之一，這是從五帝思想發展後而產生的，是周代（至早不會超過商末）的一種哲學思想，與原始部族信仰無關，所以也不會產生太早。既然黃帝的世系可能是較晚時期（周代）創造出來的，黃帝的世系也就更爲完全而廣泛，另一方面也就對於其他的傳說會有些矛盾。本篇因爲討論黃帝世系會使神話的系統變成「治絲益棼」，就不再討論這一項。

《詩經》的〈生民〉和〈玄鳥〉，恐怕是在各族的先世神話中最有價值的兩篇，一方面是詩本身和詩注都保存原來神話的面目較多；另一方面表示著后稷和契是他們兩族的始祖，他們彼此之間並無聯繫，並且也未曾有更早的祖先，因爲他們都是神的兒子。

因爲契是商族始姐，所以不僅黃帝之說不可信，即帝嚳也不是不可能是出於攀附。甲骨中的「高祖夋」有人以爲高祖嚳，實際上也可以釋爲高祖嚳或高祖契，因爲不可能有比契更早的祖先了。

中國是一個廣闊的國家，現在稱爲中華民族，是經過商、周、秦、漢幾個帝國漸次統一以後的現象，尚未統一以前，拿歐洲、北美、南美和非洲同樣面積的區域來比(記載中或現今尚在分裂中)，就知道應當如何的複雜，無論如何應當是多元的情況。以下把英雄事蹟分開來講，仍然還不夠說明上古時代非常複雜的部落分布，不過一般人所想的「一元」觀念是必需加以清除的。

在此只能就最重要的來說，即可能是眞有其人的是東方的伯益，西方的帝舜和大禹。至於帝嚳和帝堯那就大都是指主神了，尤其在古音中，如帝嚳的嚳(k'ok)[40]，太皥的皥(xog)，高陽的高(kog)，堯、舜的堯(ngiag)，以及聲母距離較遠的陶唐的陶(dog)[41]，都是可以互相通轉的，這似乎不是一個偶然的現象，而可能是這些半人半神之人王，本來都是主神的化身，原來就可能是一個名字轉化出來的，再被各族當作自己的祖先。《山海 · 中山經》說：

> 洞庭之山……帝之二女居之，是在九江之間，出入必以飄風暴雨。[42]

郭璞《注》：「天帝之二女而處江爲神，即《列仙傳》江妃二女也。《離騷 · 九歌》所謂湘夫人稱帝子者是也。」洞庭山即君山，帝之二女即《史記 · 秦始皇本紀》所說的堯女舜妃。所以堯也是天帝，不僅《山海經》是這樣說，即是晉時的郭璞

40　據董同龢《上古音韵表稿》，下同。在此「堯」和「高」，自然也可能是山神的化身。古人相信山是神秘的，山神可以有子孫。例如姜姓就被指為嶽山（岳）的後裔。《左傳》莊公二十二年，周史說：「姜太嶽之後也，山嶽則配天。」這是現代人所不能想像的。「高」即嵩高，所以堯和高陽也可能是從山的崇拜引申而成。不過我覺得還是認堯為天帝，要好一些。

41　陶有時讀若皋陶之陶（縣 giog）就音更類似了。

42　《山海經》（世界版），頁275。

也承認的。因爲帝嚳和堯一樣也是主神，所以契和后稷雖然都是一個部族的始祖，但也同時是天帝之子，也就是帝嚳之子了。

如其要追溯神的世系，那就帝嚳比一切的帝王更爲重要。《山海經》的帝俊，是一切發明和世系的重要人物，在別處（如同《史記》及《漢書·古今人名表》等）是不見帝俊的，這就表示帝俊應爲其他帝王別名。帝俊的考證，依照《山海經·大荒東經》[43]郭《注》認爲帝俊就是帝舜，這一點郝懿行在《山海經箋疏》說：

> 案《初學記》卷九引《帝王世紀》云，帝嚳生而神異，自言其名曰夋[44]，疑夋即俊也，古字通用。郭云俊亦舜字，未審何據，〈南荒經〉云帝俊妻娥皇，郭蓋本此爲說。然而〈南荒經〉又云帝夋生后稷，《大戴禮·帝繫篇》以后稷爲帝嚳所產，但經內帝俊疊見，似非專指一人，此云帝俊生中容，據《左傳》文十八年云高陽氏才子八人，內有中容，然則此經文當爲顓頊矣。經文踳駁，當在闕疑。

郝氏所說「帝俊疊見，似非專指一人」，正表示神話傳說的分化。幸虧《山海經》從來未曾被認爲鄭重的經典，未被人整齊畫一，才保存了許多原始材料[45]。倘若我們不用傳統的眼光，那樣拘謹的認爲都是信史，而是用看神話的立場去看，那這些疑點也就毫不礙事了。其中娥皇爲舜妻，最早見於劉向《列女傳》，這部書取材雜駁，其原始性還不及〈帝繫篇〉。所以在各說之中，還是以帝嚳生后稷一事比較最爲重要。此處還是認爲帝俊就是帝嚳一說是一個傳說的中心，也就是說帝俊或帝嚳的地位是中國神話中相當於「周比得」的地位。

首先日和月是帝俊妻羲和所生，〈大荒南經〉說：

> 東南海之外，甘水之間，有羲和之國。有女子名曰羲和，方浴日於甘淵。羲和者帝俊之妻，生十日。[46]

43　《山海經》（世界版），頁398。

44　此與《史記·五帝本紀》黃帝「生而神靈，弱而能言」正出於同一傳說，《史記》誠然較早，皇甫氏《帝王世紀》卻曾用汲冢佚文。

45　卻也被人竄入不少，不過大致還看得出來。

46　《山海經》（世界版），娥皇見頁411，羲和見頁419。

又〈大荒西經〉說：

> 大荒之中，有山，名曰日月山，天樞也。有女子方浴月，帝俊妻常義生月
> 十二月，此始浴之。[47]

義和即是《尚書·堯典》的義和，常義也就是嫦娥或姮娥。這是一個傳說的分支，演變到和原來的「面目全非」。但其中最偏僻而離奇的，反而可能較為原始。

在《山海經》中還有許多有關帝俊的[48]，如帝俊生中容為中容之國，帝俊生晏龍為司幽之國，帝俊生帝鴻為白民之國，帝俊生黑齒為黑齒之國（俱見〈大荒東經〉），帝俊生季釐之國，帝俊妻娥皇生三身之國（〈大荒南經〉），帝俊生后稷為西周二國（〈大荒西經〉）等等，而有關發明的事，如同：

> 帝俊生禺號，禺號生淫梁，淫梁生番禺，是始為舟。
>
> 番禺生奚仲，奚仲生吉光，吉光是始以木為車。
>
> 帝俊生晏龍，晏龍是始為琴瑟。
>
> 帝俊有子八人，……是始為歌舞。
>
> 帝俊生三身，三身生義均，義均是始為巧倕，是始作下民百巧。
>
> 后稷是播百穀，稷之孫曰叔均，是始作牛耕。[49]

所謂帝俊（帝嚳），無疑的是古代神話中的主神，而為各種發明以及各族的世系的中心。但是帝俊的世系還是太簡單了，為了把歷史拉得更長，帝王名號加得更多，於是帝俊（帝嚳）之外，還得再加。因此五行說所推出的五帝，被人注意了，五帝中的中央黃帝被用上了。到了五行的應用越廣，黃帝的傳說愈多

47　《山海經》（世界版），頁431。又十日十二月的神話卻是從古曆法的十日十二月演出來的，管東貴的〈討論射日問題〉的論文（頁82）可據。

48　參看玄珠，《中國神話ABC》（世界書局）。又這裡的常字可能為恆字所改，避諱，因為恆本指月。

49　並見於《山海經·海內經》。

[50]，以致帝俊的地位被取代了。但是黃帝傳說的思想方式，是另外一套的。在古代神話的研究與復原上不會有它的地位。

（三）主要的英雄

在英雄神話之中，正面人物是舜和禹，問題人物卻是伯益，伯益在《史記》本紀稱作柏翳，《尚書・堯典》中有他，孟子也說舜使益掌火，〈秦本紀〉稱他是佐舜調伏鳥獸，看來也算正面人物了。但從另一方面去看，益和羿（或稱后羿）工作本來很像，翳和羿又可互相通轉[51]，並且〈天問〉說「帝降夷羿，革孽夏民」[52]，而柏翳又正是東夷嬴姓之祖。再就后羿來說，《山海經》和《淮南子》的后羿也是個不小的英雄，另一方面又是一個反叛[53]，這種矛盾的性格和多采多姿的事蹟更使這個神話充分戲劇化。

《山海經・海內經》帝俊賜羿彤弓素矰以扶下國，羿是始去恤地下之百艱」，這個除地下百艱的，當然非是大英雄不可。尤其是《淮南子・本經篇》說：

> 遠至堯之時，十日並出。焦禾稼，殺草木，而民無所食。猰貐、鑿齒九嬰、大風（鳳），封豨、修蛇皆為民害。堯乃使羿誅鑿齒於疇華之野，殺九嬰於凶水之上，繳大風於青丘之澤，上射十日而下殺猰貐，斷修蛇於洞庭，禽封豨於桑林，萬民皆喜，置堯為天子。於是天下廣狹險易遠近，始有道里。[54]

但是這個英雄也就是〈天問〉所說「射夫河伯而妻彼雒嬪」[55]的羿，也就是反叛夏朝的「有窮后羿」。到了後來，他的妻子逃到月宮去了。他自己又被逢蒙射死。因為他是一個悲劇的英雄，要做成歷史教訓的時候，需要把好人和壞人分

50　雖然黃帝傳說第一步還是從帝嚳傳說分出來，杜注《左傳》文十八年，帝鴻氏釋為黃帝，這是有據的，仍依帝嚳傳說。到了五行說盛行，就變成百家皆言黃帝了。

51　《廣韻》同在霽韻。

52　《楚辭》（世界版），頁58。又按羿相傳不是一人，這也許古不避諱，可以父子祖孫同名的緣故。

53　見玄珠前引書及程璟〈后羿與海句力士〉（中央大學《文史哲學報季刊》，1943)。

54　世界版《諸子集成》本《淮南子》，頁118。

55　在這裡雒嬪（即宓妃）、湘君和嫦娥是糾纏不清的，自然最可能的是幾個故事混淆為一，也可能一個故事分化為幾個。

爲兩組，於是益和羿需要分化，而羿的本身又分化爲堯時的羿和夏時的羿。只要了解神話中的道德觀念和哲學家的道德觀念並不一致，原始人的道德觀念和文明人的道德觀念並不一致，那神話把后羿算成這種英雄就並不稀奇了。當然，益和羿可能代表一個部族，也就是夏和徐嬴相敵對，商和徐嬴爲同盟，這就相當複雜了。

帝舜可以說是一個英雄人物的代表。現在舜的事蹟主要的在《史記‧五帝本紀》，而〈五帝本紀〉是取之《孟子》和〈堯典〉。《孟子》轉述的是戰國時候的民間傳說（雖然已經受過了《尚書》一類記述的影響）；至於〈堯典〉，就是有計畫的把傳說拿來歷史化，許多地方確是以傳說作根據的。可是裝點的結果，使人完全看不出舊日傳說的痕跡。

帝舜和黃帝是同類型的英雄。所不同的是舜多了一些私人的事，黃帝沒有；黃帝多了一些發明的故事，以及有關神仙的事，舜卻沒有。這也是可以解釋的。舜有一些私人的事，是由於現存舜的事蹟是史詩性傳說的殘餘，黃帝較少私人事蹟是由於他是後來有意造出來的，不屬於史詩型的人物。至於黃帝發明的事，已經和帝俊的傳說有一部分重合了（見前），只是有關發明的傳說，對於帝俊還不是那樣集中罷了。最可重視的，是神仙的故事，這本來較爲晚出，附會到黃帝（五帝中的中央帝），自然是順水推舟的狀況，不成問題的。

關於帝舜私人的事，最具有故事性的是《孟子》中瞽瞍使舜完廩那一段，以及《尚書‧堯典》「納於大麓，烈風雷雨勿迷」那一句，這兩條故事，單獨看來是沒有多大原始趣味的，但是和日本的「大國主命」故事比較下來，顯然的和大國主命故事是一個故事[56]。在這裡沒有篇幅來敘述大國主命故事，不過只要稍一對照一下，就會發現帝舜故事，其故事性是非常豐富的。

黃帝故事，除去了發明故事不算[57]，主要的事蹟是黃帝和蚩尤的戰役。最

56　大國主命故事見於日本的《古事記》。這是一個有趣的問題，不過日本民族是經過許多波次的移民，從大陸（包括中國和韓國）到日本，而日本民族中有在史前時代（中國的史前時代）從中國到日本去的。所以大國主命的故事中日相同，本不足異，只可惜中國方面修改太甚，以致面目全非了。

57　《山海經》就不認黃帝是發明器用的中心，〈天問〉中也沒有黃帝。黃帝稱為軒轅，可見發明車子最為重要（古說是相土發明的）。按照年曆說來，黃帝在公元四千六百年

早說到蚩尤的，是《尚書・呂刑》。原文是：

> 王曰若古有訓，蚩尤惟始作亂，延及於平民。……苗民弗用靈，制以刑，惟作五虐之刑。……皇帝哀矜庶戮之不辜，報虐以威，遏絕苗民，無世在下。

這裡的蚩尤顯然是三苗之君，可是和蚩尤對敵的卻是「皇帝」而非「黃帝」。皇和黃本來同音，這正是黃帝傳說的最早根據。問題只在「皇帝」是誰，皇之意為大，皇帝即大帝，猶之皇祖即是太祖。依照《偽孔傳》認皇帝為堯，但依照《左傳》去凶人是舜的故事，再依照《戰國策・秦策》蘇秦亦說「舜伐三苗」，那就皇帝被認為舜，更為合適。

再就黃帝阪泉之戰來說[58]，據《史記》黃帝是「教熊羆貔貅貙虎」來戰，而〈堯典〉在虞官伯益之下正有「朱虎熊羆」，這兩者顯然是相同的。此外，《史記》所說黃帝另一特點是「披山通道未嘗寧居」，而舜也是時常巡狩，最後南巡狩，崩於蒼梧之野。所以把這個神話復原一下，就表示著舜和蚩尤有一次大戰，在舜這一方面，群神百獸皆來助戰，最後贏了戰爭，但是對三苗之戰，算打勝了，這個英雄卻未曾享了清福，終於在一個遠征中逝世。

舜的故事為黃帝故事，所未有的是舜妃的故事[59]。其中牽涉甚廣，不能在此篇討論。其中可以注意的是女性的水神[60]，這個故事牽涉到宓妃，甚至於到天河旁的織女星以及後代的天后。

禹的故事是另外一個英雄故事，這和舜的故事連接著，卻各人顯出各人不同的個性。舜的故事是一個戰爭的故事，禹的故事卻是一個旅行的故事。舜的故事是伊里亞德型的，禹的故事卻是奧德塞型的。司馬遷看到過那部《禹本紀》，就是一篇神話式的遊記。可惜這部書早已失傳了。

大禹治水和女媧治水是矛盾的，可能屬於兩組不同民族的神話；也非常

前，其時全世界都沒有車子。

58　《史記》(藝文版)，頁 27。按阪泉與涿鹿並在上谷，仍是一個傳說。

59　到了黃帝故事中，變成了許多下流的故事，顯然是方士偽託的，屬於後起，不在神話研究範圍之內。

60　〈九歌〉中湘君、湘夫人、山鬼均為女神，這也表示著山水均為女神，其中，如驪山女、泰山女、塗山女及貌姑射山的山神，這也關涉著一些原始的神話。

可能女媧神話是個純粹早期的神話，而大禹神話又加入巴蜀地區人工治水的神話，再傳播到中原。此外，共工一族被認爲是壞的，而共工又顯然是禹所屬的夏族，這也顯示著原來傳說不是出於一族的。

大禹的王后塗山氏是山神之女，正和舜妃爲水神相對。其中當然也包括若干古時成套的神話在內。以上所分析的，只限於神話傳說方面，至於和眞的歷史人物的關係，屬於另一個問題，不在本篇討論之中。

（四）其他神話

以上所舉是神話的主要部分，也就是神話中的構架。其中如巨人族的防風氏和長狄，雖然未曾說明和帝舜的戰爭有關，但仍然非常可能曾被牽涉進去。此外關於自然現象的神話，例如九重天，十日、十二月、十二歲等等，這都牽涉曆法和天象。關於日神又有日御和逐日的夸父。對於天河又有牽牛織女一個動人的故事，這個故事在《詩經》中已發現了，到了漢代樂府詩中，又曾說到，一直到了後代，仍是非常有趣的民間故事。

西王母的傳說也是一個早期的傳說，雖然在《山海經》中所談到的西王母並不同於《穆天子傳》的西王母，但對於西王母的神話地位都是一致的重視。漢代西王母和東王公是相對的，東王公可能是〈九歌〉的東君，是指太陽神而言，那西王母就可能是月神了。這一點又可能牽涉到羲和、嫦娥一類的問題。不過從另一個觀點來看，所謂「西王母石室」，據《漢書・地理志》是在現在青海地方，那就漢代的人曾找到了地理上的根據，似乎古代傳說是以西藏一帶以婦女做酋長的國家來做背景，那就它的來源還是相當複雜的，也就不容易做詳細的追尋了。

漢代社祀的源流

在漢簡中和漢時人民信仰有關的，只在居延簡中有幾條：

買芯冊束給社　　　　　(32·16)　(註1)

官封符爲社市買□……　　(63·34)

　　　　雞一　　　　　酒二斗

對祠具　黍米一斗　　　鹽少半斗　(10·39)

　　　　稷米一斗

第一，二條是提到社的，第三條所指的是一種祠祀，是否爲社，在本條中無從知道。不過究社祭一事在漢代民間最爲普遍這一端而言　，　自然屬於社祭的可能性較大。雖然不敢貿然下斷語，但決無法確指爲別一種的祭祀。

居延爲漢代比較邊遠之區，但『社』的信仰也隨着內地的移民而來。　這一點顯示着中國文化的勢力已經植根在這個地方了。

『社』的信仰確是在中國古代的基本民族之中一個主要的信仰。　最早的確實起源和發生的原因，我們當然不知道。　倘若完全和現存原始民族中的圖騰崇拜或自然崇拜 (Nature　Worship) 的原流來互相比較，有時也是一個危險的事。　但我們仍然不妨追溯其較早的來源和其重要性。　並且在本篇中還可和後代信仰追求其聯繫。

在相傳的文獻方面『社』可推溯到很早，在現在存在比較最早文字上的直接材

（註1）芯字不見於較早的字書，未知何物。　不過在原簡上確是芯字。

料來說，據說在殷虛甲骨已經有『社』的祭祀（註1）。 所以決不能說是後起的。

在春秋戰國的習慣用法，『社稷』一詞常來代表國家。 可見社稷確是非常重要的。 古代國家的大事在祀與戎，而祀則分爲天神地祇人鬼。 但人鬼實際上是分配到天神和地祇。 尤其比較偉大的祖先是分配在天上的。 例如詩經：

文王陟降，在帝左右。（大雅文王）

三后在天。 （大雅下武）。

秉文之德，對越在天。 （周頌清廟）。

至於大乙和傅說爲列星，也是這一類的思想。但有特殊關係的祠祀，例如山川和社稷，也是有偉大的人來配的。 關於社，實際上和社稷是一回事，即周人以稷配社的（註2）。

不過古代的祠祀是有階級上的差異的，禮記曲禮：

天子祭天地，祭四方，祭五祀；諸侯方祀，祭山川，祭五祀，歲徧；大夫祭五祀，士祭其先（註3）。

（註1）殷虛書契考釋王國維曰，『卜辭所紀祭祀，大都內祭也。 其可確知爲外祭者，有祭社二事，其一曰，「貞寮于土，三小宰，卯一牛，沈十牛」（前一卷二四葉）。 其二曰，「貞，勿寮年于拜土」（前四卷，一七葉）。 按土字卜辭假借爲社。 詩大雅，「乃立冢土」傳曰，「冢土，大社也」商頌，「宅殷土茫茫史」記三代世家引作，「宅殷社茫茫」公羊僖三十一傳，「諸侯祭土」，何注，「土謂社也」，是古固以土爲社矣。邦土卽邦社，亦卽祭法之國社，漢人諱邦，改爲國社，古當稱邦社也。』 這一點新進的甲骨文研究者，也並無反顧。

（註2）見傅孟眞先生新獲卜辭寫本後記跋（安陽發掘報告第二期），按商社相土而不及后稷，周社后稷而不及相土，乃無疑問的事。祇因甲骨未出，殷禮無徵，同時又有社配句龍一個傳說。 於是漢代鄭王諸家聚訟紛紜。 但必別社稷爲二，以社配句龍稷配后稷，而相土遂無所屬。 今按社爲地祇，鄭說爲是。 但謂周代仍以句龍配社，亦少徵證。孟眞先生云『蓋夏商周同祀土，而各以其祖配之，夏以句龍，殷以相土，周以棄稷，』此言實可破千載之惑。 又參看胡厚宣先生甲骨文所見殷代之天神（責善2·16）。

（註3）漢書郊祀志『周公相成王，王道大洽，制禮作樂，天子曰明堂辟雍，諸侯曰泮宮，郊祀后稷以配天，宗祀文王於明堂以配上帝。 四海之內各以其職來助祭，天子祭天下名山大川，懷柔百神，咸秩無文。 五嶽視三公，四瀆視諸侯，而諸侯祭其疆內名山大川，大夫祭門戶井竈中霤五祀，士庶人祖考而已。』 此段臚括諸書較具，今引於此。

所以士以下有許多神是不能祭祀的，所能祭祀的，除過自己先人以外，就算社了。

禮記祭法：

> 王爲羣姓立社曰大社，王自立社曰王社，諸侯爲百姓立社曰國社，諸侯自立
> 社曰侯社，大夫以下成羣立社曰置社。　（鄭注：『大夫不得特立社，與民族居百家以
> 上，則共立一社，今時里社是也。』）

因爲社是成羣而立的，所以士庶的集團信仰完全在社，一直到兩漢以後。

以上只是敍述一個概略，詳爲考訂，屬於治經學和上古史的人所治的範圍，所以不再詳說了。

由漢以前至漢，士庶合法的祭祀，只有社祭是在家門以外，而有團體性質的，所以『社』的重要決非其他祠祀可比。　社神的位置也就是一個團體中的保護神的位置。

在漢代里爲什伍以上的最小單位，積里爲亭，積亭爲鄉，積鄉爲縣，到縣便是中央所派的官吏了。所以國家所立的社稷到縣爲止，（註1）人民自立的社卻以里爲準。關於里社一事，禮記鄭注見前引。　其餘里社的例，如：

> 禮記郊特牲，『惟爲社事單出里』。
>
> 史記封禪書，『高祖初起禱豐枌榆社』。　注，『高祖里社』。　又『高祖
> 十年春有司請令春二月祀社稷以羊豕民里社各自財以祠』。
>
> 漢書食貨志，『社閭嘗新春秋之祠三百』。
>
> 漢書陳平傳，『里中社，分由甚均』。
>
> 蔡邕獨斷，『大夫以下，成羣立社，曰置社。　大夫不得特立社，與民族居
> 百姓以上，則共立一社，今之里社是也。』
>
> 蔡中郎集，陳留索昏庫上里社碑，『社祀之建尚矣，在昔聖帝有五行之官，
> 而共工子句龍爲后土。　及其沒也遂爲社祀，故曰社者土地之主也。』

今山東圖書館藏有漢梧臺里社刻石，所以漢代里置一社，當無多大問題。

所立的社，或用土，或用木，或用石，是不一定的。淮南子齊俗訓云：

（註1）見續漢書祭祀志下。

有虞氏社用土，夏后氏社用松，殷人社用石，周人社用栗。

其說社用石的，例如：

周禮春官小宗伯帥有司而立軍社，鄭注『社之主蓋用石爲之』。 賈疏，『案許愼云「今山陽俗祠有石主」彼雖施於神祠要有石主，主類其社，其社既以土爲壇，石是土之類，故鄭注社主蓋以石爲之，無正文故曰蓋以疑之也。』

周禮夏官量人賈疏，『在軍不用命戮於社，故將社之石主而行。』

陳祥道禮書，『鄭氏曰「社之主蓋以石爲之」。 唐神龍中議立社主韋叔夏等引呂氏春秋及鄭玄議以爲社主用石，又後魏天平中大社石主遷於社宮，是社主用石矣。』

其說社用樹木的，例如：

論語八佾篇，『哀公問社於宰我，宰我對曰，夏后氏以松，殷人以柏，周人以栗』。

墨子明鬼篇『必擇木之修茂者，·立以爲叢社。』

戰國秦策，『亦思恆思神祠神叢歟？恆思有悍少請與叢博，……勝叢，叢借其神三日，遂勿歸。』

周禮地官大司徒，『設其社稷之壇，而樹之田主，各以其野之所宜木，遂以名其社與其野。』（鄭注：『田主田神，后土田正之所依也。詩人謂之田祖，所宜木謂松柏栗也。』）

白虎通義社稷篇，『社稷所以有樹何？尊而識之也使民人望見卽敬之，又所以表功也。 故周官曰「司徒班社而樹之，各以土地所生。」 尚書逸篇曰，「大社唯松，東社唯柏，南社唯梓，西社唯栗，北社唯槐。」』

漢書陳勝傳，『又令（吳）廣之次所旁叢祠中，搆火狐鳴曰「大楚興，陳勝王。」』 沈欽韓疏證曰『古者，二十五家爲閭，閭各立社，卽擇木之茂者爲位，故名樹爲社又爲叢也。』

漢書東方朔傳，『柏鬼之庭也』注『言鬼神尚幽闇，故松柏之屬爲庭府。』

三國志注引邴原別傳，『嘗行而得遺錢，以繫樹枝，此錢不見取，繫錢者逾多，……里中逐斂其錢，以爲社供。』

大唐開元禮諸里祭社稷議，『前一日社正及諸社人與祭者各清齋一宿於家正
寢。 應設饌之家先修理神樹之下，又爲瘞埳於神樹之北方深取足容於物。
……祭日未明烹牲於廚（惟以特豕祝，以豆取牲血置於饌所，）夙興掌饌者
實祭器，（……其尊一玄酒爲上，一實清酒次之，籩實麥粟，豆實菹醢，簋
實稷黍，簠實稻粱，）掌事者以席入，社神之席設於神樹下，稷神之席設於
神樹西，俱北向。 ……』（太平御覽五三二尚有若干條，今不悉轉引。）

所以社主用石或用樹，似乎都是可以的。 若論是非當然另外是一類話，不過現在
不是考經而是考史，不是論是非，而是論是否曾經存在過。 所以那一種用的對，
現在看來並無關係，只是用神樹（Sacred Groves）的事實的確較多，而且直到唐
代（政和重修新禮無里社）。

對於中國接近的遊牧民族，也有社樹的事，漢書匈奴傳云：

『秋馬肥，大會蹛林，校人畜計。』 注服虔曰『蹛音帶匈奴秋社，八月中
皆會祭處也。』 師古曰『蹛者繞林木而祭也。 鮮卑之俗自古相傳，秋天
之祭無林木尚豎柳枝，眾騎馳遶三周迺止，此其遺法。』

匈奴八月祀神一事和漢族也是同時的；玉燭寶典引崔實四民月令云：

八月筮擇月節後良日，祠歲時常所奉尊神。 前期七日舉家母到喪家及產乳
家。 少長及執事者悉集案祠，薄掃滌務加謹絜。

漢人常所奉尊神社神竈神當然是最重要的。 所以八月所祭的神，當有社神。 這
一點並非說漢與匈奴的社祭有何等相互密切的關係。 因爲二八月（註1）是舉行太
社的時期，同時也是祭祖的時期。 中庸云，『春秋修其祖廟，陳其宗器，設其裳
衣，薦其時食，』就是一個例子。 漢與匈奴同在北緯的亞洲東部，春秋都是佳日，
此時有令節的關係，並不是費解的。

漢代民間的社神早已不是句龍，相士，或后稷了。 漢人自有配食的神。 漢

書樂布傳，云：

　　布蒶，燕齊之間皆爲立社，號曰樂公社。

又社神亦稱社公，並且相信有法術的人，還可驅使社公。

　　禮記郊特牲，『社祭土而主陰氣也』疏引五經異義曰，『今人謂社神爲社

　　公。』

　　後漢書費長房傳，『遂能醫療衆病，鞭笞百鬼，及驅使社公』。

社中更有社鬼：

　　王莽傳，『分赦城中諸獄囚，皆授兵，殺豨，飲其血，與誓曰有不爲新室者，

　　社鬼記之。』

　　以上所舉，都可以表現社對一般人的生活上是比較密切的。　自然，社以外還有若干祠祀，例如齊人的城陽景王，東漢由外國輸入的佛教。　但都不能使社的祭祀失去重要性。

　　我們要追溯漢代的信仰，無法追溯太遠，並且也不應當追溯太遠。　不過漢人禮俗因襲周秦，大致是有跡可尋的。周代的信仰，似乎在周初是有人整理過，將天神地祇人鬼的系統整理好，而歸結於上帝。　凡不在祀典的則算做淫祀。　這不能說不是一個有計劃的工作。　不過有兩個缺點。　第一，周人的宗教是政教合一的，天子祭天地，諸侯祭山川，各有所祭的範圍。　這是和封建制度聯繫的，封建制度若破壞了，宗教也就不能維持。　『季氏旅於泰山』便是一個例子。　第二，周的封建諸侯似乎也並未完全接受王室的宗教，現所知道的，除過晉魯幾個宗邦外，齊楚各公室似乎都自有其信仰。　到後來甚至伊川也有披髮而祭的了，邦畿之內也無法統制。

　　宗教對於周人確實是十分重要的，不過周的政教合一是宗教寄託在政治上，而非政治寄託在宗教上。　周人宗教的合於理性，似乎不是一般宗教所能企及（註1）。不過政治色彩太濃，到周之季世，人亡政息，宗教信仰也就不振了。　魯是周的標

（註1）關於周人的上帝觀念及人道思想，可參考傅孟眞先生性命古訓辨證第二章周初之天命無

　　常論。

準宗邦，周禮盡在魯。　但觀魚觀社，許多不是教規所許的事，也由公室做出；告朔的羊，成了周室宗教頹敗的象徵。　到了戰國，政治無主宰，而宗教也無主宰。

所以周代信仰的致命傷便是和封建制度聯繫的結果，一般人民不得崇拜上帝，上帝的信仰便隨着王室的崩潰而消失。　只有祖先的祭祀，和社的祭祀，原來准許一般人民舉行的尚存在，卽是周代宗教系統，只存下一截。　一個一個單獨的社不能成為一個有系統的宗教，自是當然的事。

周室的宗教隨着封建制度破壞了。　戰國諸子連儒墨在內都無建設宗教的宏願。墨子宗教氣息最濃，但其信仰仍寄託在政治上，而且並無一套系統化的神祇。　秦皇漢武政治上氣象雖然弘大，但宗教的信仰卻極端低陋。　從史記封禪書及漢書郊祀志看來，都只能談到巫鬼的信仰而已。

東漢以後，佛教輸入，道教長成。　帝王及士大夫表面上雖然接受着圜立方澤山川社稷的系統，但內心的信仰早已不是這麼一回事。　只有殘存的『置社』尚在社會活躍着，變為城隍和土地的信仰。

城隍神和土地神對於佛教和天師道並無相關的痕跡，和縣社里社所崇拜的對象卻完全一致。　其分合之跡現在因為史料有限無從作詳密的敍述。　只能得一個大略的概況。　趙翼陔餘叢考云：

> 按北史慕容儼鎮郢城，梁大都督侯瑱等舟師至城外，城中先有神祠一所，俗號城隍神，儼於是順人心禱之。　須臾風浪大起，凡斷其荻洪鐵鎖三次，城人大喜以為神助，遂破瑱等。　隋書五行志梁武陵王紀祭城隍神將烹牛，有赤蛇繞牛口，是城隍之祀蓋始於六朝也。　至唐則漸遍，唐文粹有李陽冰縉雲縣城隍記，謂城隍神祀典所無惟吳越有之，是唐初尚未列於祀典。　張曲江集有祭洪州城隍文，杜甫詩有十年過父老，幾日賽城隍之句，杜牧集有祭城隍祈雨文，則唐中葉各州郡皆有城隍，五代錢鏐有重修城隍神廟碑記，書大梁開平二年……陸放翁寧德縣城隍廟記所謂唐以來郡縣皆祭城隍是也。宋史蘇緘殉節邕州後交人入寇，見大兵從北來呼曰蘇城隍來矣，交人懼遂歸，又范旺守城死邑人為設像城隍以祭。　張南軒治桂林，見土地祠令毀之，曰此祠不經，自有城隍在，或問既有社，莫不須城隍否，曰城隍亦瀆也，然載

在祀典，是宋時已久入祀典也。

據宋趙與時賓退錄及五禮通考引太平府舊志稱蕪湖城隍廟建於吳赤烏二年，未爲確據，太平廣記引唐牛肅紀聞云，『吳俗畏鬼，每州縣必有城隍神，開元末宣州司戶卒引見城隍神，神所居重深，殿宇崇峻侍衞甲仗嚴肅……府君曰吾卽晉宣城內史桓彝也，爲是神管郡耳。』所以城隍的職位是管郡的。法苑珠林，『晉王文度鎮廣陵，忽見二騶持鵠頭版來召之，王大驚問騶我作何官，騶云尊作北平將軍徐兗二州刺史，王曰吾已作此官何故復召耶，鬼云此人間耳，今所作是天上官也，……王尋病薨。』法苑珠林爲唐釋道世所作，則徐兗二州刺史亦是城隍神一類。所以城隍神的祠祀在唐已經流行是確無疑問的。

不過城隍神的信仰確有地域的分配問題。最初起源的地方似乎確在長江下游至多也只在長江流域附近的地方。據宋會要卷一千二百零四所載宋代加封號的城隍和土地，大都是在長江流域和閩粵。

這一點卻不能以『吳人信鬼』一個理由來解釋的。吳人固然信鬼，但城隍神的崇拜或者是受了吳人風俗中信鬼一事的影響，卻不能說是吳越本來的信仰。城隍神的性質，照名稱方面說爲城郭之神，照職位方面說是管郡縣之神。據漢書嚴助傳稱，『臣聞越非有城郭邑里也，處谿谷之間，篁竹之中。』漢書郊祀志雖然談到越巫，似乎不能產生城隍神的信仰。況且假如吳越本地早已有此信仰，漢武帝將以『寫放六國官室』的態度來採取，何至兩漢之中，毫無痕跡，所以起源絕不至太早。

城隍神的名稱顯然是城郭邑里的保護神，這一點當然在城市發展到相當的程度以後。倘若認爲起源於長江下游，則長江下游的都市發展可以最早追溯到漢武帝山東移民七十餘萬人中到會稽移民。此後由西漢末年到東漢，長江下游日漸繁榮及孫權和東晉元帝在江南建國，江南物質上的富庶，已經超過北方，三吳的郡邑，也就常見於記載。所以城隍的名稱不應當早過這時。

關於在縣社配食的事也是在後漢以後比較普遍。後漢書孔融傳，『郡人甄子然，臨孝存，知名早卒，融恨不及之，乃命配食縣社；』後漢書宋登傳，『爲汝陰令，政爲明能，號爲神父，……卒於家，汝陰人配社祀之；』晉書陸雲傳，『出補

浚儀令，……去官，百姓追思之圖畫其形像，配食縣社。』　所以縣社在後漢及晉
時已經有人配食，並且可以有圖畫形像的地方，卽縣社不僅是壇，而且是廟了。
再就此幾條證據看來，縣社對於人民還是相當密切，並無僵化的朕兆。

　　但這是永嘉之亂以前的事，自永嘉之亂以後，海內播遷，據宋書志序說：

　　　自戎狄內侮，有晉東遷，中土遺氓，播徙江外，幽幷冀雍兗豫靑徐之境，幽
　　　論寇逆……百郡千城，流寓比室，人伫鴻鴈之歌，士伫懷本之念，莫不各樹
　　　邦邑思復舊井，旣而民單戶約，不可獨建，故魏邦而有韓邑，齊縣而有趙民，
　　　且省置交加日回月徙，寄寓遷流，迄無定託，邦名邑號，難或詳書。

在這種狀況之下，流民旣不願爲所居郡縣的人，自無從奉祀所居郡縣的社。　但
『寄寓遷流，迄無定託，』其不能僑立社稷，又可想見。　在此時期禮壞樂崩，京
師雖有一般士大夫勉強維持，但僑郡豈能徧顧。在『魏郡而有韓邑，齊縣而有趙民』
的狀況之下，社稷的信仰自然是有的；但其方式決不能和平時一樣，那是一定的。

　　現在文籍殘缺，始終未發見代替僑郡社稷是用那一種方式的明文。　現在只知
道城隍和土地爲此時江南新的祠祀。　但假若城隍土地是一種僑郡臨時社稷的話，
那就最合適沒有了。　所以不論賓退錄所說蕪湖城隍廟是否建於孫權之世，但在這
種郡縣紛更狀態之下，社稷無從固定，人民的信仰移轉到和社稷作用相等，而不必
再分僑舊的城隍神，應當是一個相當自然的事。

　　關於記載城隍神的史料，有兩段是比較早些的：其一爲北齊書所記慕容儼的事；
其一則爲隋書五行志所記梁武陵王蕭紀的事。　按慕容儼傳稱：

　　　梁司徒陸法和儀同宋莒等，率其部下以郢州城內附。　時清河王岳率師江上，
　　　……衆咸共推儼，岳以爲然，遂遣鎭郢城。始入便爲梁大都督侯瑱任約率水
　　　陸軍奄至城下。　……城中先有神祠一所，俗號城隍神，公私每有祈禱，於
　　　是順士卒之心，乃相率祈請冀獲冥祐。

據北齊書陸法和傳，事在天保六年。　卽在西魏入江陵以後。　地本梁有，後復歸
梁，所以住民仍是梁人。　郢州本爲江夏郡，郡治夏口。　宋書地理志云：

　　　汝南侯相本沙羨土，晉末汝南郡民流寓夏口，因立爲汝南縣，沙羨令漢舊縣，
　　　吳省，……後以其地爲汝南賣士。

經過幾次土斷當留有僑郡的痕跡，以前應當僑郡當不止此一處。 又接隋書五行志。

> 梁武陵王紀祭城隍，將烹牛，忽有赤蛇繞牛口，牛禍也。 ……是時紀雖以
> 赴援爲名，而實妄自尊。

按梁書武陵王紀傳：

> 授持節都督益梁等十三州諸軍事，安西將軍益州刺史……及太清中侯景亂不
> 赴援，高祖崩後，紀乃僭號於蜀。

其時和慕容儼祭郢州城隍只前五六年。 其地爲蜀。 按宋書地理志：

> 懷寧太守，秦雍流民，晉安帝立，……寄治成都。
> 始康太守，關隴流民，晉安帝立，……寄治成都。
> 宋寧太守，宋文帝元嘉十年免吳營僑立，……寄治成都。
> 宋興太守，宋文帝元嘉十年免建平營立，……寄治成都。

按劉裕實行土斷在晉安帝義熙七年，入蜀平譙縱在義熙九年，志稱晉安帝立，實卽
是劉裕平譙縱後依土斷法所改定。在東晉南渡以後僑郡的設立，定較此爲緊，是可
以推定的。 所以正史最早記載兩處有城隍的地方，正是僑郡縣所在之地。 至於
照唐人所傳吳越崇奉城隍最盛，但吳越亦是僑郡縣最多之處，凡稍留意南北朝史事
的人，不必舉例，自能明白。 卽隨便就洪亮吉的補東晉疆域志的僑郡來看，也大
致可以看出來。 所以城隍神的信仰，以時以地，都和流人的遷徙相符。 雖然現在
尙無流人如何崇奉城隍神的正史明文，但總可假定說不是偶然的事。 至於賓退錄
稱城隍廟在吳大帝時建在蕪湖，太平府舊志從之，野史稗官記一千年以前的事（吳
赤烏二年 239 ——宋嘉定十七年 1224），單文孤證，無從考核，現在證明和反駁
都說不上，只好列爲縣案。 據建康實錄黃武元年『詔揚州置牧以丹陽太守呂範爲
陽州牧，以東征將軍高瑞領丹陽太守，復自建業徙治蕪湖。』 蕪湖縣志則謂黃武
以前『故城在縣東三十里自黃武初徙縣治，故城遂廢。』 未知是否可靠。 此說若
確，頗有黃武元年徙治，至赤烏二年方立縣社之可能。 據陸雲傳晉時的縣社確有
房屋，據孔融傳，宋登傳，後漢的縣社或亦有房屋，（因爲無房屋，不大容易配
食），則蕪湖縣社亦可以原有房屋更改成後來的城隍廟。 蕪湖在晉爲豫州及上黨
郡僑治之所，假若赤烏時的縣社變成南渡後的城隍神祠，亦非甚悖。 不過現在黃

武建城，赤烏立廟，均是一個不可十分相信的事，所以這一個解釋也只好懸而不決了。

　　土地神的名稱據白虎通義社稷篇說，『王者自親祭社稷何？社者土地之神也，土生萬物，天下之所主也。』所以土地和社應當沒有多少區別的。　御覽八八二引搜神記曰：

　　　　蔣子文者廣陵人也，嗜酒好色，常自謂己骨青死當爲神漢末爲秣陵尉，逐賊至於鍾山之下，賊擊傷額因解綬以縛之，有頃遂死。　及吳先主之初其吏見子文於道，乘白馬執白羽，侍從如平生。　文曰我當爲此土地神也。　爲吾立祠。　……吳主患之，封爲中都侯加印綬立廟，改鍾山爲蔣山，以表其靈。

此爲土地神三字見於記載之始。　不過言立廟而不言立社。　此或因吳主信神。已經出乎故吏所言立社的原來希望以上了。　明太祖御製集有南京城隍蔣子文祭文。到明時已正式認蔣子文爲城隍。　所以城隍土地實有共同之點。　徐鉉稽神錄卷六：

　　　　張鋌者累任邑宰，以廉直稱，後爲彭澤令，至縣宅堂後有神祠，祠前巨木成林，烏鳶野禽羣巢其上，糞穢積於堂中，人畏其神，故莫敢犯，鋌大惡之，使巫祝於神曰：所謂土地之神當潔淨縣署以奉居人，奈何使腥穢如是耶？爾二日中當盡逐衆禽，不然吾將焚廟而伐樹矣。　居二日有數大鵰奮擊而至，盡壞羣巢。　又一日大雨糞穢皆盡，自此宅居清潔矣。

此所言土地祠和樹是有關係的，樹的祠祀當卽社樹，所以土地祠亦卽社祠。　又宋張邦基墨莊漫錄卷五云：

　　　　蔡君謨作福守日，有一書生投詩來謁……君謨異之，尋令人伺其歸，至一山下忽不見，四顧無人，惟一社屋爾，意其社神也。

社屋應卽土地祠。　又宋孫光憲北夢瑣言十二云：

　　　　彭城劉山甫自言外祖李公敬彝郎中宅在東都毓財坊，土地最靈。　家人張行周事之有應。

光憲生於唐末，所稱東都乃唐時洛陽。　所以唐時已有當坊土地。　又宋張舜民畫墁錄云：

北人信誓兩界非時不得葺理城堞。 李允則知雄州，欲展城遷由，因作銀香
爐寘城北土地堂，一旦使人竊去之，遂大喧劫，蹤跡去來。 辭連北疆紛紜
久之，因興工起築。

此爲宋初的事。 所以『土地堂』在唐末宋初的時候，已經是普遍的稱呼。 雖然
行文時尙有人叫做社屋，但實際上已經是『土地堂』了。

玉佩與剛卯

（一）　玉與佩玉

（二）　從佩玉轉變爲剛卯

（三）　剛卯的形質

（四）　剛卯的文字

一、玉與佩玉

中國古代的人對於玉是非常重視的。重視玉的原因，當然因爲玉是希有的寶物，此外還含着有一種信念，認爲玉具有神秘的力量，可以發生某一些作用。因此玉除去了市場上的高貴價值以外，還含有宗敎上以及禁忌上的成分。圭璧一類的玉器，普通是對神用來祭祀，對人表示身份以及作爲貴重的禮品，至於玉佩的用處，就更爲廣泛，因爲可以適用於各階級的私人。

禮記玉藻：

古之君子必佩玉，右徵角，左宮羽，趨以采齊，行以肆夏，周還中規，折還中矩，進則揖之，退則揚之然後玉鏘鳴也……。君子無故，玉不去身，君子以玉比德焉。

這是說玉佩與禮貌上的關係。又禮記玉藻：

天子佩白玉而玄組綬。諸侯佩山玄玉而朱組綬，大夫佩水蒼玉而純組綬，世子佩瑜玉而綦組綬，士佩瓀玫而縕組綬，孔子佩象環五寸而綦組綬。——鄭玄注：『玉有山玄水蒼者，視其文色所似也，綬者所以貫玉相承受者也，象有文現者也，環取可循而無窮。』

在這一段所見到的，是（1）佩玉是用組綬來穿上再佩帶的，（2）佩玉有一定的等級，不過再特定等級所佩之外，也可以隨個人自行佩帶。

玉佩所包含的種類較爲複雜，玉佩是許多件數合成的，每一個件數就有它的名稱。如珩、璜、瑀、衝牙之類。詩經鄭風雞鳴：『雜佩以贈之』的毛傳：

> 雜佩者，珩、璜、瑀、衝牙之類。——陸德明釋文：『珩者衡上玉也，衝昌容反，狀如牙。』

這一些雜佩，據周禮二天官玉府：『共王之服玉、佩玉、珠玉』。鄭玄注：

> 佩玉，王之所帶者，玉藻曰『……天子佩白玉而玄組綬』，詩傳曰：『佩玉上有葱衡(衡當作衡，韋昭國語晉語注引作珩，珩卽衡，可證)，下有雙璜，衝牙蠙珠，以納其間。』——賈公彥疏：『引詩傳云，謂是韓詩。佩玉上有葱衡者，衡橫也，謂葱玉爲橫梁，下有雙璜。衝牙者，謂以組縣於衡之間，頭兩組之末，皆有半璧之璜，故曰雙璜，又以一組縣於衡之中央，於末著衝牙，使前後觸璜，故曰衝牙。毛詩傳，衡璜之外，別有琚瑀，其琚瑀所置，當於縣衝牙之中央，又以二組穿於琚瑀之內角，斜繫於衡之兩頭，於組末繫於璜。云蠙珠以納其間，蠙蜯也，珠出於蜯，故言蠙珠。納於其間者，組繩有五，皆穿蠙珠於其間。故云以納其間。

這一段應當照朱駿聲說文通訓定聲，『珩』字下的解釋，較爲清楚，卽：

> 珩者，佩着橫玉。所以繫組，組有三，中組之末，其玉曰衝牙，左右組之末，其玉曰璜，而蠙珠琚瑀則貫於珩之下，雙璜與衝牙之上。

故其配列，應爲：

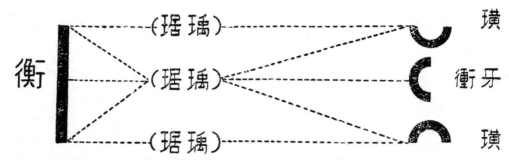

聶崇義三禮圖八，所繪佩玉之形製，與此略同。又三禮圖引舊圖云：『佩上有雙衡，長五寸，博一寸，下有雙璜，徑二寸，衝牙長三寸。』所以佩玉之中，以珩爲最大，其次爲衝牙，再次爲璜，至於琚瑀，就更小了。

因爲玉佩中以珩爲最大，所以現在所稱的古玉中『玉佩』，都指珩而言。段玉裁說文解字注（第一篇上）珩字注：

> 詩……韓傳曰『佩玉上有蔥衡，下有雙璜，衝牙蠙珠，以納其間，』按衡卽珩
> 字，晉語：『白玉之珩六雙』，注『珩佩上飾，楚語，「楚之白珩」，注，珩，
> 佩上之橫者。』玉藻：『一命再命幽衡，三命蔥衡』，注：『衡，佩上之衡也，
> 其制珩上橫爲組三，繫於珩，繫於中組者曰衝牙，繫於左右者曰璜，皆以玉，
> 似半璧而小，亦謂之牙，繫於中者，觸牙而成聲，故曰衝牙。蠙珠琚瑀貫於珩
> 之下，璜衝牙之上。故毛詩大戴皆曰『以納其間』。 云佩上玉者，謂此乃玉佩
> 最上之玉也。統言之，曰佩玉，析言之，則珩居首，以玉爲之。依玉藻所言，
> 則當天子白玉珩，公侯山元（玄）玉珩，大夫水蒼玉珩，所謂三命蔥珩，士濡
> 玟則以石。月令春蒼玉，夏赤玉，秋白玉，冬元（玄）玉，注，凡服玉，謂冠
> 飾及所佩之珩璜，則又隨時異色矣。

他的意見是（一）玉佩以珩爲主，（二）階級不同的佩玉，以珩爲代表。但他已經發現
了禮記玉藻和禮記月令兩篇對於玉的配列，互相矛盾，因此我們也可以看出古人對於
佩玉的規定，也不是那樣的嚴格。

佩玉的衡　（采自梅原末治：支那古玉圖錄）

佩玉的璜及衝牙　（採自梅原末治：支那古玉圖錄）

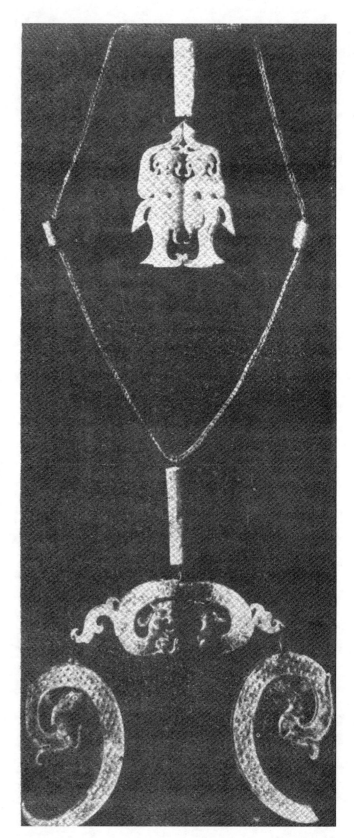

華盛頓佛里耳博物院所藏的玉佩
（采自梅原末治支那古玉圖錄）

　　此玉佩因爲裝飾的目的，已
經把舊有制度略有些改變，例如
『珩』是雕成雙人形，『瑀』爲雙
頭龍形，『衝牙』爲龍形，『琚瑀』
均爲通心圓柱形。但其中各部的
關係，還可以很清楚的看出來。

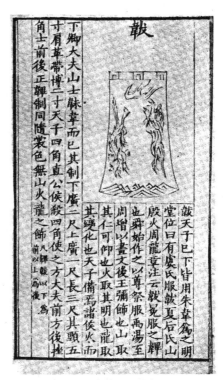

諸侯朝服　（采自三禮圖）　示佩玉之位置　　　　　　　韍　（采自三禮圖）

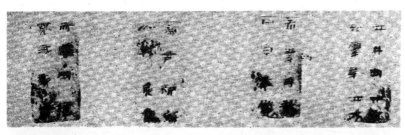

剛卯　（一）

剛卯　（二）

首句省去『旣央』二字

剛卯　（三）

以上采自黃伯川古玉圖

錄初集

二、從佩玉轉變爲剛卯

佩玉的玉質是不會那樣嚴格來代表階級的，同樣佩玉的形式，也不是那樣固定。玉藻所說『孔子佩象環五寸』當然指佩上的珩部而言，但既不是玉，也和標準橫形的珩不同，正可證明佩玉的形製，並不如何固定。玉佩各部的出土，已經很不少了。只是組綬用絲製成，皆已朽腐，看不出來各部聯結的關係。只有美國 Washington D. C. 的 Freer Gallery （華盛頓城佛里耳博物館）藏著一個玉佩，據說是在洛陽金村發現的，其製造時代當爲戰國中期或晚期。其形製爲玉佩而用金爲組綬，所以毫無損傷，使人看出各部相互的關係。其珩部是做成雙人形，衝牙和璜也加上了裝飾，琚瑀部分不用蠙珠，而用長條形的玉，用金鍊從中心穿過。這件佩玉給人許多珍貴的啓示。

假如將珩，衝牙及璜去掉，只留下了長條形的琚瑀一對，便成功了一對剛卯。這正和司馬彪續漢書輿服志相符合（後漢書卷三十），輿服服說：

古者君臣佩玉，尊卑有度；上有韍（注，徐廣曰韍如巾，蔽膝），貴賤有殊，佩所以章德，服之衷也；韍所以執事，禮之共也。故禮有其度，威儀之制，三代同之。五伯迭興，戰兵不息，佩非戰器，韍非兵旗，於是解去韍佩，留其係璲（惠棟補注曰，……爾雅曰緣綬也，郭璞云，卽佩玉之組，所以連繫瑞玉者，因通謂之緣），以爲章表。故詩曰鞙鞙佩璲，此之謂也。

韍佩既，廢秦乃以采組連結於璲，光明章表，轉相結受，故謂之綬。漢承秦制，用而弗改，故加之以雙卯（原誤作印，今從瞿中溶奕載堂古玉圖錄意見校正），佩刀之飾。

又輿服志說：

佩雙卯（原誤作印，今從瞿氏校改），長寸二分，方六分。乘輿，諸侯，王，公，列侯以白玉，中二千石以下至四百石，皆以黑犀，二百石以至私學弟子皆以象牙。上合絲，乘輿以縢貫白珠，赤罽蕤，諸侯王以下以綵，赤絲蕤。縢綵各如其卯（原誤印）質。

刻書文曰：『正月剛卯既決，靈殳四方，赤青白黃，四色是當。帝令祝融，以教夔龍，庶疫剛癉，莫我敢當』。『疾日嚴卯，帝令夔化，愼爾周伏，化茲靈殳，旣正旣直，旣觚旣方，庶疫剛癉，莫我敢當』。凡六十六字。

再據本節的劉昭注文：

前書注云，『以正月卯日作』（按見漢書十九王莽傳，『正月剛卯之利，皆不得行』下的顏師古注）。惠棟集解曰：決，一作央。說文『䰟改，大剛卯以逐鬼魅也』。左傳曰：『辰在子卯，謂之疾日』，剛卯以卯日作，故曰疾日。『愼爾周伏』漢書注作『順爾周伏』黃山曰：『前書王莽傳注，服虔說，剛卯「長三寸，廣一寸四分」，晉灼說「長一寸，廣五分，四方」，均與志異』。卯得名印者，據漢舊儀，秦以前民皆佩綬，金玉銀銅犀象爲方寸璽，各服所好，是佩印本秦俗之舊，不能驟革，故漢因而製卯，其分寸固亦難畫一，志所言持後漢官學定制耳。

在這裏有幾個問題需要討論的，第一，是『卯』字與『印』字的是非問題。印字和卯字的字形相似，這兩個字本來字形容易相混，再加上在續漢書輿服志中的部位，雙卯的後面就接着佩印的綬，地位也容易相混，因此抄字時就十分容易被抄寫的書手誤爲印字。這裏的錯誤，惠棟尚未發現，直到瞿中溶才發現出來。不過旣經指出，那就印字應作卯字是顯而易見，不成多少問題的。因爲（甲）續漢志所稱剛卯凡六十六字，照地下發現的剛卯來看，應當屬於兩個剛卯一個是三十四字，一個是三十二字，正合於雙卯之數。（乙）秦漢的人都佩有私印，這是不錯的，不過私印只有一印，不是雙印，若再加上雙卯，就成了三件，不是雙數。（丙）雙卯的『菆』和輿服志後面所說的『綬』，形製全不相同，顯然是兩件事，綬旣屬於印，那就『菆』不應當再屬於印。——所以『雙卯』的『卯』字，在輿服志誤抄作印，是不成問題的。

當然，其中還有若干變化，而卯和綬也自有其相互的關係。當佩玉時期，玉佩附於韍上，而韍自有韋帶，韋帶係腰，而另外還有一個『大帶』係腰。到了玉佩和韍並廢，只留下兩個用菆的剛卯，繫在係腰之綬上，而綬之形制部位又應爲大帶於轉變。所以菆和綬雖不同爲一物，還是互相連結的。

水經注江水注云：

江神歲取童女二人爲婦，冰以女與神爲婚，經至神祠，勸神酒，酒杯恒澹澹，冰厲聲以責之，因忽不見。良久有兩牛鬭於江岸旁，有間，冰還，流汗，謂官

屬曰：『吾鬪大亞，當相助也，南向腰中正白者，我綬也』。主簿刺殺北面者，
江神遂死。(按此事亦見於應劭風俗通)。

漢制二千石青綬（見續漢書輿服志），漢制本承秦制，太守可能在秦代也不是白
綬。不過繫綬於腰，在酈道元時代，一般人是知道的，酈氏根據通俗傳說，縱令綬色
未必切合，至於綬的部位，不會與實際不符。漢制官服不再談到大帶，則綬為大帶的
轉化，大致應當不差的。所以卯與印雖非一物，但卯與印均佩帶於腰際，是彼此有關
的。

第二，佩玉轉化為剛卯，在輿服志中已有明文。至於佩玉的那一部分轉為剛卯，
還得加以分析。現在要討論這個問題，應當根據實物才可以。關於剛卯的形製，是通
心穿的柱狀飾物，這一點和玉佩上的珩，衝牙，璜都不相類。只有琚瑀一類的珠子，
是通心穿孔。但是琚瑀應當還是圓珠子。到了戰國時期的玉佩（如同 Freer Gallery
所藏的）琚瑀部分，成為通心穿的柱形，這就正和剛卯的形製相符合了。不過兩卯相
當，同為下垂飾物，還是璜的地位，這就是由柱形的琚瑀來代替璜，其間還有一層轉
變。再從無字的柱狀飾物刻上了字，其間更多一層轉變。倘若不是有佩玉轉為剛卯的
舊說，就使人不敢隨便牽附了。

三、剛卯的形質

依照續漢輿服志，剛卯有玉，犀，象牙等材料，都是屬於比較貴重的物品。宋代
馬永卿懶眞子說：『于士人王君蒞家，見一物似玉，長短廣狹，正如中指，上有四
字，非隸非篆，上二字乃正月字也，下二字不可認，問之君求曰，前漢剛卯也，漢人
以正月卯日作，佩之銘其一面曰：正月剛卯』。這就是屬於玉類。清瞿中溶古玉圖錄
中，曾著錄一器，又稱曾見三器，皆為玉質，吳大澂古玉圖錄中著錄三器，亦皆是玉
質。黃伯川尊古齋古玉圖錄中，曾著錄八器亦均是玉質。

但是剛卯亦可以用木質的，漢書王莽傳說（漢書九十九）：

今百姓咸言皇天革漢而立新，廢劉而立王。夫劉之為字金刀也，正月剛卯，金
刀之利，皆不得行。博謀卿士，令曰：天人同應，昭然著明，其去剛佩，莫以
為佩，刀錢莫以為利。

注引服虔曰：

　　剛卯以正月卯日作，佩之，長三寸，廣一寸，四方，或用金，或用玉，或用

　　桃，著革帶佩之，今有玉在者，銘其一面曰：『正月剛卯』。

又注引晉灼曰：

　　剛卯長一寸，廣五分，四方，當中央縱穿孔，以彩絲葺其底，如冠頭纓，刻其

　　上面作兩行書，文曰：『正月剛卯既央，靈殳四方，赤青白黃，四色是當。帝

　　命祝融，以敎夔龍，庶疫剛癉，莫我敢當』。其一銘曰：『疾日嚴卯，帝令夔

　　化，順爾固伏，化茲靈殳，既正既直，既觚既方，庶疫剛癉，莫我敢當。』

注，師古曰：『今往往土中有玉剛卯者』。

　　照此來看，剛卯除玉質而外，還有金質和木質兩類，其木質是用桃木來做的。在

居延發現漢簡之中，就有兩個木製剛卯（不知是否桃木，因爲還未請森林學專家鑑

定）。骨董店中未曾見過木質剛卯，當由玉質比較值錢而木質不值錢，因已未能到收

藏家之手。

　　用玉或桃木來做剛卯，當然因爲玉及桃木都被相信具有靈異的性質，也就是有

『厭勝』的功用。關於玉，至少有以下的記載，是屬於玉的靈異性的。

　　周禮天官下：『玉府掌玉之金玉，玩好，兵器，凡良貨賄之藏，共玉之服玉，

　　佩珠玉，齋則共食玉。』（注：『玉是陽精之純者，食之可禦水寒』）

　　禮記檀弓篇：『石駘仲卒，無適子，有庶子六人，所以爲後者，曰：「沐浴佩玉

　　則兆。」』。

　　禮記玉藻篇：『君子比德於玉焉……氣如白虹天也，精神見於山川，地也。』

　　左傳昭公十七年：『鄭禆竈言於子產曰，宋、衞、陳、鄭將同日火，若我用瓘

　　斚玉瓚，鄭必不火。』

　　太平御覽八〇四引禮含文嘉：『玉石得宜，則太白常明。』

　　太平御覽八〇四引禮稽命徵：『王者得禮制，則澤谷之中有白玉焉。』

　　太平御覽八〇四引禮斗威儀：『君乘金而王，則紫玉見於深山。』

　　太平御覽八〇四引春秋演孔圖：『孔子論經，有鳥化爲書，孔子奉以告天　亦

　　俱集書上，化爲玉，刻曰：「孔提命作應法。」』

太平御覽八○四引孝經援神契：『神靈液百寶用，則玉有瑛。』

韓詩外傳：『良玉度尺，雖有千仞之土，不能掩其光。』

山海經二，西山經：『稷澤……玉膏之所出……瑾瑜之玉爲良，堅粟精密，濁澤而有光，五色發作，以和柔剛，天地鬼神，是食是饗，君子服之，以禦不祥。』

太平御覽八○四引胡綜別傳：『秦皇以金陵有天子氣，緣處埋寶物，以當王土之氣。』

在這裏可以看得出來，玉是一種重要的寶物，因爲高出一切凡品，具有通神明的功用。也就可以禦不祥，而剛卯由佩玉變來，但一種鎭驚禦邪的信念，不僅保持著，而且發展下去，更刻上了抵禦疫氣一類的文字。

剛卯用桃木來做，也是爲著辟邪的功用的。桃木本爲中國的特產。在詩經中的桃是莊嚴美麗的，例如周南，桃夭：

桃之夭夭，灼灼其華。——毛傳：『桃夭，后妃之德也』

又召南，何彼穠矣：

何彼穠矣，華如桃李，平王之孫，齊侯之子。

這都是稱讚或者比擬桃花的莊重及美麗的一方面。所謂『輕薄桃花』乃唐人以後的設想，與此原不相關。但從別一方面來說，桃花及桃樹却有其神秘性。續漢書禮儀志劉昭注引山海經說：

東海中有度朔山，山上有大桃樹，蟠屈三千里，其卑枝門曰東北鬼門，萬鬼所（所字據太平御覽九百六十七補）出入也。上有二神人，一曰神荼，一曰鬱儡，主閱領衆鬼之惡害人者，執以葦索而用食虎，於是黃帝法而象之，毆除畢而立桃梗於門上，畫鬱儡持葦索以御凶鬼，畫虎於門，當食鬼也。

此則不見於今山海經。當是今本有脫漏，王充論衡訂鬼及應劭風俗通亦均言及此事，常爲漢以前舊說，此外在太平御覽九百六十七中，還有許多舊的材料，涉及桃木的神秘性，所以剛卯也會用桃木來做。

除去玉和桃木以外，剛卯也會用金，犀角，象牙來做，這當然取其質料的珍貴，在珍貴之中，也就含著了厭勝辟邪的功用。

剛卯的形式大都是四方長條形，中有一個通心穿，據陳大年的：『剛卯嚴卯考』

（說文月刊第三卷第十二期，民國三十三年二月出版），和那志良的：『剛卯』（大陸雜誌第十一卷第十一期，民國四十四年十二月出版），都說除去四方形的以外還有六方形的，可見形製不限於四方形。再就尺寸大小來說，據漢書王莽傳，顏師古注引服虔曰：『長三寸，廣一寸四分，』又引晉灼曰：『長一寸，廣五分』，師古曰：『今往往有土中得玉剛卯者，案大小及文，服說是也』。續漢書輿服志，則稱爲：『長寸二分，廣六分』，和服虔說及晉灼說也都不一樣。吳大澂古玉圖錄說：『大澂見古剛卯，從無三寸長一尺廣者，似以晉灼之說爲長』，但說文『𣪠』字下云：『𣪠攺，大剛卯也，以逐精鬼，從殳亥聲，』又『攺』字下云『𣪠攺，大剛卯，從支已聲』。史游急就篇：『射𩰚辟邪除羣凶』，顏師古注：『射𩰚，大剛卯也；一名𣪠攺，其上有銘而旁穿孔，系以彩絲，用繫臂焉。』這幾條既然說『大剛卯』，那就也必然有小剛卯。古物的有無，不能專以目見的爲有，其未曾見到的，就指爲沒有。陳經求古精舍金石圖說：『剛卯之制，漢時必不一其式，服晉各就所見以爲注，而小顏只據目見妄以服說爲是，陋矣』。這種意見是比較上對的。

四、剛卯的文字

　　剛卯是兩卯成對的，兩卯的字數差不多，其一爲三十四字（有些剛卯將『正月剛卯既央』句中的『既央』二字省去，就成爲三十二字），另一個爲三十二字。兩個剛卯，就成爲一組，當然，漢代人也許會單用其中的一個，不過在原則上是成對的，因此就不可以把兩個剛卯認爲完全不同的兩種。

　　關於剛卯的考訂，以瞿中溶的奕載堂古玉圖錄爲最好，最近那志良的『剛卯』一文也很謹愼。陳大年的剛卯嚴卯考較多無中生有的臆斷。陳氏對於古玉，見聞上廣博，這是不錯的，不過考訂之事，不可以只憑見聞廣博，就可以隨意揣測。陳氏有若干地方，有意來出新奇的意見，而錯誤也就在這新奇的地方。

　　『正月剛卯』的卯字漢書及續漢志注都認爲『正月卯日作』，這是現存最早的解釋。宋馬永卿嬾眞子認爲『剛者強也，卯者劉也，正月佩之，尊國姓也』，剛卯原出而秦，非始於漢，民間習俗本來不管國姓不國姓的。雖其說不近情理，還有王莽傳一段可以附會上。陳大年之說認爲『正月剛日卯時作，央言卯時既中』便是一個與古無徵而完全出於揣測之辭。漢人漏刻雖分為百刻十二時，却只用夜半，平旦，雞鳴等名稱，從無子時丑時等號，而且也只說上水幾刻下水幾刻，亦無所謂『中』與不『中』。(見居延漢簡考釋下)，所謂『中』或『央』者，專指日中或日央之稱，不是用在『時』或『刻』上。所以用正月的卯日，因為正月為一歲之始，而卯日在正月(秦代雖然以十月為歲首，但十月仍稱十月，以建寅之月為正月)，按建除家之法，(見淮南子天文篇)，正月卯日當為『除』日。除有除災害之義(王莽傳『戊辰直定』則利用定國之義)，和驅除疫癉，正相符合。至於與劉氏的『卯金刀』相符，不過偶然的事罷了。

其次關於『靈殳四方』，此處之殳明言『四方』，而其下又有『既觚既方』一語，則殳刀指殳之稜角，並非指『殳書』而言。據說文云之『殳，以杖殊人也，周禮，殳以積竹，八觚，長丈二尺，建於兵車，旅賁以先驅。』則殳為有觚稜之杖，以示威嚴的。詩衛風云：

伯兮朅兮，邦之桀兮，伯也執殳，為王前驅。

自伯之東，首如飛蓬，豈無膏沐，誰適為容？

很清楚的，這是一首戀詩，作者是一個女子，所戀想的『伯』(某一家的長子)，正是一個執殳的英雄，不說他的姿容，而姿容自可想見。這也是壯士和殳，同為代表威嚴的一個舉例。論語：『觚不觚，觚哉觚哉』，注家皆以觚失觚稜，以喻王室之失政，實亦以觚稜指威嚴。漢代凡『方』，『稜』，『嚴』皆有威義，故翟方進字子威，馬嚴字威卿，馬稜的伯威，皆見兩漢書本傳。所以剛卯中的『剛』，『嚴』，『觚』，『方』，皆是威嚴的同義字，而殳和剛卯，同具稜角，亦皆所以代表威嚴。也就是剛卯上的稜角乃剛卯上應有之義，倘無稜角，也就不成其為剛卯了。

因此『剛卯』和『嚴卯』也就是同義的形，並無區別。自然不應當揣度成『剛卯』為『強劉』，『嚴卯』為『禳劉』，勉強把同義的字分而為二。這一點邢志良先生也如此主張，也就不必多為發揮了。

『赤青白黃，四色是當』，四色中獨無黑色。其無黑色，可能和秦人所祀的帝有關，漢書郊祀志云：

平王東徙雒陽，秦襄公攻戎救周，列為諸侯。自以為主少昊之神，作西時，祀白帝。……(高帝)二年冬，擊項籍而還入關，問故秦時上帝，祠何神也。對曰

『四帝，有白青黃赤帝之祠』，<u>高祖</u>曰，『吾聞天有五帝，而四，何也？』莫知其

說，於是<u>高帝</u>曰：『吾知之矣，迺待我而具五也。』迺立黑帝祠，曰北畤。

赤青白黃爲<u>秦</u>時上帝，剛卯用此四字，當是襲用<u>秦</u>時之舊。至於爲什麼只有四帝，那

在<u>漢</u>時已經『莫知其說』，現在除去認爲秦人信仰，和五行說可能有若干不同之外，

也不能作更多的解釋。

居延漢簡中有兩個剛卯，其文爲

(1)　若一心堅明

　　　安上去外英

　　　長示六□　　　（甲面）

　　　□□□□

　　　則□□□

　　　□□□明　　　（乙面）

　　　□書□亡

　　　□□□章

　　　□□□□　　　（丙面）

　　　五鳳四年

　　　□□□□

　　　□□丞光　　　（丁面）

　　此剛卯長一生的半，寬一生的

(2)　正月剛卯旣央

　　　靈殳四方　　　（甲面）

　　　赤青白黃

　　　四色賦當　　　（乙面）

　　　帝命祝融

　　　以敎夔龍　　　（丙面）

　　　庶役罔單

　　　莫我敢當　　　（丁面）

　　此剛卯長一生的半，寬九米厘

從第一個剛卯看來，剛卯是可以不必拘守一定的格局，也可另外作其他的文字。

從第二個剛卯看來，其中的文字也常有異同。再以續漢志爲標準，校對玉剛卯和木剛

卯其異文計有：

　　　『靈殳』作『靈犀』　（玉剛卯一）

　　　『帝命』作『帝令』　（玉剛卯一）

　　　『夔龍』作『龜龍』　（玉剛卯一、二）

　　　『帝命祝融』作『帝令祝松』。（玉剛卯二）

　　　『是當』作『賦當』　（木剛卯二）

『庶疫剛癉』作『庶役岡單』 （木剛卯二）

『帝命夔化』作『帝令蟲化』 （玉剛卯三）

『愼爾周伏』作『愼璽固伏』 （玉剛卯三）

『庶疫剛癉』作『赤疫剛癉』 （玉剛卯三）

都互相有異文。其中除去漢人常夔龍並稱（夔爲木石之怪），夔龍當作夔龍，不當作爲龜龍之外，其餘如祝融作祝松，剛癉作岡單，類皆音近假借，而庶疫作庶役，則釋名『疫役也，言鬼有行役也』，更是音義並通，當然是可以的。此外如瞿中溶的古玉圖錄中載一剛卯『庶疫剛癉』作『疒瘻剛瘄』，當然是誤字。而陶宗儀的輟耕錄所載：『制曰嚴卯，帝令莫忘，曰賨惟是，赤靑白黃』合併兩卯之文爲一剛卯，假如比較木剛卯一之文，則比剛卯對於續漢志之文俏比較接近。所以漢代剛卯的文字，雖然還有一個標準，但其中變化，仍可能千差萬別，就現在所知道來比較，已有不少的相互差異。這一點也可以知道剛卯文字在漢時也不是凡人都能加以解釋，其用途多少有些符籙化了。

六博及博局的演變

賭博，是一種娛樂，也是一種人類的病態生活，縱然賭博對於人類社會的影響是壞的，可是對於人類社會的重要性，却是一種事實，在中國古代賭博對於生活上所占分量，是不容忽視的。"六博"就是中國古代賭博的代表，中國古籍中許多訓詁牽涉到六博，六博的制度不明，那就許多方面的訓詁也不明。六博的風尚甚爲普徧，因而六博的形製也用在裝飾方面，漢鏡中最普通的一種，卽過去被稱做"TLV 鏡"的，自從楊聯陞先生根據"仙人六博鏡"的形製，確定爲博局的形狀以後，這個問題已經解決了。不過六博的方法，古代也有許多不同的形類，現在就現存的材料來分析，所謂"六博"並非限於一種方式的，要把這許多方式的異同分別出來，才有進一步了解的可能，本篇就是依著這一個方向，先來試作。

①　簡式的博，和"瓊"的形製

六博的形製及其用法，是比較複雜的，不過在南北朝時代，却有簡化了的賭博法，從這個簡化的賭博來看，就比較清楚了，據顏之推顏氏家訓雜藝篇說：

> 古者六博則六箸，小博則二煢，今無曉者。比世所行，一煢十二棋，數術短淺不足可翫。

這種"一煢十二棋"的博具，就比早期的六博，要簡單的多了，其中包括兩種賭具，一爲煢，另一種爲棋，現在先說煢。

煢是一種投擲采數的博具，和現在所用的"骰子"（ㄕㄞˇㄗˇ），有類似的用處，顏氏家訓盧文弨注說：

> 煢卽瓊也，溫庭筠詩"用雙瓊"卽二煢也，瓊與煢通用。

所以煢亦有時寫作瓊。列子說符篇張湛注引古博經說：

其擲采用瓊爲之。瓊夏方寸三分，長寸五分，銳其頭，鑽刻瓊面爲眼，亦名爲齒，二人互擲采行棋。

又後漢書梁商傳附梁冀傳：“性耆酒，能挽蒲，彈棊，格五，六博”，句以下，注引鮑宏簺經說：

> 簺有四采：塞，白，乘，五，是也。至五卽格不得行，謂之格五。

注又引鮑宏博經說：

> 用十二棊，六棊白，六棊黑，所擲頭謂之瓊，瓊有五采，刻一畫者謂之塞，刻兩畫者謂之白，刻三畫者謂之黑，一邊不刻者，五塞之間謂之五塞。

就上面看來，“塞”，“瓊”和“瓊”是同一的博具，只是“格五”和“六博”的方法，稍有不同。照漢書六十四上吾丘壽王傳：“年少以善格五，召待詔。”注說：

> 蘇林曰：“博之類，不用箭，但行梟散。” 劉德曰：“格五，棊行簺法，曰塞，白，乘，五，至五格不得行，故曰格五。”(按“塞，白，乘，五，當作”塞，白，黑，五。“黑字草書略近於乘字，所以易於抄錯。”)

所以格五和六博最大的異點，是六博用箭，而格五不用箭。依照用瓊擲采一點來看，那就並無分別的。至於瓊（或稱塞）的形製，也就只有四采的一種，鮑宏簺經所說和劉德所說是相同的，被引的鮑宏博經所說“瓊有五采”五字顯然是一個錯字，隸書四字常作三，很容易和隸書五字作乂的相混（因爲注文較小，而且古卷子的紙張容易漫漶），“瓊有五采”實際上是“瓊有四采。”

綜合上文來看瓊的形製，應當是一個六面體，除去兩面各有一個尖頭以外，還剩四面。在這四面之上是：

第一面刻一畫——叫做塞

第二面刻二畫——叫做白

第三面刻三畫——叫做黑

第四面不刻——叫做五

這個“五”也就是“五塞之間謂之五塞。”因爲“塞，”“白”“黑”都有他正面的價值，第四面叫做“五”的却不是。他沒有贏的數字，只有輸的數字，也就是說他沒有正的數值，只有負的數值。其負的數值，是照其他五面來算的，換言之，這一面的數值是負五，所以不稱爲四而稱爲"五，"或稱爲"五塞。"

這種四面的投子（骰子）不論在中國或者在中東，都是較爲古老的辦法，其六面的投子，却是從這種四面的投子變化而來的。不僅如此，四面的投子也未曾完全廢棄，直到如今，陞官圖所用的投子，還是四面的。其中"德"、"才"、"功"三面，代表正的數值，而第四面"贓"代表負的數值，正和古代的"瓊"是一致的。所稍有不同的，只是古代的瓊有兩面尖頭，而陞官圖用的只有一面尖頭，另一面改爲一個小柄，以便持柄來轉，和陀螺一樣的轉，來定采值罷了。

②　博局中的"棋"的形製

棋是棋局上或博局能够移動的小標幟，圓形的棋如中國象棋或圍棋固然是棋，可是其他形狀，能够在局上移動的，例如陞官圖上的碼子，也是屬於棋的一種。（日本將棋棋形作長方形，當然也算做棋）。博局的棋大致是長方形的，不是圓形的。列子說符篇張湛注引古博經說：

> 二人互擲行棊，棊行到處卽竪之，名曰驍。

"互擲"局是輪流來擲投子。依照采的大小來定行棋的步數，到達終點以後，就成爲驍棋（或稱梟棋，驍和梟二字通用，所以驍雄亦稱做梟雄），把他直立起來表示分別。其未成驍的棋，就稱爲散棋（梟散並稱見戰國策秦策"一驍之不勝五散亦明矣。"因爲一個驍棋，實際上不如五個散棋的取勝機會更多一些）。驍棋可以攻擊別人的驍棋，也可以放棄走的機會不動，散棋却是不能的。這和西洋的"王棋"（checkers）有點相類似。王棋中到達對方邊界的棋子，上面再加上一個棋子，這就時古人所謂"驍"。王棋中成王的棋，可以前進，也可以倒退，不成王的棋不能，這也是驍棋和散棋的分別。

古代的中國瓊尙未被發現，只有就文獻上的記載，和現在的各種投子，以及國外發現的古代投子，來推斷他的形製，大致是可以斷定的。至於古代博局上的棋，那就更容易用地下實物來比證了。從楊聯陞先生"再志古代六博"（An Additionol Note on the Ancient Game Liu-po, Harvard Journal of Asiatic Studies 1952）附圖版兩幅來看，都可以知道棋的形製，這兩種圖版，一爲日本水野精一先生在山西陽高發現的，另一種是倫敦大英博物院（圖版三）收藏的，陽高發現的是一種長方形的骨器（圖版四），大英博物院收藏的却是畫鳥獸花紋的木塊。那些骨器和木塊只有認爲是棋，才好解釋，尤其大英博物院那四塊木塊，凡一面畫鳥就全部都畫鳥，凡一面畫獸也就全部畫獸。所畫的是那種鳥，或那種獸，似乎並無特殊意義，只爲的表示畫鳥的是代表一方，畫獸的又代表另一方，這用鳥獸來表示，和一方用白，一方用黑的功用完全一樣，至於都用長方形，顯然的爲著平放和豎立是一樣的方便，平放可以代表散棋，豎立可以代表驍棋，（近世牙牌麻雀牌之類，雖無驍散之分，却仍然沿襲長方的形式）。

此外認爲長方塊是棋的，還有一個證明，就是大英博物院所藏的漢代陶俑（圖版二）經楊先生指爲博戲的，他的博局上有長條形，和長方塊形，對于這兩種博具，我們只能認前者是博籌（解釋見後），而後者是博棋。這個博棋正和陽高的骨製長方塊及大英博物院藏的木長方塊形狀相同。這就更增加了對於博棋形狀的認識。

③　博局的形製和行棋的棋道

依照漢鏡的構圖，再根據武梁祠石刻及四川漢代浮雕（圖版五），博局都應當是TLV 形式的，雖然魏晉以後可能有別的形式，這却是以後的發展。

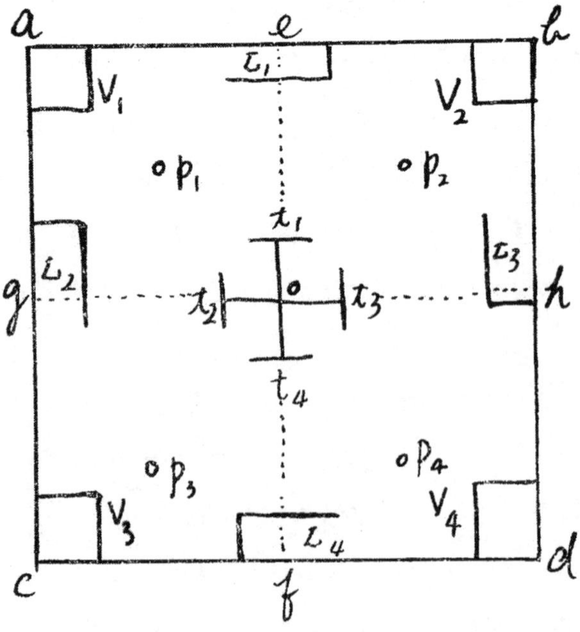

附圖一

TLV 的博局，具如左式：博局爲正方形 abcd、博局的中點爲 o，四邊中點的垂線 ef 和 gh 將博局分成爲四個小的正方形。

在博局的四角有 V_1，V_2，V_3，V_4四個小的區域，（卽所謂 V 的所在），博局四邊的中部有L_1，L_2，L_3，L_4 個小直線（卽所謂 L

的所在），而中心的周圍又　t_1，t_2，t_3，t_4　四個小區域（卽所謂 T 的所在），這些都應當是放置博棋的地方。此外在分成四個小四方形的中部，還可定上 p_1，p_2，p_3，p_4 四點。這是依照四川漢代浮雕去加上的。

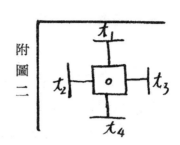

附圖二

博局中心部分依照四川浮雕，四個 T 形是相接的（如附圖一），但依照"仙人六博鏡"却是中心還有一個方塊（如附圖二），仙人六博鏡要早一些，這種有方塊在中心的，應當是早期的形式，也許更是標準的形式。只是前者較簡單一些。所以被後來的人採用了。

當兩人對博的時候，兩方的棋，每方六個，都擺在自己前面 "L" 範圍之內，這是從梁武祠石刻畫像前石室第七石看出來的（附圖三）。此時六個棋子都在 "L" 形限制以內，出棋時候只能一個一個的魚貫而出。並且 "L" 形的出口都在各人的右手方，所以出棋的時候是從右手方依次出來的。

出棋的時候，每次可能有一定的步數，不能超過。並且步數的多少，是從擲瓊的點數來規定的。擲得高點的人，走棋的步數可以多些，擲得低點的就少些。擲得最壞點數的便只能停止不動。這樣的輪流前進，誰的棋子達到對方邊界線上的，便可算爲梟（或稱驍），梟棋是直立起來的，行動較未成梟的比較少些限制。可以囘頭吃掉別人，也可以囘到自己陣地中來。等到一方有兩個梟時，就算勝利，其勝利的大小，再擲瓊來依照點數決定。

現在看來，博局的形式頗爲複雜。不過分析起來却只有三種形式爲著放置棋子的。卽：

　　1　封口的，卽 V 形。

　　2　開口的，卽 L 形和 T 形。

　　3　無界線的，卽四個小方形中心的 P 點。

V 形旣然是封口的，一定有一種封閉的意思存在著，也就是和所謂 "下逃於窟" 的窟的作用相符，逃到窟中的棋子，不再受對方的攻擊，可是要攻擊對方的棋子，也得從窟中出來才可以，不能從窟中直接攻擊對方。因此在行棋的時候，就要受到限制，不擲得高采，就不能利用窟內的棋。爲著怎樣才可以爭取先贏的機會，兩方博者就多出了複雜的考慮。

　　T形和L形同樣是開口的，可是L的區域較長，T形每邊較短，L形只有一邊，T形却可以有兩邊，這就意識到形L可以容納許多棋子，T形每邊容棋較少，可能就只能容納一子。L形是原來停放棋子的地方，而T形却應當是棋子休息的地方。T形所不同於P點的，應當是T形只能一面進出，比較有防衛的意義，而P點則四方受敵，情況不同了。

附　圖　三

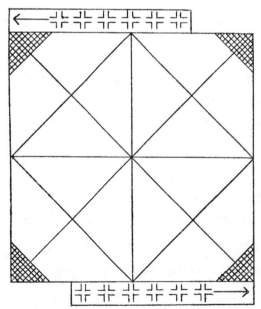

附　圖　四

武梁祠前石室第七室的六博圖，（轉載自三十七年一月二十一日上海中央日報文物周刊，楊寬：六博考附圖，因為此圖由於轉摹比較清楚。又按楊寬文搜集材料不少，只可惜他未見楊聯陞文。）

　　從上來看，博局是非常複雜而且非常離奇的，若就博言博，似乎無此複雜而離奇的必要，照現在推測，是應當溯源於過去的傳統游戲，並非賭博本身上的需要（解釋見後文）。假如這個看法不錯，那為容易明瞭起見，博局是可以簡化的。左面就是簡化的假設。

以上表示的博局，分為四區，四區的分配是兩區靠著自己，兩區靠著對方。每一區都畫有對角線，而相交於四區的中心。四區緣邊之線及對角線，都是行棋的道路。在每方靠自己緣邊之處，另外畫出一個地方，作為排列棋子之用。在這一區域的棋子，一共六個，只能依次從右方出去。在未出去以前，不受別人的攻擊，也不能攻擊別人（這是漢鏡中的L區域）。從這個區域出發，即到轉角的地方（附圖三畫黑三角地方，亦即漢鏡中的V區域），仍是一個封閉區域，不能作戰。直到從這個區域再出來，才能發生戰鬥。這可能為保護L區的棋子以及從L區出來的棋子，都是散棋（即未成為梟的棋），免得受對方梟棋的攻擊，有一些藏躲的地方。

從博局自己緣邊右下角出發的"散棋"，前進的目的地是對方的緣邊，然後再成梟回來，每次輪流到行棋的步數，由擲瓊決定。所以行棋的路線，要找最經濟而且最安全的路線，還要乘機攻擊敵方，這就成博局上的戰略問題了。西京雜記載安陵許博昌六博之術為：

　　　方畔揭道張，張畔揭道方；張究屈玄高，高究屈玄張。

　　　張畔揭道方，方畔揭道張；張究屈玄高，高究屈玄張。

這實在是非常費解的，只有楊聯陞先生的解釋最為清楚，現在以楊先生的解釋為主，稍加補充，說明如下：

　　　"方畔揭道張"是"從方形以區域的邊緣起，有條路通至伸張的區域。"

　　　"張畔揚道方"是"從伸張的區域的邊緣起，有條道路通到方形的區域。"

"方形的區域"應當指從自己地方出發的區域，即右下角區域，"伸張的區域"應當指比方形的區域較遠的區域，即右上角區域，這兩句說從右下角區域出發，成為梟棋之後，仍從右上角區域轉回來，不必經左方的區域。——這是行棋的基本形式。

其次"張究屈玄高，高究屈玄張"兩句確實費解一些，不過楊聯陞先生已經解釋"屈"為窟（註一）。而"究"字亦當指箭或瓊而言。那就"玄"和"高"當算作兩個地

玄	張
高	方

區，與上方所說的"張""方"兩區共為四個地區，則此四個地區應為。"因此"張究屈玄高"應為從"張"區出發，可以經"玄"區而回到"高"區，"高究屈玄張"則為從"高"區出發，可以經"玄"而回到"張"

（註一）　HIAS；1952，葉135。

區，其中可能有時逃入窟中，並且還要利用擲瓊的點數，這都要靠戰術上精密的斟酌。

④ 六 博 與 投 壺

以下，依次討論到箸（也就是箭），壺，以及分曹的博戲：

複雜的六博，是要用到箸的。顏氏家訓雜藝篇說；"古爲六博則六箸，小博則二熒，今無曉者。"顏氏言當時只用一熒，已不用箸。不過我們却可從各方面記載來歸納，凡古代的博戲，大致用熒就不用箸，用箸就不用熒，箸和熒可是以相互代替的。爲的是箸和熒都是投擲出來一個數目，作爲行棋之用(註一)。

韓非子外儲左上說：

秦昭王令工施鈎而上華山，以松柏之心爲博箭，長八尺，棋長八寸，而勒之曰："昭王嘗與天神博於此矣。"

這次博戲是用博箭，不是用熒；至於戰國策秦策所說：

亦思恆思神叢歟？恆思有悍少請與叢博，……左手爲叢投，右手自爲投，勝叢。

這種兩手分投應當是用熒的，兩者比較，似乎用箭的比較複雜，而用熒的簡單一些用箭的博戲可能和投壺有關，史記一二六滑稽列傳淳于髡傳說：

乃州閭之會，男女雜坐，行酒稽留，六博投壺，相引爲曹，握手無罰，目眙不禁。

這裏的"六博"和"投壺"，可能爲兩件事，也可能是一件事。憑著史記本文雖然不能決定。可能根據倫敦大英博物館 (British Museum, London) 所藏的漢代陶俑(註二)。就是六博的博具旁邊擺著一個壺，這個壺的性質是不容易解釋的。對于這個陶俑，魯德福先生 (Prof. R. C. Rudolph) 認爲和投壺有關(註三)。這是不錯的。我們從這裏看出來六博和投壺間的連繫。使得對於淳于髡傳有一個比較清楚的了解。

(註一)　直到近世的麻雀牌，還是先擲骰子，再打牌。擲骰就是擲熒，打牌就是行棋，雖然和六博面目全非，可是仍然淵源有自的。

(註二)　Illustrated London News, 13 May, 1933.

(註三)　R. C. Rudolph: The Antiquity of Tow Hu--Antiquity 34, 1950.

如認為投壺可以為六博進行中的一種程序。那博箭就是投壺的箭，在進行六博戲的時候，先用投壺的方法來決定點數，再按著點數行棋。經過的手續是比較繁複一些，不過許多遊戲是要依靠繁複的程序來增加趣味，這並不算怎樣不合理的。

用箭和用煢的程序和形式雖然不同。但是行棋的方法應當大致差不多的。行棋得到結果以後，才能決定輸贏，大致需要一個比較長的時候。因此，為熱鬧起見，六博投壺也就不是兩個人對博，而是分為兩組的遊戲，兩面各有許多人認定，這就是所說的分曹了。

楚辭招魂說：

　　菎蔽象棋，有六博些，分曹並行，遒相迫些，成梟而牟，呼五白些。

王逸注"菎，玉；蔽，博箸；以玉飾之也。或言蔽蘆，今之箭囊也。"以玉飾箸，是不可想像的。不過"菎蔽"解釋為玉煢（或玉瓊）那就比較明顯了。"成梟而牟"據王逸注"倍勝而牟"意指成梟而後，便成倍勝。而所以能成梟，卻由於"五白"的出現。但是"五白"是煢的采，非箭的采。以後證前，更可知"菎蔽"非解釋做"玉煢"不可了。

關於五白的解釋，顏氏家訓風操篇說：

　　凡避諱皆須得以同訓以代換之，桓公名白，博有五皓之稱。

這是說在春秋時期已有"五白"的一種博采，和戰國時相同。

依照唐代李翱的五木經及唐代李肇的國史補(註一)，唐時的擲點法是用五瓊（即五煢），每瓊四齒，一齒全白，稱為"白"，一齒全黑，稱為"黑"，一齒黑而刻二，稱為"牛"（或犢），一齒白而刻二稱為"雉"。擲得貴采的得連擲，並得行馬（即行棋）(註一)，其采的算法，是：

(註一)　李翱五木經見四部叢刊李文公集，李肇國史補見太平廣記二二八卷。

(註二)　禮記四十投壺"請賓曰：'順投為入，比投不勝，勝飲不勝者。正爵既行，請為勝者立馬，三馬既立、請慶多馬。'請主人亦如之。正爵既行請徹馬"鄭注"馬，勝筭也，謂之馬者，若云技藝如此。任為得帥乘馬也。(鄉)射投壺，皆所以習武，因為樂。所以馬是指筭籌而言。
　　　　此處指行棋為"行馬"應即溯源於投壺制中的立馬。其後唐宋的六博變為打馬（見李清照打馬圖經），"馬"字的使用當然和這事有關，到了現代的賭局仍然把賭籌稱做"籌碼"。碼字的來源，也應毫無問題的從投壺舊制中稱筭籌為馬的習慣而來。引申到金融名稱，稱通貨為籌碼，又是從賭局的籌借用的。

貴采：

1. 盧——五瓊均黑，十六采。

2. 白——五瓊均白，八采。

3. 雉——兩雉三黑，十四采。

4. 牛——兩牛三白，十采。

雜采：

1. 開——一雉，一牛，三白，十二采。

2. 塞——一雉，一牛，三黑，十一采。

3. 塔——二雉，二白，一黑，五采。

4. 禿——二牛，二黑，一白，四采。

5. 撅——三白，二黑，三采。

6. 梟——三黑，二白，二采。

這裏的"白"顯然的就是春秋戰國時的"五白"。不過"白"雖列入貴采第二，采數却不多，那就又是經過了後代的改變的。而且再按照出現的或然性來說，五瓊均雉以及五瓊均牛的可能也不大，那就雉當為五瓊均雉，牛應為五瓊均牛才對。其兩雉三黑，以及兩牛三白，當屬於雜采而非貴采。卽令不是抄寫中的錯誤，也應當屬於較後時期的改變。無論如何，"五白"為戰國時貴采中采數較多的，當無疑義。

據楚辭招魂，分曹的博戲，在戰國時已經有了，因為加入博戲的人各人認定各人的組，因此各個人的賭注就放在賭局上面。這種賭注就叫做壓。（說文"鎮"博壓也。"博壓就是賭注"。）所以博戲本是以兩人為主，到了兩方都有人放置賭注，就成為分曹的局面了。李商隱詩："隔坐送鉤春酒煖，分曹射覆蠟燈紅，"射覆之戲是一種猜對方覆蓋的東西來打賭的（見漢書六五東方朔傳）。射覆也是分為兩方，所以也可以有分曹的形式，和六博之戲成為類似的分為不同的組合。

如博戲不用瓊而用箭，那就應當和投壺有若干的關係。投壺可以說是小型的鄉射，鄉射又是小型的大射，從大射以至於投壺，都是古代重要的典禮，並且這些典禮，又顯然的和古代狩獵有關的。從六博中擲采的命名來看，盧就是獵狗，雉和犢也都是狩獵中獵取的對象，也可以想像到它的來源也可能和狩獵多少有些關係。

其次六博所以稱爲六博，也似乎和射藝直接有關，因而間接可以涉及狩獵，據楚辭招魂王逸注稱：

投六箸，行六棋，故爲六博也。

投六箸，卽投六箭，正和秋射時射六箭是一致的，居延漢簡：

功令第卅五，士吏，候長，烽燧長常以令秋試射，以六爲程，過六賜勞矢十五日（居延漢簡圖版 371 頁）。

這是說漢代正式秋射，是以六發爲度，中了六矢的人，再給予獎勵。這種以六矢作爲一個單位來計算的方法，正和六博的六箭數目相符。再向前追溯儀禮的鄉射和大射，也都是兩人一組各發三矢，合爲六矢，也和漢朝秋試共發六矢有因革的關係。

大射鄉射以及投壺其根本的原則是出於習武及校獵。所不同的只是規模上和身份上因時因地而制宜的區別。所以不論在野外或在庭中，其中根本原則上有彼此互相類似之處。等到由校射變爲投壺，其形式上和六博已經甚爲接近。所不同的，投壺還是鄉黨中行禮式的娛樂，而六博就成爲金錢上的賭博。投壺因爲古代社會組織上的限制，只是專爲男子而設的娛樂，六博就從來不限男女的性別，這就表示春秋戰國的社會已經和舊有的氏族社會有了變化了。

因此，對於六博的博局也就可以做一個假定的解釋。就是說博局的布置是以古代宮室的形式爲基礎的，依照殷虛的發掘，以及早期青銅器亞字形的標記，可以推測出來，古代宮室的基本形式是亞字形，這種亞字形排列的方式，就是現在中國四合院房屋的早期形式，王國維的明堂廟寢通考（觀堂集林卷三）雖然尚有應當修正之處，不過他的以四合院爲基本形式這一個原則，却是正確的。所謂"四合院"實際上是用四所建築，拼湊起來，把中間做成了一個中庭或現在所謂"天井"。因此依照了四合院形式，就可畫成右邊的平面圖（附圖五）。

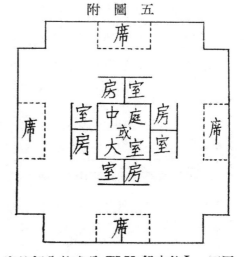

附 圖 五

照這圖來看，房和室就成爲 TLV 鏡中的 T，席的部分就成爲 TLV 鏡中的 L，而四個空角就成爲 TLV 鏡中的 V，按照禮記投壺篇，席的位置是在兩楹之間，正是客人的坐位。再以博局來看，也正是六個棋子排列之處，所以六博不僅要採用投壺的方法，而且博局也是從宮室的式仿效而來。這就不難找出六博創始時所用的根據了。

⑤　魏晉以後十二道的博局

TLV 形的博局是漢代或漢代以前採用的。到了漢代晚期至魏晉時代，顯然在博局形式上起了一個變化，這種變化是把繁複的博局簡化了。列子說符篇：

> 虞氏者梁之富人也，家克殷盛，錢帛無量，財貨無訾，登高樓，臨大路，設樂陳酒，擊博樓上，俠客相隨而行，樓上博者射，明瓊張中，反兩搤魚而笑。

張湛注引古博經云：

> 博法二人相對坐，向局，局分十二道，兩頭當中名爲水，用碁十二，故法六白六黑，又用魚二枚，置於水中，其擲采以瓊爲之。……二人至擲采行碁，碁行到處卽竪之，名曰驍，碁卽入水食魚，亦名牽魚。每牽一魚獲二籌，翻一魚，獲三籌。若已牽兩魚而不勝者，名曰波翻雙魚，彼家獲六籌爲大勝也。

又張湛注說：

> 凡戲爭能取中皆曰射，亦曰投。裴駰曰：“報采獲魚也。”

張湛注又說：

> 明瓊，齒五白也，射五白得之，反兩魚故大笑。

列子及列子注有兩件事可以特別提出的，第一，是棋局中心的空白處，被稱水的部分。第二，是“明瓊”或“五白”的采，到張湛時尙存在。

張湛注引古博經所說的“水”，這種形式還保存在象棋中的“界河”裏。中國的象棋本出於印度、印度象棋和西洋象棋都並無所謂界河，界河本是中國獨創的制度。而把界河加到象棋局上，却是從一種博局中採用過來的。

其次，關於“明瓊張中”一語來看，“張”應卽西京雜記所說的“張”，當指對方局內。明瓊張中，就是擲瓊時瓊擲到博局內，並且在對方的博局中。再依照張湛注明瓊卽“五白”，可見著列子時，“五白”仍受重視，據唐國史補，五白仍爲貴采。不過不算貴采中的高采。可見列子成書時采的算法和唐代應當不一樣。

　　至於西京雜記所記，和漢代的博局相符，似乎比列子所記還要更早一點。西京雜記是一個後出的書(註一)，比列子成書爲晚，不過所用的材料，除過有些是作者杜撰的而外，還包括有眞的漢代遺文。所以較早方式的六博出現在西京雜記書中，並非一個不合理的事。此外，凡是游戲的事，一定有許多不同的形式存在著。當西京雜記的時代，並非不可能還有一種較古形式的博局。例如顏之推所說的是"一梟十二棋"，可是五木（卽五梟）的辦法到唐代還流行，可見博戲的形式，決不是在某一個時代只有一種。

　　雙陸的游戲，實是從六博變來，所謂雙陸，解釋尚不一定。不過按照雙陸所用的棋子，每方爲十二或十五（十五棋子實際上也只有十二棋）。數目爲六博所用的二倍（而行棋時也是每次行二棋）。"雙"的得名可能由於棋子二倍而來，據錢稻孫"日本雙陸談"(註二)，說：

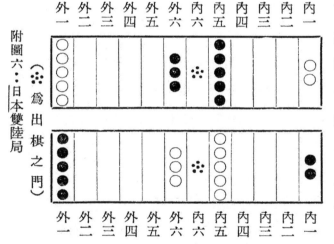

附圖六：日本雙陸局

（※為出棋之門）

古法大致不殊譜雙所云："日本雙陸，白木爲盤，闊可尺許，長尺有五，厚三寸，刻其中爲路。置二骰子於竹筒中，撼而擲諸盤上，視采以行馬。馬以靑白二色，琉璃爲之。如中國棋子狀，馬先歸一處者爲勝。"

又說：

盤不必白，筒不必竹，馬不必琉璃。盤之尺寸亦未確，然無大差。刻本之圖則殊不類，今圖其布局如左。十二格分內六外六，皆謂之地，俱相對。內六通常有門，蓋譜所謂雙門。或亦無之，俾隨地定內外陣。依法設席必外陣在外而內陣在內，視室而定也。二人對局，一人以右的內，一人以左爲內。行馬俱由此內陣出，歷外陣而入人之內陣。馬謂之駒，呼 koma，亦謂之石，呼 ishi，視

（註一）　見勞榦"論西京雜記之作者及成書時代"（史語所集刊三十三本）。

（註二）　民國二十四年四月清華學報十卷二期。

采行馬，分行爲本。例如得采四與六，則一馬行四地，一馬行六地。必無可分，乃行一馬四地，再行六地，或先六後四。舉筒而撼必齊胸。撼時有所禱采，謂之乞目 (koime)，乞目不必大采，有時而乞其小。蓋孤駒有被切 (kiru) 之虞，敵衆有莫入之患。一地有敵二駒，則敵衆不敢入。孤駒獨居一地，敵至輒被切。切之言猶打，被打則置之溝中。得采還歸己之內陣。還陣必得其間，已有二駒無論敵我輒不得還。如是互行，輪駒入人之內陣，地各塞以二駒爲勝。故駒之數十有五，其用十二而已，行之視所緩急先後，一在乎籌之熟，計之確，尤在乎遇之巧。對局極重禮貌，不得論敵是非，不得乞不利人之目，不得悔。撼筒不得隱於盤下，不得以筒觸盤，不得以指入筒口傾骰，不得使筒口向上。傾骰落盤外，謝而不行。拾人之骰必讀其采而後取。徒然草敎人雙六毋求勝，但求無負。必計如何輒速負，雖爭一目亦求後負，其言雋永，不啻淮南。

顯然的，錢稻孫這篇論文的原意是想使人懂，並非存心使人不懂，不過他這篇文章做的失敗了。他受到了舊文章的表現法太深，此篇竟成爲無法了解的文章。只是看到了其他有關六博的材料以後，他的這篇雖然不能全懂，大部分還可以猜得出來，使得我們意識到日本雙陸還和六博大同小異，對于古代六博還是一種重要的參證。

從上文來看，可知六博一事牽涉到的是如何的廣泛。向前會涉及古代的狩獵生活，以及大射，鄉射，投壺等等各種禮節。向後涉及骰子，中國象棋，以及後世種種賭博的形式，並且間接可能和近東及歐洲的賭博發生若干關係。（歐洲的紙牌還可能是中國傳去的，又和印刷術的發展有關），這些事牽涉太廣，不屬於本篇範圍以內。不過無論如何，六博在中國人古代生活中，確占一顯著位置，是不容懷疑的。例如唐宋以來設想中的仙人娛樂，是圍棋；而在漢代，根據漢鏡和漢畫來看，却是六博，這一個轉變，使人更意識到六博在古代社會中的重要性了。

⑥ 唐代以後的投子

古代瓊（或䓔）的體製，在近世已經甚少看到，現在通行的都是六面的投子，這在第一段中已經說到。至於在什麼時代才開始變化呢？據程大昌演繁露，他說是起於唐代。演繁露卷六：

博之流爲樗蒱，爲握槊（卽雙陸也），爲呼博，爲酒令，體製雖不全同，而行塞勝負，取決於投，則一理也。蔡澤說范睢曰“博者或欲大投”，班固奕指曰：“博懸於投，不必在行”，投者擲也。桓玄曰：“劉毅樗蒱，一擲百萬”皆以投擲爲名也。古惟斲木爲子，一具凡五子，故名五木。後世轉而用石，用玉，用象，用骨。故列子之謂投瓊，律文之謂出玖，凡瓊與玖，皆玉名也。蓋謂博者借美名以命之，未必眞皆用玉也。御覽載繁欽威儀箴曰：“其有退朝，偃息閑居，操槩弄棊，文局樗蒱，言不及義，勝負是圖。”注：“槩，瞿營反，博子也。”槩之讀與瓊同，其字仍自從木，知其初制本以木爲質也。唐世則鏤骨爲竅，朱墨雜塗，數以爲采。亦有出意爲巧者，取相思紅子，納實竅中，使其色明現而易見。故溫飛卿艷詞曰：“玲瓏骰子安紅豆，入骨相思知也無？”凡此二者，卽今世通名骰子也。本書爲投，後轉爲頭。北史周文帝命丞郎擲樗蒱頭，則昔云投者逐轉爲頭矣。頭者，總首之義，自鏤骨爲骰以後，不惟五木舊制，壞沒不傳，而字直爲骰，不復爲投矣。若其體制，又全與用木時殊異矣。方其用木也，五子之形兩頭尖銳，中間平廣，狀似今之杏仁。惟其尖銳，故可轉躍，惟其平廣，故可以鏤采也。凡一子悉爲兩面，其一面塗黑，黑之上畫牛犢以爲之章，犢者牛子也。一面塗白，白之上卽畫雉，雉者，野雞也。凡投五子皆現黑則其名盧，盧者黑也，言五子皆黑也。五黑皆現，則五犢隨現，從可知矣。此在樗蒱爲最高之采，按木而擲，往往叱喝使致其極，故亦名呼盧也。其次五子四黑而一白，則是四犢一雉，則其采名雉，用以比盧，降一等矣。自此而降，白黑相雜，每每不同。故或名爲梟，卽鄧艾言云，六博得梟者勝也。或名爲犍，謂五木十擲輒犍，非其人不能是也。凡此采名樗蒱，雖經皆枚載，然反覆推較，率多駁而不通也。至於骰子之制，固知祖襲五木，然而詳略大率不同也。五木只有兩面，骰子則有六面，故骰子著齒自一至六，爲采亦益多。率其大者而言之，則是裁去五木兩頭尖銳而蹙長爲方，既有六面，又著六數，不比五木，但有白黑兩面矣。五木之制，至晉世猶復用木，然列子已言投瓊，則周末已嘗改玉骨也耶？或者形製仍同五木，而質已用玉石也。今世蜀地織綾，其文有兩尾尖削而中間寬廣者，旣不象花，亦非禽獸，乃遂名爲樗蒱。豈古制流於機織，至此尙存也耶？

古書言六博和樗蒱之制的，應以演繁露爲最詳。在演繁露中說明變盧雉爲一至六的數目始於唐代。這是一個非常珍貴的啓示，因爲盧雉和一至六的數目顯然是屬於兩個系統，唐代投子整個系統的轉變，應當不是逐漸轉換而成的，而是受了外來的影響。據現在可能知道的，大致用數目作點的投子，是從西方傳入的。等到六面而用點的投子採用以後，較爲簡明，原來盧雉的投子就再不爲人所採用了。

程氏依據詳明，只是有幾個誤解。古投子是四面的，他却認爲只有兩面，這種誤解一經發生，對於古樗蒱經改正的地方，就很有問題了。程氏引古樗蒱經只有四木（卽四個投子），程氏改爲五木，改爲五木是可以的，不過用四木也不見一定不對，因爲古代賭博的方法相當繁多，決不僅一種而止的。至於列子爲魏晉時人的書，程氏當時還不知道，因而對列子投瓊之說，不能得到適當的解釋。但他對於列子和其他史料的矛盾，已有相當的注意了。

附記：此篇承金發根先生精心校對，並提出意見，特此志謝。

仙人六博鏡

圖版一　日本梅原末治先生紹興古鏡聚英

圖版二　　倫敦 大英博物院 藏六博陶俑

圖版三　　　倫敦 大英博物館藏六博用的棋

圖版四　　四川 漢塼畫像

十、其他

論漢代的游俠

一　漢代的游俠與黃老的關係

關於游俠的概述，最好在史記游俠列傳來看（到漢書游俠傳和游俠傳序便和史記不同了）。我們可以想到，一種在社會上可以表現出來的形式和內容，都可以隨時代的變遷而有不同。在司馬遷的史記，游俠所代表的內容和形式，與後來班固所續載的並不完全相同。但班固在這一點所述，並未加區別。他只認爲他所說的游俠仍和從前一樣。但是他的態度和立場，便顯然的和司馬遷有些出入了。

史記游俠傳序說：

韓子曰：『儒以文亂法，而俠以武犯禁』，二者皆譏，而學士多稱於世云。至如以術取宰相卿大夫，輔翼其世主，功名俱著於春秋，因無可言者。若季次、原憲，閭巷人也。讀書懷獨行君子之德，義不苟合，當世亦笑之。故季次、原憲終身空室蓬戶褐衣蔬食不厭，死而已。四百餘年而弟子志之不倦。今游俠其行雖不軌於正義，然其言必信，其行必果，已諾必誠，不愛其軀，赴世之阨困旣已存亡死生矣，而不矜其能，羞伐其德，蓋亦有足多者焉。……鄙人有言曰，『何知仁義，已饗其利者有德』，故伯夷醜周餓死首陽山，而文武不以其故貶王，跖蹻暴戾，其徒誦之無窮。由此觀之，『竊鉤

者誅，竊國者侯，侯之門，仁義存』，非虛言也。今拘學或抱咫尺之
義久孤於世，豈若卑論儕俗，與世沈浮而取榮名哉？而布衣之徒，
設取予然諾，千里誦義，爲死不顧世，此亦有所長非苟而已也。故
士窮窘而得委命，此豈非人之所謂賢豪者耶？誠使鄉曲之俠，予季
次、原憲比權量力，效功於當世，不同日而論矣。要以功見言，信俠
客之義，又曷可少哉？古布衣之俠靡得而聞己，近世延陵、孟嘗、
春申、平原、信陵之徒，皆因王者親屬，藉於有土卿相之富厚，招
天　賢者，顯名諸侯，不可謂不賢矣，此如順風而呼聲非加疾，其
勢激也。至如閭巷之俠，修行砥名，聲施於天下，莫不稱賢，是爲
難耳。然儒墨皆擯不載。（班固游俠傳序文繁不引）

從上一段來看，所謂『游俠』的社會關係，顯然是『出於閭里』。亦即是
這一般人都不是（一）藉着帝王之親，卿相之勢，（二）田連阡陌之富豪，
（三）結駟連騎之游賈。同樣他們也不是過去之齊諸田，楚昭屈景。他們
假如以身分言，他們只是閭巷之細民；他們假如以貲財言，那就如魯朱家
之『家無餘財，衣不完采，食不重味，樂不過軥牛』，輕郭解的『家貧不
中眥』。又如河南劇孟『劇孟死，家無餘十金之財』，然而他們却有他們
社會上的威權，『天下騷動，宰相得之　若一敵國云』。卽是他們不倚賴
着金錢和權勢，但他們却有支配社會的力量。

　　他們的社會背景和一般有地位的人不同　，　所以他們的道德觀念也不
同；在有地位的人認爲道德的，他們會認爲不道德；在有地位的人認爲不
道德的，他們會認爲是道德。因此『何知仁義，已饗其利爲有德』，『竊鉤
者誅竊國者侯；侯之門，仁義存』，成了漢代初年的諺語。這是顯然的，
根據了另外一種的認識。從這一點認識出發，便在當時社會出現了許多特
殊的行爲，在他們自己當然是一貫的　，但在一般社會的信條上　，顯然不
合。假若說明社會立場之不同，那就用不着奇怪了。

自然，標準的俠者是閭里細民，但閭里細民却不定都是游俠。閭里細民之中仍然有商賈，有富有田宅之農民，有薄有田宅可以自給之農民，以及胼胝終年僅得一飽之農民，還有讀書懷獨行君子之德的士人。而在士人之中，又要算儒、墨兩種『顯學』的分子爲最多，這都是並看不起游俠的。在以上的各種人，游俠似乎任何類都不是。固然也有不少業餘的游俠，但最重要的游俠除去職業的游俠以外，似乎並無他種可能。因此，假若要說標準的游俠是一囘甚麼事，那就可以說他們是城郭中流動而頑强的閭里細民。憑着放縱的生活，不調協的精神，在禮法的空隙，走到另外的立場。

在漢代的游俠，顯然和黃、老之術有若干因緣，例如：

　　讀書陳平傳：少時家貧，好讀書，治黃帝、老子之術。……家迺負郭窮巷，以席爲門，然門外多長者車轍。

　　史記田叔傳：叔喜劍，學黃、老術於樂巨公所。叔爲人刻廉自喜，喜遊諸公，正義，諸公謂丈人行也。

　　史記汲黯傳：黯學黃、老之言……好學游俠，任氣節，內行修，好直諫，常犯主之顔色。

　　史記鄭當時傳：鄭當時字莊，孝文時，鄭莊以任俠自喜，脫張羽於尾，聲聞梁、楚之間。……莊好黃、老之言，其慕長者，如恐不見。

從以上幾條看來，游俠與黃、老有若干因緣，殊不可解。但假若明瞭黃、老爲民間的學術，正與游俠爲民間行誼相符合，那就不難解釋了。

　　游俠本爲閭里之雄，那在史記游俠傳及游俠傳序可以看得很明白。至於黃、老亦爲民間的學術，那也可以證明的。漢書儒林轅固傳：

　　竇太后好老子書，召問固，固曰：『此家人言耳』。太后怒曰：『安得司空城旦書乎？』

這裏所謂『家人言』，注家沒有確切的解釋，按史記魯周公世家云：『楚考烈王伐滅魯，魯頃公遷於下邑，為家人，魯絕祀』。漢書欒布傳：『彭越為家人時，嘗與布游』。注：『師古曰：家人言編戶之人也』。漢書武五子傳：『王莽時皆廢漢藩王為家人，（燕王）嘉猶以獻符命封扶美侯，賜姓王氏』。漢書中山衛姬傳：『王莽篡國，廢為家人，後歲餘卒』。所以『家人』就是『老百姓』；『家人言』就是閭巷市井的話，不是君相貴冑之間所應說的。——至於太后所說的『安得司空城旦書乎』？注引服虔曰：『道家以儒法為急，比之於律令也』，沈欽韓疏證曰：『說文：「獄司空也」，御覽六百四十三引風俗通曰：「詩云，宜犴宜獄，犴司空也」，漢以司空主罪人，故賈誼亦云：「輸之司空」』。沈注係釋服虔之說的，不過服虔是說錯了，沈注用的材料反而是對的。因為轅固看不起黃老，說他們是居民閭里之書；太后和他針鋒相對：『說既然不要平民之書，難道還要奴隸之書嗎？』司空就是刑獄，就是犯罪的刑徒或奴隸。沈氏用的材料是正對的，不過以釋服虔的話，那就有些不切當了。又城旦亦指犯罪的人而言，漢書惠帝紀：『當為城旦舂皆耐為鬼薪白粲』，注應劭曰：『城旦，旦起治城，婦人不豫外徭，但舂作米，四歲刑』。後漢書韓稜傳注：『前書音義曰：「城旦輕刑之名也，晝日伺寇，夜暮長城，故曰城旦」』。這也正和司空為刑徒有同樣的意義，倘若釋為法令之書那　有些費解了。

　　關於黃、老之學源於諸子中的老子，這件事可以不必多為爭辨。不過游俠在道家或黃老的教義之中，並未看出有多少的相關。倘若不就游俠之士和冶黃老之術者兩種人的社會地位來看　，　那就永遠不能解釋以前所引史記和漢書中所載的幾種現象。因此，我們從游俠和黃老同屬於社會中較低階級，即同屬於閭里及市井中人，那就對於這個看去不倫不類的現象得着一個假定的解釋了。

　　不過現在搜求游俠與黃老結合的材料，最早只能推溯到陳平。陳平讀黃老好游俠一事自然在其仗劍從軍之前。則其時期或可及於戰國的末期。因為陳平本為魏人，從秦滅魏至秦的滅亡共為十五年（始皇二十二年至二世二年）。陳平死於孝文二年，當時和陳平年輩相同的多已死去。假如他七十歲死去，則魏國亡時為三十歲，假如六十歲死去，則魏國亡時為二十歲。所以陳平見到魏國末年的游俠，應當是不成大問題的。

　　然而這種游俠與黃、老結合之風，只能到武帝時代為止。在武帝時代只有汲黯和武帝有舊恩，他才能做一個特殊的人物，在武帝時代存在下去。其餘的人就不再有相類的現象了。誠然武帝以後不是沒有黃、老學者，更不是沒有游俠，但却不見黃、老與游俠結合下去。這是黃老在漢初本為家人言，文帝以後就已漸漸的貴族化了。游俠本也是從戰國貴族養士之風衰熄以後就寄託在民間，但從景帝、武帝以後極端壓制，非倚賴貴族也不能自存。這兩支民間的學說和行動，都一變而寄託在非民間的基礎上，那就和寄託在非民間基礎上別的事情一樣，就用不著彼此常常結合了。

　　史記游俠傳序稱：『儒墨皆排擯不載』，可見游俠既非儒，亦非墨。亦即是游俠的行動並不要任何學術或思想做基礎。所謂或以為韓非言『儒以文亂法，俠以武犯禁』，而認為墨出於俠，是並無根據的。不過俠雖與道家並無思想上相承之序，却有若干思想上溝通之處。因為游俠本是一種傳奇式（romantic）的行動，出發點是任情適性，而不是在清規下的嚴肅生活，所以與儒墨俱不類，只有在道家之中可以適合。例如莊子的盜跖篇雖然是否莊周之言尚有爭執，但游俠行動的極致，也是如此。因此我們可以說游俠和黃老之結合，雖有偶然的成分，但游俠及黃老不相衝突却顯然的存在著。這種彼此的關係，到了三國的嵇康仍『好言老莊而尚奇任俠』，雖然他已不是平民了。

二　漢代游俠者與吏治

民間游俠的流行和黃老的得勢，都是漢代初年的狀況，但是這種情形，在當時已經有人不滿了。漢書賈誼傳：

今其甚者，殺父兄矣。盜者剟寢戶之簾，搴兩廟之器，白晝大都之中，剽吏而奪之金。矯偽者出幾十萬粟，賦六百餘萬錢，乘傳而行郡國，此其亡行義之先至者也。

注：師古曰：『此又言矯偽之人詐爲詔令，妄作賦斂，其數甚多，又詐乘傳而行郡國也。』王先謙補注曰：『案以上數事皆實有之。故誼臚舉以爲民亡行義之證。顏說近之。漢世奸俠橫行，談貨殖、游俠兩傳可以概見，不必執今疑古。酷吏傳，胡倩詐稱光祿大夫，言使督盜賊，止陳留傳。公孫勇衣繡衣乘駟馬車，亦其比也。』所以在漢初游俠的犯禁令，並不是一個如何罕見的事。然而這種對於游俠的禁令却一步一步的嚴下去。

以上所說的，是黃老與游俠並無相承之點，却是可以並容。但在儒家禮治和法家法治主張之下，決不容許游俠存在的。所以游俠在文帝時代已經開始被制裁，到了武帝時代政府就要和游俠顯著的敵對了。

文帝自己本人雖然是一個黃老學的信仰者，但從對於賈誼的尊重看來，就很有一個儒家或法家的趨勢。據史記游俠傳稱：『郭解，軹人也，解父以任俠，孝文時誅死。』可見文帝時國法還是不容許游俠的。在景帝時代據史記游俠傳所記，有符離人王孟、濟南人瞷氏、陳人周庸，都被景帝使人誅死，亦即是景帝對於游俠更不姑息。到了武帝時代，那就更顯然的，有若干可以作代表的例證。

在武帝時代，關東的豪富是要徙入關內的，名義上是守衛園陵，實際上是將地方勢力讓他們離開本土，並且容易監視。當時關東大俠郭解亦在徙中。史記游俠傳：

及徙豪富茂陵也，解家貧不中訾（索隱：案訾不滿三百萬以上為不中。）吏恐不敢不徙。衞將軍爲言郭解家貧不中徙。上曰：『布衣權至使得軍如言，此其家不貧，』解家遂徙。諸公送者出千餘萬。……解入關，關中賢豪知與不知聞其聲爭交權。……解爲人短小，不飲酒，未嘗有騎，已又殺楊季主，楊季主家上書，人又殺之闕下。上怒，乃下吏捕解，……窮治所犯，爲解殺者皆在赦前。軹有儒生侍使坐，客譽郭解。生曰：『郭解專以姦犯公法，何謂賢？』客聞，殺此生，斷其舌。吏以責解，解實不知，殺者亦莫知爲誰。吏奏解無罪，御史大夫公孫弘議曰：『解布衣，爲任俠行權，以睚眦殺人，解雖弗知此，罪甚於解殺之，當大逆無道。』遂族郭解。自是之後，爲俠者極衆，敖而無足數者，然關中長安樊仲子、槐里趙王孫、長陵高公子、西河郭公仲、太原鹵公孺、臨淮兒長卿、東陽田君孺，雖爲俠而逡逡退讓有君子之風。至若北道姚氏、西道諸杜、南道仇景、東道趙他、羽公子、南陽趙調之徒，此盜跖居民間者耳，何足道哉？此乃鄉者朱家所羞也。

郭解是游俠中稱爲領袖的；所以武帝一定要解決他，而公孫弘是儒生而兼法術的，亦必要族誅郭解而後快。在這二段記載之中，司馬遷對於游俠是同情的，只有下流的游俠他才指斥，因此可所看出他對於郭解的被殺是不滿意的。審問郭解的法吏是站在純法律的立場的，郭解殺人的證據不足，所以認爲應當無罪。但公孫弘却站在政治的立場，認爲郭解的罪不在尋常法律範圍之內，卽他的罪不僅在『任俠』，而更在『行權』，布衣行權，當大逆無道，於是郭解便伏最重的罪了。照此看來，任俠是當時一種風氣，勢難盡誅　只能誅游俠中的勢力最大，而侵犯了天子的威權的。因此在武帝時雖誅游俠而誅之不盡。

　　除去郭解之外，各地的地方主官在原則上是可以盡量誅游俠的。在漢書酷吏傳中，就頗有誅戮游俠的。以下便是酷吏傳中的幾則。

　　周陽由……所居郡必夷其豪。

　　義縱……遷爲河內過尉，至則族滅其豪穰氏之屬。……寧成……歸家，稱曰：『仕不至二千石，賈不至千萬，安可比人手？』迺貰貸陂田千餘頃假貧民，役使數千家，數年，會赦，致產數千萬，爲任俠，持吏短長，出從數十騎，其使民威重於郡守。……義縱自河內遷爲南陽太守，聞寧成家居南陽……至郡，遂按寧氏，破碎其家。成坐有罪，及孔暴之屬皆奔亡。（注師古曰：『孔氏、暴氏二家素豪猾者』，按宛孔氏見史記貨殖列傳。）

　　王溫舒……遷爲河內太守，素居廣平，皆知河內豪姦之家，……捕郡中豪猾，相連望千餘家。

　　嚴延年……爲涿郡太守，時郡比得不能太守，涿人畢野白等由是廢亂，大姓西高氏，東高氏，自郡吏以下皆畏避之，咸曰：『寧負二千石，無負豪大家』賓客放爲盜賊，發輒入高氏，吏不敢追浸浸日多，道路張弓拔刃然後敢行，其亂如此。……吏遣吏分考兩高，窮竟其姦，誅殺各數十人，郡中震恐，道不拾遺。

　　尹賞……以御史擧爲鄭令，永始、元延間，上怠於政，貴戚江陽（侯立）長仲兄弟交通輕俠，藏匿亡命，而北地大豪浩商等報怨，殺義渠長妻子六人，往來長安中，丞相御史遣掾求逐黨與，詔書召捕，久之乃得。長安中姦猾浸多，閭里少年羣輩殺吏，受賕報讐。相與探丸爲彈，得赤丸者斫武吏，得黑丸者斫文吏，白者主治喪。城中薄暮塵起，剽劫行者，死傷橫道，桴鼓不絕。賞以三輔高第選守長安令，得一切便宜從事。賞至修長安獄，穿地深各數丈，致令辟爲郭，以大石覆其口四名爲虎穴，乃部戶曹掾史與鄉吏、亭

長、里正、父老、伍人，雜舉長安中輕薄少年惡子，無市籍商販作
務，而鮮衣凶服，被鎧持人刀兵者，悉籍記之，得數百人，賞一朝
會長安吏，車數百輛，分行收捕 ， 皆劾以爲通行飲食羣盜。 賞視
閱，見十置一，其餘畫以次內虎穴，百人爲輩，覆以大石，數日壹
發視，皆相枕藉死。……賞所置皆其魁宿，故故吏善家子，失計隨
輕點，願自改者，財數十百人。皆貫其罪會立功以自贖。盡力有效
者因親用之爲爪牙，追捕甚精，甘者姦惡，甚於凡吏。

此外在漢代一般能吏之中，也可看見不少的人制來裁游俠。

又漢書趙廣漢傳：

察廉爲陽翟令，以治行尤異遷京輔都尉。守京兆尹，會昭帝崩，而
新豐杜建爲京兆掾，護作平陵方上。建素豪俠，賓客爲姦利。廣漢
聞之，先風告建不改，於是收案陵法。中貴人豪長者爲請無不至，
終無所聽。宗族賓客謀欲篡取，廣漢盡知其計議，主名，起居。使
吏告曰：『若計如此，且并滅家，令數吏將建棄市，莫敢近者，京
師稱之。……遷潁川太守。郡大姓原褚宗族橫恣，賓客犯爲盜賊，
前二千石莫能禽制，廣漢既至數月，誅原褚首惡，郡中震栗，先是
潁川豪傑大姓，相與爲婚姻。吏俗朋黨，廣漢患之，屬使其中可用
者受記，出有案問既得罪名行法罰之 ， 廣漢故漏泄其語， 合相怨
咎。又教吏爲詐莆，及得投書，削其主名，而託以爲爲豪傑大姓子
弟所言。其後疆宗大族，家家結爲仇讎，姦黨散落。……廣漢爲人
彊力，天性精於吏職……郡中盜賊，閭里輕俠，其根株所在，及吏
受取謂求，銖兩之姦皆知之。

漢書尹翁歸傳：

東海大豪、鄭、許仲孫爲姦猾亂吏治，郡中若之，二千石欲捕者，
輒以力勢變詐自解，終莫能制，翁歸至，論棄仲孫市一郡怖栗，莫

敢犯禁。

漢書王尊傳：

三老公乘興上書曰：（王尊）拜爲諫大夫守京輔都尉，行京兆尹事。尊盡節勞心，夙夜思職，卑體下士，屬奔北之吏，起沮傷之氣，二旬之間，大黨震壞，渠率效首。……長安宿豪大猾，東市賈萬，城西萬章，翦張禁，酒趙放、杜陵楊章等、皆通邪結黨，挾養姦執，上干王法，下亂吏治，幷兼役使，侵漁小民，爲百姓豺狼，更數二千石，二年莫能會討。尊以正法案誅，皆伏其辜。姦邪銷釋，吏民悅服。

漢書孫寶傳：

徵爲京兆尹，故吏侯文以剛直不苟合，常稱疾不肯仕。寶以恩禮請……以立秋日署文爲東部督郵，入見，勑曰，『今日鷹隼始擊，當順天氣取姦惡以成嚴霜之誅，掾部渠有其人乎』。文曰：『無其人不敢空受職』。寶曰：『誰也』。文曰：『霸陵杜穉季』。寶曰：『其次』。文曰：『豺狼當道　不宜復問狐狸』。寶默然。穉季者大俠，與衞尉淳于長下鴻臚蕭育等皆厚善。寶前失車騎將軍與紅陽侯有郤，自恐見危。時淳于長方貴幸，友寶，寶亦欲附之。始視事而長以穉季託寶。故寶窮無以俊應文。文悟寶氣衰，知其有故。因曰：『明府素著威名，今不敬取穉季，當且闓閤勿有所問、如此竟歲，吏民未敢誣明府也，卽度穉季而譴它事，衆口讙譁，終身自墮。』寶曰：『受教』。穉季耳目長，聞知之，杜門不通水火，穿舍後牆爲小戶，但持鉬自治園，因文所厚，自陳如此。文曰：『我與穉季幸同土壤，素無睚眥，顧受將命，分當相直，誠能自改嚴，將不治前事。卽不更心，但更門戶，適趣禍耳。』穉季遂不敢犯法，寶亦竟歲無所譴。明年穉季病死。寶爲京兆尹三歲，京師稱之。……種季子杜蒼，字君敖，名出種季右，在游俠中。

漢書何並傳：

舉能治劇爲長陵令，初邛或大后外家王氏賞，而侍中王林卿通輕俠，傾京師。坐法免，賓客愈盛。……先是林卿殺婢壻，埋冢舍，並具知之，以非已時，又見新免，故不發舉，欲無留界中而已。即且遣吏奉謁傳送。林卿素驕，慚於賓客，並度其爲變，儲兵馬以待之。林卿既去，北度涇橋，令騎奴還至寺門。拔刀剟其建鼓。……並……收傳冠奴，叱吏斷頭，還縣所縣鼓，署曰：『故侍中王林卿，坐殺人埋冢舍，使奴剟寺門鼓』。吏民驚駭，林卿因亡命。

又何並傳：

(鍾威)爲椽臧千金。陽翟趙季李款多畜賓客，以氣力漁食閭里，至姦人婦女，持吏長短，縱橫郡中，聞並且至皆亡去。並下車，求勇猛曉文法吏且十人，使交吏治三人獄，武吏往捕之，各有所數。數曰：『三人非負太守，迺負王法，不得不治，鍾威所犯多在赦前，驗使入函谷關，勿令汙民間，不入關。乃收之。趙李桀惡，雖遠去，當得其頭以謝百姓。』

從以上所引的各節看來，游俠們很顯然的與法吏相衝突。即游俠們所活動的理想世界，另外是一個範圍，而和法治是完全違背的。但是在維持綱紀的原則下，雖然盡量的消滅游俠，而政府的力量却仍然不能將游俠消滅淨盡。推其原因，不外：

(1) 游俠的活動範圍太廣了，而安心消滅游俠的只是少數的酷吏或幹吏。其餘軟弱些的官吏多只能讓游俠橫行。

(2) 即在酷吏或幹吏之中，亦僅能除其尤者，而不能將游俠的風氣完全熄滅。

（3）游俠之流往往和政治上最有勢力的人互相句結。

（4）游俠往往是世爲游俠。

以上幾點在以上所舉各例之中，可以看的清楚，無需多爲徵證，但還有一個重要之點，即最高政權當然和游俠不能相容。但遇見臣下與君上的衝突，其嚴重性超過游俠的嚴重性，那就君主有時可以對於游俠作爲姑息的考慮。例如漢書公孫賀傳：

> 賀子敬聲代賀爲大僕，父子並居公卿位。敬聲以皇后姊子驕奢不奉法，征和中，擅用此軍錢千九百萬，發覺下獄。是時治捕陽陵朱安世，不能得，上求之急。賀自請逐捕安世以贖敬聲罪，上許之。後某得安世。安世者，京師大俠也。聞賀欲贖子，笑曰：『丞相禍及宗矣。南山之竹不足受我辭，斜谷之木不足爲我械』。安世遂從獄上書，告敬聲與陽石公主私通，及使人巫祭祠詛。上且上甘泉，當馳道理偶人，祝詛有惡言。下有司案驗賀，窮治所犯，遂父子死獄中，家族。巫蠱之禍起於朱安世，成於江充，遂及主公、皇后、太子皆敗，語在江充戾園傳。（又見劉屈氂傳詔）。

巫蠱之禍爲武帝時一件大事。自然原來的動機是迷信而可笑的，但是皇帝確認爲是一個非常嚴重而損害及於皇帝本身的情態，因此便不能不放鬆游俠而着重於巫蠱了。不過這却是一個偶然的特例，不屬於一般的狀態的，就大體而言，『自魏其、武安、淮南之徒，天子切齒』，自武帝以後，游俠之徒，就決不能像漢初那樣的可以特立獨行了。

三　漢代游俠者的生活

游俠之徒差不多都是不事生產的分子，他們之中最著名的都是『家無餘財』，例如：

史記游俠傳：魯朱家……先從貧賤始，家無餘財。

又：劇孟行大類朱家而好博，多少年之戲。然劇孟母死，自遠方送葬者蓋千乘，及劇孟死，家無餘十金之財。

又，郭解……及徙茂陵也，解貧不中訾。

因此，在游俠之徒，一定有一種辦法來維持生活和施濟別人，決不會像『季次、原憲終身空室蓬戶，褐衣蔬食不厭死而已』，因爲照這樣關起蓬門而獨善其身，決不會發生力量的，漢代游俠既能發生力量，必有其經濟的來源。照司馬遷所說：『古布衣之俠，靡得而聞已，近世延陵、孟嘗、春申、平原、信陵之徒，皆因王者親屬，藉於有土卿相之富厚招天下賢者，顯名諸侯』。這就是說，據司馬遷所知道的，游俠之徒，在延陵季及戰國四公子時已經開始，亦卽春秋、戰國之際，有一部分貴族，憑着他自己的貴族收入，養了若干的俠士。這一種類型後來是有的，如秦時的呂不韋，漢時的吳王濞、淮南王安、魏其侯竇嬰、武安侯田蚡之流，以至於漢末的王氏五侯，都屬於這種類型之下。然而漢代假認正宗的游俠，却屬於司馬遷所稱的：『自秦以來，匹夫之俠湮滅不見，余甚恨之。以余所聞，漢興有朱家、田仲、王公、劇孟、郭解之徒，雖捍當世之文罔，然其私義廉潔退讓，有足稱者，名不虛立，士不虛附。至如朋黨宗彊，比周設財，役貧豪暴，侵凌孤弱，恣欲自快，游俠亦醜之。余悲世俗不察其意而猥以朱家、郭解等令與暴豪之徒同類而笑之也』。在游俠傳中所記，游俠中的『長者』，與豪暴之徒也看不出太大的差異。只有一點是不同的，卽正宗游俠是『修行砥名』，『廉潔退讓』，而豪暴之徒則爲『比周設財，役貧豪暴』。亦卽正宗的俠是出發點不是爲着自己的錢財與享受，爲的是重取予，尊然諾，救人之急，不避禍難。至於爲達到這個目的的手段，那就決不要循着公認的道德及法律的標準，但看四公子的列傳和游俠列傳便可曉然。並且我們可以看的很清楚，凡是游俠的領袖，他們並不屬於士農工商中的某種職業，他們却屬於職業的游俠者。他們除去簡單而節儉的生活以外，需要大量的收入才可應付大量的支出。這些大量的支出，和鄭當時行千里不裹糧一樣（據史記汲鄭列傳，鄭亦游俠者），都是從朋友們送來的。至於朋友們的錢從何而來，游俠之中並無『不飲盜泉』的信條，當來就不問所由來了。

　　游俠之徒是以游俠爲職業的，至少也是以游俠當做一種事業來看。因此他們的收入也是同情於他們的人來餽贈。例如郭解傳：『解家逐徙，諸公送者出千餘萬』，萬章傳：『石顯貲巨萬，當去，留牀席器物數百萬直，欲以與章。』樓護傳：『護坐免爲庶人，其居位爵祿賂遺，亦緣手盡』。都可以看出其中的消息。不過游俠之徒，不事家人生產作業，其生活所需究竟是一小部份，在游俠者支出之中不算占很大的地位，所以也就未爲記載的人所注意。至於餽贈的人當然也就是平時養客的人，除過貴戚、達官、豪右之外，還有養客的商人，例如蜀的卓氏。到這幾種都沒有時，就可能如郭解傳所說：『藏命作姦，剽攻不休，及鑄錢掘冢』了。這些事情在郭解一類的游俠，晚年是不做的，因爲他已成名，不需要此；但是假若這一類的人真是要餽贈他，他是不是拒受呢？在此，便不能以公認的道德來量度了。

　　在史記游俠傳中，游俠之著者如朱家、田仲魯人，劇孟周人，郭解河內人，其餘如長安樊仲子、槐里趙王孫、長陵高公子俱關中人　魯、周及河內似乎和當地的經濟發展有關。關中首善之區爲貴戚王侯之所在。至後『州郡之豪傑，五都之貨殖，三選七遷，充奉陵邑』，於是五陵（見漢書原涉傳注）更爲游俠之會，其中家風世尙，在在相因，但已經決不是舊時的不事王侯了。

　　至於北邊之俠如西河郭公仲、太原鹵公孺之流，則又如史記貨殖傳所稱：『地邊胡，數被寇，……好氣任俠爲姦，不事農商；然迫近北夷，師旅亞住，中國委輸，時有奇羨』，則是任俠之徒亦自有其經濟的來源，可以供應其必要的開支了。

游俠之徒彼此當然互有聯繫，但還說不上堅強的組織。史記郭解傳：『然其自喜爲俠益甚，旣已振人之命不矜其功，其陰賊有於心本，發於睚眦如故云。而少年慕其行，亦輒爲報仇，不使知也』。又朱家傳：『田仲以俠聞、喜劍、父事朱家』，在此可以看出游俠們對於前輩是如何的尊敬和致力。不過游俠與游俠彼此間不過只有友誼上的關係而無組織上的關係。但看竇嬰、灌夫、汲黯、鄭當時的賓客，可去可留，其間並無若何的拘束。只是交誼範圍旣廣，雖無一定的組織，也自然形成了一個社會結構，但憑着人與人的關係，也可以發生很大的力量。況且在這個社會包括了許多亡命之徒，當然力量更要大些。此外在漢代游俠之中，雖然找不到任何大的組織的痕跡，但在若干小團體之中仍然有其組織，例如張敞傳中所記偸盜的會長。

游俠旣然屬於民間的習俗，在當時只發展到一種小的組織，而並無大的結合，所以到西漢末年民間勢力蜂起的赤眉和平林，也只有比較小的組織一擴張到比較大的範圍，便窮於應付了。這雖然和游俠不完全相關，但假如已經有了游俠的組織，不會不充分應用的。（例如當時起兵中最以謹慎著稱的漢光武帝，便有游俠的現象存在着。後漢書董宣傳稱湖陽公主謂『文叔爲白衣時，藏亡匿死，吏不敢至門，今爲天子，威不行一令乎』，藏亡匿死便是游俠的行爲。但看起兵時的光武對於民衆的組織並無貢獻，只是後來儘量政治上的組織，便可見民間社會自己並無政治以外的任何組織的。）但是到了太平道及五斗米道組織就嚴密些了。這就顯示著，民間祕密社會組織是隨著宗教的發展而發展的。從後來道教儘量的抄襲佛教看來，這種現象也許就是因爲東漢以後佛教傳入中國，因之太平道和五斗米道的組織也多受少了若干影響。我們還可以說游俠雖然在西漢前期到西漢後期已經有些變質，但是從西漢到東漢，到魏晉，到唐，雖然時代越長越會變質，却仍然保存着若干類似之點。此外佛教和摩尼教的組織却隨着時代的進展而深深印在市井閭里之間。從這兩點發展下去，又可形成爲種種的因素，這些種種因素配列和組合起來又可成爲種種現象，我們雖然因爲材料不够不能十分確指，但對於紅巾和白蓮教種種組織，似乎可以從此得到若干的啓示。

西漢的游俠作成民間社會中的領袖的這件事實，雖然在武帝時代被摧毀了。但游俠的若干行動，仍舊保存下來。不僅在西漢晚期，如豪爽、輕財、藏亡匿死、結客、報仇，甚至於作姦犯科，都是仍舊的流行著，就到了東漢仍然還是很流行著。只有陰興等少數人的『門無俠客』，爲世所稱。而東漢親貴如竇融、馬援且都曾有游俠的痕迹。試看一看後漢書中，如馬武、竇憲、趙喜、桓譚、翟酺、申屠蟠、郅惲、虞章、鍾離意、魏朗、郭太、賈游、許荆、陽球、周黨各傳，便知復仇的事，在東漢一代是如何的被重視。同樣再看一看東漢一代門生故吏的忠於府主，不計死生，也顯著然仍是游俠的遺風，所以武帝之　，雖然法網頗密，使得閭里中人不敢過分的以游俠自居，使得漢書游俠傳中後續的游俠，有些變質。然而只要社會上有這一種需要，那就這一種的現象便會有一天的保存著。

論漢代陸運與水運

兗、冀、靑、徐為中國古代文化發揚之地。嶢函以西故為戎狄之所薦居。自春秋、戰國以迄於漢，猶可於典籍中窺見邦國之富庶，人才之茂美，皆東勝於西。惟秦起西陲，以河渭之間為國家根本，集東方之財富以實西方。漢繼秦規，一循前代強幹弱枝之術。讀史者遂覺西方富實堪與東方相埒。況西北高原對河濟文化之區勢成居高臨下，農藝之民艱於守禦，有國者不得不悉其國力以防胡虜之南侵。於是邦國之政事與軍備皆北重於南，陸重於海；而西北之區遂為國家首善。然以民族發展之方位言之，則經濟發展之趨向在南而不在北，國防發展之趨向在北而不在南。當茲紛紜矛盾交織之中，使民族前途陷於彷徨無主之岐路。對北對南遂咸不能開發盡致。

漢代為擁有人口六千萬之大國，其國力之充沛富實，並世無兩。若就其國力以從事發展，自宜無往不捷。第以匈奴亦為同時大國，雖富庶弗如，而強毅善戰。漢憑其有效之國家組織與其富庶之國力，積數世經營之力，僅乃克之，而使單于伏闕稱臣。徒以塞上苦寒，不便耕殖，飛芻輓粟，艱苦百端。雖王師屢絕大漠，而郡縣之設，但到漠南。於是漠北雄區常為胡人休養生息之地，北邊烽候亭障之防，無復已時。此數千年來所為致慨於平戎無上策也。今於漢世水陸交通略述其大要，以見漢朝帝國雖賴陸運以維持國家之完整，供給國防之軍資，而緣海之地則海運常重於陸運。漢人非不明海事，徒以陸上危機大於緣海。其間不能不有所輕重。此所以海南諸國，一葦可航，而卒不能成為『中朝』內地也。

(甲)陸運

西漢京都雖在長安，然人口集中之處，實在關東。故以發號施令言，則天下之道集中於京師。自京師以西，則自渭城經天水、隴西、金城以及河西四郡，度玉門而至西域。京師西北，則自渭城、雲陽以至安定、北地。京師以北則自櫟陽、上郡、西河、以至五原。京師東北則自華陰渡河以至河東、太原、而北至燕、代。京師以南，則自鄠以南爲斜谷道，自陳倉以南爲陳倉道，自杜陵以南爲子午道，皆會於南鄭，經劍門入蜀。而京師之東則關東道路咸集於洛陽經函谷以至於京師，故宏農、河南爲天下重鎮。此西漢時京師與天下交通之大凡也。至於東漢，則洛陽爲京師，京師財富惟關東是賴。長安爲陵墓所在，保有三輔舊名，然其重要不在財富而在國防，方之西漢洛陽，爲稍減矣。

然此特就國家行政之道路而言耳。以當時貨殖之道路而言，則此猶未盡也。當時天下之財富在關東，關東之財富湊於齊、梁，而道路之中樞，實在梁國。韓、魏風稱天下之樞（戰國策）。張儀說魏王，謂爲『地四平，諸侯四通，條達輻湊，無名山大川之險。』陶在戰國及漢初爲魏邑，而史記貨殖傳謂范蠡『之陶爲朱公，朱公以陶爲天下之中，諸侯四通，貨物所交易也。』戰國時魏冉爲秦穰侯，執秦政柄，獨以陶爲封邑（史記穰侯列傳）。漢高帝平項羽，卽天子位，亦獨在陶（漢書高帝紀）。及西漢時，濟陰一郡，爲全國人口最密之處。可知西漢之世，天下之湊在定陶而不在洛陽。

若以陶爲中心而衡論之，則其東北爲臨菑，故爲齊都；西漢初年巳至十萬戶（漢書高五王傳）。西北爲邯鄲，故爲趙都；邯鄲之北則爲涿與薊；其南則壽春，故爲楚都，其西則洛陽。其西南則爲南陽之宛與潁川之陽翟，地理志稱宛有四萬七千五百四十七戶；稱陽翟有四萬一千六百五十戶，十萬九千口。此皆河濟間大平原之都會也。若自此而南，見於史記所記者，則若成都，若江陵，若會稽，若合肥，若番禺（並見史記貨殖傳），亦稱要地矣。

漢書賈山傳云：

> 『爲馳道於天下，東窮燕、齊，南極吳、楚。江湖之上，瀕海之觀畢至。道廣五十步，三丈而樹。厚築其外，隱以金椎，樹以靑松，爲馳道之麗至於此。』

此所言爲秦之馳道，或有辯士誇飾之言，未敢卽引爲信據。卽令有之，亦始皇巡幸時方有此制，非平時所應有。觀漢武巡幸朔方，事出偶然，卽或千里無亭障（漢書武帝紀）。又當漢武有疾，義縱且不治甘泉道（漢書酷吏傳）。始皇雖濫用民力，然謂通秦之世，通天下之馳道皆如此，恐未必然也。惟秦世於道路固嘗致力，則從西南夷之開發，略可概見。史記西南夷列傳云：

> 『始楚威王時將軍莊蹻將兵循江上，略巴蜀黔中以西。……秦時常頗略通五尺道，諸此國頗置吏焉。』

此所謂『五尺道』卽秦通西南夷之道，索隱云：『謂棧道廣五尺』其言是也。至漢高所焚之斜谷棧道，尤顯屬故秦時所開，事有明徵，可不待論。

迄於漢代，道路之開闢與增築，歷見於史籍碑銘。如蜀郡太守蜀郡何君開閣道碑云：

> 『蜀郡太守平陵何君遣掾臨邛舒鮪，將徒治道，造尊楗閣，袤五十五丈，用功千一百九十八日。建武中元二年六月就道。史任雲陳春主。』（隸釋四）

又漢中太守鄐君開襃斜道碑云：（據歷史語言研究所藏拓本，下同。）

> 『永平六年，漢中郡以詔書受廣漢蜀郡巴郡徒二千六百九十人開通襃余道，大守鉅鹿鄐君，部掾治級王弘，史苟茂，張宇韓岑等興功作。大守丞廣漢楊顯將。相用始作橋格六百二十三間，大橋五，爲道二百五十八里。郵亭、驛置，徒司空，襃中縣官寺，幷六十四所。凡用功七十六萬六千八百餘人。凡卅六萬九千八百四器用錢。百四十九萬九千四百餘斛粟。九年四月成就，益州東至京師，去就安隱。』

又析里橋郙閣頌云：

> 『惟斯析里，處漢之右……緣崖鑿石，處隱定柱，臨深長淵，三百餘丈，接木相連，號爲萬柱。過者慄慄，載乘爲下。常車迎布，歲數千兩，遭遇隤納，人物俱隕。沈沒洪淵，酷烈爲禍，自古迄今，莫不創楚，於是太守漢陽阿陽李君諱翕字伯都……乃俾衡官掾下辯仇審，改解危殆，卽便求隱，析里大橋於今乃造。校致工堅，□□工巧；雖昔魯班，亦莫擬象，又醳散關之嶔嶔，從朝陽之平燥，減西□□高閣，就安寧之石道。……』

在前各則中可以見工程之鉅，用時之久，在後一則中可見當漢世中已漸從棧柱改爲石道矣。此其例也。

就兩漢書所記，治道之事尤多。漢書武帝紀元光五年：

『夏，發巴蜀卒治南夷道；又發卒萬人治雁門阻險。』

又漢書武帝紀元封四年：

『行幸雍，祠五時，通回中道。』

後漢書順帝紀延光三年：

『十月，乙亥，詔益州刺史罷子午道，通襃斜路。』

後漢書王霸傳：

『十三年，盧芳與匈奴烏桓連兵，寇盜尤數；緣邊愁苦。詔霸將施刑徒六千

餘人。與杜茂作飛狐道，堆石布土，築起亭障。』

後漢書杜茂傳：

『作飛狐道，堆石布土，築起亭障，自代至平城三百餘里。』

皆為築道之事，至於後漢書衛颯傳稱在含洭，湞陽，曲江，三縣，『鑿山通道五百

餘里，刋亭障，置郵驛』又後漢書鄭弘傳：『奏開零陵，桂陽嶠道，於是夷通，至

今遂為常路。』則皆以陸路代水運之事。然特於中原嶺南之間增一通路，較為便利

而已，水運固始終未廢也。

漢代之道路既於其境域之中無所不達，故凡陸路大都可以行車。巴蜀之道素稱

天下之險，然行車之事，亦固其常。前引析里橋郙閣頌云『常車迎布，歲數千兩』

可見蜀中來往，車乘之繁。又漢書王尊傳云：

『先是王陽為益州刺史，至邛崍九折阪，歎曰：「奉先人遺體，奈何數乘此

險」。後以病去。及尊為刺史，至其阪，問吏曰：「此非王陽所畏道耶」？

吏對曰：「是」。尊叱其馭曰：「驅之！王陽為孝子，王尊為忠臣。」』

漢書司馬相如傳：

『上拜相如為中郎將，建節往使。副使者王然于，壺充國，呂越人，馳四乘

之傳，因巴蜀吏幣物以賂西南夷。至蜀，太守以下郊迎。』

後漢書張堪傳：

『蜀郡計掾樊顯進曰：「漁陽太守張堪昔在蜀漢，仁以惠下，威能討姦。前

公孫述時，珍寶山積。捲握之物，足富十世。而堪去職之日，乘折轅車，布
被囊而已。』』

此蜀中之車也。漢書朱買臣傳：

『買臣隨上計吏爲卒將重車至長安。』

『會稽太守且至，發民除道，縣吏並送迎，車百餘乘入吳界。』

後漢書趙曄傳；

『會稽人也，少嘗爲縣吏，奉檄迎督郵。曄恥於斯役。遂棄車馬去。』

此會稽之車也。漢書南越王趙佗傳：

『佗乃乘黃屋左纛，稱制與中國侔。』

此南海之車也。後漢書循吏傳：

『孟嘗遷合浦太守被徵當還 。 民攀車請之 。 嘗既不得進，乃載鄉民船夜遁
去。』

此合浦之車也。後漢書臧宮傳：

『將兵屯駱越，……越人謀畔從蜀，宮兵力少，不能制。會屬縣送委輸車數
百乘至，宮夜使鋸斷門限，令車聲回轉出入，至旦，越人候伺者聞車聲不絕
而門限斷，相告以漢兵大至。』

駱越在南郡，此南郡有車也。

故漢代漢人所至，亦卽車之所至。此與後世江淮以南鮮用車者頗異。惟嶺嶠之
間 ， 路初未闢，故漢書嚴助傳云；『今發兵行數千里，資衣糧入越地，輿轎而隃
嶺。』是則非可以行車者。然至後漢時亦漸開通。後漢書鄭弘傳云：

『建初八年代鄭衆爲大司農。舊交阯七郡，貢獻轉運皆從東治泛海而至，風
波艱阻，沈溺相係。弘奏開零陵桂陽嶠道，於是夷通，至今遂爲常路。』

此路既通，故嶺嶠之間，遂有車騎以返中原。後漢書吳祐傳云：

『父恢爲南海太守，祐年十二，隨從到官。恢欲殺靑簡以寫經書，祐諫曰：
「今大人踰越五嶺，遠在海濱，其俗誠陋。然舊多珍怪，上爲國家所疑，下
爲權戚所望，此書若成，則載之兼兩。」』

祐之仕宦在安、順時，其十二歲當在和帝時，是嶺嶠之道路固已通達，故云『載之

兼兩』矣。

凡山區之縣邑道路，亦有至東漢方始開闢者。後漢書循吏衛颯傳曰：

> 『先是含洭，湞陽，曲江三縣，越之故地。武帝平之，內屬桂陽。民居深
> 山，濱溪谷，習其風土，不出田租，去郡遠者，或且千里。吏事往來，輒發
> 民乘船，名曰傳役，每一吏出，徭及數家。百姓苦之。颯乃鑿山通道五百餘
> 里，列亭障，置郵驛。』

此嶺南縣邑中有至後漢方始開通者。然關西亦有竟不得開通而用水運者。後漢書虞
詡傳：

> 『遷武都太守。……先是運道艱險，舟車不通。驢馬負載僦五致一。詡乃自
> 將吏士，案行川谷。由沮至下辯數十里，皆燒石剪木，開漕船道。以人僦直
> 雇借備者。於是水運通利，歲省四千餘萬。』

則僻處之區，不足以國道論矣。

漢世道路之在平原者，仍爲土路。若遇大雨，難以通行。陳勝吳廣爲秦屯長，
天大雨失期乃舉事（史記陳涉世家）。則自秦已然。蔡邕述行賦云；

> 『余有行於京洛兮，遷淫雨之經時。塗迤邐其蹇連兮，潦汙滯而爲災。……
> 路阻敗而無軌兮，塗濘溺而難遵。……佇淹留以候霽兮，感憂心之殷殷。』

此平原大雨，道不能通也。又三國魏志曹眞傳：

> 『眞以八月發長安，從子午道南入。司馬宣王泝漢水，當會南鄭。諸軍或從
> 斜谷道，或從武威入（按威當作都，本傳誤）。會大霖雨三十餘日，或棧道
> 斷絕，詔眞還軍。』

是則山中之棧道當大雨時亦不能通行。不僅平原爲然矣。

漢世在京師與郡國，以及郡國之間，皆有驛傳。驛傳之用，驛以通郵書，傳以
發車乘。漢書高帝紀注如淳引漢律曰：

> 『四馬高足爲置傳，四馬中足爲馳傳，四馬下足爲乘傳，一馬二馬軺傳，急
> 者乘一乘傳。』師古曰：『傳者若今之驛，古者以車，謂之傳車。其後又單
> 置馬，謂之驛騎。』

其驛騎之置則漢世三十里一置（續漢書輿服志）。惟南海獻龍眼荔枝，『十里一置，

五里一候』爲特例（後漢書和帝紀）。有急，則一日可行四五百里。漢書王温舒傳云：

> 『遷爲河內太守，⋯⋯令郡具私馬五十匹爲驛，自河內至長安⋯⋯奏行不過
> 二日，得可，事論報。』

據續漢書郡國志注，河內去洛陽百二十里，洛陽去長安九百五十里，凡河內至長安一千七十里。奏行二日，是每日可行五百里也。又漢書趙充國傳云：

> 『六月戊申奏，七月甲寅，璽書報從充國計焉。』

洪邁容齋四筆曰：

> 『金城至長安一千四百五十里，往返倍之。中間更下公卿議臣，而自上書
> 得奏報，首尾纔七日爾。案初學記二十，漢舊儀云，「驛三騎行日夜千里
> 爲程。」』

若以公卿議一日，往返六日計之，則一日當行五百里矣。漢書霍光傳：

> 『蓋主，上官桀，安，及弘羊皆與燕王旦通謀，詐令人爲燕王上書。⋯⋯
> 上曰「⋯⋯朕知是書詐也，將軍亡罪。」光曰：「陛下何以知之。」上曰：
> 「將軍之廣明，都郎屬耳。調校尉以來，未能十日，燕王何以得知之？」』

按續漢郡國志注，薊在洛陽東北二千里，長安在洛陽西九百五十里。自燕至長安往返約六千里。每日行千里則六日可畢。今昭帝以未及十日不能往返，是驛騎在平時決無一日行千里之事。若以每日行五百里計，十二日始行六千里，不及十日不能達到。如此，與昭帝之語意方能切合。然則初學記所引漢舊儀，驛三騎行日夜千里爲程，不合於漢世實際情況矣。（以上之里俱指漢里）。

居延漢簡中有『以亭行』，『隧次行』，『以郵行』，『吏馬馳行』者。如

『甲渠鄣候以亭行』（三三、二八）

『肩水□隧次行』（二八八、三〇）

『肩水候以郵行（張掖都尉更九月庚午卒孫惠以來）』（七四、四）

『肩水候官吏馬馳行（甲辰十二月丙寅盡□〇入卒外人以來）』（二〇、一）

其以亭行或以隧次行者，則就亭隧而傳遞。以郵行當由驛馬傳遞，而云吏馬馳行，則緊急公文矣。漢世凡公文之緊急以赤白爲囊，謂之奔命書，見丙吉傳，則所謂馳

行者，殆即是矣。

官家所發之車曰傳車，已見前引高紀如淳注。今按傳即符，漢世或曰傳，或曰符，見居延漢簡。漢書宣帝紀本始四年『民以車船載穀入關者，得毋用傳。』注師古曰：『傳符也』。漢書文帝紀二年九月：『初與郡守爲銅虎符』。注應劭曰：『銅虎符第一至第五，國家當發兵，遣使者至郡合符，符合乃聽受之。竹使符皆以竹箭五枚，長五寸，鐫篆書第一至第五。』又注，師古曰：『與郡守爲符者，謂各分其半，右留京師，左以與之。』此太守取自京師，爲發兵之符也。藝文類聚職官部引漢官解詁『衛尉主宮闕之內，……皆施籥於門……皆復有符，符用木長二寸（案當作尺二寸），以當所屬兩字爲鐵印，亦大卿兵符，當出入者。』此宮廷門禁之符也。後漢書陳蕃傳：『刺史周景辟爲別駕從事。以諫爭不合，投傳而去。』注：『投棄也，傳謂符也。』此郡縣之符也。居延漢簡：『□居延都尉，行塞藿隧，移過所』（四五、二八），過所者，周官司關鄭注云：『傳如今移過所文書』。又馬縞中華古今注卷中：『程雅問，「傳者云何？」答曰：「傳以木爲之。長一尺五寸，書符信其上，又一板封以御史印章，所以爲符信，即今之過所也。」』此行旅之符也。本作傳，傳車之傳即從此而言。至於東漢，遂廢傳車。晉書刑法志引魏新律序『秦世舊有廄置，乘傳副車食廚，漢初承秦不改。後以費廣稍省，故後漢但設騎置，而無車馬，律猶著其文，則爲虛設。故除廄律，取其可用合科者以爲郵驛令。』故漢世之季惟通行過所之名，傳之稱轉廢，而鄭氏云：『傳如今移過所文書』矣。漢書王莽傳：『徵天下通知逸禮，古記，天文，歷算，鍾律，小學，史篇，方術，本草，以及五經，論語，孝經，爾雅，教授者，在所爲駕一封軺傳。』注，如淳曰：『律，「當乘傳及發駕置傳者，皆持尺五寸木傳信，封以御史大夫印章。其乘傳參封之。」參三也。有期會累封兩端，端各兩封，四封也。乘馳驛傳，五封也，兩端各二，中央一也。軺傳兩馬再封之，一馬一封也。』師古曰：『以一馬駕軺車而封傳』。故以前引高紀如淳注對照言之，則馳傳五封，謂四馬高足也，期會者四封，謂四馬中足也；發駕置傳者三封，謂四馬四足也。此皆就馬之優劣以爲區別者也（漢驛馬分爲上中下三等，就馬籍中各馬分別標出之，見後引居延簡）。皆封以御史大夫以爲信。其二馬之軺傳，亦封以御史大夫印章。至在所爲駕一封軺傳，則由郡縣之印封之，不必用御史印章矣。居延漢簡云：

『告尉爲傳』（二一八、四三）。

『元延二年十月乙酉，居延令尙，丞忠，移過所縣道河津關，遣亭長王豐以詔書買騎馬酒泉、敦煌、張掖郡中，當言舍舍，從者如律令。一守令史謝，佐褒。十月丁亥出。居延令印，十月丁亥出』（一七〇、三）。

此傳或言『告尉』，或以縣印一封之。則亦當爲駕一封軺傳也。

簡言『當言傳舍』傳舍卽郵亭。可以止宿者。漢書灌夫傳：『乃戲縛夫，置傳舍。』霍光傳：『去病……爲驃騎將軍擊匈奴，河東太守郊迎，置平陽傳舍』。薛宣傳：『至陳留，其縣郵亭橋梁不修。』注，師古曰：『郵亭行書之舍，亦如今之驛及行道館也。』翟方進傳附翟義傳：『義行太守事，行縣至宛。丞相史在傳舍，立持酒肴，謁丞相史。』魏相傳：『御史大夫桑弘羊詐稱御史至傳。』田廣明傳：『故城父令公孫勇，與客胡倩等謀反。倩詐稱光祿大夫，言使督盜賊止陳留傳舍，太守謁見，欲收取之。廣明覺知，發兵皆捕斬焉。』嚴延年傳：『母從東海來，到雒陽，適見報囚。母大驚，便止都亭，不肯入。』黃霸傳：『吏不敢舍郵亭，食飲道旁，烏攫其肉。』司馬相如傳：『於是相如舍都亭。』後漢書光武紀：『光武乃自稱邯鄲使者入傳舍。傳吏方進食。從者饑，爭奪之。傳吏疑其僞，乃椎鼓數十通。』郭伋傳：『行部旣還先期一日，伋爲違信於諸兒，遂止於野亭中，須期乃入。』謝夷吾傳注引謝承書曰：『行部始到南陽縣，遇孝章皇帝巡狩，有詔刺史入傳，錄見囚徒。誠長吏勿廢舊儀，朕將親覽焉。上臨西廂南面，夷吾處東廂，分帷隔中央。夷吾所決一縣三百餘事，事與上合。』李郃傳：『縣召署幕門候吏。和帝卽位，分遣使者皆微服單行，各至州縣，觀采風謠。使者二人當到益部，投郃候舍。』趙孝傳：『嘗從長安還，欲止郵亭。亭長先時聞孝當還，以有長者客，掃洒待之。孝旣不自名。長不肯內。因曰：「聞田禾將軍子當從長安來，何時至乎？孝曰：「尋至矣」。於是遂去。』衛颯傳：『颯乃鑿山通道五百餘里，列亭傳，置郵驛。』任文公傳：『遣五從事檢行郡界，僭伺虛實，共止傳舍。』三國志魏志張魯傳：『諸祭酒皆作義舍，如今之亭傳。』御覽一九四引風俗通：『謹案春秋國語，置有寓室，謂今亭也，民所安定也。亭有樓，從高省，丁聲也。漢家因秦，大率十

里一亭。亭留也。今語有亭留，亭待，蓋亭行旅宿食之所館也。』御覽六九三引桓
譚新論：『余從長安歸沛，道病。蒙絮被，絳罽襜褕，乘驛馬，宿於下邑東亭中，
亭長疑是賊，夜發卒來攻，余令吏勿鬪，乃相問，解而去。此安靜自存也。』周禮
遺人：『凡國野之道，十里有廬，廬有飲食。三十里有宿，宿有路室，路室有委。
鄭玄注：『廬，若今野候有屋也。宿，可以止宿，若今亭有室矣。』漢書尹賞傳注
如淳曰：『舊亭傳於四角面百步，築土四方，上有屋，屋上有柱出，高丈餘，有大
板貫柱四出，名曰桓表。縣所治夾兩邊各一。』師古曰：『卽華表也。』說文：『桓
郵亭表也。』御覽二九七引崔豹古今注：『今之華表以橫木交柱頭，狀如華，形似
桔橰。大路交衢悉植焉。或謂之表木，以表王者納諫。亦以識衢路。』此皆漢魏言
亭傳者之例證也。今綜合上文，具得下列諸義；

一、郵亭之制與亭隧之亭相通。

二、郵亭有屋，可以止宿。

三、郵亭在都邑者爲傳舍，有傳吏可以具飲食。

四、郵亭之設以內官吏及其家屬爲準則。平民行旅欲入郵亭者必待無官吏及
　　其家屬止舍時方能投宿。

故漢世亭傳之設，所以供國家之急，達施政之宜。今按居延亭隧所記，則公私車馬
之出入，咸有記錄。今就其例證之顯著者，舉列於次：

一、傳車：

□□充光謹案曰藉在宮者弟年五十九毋官獄徵事，願以令取傳乘所占用馬。
八月癸酉居延丞奉光移過所河津金關毋苛留止。如律令。掾承。（二一八、二）

☑十月盡九月傳馬四☑

□□諸吏□□傳車二兩。（三一、一五）

右新陽符一，車十二。（五一五、一六）

告尉爲傳（二一八、四三）

自言具傳（二一二、五八）

傳馬十二匹，傳車一乘。（二一二、六九）

二、軺車

弩一矢廿，軺車一乘，馬二匹。（三六、六）

牛車二兩，軺車☒（五四、一一，五四、一三）

敦煌效穀宜王里瓊陽年廿八。軺車一，乘馬四。閏月丙午南入。（五〇五、一二）

登計掾衛豐。子男居延平里衞良年十三，軺車一乘馬一匹，十二月戊子北出（五〇五、一三）

☐☐長☐里張信，軺車一乘用馬一匹，十二月辛卯北出。（五〇五、九）

軺車一乘，馬一匹，騧牡，長九尺，高六尺。☐☐☐輔入。（五〇六、三）

南馬二匹，軺車一乘。（四四、一五）

徐黨年三十七。軺車一乘，用馬一匹。八月庚子出，九月甲戌入。（二五、二）

居延爲檄，寧當。軺車一乘。（五一、六）

三、方相（方箱）車：

☒二，方相車一乘。（三三五、一五）

奉明善居里公乘丘誼年六十九。居延丞付方相車一乘，用馬一匹，騂牡齒十歲，高六尺。閏月庚戌☐（五三、一五）

長安宜里閻常字仲兄。出。乘方相車，駕桃（花）牡馬一匹，齒七八歲，龐牡馬一匹，齒八歲。皆十月戊辰出。已。（六二、一三）

向壽☐年廿二，池，無方相車馬齒六歲。（六二、三二）

☐方相一乘，騧牡馬一匹，齒八歲，子穎。（四三、九）

四、牛車：

京兆尹長安棘里任尋方。弩一，矢廿四，劍一。牛車一兩挾持，庫丞印封隔。（二八〇、四）

☒書佐忠時年廿六長七尺三寸黑色。牛一車乘。第三百九十八。出。（二四九、二）

☒牛車二兩，軺車☒。（五四、一一，五四、一三）

☒市酒泉持牛車二兩，桼毌☒。（四〇三、一二）

牛車一兩，牛二頭，二月甲戌南入。（四一、二八）

□□牛車一兩。尉史亮。（二○六、三）

發牛車各繫一兩。（二六八、三九）

入牛車一兩。（三七、三○）

□牛車一兩，弓一，矢廿四，劍一，三月己丑，出大麥。（三七、六，三四○、三八）

□部吏陽里大夫封□年廿八，長七尺二寸，黑色，牛車一兩。五月戊戌□（四三、一三）

□□子鄭安自言持牛車一□，⊘官獄徵事，官德⊘（二一八、四五）

五、各地運輸之車：

戍卒梁國睢陽第四車父，宮南旦，一馬廣，鑡二，承□二破。（三○三、六）

賣羊三十頭，不出。右第三車。（七四、二二）

將車河南郡第⊘。（三四六、三九）

右第二車。（一五、一七）

新野第一車父連⊘。（一四五、四）

戍卒酇東利里張敞第卅車。（二八、一○）

冠軍第二車吳湯□□。（一八○、八）

右第八車父杜□□守父斬子衡，身一人。（一八○、四○）

第十車（五一四、五○）

右第六車卒廿人。（二三○、一○）

第一車閏月甲辰居延⊘。（五四、二四）

霣陽第十車父羔陽里郭□。（二八七、二一）

元城第八車卜廣，□□出。（三一一、三○）

內黃第五車入，魏郡⊘。（一○一、二九）

戍卒□□曾里石尊，第卅車五人。（四七七、四）

元康四年二月己未朔乙亥，使鄯善以西校尉吉，副衛司馬富昌，丞慶，都尉□重卽⊘通元康二年五月癸未，以使都護檄書，遣尉丞赦將扡刑士五千人送

致，將車□□□。（一一八、八七）

六、驛馬。

馬一匹，白，牡，齒七歲，高六尺。（六五、一二）

馬一匹，騂，□生□，齒九歲，高五尺。（五一〇、二七）

驛馬騂一匹。（一〇、一八）

一□□亡驛馬□□。（五一三、二一）

候馬二匹。（五一五、四五）

驛馬一匹□□牡齒□歲，高五尺八寸。上。調習。（一四二、二六）

官□驛馬一匹□駿牡□□齒十四歲，高五尺八寸。中。（二三、一三）

一月中馬二⊘。（四八五、二七）

候馬九匹。（九〇、三〇）

從以上諸例觀之，塞上傳車驛騎，亦同於內地。而運輸之車運至塞上者，且遠自梁國魏郡諸境。漢書主父偃傳：『秦又使天下飛芻輓粟，起於黃腄琅邪負海之郡，轉輸北河，率三十鍾而致一石。』案自龍門而上，黃河不可牽挽，則塞北轉輸固賴車運。鄒陽傳云：『闕城不休，救兵不止，死者相隨，輦車相屬。轉粟流輸，千里不絕，』卽其事也（惟至關中可用船，故宣紀本始四年云『以車船載穀』）。今據漢簡之文，山東之車牽以若干車編爲車隊，行數千里，轉運之難，大略可想。則漢世不能越大漠而收郡縣，雖爲千古可惜之事，然亦可知其由矣。又據漢簡其他諸則，戍卒之布帛衣物，亦從山東來，固不必悉爲糧秣也。

(乙)水運

中國之海上交通，若依地下遺物文化之分布定之，或竟在有史以前，已有相當發達。迄於春秋戰國，記載舟運之事，頗有可述者。而漢書藝文志所載天文書中亦有：

海中星占驗十二卷

海中五星經雜事二十二卷

海中五星順逆二十八卷

海中二十八宿國分二十八卷

海中二十八宿臣分（區分）二十八卷

海中日月彗虹雜占十八卷

以上諸書皆標明『海中』，則其為舟行所記，可得而言。海中用及天文，在後世本為尋常而必需之事。今漢志記先漢海中天文之書其多如此，則其時海上交通固可以想見也。海上行船所用之觀測，其在古昔本與方術相通。故史記封禪書云：

> 『自齊威宣之時，騶子之徒論終始五德之運。及秦帝而齊人奏之。故始皇採用之。而宋毋忌，正伯僑，充尚，羨門子高，最後皆燕人。為方僊道形解銷化，依於鬼神之事。騶衍以陰陽主運顯於諸侯，而燕齊海上之方士傳其術不能通。然則怪迂苟合之徒自此興不可勝數也。自威宣燕昭使人入海求蓬萊方丈瀛洲，此三神山者其傳在勃海中，去人不遠，患且至則船風引而去。……及至秦始皇幷天下……使人乃齎童男女求之，船交海中，皆以風為解。』

可知神仙雖未得，而齊燕方士固曾至海中也。後漢書王景傳云：

> 『王景字仲通，樂浪讘邯人也。八世祖仲，本琅邪不其人。好道術，明天文。諸呂作亂，齊哀王襄謀發兵而數問於仲。及濟北王興居反，欲委兵師仲。仲懼禍及，乃浮海東奔樂浪山中，因而家焉。』

按漢書高五王傳，濟北王興居以文帝二年立，『歲餘，匈奴大入邊，漢多發兵，丞相灌嬰擊之。文帝親幸太原。興居以為天子自擊胡，遂發兵反。上聞之，罷兵，歸長安。使棘蒲侯柴將軍擊破虜濟北王，王自殺。』據文帝紀事在文帝三年五月。濟北王發兵反，欲襲滎陽。使棘蒲侯柴武為大將軍，將四將軍十萬衆擊之。八月虜濟北王興居，自殺。赦諸與興居反者。此興居謀反時，規模固甚大也。又按王仲為琅邪不其人，而濟北後為泰山郡地，與琅邪不相接。當時濟北反而琅邪所屬之齊未反。其勢不能相強。則仲當興居反時，固當與興居之事，而在赦前逃至朝鮮，史文據王氏之家乘，因之有所回護也。然王氏之適朝鮮則自由於方術之士早已有至其地者，否則又何得盡室以行乎？

漢書伍被傳：『（始皇）又使徐福入海求仙藥，多齎珍寶童男女三千人，五種百工而行。徐福得平原大澤，止王不來』。所謂平原大澤者今尚不敢確指其地，然自燕齊泛海而東，得海外之地而居之，則可知也。後漢書東夷傳：『辰韓耆老，自言秦之亡人避苦役適韓國，馬韓割求界地與之。其名國爲邦，弓爲弧，賊爲寇，行酒爲行觴，相呼爲徒，有似秦語，或名之爲秦韓。』辰韓在朝鮮半島之東南，約當於後世新羅地。自中國前往，無論經由馬韓或直赴，皆非由舟船不能。又傳言其語有似『秦』人，此所言『秦』當承上文之秦而言，乃指關中，非指全中國。則『秦之亡人』云者，竟是秦之戍卒戍於燕齊者，此可徵泛海東指，不僅燕齊方士矣。

中國沿海之交通，其開展蓋已甚久。左傳哀公十年：『徐承帥舟師，自海入齊，齊人敗之，吳師乃還。』國語越語：『越之入吳也，范蠡古庸帥師自海詣淮以絕吳路』史記越王勾踐世家：『范蠡浮海出齊，變姓名自稱鴟夷子皮，耕於海畔』禹貢：『浮於江海，達於淮泗，』此皆遵海而北者也。孟子：『齊景公問於晏子曰，吾欲觀於轉附朝儛，遵海而南，放於琅邪。』此則遵海而南矣。琅邪山在青島西南，凡膠東半島南岸諸港，爲中國緣海自北而南之要衝。晉世法顯歸來隨風飄蕩，竟至青州長廣縣界，亦其地也。吳越春秋言：『越王勾踐二十五年，徙都琅邪，立觀臺以望東海，遂號令秦晉齊楚，以尊輔周室』據史記勾踐世家謂勾踐平吳乃以兵北渡淮，既去而以淮上地與楚，是徙都之時不長。然史記秦始皇本紀，始皇巡狩東土，徙黔首三萬戶琅邪臺下，立石頌德。始皇立石之地凡七，而徙民者獨此，則琅邪之重於當時，亦可知矣。

漢書司馬相如傳子虛賦：『且齊東陼鉅海，南有琅邪，觀乎成山，射乎芝罘，浮渤澥，游孟諸，邪與肅慎爲鄰，右以湯谷爲界。秋田乎青邱，徬徨於海外』注：『服虔曰，青丘國在海東三百里。』又上林賦：『今齊列東藩而外私肅慎，捐國踰限，越海而田，其於義未可也。』注：『師古曰捐棄也，謂田於青丘也。』此雖辭賦誇飾之言難爲論證，然齊國當時越海而田青丘，交肅慎，自亦無所不可也。

武帝征四夷，於胡則用騎士，而於兩粵及朝鮮則皆兼用樓船浮海以征之。漢書閩粵傳：『餘善刻武帝璽自立，詐其民爲妄言。上遣橫海將軍韓說出句章，浮海從東方往。樓船將軍僕出武林，中尉王溫舒出梅嶺。粵侯爲戈船下瀨將軍出如邪白沙，元封元年冬，咸入東粵。』又朝鮮傳：『天子募罪人擊朝鮮，其秋遣樓船將軍楊僕從齊浮渤海，兵五萬；左將軍荀彘出遼東。』皆可證水陸並出也。漢書朱買臣傳云：『買臣因言故東越王居保泉山，一人守險，千人不得上。今聞東越王更徙處南行，去泉山五百里，居大澤中。今發兵浮海，直抵泉山，陳舟列兵，席卷南行，可破滅也。上拜買臣會稽太守。……居歲餘，買臣受詔將兵，與橫海將軍韓說等俱擊破東越。』則武帝以買臣爲會稽太守，所以領會稽之卒以破東越者。朝鮮傳已記楊僕帥領者爲齊卒，而韓說出句章之兵亦可證明以會稽之卒爲主矣。

漢代自定兩越而後，舟船之利益溥，於北則齊與樂浪：於東則會稽與東冶，於南則南海合浦以至日南，皆大漢舟船之會也（見本篇前後各節）。史記貨殖傳云：『舫長千丈（漢書注，師古曰總積舫之丈數也。）木千章，竹竿萬个，軺車百乘，牛車千兩……亦比千乘之家。』故以運輸之利言，舟車固相同矣。楊僕出師率取齊卒，韓說出師亦用會稽之卒，並已見前，可知齊地諸郡與會稽之人當以舟行，故遂可以爲樓船卒。宋錢文子補兵志謂漢世江以南多樓船卒，雖其言誠是而未盡也。

漢世都於長安，處渭水之南，橫橋南渡以法牽牛。長安之糧賴漕渠轉運之事如漢書張良傳言：『關中……阻三面而固守，獨以一面東制諸侯，諸侯安定，河漕輓天下西給京師，諸侯有變，順流而下足以委輸。』此漢世建都之初即以漕運之利爲建都之經要矣。史記河渠書，漢書溝洫志亦皆屢言此後通漕轉運之事。是知河域舟船在漢固所常用也。

其在江域，向便行舟。漢書高帝紀二年：

『發使告諸侯曰，……悉發關中兵，收三河士，南浮江漢以下，願從諸侯王擊楚之殺義帝者。』

又漢書酈食其傳：

『諸侯之兵，四面而至，蜀漢之粟，方船而下。』

又漢書淮南王安傳：

『伍被言吳王上取江陵木爲船，一船之載，當中國數十兩車，國富民足。』

後漢書岑彭傳：

『裝直進樓船冒突露橈數千艘，……彭與吳漢及誅虜將軍劉隆，輔威將軍臧宮，驍騎將軍劉歆，發南陽，武陵，南郡兵；又發桂陽，零陵，長沙委輸棹卒凡六萬人，騎五千匹，咸會荊門。』

後漢書第五倫傳：

『拜會稽太守……坐法徵……老小攀車叩馬，嘑呼相隨。日裁行數里，不得
前。倫乃僞止亭舍，陰乘船去。』

後漢書衞颯傳：

『先是含洭，湞陽，曲江三縣，……內屬桂陽。……吏事往來，輒發民乘
船。』

華陽國志巴志：

『永興二年，巴郡太守望疏曰：「郡治江州，結舫水居五百餘家，承三江之
會，夏水漲盛，壞敗顚溺，死者無數。」』

隸釋引熹平三年桂陽太守周憬功勳碑：

『郡又與南海接比，商旅所臻。至瀑亭至乎曲江，壹由此水源也……府君乃
命良吏……順導其經脈，由是小溪乃平直，大道允通利，抱布貿絲，交易而
至。』

此皆大江以南之舟船。足以證漢世水道運輸之重要者也。至於海運，則自長江流域
以至嶺南，幾皆惟此是賴。後漢書鄭弘傳所稱：

『建初八年代鄭衆爲大司農。舊交阯七郡，貢獻轉運，皆從東冶泛海而至。
風波艱阻，沈溺相係。弘奏開零陵桂陽嶠道，於是夷通，至今遂爲常路。』

東冶卽今福州。故交州大道乃經福建以至江南，更轉至洛陽。在鄭弘之前，固以海
上爲大道。在鄭弘以後，亦誠有經五嶺嶠道而至中州者。然海上往來亦固其常也。

後漢書桓曄傳：

『初平中天下大亂，避地會稽。遂浮海客交阯。越人化其節，閭里不爲訟。』

後漢書袁安傳：

『乃天下大亂，（袁）忠棄官客會稽上虞。一見太守王朗，徒從整飾，心嫌
之，遂稱病自絕。後孫策破會稽，忠等浮海南投交阯。獻帝都許，徵爲衞
尉，未到，卒。』

太平御覽六十引謝承後漢書：

『汝南陳茂爲交阯別駕，舊刺史行部不度漲海。刺史周敞涉海遇風，船欲

覆。<u>茂</u>拔劍呵罵水神，風卽中息。』

<u>王國魏志王朗傳</u>：

　　『舉兵遂與<u>策</u>戰，敗績。浮海至<u>東冶</u>，<u>策</u>又追擊，大破之。<u>朗</u>乃詣<u>策</u>，<u>策</u>以儒雅，詰讓而不害。』注：『<u>獻帝春秋</u>曰：「<u>孫策</u>率軍如<u>閩越</u>討<u>朗</u>，<u>朗</u>泛舟浮海，欲走<u>交州</u>，爲兵所逼，遂詣軍降。」』

<u>三國吳志虞翻傳</u>引<u>吳書</u>：

　　『<u>翻</u>始欲送<u>朗</u>到<u>廣陵</u>。<u>朗</u>惑<u>王方平</u>訊言……故遂南行，旣至<u>候官</u>，又欲投<u>交州</u>。』

又<u>三國志王朗傳</u>：

　　『自<u>曲阿</u>展轉<u>江海</u>，積年乃至』。注：『被徵未至，<u>孔融</u>與<u>朗</u>書曰：「……主上寬仁，貴德宥過；<u>曹公</u>輔政，思賢並立。策書屢下，殷勤款至。知擢舟浮海，息駕<u>廣陵</u>，不意黃能突出<u>羽淵</u>也。」』

<u>三國吳志孫皓傳</u>：

　　『<u>建衡</u>元年遣監軍<u>徐存</u>從<u>建安海道</u>，就<u>合浦</u>擊<u>交阯</u>。』

凡此皆可證自<u>鄭弘</u>開嶠道之後，<u>吳會</u>與<u>交州閩廣</u>間交通，仍爲舟運也。至於<u>三國志孫權傳</u>稱<u>黃龍</u>二年正月，遣將軍<u>衞溫諸葛直</u>將甲士萬人，浮海求<u>夷州</u>及<u>亶州</u>。雖因浮海失道，但得<u>夷州</u>數千人而還。然其時入海規模之大，自亦不難明曉也。

　　<u>漢</u>世<u>齊</u>人有爲樓船卒者，已見前引<u>漢書朝鮮傳</u>。今更就大江以北之緣海交通，略申述之。<u>後漢書包咸傳</u>：

　　『<u>會稽曲阿</u>人也。少爲諸生，受業<u>長安</u>。……<u>王莽</u>末，去歸鄉里。於<u>東海</u>界爲<u>赤眉</u>賊所得……遣之。因住<u>東海</u>教授。』

自<u>長安</u>至<u>會稽</u>之陸道當經<u>丹陽</u>而不經<u>東海</u>，此則赴<u>東海</u>，爲自海道而達<u>會稽</u>也。至<u>吳</u>時與<u>公孫</u>氏往來賂遺，亦經此道。<u>三國志公孫度傳</u>：

　　『<u>明帝</u>卽位，拜<u>淵</u>揚烈將軍，<u>遼東</u>太守。<u>淵</u>遣使南通<u>孫權</u>，往來賂遺。』注，<u>魏略</u>曰：『國家知<u>淵</u>兩端而恐<u>遼東</u>吏民爲<u>淵</u>所誤，故公文下<u>遼東</u>，因敕之曰：「告<u>遼東玄菟</u>將校吏民，逆賊<u>孫權</u>，遭遇亂階，因其先人，劫略州郡。遂成羣凶，自擅<u>江表</u>。……比年以來，復遠遣船越度大海，多持貨物，誑誘

邊民。邊民無分，與之交關。長吏以下，莫肯禁止。至使周賀浮舟百艘，沈

滯津岸，貿遷有無。既不疑拒，齎以名馬。」』

三國志明帝紀：

『太和六年，冬，十月。殄夷將軍田豫討吳將周賀於成山，殺賀。』

三國志田豫傳：

『太和末，公孫淵以遼東叛。帝欲征之而難其人。中領軍楊暨舉豫應選。乃

使豫以本官督青州諸軍，假節討之。會吳賊遣使與淵相結。帝以賊衆多，又

以渡海，使豫罷軍。豫度賊船垂還，歲晚風急，必畏漂浪。東隨無岸，當赴

成山，成山無藏船之處輒便循海，案行地形及諸山島，徼集險要，列兵屯

守。自入成山，登漢武之觀。賊還，果遇惡風，船皆觸山，沈沒波蕩，無所

逃竄，盡虜其衆。』

次年吳遣太常張彌，金執吾許晏，復浮海使公孫淵，遂爲公孫淵所殺，亦由此道

也。

自遼東以至吳會，可以海行，則從青齊以至遼東，海行尤易。三國志邴原傳：

『黃巾賊起，原將家屬入海，住鬱洲山中。時孔融爲北海相，舉原有道。原

以黃巾方盛，遂至遼東，與同郡劉政俱有勇略雄氣。遼東太守公孫度畏惡欲

殺之。盡收捕其家。政得免，度告諸縣敢有藏政者與同罪。政竄急往投原。

原匿之月餘。時東萊太史慈當歸，原因政付之。……原又資送政家，皆得還

故郡。……後得歸太祖，辟爲司空掾。』

三國志管寧傳：

『天下大亂，聞公孫度令行於海外，遂與原及平原王烈等至於遼東，度虛館

以候之。……中國少安，客人皆還，唯寧晏然，若將終焉。黃初四年，詔公

卿舉獨行君子，司徒華歆薦寧。文帝即詔徵寧，遂將家屬浮海還郡。公孫度

送之南郊。』注：『傅子曰：寧往見度，語唯經典，不及世事。還乃因山爲

廬，鑿坏爲室，越海避難者，旬月而成邑。』

而魏之攻公孫氏，亦用舟師。三國志蔣濟傳注引司馬彪戰略：

『太和六年，明帝遣平州刺史田豫乘海渡，幽州刺史王雄陸路，并攻遼東。

　　蔣濟諫，……帝不聽，豫行竟無成而還。』

自後司馬懿遂用陸路自遼西而出。然據此節，魏固先曾用海上之師。惟司馬氏奇兵獨出，克奏膚功。而田豫則不然，固非失之於海道也。

　　就以上所論凡中國江海之區，皆有水上交通爲昔人所利用。御覽七七一引郭璞江賦曰：

　　　　『舳艫相接，萬里連檣；泝洄沿流，或漁或商。』

又御覽七七〇引孫綽望海賦曰：

　　　　『商客齊暢，隨流往還；各資順勢，雙航同懸。』

皆可從之以想像漢魏以來江海之盛況。

　　自漢以來，南海交通要道，出於東冶，已見前引王朗傳。又後漢書東夷傳言：『倭在韓東南大海中，依山島爲居，凡百餘國……其地大較在會稽東冶之東。』此東方夷境，亦以會稽東冶爲準也。若南方諸國，則更以南海之番禺爲交易之都會。漢書地理志云：

　　　　『粵地處近海，多犀象，毒冒，珠璣，銀銅，果布之湊。中國往商賈，多取
　　　　富焉。番禺者，一都會也。自日南障塞，徐聞，合浦船行可五月有都元國，
　　　　又船行可四月有邑盧沒國，又船行二十餘日有湛離國，步行可十餘日有夫甘
　　　　都盧國，船行二月餘有黃支國，民俗略與珠崖相類，其州廣大，戶口多，多
　　　　異物。自武帝以來皆獻見，有譯長屬黃門，與應募者俱入海市明珠，流離，
　　　　奇石，異物，齎黃金，雜繒而往，所至國皆廩食爲耦，蠻夷賈船，轉送致
　　　　之。……自黃支船行可八月到皮宗，船行可二月到日南象林界云，黃支之南
　　　　有已程不國，漢之譯使自此還矣。』

所記者最遠莫如黃支。其由中國往黃支計爲：

　　　合浦至都元國——五月

　　　都元國至邑盧沒國——四月

　　　邑盧沒國至湛離國——二十餘日

　　　湛離國至夫甘都盧國——步行十餘日

　　　夫甘都盧國至黃支國——二月餘

　　　　　約計共十二月餘至十三月餘

若由黃支往中國，則爲：

　　　黃支國至皮宗國——八月

　　　皮宗國至日南象林——二月

　　　　約計十月

去程自徐聞合浦，在東；而歸程至日南象林，在西。故所取之路乃向東南，更折而西，復從北歸，略同時鐘方向。然則其路徑當爲由菲律濱而婆羅洲，而爪哇或蘇門答臘，更經交阯支那以至安南也。卽都元或當在菲律濱境，邑盧沒，諶離，及夫甘都盧或當在婆羅洲境，而黃支或當在蘇門答臘或爪哇矣。其所記月日或較實際航海所用之月日爲長，蓋海行多歷風險，不得不從長估計也。漢志所記自中國至黃支往返各有一路，不相重複，故其所記之地，決不能踰新加坡而西。若越新加坡而西，則往返之途不能不互相重疊，而皮宗象林間亦不能僅二月之期便能達到矣。前此論證漢志此節，其著者如法之費瑯（G. Ferrand）及日本之藤田豐八，皆認爲西漢使節曾達新加坡以西，且至印度。並列舉對音以證之。今並不取。惟洛佛（B. Laufer）據後漢書南蠻傳『元始二年日南之南，黃支國來獻犀牛』以爲當在馬來，或去事實不遠耳。蓋古蹟難明，但能取諸本證，若博引對音，轉滋聚訟，難言徵實，非所尙也。漢史所述黃支之事甚少，惟地理志所記『民俗略與珠崖相類，其州廣大，戶口多，多異物』及『平帝元始中，王莽專政欲耀威德，厚遺黃支王，令遣使獻生犀牛。』獻犀牛事又見於王莽傳。今據此處所言『民俗略與珠崖相類，』則似在南洋而不在印度。又云『其州廣大』，則似在島嶼而不在大陸，至於產犀牛一事，則爪哇及蘇門答臘並皆有之，卽所謂 Javan rhinoceros 及 Sumatran rhinoceros 者，原不必踰重洋而取之印度也。凡爲考證，平實爲先，據現有史料論，至西漢晚年中國使節尙未踰新加坡至印度洋，陸路則亦僅有『身毒乘象以戰』之傳聞（張騫傳）似未曾與印度發生直接關係也。

　　東漢明帝時佛教已入中國，章帝建初時之滕縣石刻亦有佛教故事之六牙象。然印度與中國之交通，亦僅在西域而不在南海。後漢書西域傳云：

　　　『天竺國一名身毒……和帝時數遣使貢獻，後西域反叛，乃絕。至桓帝延熹二年，頻從日南徼外來獻。』

故天竺與中國之海道交通，乃開發於和帝以後，桓帝以前之時期，和帝以前則經由
陸路也。按自安帝永初元年（一〇七年）罷西域都護，至桓帝延熹元年（一五八年）
中凡五十年，中印海道溝通，即在此五十年中。自此路交通後，至桓帝延熹九年，
大秦國王安敦乃『遣使自日南徼外獻象牙，犀角，瑇瑁』（後漢書西域傳）。於是
交廣兩地遂成東西市易之場。吳志士燮傳云：

> 『燮兄弟並爲列郡，（燮領交州，弟壹合浦太守，䵋南海太守。）雄長一州，
> 偏在萬里，威尊無上，出入鳴鐘磬，備具威儀，笳簫鼓吹，車騎滿道，胡人
> 夾轂燃香者，常有數十。』

依漢人通習，南海之人稱曰蠻人而不稱曰胡人。胡人者特指西域之人而言，王氏國
維西胡考所述，可據也。此言胡人，當指西胡之人，若身毒，條支，安息之屬。而
燒香一事亦原爲奉佛之俗。此三國初年之南海交通也。又梁書西域傳云：

> 『大秦……國人行賈，往往至扶南，日南，交阯。其南徼諸國人少有到大秦
> 者。孫權黃武五年，有大秦賈人字秦論來到交阯。太守吳邈送詣孫權，權問
> 士方謠俗，論具以事對。時諸葛恪討丹陽，獲黝歙短人。論見之曰：「大秦
> 希見此人」，權以男女各十人，差吏會稽劉咸送論。咸於道物故，論乃迴還
> 本國。』

又太平御覽七七一引吳時外國傳曰：

> 『從加那調州乘大伯舶，張七航，時風一月餘日，乃入秦，大秦國也。』

亦可證吳以後對遠西之南海交通矣。故中國在南海上之往來開始於西漢，發展於東
漢，至吳已臻於繁盛。而和帝至桓帝之五十年間，西域陸道隔絕，尤爲海上交通進
展之時期。自此而後，貿遷之事，未嘗斷也。若就海軍而言，則自東漢以還如馬援
（後漢書本傳），宗慤（宋書本傳），劉方（隋書本傳），皆能率領舟師遠征不庭
而所向克捷。就造船之技術與軍隊之作戰能力言，皆當有過人之處。然中國外患若
就東南與西北比較言之，固在彼而不在此。其出發固非傾國之師，其克捷除馬援之
外，亦鮮計及經營之道。此由不願疲中國以事遠略，非力之不逮也。

附記：本篇附印以後有應爲補入者二事，今附列於後。

（一）接到王毓銓先生來函云：

在兩漢時代，『傳舍』不是『郵亭』；而『郵亭』和原來的『亭』也不盡相同。『傳舍』是三十里（大致說來）一置，而『亭』則十里一置（此『里』非里居之里，下面有解釋）。『傳舍』是供官吏乘傳止宿之用，而『亭』之設則原爲徼巡禁盜賊。『亭』有樓，用以觀望。平時無事，可供行旅止宿。但止宿行旅，不是它本來的職掌。止宿『亭』不須要有『符』或『傳』，止宿的人不必然是政府的官吏；兩漢書，風俗通均載有平民止宿『亭』的事。至於『傳舍』，那是專爲政府官吏設備的。偶有平民止居『傳舍』，但非有特別理由不行。而且『傳舍』有副車，傳馬，廚，供傳馬，驛馬，和乘傳官吏飲食之用，而『亭』沒有這些設備。西漢末傳車漸廢，代以驛馬，距離間仍是三十里，而『亭』的距間也沒變，仍爲十里。看來兩事沒有合併爲一。漢代的『郵』，好像是另一傳遞消息或信件的設置，分佈也比較密。應劭說是『五里一郵』。有若干亭可藉作郵，所以有了『郵亭』，不過好像不可把『郵亭』看作完全和『亭』是一樣的東西，雖然事實上不行郵的亭怕是很少。還有一點應該注意的是驛馬只有『驛置』上有，亭上沒有。

與鄙意略有出入，但有可以補充鄙說者。

（二）關於『海中』二字，鄙意以爲與『海內』含義不同。陳槃厂先生以爲顧炎武旣有異義，而王先謙復有辨證，應爲補錄，其義始明，茲列於下：

王應麟曰：『後漢書天文志注引海中占，隋志有海中占星圖，海中占各一卷，卽張衡所謂「海人之占」也。唐天文志開元十二年詔太史，交州測星以八月，自海中南望老人星殊高，老人星下衆星粲然，其明大者甚衆。』顧炎武曰：『海中者，中國也，故天文志曰，甲乙海外日月不占。』沈欽韓曰：『海中混茫，比平地難驗，著海中者，言其術精。算法亦有海島算經。唐封氏見聞記云：齊武成帝卽位，大赦天下，其曰設金雞，宋孝王不識其義，問於光祿大夫司馬膺之。答曰，案海中星占天雞星動必有赦。』先謙曰：『王，沈說是。』（漢書補註三十）

此二則因版已排就，未能補入，附列於此，並向王陳兩先生致謝。

漢代黃金及銅錢的使用問題

㈠ 遠古銅幣的演進和圓錢的建立

關於中國經濟史有關貨幣的使用尤其有關漢代貨幣的使用，過去曾有不少人討論過。但是到如今還有不少的誤解，爲著淸除這些誤解，現在把這些問題再提出來討論，依照我自己的意見來批評，來解釋。

人類的文明是從創造工具開始的，但是工具的使用價值形成了以後，工具的應用只要不限於製造工具的人，那就工具的交換價值也立刻顯現出來。無疑的，工具的需要是甚爲普徧的，也就形成了工具交換的頻數性，工具是比較其他物品爲耐久的，也就形成了工具交換的固定性。早期的工具當然是石製的，和工具質料及性質類似的，還有石製骨製或介殼製的裝飾品，這也發生類似的交換應用。更進一步，這些工具及飾物不僅來直接交換，並且也很方便的作爲間接交換的媒介物，這就形成了貨幣上的意義。不僅如此，直到後來鑄幣，還是仿傚著古代工具的形式或者仿傚著古代飾物的形式。

當著商代及周代初期，從石製工具延伸出來的圭和璧，誠然是非常重要的貨品，代表較高的價值。而平常交換的物品，可能石刀、石斧、石鏟等會用得著，因爲後來的銅錢，有些是仿傚他們的形式而鼓鑄的。如其不曾使用過當作交換媒介，採用這些形式就毫無意義。此外工具的製作是早期的事，作爲交換價值來應用，在現存石器時代的人類中，是一個普徧的事。如其中華古代民族曾經把他仍當作交換的媒介，也就一定要追溯到新石器時代以至於舊石器時代，決不可能在鑄錢的前夕才有這種事實發生。所以把工具當作交換媒介，在中國的遠古是一個存在的事實，這一點文獻的記載是不夠的，實物的遺留更可以證明這個事實。

就中貝殼來做交換媒介一事，那是文獻上記載分明的，在文獻上爲什麼以貝殼來做標準而不以圭璧或石刀石鏟做標準。大概是並非圭璧或石斧石鏟之類不能做交換媒介，而是因為任何一種玉器或石器都不够標準化。每一個石器的交換價值，會隨著它的品質，大小，精粗而發生變異。只有貝殼，尤其是古代中國人認為貨幣的『子安貝』，每一個的差異都不大，因此就被認為是有標準性質的。十個貝算做一朋，十朋或百朋就被認為是一個較大的貨幣數量(1)，這是在甲骨，金文以及詩經中都有明顯的記載。這裏並非說古人交換，一定非用子安貝不可，而不能用其他物品，例如石刀，石斧之類來代替，而是說貝與積貝而成的朋，是衡量價格的標準。其他物品如有交換價值，也就依其質和量來議定，照朋的標準來核算。所以不必記錄作交換用的其他實物，而一律以朋的名稱來概括了。

做貨幣用的貝是子安貝，已有不少出土，這種貝殼只產在臺灣以南的海水中，而不產於大陸緣海各地。商周時代用這種貝殼來做貨幣並不代表那時中國大陸緣海當產這種貝殼。如其認為是從海上運來，在論證上還比認為古代在大陸緣岸漁獲容易的多。因為這樣就不必牽涉到洋流變化或生物分布變化上的問題。專講古代海上交通，那卻是幾千年來已經存在的事實。不僅印第安人到美洲及馬來人到馬拉加西是史前時代的事，即就現代有些玻利尼西亞人仍然保持史前的生活來說，他們仍然是優秀的航海技術者。所以就商代一般狀況說，海洋的交通是可能的，所以子安貝的輸入，用不著太多的疑問(2)。

用貝殼來做貨幣究竟是一個在不得已求得的一個辦法。貝殼究竟是一個天然物品，非人力所能控制，因而不算一個最好的辦法。用實物來做貨幣（除去完全靠人為的維持的紙幣以外），沒有比金屬更好的。因為金屬有其耐久性，和隨意等分的可能與其標準性，都非其他物品所能及。就遠古來說，貝殼的耐久性及標準性，都有一點類似金屬。但其供求量就會有時過多，有時過少，完全不能控制。這就無法樹立一種貨幣制度。自從銅的功用發現以後，銅鑄的貨幣就自然的會取貝殼來代替。

據國語說周景王鑄大錢，一般認為是鑄錢做貨幣的開始。不過根據國語的本文，單穆公諫周景王，認為鑄大錢是『廢輕用重』。也就是鑄一種一錢當數錢的大錢。據國語韋昭注(3)及漢書食貨志的顏師古注(4)，也都是同樣的發揮這種意見。所以周景王鑄大錢並非是鑄幣的開始，而是在周景王以前早就有一種小型銅錢的存在。這自然可以推到春秋以前或者甚至到西周時代。只是所謂太公的九府圜法（漢書食貨志）是根據周禮中的太府、玉府、內府、外府、泉府、天府、職內、職金、職幣共九府而言。這種制度是否是周初的制度那是十分有問題的。對於這一項，不應當做為根據。但無論如何，就周禮完成的時代（戰國初期）來說，顯然的已有金屬貨幣了。

周景王鑄的大錢，國語中未說到它的形狀，漢書食貨志卻說『文曰寶貨，肉好皆有周郭』。這是國語原文中沒有，經班固加上去的。這一點吳韋昭注國語也不置信的，他說：

唐尚書云，『大錢重十二銖，文曰大錢五十』。……王莽時錢……文曰大泉五十唐君所謂大泉者乃莽時錢，非景王所鑄明矣。戰國秦漢，幣物改轉不相因。先師所不能紀。或云大錢文曰寶貨，皆非事實(5)。

這是韋昭駁班固的話。今案文曰寶貨的圓錢，確有此物，班氏想也曾看到。不過這種寶貨，並不能算做大錢的證據，也沒有屬於周景王所鑄的任何證據。附之於周景王是不適宜。韋氏的意見是不錯的。

在鑄銅質的貨幣初期，似乎各種性質的錢是同時並行的。指圓錢的鍰字始見於呂刑。呂刑所說的『王享國百年』據說是周穆王事（堯典的『金作贖刑』寫定時應當更晚，所以不能引用），那就這篇最早的限度可以推到西周中葉。不過拿春秋時鑄刑書鑄刑鼎那些事當受人議議，呂刑中表現的頒布成文法的觀念不會太早。也許呂刑至早就是春秋晚期的作品。所以一定說周人在西周時已經用了圓錢，確實證據還不夠。

因此周景王所鑄的錢，是圓錢或者不是圓錢，仍然大成問題。就錢字和鍰字兩個字來說，鍰字是專為圓錢來造的，錢字卻本意為農器中的鏟子。詩經『庤乃錢鎛』(6)，錢就和鏟字命意相同。但為什麼錢字通行而鍰字反而廢置？這裏的原因應當是錢字來指金屬貨幣早已通用，鍰字後起，難以破除已通用的習慣把錢字取代。如其錢字應用較早，那就表示最早通用的錢應當是鏟形的貨幣而不是圓錢。所以周景王鑄的大錢，就可能是大型的鏟形錢而不是大型的圓錢。

現在被發現過的春秋晚期以至戰國的錢應當有這幾種(甲)蟻鼻錢，就是用銅製的仿子安貝(乙)鏟形錢，王莽的貨布就是漢代人仿鏟形錢的形式，因此後人就把這種叫做布。(丙)刀形錢。(丁)圓形錢。其中鏟形錢的變化最多，分布也最廣。刀形錢只限於齊國附近一個特殊區域，蟻鼻錢出土的並不多，圓錢大致比較屬於後期的。就這幾種現象來說，表示其中幾種銅貨幣的相關性。

事實表現出來，鏟形錢和刀形錢應當是平行的，早期鑄造的兩種錢。也可能是地域的分別，齊國及齊國以外的區域同時鑄造。漢詩中的『何用錢刀爲』(7)正是戰國古語表示並用的兩種貨幣。蟻鼻錢是戰國時代的錢，並不早於鏟形錢。可能的是初期鼓鑄鏟形錢時，子安貝仍然並用，並且有輔幣的功用。爲著流通上的需要，子安貝是不敷應用的，所以有鼓鑄銅子安貝的必要。但是後來也分鑄小型鏟形錢以及圓錢。這樣就用不著再鑄一種鑄造及携帶都不方便的蟻鼻錢了。至於圓錢，當然是最方便的一種錢，也就是最後成功的形式。

從發展的經過來看，鏟形幣無疑的是中國銅幣發展經過上的主要貨幣，這也是毫無疑問的，把鏟形幣的名稱『錢』變成了貨幣總稱的原故。『空首布』(8)正是最早的鏟形錢，還遺留下鏟柄的形製，後來不僅柄部只留一點痕跡，下面的兩個尖端也漸漸變圓了。這種演進的趨勢自然是最後走到圓的設計按照鏟形的結構是不穿洞的，其後來穿洞的鏟形錢，又是受到了刀形錢及蟻鼻錢的影響。

如其圓錢早已使用，或者圓錢是和鏟形錢及刀形錢同時平行的出現，那圓錢早就應該替代其他不規則形態的錢了。然而事實上並不這樣簡單。人類文化的進步，往往兜著不必要的圈子，憑著許多錯誤和改正，才走上了應當走的路。圓錢誠然是一個非常簡單的設計，可是從鑄別的形式的銅幣，到使用圓錢，似乎也費了至少一二百年的時間，到現在還不知道如何開始的。有人猜測是從璧或環縮小來轉變的，那麼就應當很早，不會畸形的鏟形錢那樣通行。有人猜測是從齊國刀錢的環變成的，這也不太對，因爲圓錢是從西方(二周及秦)開始的，其錢孔的應用，也許受到齊刀的影響，但說到從齊刀直接簡化而成，卻又不像。因此我懷疑圓錢的產生是從許多複雜因素促成的(甲)現在圓錢具有國名的有東周和西周(9)，這是舊日天子的王畿而號稱爲『天下之中』。雖然周室政權已經微弱，但洛陽的繁榮仍然繼續。洛陽附近的住民本來除去殷商遺民只有靠商賈爲生以外，其中所謂『王室親姻』(10)的，無非在封建組織之下依靠『土田』的收入。及至周室國力衰微，不能再保證他們的財產，他們就只有轉業爲商了。在這個中原區域，洛陽再加上陽翟和陶，就成爲東西南北貨物集散之地。這個區域正是鏟形錢的區域（當然齊刀也會因貿易而流入的），也正是圓形錢開始發展的區域，其中演變因革的原因自然是因爲銅錢的計數和運輸，只有標準化的圓錢最爲方便之故。鏟錢鼓鑄的趨向，是走向標準化，而標準化的極致，就非用圓形不可。(乙)鏟形錢除去依照工具交換的傳統以外，不代表什麼意義的；到戰國中葉以後，因爲天文學的發展，渾天蓋天諸說逐漸盛行。『天圓地方』就是一個蓋天的傳統，這也可能影響到鑄錢。(丙)戰國時對西域方面當無直接的交通，所知不多。不過間接的交通，確實是有的。而西域的玻璃珠，也曾鑲嵌到戰國銅鏡之上。西域的貨幣一定也會到戰國人的手中。從這個觀念下的影響，也會覺到圓錢更爲方便而鑄圓錢。這一點從圓錢開始在中國比較西部地方，也正可支持這一個可能。

戰國時雖然已經開始有圓錢，而且圓錢也逐漸增多。不過一般貨的使用，還是非常雜亂的。除去蟻鼻錢量數太少不計外。其他的各種錢，如周秦的標準圓錢，齊國的標準刀錢，以及各種形式（包括各種標準化及非標準化的）鏟形錢，一定是同時在各國的市面流通。而在各國的市面上也一定有公認的比值。也許還有若干地方性的差異。這樣複雜的幣制，很容易使商人上下其手。到了最後沒有辦法時，便只有將貨幣也用衡量來稱（當然比生銅的價值高些）。所以最後秦的半兩錢就是這樣來的。既已標明半兩，就可以每個以半兩計，不必再稱。結果半兩錢是用數目來數的，別的錢仍用衡秤稱的。所以半兩錢決不是秦統一天下才有，六國時的秦就已開始用了。

㈡　秦代圓錢的進展

秦始皇統一天下，把一切制度有計劃的標準化。當然這並不是秦始皇的創意，周代的『周道』⑾和『雅言』⑿已對於標準化做過初步的努力。只是在周初時期那時政治發展並未成熟，標準化的時機未至。秦始皇統一六國以前，六國國內都已經漸次樹立了統一的規模，等到一個更大的統一來到，對於制度的標準化就容易更有效的執行了。這項標準化的範圍是相當廣泛的，史記上雖然舉出來一些，如同文字的統一，度量衡的統一等等，但是更重要的還有法律的統一，政治制度的統一以及幣制的統一。自從秦代把半兩錢定爲唯一的標準貨幣，所有舊的錢幣如同刀形錢鏟形錢等，顯然的是政府收回改鑄。所以除去既有出土的錢幣，可算得秦時漏網之孑餘以外，其中大部分六國錢幣，經秦代鎔化改鑄的，一定不在少數。

誠然，秦代怎樣處置六國舊幣，史記上未曾說過。不過除去有計劃的收回再改鑄發行以外，似乎還沒有其他辦法。因為中國對於銅的出產，並不豐富。秦時除去豫章(13)（應當是今安徽境內的銅鑛）及巴蜀的銅鑛外，境內的銅產，並不太多。秦代併吞六國，發展的很快，秦軍到了一個地方，最重要的事項，便是控制政治，安定經濟，這才可以真正化六國為秦。如其要安定經濟，就得要整理市面，供給通貨。六國原有的雜牌貨幣既然在法律為半兩錢所取代。那就得供給市面足夠的半兩錢。但半兩錢是實物，必需準備充分的原料才可以。如其不利用舊幣，那就天下之廣，雖然豫章巴蜀加緊的開採，也不能在一個不太長的時期，供給天下的需要。其次，舊幣如其不用，就必需有一個處置方法，否則就等於凍結國富。處置的方法，就只有改鑄別的。一般民用器物，如錫釜之屬，就當時政府的立場來說，還不如由政府收回改鑄半兩錢為合算。所以在當時統一錢幣政策之下，除去用半兩錢換回舊錢，再把舊錢改鑄半兩錢以外，不可能有別的方法。

戰國時代是中國境內各區域的經濟狀態充分發展的時代。生產工具方面已由青銅器時代轉變為鐵器時代，生產技術的進步及資本的蓄積也無疑的有長足的收穫。所謂『戰國』一辭，是由『四海之內戰國七』(14)一語而來的，戰國是指有足夠的國力可以攻戰和防禦而言，所以也就是強國或列強的同意語。用戰國一辭來指這個時代，也就等於說當時並無一個統一的政府而由強國共同維持的一個時代。戰國一辭就一般的想像是一個整天打仗的時代，但就史記六國年表分別來看，各國的和平時期遠比戰爭時期為多。這些和平的段落，就是各國國內經濟發展的時期。自然，戰國時幾次大規模戰役，也確實的嚴重損害幾個城市的經濟發展，不過確也有些城市未曾經過戰禍或很少經過戰禍，例如洛陽、成都、長沙、吳(15)，以及晚期數十年中的臨淄便很少受到戰禍的波及。這就戰國經濟發展來說，很有幫助。其最阻礙經濟發展的，還是各國各自為政，築起來關稅的壁壘，如同孟子所說：『古之為關也將以止暴，今之為關也，將以為暴』以及孟子所設想的『關市譏而不征』(16)，都是針對戰國時局面而發的。到了秦統一天下，國與國間的境界破除了。除去函谷關以外其他無數的關塞不再發生作用，這件事再加上幣制的劃一，都會很大的裨益於經濟的發展。史記貨殖傳所舉少數富人便屬於秦時候的。這只是一點選樣，秦代成功的富人當然不只這一點。

　　秦代政治是純法家的政治也就是以暴政見稱的。不過也看就那一方面來說。法家政治的壞處是後面沒有一個價值觀念來指導，所走的完全是一個冷酷的路。結果會造成一種官僚政治，一切都只有一個形式的軀殼，以致終於腐爛掉。但是在其有效時期，確能做到道不拾遺，夜不閉戶，這對於國民經濟的發展確有好處。法家原則是限制每個人的政治自由卻未曾限制每個人的經濟自由。可是對於商人方面，在政策上卻有進退失據之處。法家賤商人，因為商人的財富太過，可能威脅政權。但另一方面國家要發展財富，卻要倚賴商人。所以一方面要發展商人的財富，另一方面卻要商人能以了解並且安於財富不是提高社會地位的條件，尤其是財富決不能構成干預政治的條件。但是秦代對於這件事已不能堅守立場，史記貨殖傳中的烏氏倮和巴寡清就以資財受到褒寵。漢高帝不准商人衣絲和坐馬車（只允許坐牛車）一定也是沿襲秦的政策，不過不久也成具文。所以賈誼說：『美者黼繡，是古天子之服，今富人大賈，嘉會召客者以被牆』[17]，這就表示著法家賤商政策的成功性是非常有限度的。惟其如此，就開新方面來說，法家政策做『創業垂統』的大經，實在很不夠的，可是就原有的狀況來說，法家對於經濟基礎卻也照舊維持一點也不會破壞。所以秦併天下以後各城市中的市場不僅維持了過去的繁榮，還會更進一步的繁榮。這一點對於半兩錢的功能方面去看，是成功，不是失敗。

　　半兩錢在漢人看來，是太重了。不過半兩錢的鑄造，是代替六國雜牌各種錢的。不論鏈錢或刀錢，其重量大率都比半兩錢重，也就是說六國時銅幣代表的單位比較大。半兩錢既然來代替這些稍大的單位，那就半兩錢不能太輕。也就是說半兩錢一個錢的購買力，是應當超過漢代及後代一錢的購買力許多的。食貨志引李悝說：『戰國時米石三十錢』[18]，秦代應當是一樣的。

　　在秦時半兩錢是鏈錢及刀錢代替品，這是依照舊時傳統而來，其購買力之高，非後人所能想象。漢書蕭何傳說：

　　　　高祖以吏繇咸陽，吏皆奉錢三，何獨以五[19]：

奉錢三，明明是送給三錢，何獨以五，明明是蕭何送五個錢。顏師古就不能明瞭此事，注說：

去錢以資行。他人皆三百，何獨五百。

顏師古對於漢代史事，是十分熟悉的。這個出錢的規矩，見於漢書昭帝紀元鳳四年(2)，詔賜三年以前逋更賦未入者皆勿收。章懷太子注引如淳曰：

> 古者正卒無常人，皆當迭爲之，一月一更，是謂卒更也。貧者欲得顧更錢者，次直者出錢顧之，月二千，是謂踐更也。天下人皆直戍邊三日，亦名爲更，律所謂繇戍也。雖丞相子亦在戍邊之調。不可人人自行三日戍，又行者當自戍三日，不可往便還。因便往，一歲一更，諸不行者，出錢三百入官，官以給戍者，是謂過更也。

史文云『高祖繇長安』正合於繇戍一條。亦即當時劉邦在戍邊之調，到咸陽去擔任戍卒。這一點就漢制論秦制，大概是不錯的。若就錢數來說，一月二千，三日三百，若以昭宣時所寫的漢簡來核對，那就不僅不能對秦代標準適合，竟然連西漢時的標準也不是。如淳所引漢律，顯然就東漢時的漢律做準則的（東漢時已廢都試及普徧徵兵。但在有些特殊情況下當有正卒及戍卒，所以此律未廢只就當時薪水標準隨時調整）。所以說一般吏人送劉邦三百而蕭何五百是不適合秦制的。這一點牽涉計算問題，且放下不論，而另一問題也同樣發生。這就是所謂『吏奉錢』所指的是什麼的問題。因爲如其蕭何及其他吏人也當值戍，則所給的錢是『過更錢』而不是『吏奉錢』。今稱做吏奉錢，顯然是過更錢以外的『餽饋』而不是過更的本身。再說過更錢是給官，官再給戍者，而此『吏奉錢』係直接送達，更非過更錢之比。既然是餽饋，那就要接著送禮人的景況和送禮人與收禮人的關係來決定的，劉邦和蕭何都是縣吏，比一般平民的景況好些（當然比起來薛公致孟子的餽饋一出手就幾十鎰就差遠了），這種標準可以拿當時縣吏的月薪作爲大致的估量。縣吏大致都是『百石吏』每月的收入大致八石稍多一點，以每石三十錢計，每月大約是二百四十多錢，若按照漢制上推，漢制半錢半米，每月應當是一百二十餘錢。送三錢是月薪百分的二點五，送五錢是月薪百分的四點一七。照送禮講都不算過分。

照這樣說，秦代一錢却具有其購買力，漢代情形，照漢書竇田灌韓傳說，灌夫『平生毀程不識不直一錢』。正是表示一錢是最小的貨幣單位，對於一般人的應用，一飯一錢已經夠用了。

㈢　漢代初期的錢幣問題

　　這樣情形下的物價，是相當低廉的。不過錢既然是最小的單位，還可以買一個相當數目的食物或物品，那在值一錢貨物之中，就無法再分別精粗美惡，至於找零的問題，更無法解決，這就形成了輔幣單位太大的問題。也就是漢書食貨志所謂『漢興，以爲秦錢重難用』(21)。這點確實不錯的，不過下接『更令民鑄莢錢』却是另外一回事。如其嫌錢重難用，更鑄別一種補助的錢來和半兩『子母相權』可算做一種經濟政策。如其鑄莢錢（或楡莢錢）以致通貨膨脹，再由通貨膨脹發生了商人屯積居奇的事，這是戰時病態，和經濟政策全不相干。半兩錢重是事實，不過漢代政府却未曾做過任何補救的政策，只有楚漢戰爭時有過通貨膨脹的現象。

　　這種通貨膨脹情勢的發生，當然由於政府的濫鑄。不過如其要追究責任，恐怕還相當複雜。也許漢王的政府負一部分責任，也許漢王政府完全不負責任。自秦政府崩潰以後，到處諸侯據地稱王。他們都是以獨立王國自居，鑄幣之權是不會放棄的，漢王當時也不過諸王國之一，在平定項羽之前，沒有人把他當做天子。如其漢王鑄幣，實際上也和其他王國一樣。秦的半兩久已通行，已經是一種成功的貨幣。諸侯鑄幣一定也是鑄圓錢，其影響到半兩幣值，不論上面鑄半兩二字或鑄上別的字，結果是一樣的。所以更令民鑄莢錢一語，依照戰時經濟政策來說，是違反政府原則的。現在居然漢王有『令』聽民私鑄，其中當然有不得已的複雜原因在內。現在想到的可能原因，第一、可能鑄楡莢錢是一個已經存在的事實，基於經濟上的理由，非承認不可。第二、可能漢王政府自已也在鑄楡莢錢，也就不能拿半兩錢的正常標準來衡量所有的錢幣。

　　從兩周戰國以來，錢根本是由交換的工具演變而來的，似乎根本就沒有把貨幣鑄造之權，一定完全歸到政府的必要。據食貨志引賈誼說『法使天下公得顧租，鑄銅錫爲錢，敢雜以鉛鐵爲它巧者，其罪黥』這裡所說的『法』是漢高帝『禁盜鑄錢令』以外的『法』，也就是漢代承用的秦法。這裡所引的是秦法中對於鑄錢方面質的標準，當然也一定還有量的標準，就是『半兩』。秦代依照了這個標準（銅錫合金的半兩）來控制天下的鑄錢，當然是公也鑄私也可以鑄。秦自始皇統一天下，政治已上軌道，如有敢偷工減料鑄錢的，也不難發現。但是在楚漢之際，甚至於到了漢高帝平定天下以後，鑄錢的標準已經混亂，再按照舊的法律來辦，就不易推行了。這就是漢高帝平定天下後，將所用鑄錢之權收歸國有，嚴禁私鑄的原因(22)。

漢高帝雖然禁私鑄，實際上客觀的環境仍然無法把秦半兩舊制完全恢復。第一、從高帝到文帝並未曾把半兩的量恢復起來，高帝所鑄名爲半兩，仍是輕錢，史記索隱顧氏案古今注云『莢錢重三銖』(23)。照食貨志說孝文時『錢益多而輕』正可見眞正的半兩未曾恢復，僅僅把鑄幣之權收歸官有罷了。第二、卽使收回官有，中央政府對於諸侯王仍無力限制，而且輕錢是旣成事實，不曾銷毀，對於私鑄小錢也不能有效的完全禁止，以致形成了幣制的混亂。照賈誼所說是：『民用錢郡縣不同』，『或用輕錢，百加若干；或用重錢，平稱不受』(24)。是說用錢的標準隨地方性的習慣而異。有的是可以接受輕錢，但是每百錢之中，必需要搭上定數的標準半兩，才能交易；另外一種是以標準半兩錢計數，如用輕錢，就得過稱來稱；並且還要比稱桿的標準高些，卽令稱桿是平的，仍然不夠，一定要補的多一點才受。所以當時在市場之上形成了不同的習慣，爲著整頓起見，確有重訂新辦法的必要。這就文帝五年廢除盜鑄錢令（只保存秦鑄錢標準法），同時也減輕錢的標準重量，從半兩改爲四銖的原因。

文帝的改革在原則上是無可非議的。賈誼和賈山曾反對過。賈山傳中的意見，除了認爲不應當變更先帝舊法以及鑄錢爲『人主之操柄』(25)不可與人以外，不見其他。賈誼意見除見於漢書食貨志尙見於賈子新書，所以還可以看出他大致的意見來。不過賈誼的意見，似乎並未針對漢文帝當時政策的需要，其不見聽是有理由的。

鑄幣之權所以要掌握在中央政府手中的原因，並非因爲這是『人主的權衡』而是因爲貨幣只是一種市場的籌碼，應當按着需要來調整，在調整時，對於整個國家的經濟是非常有用的，並且調整適宜對於國家稅收也只有好處。但專就調整的機關本位來說，是不應該有盈利可說的；就國家來說，也不可以憑鑄幣來賺取盈餘。就製造的成本來說，官營的作坊或工廠一定較私營的成本稍高。官營的可以做到精工，但很難做到節省。文帝爲人是主張減刑薄賦，節省民力的。而且依照『無爲』的觀念，政府應當做事越少越好。所以他的改鑄四銖錢，立下標準，開放錢禁的主張，在原則上是無可非議的。當然執行起來，卻有技術的困難，文帝也不見得不知道。只是這些困難是可以解決的，還是無法解決的，就成爲爭執的中心問題。

　　再就漢初的情形來說，當時商業誠然已經有某種程度的進展。不過市場中供求的
變動，究竟不大。當時對於通貨的需要顯然的是隨時可以補充新鑄的錢幣，而不是估
計市場的需要來調整錢幣的數量。如其只爲供給定時定量的錢幣，那就官鑄或私鑄，
結果可以無甚分別的。文帝把錢的重量定爲四銖，再按照舊以質的標準爲銅錫合金，
當時一定計算過，在某些地區人民按這個標準去鑄，一定可以多少有些餘贏的。賈誼
所說『然鑄錢之情，非殽雜爲巧，則不可得贏』[26]。可能只是某些地區是這樣的，決不
是一個普徧存在的事實。但也一定有些地區，贏利在成本之中，變成了臨界的狀態，
稍雜一點鉛鐵，就有贏利，否則就沒有。當時化學分析的方法是不知道的，檢查成品
很難斷定出來銅錫的純度，因而問題就會發生了。這就是賈誼所指出的，吏如認眞，
那就到處是犯罪的，吏如不認眞那就錢法會壞下去，就不如簡單的禁鑄，反而是一個
簡捷明瞭的辦法，這個意見確實接觸了實際問題。不過終文帝之世不改這種政策，直
到景帝中六年才再禁止私鑄，而文景之世又是著名的盛世。所以文帝的辦法誠然一定
有其缺點，但如一定說一點優點也沒有，卻又是不見得的。

　　依照賈誼的意見，不僅應當禁私鑄錢，還應當國家對銅加以管制。依照食貨志引
賈誼的建議說（賈子新書略同）[27]：

> 姦數不勝而法禁數潰，銅使之然也，故銅布於天下，其爲禍博矣。今博禍可除
> 而七福可改也。何謂七福？上收銅勿令布，則民不鑄錢，黥罪不積，一矣。僞
> 錢不蕃，民不相疑二矣。采銅作者，及於耕田，三矣。銅畢歸於上，上挾銅積
> 以御輕重，錢輕則以術斂之，重則以術散之，貨物必平，四矣。以作兵器，以
> 假貴臣，多少有制，用別貴賤，五矣。以臨萬貨，以調盈虛，以收奇羨，則官
> 富實而末民困，六矣。制吾棄財以與匈奴爭其民，則敵必懷，七矣。故善爲天
> 下者，因禍而爲福，轉敗而爲功。今久退七福而行博禍，臣誠傷之。上不聽。

這個意見是一個很極端的意見，也可說是一個革命性的意見，從來沒有人想到這樣
做，更沒人敢這樣做的。因爲依照他的辦法，是只許官家採銅，而嚴禁私採。這樣採
銅的人就減少了（卽所謂『采銅作者，及於耕田』），銅的生產量也就大減。從秦到
漢，錢的法定重量從十二銖（半兩）減到四銖，正表示銅量不敷鑄造流通貨幣之用。

若再減少銅的生產量，國家還是要鑄幣的，一定發現了銅荒，而不是像賈氏那樣的如意算盤，國家控制了充分的銅量可以運用。這種類似的意見，到漢武帝時用來做管制鐵器，卻未曾用來管制銅。顯然的大致用了賈氏的思想，只因爲管制鐵是可能的，管制銅就有事實上的障礙了，仍然比較賈氏爲緩和的。

我總覺得中國君主之中，漢文帝是一個智慧極高的統治者。不僅就文帝一代統治的成績看得到一點，從對於賈誼的關係上也可以看得出來。賈誼當然是一個很有學問而且不多見的思想家。不過檢討賈誼的議論，其中啓發性遠過於實行的可能。漢文帝確實欣賞賈誼，因爲和他討論得到不少的啓發。但如其要言聽計從，那就只有宋神宗那樣朝乾夕惕，懷抱大志，而智慧只有中才的君主才會的。依照賈誼傳中所記，漢文帝說：『久不見賈生，自以爲過之，今不及也』(28)。漢文帝的智力、判斷力，不在賈生之下，那是眞的，決非誇辭。不過一個日理萬幾的君主，當然不會有那麼多的時間，去學，去思。他說『今不及也』也是實話。他任賈生爲二千石，却又任賈生爲二千石中的閒職，其中當然有分寸的。他是要等著適當機會才用賈生。可惜賈生來不及任用就死了。

依照漢書食貨志說：文帝五年『乃更造四銖錢，其文爲半兩』(29)但現在出土的錢確有其文爲四銖的，但卻不合標準，這是爲什麼呢？照現在的解釋，四銖錢文爲半兩食貨志並不會錯。不過文帝當時的法令，決不會說今更造四銖錢，仍用半兩爲文，那樣自相矛盾的詔書，而是只說造四銖錢，未明定所用的文字。鑄造的時候，可能就有人用四銖爲文，也有人用相承的半兩爲文（因爲楡莢錢重三銖，也是用半兩爲文）。當時是可以私鑄的，吏員檢查時只檢查是否合於標準，卻不曾管上面的文字，因而上面的文字就兩者並用。食貨志只用半兩一種，所以說其文爲半兩了。

（四） 景武時期的錢幣改革

因爲漢朝初期，漢天子不能十分有效的控制諸侯王，對於鑄幣的法令不論禁私鑄或不禁私鑄，都是沒有好辦法把各地紛亂的情形改正。幸虧是當時天下已經長期太平，卽令各地地方性的幣制比較混亂一點，卻也對於國內經濟的繁榮，尙無大礙。到了景帝平定了七國之亂，中央收囘了對諸侯王控制之權，對於整頓幣制的確掃除了一番障礙。不過景帝時對於錢幣問題並非七國平定就處理的，而是要等到九年以後的中元六年才開始做。但看一看漢書景帝紀，中四年罷諸侯御史大夫官，中五年，更名諸侯丞相為相，是損抑諸侯之權到中五年才告一段落。到了中六年，定鑄錢，偽黃金棄市律，顯然的，和損抑諸侯權有連帶之作用。

　　這一個『鑄錢偽黃金棄市律』和高帝時的『盜鑄錢令』是略有不同的。雖然都是把私鑄錢的處死刑。不過高帝時是『令』，景帝時的是『律』。令是比較臨時性的，秦律有關的條文並未廢止，只是在令未廢時，照令來補充律文。至於景帝時的却是改定律文。過去有關的律文不再有效，完全照新定的律文為準。其次舊律只有鑄錢一項，不及偽黃金，如有偽作黃金的，只能比照鑄錢辦理。這條新律却是鑄錢及偽黃金都定上去了。當然比較舊律要嚴格多了。

　　關於這條律文的解說，在漢書顏師古注中曾討論過。注文說[30]：

> 應劭曰：「文帝五年，聽民放鑄，律當未除。先時多作偽金，偽金終不可成。而徒損費，轉相誑耀，窮則引起為盜賊，故定其律也。」孟康曰：「民先時多作偽金。故其語曰：金可作，世可度，費損甚多而終不成。民亦稍知其犯者希，因此定律也。」師古曰：「應說是。」

實際上這個律牽涉兩部分，鑄錢，私偽黃金，應孟兩氏只說到第二部分。定律的原因是由於鑄黃金者多而非由於犯者漸希。當以應說為是。不過應氏所說的『文帝五年，聽民放鑄，律當未除』，數語非常含混。律和令的分別，應氏當然是明白的。高帝禁鑄是令，文帝放鑄也是令，律當然指秦律而言。此所謂『律尚未除』乃指聽民放鑄，而不合標準的，則加以黥罪。至此改定前法，舊律始除。凡私鑄者處死。意思是這樣的。其中意義不明之處，可能是應注被刪削的原故。

　　景帝雖然對於私鑄的事把法律加嚴，盜鑄並未曾禁絕，也沒什麼顯著的成績，通行的官鑄四銖錢，和文帝時並無多大的分別。不過武帝初年，府庫中是盈餘的，這不僅由於文帝的積蓄，主要的還是景帝時的積蓄。

　　大致說來，這種以四銖錢為主，照地方性習慣，把成貫的錢，有條件的增加小錢數目，或用稱來稱，對於貨幣使用，妨害並不甚大，也就是對於經濟上的阻礙，還不算十分大。而其中最成問題的，還是涉及到治安問題。在景紀這段的應劭注已經接觸到治安問題，其實治安問題還不止此。如放任鑄錢，到處商人作僞，攙雜種種大小不等的錢，犯罪罪的到處都是。這些犯過罪的人，管理起來就相當費事，而影響到社會的平定。如其嚴禁鑄錢，犯小罪的固然減少了，但犯大罪的更難得管理。這般人就成了亡命之徒。史記貨殖傳稱[31]：

> 富者人之情性，其在閭巷，少年攻剽，劫人作姦，掘冢鑄幣，任俠並兼，借交報仇，篡逐出隱，不避法禁，走死若騖。其實皆爲財用耳。

所以鑄造私錢和當時游俠及盜賊都是相連的[32]。從這裡也就可以了解游俠傳中許多人物，所以能形成一個組織，其中經濟背景，就靠這些不法行動的收穫來支持。而這些行動之中，鑄私錢當然是其中一個極重要的來源。景武以來酷吏傳中一些酷吏攻擊的對象也主要是這類的人[33]。

錢種龐雜，良幣及劣幣同時並用，不夠標準的私鑄錢是極容易混入錢中雜用的。最有效的辦法，當然把劣幣全部收回改鑄，只以標準的四銖錢爲準才可以。武帝時五銖錢所以能够成功不僅靠錢的精工，也靠盡毀舊錢，專用五銖作通用錢幣。這一點文景兩代因爲還未形成太大的問題，所以沒有決心去做。

文景兩代貨幣上都有問題。做的都不澈底。這是由於當時天下太平，不希望過於煩擾。文景兩帝也未嘗不知道當時政治漏洞甚多。只是眞的澈底去做也不見得做得好，反而不如照他們只做一半的作風，倒可以天下豐盈人民安樂。所以在武帝初卽位時，天下庫藏，有一筆可觀的蓄聚。

武帝征伐匈奴是十分消耗國力的，元狩四年，武帝卽位的第二十二年，開始做第一次失敗的幣制改革。將原有四銖錢取消，改爲不同的等次。除去黃金一斤爲單位是一個主要單位，不曾變動以外，在金與銅單位之間，再鑄三種銀幣。其等次爲[34]：

(1)龍幣一重八兩直三千。

(2)馬幣—照食貨志（平準書同）說直五百，當就幣六分之一，而和次一級的龜幣，如三比五，不能互相兌換。古代幣制的原則是子母相權，若不能子母相權，那就一定有誤。大約平準書原脫『一千』二字，食貨志直抄未校正。所以馬幣實應直一千五百重四兩爲龍幣二分之一，爲龜幣的五倍，二進與五進與通常的習慣也是相合的。

　　(3)龜幣一直三百，當重19.2銖，可能把成色減些，重二十銖。

古代銀比後代銀貴些，大致比例是金的一半。如其金一斤（十六兩直一萬）那就金八兩直五千。銀八兩只應直二千五百。但武帝的銀幣，重八兩直三千，多出五百，並且還要攙入錫，成色不佳，按照武帝的原意是當主幣用，不是當輔幣用。主幣必需成色夠，可是開始設計就不曾顧到，無怪終於失敗了。

　　這種鑄銀幣的觀念，中國是一直沒有的，大約是受到張騫回來，帶回西域銀幣的影響。但作爲主幣，應當存量夠通行之用。中國不是產銀國家，漢時外來的銀也不多，再加上成色不夠，和黃金的比例不合理，所以食貨志說（元鼎二年）：『白金稍賤，民弗寶用，縣官（中央政府）以令禁之，無效』。只好把白金罷去。

　　白金幣（銀幣）的不能通行，大約是事實上的限制，而非造意上的問題。和白金同時發行的白鹿皮皮幣，那就是否可以算做貨幣就有問題了。食貨志說：

> 有司言曰：古者皮幣，諸侯以聘享，金有三等，黃金爲上，白金爲中，赤金爲
> 下。……乃以白鹿皮方尺，緣以繢，爲皮幣，直四十萬。王侯宗室朝覲聘享，
> 必以皮幣薦璧，然後得行。

　　這裏所說的幣，觀念是不清楚的。所謂幣，本義是做禮物的，至於當作市場的籌碼用，是社會發展以後，一個後起之義。漢代用幣字，當交換媒介的意義超過了禮物的意義，但是漢代在二者不同的觀念中，界線並未劃清。那時的執掌官吏（有司）忽然爲著方便籌款起見，把禮物的原義擡了出來。所以表面上是錢幣，而功能上卻是天子專賣的一種貴族間的禮物。如其專作禮物使用，並沒有任何市場上的媒介功用，那就只是一種商品而不能算做貨幣。所以皮幣始終只限於朝覲時使用，始終未曾在市場流通過。講漢代貨幣的發展時是不必將它算入的。

　　當然，皮幣以相當少數的價格貨品來代表較高的價格，這和紙幣多少有些類似。不過紙幣是要在市場流通的。並且紙幣並非先從紙幣的觀念演繹出來，而是從飛錢、交子、會子一步一步的從滙票變爲紙幣，這是從事實上所需要演變而成的。和漢代的皮幣並無觀念上或因革上的聯繫，所以追溯紙幣的發展也不應當追溯到皮幣。

　　不論銀幣或皮幣對於幣制的進展，關係都很小。只有和銀幣同時發行的三銖錢，再從三銖變爲五銖錢，才在中國幣制史上有極重要的意義。

　　三銖錢是元狩四年開始鑄造的，到元狩五年又改爲五銖錢。從文帝五年開始用四銖錢，對於私鑄雖然原來是放任的，到景帝中葉禁止。但四銖錢法的定制始終不改。經過了五十七年，直到元狩四年，才因運費太多，再加七十二萬五千貧民要遷徙到北邊和會稽，用度不足，除去造白金及皮幣以外還把四銖錢改爲三銖錢，這就是說要減輕錢的重量，要在鑄幣上政府賺一些錢來支付開支。

　　當然這一個基本觀念是錯誤的。凡是任何一種幣制，不能建立幣信，一定失敗，而這種形態下的幣制，實際上是通貨澎脹，一開始就無幣信可言。再加上鑄造輕錢更是鼓勵盜鑄的一項漏洞。結果是如食貨志所說：『吏民之犯者不可勝數』。以致國家毫無利益可言，更增上財政的恐慌，到了匱乏的程度。

　　到了元狩五年三銖錢的設計完全失敗，就不能不再爲更張。成爲中國二千多年標準的五銖錢就是在這種恐慌環境之下，勉強的產生出來的。五銖錢的原則，是政府在事實上承認了鑄錢的目的只是創造一種通用的籌碼，一點藉錢去籌款的目的也沒有。如要籌錢只有在別的方面設法。這就使發行錢幣的目的變的單純化，而五銖錢的成功就在這一點。

　　當三銖錢失敗時，未嘗不可以恢復四銖錢的。如其政府完全把雜錢收回，只鑄一種非常精工的四銖錢，一定也可以和五銖錢收到類似的效用。這種辦法更簡單些，那時管理財政的人們也一定考慮過，所以不恢復四銖，反而在那個緊急恐慌的時候鑄造較四銖爲重的五銖，大致是就當時的成本來說，鑄四銖還可以多少有些贏餘利益，如鑄五銖那就幾乎不可能有贏餘。因爲私鑄錢的人太多了，如以四銖錢爲標準，還不能杜絕私鑄，如以五銖錢爲標準，就可以減少私鑄到一個極限。所以最後還是以五銖爲定制。

　　雖然五銖錢的本意專顧到經濟上而不在財政上，財政上卻另外有些極端的辦法，如同算軺車，告緡錢等等。但仍然是不足用的，到元鼎初年，『公卿請令京師鑄鍾官赤仄，一當五，賦官用非赤仄不得行』（據食貨志，惟鍾官赤仄前的鍾字，據平準書）。這又是一件把鑄錢當財政上手段的辦法，當然結果上一定是失敗的。食貨志言其後二歲（當在元鼎四年），赤仄錢賤，民巧法用之，不便，又廢。這是一個必然的結果。

　　赤仄據平準書作赤側，依照各家的注，所謂赤仄卽是赤色的邊緣（亦卽錢的『肉好』為赤色）。這件事近代做中國經濟史的各家，均討論過。其中有關赤仄錢是否即以五銖錢作底的問題，我覺得赤仄錢是一種『大錢』，但一般鑄大錢的，其量也少於標準錢的總和（若等於標準錢的總和，就不必鑄大錢了）。所以照半兩錢的重量十二銖，或者照五銖錢的重量五銖，都可以的。平準書所以未說到錢文的原因，就是錢文仍為半兩。無甚特殊，所以不記。其次還有不少人討論過赤仄是『加工』或者『減工』的問題，就是說從半兩或五銖錢之上加一點什麼質料或減一點什麼質料。我覺得『減工』是不可能的。因為武帝不恢復四銖用五銖，就已經為的是質重以防私鑄，若再就已有的錢減一點，那就到處私鑄的人可以不用一點錢料的成本，只稍稍加工，便可將通用的錢改為大錢了，這簡直是一個不可思議的事。所以加工一說，也許可能。不過按照史文，明說是令京師鑄鍾官赤仄，是由鍾官鑄的，不是由鍾官改的。就工程做法來看，大量的工作，新做比改舊的要省工些。當時不會用那種不經濟的方法去改，所以必然是新鑄的。和舊錢不同的，是舊錢攙雜銅錫，是合金的錢，即使錫量不多，色彩也變成稍青的顏色。只有用較純的銅，才能在邊緣部分打磨成赤色。所以赤仄是特鑄純銅當五的半兩錢。這種錢比較特殊（當然也特別精工些）不會和舊錢外表相混的。

　一般錢譜是不著錄赤仄錢的，其實赤仄錢布滿天下，決不會沒有存留。所以不曾著錄。是因為無法辨別赤仄錢的形狀。如其尋繹史文，赤仄錢亦自不難辨認。因為秦錢是沒有周郭的，武帝錢有周郭，可是除赤仄以外最重不過五銖。但錢譜中確有周郭的半兩錢，並且其大小也和五株同大。這種有周郭的半兩錢，除去認為赤仄以外，那就無類可歸了。至於錢譜中認為係三分錢（即四銖錢），那是錯的，因為武帝元狩時才用周郭，未鑄四銖錢，而且錢的大小同於五銖，大於四銖，所以不是四銖。

　史文未曾說到赤仄錢始鑄的年代，但食貨志把鑄赤仄序在博士褚大等循行天下之後。循行天下事紀文在元狩六年，鑄赤仄只可能在元狩六年或元鼎元年。這種當五錢是不受歡迎的。功臣侯表曲成侯蟲達曾孫皋柔元鼎二年坐為汝南太守，知民不用赤側錢為賦，為鬼薪的。（鬼薪二歲刑）侯爵被革除。鑄赤仄至多不過兩年多，便已經被人拒用。可見赤仄的幣信始終未立。再過二年元鼎四年赤仄果然只好廢棄了。

到了赤仄不再能使用，只能通用五銖，並且因爲五銖錢的鑄造各地精粗不等，所以食貨志說(36)：

> 其後二歲赤仄錢賤，民巧法用之，又廢。於是悉禁郡國毋鑄錢，專令上林三官鑄，錢旣多而令天下非三官錢不行。諸郡國前所鑄錢皆廢銷之輸入其銅三官，而民之鑄錢益少，計其費不能相當唯眞工大姦迎盜爲之。

上林三官據殿本漢書齊召南的考證，是水衡都尉之下，均輸，鍾官和辨銅三令。到那時就集中鑄錢的業務交給水衡屬下的三官。這樣錢才可以鑄的一致。不過就國家方面來說，把天下的舊錢毀了再鑄，不僅過去鑄錢的工浪費了，而且把天下的舊錢運到長安，再從長安運到各處，除去長安以東有一條運河以外，其他地區完全靠車馬運輸，這筆運費實在可觀。這種爲錢法不計成本的辦法，眞是只有漢武帝那樣絕對集權的政府才可以做到。當然這就樹立了中國錢法的規模，但就當時人民負擔來說，是很難想像的。

從漢武帝以後，直到王莽，錢法始終不變，其劇變是在王莽的時代。

漢武帝每一種貨幣上的措施，不論是結果成功或失敗；不論漢庭是否有意的訂立貨幣政策。但總可以說，任何一種經濟措施，都是針對現實的。但是王莽的經濟措施卻不是循著這個方向。我們雖然不能說王莽的政治完全沒有一些理想，但王莽的貨幣政策卻是一點眞實的客觀背景也沒有，完全拿全國的經濟基礎，做爲裝飾上的試驗品。這一種虛浮的，裝飾的心理，不僅和漢代初年文景時代走上了兩個極端，並且還使人感覺到，是否是成人的成熟心理狀態下的產物。非常可能王莽少時是生在鮮車怒馬的五陵少年環境之中，因爲他父親早死不封侯，在從兄弟中最爲孤貧，一切都不能和別人比。他勉強折節向學，在心理狀態中是被壓抑的，一朝得志，所表現出來的，還是五陵少年式的把國家制度當成鮮車怒馬來裝飾。表面上好像有一種理想，實際上是爲著補償從前五陵少年的心理狀態。所以他的動機談不到如何高級。

王莽許多制度，都是滿足他自己心理上的補償，值不得細爲分析的。只是爲著敍述漢代錢制的演變，所以在此大致說一下(37)：

> 1.王莽居攝，用四品並行制，甲，錯刀，直五千；乙，契刀，直五百；丙，大錢，重十二銖，文曰大泉五十；丁，五銖錢仍舊。

2.王莽始建國元年，罷錯刀，契刀及五銖錢定為金、銀、龜、貝、泉、布、
為泉，布均為銅鑄，故稱為五物，六名，二十八品。布為鏟形錢，泉為圓
錢。泉分為六品，甲，大泉五十；乙，壯泉四十；丙，中泉三十；丁，幼泉
二十（重五銖），戊，幺泉一十（重三銖），已，小泉直一（重一銖），但
黃金一斤，仍為直泉萬，可是從前是直五銖錢萬，那時成為直一銖泉萬，在
市面上一定不會看見黃金的。

3.這種混亂的錢法實行不久，經濟混亂，但行大泉五十及小錢直一。

4.天鳳元年，又罷大小泉。但行兩種，貨布及貨泉。貨布重二十五銖直貨泉二
十五，貨泉重五銖。前作大泉五十與貨泉同值一。

這種貨幣混亂的情形，完全是人為的。那時老百姓但求恢復五銖，後漢書五行志所記
蜀童謠的『黃牛白腹，五銖當復』⑶，當然說不上預言，只是代表一般願望。到了東
漢光武的建武十六年再復五銖錢。雖然因為有些地區錢數不足，夾用布帛，但五銖
的標準，還是一直維持下去的。這種五銖的標準，一直適用於唐代的開元通寶，宋、
元、明和清代的各種年號錢，直等到清末鑄造銅圓以後，才形成了另外的標準。這就
可以看出來漢代五銖錢影響的鉅大。

但是王莽時的雜型錢幣到光武時改變到五銖，也不是那樣容易改變，而是經過了
一些周折的。當光武建國之初，對於鑄錢一事還和更始時期一樣，沒有一定的計畫。
在建武十一年時以馬援為隴西太守，委託他以整理西方的責任。他到了隴西以後，上
書建議應當如西漢舊法鑄五銖錢。光武將此事下太尉，司徒，司空三府會商，三府奏
以為未可施行，鑄錢事遂被打銷。等到建武十六年，馬援徵入為虎賁中郎將，再從公
卿求得前奏，共計駁議十三條，也一一駁正，再行表奏。光武竟從了馬援的意見，
如是又重新恢復五銖錢的鼓鑄，奠定了中國錢幣的基礎⑶。

這裡最大的問題，還是中國銅的產量究竟不甚豐富，在西漢時已經有用縑帛代錢
使用的記錄。本來在文帝時已經有『賜三老，孝者人五匹，悌者力田二匹，廉吏二百
石以率百石者三匹』，用縑帛代錢的事。到昭帝元年『賜郡國所選有行義者，涿郡韓
福等五人帛，人五十匹』，大量用縑帛賜少數的人，更顯明的把縑帛當貨幣使用。因
為五十匹的縑帛，對於一個人的衣著，實在大多了，只有當作貨幣看，才有意義的。

到了宣帝時期，更把縑帛賜給公卿大臣。五鳳元年，『皇太后賜丞相，將軍，列侯，中二石帛百匹，大夫人八十匹』。到甘露三年，又賜汝南太守帛百匹（因為鳳皇見於汝南）。這些都顯示著因為金屬錢幣不够用，已經漸次在某一些機會下，用縑帛賞賜來代替貨幣的賞賜。只是西漢後期，錢制並未曾破壞，所以賞賜時用縑帛來代替現錢的事，不致影響到錢幣的使用。

在東漢時代似乎和西漢時代已經有些不同，把縑帛和穀當作錢幣的事，已經比西漢更為常見。這大概由於王莽把幣制攪亂之後，五銖錢的基礎已經不如西漢的穩固。再加上金銀數量的減少及銅產的不足，更影響到貨幣的流通。還有一個原因似乎也影響東漢的錢制，那就是東漢時代南方的開發。南方的開發和王莽時期的混亂，大約有相當的關係。因為王莽時的混亂，只限於黃河流域，而長江流域各處，大都未曾受到影響。這就使得黃河流域的難民，大量向長江流域移動。長江流域接受了這些大量的難民，自然形成了開發的原動力。但是長江流域新開闢的地區，銅礦並不豐富。這就使得地方愈開闢，銅錢愈不足用。再加上地方開闢了，交通線延長了，從前用上林三官專鑄銅錢的舊制愈難行得通。所以東漢時代五銖錢的舊制還能勉強維持，而對於其中的漏洞，補苴起來也就開始發生困難了。

在安帝建光元年，許冲上書獻說文解字，詔賜布四十匹(40)，這是一個非常著名賜布的例子，倘在西漢初年，那就要賜現錢了。東漢時因為錢數不够，有時將錢雜用縑布，有時專用縑布，意識到縑布也當作貨幣來用了。其見於後漢書的，例如：

明帝紀中元二年，十二月甲寅詔曰：『天下亡命殊死以下，聽得贖論。死罪入縑二十匹，右趾至髡鉗城旦舂十匹，完城旦舂至司寇作二匹』(41)。

郭后紀『以太牢上郭主塚，賜粟萬斛，錢五十萬』(42)。

馬皇后紀，『帝崩，肅宗卽位，太后感析別之懷各賜王赤綬，加安車駟馬。白越三千端，雜帛二千匹，黃金十斤』(43)。

又買貴人傳：『及太后崩乃策書加貴人王赤綬，安車一駟，永巷宮人二百，御府雜帛二萬匹，大司農黃金千斤，錢二千萬』(44)。

鄧后紀：『賜周馮貴人……黃金三十斤，雜帛三千匹，白越四千端』(45)。

曹后紀『聘以束帛之縭五萬匹』(46)。

韋彪傳：『彪遂稱困篤……受賜錢二十萬。永元元年卒。……賜錢二十萬，布百匹，穀三十斛』(47)。

劉般傳：『賜般錢百萬，繒二百匹』(48)。

梁商傳：『賜錢百萬，布三十匹，皇后錢五百萬，布萬匹』(49)。

劉愷傳：『卒於家，詔使書護喪事，賜東園秘器，錢五十萬，布千匹』(50)。

祭肜傳：『賜縑百匹』(51)。

張奐傳：『董卓慕之，使其兄遺縑百匹，奐惡卓為之，絕而不受』(52)。

夏馥傳：『乃自翦須，變形入林慮山中，隱匿姓名為冶家傭，親突煙炭，形貌毀瘁，馥弟靜，乘車馬，載縑帛，追之於涅陽市中』(53)。

歐陽歙傳：『賻縑三千餘匹』(54)。

周黨傳：『賜帛四十匹』(55)。

董卓傳：『拜郎中，賜縑九千匹。卓曰「為之則已，有之則士」。乃悉分與吏兵，無所留』(56)。

東海恭王傳：『元初中，恭王嗣孫肅上縑萬匹以助軍費』(57)。

又任城王尚傳『順帝時，尚嗣孫崇上錢帛在邊費』（按任城國亢父縑見敦煌漢簡）(58)。

東夷高句驪傳『安帝詔許高句驪新附送還所掠生口者，皆與贖直。縑人四十匹，小口半之』(59)。

縱以上的各種材料來看，東漢時期布帛和現錢雜用來完成貨幣的功用，情形非常普遍。當然布帛作為貨幣來使用，並非一個好的辦法，所以要參雜使用的，顯然因為籌碼短缺的原因。而籌碼短缺的原因，可能因為市場增大，而籌碼並未配合市場的需要。籌碼之中，黃金可能因為外流而消失（此事下面再為討論），而銅錢除去王莽時一陣混亂之外，可能還有因為銅價偏高以致形成私銷的情形。這些都使執政者窮於應付，只好參用布帛，也就藉此緩和了銅錢短絀的危機。當然東漢時銅錢還夠作輔幣之用，縑帛和布都以匹為單位，還不至於像三國時情形那樣的嚴重。

布帛和錢幣，實際上在東漢前期（章帝時）已發生一種並用的現象了。後漢書朱暉傳說(60)；

是時穀貴，縣官經用不足，朝廷憂之。尙書張林上言，穀所以貴，由錢賤故也。可盡封錢，一取布帛爲租以通天下之用。……於是詔諸尙書通議。暉奏據林言不可施行，事遂寢。後陳事者復重述林前議，以爲於國誠便，帝然之，有詔施行。暉復獨奏……布帛爲租，則吏多姦盜，誠非明主所當行……寢其事。

這種布帛銅錢並用的事一直到桓帝時代，那時錢賤的事實發生，當然是由於私鑄橫行，劣幣驅良幣的原因，據後漢書劉陶傳(61)，有人上書以爲貨輕錢薄，故致貧困，宜改鑄大錢。(此所謂大錢，依原有辭意，並非指當五或當十的錢，而是朝廷鑄合於標準的五銖錢，比較一般通行的爲重)。事下四府羣僚(四府指大將軍及太尉，司徒，司空)，及太學能言之士。陶以爲『民可百年無貨，不可一朝有饑，故食爲至急也。議者不達農殖之本，多言鑄冶之便，………蓋萬人鑄之，一人奪之，猶不能給，況今一人鑄之，萬人奪之乎？(因爲當時『良苗盡於蝗螟之口』的原故)，帝竟不鑄錢』。這是說當時的客觀形勢，已經不是鑄標準的錢幣所能挽救。到了獻帝初平元年，董卓壞五銖錢，悉取洛陽長安銅人，鍾簴，飛廉，銅馬之屬去鑄小錢，由是錢賤物貴，穀石數萬，錢貨不行，就形成三國兩晉以後用穀帛爲通貨的局面。

但是無論如何，用穀帛做通貨是十分不正常的。所以在中國縱然銅少，不能應付充分鑄錢的需要，也得被環境強迫的，非鑄錢不可。晉書食貨志(62)：

黃初二年，魏文帝罷五銖錢，使百姓以穀帛爲市。至明帝世，錢廢穀用旣久，人間巧僞漸多，競濕穀以爲利，作薄絹以爲市，雖處以嚴刑，而莫能禁也。司馬芝等舉朝大議，以爲『用錢非徒豐國，亦所以省刑，今若更鑄五銖錢，則國豐刑省，於事爲便。』魏明帝乃更立五銖錢，至晉用之，不聞有所改制。……晉自中原喪亂，元帝過江，用孫氏舊錢，輕重雜行。大者謂之比輪，中者謂之四文。吳興沈充又鑄小錢，謂之沈郎錢，錢見不多，由是稍貴。孝武太元三年詔曰『錢國之重寶，小人貪利銷壞無已，監司者當以爲意。廣州夷人寶貴銅鼓，而州境素不出銅，聞官私賈人皆於此下貪比輪錢斤兩差重，以入廣州貨與夷人，鑄敗作鼓，與重爲禁制得者科罪』。安帝元興中，桓玄輔政，議欲廢錢用穀帛。孔琳之議曰……『洪範八政，貨爲食次……穀帛爲寶，本充衣食，分以爲貨，則殘損甚多。又勞毀於商販之手，耗棄於割裁之用，此之爲幣著於自囊』。……朝議多同琳之，故玄議不行。

這種情形也見於晉書張軌傳：

> 愍帝即位，大府參軍索輔言於軌曰：『泰始中河西荒廢，遂不用錢，裂匹以爲
> 段數，縑布既壞，市易又難，徒壞女工，不任衣用，弊之甚也』。

所以三國兩晉以後，把布帛當做通貨使用，只是因爲金屬貨幣缺乏，採用一種萬不得已的辦法。凡是有銅可以鑄錢，不論是政府，不論是人民，沒有願意使用米粟布帛的。只有魏代當魏文帝初年，在金屬貨幣十分缺乏之時，才採用廢錢用穀帛的辦法。但是過了四十年，仍從司馬芝的意見，恢復用錢。吳國是始終用錢的，只是間或鑄造大錢，使得幣制混亂，蜀國是用錢的，但因銅料缺乏，劉備至取帳鉤銅鑄錢（南齊書崔祖思傳）[63]。直到諸葛亮平定南中，才解決了銅料的問題[64]。但是晉平蜀以後，南中竟成半獨立的狀況，對於銅料未聞有所補助。所以劉宋時沈演之說『錢少由于採鑄久廢』（宋書何尚之傳），並且國內只有貧鑛，採取也不敷成本。在南齊武帝永明八年，劉悛採蒙山銅（今四川雅安）鑄錢千餘萬，卒因功費多乃止（南齊書劉悛傳）。這些事實上的限制，使得鑄錢的事無法貫徹，而參用穀帛的問題，一直拖下去。隋唐時代雖然情形好轉，但殘餘的習慣尚未能完全去掉。一直要等到大量的白銀來到中國，才改掉這種經濟上不合理的負荷[65]。當然唐宋以來交鈔的發明，可以作爲通貨使用，也是廢除穀帛一個因素。

穀帛的使用並非因爲穀帛有任何便利之處，更不是像迂腐老生的想法，使用穀帛爲的是重農，是重視穀帛（實際上的結果是浪費穀帛），而只是因爲市場上的籌碼不夠，要找一種東西當籌碼來使用。如其有一種高價而性質不變的物質，這個問題當然就解決了。銅，當然也算比較上可用的物質，只是銅的價值並不算高，而用途卻非常廣，經常日用缺不了銅。所以銅總會在貨幣和器用之間擺動。拿銅來鑄成幣，所代表的是貨幣的價值而非是銅的價值，既然價值在交換方面，而非使用方面，和銅的市價當然有一個距離。如其以銅爲主幣，當然會發生困難問題，即銅貴則會私銷，銅賤又會私鑄。並且如其銅錢不能標準化（把不合標準的廢棄不在市場上通用），那就即令銅價不賤，私鑄也無法防止。終於幣制敗壞，市場不能安定。

西漢時代被注意到的問題是私鑄，而私鑄出來的錢一定都是不合標準的小錢。雖

然和標準錢相差的程度各不相同，但私鑄的錢不能切合標準，卻是不容疑問的事。其所以造成大量私鑄，而無法禁止的原因，大致由於下列各種關係：

（甲）半兩錢的傳統，就是從戰國時各種圓錢改換而成的。原來在戰國時，一定就是把許多種不同的圓錢，混雜起來使用。到了秦併天下，進展相當迅速。決不可能把秦的半兩錢普及到天下市場，而把舊有的圓錢全部廢棄，一定用一種逐漸用半兩錢代替舊錢的方法。秦統一天下不過十二年，天下卽重歸於動亂，所以半兩錢是否當時卽已全部把舊錢替代，尚未可知。就算在始皇時半兩錢全部代替舊錢已經成功，但人民雜用舊錢的記憶尚在，並且再遭動亂，私錢充斥市場。經過漢高帝、惠帝、呂后、文帝、景帝、直到武帝元狩五年經過了九十年之久，才開始鑄五銖錢，有計畫推行標準的錢制。但這仍然是逐漸代替的，到平帝元始中，京師上林三官總鑄五銖錢二百八十餘億萬（食貨志，案億萬當作萬的自乘方來解釋），這是一百一十年總鑄錢的數目。除去私銷以外，應當大致夠用，足以建立標準化的錢制。自從王莽時一個人為的擾亂，從此中國各朝就不會再有機準的銅錢制度了。若就清末到民國初年的制錢情況來說。當時的制錢大致是以清代官鑄錢為主，但清錢的大小輕重也不一致，順治、康熙、雍正的錢最合標準，乾隆和嘉慶的官鑄錢已經減小，咸同以後更加減縮，並參雜一些私鑄小錢。除此以外至少有十分之一是半兩，五銖，大泉五十，貨泉、開元通寶，宋元明年號錢，日本的寬永錢，再偶然加上極少永昌錢及太平天國錢。這些不同形製的各種錢一樣雜用，只要錢數夠就算可以通用了。這種混雜不純的錢貫制度，實在是一個非常久遠的傳統，也就是歷代私鑄不能根絕的一個重要原因。

其次，自戰國、秦、漢以來，黃金和錢並用，而且漢時還定了黃金和錢互換的比例，但黃金與錢之間，並無主幣輔幣的區別（至清代，甚至民國初年，都還未將制錢及銅圓算做正式的輔幣。只因銅圓携帶及使用都不方便，而市場上銀兩及銀圓已夠用，銅圓已漸形成輔幣了）。主幣是市場上的貨幣單位，交易用主幣來計算，輔幣只為找零而使用，大量的輔幣，市場上得拒絕接受。就漢時情形來說，黃金一斤的單位太大，在市場交易上很少用到，只有用錢來計算。所以銅錢在事實上就成為主幣。但這個單位又嫌太小，一般的交易，以百錢千錢計算是常事。在漢代時百錢一貫已經習為故常，也就是百錢一貫才是正式的單位。依照後漢書百官志注引荀綽晉百官表，東漢時俸半錢半米。其中俸錢數從中二千石至百石，是以九千，六千五百，五千，四千，三千五百，二千五百，二千，一千，八百為差。百是最小單位，其下再無奇零。這就是因為百錢一貫，自成單位的原故（清代雖然千錢一貫，但其中每百錢自成一節，此亦沿襲百錢一貫舊制）。百錢一貫既成一單位，就一般情形而論，只檢查錢數，並不嚴格一一檢查各錢是否都合於標準，只要大致都是大錢，就不將較小一點的剔出。這一種情況，就是說對於把持銅錢的標準，從來就無法做到嚴格。市場上也不會有那樣的時間去把制錢一一審核。這也是給私鑄者一個漏洞。西漢錢貴，交易時用的錢數較少，審核時可能做到嚴格一點。（也不是絕對的）所以私鑄五銖錢惟『真工大姦』乃能為之。到王莽把幣制破壞，幣制雜亂起來，從東漢開始，直到明清，大概沒有一個時期可以真正後的那樣嚴格了。在這裏不必多為引據，但看文獻通考卷八和卷九，就可知道從六期到宋末的情形，元代固不必說，明清兩代是明不如清，而清代也始終未曾拿出來統一錢幣標準的辦法。

（四）漢代黃金的使用

依照漢書食貨志，『秦兼天下，幣為二等，黃金以溢為名上幣，銅錢如周錢，文曰半兩，重如其文。而珠玉，龜、貝、銀、錫之屬，為器飾寶藏，不為幣，然各隨時而輕重無常（此段只食貨志有，不見史記平準書）。漢興，以為秦錢難用，更令民鑄莢錢，黃金一斤（此段與平準書同，但平準書作一黃金一斤）』。這是說從秦開始把黃金和銅錢定為法定的貨幣。除此以外，在法律上都不算貨幣。這當然是進步而合理的辦法，不過依照戰國時的記載用金用溢（或鎰），用錢也已經普遍，而龜貝等物也早已廢止。所以這種複本位的辦法實已在戰國施行，秦不過只做一些整齊畫一的功夫罷了。

漢代黃金和銅錢是兩個不同的單位，但是還是可以互稱的，有時在公文上稱金也有時在公文上稱錢。漢書惠帝紀⑯：

> 五月丙寅，太子即皇帝位。尊皇后曰皇太后，賜民爵一級，中郎，郎中滿六歲爵三級，四歲二級，外郎滿六歲二級，中郎不滿一歲一級，外郎不滿二歲賜錢萬，宦官當食比郎中。……賜給喪事者二千石錢二萬，六百石以上萬，五百石

二百石以下至佐史五千。視作斥上者將軍四十金，二千石二十金，六百石以上六金，五百石以下至佐史二金。

據漢書顏師古注：

鄭氏曰『四十金，四十斤金也』。晉灼曰：『近上二千石賜錢二萬，此言四十金實金也。下凡言黃金眞金也，不言黃謂錢也。食貨志，黃金一斤直錢萬』。

師古曰『諸賜言黃金者，皆興之金，不言黃者，一金與萬錢也』。

給喪事和作斥上都是服務，但作斥上的工作可能要艱難些，所以獎勵金錢的數目就很有差別。不僅數目上大有懸殊，在賞賜的貨幣種類上也有區別。論起來如眞黃金和銅錢能公開的兌換，那就不應當有所差別的，但在此處記載之中，同時的賞賜卻是貨幣種類上不同，那就顯然給錢是給與銅錢，而給金是給與黃金，不是賜黃金的只名義上賜黃金，實際上用錢來折合。爲什麼要用這樣方法去做呢？這段史料應該表現出來漢代初年黃金和銅錢之間已經發生了黑市。漢代萬錢值黃金一斤是指標準錢而言的，高惠之間流行的是楡莢錢，在市場上並不能照市價買到黃金，當時朝廷重視斥上的工作，特給予眞的黃金。所以兌換率的維持，要等到文帝以後，甚至要等到武帝元狩以後。

漢代官定比例黃金一斤直錢萬應當不會有多少問題的。因爲漢律都是以黃金爲標準（據九朝律考所輯各條），而黃金和錢的折合數目，卻是不可以輕易變更的[67]。如其曾經把比例變動過，那就將成爲非常重大的事件，不可能既在食貨志不載，也在各帝的本紀中不載的。

漢代黃金一斤直錢萬本來是一件極普遍的事，應該在漢律中就有規定。可惜現在漢律已亡，諸書用漢律各條未曾引到，所以也不見於輯佚。晉灼注漢書，只據漢書食貨志，而食貨志中記載的是王莽卽眞以後，亦卽始建國元年以後的制度，當時雖然也是『黃金重一斤直錢萬』，可是這裏的謂『直錢萬』的錢是『小泉直一』的小錢，而這種小錢，卻只有一銖，因此就可以有兩種解釋。第一種是『黃金一斤直錢萬』，本來是漢代相承的制度，在始建國元年以前，不曾鑄造減料的『小泉直一』時卽已存在。等到始建國元年，銅錢實質上已經貶值，可是這個『黃金一斤直錢萬』的虛設比例尚存，在市場上一萬小錢是換不到一斤黃金的。第二種是『黃金一斤直錢萬』是王莽時按一銖錢的銅重來核算的，也就是小泉直一只能算五銖錢的五分之一。西漢時黃金一斤應當值二千，王莽把錢的質量縮小，所以把黃金的價格也提高了。現在既然可以有兩種假設，所以應當批判一下。

先說第二種。王莽鑄的『小泉直一』明明認爲是『直一』，卽在他法律之下，是認爲和五銖錢有同等價值的。他決不可能鑄一種新錢而承認比舊錢的價值低的。若眞是這樣去做，那就毫無意義，不如不改了。所以此說不合理。而且王莽傳明說禁列侯以下挾黃金，這就表現一萬個個小泉不能兌換到黃金的。再參酌王莽的記載，其中一段說：

有司奏故事，聘皇后黃金二萬斤，爲錢二萬萬。莽深辭謝，受四千萬，而以其三千三百萬予十一媵家。

這是平帝元始三年春的事，去王莽始建國元年，還要早七年。那時不僅沒有小泉直一，並且去居攝元年也尙有三年。居攝元年王莽才鑄大泉五十與五銖錢並行，在元始三年時只有五銖錢一種。所以那時以錢二萬萬折合黃金二萬斤，毫無疑問的是五銖錢。也就毫無疑問的『黃金一斤直錢萬』是西漢時代一貫的制度。

漢代一般使用錢幣雖然號稱用金，仍多以錢折合，並不見都拿眞黃金使用。不過漢代黃金的數量，確也不少。尤其等到漢代末期，雖然武帝征伐四方一度大加浪費。等到昭宣以後又漸次積存下來。直到王莽之亡，仍然還有一個極爲可觀的數目，存在內庫。到東漢以後，一直就沒有那樣的積蓄了。顧炎武日知錄卷十一說⑱：

漢時黃金上下通行，故文帝賜周勃至五千斤，宣帝賜霍光至七千斤，而武帝以公主妻欒大，至齎金萬斤。衞青出塞斬捕首虜之士，受賜黃金二十餘萬斤。梁孝王薨藏府餘黃金四十餘萬斤。館陶公主近幸董偃，令中府曰；董君所發，一日金滿百斤，錢滿百萬，帛滿千匹，乃白之。（案此亦可以證黃金百斤與錢百萬爲等值）。王莽禁列侯以下，不得挾黃金，輸府受直。及其將敗，省中黃金萬斤者爲一匱，尙有六十匱，黃門，鉤盾，中府，中尙方處，處各有數匱。而從漢書光武紀，言王莽末，天下旱蝗，黃金一斤，易粟一解，是民間亦未嘗無黃金也。董卓死，塢中有黃金二三萬斤。銀八九萬斤。昭烈得益州，賜諸葛亮，法正，關羽，張飛金各五百斤，銀千斤。南齊書蕭穎胄傳，長沙寺僧業富沃，鑄黃金數千兩爲龍埋土中，歷相傳付，稱爲下方黃鐵，莫有見者。穎冑起兵乃取此龍以充軍實，梁書武陵王紀傳，黃金一斤爲餅，百餅爲籯，至有百籯，銀五倍之。自此以後，則罕見於史。尙書疏，漢魏贖罪皆用黃金。後魏以金難得，令金一兩收絹十匹。今律乃贖銅。

宋太宗問學士杜鎬曰：『兩漢賜予多用黃金，而後代逐爲難得之貨，何也？』對曰『當時佛事未興，故金價甚賤』。……古來用金之費，如吳志劉繇傳『笮融大起浮圖祠，以銅爲人，黃金塗身，衣以錦采，垂銅盤九重』。何姬傳注引江表傳，『孫皓使尙方以金作華燧步搖假髻以千數，會宮人著以相撲，朝成夕敗，輒出更作』。魏書釋老志，『興光元年勑有司於五緞大寺內，爲大祖已下五帝，鑄釋迦立像五，各長一丈六尺，都用赤金二萬五千斤。天安中於天宮寺造釋迦立像，高四十三尺，用赤金十萬斤，黃金六百斤』。齊書東昏侯本紀，『後宮服御極選珍奇，府庫舊物不復周用貴市民間金銀寶物，價皆數倍京邑。酒租皆折使輸金，以爲金塗，猶不能足』。唐書敬宗紀，『詔度支進銅三千斤，金簿（原注，即箔字）十萬，翻修淸思院新殿，及昇陽殿圖障』。五代史周世家，『王昶起三淸臺三層，以黃金數千斤，鑄寶皇及元始天尊，太上老君像，宋眞宗作玉淸昭應宮，麗拱欒楯，全以金飾，所費鉅億萬，雖用金之數亦不能全計』。金史海陵本紀，『官殿之飾，編傅黃金，而後間以五采，金屑飛空如落雪』。元史世祖本紀，『建大聖萬安寺，佛像及窗壁，皆金飾之。凡費金五百四十兩有奇，水銀二百四十斤。又言繕寫金字藏經凡糜金三千二百四十兩』（原註，吳澄傳，言粉黃金如泥，寫浮屠藏經。泰定帝紀，泰定二年七月庚午，以國用不足，罷書金字藏經）。此皆耗金之由也，杜鎬之言頗爲不妄，草木子云，金一爲箔，無復再還元矣。故南齊書武帝紀，『禁不得以金銀爲箔』。

趙翼二十二史劄記卷三『漢多黃金條』說69：

古時不以白金爲幣，專用黃金，而黃金甚多。尉繚說秦王，賂諸侯豪臣，不過三十萬金，而諸侯可盡。漢高祖以四萬斤與陳平使爲楚反間不問其出入。婁敬說帝都關中，田肯說帝當以親子弟封齊，卽各賜五百斤。叔孫通定朝儀，亦賜五百斤。呂后崩遺詔賜諸侯王各千斤。陳平交歡周勃，周五百斤。文帝卽位，以大臣誅諸呂功，賜周勃五千斤，陳平，灌嬰各二千斤，劉章、劉揭各千斤。
吳王濞反，募能斬漢大將者，賜五千斤，列將三千斤，裨將二千斤，二千石一
千斤。梁孝王薨有四十萬斤。武帝賜平陽公主千斤，賜卜式四百斤。……可見
古時黃金之多也。後世黃金日少，金價亦日貴，蓋由中土產金之地，已發掘淨
盡。而自佛敎入中國後，塑像塗金，大而通都大邑，小而窮鄉僻壤，無不有佛
寺，卽無不用金塗，以天下計之，無慮數千萬萬。此最爲耗金之蠹，加以風俗
侈靡，泥金寫經，帖金作榜，積少成多，日消月耗。故老言黃金作器，雖變壞
而金自在，一至泥金塗金，則不復還本，此所以日少一日也。

顧炎武和趙翼的看法差不多。只是顧炎武用宋杜鎬的意見，而趙翼是他自己的看法，
以現在的看法看來，漢代黃金的量數確實很充足。尤其王莽傳所記的庫藏數量，更是
以後歷代都未曾達到過，不僅未曾達到過，　而且都差的很遠。　佛寺鑄像用黃金箔包
裝，因而消費掉黃金，固然是一個解釋。不過據顧炎武所擧的造像規模最大的是北魏
文成帝興光元年一次及北魏獻文帝天安元年一次。只是所說的赤金實在是純銅，而黃
金才是眞金。天安中的大像用銅十萬斤，用金六百斤，按照比例與光那次五像共用銅
十二萬五千斤，用金就應當合七百五十斤。以後元代建萬安寺用金五百四十兩，寫藏
經用金三千二百四十兩，都比北魏時代所用的金少（北魏比元衡制較小，卻少不到二
分之一）。至於孫皓屢次鑄宮人的華燧步搖，齊東昏侯爲後宮買民間飾物，以及五代
閩王氏鑄三清像，都是用純金鑄造，後來毀掉，仍是純金，不損失全國純金的總量。
又金極富於展性，四十三尺的大像，如用金箔去包，至多六百兩實已夠用，用不著六
百斤。此處所說六百斤，只有用誤字來解釋，如其不是誤字，就是當時經手人大量盜
竊，以少報多，金的實際消耗，要比此數爲少。就算當時的確費了那麼多的黃金，至
多也不過王莽時一匱的十分之 1.8（因爲隋開皇時以古稱三斤爲一斤，大業初依復古
稱。魏文成及獻文時尚在開皇時一百多年以前未經歷次政治上大變動，比較小些），
也就是六十匱全數中六十分之 1.8，而且這還是比較上特殊的例子。現在尚存的北魏
佛像之中，敦煌和麥積山尚有不少，佛像上的彩繪亦至今存在，卻沒一尊佛像是塗金
的，並且佛像上和壁畫上用金處也很少。若說漢代那麼多的藏金都被修築佛寺及裝塗
佛像用的淨盡，卻也很不對題。再說從漢明帝時佛敎入中國，直到笮融才開始大修寺

院這一百多年之中，並無大修寺院的記載，但東漢時期眞正賜黃金之事卽已不多。董卓盡量搜取，塢中也只有二三萬斤，僅合王莽時的二三匱，旣未曾有大量佛寺裝金的事情，這些大量的黃金那裏去了？只有在佛寺裝金以外去找事實，才能有合理的解答，否則卽令是古今公認的意見，仍然不足取信的。

　　從王莽以至東漢末期，大量的黃金確實消失了，旣不可以用寺院的消費來解釋，就不如用對外貿易輸出黃金那一件來解釋更爲合理一些。因爲如其把黃金運到國外，也自然而然的，將來在國內不能出現的，現在在漢書中去找，就有兩段是把黃金輸出的。

　　　　漢書地理志：『自日南障塞船行可五月有都元國，又船行可四月有邑盧沒國，又船行二十餘日有諶離國，步行可十餘日有夫甘都盧國，自夫甘都盧國船行可二月餘有黃支國，民俗略與珠崖相類，其州廣大，戶口多，多異物。自武帝以來皆獻見。有譯長屬黃門，與應募者俱入海市明珠，璧，流離，奇石異物，齎黃金雜繒而往。

　　　　漢書西域大宛傳：『得漢黃白金，輒以爲器，不用爲幣。自烏孫以西至安息，近匈奴。匈奴嘗困月氏，故匈奴使持單于一信到國，國傳送食，不敢留苦，及至漢使，非出幣物不得合，不市畜不得騎，所以然者，以遠漢而漢多財物，故必市乃得所欲。及呼韓邪單于朝漢後，咸鲁漢矣。

　　這兩段之中，地理志所說的是有關南海方面對於黃金的出口，西域傳所說的是有關西域方面對於黃金的出口。西域傳方面指的是漢廷使節携往的黃金，而南海方面，卻是黃門署與應募的人入海去用黃金和雜繒去購買珠寶。除去宮廷派人去以外，還有商人在內。所以南海方面更爲重要，再據地理志說『粵地………處近海，多犀，象、珠，璣，銀，銅，果，布之湊，中國往商賈者，多取富焉。番禺，其一都會也』。犀是指犀角，象是指象牙，和珠璣等物都以番禺爲集中地。這許多高價的進口貨物，當然是由中國出口的黃金和各種絲織品換來。這些黃金，年年向外疏出，拿幾十年或幾百年的數目總計起來，可以變成一個非常鉅大的數目，決非寺院所消耗的所能比擬(70)。這裡並非說寺院不消耗，而是說黃金出口所占的數目更大。因爲寺院並非年年都有消耗，但在中國各處淘沙出金的，雖然數量有限，總可以大致抵補消耗。至於對外貿易所用的黃金，卻是只要商人能夠拿到手，就可以無限制的出口去買犀象珠璣各種高價品而大賺一番錢。周秦以來，中國每年產金數量誠然不算太多，但漢代以前，南海貿易不大繁盛，黃金經年累積，自然成爲一個可觀的數目，這就是漢代『多黃金的』原因。等到漢代以後，海道貿易大通，國內產的黃金不再可以在國內長期累積，這就自然而然的表現出來黃金的量不夠了。

中國人口集中內陸，表面上是一個自給自足的整體。尤其從秦代以後，受到了法家農戰主義的影響，所以把視線全集中到農業上，縱然對外貿易對國家經濟的影響極大，也一點不知道重視。黃金的集散，明明是一個經濟問題，最先一步就應在經濟問題，尤其要在貿易進出口問題去求解答。只爲了傳統上忽視對外貿易的關係，從宋代杜鎬以來，就未曾想到對外貿易的重要性。他只能想到次要問題，佛像的裝金問題上。一直使得中國的黃金問題，在謎的世界之中，過了二三千年沒有適當的解答。

附　注

（ 1 ）詩經菁菁者莪（藝文本 353 頁），『錫我百朋』鄭箋引三家詩以五貝爲朋，而漢書食貨志王莽則以二貝爲朋，今按朋字早骨作 拜 顯然爲一朋二系，一系四五貝，所以一朋應爲十貝。見王國維釋朋（觀堂集林三，24，藝文本）。

（ 2 ）不僅玻利尼西亞人是傑出的航海者，亞洲土人移殖到南太平洋各島，也是史前時期用的原始性舟船。

（ 3 ）四部叢刊國語卷三、頁十四。

（ 4 ）漢書食貨志（藝文補注本 522 頁），師古注引應劭曰：『大於舊錢，其價重也』。

（ 5 ）四部叢刊國語卷三、頁十三。

（ 6 ）詩經，周頌、臣工（藝文本 724 頁），毛詩云：『庤，具；錢，鎛』。孔穎達疏云：『說文云錢銚古田器，世本云，垂作銚』。

（ 7 ）古樂府皜如山上雪，全漢三國晉南北朝詩藝文本 186 頁。

（ 8 ）空首布的形製是 𠙹 爲鐈形，柄首空處是縱裝木柄的形狀變來，參考古錢大辭典49至97頁。

（ 9 ）周爲徹底的封建制度，周考王封其弟揭於洛陽王城，是爲西周，而西周又分封其子於鞏，是爲東周。以後周王要通過二周公室，才算有領土。東周錢見古錢大辭典 252 頁。

（10）左傳僖公二十五年（藝文本 263 頁）。晉（文公）於是始啓南陽。陽樊不服，圍之。倉葛呼曰『德以柔中國，刑以威四夷，宜吾不敢服也，此誰非王之親姻，其俘之也』。乃出其民。

（11）詩經小雅大東『周道如砥，其直如矢，君子所履，小人所視』（藝文本 438 頁）。

（12）論語述而第七（藝文本62頁）何注引鄭（玄）曰：『讀先王典法，必正言其音，然後義全』。按雅言即中夏之言，也就是標準的讀法。

（13）豫章見於史記吳王濞傳（藝文本1151頁），『吳有豫章郡銅山……益鑄錢……國用富饒』，其地當在安徽繁昌一帶。亦卽江西與安徽南部爲一郡，可能稱爲豫章郡，也可能稱爲九江郡。

（14）戰國策趙策三，趙奢答田單曰，『且古者四海之內，分爲萬國……今所　古之萬國者，分爲戰國七，能具數十萬之兵，曠日持久數歲』（商務印書館排印本，卷二十、頁　）。

（15）洛陽在漢代是重要都市，是繼承周代的繁榮的。其成都、長沙、吳三縣在漢代獨有縣令，其他長江各縣都爲長，這也可證明其繁榮的程度。

（16）見藝文翻吳志忠孟子集注二、第七頁。

（17）漢書賈誼傳（藝文補注本，1072頁）。

（18）漢書食貨志（藝文補注本，514頁）。

（19）漢書蕭何傳（藝文補注本，989頁）。

（20）漢書昭帝紀（藝文補注本，107——108頁）。

（21）漢書食貨志（藝文補注本，523頁）。

（22）漢高帝所頒布的只是『禁盜鑄錢令』，而不是『禁盜鑄錢律』，是秦法中並無此律。至景帝中二年始定『鑄錢，僞黃金棄市律』（漢書補注藝文本82頁），後來劉向卽坐此律幾死，遇赦，始以減死論（漢書補注藝文本965頁）。

（23）史記平準書（藝文影殿本，562頁）。

（24）漢書食貨志（藝文補注本，523頁）。

（25）漢書賈山傳（藝文補注本，1106頁）。

（26）漢書食貨志（藝文補注本，523頁）。

（27）漢書食貨志（藝文補注本，524頁）。

（28）漢書賈誼傳（藝文補注本，1068頁）。

（29）漢書食貨志（藝文補注本，523頁）。

（30）漢書景帝紀（藝文補注本，82頁）。

（31）史記貨殖傳（藝文影殿本，1342——1343頁）。

（32）史記游俠傳（藝文影殿本，1302頁）。『郭解少時……藏命作姦，剽攻不休，及鑄錢掘塚』，又居延漢簡，『元康元年十二月辛丑朔，壬寅，東部候長生敢言之。候官官移大守府所移河南都尉書曰，詔所名捕及鑄僞錢，盜賊，凡未得者牛延壽高建等廿四移……』（20‧12）。此卽盜賊與鑄僞錢相關之例。

（33）參看史記酷吏傳（藝文影殿本，1279——1287）及游俠傳（藝文影殿本，1301——1304）。

（34） 漢書食貨志（藝文補注本，527頁）。

（35） 史記高祖功臣表（藝文影殿本，362頁）。

（36） 漢書食貨志（藝文補注本，529頁）。

（37） 漢書食貨志（藝文補注本，532頁）。

（38） 後漢書五行志（藝文集解本，1185頁）。晉書食貨志（藝文斠注本，583頁）。

（39） 後漢書馬援傳（藝文集解本，312頁）。

（40） 說文解字序附許沖上表（藝文影殿注本，795頁）。

（41） 後漢書明帝紀（藝文影集解本，66頁）。

（42） 後漢書皇后紀（藝文影集解本，165頁）。

（43） 後漢書皇后紀（藝文影集解本，158頁）。

（44） 後漢書皇后紀（藝文影集解本，159頁）。

（45） 後漢書皇后紀（藝文影集解本，162頁）。

（46） 後漢書皇后紀（藝文影集解本，173頁）。

（47） 後漢書韋彪傳（藝文集解本，339頁）。

（48） 後漢書劉毅傳（藝文集解本，470頁）。

（49） 後漢書梁商傳（藝文集解本，423頁）。

（50） 後漢書劉愷傳（藝文集解本。472頁）。

（51） 後漢書祭肜傳（藝文集解本，279頁）。

（52） 後漢書張奐傳（藝文集解本，766頁）。

（53） 後漢書夏馥傳（藝文集解本，788頁）。

（54） 後漢書儒林傳（藝文集解本，911頁）。

（55） 後漢書逸民傳（藝文集解本，986頁）。

（56） 後漢書董卓傳（藝文集解本，830頁）。

（57） 後漢書光武十王傳（藝文集解本，511頁）。

（58） 後漢書光武十王傳（藝文集解本，517頁）。又敦煌漢簡：『任城國亢父縑一匹，幅廣二尺二寸、長四丈，重廿五兩，直錢六百一十八』。（沙畹簡號539）。

（59） 後漢書東夷傳（藝文集解本，1005頁）。

（60） 後漢書朱暉傳（藝文集解本，524頁）。

（61） 後漢書劉陶傳（藝文集解本，685頁）。

（62） 晉書食貨志（藝文斠注本，584頁）。

（ 63 ） 南齊書崔祖思傳（藝文本，251頁）。

（ 64 ） 華陽國志（四部叢刊本，卷四、28頁）諸葛亮平定南中，『出其金、銀、丹、漆、耕牛戰馬，給軍國之用』。金銀包括金屬，雲南盛產銅，故銅當然在內。

（ 65 ） 中國市場大量用銀，宋代已開始，元代以後更為顯著。這和對外貿易輸入銀兩有關。至於紙幣的發明，在人類的文化史上，實有非常重大的意義，不下於指南針，火藥，印刷術的重要性。但如加以推測，是由於中國中古的經濟，已有高度的進展，而籌碼不足應付，才推衍出這種代用的辦法。紙幣初期的形式，飛錢，嚴格說來，當然還不算紙幣，卻屬於信用的充分利用，這也是商業經濟在高度發展後的成果。

（ 66 ） 漢書惠帝紀（藝文補注本，60頁）。

（ 67 ） 彭信威中國貨幣史（1965上海版）157頁附注說『九章算術卷六，今有人持金十二斤出關，關稅之，十分而取一。今關取金二斤，償錢五千，問一斤值錢幾何？答曰六千二百五十』。李儼中國古代數學史料一九五六版第一○九頁，說是指白金，並引武帝的白金幣為證。白金幣的白撰確是八兩值三千，不是真正的銀價。如果當時銀價每斤值六千二百五十，而武帝反以半斤作價三千， 政府豈不賠本？——今按武帝時的銀幣，是銀錫的合金，成色不純。所以比純銀的市價反而低一點。所以李儼把值錢六千二百五的是指銀，不是不合理的、又九章算術卷七，『今有共買金，人出四百盈三千四百，人出三百盈一百，問人數金價幾何？答曰三十三人，金價九千八百』。則與一斤萬錢之數甚為接近。不過此種當指成色不足的生金（如漢中出金，至現在尚然，可是含銀量甚高，成色不佳），所以較規定的一斤萬錢反而低一點。

（ 68 ） 商務印書館國學基本叢書本，卷二下，77頁。

（ 69 ） 世界書局排印本，第39頁。古代不是絕對不以『白金』為幣， 漢武時即用過『白金』只是中國不產銀，無法大量採用，唐宋以後，銀係外來的。具見加藤繁所考證。

（ 70 ） 彭信威的中國貨幣史（1965上海版），第145頁說：『數量的減少，是由於黃金外流，西漢因為普徧採用黃金為支付手段，所以一定有相當大的數量流到外國去。………他派張騫到西域去招徠大夏的屬國，也用黃金縑幣，這也是黃金的一條去路，但最重要的還是入超』。『西漢時已有若干對外貿易。如武帝向大宛買馬，向海外買明珠、璧流離，都曾輸出黃金。……史記大宛傳說「得漢黃白金，輒以為器，不用為幣」，這也是金銀外流的確證』。這個見解是不錯的。不過他卻未曾指出漢書地理志那一段， 所以沒有找到貿易上直接證據， 而且對於最重要的南海貿易也沒有找到中國的材料去解答。——又本篇以上各則，並參考李劍農中國經濟史，楊聯陞中國貨幣史（英文本）及全漢昇中古自然經濟。

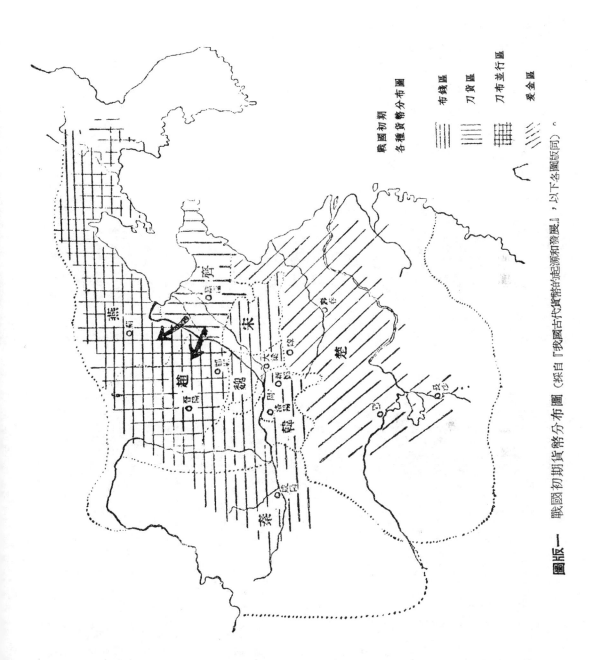

圖版一　戰國初期貨幣分布圖（採自『我國古代貨幣的起源和發展』，以下各圖版同）。

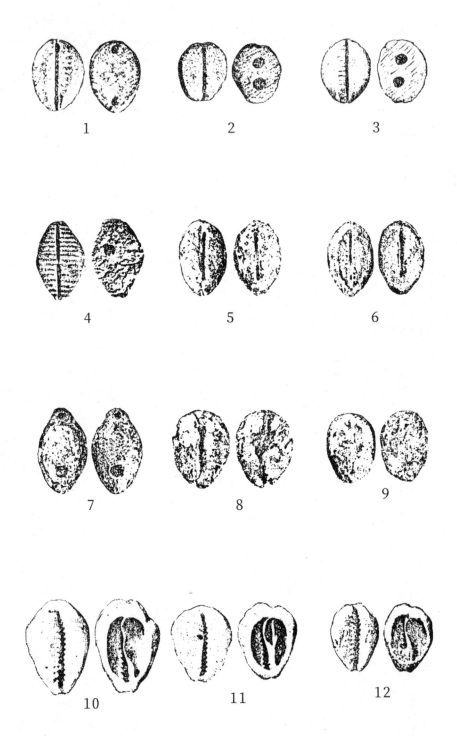

圖版二　1.2.3.貝　4.5.7.骨貝　8.9.10.銅製貝　11.12.包金銅貝

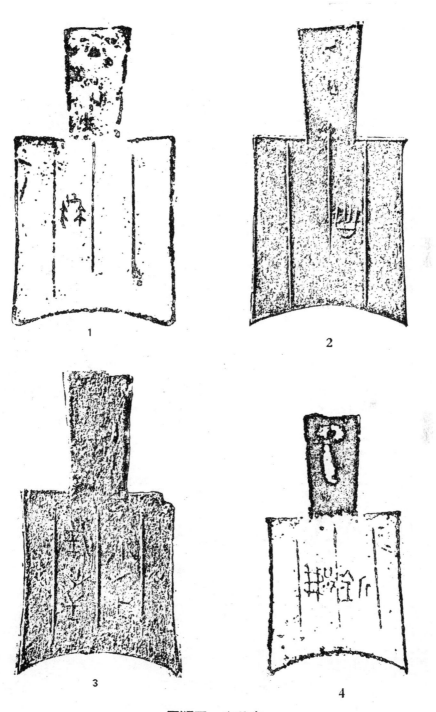

圖版三　空首布

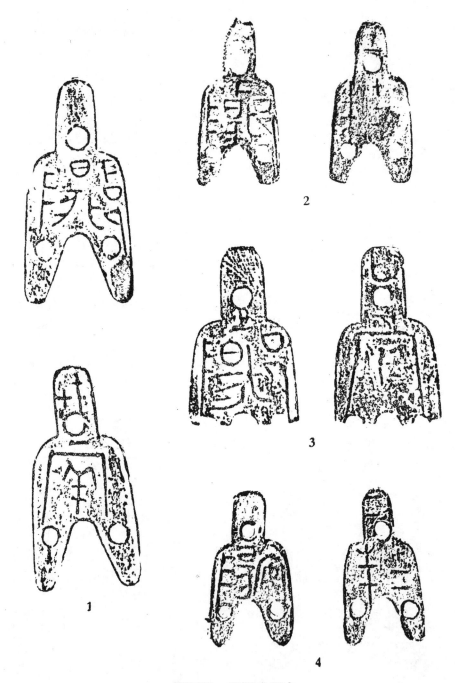

圖版四　戰國晚期布

圖版五　齊刀

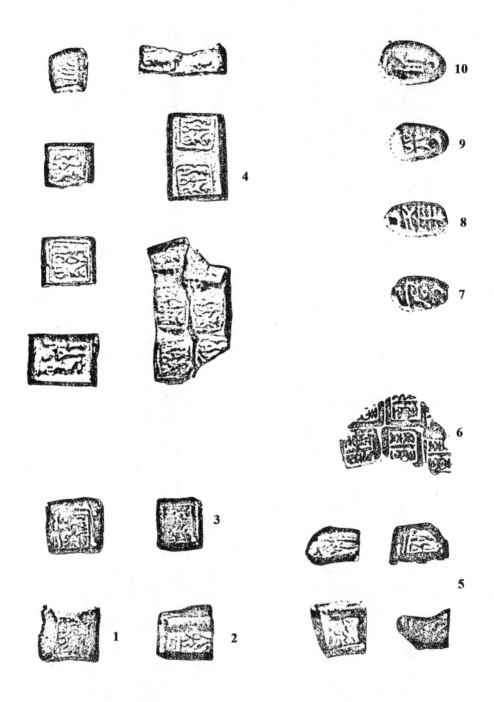

圖版六　1—5郢爰　6 陳爰　7—10蟻鼻錢

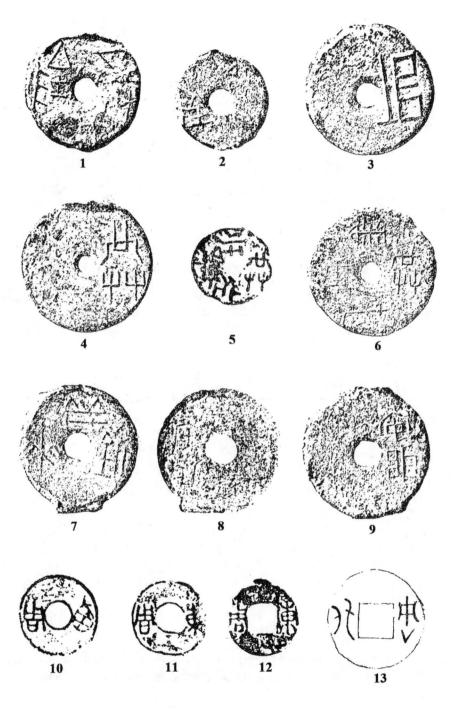

圖版七　戰國時圓錢

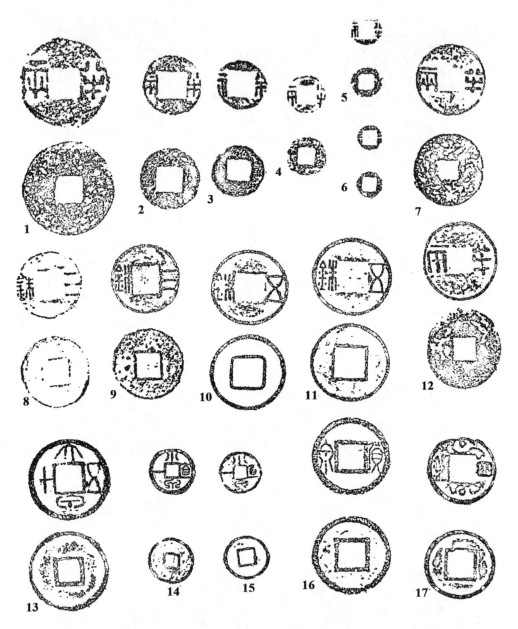

圖版八　秦漢圓錢（據古錢大辭典）

1.半兩。　2—6楡莢。　7.四銖半兩。　8.9.三銖。　10.11.五銖。　12.有周郭半兩。　13.大泉五十。

14.15.小泉直一。　16.貨泉。　17.四銖（或係劉末時鑄，不過據此可以了解四銖的大小）。

〈漢代黃金及銅錢的使用問題〉英文摘要

THE PROBLEM OF THE USES OF COPPER COINS AND GOLD PIECES IN HAN TIME

English Summary

Kan LAO

In ancient China various kinds of materials were used as the medium of currency. Cowries were the most popular kind among them. That cowries were highly valued by the ancient Chinese and widely used as money had been shown as early as on the oracle bones. The cowries found at Anyang ruins are similar to the fresh ones found on the Taiwan coast. This fact shows that ancient cowrie shells were transported through a long way from the East China Sea to the center of the China mainland.

The original use of cowries might be similar to the use of pearls for necklace which is so common as found in the primitive societies and among the civilized people. In ancient time a string of cowries was called a "pêng" which might be used both as ornaments of personal adornment and as a medium of exchange. The cowries are quite beautiful and very much alike and there is every indication that one of them had the same value as another. Thus we found that in the inscriptions on bronze vessels it is said that the lords have often given cowrie strings to their subjects as reward for service or as a mark of esteem.

In a long ranged term cowries ceased to be used as currency. Firstly , due to the wide use of bronze, imitation cowries were cast in place of the natural ones. Secondly, bronze tools such as spades and knives became the main medium of exchange. During the time of the Warring States, copper coins cast in the shape of the spades and the knives bearing inscriptions were used. Later, round coins were cast and circulated. The round coins proved to be most convenient in carrying as well as in counting. In consequence they became the last from having been used throughout the period of dynasties in China.

After the unification of China by the Ch'in dynasty all the rules imposed by the Six States were adjusted according to the standard regulations set by the Ch'in court. The shape and the size of the copper coins were not exceptional. Half ounce coin, or half tael coin (or panliang chien) was cast. When the Han court began its sovereinty, almost all the regulations were duplicated from those of the Ch'in dynasty. The cast of half ounce coin also followed the Ch'in system. But the newly established Han court was not as efficient as the Ch'in court had been. Illegal coinage was frequently found in the newly appointed princedoms and even in private factories. Because the illegal coins could not be controlled by the government, the number of coins grew and grew and overflowed the market with a decrease in size and weight to such a degree that they resembled elm-seeds. Those facts showed that there were inflations which had caused the living expenses running high and had compelled the government changing its monetary policy to solve the new problem.

In 175 B. C. (the thirtieth year from the establishment of the Han dynasty) the Han government issued a new coin known as ssu-chu chien or ssu-shu chien (or four twenty-forth ounce coin). The size is medium comparing to the standard pan-liang chien and the illegal elm-seeds. On the other hand, the government repealed the law prohibiting illegal coinage. This was done in order to root out false coining.

The result of this policy was good; the coinage got in order. But since the government gave up the privilege of the coin monopoly, the wealthy lords and the wealthy individuals became more wealthy by means of coinage. It became the menace of the imperial power. Thus the new policy was opposed by the famous philosopher Chia Yi.

In 140 B. C. Han Wu–ti took his throne. He was the most aggressive emperor in the line of his heredity. He changed many laws basing on his new ideas. He reformed both the political system and the economic system with an intention to control his domain efficiently. He also made several amendments in his economic and financial policies in order to provide his army with sufficient food and equipments during the time of military expeditions. Certainly the monetary system was most important to him. He failed several times in reforming the system, but finally he succeeded by setting up the Wu–chu chien or five twenty–forth ounce coin system.

Wu–chu chien was lighter than half ounce coin but heavier than the four twenty–forth coin. It proved to be a convenient unit of cash. The major difference between this policy and the former ones was that the coinage of wu–chu chien was monopolized by the central administration. No feudal lords, no wealthy people and not even the local administrations were allowed to cast coins. Only limited mints in the suburb of the capital Chang–an were used to cast the special coin with specific techniques. Under the control of material and technique, counterfeiting became nearly impossible. In consequence it proved to be even more stable than the ssu–chu coin. The wu–chu coin lasted for quite a long period of time until it was abolished by the usurper Wang Mang.

The monetary system established by Wang Mang was complicated and unpractical which caused serious inflations. The people dissatisfied with the system and prayed for the return of wu–chu coin which was expressed in popular folk ballads, such as

"Yellow ox with white belly,
Let the 5–shu coin return."

When the Latter Han was established, the old wu–chu coin system was recovered. It lasted about two hundred years until the other usurper Tung Cho abandoned it to cast small coins. However it remained the basic unit throughout the Three Kingdoms and the Six Dynasties, though coins of different sizes and of large denominations were in circulation.

In ancient time gold was discovered and used in China as well as in other parts of the world. However, in Chinese the term for gold *chin* (or in ancient speech *chim*) was confused in interpretation because it has three meanings, namely, gold, copper, and metal in general. We may trace back to the construction of the archaic form of the character *chin* which is a pictograph showing the process of metal casting. Later the meaning of this character changed and denoted any kind of metal including gold, silver, copper, etc. To distinguish the meanings of *chin* is rather difficult. Only rarely does the context furnish a clue. In the time of the Warring States *yi* was used as a unit of gold which indicates that gold, for the first time, was used as currency.

The term *chin* (*chim*) used for gold specifically was rather late, but to use huang–chin or yellow metal for gold dated back as early as the time of Yi–ching compiling. It might be around one thousand B. C. At the ruin of Anyang, bronze vessels plated with gold have been found. This shows that gold was already in use in the Shang time, but strangely no special name was given. It was mentioned in Yü–kung, or the Tribute under Yü's Management in the Book of History, that three ranks of metal were presented as tribute by the people of the Delta of Yangtze. The three ranks of metal certainly referred to gold, silver, and copper. Most scholars believe that Yü–kung was compiled in the beginning of the Warring States. We may thus conclude that down to the period of the Warring States the term *chin* (*chim*) represented three kinds of metal, i.e. gold, silver, and copper.

Yi was a unit for gold used as currency with a weight of twenty ounces in the time of the Warring States. However the word *chin* "catty" (not to be confused with *chim* "metal") became the unit for gold in the Han time with a weight of sixteen ounces only.   Meng–tze, Chan–kuo–tse, and Shih Chi all contain references to the fact that *yi* was primarily used as a unit for gold throughout the Warring States.   But we do not know the ratio of gold to copper coins.

Ku yen–wu was the first scholar who discussed the problems of gold in his outstanding work Jih–chih Lu.   Chao Yi, an eminent historian of the eighteenth century, in his "Nien–ê–shih–cha–chi" also pointed out the problems of gold in the dynasties of China.   He stated that there must have been a great amount of gold in the time of the Han dynasty for the emperors always bestowed gold upon their subjects.   Also, when the regime of Wang Mang was overthrown, as much as six hundred thousand *chin*, or catties of gold was found in his treasury. But in the later dynasties the quantity of gold in circulation was not so immense. In Chao Yi's opinion the gold mines in the Chinese territory had been exhausted and the gold which circulated in the earlier dynasties was dissipated by the gilding of Buddhist images.

His assumption is remarkable but the cause of the vanishing of the gold is not so simple.   Gold leaf with a thickness of one hundredth millimeter can be made for gilding, therefore not very much gold is required for gilding a big Buddhist image.   Moreover, when I visited the caves at Tunhuang I found that none of the images cast during the time of the Northern Wei and the T'ang dynasties were ornamented with gold leaves.   This shows that gilding Buddhist images was not very common at that time; thus it cannot be the primary cause of the dissipation of gold.

So much gold reserved in the imperial treasury during the time of Wang Mang was quite unusual in Chinese history.   Most of this collection vanished during the Latter Han and the Three Kingdoms.   And we know that not until the Southern and Northern Dynasties did Buddhist temples become popular in Chinese society. Therefore better explanation should be found for the vanishment of this great amount of gold.

Ti–li–chih or the Geographical Record in Han Shu mentioned the commercial relations between China and the South Sea world.

"The Nan–hai(province)…is situated by the sea. It is the center of rhinoceros' horn, ivory, tortoise–shell, various kinds of pearl, silver, copper, fruit and cotton. Most of the merchants from mainland become rich by the South Sea trade. Pan-yü is one of the main ports…Huang–chih…is the largest island with a large population and special treasures. From the time of Wu–ti people in those countries always come to the court with tribute. The chief interpreter who belongs to the eunuch office navigated with voluntary employees carrying gold and various kinds of silk to trade for bright pearls, glass beads and other precious stones."

From this paragraph we know that ivory, rhinoceros' horn, pearls, precious stones and even glass beads were the principal imports from the South Sea world, whereas gold and silk were used as currency. This kind of trading had continued for quite a long period of time from Han to the Southern and Northern Dynasties. Obviously an immense amount of gold was exported through the trade. Therefore this should be the major fact which caused the exhaustion of the gold reservation in the imperial treasury.

The legal ratio of gold to copper coins was one catty of gold to ten thousand coins. Gold was the main standard currency and copper coin was the auxiliary currency during the time of Han and Wei–Chin dynasties. Since gold became rare and could not be found in the open market, rolls of silk and cotton became the standard currency in the time of the Southern and Northern

Dynasties.　Undoubtedly the silk–cotton standard was very inconvenient. Therefore, when a considerable amount of imported silver was accumulated towards the middle period of the T'and dynasty, silver standard was naturally established in place of the silk–cotton standard.　This standard had continued in the following dynasties up to the twentieth century before the Second Sino–Japanese war.

漢代常服述略

漢簡中多有記載衣服的，今略舉數例，以見其餘。居延簡：

『昌邑國邸良里公士費塗人年廿三　袍一領　枲履一兩　單衣一襲，絝一兩』

(19.36)

『陽綺裏直百　　□安世官絝』　　(233.52)

『襲八千四百領　　絝八千四百兩　　右六月甲辰遣□……常韋萬六千八百……··』　(41.17)

『田卒淮陽郡長平長平里公士李休年廿九　　襲一領　絝一兩　犬緤一兩　私緤一兩　自取』　(303.34)

『田卒淮陽郡長平容里公士稺絹年卅　　襲一　絝一　犬緤一　介史貫贅取』

(303.46)

『田卒淮陽郡長平北朝里公士李宜年廿三　　襲一　絝一　犬緤一　貫贅取』

(509 6)

『田卒淮陽郡長平東洛里公士尉充年卅　　襲一領　絝一兩　私單絝一　私絝練　犬緤一兩　私緤二兩　貫贅取』　(509.7)

『……一編復襲布複縛布單襜褕各一領幸單絝布牆革履枲履各……』　(82.34)

『十月十日鄣卒張中功貰買卓布章單衣一領，直三百五十三，墆史張君長所。錢約至十二月，盡畢己，卒史臨，掾史解子房知券。□』　(262.19)

『魏華里大夫曹□　　卓布複袍一領　卓布□襌衣一領　練複襃襲一領　卓布複絝一兩』。　(101.23)

『官章單衣一領　官布複絝一兩　官布枲一　官枲履一兩　私韋單絝一兩　私布枲一　官□二封□□□□』　(37.30)

以丄所舉的為居延簡，至於敦煌簡中，也有見到的。

　　　『李龍文袍一領　直三百八十一　襲一領　直四百五十』　　（流沙墜簡器物三十六）

　　　『……封里段千脩袍一領』　　（同，器物三十七）

　　　『布復袍一領……練復襲一領　……枲履襲一領　枲履……』　（同，器物三十八）

　　　『卒趙裏　單衣一見　十月乙丑出』　　（同，器物三十九）

流沙墜簡器物類，王國維考釋曰：

　　　『古四簡雜記衣服事。袍者，衣之有著者。玉藻（禮記）「纊爲繭，縕爲袍」是

　　　也。衣之有著者必具表裏，其無著則有複有單，複者謂之襲，謂之褶，單者謂

　　　之綯，亦謂之襌衣，單衣卽襌衣也。絑與韤同，淮南子說林訓，「均之縞也，一

　　　端以爲冠，一端以爲絑，冠則戴致之，絑則屨履之」。後漢書禮儀志：「絳袴韤

　　　絑」，皆作絑。釋名：「襪末也，在腳末也」。二兩者，一雙，古人履與韤皆以兩

　　　計也。』

我們根據以上居延漢簡和敦煌皇漢簡之中所說的，再照王國維的叙述，可以作以下的

分類：

```
         ┌有著的───袍
         │              ┌單衣
上衣 ┤          ┌單層┤禮襦
         │無著的┤      └褸
         └      └複層──襲（或稱爲褶）

         ┌袴
         │襪
其他 ┤履
         └韈
```

以下再根據上表，再來加以叙明和分析。

　　按古代的衣服制度，據三禮注疏及諸史與服志及注，大別可分爲兩類，卽 (1) 弁

服，(2) 深衣。弁服是屬於禮服部分的，深衣是屬於常服部分的。關於禮服一類，漢簡

中旣未曾提到，在本篇中也就不爲叙到。本篇所注意的，爲常服部分，亦卽『深衣』

部分。

　　歷來討論深衣制度的，大率都以三禮中遺說爲根據，和漢代制度不能盡同。卽謂

爲根據周制，也不能證明是否盡合。不過將古代制度正確的復原是一回事，根據前人

研究的結果，作爲解釋漢代制度的參考，又另外是一回事。本篇的設計和命意只是假借深衣制度作爲推測漢代常服根據的一部分，所以只略舉其大綱，而不再條辨其細目。

關於深衣制度，歷來折衷衆說，考證精審的，當推清代漢學家江永的深衣考誤和任大椿的深衣釋例。大概江氏發其大凡，任氏更加推演。當然無論如何精審，也只做到一個『標準制度』。凡是根據三禮做出來的所謂『標準制度』，都是現代考古學中的重要參考，並無疑義；但是古人的實際生活，並不那樣的標準，因此所有的『標準制度』，和實際生活，仍然有一個很大距離。以下，只是毫不增改的將清人結論重述，重述之後，再用漢制解釋。

深衣和弁服的區別，是深衣的上衣下裳連綴在一處；弁服是將衣和裳分割爲二。深衣用布二幅，共二尺二寸；兩袖（卽袂）各用布二幅，共用布四幅。袖口（卽袪）尺二寸，袖肩仍布二尺二寸。因此兩袖的前端下面，因斜裁的關係而成爲半圓形。襟分內部和外部，兩襟相交，便成方領。腰圍全部七尺二寸，每圍三尺六寸。下擺（縫齊）四周全部爲一丈四尺四寸。

自腰至下擺爲裳的部分，前後各用布六幅，共爲十二幅。每幅的寬爲半幅布，在腰部和上衣連處用布四幅，兩旁左右又各綴布兩幅，謂之『衽』。衽上寬四寸，下寬一尺八寸。裳在腰帶以下的約四尺五寸，下距地約四寸。衣裳各有緣邊，稱之爲『純』，衣裳的緣邊均有寸半，領的緣邊則爲二寸。

深 衣 的 裁 製 法

我們看到這種制度的敘述之後，可以得到一個印象，就是：『深衣是一種擁腫而費材料的長袍』。——但這是古代常服的基礎，以下再分類來叙述。

（1）禪衣——禪衣就是單層的長袍。也就是所謂『絅』。說文：『禪衣不重』，大戴禮及黄小正傳：『禪單也』，所以是單層的。楊雄方言：『禪衣，江淮南楚之間謂之襝，關之東西謂之禪衣，有深裏者，趙魏間謂之袿衣（裏，郭注，「前施裏囊也」）。無裏者謂之裎衣，古謂深衣』。所以禪衣和深衣是最接近的。又稱爲單衣，後漢書馬援傳：『公孫述更爲援制都布單衣』章懷注卽引楊雄方言爲說，故『單』字亦卽是『禪』的省字。

但深衣和禪衣究竟還略有區別，因爲深衣是一種標準制度，而禪衣並不定要完全合於標準。急就篇：『禪衣蔽郯布母縛』。顔師古注：『禪衣似深衣而裏大，亦以其無裏，故呼爲禪衣』。在此已經說明禪衣及深衣不必盡同。至任大椿深衣釋例則云：

> 又案士喪禮『浴衣用篋』注，其制如今通裁，正義如今通裁者，以其無殺，卽布單衣上下通直，不別衣裳，故得通裁之名。後世單衣與通裁同制，若深衣則猶別衣裳，特縫之不使殊耳。此布單衣與深衣又大同而小異耳。

這個分析比顔師古急就注，還要清楚些。我們在此可以得到更深的印象，就是古人衣服，原則上本是上衣而下裳，爲方便起見，衣裳至相縫接這就成爲深衣。再進一層，裁的時候，就上下相通，不要裁斷，成爲完整的長袍，這就成爲一般的禪衣了。與其說是衣服標準的不同，還不如說這是在衣服的設計中，爲著便於裁製，爲著便於穿著，一種自然的衍進。

（2）襜褕——襜褕是禪衣的一種，但可能比一般的禪衣更講究一些。釋名釋衣服曰：『褕，屬也。衣裳上下相連屬也。荆州謂禪衣曰布褕。亦曰襜褕，言其襜襜宏裕也。』

史記武安侯列傳：『坐衣襜褕入官不敬』，索隱：『謂非正朝服，若婦人衣也』。

——按詩碩人：『碩人其頎，衣錦褧衣』，箋；『褧禪也……尙之以禪衣』，褧卽絅，古婦人服不殊衣裳，禪衣亦不殊衣裳，所以索隱說『若婦人衣』了。

據任大椿深衣釋例

> 襜褕一衣，各異其質。張衡四愁詩：『美人贈我貂襜褕』。東觀漢紀：『耿純與從昆弟率宗族賓客二千餘人，皆衣縑襜褕奉迎世祖』，桓譚新論：『余從長安歸，

道病，蒙絮被，襲襜褕，宿於下邑亭中』，曰貂，曰縑，曰罽，與布單衣不同，然則襜褕乃單衣之加飾者也。荀子子道篇，孔子云：『由是裾裾者何』，注『裾裾衣服盛貌』。說苑裾裾作襜襜，裾裾襜襜同訓，皆言其盛也。釋名襜褕亦取義於襜襜，然則襜褕爲單衣之褒大者矣。

照這上面來說，襜褕和襌衣的不同處，共有兩點。第一，是由於質料的不同；第二，是由於形式上的不同。就質料方面來說，還可以包括兩點（甲）是所用的原料，如縑（厚的絲綢），如罽（毛織物），都是比較厚重的（乙）是外加的裝飾，如貂皮（因爲貂襜褕，只是貂的裝飾，借若是全貂就不是襜褕而是祝裘了）。至於第二點，從襜襜來訓襜褕的襜字爲宏闊，證據上尚嫌不夠。不適再從釋名『襜襜宏裕』來說，則任氏亦是說對了。但襜褕和衣裾有關大致是不錯的，裾就是衣服的前襟。

說文：『直裾謂之襜褕』

在漢書的顏師古注中在外戚恩澤侯表武安侯下及雟不疑傳，又在急就篇的顏師古注中，均作『直裾襌衣』。但漢書母將隆傳及何並傳的顏師古注，却作：『曲襌裾衣』。直裾和曲裾是不相同的，不應忽而直裾，忽而曲裾。同出一人之手而所指不同，必有一誤，不過說文爲漢代人的著作，應當以說文爲準，認襜褕爲直裾的襌衣，或者比較好些。自然，還不能說凡是直裾襌衣都是襜褕，但可說凡是襜褕都應當是直裾。直裾，就是直前襟之下是直垂的，而不用『續祍鉤邊』的袥，這樣腰部就要粗些，也就自然顯得更爲宏裕了。這一種宏博的衣服，應當作爲外衣之用，這也就成爲用厚料，加皮質裝飾理由。

（3）襦——『襦』及『衫』同爲短製內衣。『衫』爲單的，而『襦』爲夾的。潛夫論：『裙襦衣被，費繒百縑』。廣韻鐸韻：『襦，短夾衫』，類著：『襦，短衫也』，方言注：『今或呼衫爲襌襦，……襌襦卽衫也』（襌襦卽單的襦，襦爲短衣）。所以襦和衫的不同在單或夾上面。又釋名：『衫芟也，末無袖端也』，古人的袖端有特殊的裁製，第一是袖端要特加邊緣，第二是袖特大而袖端才收小，末無袖端便是和今人的中國式衫相類，不再這樣複雜了。襦本爲夾衣，簡中又有『複襦』一個名稱，那就是夾衣之中更加襯布，或者就是習慣上義字疊用了。廣雅：『複襂謂之裯』，王念孫疏證曰：『此說文所謂重衣也，襂與衫同。方言注以衫爲襌襦，其有裏者則謂之裯，裯重也』，那就裯和襡當爲同義字。

（４）襲——釋名:『襲襲也，覆上之言也』，所以褶襲音義並同。禮記玉藻:『帛
爲褶』，注:『謂有表裏而無著』，所以褶也是一種夾衣。急就篇:『襜褕袷複褶袴褌』
注:『複謂重衣之最上者，其形若袍，短身而廣袖，一曰左衽之袍也』。禮記內則:『寒
不敢襲』，注:『謂重衣』，從上更可以看出襲爲夾衣的一種。

再綜合上列各條，更知道襲或褶更含有以下各種特質:

（１）有表有裏的夾衣。

（２）最外之衣。

（３）短身之衣。

（４）左衽。

以上四點，尤其是第（４）點，更和胡服相近。固然，襲的原名雖不是指胡服，如士
喪禮:『襲者以褶，則必有裳』，褶和裳對舉，明褶加於端衣之上，而衣下尚垂有裳，
仍是中國服裝，並非胡服。但此衣既與胡服有共同之點，則胡服的外衣，自用『襲』
或『褶』來稱呼較爲合適。軍服本以胡服爲便，因此軍服也就以『褶袴』爲稱，具見
王國維觀堂集林胡服考，及流沙墜簡補遺考釋第三十七簡之下。

褶雖然是夾衣，但也有用絲綿絮的，如居延簡:

> 五十六五練襲一領，表裏用帛一匹，糸絮。　　（203.45）

那就短製的褶，也有實絮的了。

（５）袍——禮記玉藻:『纊爲繭，縕爲袍』，注:『纊新綿，縕舊絮』，同是一樣
的，只以新舊來分。論語:『衣敝縕袍，與衣狐貉者立，而不耻者，其由也歟』？左傳:
『三軍之士，皆如挾纊』，正表明新舊之別。詩無衣章:『豈曰無衣，與子同袍』。毛傳:
『袍繭也』，又爾稚釋言及方言也都說:『袍襺也』，那就新舊之稱亦不是那樣嚴格到不
能互用。

袍的制度大概也是爲深衣之屬，禮記儒行:『孔子在魯衣逢掖之衣』，注:『逢猶大
也，大掖之衣，大袂襌衣也』。續漢書輿服志云:『周公抱成王安居，故施袍，禮記，
孔子衣逢掖之衣，逢掖其袖合而縫大之，若近今施袍者』，故逢掖爲大袖的單衣，而漢
世的袍也是這種形製。但漢代一般的袍又是專指綿袍而言。再據急就篇:『袍襦表裏曲

裕裙』，顏注：『長衣曰袍，下至足跗，短衣曰襦，自膝以上』，正是袍和襦不同之點，據長短來分別。

因此，我們可以就漢代衣服的分別，大致做以下的分類：

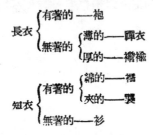

其他絝，履，絑，在種類上大致均無甚問題，只是形製的問題罷了。至於幨字，不見於說文，但廣雅及釋名，均釋作車幔，可能是帳子一類的用具，或者是和衣服同橐所裝的車幔，因爲收藏的關係，所以記載在同一的木簡上。

漢晉時期的帷帳

一　宮室和帷帳之關係

　　帷帳是漢代宮室中的一個重要陳設。在漢代宮室之中，並沒有用到玻璃窗，也沒有用到紙（註一）。因此帷帳是廣泛的使用着。帷帳的種類也因為使用的性質不同，使得有種種不同的形式。

　　在秦漢以還的宮室中，幬帳是其中的最普遍，並且是最觸目的，最奢麗的。因此談到富麗宮室中的陳設，就先要談到帷帳。在以下各段中，可以看得出來。

　　漢書賈山傳：『秦……起咸陽而西至雍，離宮三百，鐘鼓帷帳，不移而具。』

　　漢書陳勝傳：『其故人嘗與傭耕，聞之，之陳，叩宮門曰：吾欲見涉。……勝出，遮道而呼涉，迺召見，與歸。見殿屋帷帳。客曰，夥，涉之爲王沈沈者。』

　　漢書張良傳：『沛公入秦，宮室，帷帳，狗馬，重寶，婦女，以千數。』

　　漢書劉澤傳：『田生如長安，不見澤，而假大宅，令其子求事呂后

> 所幸大謁者張卿。居數月，張卿親臨修具。張卿往見田生，帷帳具
> 置如列侯。張卿驚。酒酣乃屏人說張卿曰……太后欲立呂產爲呂
> 王，王代，呂后又重發之。

在以上幾個例證之中，便可以大略看出在一般富麗宮室的中間，帷帳在裝飾中，要占著一個重要的地位。

在這裏，爲的要更明瞭帷帳對的宮室的關係，因此先將漢代宮室的結構叙述一個大致。漢代的房屋和經注中的宮室結構應當是屬於同一系統之下。自然漢代的房屋決非都是千篇一律，就是在陶製明器中的房屋也是一個與別一個並不完全相同。但是凡在同一系統下的東西，仍然很容易發現他們相同的一點，所以在此是不妨舉出來。經注中的宮室結構，從宋代的李如圭到淸代的黃以周以及民國時代的王國維都各有他到意見，但是中國式房屋總是中國式房屋，他的基本相同點仍然是存在的。爲看簡單明瞭起見，在此先引一段陳奐的毛詩傳疏，以後再略爲解釋。

> 詩豳風七月疏：『凡屋前有堂，後有房有室。房在東有南戶，室在
> 西有南牖。房之北有北堂，北堂之下有北階，房室之間亦有戶相
> 通，室之北有北牖，此燕寢制也。』(註二)

這是房屋中的最簡單的形式，也就是房屋中的基本形式。將這個形式擴大做成一個四面對稱的形式，就是四合頭院。將這個形式兩側加上耳房，也可以變成東堂西堂或則是東閣西閣。再擴大些還可做成千門萬戶的宮殿。但就他的基本條件來說，却是堂是宮室最主要的部份，再便是所謂『內』，『內』分做『房』和『室』附屬在堂之後面。

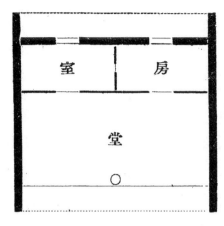

簡單的建築，所謂
『一堂二內』的建
築。（一堂二內，
見漢書晁錯傳。）

這種前兩大間空着中間有一個柱子，後面再有兩小間的形式，在彭山
的漢代崖墓中，還有不少(註三)。彭山的漢代崖墓，雖然已經不是木構，但
却很清楚的是仿做木構的形式和布置。正可以作爲一個旁證。不還這種只
是一個最簡單的舉例，爲的是要知道前面的堂是空敞的，後面的房和室才
有間隔。在本篇所要討論的房屋凡是涉及帷和帳的，他的規模都比較這一
種的形式大得多。堂的間架要至少在三間以上，因此後面的三間也變成了
東房，西房，和室。

堂的前面既然是開敞的，在比較簡單的房屋，卽農家的房屋，可以用
來放農具，囤糧食，自然堂用不著任何的遮蔽。但是在一般帝王的殿和士
大夫的堂中，堂是用來行禮，和宴會，決不能和農家一樣的簡陋，因此帷
帳是用得着的，所以幛帳住住和堂殿互相題到。

後漢書馬融傳：『融才高博洽，爲世通儒。教養諸生，常有千數。
涿郡盧植，北海鄭玄，皆其徒也。善鼓琴，好吹笛，達生任性，不
拘儒者之節。居處器服，多存侈飾。常坐高堂，施絳帳，前坐生
徒，後列女樂，弟子以次相傳，鮮有入其室者。』

晉書元帝紀：『有司當奏太極殿廣室施絳帳。帝曰：漢文集上書皁
囊爲帷，遂令冬施靑布，夏施靑練帷帳。』

晉書穆帝紀：『永和元年春，正月，甲戌朔，皇太后設白紗帷于太

極殿，抱帝臨軒改元。』

在這裡我們可以理會到的，帝王的殿和士大夫的堂是具有同樣的性質。因為殿堂是開啟的，需要一種遮蔽風日的物件。這種物件便是帷帳。帷帳可以用精細的絲織品來做，也可以用粗糙的麻織品來做。帷帳的地位據山東嘉祥縣和兩城山等處漢畫，可以看出來是懸掛在簷內兩柱間的橫楣上，並且時常將帷帳捲起來的。但據馬融傳，帷帳似乎不僅在簷內兩柱之間施有帷帳，並且在堂內還施有很講究的帷帳，將堂分為前後二部，前列生徒，後列女樂。這雖然是一個比較特殊的例子，但可以看出帷帳的廣泛應用。帷和帳是同屬一類的兩種物件。但在漢魏却將帷帳二字常常指帷帳兩物的通名，並且也有時互稱的。例如：

漢書高帝紀十二年：『沛中空縣皆之邑西獻，上留止張飲三日』注：『張晏曰，張帷帳也。』

漢書外戚李夫人傳：『方士齊人少翁言能致其神，乃夜張燈燭，設帳帷，陳酒肉，而令上居他帳。遙望好女如李夫人之貌，逐幄坐而步，又不得就視。』

漢書郊祀志：『齊人少翁以方見上，上有所幸李夫人，夫人卒，少翁以方，蓋夜致夫人及竈鬼之貌云。天子自帷中望見焉，廼拜少翁為文成將軍。』

後漢書宣秉傳：『帝嘗幸其府，見而歎曰：楚國二龔，不如雲陽宣巨公，卽賜布帛，帷帳，什物。』（注：『周禮幕人掌帷帟幄幕。鄭玄曰：在旁曰帷，爾雅幬謂之帳。』）

後漢書翟酺傳：『安帝始親政事……元舅耿寶及皇后兄弟閻顯等並用威權，酺上疏諫曰……文帝愛百金於露臺，節帷帳於卑囊，或有譏其儉者，上曰：朕為國家守財耳。』（註：東方朔曰文帝集上書囊以為殿帷。）

太平御覽六九九引益部耆舊傳：『鼂酺上事，漢文帝連上書囊以爲帳惡聞紈素之聲。』

左思吳都賦：『張組帷，搆流蘇，開軒幌，鏡水區。』

從以上各例看來，帷和帳固然各有各的意義，但是帷帳或帳帷二字連用是指一切帳類的總名，並且帷和帳二字的界限也並不如何的嚴格，這兩個字是隨時可以混用的。

二　帷帳的種類

照着鄭玄周禮幕人注：『在旁曰帷』和釋名的解牀帳：『帷圍也，所以自障圍也。』『帳張也，張施於牀上也』顯然的帷和帳是有區別的，帷的功用是宮室中的障蔽，帳的功用是牀上的籠罩，所以形製應當不同，帷大而帳小，帷大率爲單面的隔開，帳大率要四方的覆蔽。但帷的種類很多，帳的種類也很多，因此就形成了種種的名稱。

（甲）　帷

帷本是在帷帳中一個廣泛的名稱。但有一個最狹的意義，是指車的帷裳。詩衞風氓：『淇水湯湯，漸車帷裳』。毛傳：『帷裳，婦人之車也。』陳魚疏：『箋：「帷裳，童容也」。鄭司農注：「巾車作潼容」。士昏禮，「婦車亦如之」。「有裧」註：「裧車帷裳」，裧與襜通。列女傳貞順篇：「齊孝公使騶馬立車載姬以歸，姬使傅御者舒帷以自障蔽，而使傅母應使者曰：「妾聞妃后野處，則帷裳擁蔽，所以正心壹意，自歛制也。今立車無輧，非所以受命也，野處無衞，非所敢久居也。」君子謂孟姬好禮，婦人出，必輜輧，是帷裳又名輜輧也。」按輜輧和立乘的男子車均有帷，只是輜輧的帷更大更長。因爲鄭箋：『帷裳，童容也』，童容卽襠襦，釋名釋衣服：『襠襦，言其襜襦宏裕也。』這就是談輜輧的帷更大些罷了。禮記曲禮：『仲尼之畜狗死，使子貢埋之，曰：「吾聞之也，敝帷不棄爲埋馬也，敝蓋不棄，爲埋狗也。丘也貧無蓋，於其封也，亦爲之席，毋使其首陷焉」。路馬死，埋之以帷。』這裏所言的帷，與蓋連稱，當然也是指車帷而言。在後漢書也有關於車帷的事。例如：

趙岐傳：『自匿姓名賣餅北海市中。時安丘孫嵩年二十餘，游市見岐，察非常人，停車共載。岐懼失色，嵩乃下帷，令轉屏行人。』

賈琮傳：『以琮爲冀州刺史，舊典傳車驂駕垂赤帷裳（續志大使車之乘，駕駟赤帷，持節者重導）。迎於州界及琮之部，升車言曰：「刺史當廣聽糾察美惡，何有反垂帷裳以自掩塞乎？乃命御者闓之。」

這兩個例子都是男子坐的帷車，不是女子坐的輜車，所以漢代車帷是不限於女子車的。此外喪車也有裳帷的。例如：

禮記雜記上：『諸侯行而死於舘，則其復如其國。如於道，則升其乘車之左轂，以其綏復。其輤有裧，緇布裳帷。素錦以爲屋而行。……大夫以布爲輤而行，至於家而說輤，載以輲車。……士輤，葦席以爲屋，蒲席以爲裳帷。』

在這一段並且還可以看出來，蒲席的裳帷是不便於褰開的，因此在車上的帷只爲的是分隔，並無十分固定的質料和形式。

同樣在一般宮室中所用的帷，主要的也是爲的分隔。周禮天官掌舍：『爲帷宮，設旌門。』鄭玄注：『王若食息，張帷爲宮，則樹旌以表門。』這是說天子遇出巡的時候，就食和休息的所在，是用帷來分隔的。禮記檀弓：『尸未設飾故帷堂，小歛而徹帷。』這是說在堂上特設的喪帷來掩隔死尸。以上還都是特殊的例子。至於禮記曲禮：『帷薄之外不趨。』注：『帷幔也，薄簾也。』正是平時分隔內外的。漢書賈誼傳：『古者大臣有坐不廉而廢者，不謂不廉，曰簠簋不飾。坐汙穢淫亂，男女亡別者，不曰汙穢，曰帷薄不修。坐罷軟不勝任者，不謂罷軟曰下官不職。故貴大臣定其有罪矣，猶未斥然正以呼之也。』這也表示着帷是在平時用來分隔內外的帷幔。

在此，我們可以很清楚看出帷的用處是分隔內外，所以馬融的絳帳，也就是絳色的帷幔。在一個類似的例子，還在漢書張禹傳可以看出來：

> 『禹成就弟子淮陽彭宣至大司空，沛郡戴崇至少府。宣爲人恭儉有法度，而崇愷弟多智。二人異行，禹心愛崇，敬宣而遠之。崇每候禹，常責師宜置酒設樂，與弟子相娛。禹將崇入後堂，飲食男女相對。優人筦絃鏗鏘極樂，至昏夜乃罷，而宣之來也，禹見之於便坐，講論經義。日宴賜食不過一肉，巵酒相對。宣未嘗得至後堂，及兩人聞知各自得也。』

這裡所謂『後堂』，在一般的解釋，應當卽是婦人所坐的『北堂』，在東房之後。爲的是要從堂上分隔內外，應當有一層帷幔的。又這裡所謂接待彭宣的『便坐』，那是指不在一般接待賓客的正堂上。照顏師古解釋『便坐』二字說：『便坐謂非正殿，於旁坐可以延賓者也。』爲甚麼延在『便坐』，當然可以有許多解釋。但照張禹傳來說：『禹姓智知音聲，內奢淫，身居大第，後堂理絲竹筦絃。』後堂卽在堂後，所以他不在正殿來接應客人，而去到一個偏僻而淸靜的『便坐』。當然，張禹旣然在一個『大第』，後堂不一定便接近正殿。但是也可以這樣解釋，就是；在漢代一般建築之中，正寢（或正殿，前殿）是第宅中一個主要的建築，也是一個最大而且最華麗的建築。所以宴會或奏樂，也在此處。但看後漢書馬融傳的高堂，也就是主要的建築，也就是女樂演奏之處。兩相比較，可以用不着多少懷疑了。

在禮記曲禮著，鄭玄注用『幔』來解釋帷字。據說文『幔幕也』。段注改爲『幔帳也』『帳各本作幕，由作羃而誤耳。今正。（說文，『帳，幔也』)。凡以物冡其上曰幔，與帴雙聲而互訓，釋名，玉篇以帷幔釋之，今義非古義也。』但段氏所謂『今義』仍是漢人之義，『古義』乃周以前之義。許氏說文中不合古義者正多，似不必一一盡以意改正。現在但取漢以後人認幔爲帷帳便已經够了。

　　除去帷以外尙有簾一物，簾亦卽帷薄之薄。許愼分帴簾爲二字。說文：『帴帷也』段注：『釋名曰「簾廉也，自障蔽爲廉恥也，戶箕施之於戶外也。按與竹部簾異物。帴以布爲之，簾以竹爲之。』所以簾和帷是一類的。此外關於簾的，例如：

　　漢書周勃傳：『以織曲爲業』，注：『蘇林曰：薄一名曲也。』

　　漢書王吉傳序：『蜀有嚴君平………卜筮於成都市……得百錢足自養，則閉肆下簾而授老子。』

　　太平御覽六九九引服虔通俗文：『戶帷曰簾。』

　　太平御覽六九九引漢武故事：『甲帳居神，以白珠爲簾箔，玳瑁押之。象牙爲篾。』

　　西京雜記：『漢諸陵皆以竹爲簾，簾皆以水文及龍鳳像。』(註四)

　　太平御覽六九九引晉東宮故事曰：『簾箔皆以靑布緣純。』

所以簾和帷是一類的，只是簾小而帷大，簾或用布製，或用竹製，帷只是用絲質品或布製罷了。簾是施於戶的，戶是半扇的門，在開的時候便要用簾遮蔽。但是戶不一定都是全幅的木板。漢書元后傳：『曲陽侯根驕奢僭上，赤墀靑瑣』。注：『師古曰：靑瑣者，刻爲連環文而以靑塗之也。』這種類似刻鏤，現在還可看到從宋到淸，大的廟宇中的殿戶和殿牖。當然也是好的採光的方便。但是還需要綾綺糊上去，光線不太好，平時仍然要打開，再加上戶簾或窗簾的。

　　在漢代普通人的窗子，是用木條做成格子的。說文：『窗，穿壁以木爲交窗，所以見日也。』『牖，窗櫺閭子也。』所以除非最簡陋的『甕牖，』

照例是有格子的。在漢代明器中，陶製房屋的牖是許多條的長條。這是表示着直格形的窗格，這種用一條一條木條做成的窗格，現存實物中在唐代廟宇中就有這種形式（例如五臺的佛光寺，以及敦煌的唐代廊子）， 一直到現在中國北部尚有這種窗格。 這種窗格爲着冬天遮蔽風，夏天遮蔽蚊蚋，當然簾子還是紙用得着。（註五）

（乙） 帳

帳字和張字是同源的，釋名：『帳張也，張施於牀上也，小張曰斗，形如覆斗也。』和帷不同之處是帷是一方的，帳是籠罩四面的。因此帳不僅限於牀上，凡有頂的帷幕都可稱爲帳。例如：

史記汲鄭列傳：『丞相公孫弘燕見，上或時不冠，至於汲黯，不冠不見也。上嘗坐武帳中，黯前奏事，上不冠，望見黯，避帳中，使人可其奏，其敬禮如此。』

漢武故事：『上以琉璃，珠，玉，明月，夜光，錯雜天下珍寶爲甲帳；其次爲乙帳，甲以居神，乙以自居。』

御覽六九九引東觀漢記曰：『馮魴，永平中，上行幸諸國，勅魴車駕發後，將緹騎宿玄武門複道。上詔南宮複道多惡風寒，老人居之且病痱。若向南者名曰帷帳，東西完塞諸窗，望合緻密。』

魏志四夷傳論注引魏略：『大秦國……非獨用羊毛也，亦用木皮或野繭絲織成氍毹罽帳之屬。』

世說新語雅量：『許侍中（璪）顧司空（和）俱作丞相從事，爾時已被遇，游宴集聚，略無不同。嘗夜至丞相許戲。二人歡極，丞相便命使入己帳眠。顧至曉回轉不得快孰。許上牀便咍臺大鼾。丞相顧諸客曰：「此中亦難得眠處」。』

世說新語雅量：『桓宣武與郗超議芟夷羣臣。條牒既定，其夜，同宿。明晨起，呼謝安，王坦之入，擲疏示之。郗猶在帳內，謝都無

言。王直擲還示多。宣武取筆欲除，都不覺竅從帳中與宣武言。謝含笑曰：「郗生可謂入幕之賓也」。』（註六）

世說新語寵禮：『卞範之爲丹陽尹，羊孚南州暫還，往卞許，云：「下官疾動不堪坐」。卞便開帳拂褥，羊經上大牀，入被須枕。卞同坐傾睞，移晨達莫。羊去。卞語曰：「我以第一理卿，卿莫負我」。』

世說新語排調：『許文思往顧和許，顧先在帳中眠，許至，便經就牀角枕共語。既而喚顧共行，顧乃命取枕上新衣，易已體上所著。許笑曰：「卿乃後有行來衣乎」？』

世說新語假譎：『王右軍（王羲之）年減十歲時，大將軍，（王敦）甚愛之，恆置帳中眠，大將軍當先出，右軍猶未起。須臾錢鳳入，屏人論事，都忘右軍在帳中，便言逆節之謀。右軍覺，既聞所論，知無活理，乃剔吐汙頭面被褥，詐孰眠。敦論事造半，方意右軍未起，相與大驚曰：「不得不除之」及開帳，乃見吐睡縱橫，信其實孰眠，於是得全。于時稱其有智。』（註七）

北堂書鈔一三二引鄴中記：『石虎冬月纏大明光錦絮以房子綿一百二十斤，白縑爲裏，名複帳。帳之四角，安純金銀鑿鏤香爐，以石墨燒集和名香，帳頂上安蓮花，中縣金薄織成椀囊……盛香。帳之四面上十二香囊，采色亦同，但小囊耳。』

北堂書鈔一三二引鄴中記：『春秋但施錦帳，表以五色絲爲複帳，惟夏用單紗，羅，或綦文單羅，或縠文羅爲單帳。』

從以上各節來看，帳和帷是有區別的。帷是一種單幅的帷幔。帳却是四面罩在牀上的。罩在牀上的方法，和現在所存舊式牀上的方帳應當有若干類似。尤其在世說新語中說到的帳，更顯然和現存的方帳是屬於同式。只是史記汲鄭列傳所說的武帳，也許和一般牀上的帳有若干的區別。因爲一般的牀帳是在室內，而武帳却在宮廷會集之所。漢書霍光傳云：

> 『頃之，有太后詔召王（昌邑王），王聞召意恐，廼曰：「我安得罪而
> 召我哉？」太后被珠襦，盛服坐武帳中，侍御數百人皆持兵，期門
> 武士陛戟陳列殿下，羣臣以次上殿。』

在這裏可以看出來的是武帳應當是殿上御坐的帳。殿上的武帳是要裝飾
的，所以太平御覽六九九引晉後略曰：

> 『張方兵入洛，御室織成，流蘇，武帳，皆割分爲馬韉矣。』

然而裝飾是有限度的，這度的裝飾也就有些不像樣。晉書桓玄傳：

> 『小會於西堂，設妓樂，殿上施繹綾帳。鏤黃金爲顏，四角作金龍
> 頭，銜五色羽葆旒蘇。羣臣竊相謂曰：「此頗似輼車，亦王莽仙蓋
> 之流也」。』

這是說殿上的帳，還只是一個好的帳子，在一般說來，仍然並無過分的裝
飾的。

　　此外，行軍時是用到帳幕的，這種行帳，卽李廣傳：『幕府省文書』
的幕。但也有稱做帳的，例如，

> 三國志呂布傳注引英雄記：『布自以有功於袁氏，輕傲紹下諸將，
> 以爲擅相署置，不足貴也。布求還洛，紹假布領司隸校尉。外言當
> 遣，內欲殺布。明日當發，紹遣甲士三十人，辟以送布。布使止於
> 帳側，僞使人於帳中鼓箏。紹兵臥，布無何出帳去而兵不覺。夜半
> 兵起，亂斫布牀被，謂爲已死。明日紹訊問知布尚在，乃閉城門，
> 布遂引去。』

> 三國志呂布傳：『太祖乃盡收諸城，擊破布於鉅野，布東奔劉備。』
> 注引英雄記：『布見備，甚敬之。謂備曰：「我與卿同邊地人也，
> 布見關東起兵，欲誅董卓　布殺卓東出，關東諸將無安布者，皆欲
> 殺布耳。」請備於帳中坐歸牀上，令歸向拜，酌酒飲食，名備爲

弟。備見布語言無常，外然之而內不悅。』

魏志典韋傳：『拜韋都尉，引置左右，將親兵數百人。常遶大帳。韋旣壯武，其所將皆選卒，每戰鬭常先登陷陣，遷爲校尉。性忠至謹重，常晝侍玄終日，夜宿帳左右，稀歸私寢。』

這裡說到的帳，都是營中的帳幕。同例，據梁書西北諸戎河南王傳吐谷渾傳）說：

『其國多善馬，有屋宇，雜以百子帳，而穹廬也。』

這是稱穹廬爲帳的。穹廬所以稱做百子帳的原因，大約是因爲和結婚時的青廬類似的原故。宋程大昌演繁露：

『唐人昏禮多用百子帳，特貴其名與昏宜，而其制度則非有子孫衆多之義。蓋其制本出戎虜，持穹廬拂廬：具體而微者耳。椶柳爲圈，以相連鎖。可張可闔，爲其圈多，故以百子總之。亦非眞有百圈也。其施張旣成，大抵如今尖頂圓亭子，而用青氈通冒四隅上下，便於移置耳。』

程大昌說和戎虜的穹廬有關，是不錯的，不過這個制度却不是在唐才開始，唐段成式酉陽雜俎：

『北朝婚禮，青布幔爲屋，在門內外，謂之青廬。於此交拜迎婦。』

和程大昌所說的雖然青氈和青布不同，仍然還屬於一類。但是青廬這一種制度，可能還更早些，古詩孔雀東南飛：

『其日牛馬嘶，新婦入青廬。』

這首詩雖然說的是建安時事，但成詩時代還有問題。不過據世說新語假譎篇：

『魏武少時，嘗等袁紹好爲游俠，觀人新婚，因潛入主人園中。夜叫呼云：「有偸兒賊。」青廬中人皆出觀。魏武乃入，抽刄劫新婦。等紹還出，失道墜枳棘中。紹不能得動，復大叫云：「偸兒在此。」

紹遽迫自擲出，遂以俱免。』

這件事的可靠性仍然還成問題。不過世說新語的著作者劉義慶却是南朝人，不是北朝人。因此青廬的制度，至少在南朝也是有的。至於屬於這一條的時間性和地域性的演變，當然也是有的。只是材料不夠，不能詳細說明罷了。

（註一）西京雜記：『昭陽殿窗戶扇多是綠琉璃，皆照逼毛髮不得藏焉。』此雖言漢代的琉璃窗，但西京雜記一書本不可信。此書舊題晉葛洪撰，但酉陽雜俎語資篇，言庾信作詩用西京雜記事，旋自追改。曰『此吳均語，恐不足信。』吳均梁時人，更較葛洪爲後。據魏書大月氏傳云：『世祖時，其國人商販京師，自云能鑄石爲五色瑠璃，於是採礦山中，於京師鑄之，既成，光澤乃美於西方來者。乃治爲行殿，容百餘人，光色映徹，觀者見之，莫不驚駭，以爲神明所作。自是中國瑠璃遂賤，人不復珍之。』世祖卽魏太武帝，與宋文帝同時。在此以前中國的玻璃窗是一個經絕沒有的事。因此西京雜記不惟不是漢代的人所作，並且也不可能是晉代的葛洪所作。段成式記庾信的話頗有可以令人相信的理由。

紙爲後漢順帝時蔡倫所造。但一直到西晉使用還不很普徧。紙窗的使用現在知道最早或在唐代。說郛引馮贄記事珠：『楊炎在中書，後閣糊窗用桃花紙，瑩以冰油取其明甚。』又：『段九章詩戒，無紙就窗裁故紙，連綴用之。』（馮贄爲宋王銍化名）。到了宋代造紙更多，不僅有紙窗，並且還有紙被和紙帳了。

（註二）參看禮經制度與漢代宮室（北京大學四十四週年紀念論文集）

（註三）參看色伽蘭：中國西部考古記（V. Segalen Premier Exposé des Résutats Archeologiques obtenus dans la Chine Occidentale par la Mission Gilbert de Voisins）

（註四）西京雜記不可信已見前，但漢武故事荒誕不經又在西京雜記之上。舊題班固撰，甚妄。晁公武郡齋讀書志引張束之洞冥記跋，謂出南齊王儉，庶乎近之。隋書經籍志已著錄此書，當然爲六朝舊籍。則西京雜記及漢武故事至少所記爲六朝名物，故今據之。

（註五）帷亦稱爲幔，御覽六九九引東觀漢記曰：『岑彭與吳漢圍隗囂，壅谷水以縑幔盛土，爲堤灌城。』南史柳元景傳附柳悆傳：『悆甚重婦，頗成畏憚，性愛音樂，女妓精麗略不敢視，僕射張稷，與悆狎密，而爲悆妻賞敬。稷每詣悆，必先相問夫人。悆每見妓，但因稷請奏，其妻隔悆坐然後出，悆因得留目。』晉書列女傳：『韋逞母宋氏……傳其父業，得周官音義，……年八十，視聽無闕，……於是就宋家立講堂，隔絳幔而受業。』此外還有步障，亦是帷幔之類。晉書石崇傳：『與貴戚王愷，羊琇之徒，以奢靡相當，愷以飴澳釜，崇以蠟代薪。愷作紫絲步障四十里，崇作錦步障五十里以敵之。』

（註六）　按御覽六九九引世說曰：『郗超為桓溫參事，時謝安王坦之嘗詣溫，令超帳中臥，聽論事，風動帳開，安笑曰：「郗生可謂入幕之賓」，』與此節文字大異。惟晉書郗鑒傳附郗超傳與此節文略同，僅小有出入，所以此節應當是從十八家晉書節取。御覽誤題為世說。

（註七）　按王羲之當王敦及錢鳳謀逆時，在王敦帳中，事當不誣。敦本無子，羲之是王敦從子中的優秀者，和王敦嗣子王應的親疏略同。似乎王敦的逆謀，並無一定要迴避羲之的必要。世說言王敦說：『不得不除之』，和羲之大吐之事，並不太盡情理，假如真要除羲之，也不是大吐所能掩飾。則是此節大吐的故事，應當是王敦敗後，王家為脫免王羲之的原故來假造出來的。晉書不載此事，頗有史識。不過不論此事的真偽，還可以來作為晉代帳子的例證。

論中國造紙術之原始

紙是中國人的發明，和埃及紙草的紙，在文獻上或理論上，並無任何的相關。因為中國人是發明蠶絲的民族，紙的製造，就從蠶絲衍化出來。中國的蠶絲，發明甚早，李濟之先生在西陰村遺址，已經發現過半個蠶繭。這是很清楚的，將破碎的蠶繭，黏着到一塊兒，遠較將蠶絲抽出來織成縑帛爲價廉。紙的發見和製造，就應當從這一個原理出來。

紙字是絲，顯然的和蠶絲是有關係的。說文糸部：

> 紙，絮一笘也。從糸氏聲。

段玉裁注云：

> 笘應作苫，笘下曰澈絮簀也；澈下曰於水中擊絮也。……按造紙昉於漂絮，其初絲絮爲之，以笘荐而成之；今用竹質木皮爲紙，亦有緻密竹簾荐之是也。

關於漂絮這一件事，又見於莊子逍遙游。

> 宋人有善爲不龜手之藥者，世世以洴澼絖爲事。

郭象注云：

> 其藥能令手不拘坼，故常漂絮於水中也。

陸德明音義云：

> 澼普歷反，絖音曠。小爾雅云：『絮細者謂之絖。』李云：『洴澼絖者，漂絮於水上，絖絮也。』漂四妙反，韋昭云：『以水擊絮爲漂。』

史記淮陰侯列傳：

> 信釣於城下，諸母漂，有一母見信飢飯信，竟漂數十日。

集解引韋昭曰：

以水擊絮爲漂，故曰漂母。

照這樣看來，漂絮是一種長期的或臨時的職業。

漂絮既然是一種職業，可見這一類的事，在當時需要比較普遍，那就不得不從絮的性質上來求解釋。說文糸部：

絮敝緜也，從糸如聲。（大徐本作絮）

段玉裁注云：

緜者聯敝也，因以爲絮之偁。敝者敗衣也，因以爲敦之偁。敝絲，敦緜也。是之謂絮。凡絮必絲爲之，古無今之木緜也。以絮納袷衣爲袍曰襺，亦曰裝襺，以作著，以麻縕爲袍亦曰襺。

又說文糸部：

纊絮也，從糸廣聲。春秋傳曰：『皆如挾纊。』絖，纊或從光。

段玉裁注云：

玉藻『纊爲繭』，注曰：『纊今之新緜也。』按鄭釋纊爲新緜者，以別於縕之爲新緜及舊絮也。許則謂纊爲絲絮，不分新故，謂縕爲麻紼，與鄭絕異，

又說文糸部：

絮治敝絮也。從糸店聲。

又說文糸部：

絮絮䋏也，一曰惡絮，從糸敫聲。

段玉裁注云：

一曰猶一名也。絮䋏讀如貉絫，疊均字轉爲絲絖，絲苦堅切。廣均十二齊一先皆曰『絲絖惡絮』是也。釋名曰：『煮繭曰莫，莫幕也。貧者著衣，可以幕絮也。或謂之牽離，煮熟爛牽引使離散如絮也。』……大徐本古諧切非也。此字之本音見周易釋文云：直作敫下糸者，音口笑反。集均絮牽奚切，引說文『絮䋏今惡絮』，陸德明，丁度非不言之憭然也。而六朝以後，舍系不用，而叚絮爲系，遂使絮之本義，聲蘊終古。至鼎臣奉敕校定此書，亦緦云古諧切，何淺牽若此，倘自謂用唐均，不知唐均齊均之絮，非許書之絮也。十六部。

又說文糸部：

　　緆繫繋也，從糸虒聲，一曰維也。

以上和漂絮，絮，及敝絮有關的字，共有：絮、繢、紙、絬、繫、繳六個字。在說文中，便是按着絮、繢、紙、絬、繫、繳六個字先後的次序排列着。說文中各字次序的排列，大都是有意義的。紙字在這幾個字的中間，顯然和其他的五個有若干的關聯。

　　照明宋應星天工開物說：

　　凡取絲必用圓正獨蠒繭，則緒不亂。若雙繭，併四五蠒共爲繭，擇去取綿用。或以爲絲，則粗甚。

　　凡雙繭，并繅絲鍋底零餘，併出種繭売，皆緒亂不可爲絲，用以取綿。用稻灰水煮過（不宜石灰。）傾入清水盆內。手大指去甲淨盡，指頭頂開四箇。四四數足，用拳頂開。又四四十六拳數，然後上小竹弓，此莊子所謂洴澼絖也。湖綿獨白淨清化者，總緣手法之妙。上弓之時惟取快捷，帶水擴開。若稍緩水流去，則結塊不盡解，而色不純白矣。其治絲餘者，名鍋底綿，裝綿衣衾內以禦重寒，謂之挾纊。凡取綿人工，難於取絲八倍，竟日只得四兩餘，用此綿墜打線織湖紬者，價頗重。以綿線登花機者，名曰花綿，價尤重。（按宋應琂裳書已有『炎蠒作絮』之語，又元王禎農書及明徐光啟農政全書亦略與宋說同。）

這是明代的造絮法，現在還差不多。只是他有幾個誤會。

　　第一、洴澼絖是漂絮，據淮陰侯傳，漂絮是在城下的河中，和宋氏所說的清水盆中，並不一樣，所以古代不見得是用手指、拳、和竹弓來頂。

　　第二、鍋底的絮不是繢。說文別有一字，卽：『絓，繭滓絓頭也。從糸圭聲。一曰以囊絮澆也。』與此不同。

所以還不敢說明代以來做法，是與古代相同。只能從明代的做法，來推想古代的大致。因爲蠒繭有膠，非煮不能撕開，明代如此，古代亦必如此。但明代和現代是在盆內用手來撕，而古代卻是在河內放在蓆子上來擊（見前紙字段玉裁注。）現代用手來撕的絲綿，當然是輕而煖，古代放在蓆子上來擊的絲綿，當然比較重而疑凍了。並且在蓆子上來擊，剩下的殘餘黏在蓆子上的，從水裏取出蓆子之後，一定有一片一片的薄片，這就是說文所說的紙了。

在西漢時代，傳說已經有紙了。漢書九十七下趙皇后傳：

兒生八九日，後三日，客復持詔記，封如前予武。中有封，小綠篋，記曰：『告武以篋中物書，予獄中婦人。武自臨飲之。』武發篋中有裹藥二枚赫蹏書，曰：『告偉能努力飲此藥，不可復入，女自知之。』偉能即宮……宮飲藥死。顏師古注云：

孟康曰：『蹏，猶地也，染紙素令赤而書之。若今黃紙也。』鄧展曰：『赫音兄弟鬩牆之鬩。』應劭曰：『赫蹏薄小紙也。』晉灼曰：『今如薄小物爲鬩蹏，鄧音應說是也。』師古曰：『孟說非也，今書本赫字或作擊。』

王先謙補注云：

沈欽韓曰：『玉篇幟䏠赤紙也。』周壽昌曰：『據此西漢時巳有紙可作擊炙。赫狀其色赤，蹏狀其式小，孟說未爲非也。』

顏師古只說孟康的解釋不對，卻未曾說出所以然。因此周壽昌要來替孟康辯護。現在看來，孟康的解釋大概是錯誤的。因爲赫蹏即擊蹏，又即鬩蹏。這和說文的繫蹏顯然同爲一物。擊與繫都從毄得聲，蹏與䏠都從虒得聲，其可以互通當無問題；又鬩與繫本屬同部，聲類亦近，應可互通；赫與繫雖相去稍遠，但均爲收k之入聲；且有鄧展注出音鬩之音，亦可證明漢人的音讀，耤知和繫字相關。因此，要解釋漢書的赫蹏，不如認爲即係說文所說的惡絮（亦即敝絮）做的紙比較清楚些。赫蹏之原義既當爲敝絮，那就『蹏』訓地，『赫』訓赤，是孟康的望文生義，而顏師古所說的『孟說非也』是對的了。

紙既由絮造成，所以御覽六百五引服虔通俗文『方絮曰紙。』正是紙的初義。方絮亦即方形的繫繕，亦即方形的赫蹏。絮作成方形是黏成的，帛作成方形是織成的，所以方絮不是方帛而是方紙。（又劉熙釋名：『紙砥也，平滑如砥石也。』釋名全書好以音爲訓，在此處紙砥也一語，在古音是不能相通的，這一處所用的只是漢人平常所用較寬的韻讀，未足據爲典要。但平滑如砥石一語，卻可證明漢人的紙是求其光滑。）因此我們可以意想到漢成帝宮中的赫蹏，是一種壓緊或者是黏緊的方絮，寫上字再包上藥，裝盛匣子裏面的。此物爲大內之物，非出寒素，也可見到是加工的廢絮，而精美到可供奢侈君主漢成帝的御用了。

到了後漢時代，紙已經漸漸的不僅用在包裹藥品等小的用途上。經傳也用紙來寫了。後漢書六十六賈逵傳：（按此文僅見於後漢書，是否被范蔚宗增飾，待證。）

> 肅宗立，降意儒術，特好古文尚書左氏傳。建初元年（七六年）詔逵入講北宮白虎觀，南宮雲臺。帝善逵說，使出左氏傳大義，長於二傳者。逵條奏之。……書奏，帝嘉之，賜布五百匹，衣一襲。令逵自選公羊嚴顏諸生高才者二十人，教以左氏與簡紙經傳各一通。（注：『竹簡及紙也。』）

許慎是賈逵的門徒，許沖上說文書曰：『臣父故大尉南閣祭酒慎，本從逵受大學。』所以賈逵用紙來寫的左氏，許慎不應該不知道。但說文解釋紙字，只有『紙，絮一苫也』一個意義，並無縑帛的解釋，可見賈逵所有的傳文紙質，也就是許慎所解釋的紙質，亦卽賈逵同時的紙，和漢成帝時的紙，同樣的是黏的絮，而不是織的帛。

說文成於和帝永元十二年（一〇〇年），其時已有紙字，並有『紙絮一苫也』的解釋，再加上成帝時的證據，可知西漢末年，東漢初年，已經有紙了。中國有紙相傳為蔡倫所造，蔡倫在元興元年（一〇五年）才正式奏上所造的紙，因而天下才應用蔡倫的紙，事在說文成書之後的第六年，所以蔡倫對於紙，應當是改進的人而不是始創的人。再參考西洋人現代的發明史，最後成功的人大多不是草創的人，那蔡倫的紙以前還有一個前期，那也不足怪了。

敍述蔡倫事蹟最詳的是范曄的後漢書，范曄死於元嘉二十二年（四四五年），此書列傳的寫定在元嘉二年間（四二五年。）其後漢書七十八宦者傳說：

> 蔡倫字敬仲，桂陽人也。……建初中（七六年──八三年）為小黃門。及和帝卽位，轉中常侍。倫有才學，盡心敦慎，數犯顏匡弼得失。後加位尚方令。永元九年（九七年），監作祕劍及諸器械，莫不精工堅密，為後世法。自古書契多編以竹簡，其用縑帛者謂之紙，縑貴而簡重，並不便於人。倫乃造意用樹膚，麻頭、及敝布，魚網以為紙。元興元年（一〇五年）奏上之，帝善其能，自是莫不從用焉。故天下咸稱『蔡侯紙。』

但這一段是從幾個來源來的。太平御覽六百五云：

> 東觀漢記曰：『黃門蔡倫典作尚方作紙，所謂蔡侯紙也。』（類聚五十八

同，書抄一○四引東觀記云：『蔡倫典作尚方作紙』）

蓲巴記曰：『東京有蔡侯紙卽倫（脫一紙字）也。用故麻名麻紙，木皮名穀紙，用故魚網作紙，名網紙也。』

王隱晉書曰：『魏太和六年，博士河間張揖上古今字詁，其巾部「紙今（脫一帋字）也，」其字從巾。古之素帛，依舊長短，隨事截絹。枚數重沓卽名幡紙，此形聲也。後和帝元興中，中常侍蔡倫以故布擣剉作紙，故字從巾，是其聲雖同，系巾爲爲殊，不得言古紙爲今紙。』

又北堂書抄一百零四引張華博物志：

漢桓帝時（絫桓字誤），蔡倫始擣故魚網以造作紙。

初學記三十一紙部敍事：

釋名曰『紙砥也，謂平滑如砥石也。』古者以縑帛依書長短，隨事裁之，名曰幡紙，故其字從系，貧者無之，或用蒲寫書，則路溫舒截蒲是也。至後漢和帝元興，中常侍蔡倫剉故布擣抄作紙。又其字從巾。東觀漢記云：『黃門蔡倫典作尚方作帋，所謂蔡侯紙是也。』又魏人河間張揖上古今字詁，其巾部云：『紙今帋』則其字從巾之謂也。（見漢記及王隱晉書。）一云倫擣故魚網作紙名網紙。後人以生布作紙絲緻如故麻紙，以樹木皮作紙名穀紙。（見蓲巴記及博物志。）

從以上各條看來，太平御覽條分縷析，最爲清楚。但是頗有誤字，並漏去博物志中一條。初學記將材料混到一塊兒，使人看不出史料原來面目，但是誤字甚少，可以校正御覽和書抄之誤。現在看來，各書所引的東觀記，只有『黃門蔡倫典作尚方作紙，所謂蔡侯紙也』一語。因此在東觀記中的本文無論如何省略，蔡倫作紙時只是小黃門加尚方令而非中常侍加尚方令。據司馬彪的百官志，尚方令只是六百石官，和小黃門同秩。小黃門加尚方令是一個榮譽，而中常侍就不需此了。當然蔡倫後封龍亭侯，其時必已爲中常侍，但造紙時卻未必任中常侍。這一點異文，范蔚宗應當是據他家後漢書，而不是據東觀記的。因此東觀記可能未給蔡倫立傳，後漢書蔡倫傳中的文字，一定有若干竄改和增定，出於魏晉以來的史家，不當屬於東觀記的原文。再看以下的一段，卽：

自古書契多編以竹簡，其用縑帛者謂之紙。縑貴而簡重，並不便於人。倫乃造意用樹膚麻頭及敝魚網爲紙。

關係於造紙的歷史，非常重要。假若東觀漢記果有此文，那就類書中關涉及於造紙的應當首先徵引到。然而卻不如此，只引些『黃門蔡倫典作尚方作紙，所謂蔡侯紙也』一段。語氣輕重顯有不同，可見並非東觀記的原文。再對照王隱晉書，便知『其用縑帛者謂之紙』，是出於王書的『古之素帛，隨事裁絹，枚數重沓，即名幡紙』一段，而對照董巴輿服志，便知『倫乃造意用樹膚麻頭及敝魚網爲紙，是出於董記的『東京有蔡侯紙，即倫也。用故麻名麻紙，木皮名穀紙，用故魚網作紙，名網紙也』一段。范蔚宗的後漢書誠然比東觀漢記多加了史料，但可惜的是王隱晉書已經有了誤會，范蔚宗作史時再加上史筆和潤色，因此這一篇的可信程度就不免打一個折扣了。

綜上所述，關於紙的發明一件公案，可以作下列的假定：

甲、早期的紙是用絲絮黏成的，也就是所謂赫蹏，在西漢的晚年已經有了。

乙、在明帝時經傳已經用紙來寫，這當然不是薄小紙的赫蹏，而是赫蹏以外的紙，很可能已經用絲以外的材料造紙了。

丙、到和帝的晚年，蔡倫爲尚方令，始採用魚網造紙之法。因此造紙之法更加進步。

這樣對於一切的史料才不致互相衝突的。

此外還有一個很重要的證據，便是後漢紀和帝紀：

永元十四年，冬，十月辛卯，立皇后鄧氏。……初陰后時諸家四時貢獻以奢侈相高，器物皆飾以金銀。后不好玩弄，珠玉之物不過於目。諸家歲供紙墨，通殷勤而已。

此段在通鑑中曾經援引，只稍爲改動了一些：

永元十四年冬，十月，辛卯，立貴入鄧氏爲皇后，后辭讓不得已，然後卽位。郡國貢獻悉令蔡絕（原注：漢郡國貢獻，進御之外，別上皇后宮。）歲時但供紙筆而已。

胡三省注引毛晃的話說：

楮籍不知所始。後漢蔡倫以魚網木皮爲紙。俗以爲紙始於蔡倫，非也。案前書外戚傳已有赫蹏矣。

這和史繩祖的學齋拈畢說：

> 蔡倫乃後漢時人，而前漢書外戚傳云：趙偃伃，赫蹏書，注謂『小紙也』（原書應劭注），則紙已見於前漢，恐非始於蔡倫，但倫所造精工於前世，則有之耳。

也和這意思差不多。

今按鄧后立時的永元十四年（一〇二年），正是蔡倫奏上所造紙永興元年（一〇五年）的前三年，這時鄧后罷免一切的供奉（見後漢書十鄧皇后紀），只留了紙墨也可見鄧后對於紙墨是有特別愛好的。（范蔚宗鄧后紀記載鄧后事較詳，只是對於紙墨卻一字不提，那是范氏以前的後漢書爲袁宏所據的曾經說到紙墨，到范氏因爲和蔡倫造紙一說衝突，將這兩字刪去了，這正是所謂史裁。由此看來修的好的史書有時反而不能保存史料的原狀，這也就是新唐、新五代、新元、遠不如舊書的大原因。以此而推也可見後漢書有時頗不足恃了。）因此蔡倫造紙的成功，很可能的鄧后的好尚有若干關係。

中華民國三十一年的秋天，我和石璋如先生在額濟納河沿岸清理 Folke Bergman 所發掘過的遺址，在 Bayan Bogdo 山南，名叫 Tsakhortei 的烽燧下，掘出了一張漢代的紙，這張紙已經揉成紙團，在掘過的坑位下，藏在未掘過的土裏面。到了李莊之後曾經請同濟大學生物學系主任吳印禪先生審定，認爲係植物的纖維所作。

根據中瑞考察團報告第四冊 (The Sino-Swiden Expedition, Book IV.) 第一百四十面，F. Bergman 先生說 Tsakhortei 就是他發現過七十八根漢簡卷子的地方。這七十八根簡其中大部分是永元五年至永元七年的兵器簿，還有別一根是永元十年正月的郵驛記錄。其文爲：

> 入南書二封　居延都尉九年十二月二十七二十八日封詣府封完　永元十年正月五日蚤食時時狐受孫昌

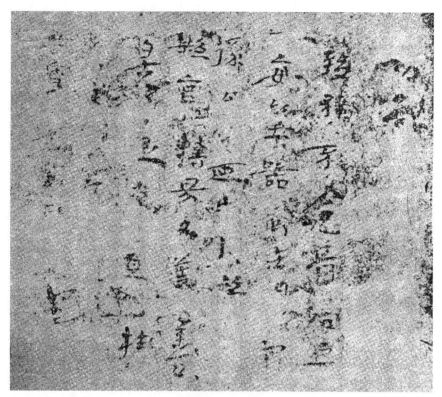

在居延發見的漢紙

這一張紙是在坑位下面的，即其埋到地下比永元十年的簡要早些。不過永元十年的木簡不一定就是永元十年埋到地下，當然還有再後的可能。這一張紙既然和永元的木簡在一個地方，那就他的時代也是永元十年的前後。

永元一共十六年，蔡倫的紙是元興元年造成的，假若這張紙也是永元十年的，那就在蔡倫造紙七年以前。然而七年以前的紙到七年以後才埋到地下，雖然烽燧中事簡，按情理不應當有，卻也不是不可能。假若真像過去傳說一樣，元興元年以前並無紙的痕跡，到這一年蔡倫才創造出來。那麼在京師的朋友，用了新發明的事物，寫信給邊塞屯戍的朋友，送給他見一見『市面』，那就也沒有什麼不可以。所以這張紙當然有在蔡倫造紙以前的可能性，但是也不是沒有在蔡倫造紙以後的可能性。只是大致就時代說，可以說是和蔡倫同時的。所以這張紙發現的意義，在他的本身，並不足為蔡倫造紙以前便已經有紙的充分證明，可是除這張紙以外尚有其他證據，那就對於這種證據可以加強些，而在紙質方面因為這張紙是粗、厚，而簾紋不甚顯著的，也許對於早期的紙更進一層了解。從前斯坦因在敦煌烽燧曾發現過用中國字的紙，但是字很少，而 Bergman 報告中所稱的漢紙，按着照片分明有『亦集乃路』字樣，那就時代很晚了。

綜合上面所有的材料來說，在西漢晚年已有原始的絮紙「赫蹏」，到東漢以後，便有可以寫書的大型『紙』了。假若再有新的材料出現，也只能再推到西漢晚年或者有大型的紙，而不能否認蔡倫之前是有紙的。這是一個很普通的例子，凡一個大發明的前身一定有若干未成熟的發明來做他的基礎。因此在蔡倫發明紙的一〇五年以前，當然可以有紙的製造。唐張懷瓘書斷云：

> 左伯，字子邑；東萊人，甚能造紙。漢興，用紙代簡， 至和帝時蔡倫工悟之。而子邑尤行其妙。

這是說前有蔡倫，後有左伯，都是推進造紙方法的人。他的話可以說還是有分寸的。也可見在唐代已經有蔡倫以前尚有紙存在的認識了。

附記：此篇曾由韓鴻庵先生夏作銘先生石璋如先生周子範先生閱過。又夏作銘先生和周子範先生並以 Journal Asiatique 1915 見示，其中 E. Chavannes 的 Les Livres Chinois avant L'invention du Papier 一篇曾提到絲絮和紙的關係。並此向諸先生致謝。

此外，在中國大陸發現的『灞橋漢紙』據說是西漢時代的，似乎較居延漢紙的時代為早。不過上面沒有字，只是具有紙的形狀，並且也是植物纖維組成的。因此，這種紙是否當時作為書寫的用途，甚有問題。非常可能的，這種紙還是作為縕袍的著，而不是用作書寫上的用途的。

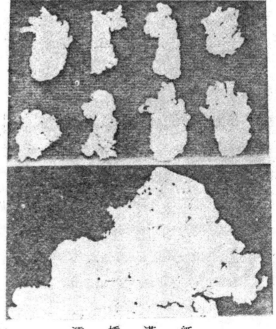

灞 橋 漢 紙

又附：

周法高先生『論中國造紙術之原始』後記

Horn 以為波斯文中的漢語借字，也許有 "kāgad 或 kāgid（"紙"）。Hirth 曾說從波斯文得來的阿剌伯字 "kāghid"（"紙"）可以回溯到漢文的" 穀紙"。（古讀 ǝk-dz）。此說為 Karabacek 和 Hoernle 所採。Laufer 反對此說。他認為這個 波斯－阿剌伯字（Persian-Arabic word）是借自一種突厥語（Turkish language:）: Uigur "kagat" 或 "kagas"; Tuba, Lebed, Kumandu, Comanian, "kagat"; Kirgiz, Karakirgiz, Taranči 和 Kazan, "kagaz"。這個字的來源可以從突厥語 得到解釋；因為在 Lebed, Kumandu 和 Šor, 我們有 "kagas", 解作 "樹皮"。 此外，在印度（Indian）語中：Hindi "kāgad", Urdu "kāgaz", Tamil "kāgidam", Malayalam "kāyitam", Kannada "kāgada", Kāçmīrī "kākaz"; 在印度支那（Indo-Chinese）語中：Siamese, "kadat," Kanaurī, "kaglī"。（註一）唐禮言梵語雜名： 紙，迦迦里 kakari", 一本 ri 作 li, 義淨梵語千字文："kākali 迦引 迦哩，紙"。 （註二）

以上諸語，恐與漢文 "赩㲲" 諸詞有關。廣雅釋器："㡓㲳謂之幝", 王念孫疏

廣韻引埤倉云："㡓㲳，赤紙也"。漢書外戚傳，"赩㲲書"。應劭注云：" 赩 㲲，薄小紙也"。顏師古注云："今書本赫字或作㡣"。說文 "緐" "縴" 二字

（註一）以上見 Laufer, Sino-Iranica P. 557—559, P. 610.

（註二）見大正藏第五十四卷 P. 1233, P. 1201, 參看 Bagchi, Deux lexiques sanskrit-chinois P. 287, 伯希和 (p.p.) 加按語云：『古畏吾兒語（l'ouigour ancien）好像是 kāgda. 蒙古語（le mongol）"qayudasun", "紙頁"（feuille de papier）應該也很 好地加入這一組。』

注，並云"縈繞也"。赫毓、聲毓、縈繞，並與檕𥷚同。

案廣韻陌韻，"檕，赫"並"呼格切"；錫韻，"聲，古歷切"；霽韻"縈，古詣切，又口奚胡計二切"。齊韻，"幭，杜奚切，又呼雞切"；"毓，杜奚切"；"繞，郎奚切"。此語上字都是舌根音的聲母 k 或 x，檕，赫又都為收 k 之入聲字，"幭繞"則為 d- 或 l-聲母。周秦音："縈，毓，繞"收-ieg，"聲"收-iek，皆在支部；"赫"收-ǎk，在魚部。"幭，毓"有複聲母 dl- 的可能。（註三）kiek（或 xak）-diei（或 liei）與上述諸語音也相近。諸語後一音或為 d, t, 或為 l, 也恰與漢文的情形相同。拿 ka 對 -k 尾，也很常見，如梵文 "kāsyapa"譯作"迦葉"以 -p 對 pa，"tusita"譯作"兜術"以 -t 對 ta；"kauśika" 譯作"拘翼"，以 -k 對 ka；"brahmā"，譯作"梵"以 -m 對 mā，皆其例也。

至於此語來源如何，我還不敢斷定，說文解作"惡絮"，漢書注解作"紙"、Laufer 引突厥語，解作"樹皮"，其原始意義也不敢確定。不過此語已見於漢代的記載，而紙又是中國所發明，漢語中用雙聲或疊韻連語為事物之名的也是數見不鮮。（註四）再說"紙"：廣韻"諸氏切"隋唐音：tçiě，聲母 tç- 可能從上古 ȶ 或 t 變來。牠和"毓幭"等都屬上古音的支部。漢語中連語和單詞的轉變，也相當常見。若是沒有別的證據，我們似乎還無法假定漢語是借自以上諸語。在目前，假定諸語是自漢語假去，似乎可能性較大。

貞一先生囑為短跋，忽忽不及詳考，不知別人已有此說否，尚祈指正！

（註三）參看同蘇上古音韻表稿。

（註二）集韻齊韻『檕幭』條下即有『楚人訓絮曰檕幭』一條。

中國丹砂之應用及其推演

　　化學的發展，本來有兩個來源。在理論方面啓發於希臘的哲學家，在實驗方面出於中世紀點金的術士（Alchemist）。鍊賤金屬爲貴金屬雖然埃及時已有此思想，巴比倫、腓尼基、印度，也有許多應用的實驗，Chemistry 一字語根也是埃及的意思。但發揚光大傳到歐洲乃出於阿拉伯人，其時當中國的宋代（十一世紀）到明代的中葉（十五六世紀），遠在中國鍊金術士以後。中國和其餘民族一樣，在舊石器時代，已經重視丹砂，但希望從丹砂鍊出黃金，據紀載漢時不惟有此思想，而且有詳細的方法，阿拉伯的術士與中國的關係，一時雖不能爲詳確的證明，但中國的製鍊丹砂，確經過長時期的單獨發展，乃不容否定的事。現在就與丹砂有關的史料敍其推演的經過如下。

一　尙赤與丹砂的關係

　　中國後代的尙黃是沿襲隋代的事，以前大都尙赤的，秦人據說曾經爲五行的關係而尙黑，但詳細制度難考。禮記檀弓稱『夏后氏尙黑，殷人尙白，周人尙赤』，乃據漢人的三統說而言，未足爲信。從各方面看來，只有周人尙赤是正確的。夏代不能考見，殷人則不惟不尙白，反有尙赤的可能。我聽見梁思永先生說在安陽殷虛，一切儀仗采繪都以紅色爲主，可見檀弓的話不盡合。周人尙赤的事，因爲時代較近，所以三統說不能違反不遠以前的事實。現在將周人尙赤的事，舉例如下：

(1)衣服

　　方叔率止，約軝錯衡，服其命服，朱芾斯皇。（詩小雅采芑·）

　　四牡奕奕，赤芾金舃。（詩小雅車攻。正義「天官履人注舃有三等，赤舃爲上……此云金舃，則禮之赤舃也。）

朱芾斯皇，室家君王。 (詩小雅斯干。箋：「芾者，天子純朱，諸侯黃朱。」)

錫汝玄衣黻純，赤芾朱黃。 (頌鼎。又趙鼎，師毛父段，毛公鼎，師艅段，揚段，番生段，休盤，均有錫朱芾之事。)

士玄衣纁裳，天子之冕朱綠藻。 (禮記禮器。)

繡黼丹朱中衣，大夫之僭禮也。 (禮記郊特牲。)

玄冠朱組纓，天子之冠也；緇布冠繢緌，諸侯之冠也；玄冠丹組纓，諸侯之齊冠也；玄冠綦組纓，士之齊冠也。 (禮記玉藻。)

韠，君朱，大夫素，士爵韋。 (禮記玉藻。)

天子袾裷衣冕，諸侯玄裷衣冕，大夫裨冕，士皮弁服。 (荀子富國。高注，『袾古朱字，裷與衮同，畫龍於衣謂之衮，朱衮以朱爲質也，衣冕猶服冕也。』)

(2)宮室及其他：

若作梓材，既勤樸斲，惟其塗丹雘。 (書，梓材)。

莊公二十三年 ，丹桓公楹 。 二十四年刻桓公桷。 (見春秋經，杜注，將送夫人故爲盛飾。)

丹漆雕幾之美。 (禮記，郊特牲。)

紅壁沙版，玄玉梁些。 (楚詞招魂。王逸注，紅赤白色，沙丹沙也。)

諸侯垣有黝堊之色，無丹青之采。 (御覽一八七引新序。)

彤弓一，彤矢百。 (書文侯之命。)

彤弓天子賜有功也。 (毛詩彤弓序。箋『諸侯設王所慨而獻其功，王饗禮之。於是賜彤弓一，彤矢百，· 弓一，玈矢千。凡諸侯賜弓矢，然後得專征伐。』)

彤弓虎賁，文公受之，以有南陽之田。 (左昭十五年)。

公車千乘，朱英綠縢。 (詩閟宮。)

古者后夫人必有女史彤管之法，史不記過，其罪殺之。……彤管筆赤管也。 (詩靜女箋。)

從其有皮，丹漆若河？ (左宣二年。)

牲用騂尚赤也。 (禮記郊特牲。)

從上看來，衣服的赤色，是用來表示尊貴的；宮室及其他用具的赤色，是用來示盛美的。在染料之中，除去衣服的顏色，現在無從知道外；其餘主要染料或塗料還是丹沙。因此便以丹來代表紅色，如詩經『顏如渥丹，其君也哉』？卽其一例。重視紅色的原因，現在尚不能尋出較早的史料。據漢人的說法，大抵由於拜火或拜日，太平經：（道藏太平部）

> 丙午丁巳火也，赤也。丙午者純陽也，丁巳者純陰也。陰陽主和，陽氣復和合，天下與也。爲者爲利。（二，二十三。）

> 五書中善者使靑爲下而丹字，何乎？吾道乃丹靑之信也。靑者生，仁而有心；赤者天下之正氣。吾道太陽仁政之道不欲傷害也。（四，十一。）

> 以赤心，心生於火，還以付火，爲治象。是則延年益算，萬不失一，吾不欺子也。（七，六。）

> 吾書中善者悉使靑首而丹目，何乎？吾道乃丹者之信也。靑者生，仁而有正；赤者太陽，天之正色也。（七，二十七。）

> 東方者好生，南方者好養，夫不仁用心不可與長共事，不明不可以爲君長，故東方者，木仁有心，南方者火明也。（六十九，二。）

> 夫太陽上赤氣乃火之王精也，火之王者乃光，上爲日月者乃照察姦惡人。（一一九，八）。

用這些材料來解釋後世道敎尙赤的原因，較爲確切，來解釋上古尙赤的原因，當然尙有問題。但道士的重視丹砂沿襲自上古；其重視赤色，自亦有襲自上古的可能。在尙未有確切解釋以前，固可存此以備一說也。

因爲丹砂是貴重的塗料，所以周人非常重視，庚嬴卣云：

> 隹王十月旣望，辰在己丑，王格於庚嬴宮，王蔑庚嬴歷。錫貝十朋，又丹一枡。庚嬴對揚王休，用作㣇文姑寶尊彝，其萬年子子孫孫永寶用。

周代以貝爲錢幣，丹與並稱，可見丹的貴重。禹貢荆州的貢品有礪砥砮丹，荀子中紀載丹砂，也認寶貴物品或裝飾，王制篇云：

> 南海則有羽翮齒革曾靑丹干焉，然而中國得而財之；東海則有紫結魚鹽焉，然而中國得而衣食之。

又正論篇云：

孔子曰，天下有道盜其先變乎？雖珠玉滿體文繡充棺，黃金充椁，加之以丹
矸，重之以曾青，……人猶相莫之扣也。（高注丹矸丹沙也。曾青銅之精，形如珠，其色
極青，故謂之曾青。加以丹矸，重以曾青，言以丹青采畫也。）

都可證明丹砂的貴重。

再從地下的新發現看來，也是自然的。董作賓先生甲骨文斷代研究例云：

將已刻文字的甲與骨，加以朱或墨的裝潢塗飾，這是武丁時代的一種特色。
……像書契精華式的大字，無論甲、骨，許多都塗過硃砂（塗墨的較少，字也細小一
些。）我記得最清楚的一段有經驗工人的談話：『村子裏也出大的骨版，但是
太稀疏，字也小，永沒見過十四畝地（在第一區）出的那樣骨版，滿刻着紅鮮的
硃砂大字』。（蔡元培先生六十五歲論文集。）

此外在墓葬中用丹砂，還可以從安特生甘肅考古記，李濟先生俯身葬（本所安陽發掘
報告三期），馬衡先生新鄭古物調查記（東方雜誌二十二卷一期），知道應用的普遍。漢書佞
倖傳，孔光奏徙董賢家屬云：

乃復以沙畫棺，四時之色，左蒼龍，右白虎，上著金銀，日、月、玉衣、珠
璧，以棺至尊無以加。

又壽縣所獲的楚王棺板，上亦有金及朱的文飾，可證自上古，戰國，至漢都以丹砂為
貴重塗飾。所以史記貨殖傳稱，『巴寡婦清，其先得丹穴，而擅其利數世，家亦不
訾』，自非重視丹砂之時不致如此。又楊雄蜀都賦：『其中則有玉石嶜岑，丹青玲
瓏』。易林乾之咸『三人求橘，反得丹穴，女貴以富，黃金百鎰』，大抵皆是指此。

二　丹　書

不惟商代重要文籍塗朱，周代也是一樣，一貫的承受，一直到漢猶然。大戴記武
王踐阼云：

武王踐阼三日，召士大夫而問焉。曰『惡有藏之約，行之行萬世，可以為子子
孫孫常者乎？』……師尚父曰：『在丹書，王欲聞之，則齋矣』。（孔廣森補注云
『丹書古策府之遺典』。）

左傳襄二十三年云：

> 斐豹隸也，著於丹書。欒氏之力臣曰督戎，國人懼之。斐豹謂范宣子曰：『苟
> 焚丹書，我殺督戎。』宣子喜曰：『而殺之，所不請於君焚丹書者，有如日』。

晏子春秋內篇雜上：

> 景公游於紀，得金壺，乃發視之。中有丹書曰：『食魚無反，勿乘駑馬』。

漢書高紀：

> 又與功臣剖符作誓，丹書鐵契，金匱石室，藏之宗廟。

漢書高忠功臣表序：

> 封爵之誓曰：『使黃河如帶，泰山若厲，國以永存，爰及苗裔』。於是申之以
> 丹書之信，重之以白馬之盟。

據以上諸則，凡傳世的典則，在奴隸的契約，傳後的箴銘，功臣的符契，都要用丹書
以示鄭重，至漢猶然。但鄭重的極致，歸於神祕，所以神祕的事也要用丹書來表示。

漢書王莽傳：

> 平帝崩……前煇光謝囂奏，武功長孟通浚井得白石。上圓下方，有丹書著石，
> 文曰：『告安漢公莽爲皇帝』。符命之起，自此始矣。

此外在緯書中，可以尋出許多關於丹書的話。大抵在緯書中認爲凡應世帝王都有符
命，而所有符命均係丹書。其丹書或自鳳皇之類銜來，如詩文王序正義引春秋元命苞
云：

> 鳳皇銜丹書，遊於文王之都。西伯既得丹書，於是稱王，改正朔，誅崇侯虎。

又引尚書中侯云：

> 季秋之月，甲子，赤雀銜丹書，入豐，止於昌戶，再拜稽首受。

又引易是類謀：

> 文王比隆興始霸，伐崇，作靈臺，受赤雀丹書，稱王制命。

或以龍負出，御覽七九引尚書中侯握河紀：

> 黃帝幽洛，河出龍圖，洛出龜書。白威赤文像字，以授軒轅。

御覽八〇引尚書中侯握河紀：

> 帝堯……龍馬銜甲，赤文綠地，自河而出。

御覽八一引尙書中侯考河命：

> 舜沈璧，黃龍負卷舒圖，出水壇畔，赤文綠錯。

或有魚出，魚有赤文丹書御覽九三六引河圖挺佐輔：

> 黃帝遊於洛，見鯉魚長三丈，青身無鱗，赤文成字。

詩商頌譜正義引尙書中侯：

> 天乙在毫東觀於洛，黃魚雙躍 ，出濟於壇，黑鳥以雛隨魚亦上 ，化爲黑玉赤
> 勒。

御覽八四引尙書中侯：

> 武王……渡於孟津，中流受文， 命待天謀。 白魚躍入王舟， 王俯取魚。 長三
> 尺，赤文有字。

或有龜出，龜負赤文丹書。開元占經一八〇引尙書中侯握河紀：

> 堯勵德匪懈，萬民和欣，則色龜背袤廣九寸，五色，領下有文，赤文似字。

御覽九三一引尙書中侯：

> 堯沈璧於洛，玄龜負書，出於背上，赤文朱字，止壇場，沈璧於河，黑龜出赤
> 文題。

又云：

> 周公攝政七年，制禮作樂，成王觀於洛， 沈璧， 禮畢， 王退。 有玄龜青純蒼
> 光，背甲刻書，上臍於壇，赤文成字，周公寫之。

酈元注水經洛水隱括其事曰：

> 黃帝東巡河過洛，俯壇沈璧，受龍圖于河，龜書於洛，赤文綠字，堯帝又俯壇
> 河洛，擇良卽沈，崇光出河，綠氣四塞，白雲起，迴風逝，赤文綠色，廣袤九
> 尺，負理平上有列星之分， 七政之度， 帝王錄記， 興亡之數， 以授之堯。 又
> 東；書于旦稷，赤光起，玄龜負書，背甲赤文成字，遂禪于舜。舜又習堯禮，
> 沈書于日稷，赤光起，玄龜負書，至于稷下，榮光休至 ， 黃龍卷甲， 舒圖壇
> 畔，赤文綠錯以禪舜。舜以禪禹。殷湯東觀于洛，習禮堯壇，降璧三沈，榮光
> 不起。黃魚雙躍，出濟于壇，黑鳥以浴，隨魚亦上，化爲黑玉赤勒之書，黑龜
> 赤文之題也。湯以伐桀。

以上除文王的赤雀銜書以外，其出赤文的地方非河卽洛，當然指河圖洛書而言。易繫辭：『河出圖，洛出書，聖人則之』，正義引鄭康成說，卽指龍圖龜書而言。惟尙書僞孔序以河圖爲八卦，洛書爲九疇，自是後起之義，不足以代表漢人的說法。在經籍除易以外，較早的史料中只有論語『鳳鳥不至，河不出圖，吾已矣夫。』有點神祕的意義。然而在這唯一有神祕性質的一條上，還要附着丹書赤文的話上去，可見古代人對於硃沙字是有神祕的感覺的。至於有朱字的卜辭或册書，周漢兩代是否在河洛有所發見，而引起許多神祕的話，則現在無從考究了。

丹書旣有神祕的意義，道教的術士所用的符籙自然要用丹書了。符本指符節的符，如周禮門關用符節，孟子離婁『若合符節』，荀子儒效『曣然若合符節』，史記信陵君傳『晉鄙兵符在王臥內』，都指符節之符。其他若符瑞，符兆等抽象的意義，也只由此引申而出。符籙之符最初當亦由符節之符變來，如類聚帝王部引尙書璇機鈐：

> 湯受金符帝籙，白狼銜鉤入殷朝。（注金符禹籙，縛束之要，明湯得天下之要也。）

此所謂符籙卽符命之意。及後漢書方術費長房傳云：

> 老翁又作一符曰：『以此主地上鬼神』……遂能醫療衆病，鞭笞百鬼，及驅使社公，……後失其符爲衆鬼所殺。

則符雖爲劾鬼之用，但由神仙手授，而不是凡人可以自作，仍與後來的符相差一間。只方術解奴辜傳：

> 河南有麴聖卿，善爲丹書符劾，壓殺鬼神而使命之。

則與後來的符無異了。自然劾鬼之法不始於東漢，漢志有執不祥劾鬼八卷，惠棟在後漢書方術補注中引淮南子高誘注也如此說。但無論如何不能磨滅符籙和符命的相關之義。而解奴辜傳所稱丹書劾鬼，與緯書所稱帝王受命的丹書多少總有些關係，是不容置疑的事。至以丹書爲符自漢已然，藝術叢編所刊載的鳳翔陶瓶，周漢遺寶所刊載的陶瓶，和中央博物院所藏的藍田陶瓶（以上幾件是張政烺和高去尋兩先生告我的），皆用爲鎮墓，而字則丹書。又抱朴子登涉第十七所刊各符，後均說明要丹書桃板或丹書帛上。

三　丹沙之製鍊和服食

丹書的神祕性是一方面，其另一方面，丹沙的本身性質也從寶貴轉爲神祕。神仙

中 國 古 代 金 丹 家 煉 丹 圖

轉 載 科 學 雜 誌 十 七 卷 第 一 期
曹 元 宇：中 國 古 代 金 丹 家 的 設 備 和 方 法

的傳說，戰國時已有，史記封禪書：

> 自威、宣、燕昭，使人入海求蓬萊、方丈、瀛洲，此三神山者，其傳在勃海
> 中，去人不遠，患且至則船風引而去。蓋嘗有至者，諸仙人及不死之藥皆在
> 焉。其物禽獸盡白，而黃金銀爲宮闕。未至望之如雲，及到三神山反居水下。
> 臨之風輒引去，終莫能至云。世主莫不甘心焉。

此所謂不死之藥，尚須『求』而不是『鍊』。張良傳所稱避穀與赤松子遊，亦未言
『鍊丹』及『服餌』，似與鍊丹尚無關係。但海上求而不得，當然向內陸求之，所以
在漢武淮南的時代，『鍊』的方法便開始了。鍊的方法爲鍊丹砂成黃金，藉丹沙所成

的黃金以求仙藥，並非如後世的人直接將丹沙吞到腹內去。史記封禪書：

> 少君言上曰：『祠竈則致物，而丹沙可化爲黃金；黃金成以爲飲食器，則益壽；益壽而海中蓬萊仙者皆可見；見之封禪則不死，黃帝是也。

漢書劉向傳：

> 宣帝修武帝故事……復興神仙方術之事，而淮南有枕中鴻寶祕書；書言神仙使鬼物爲金之術及鄒衍重道延命方。世人莫見，而更生父德武帝時治淮南獄得其書。更生幼而讀誦，以爲奇，獻之。言黃金可成，上乃令典尙方鑄作事。費甚多，方不驗，上乃下更生吏。

據劉奉世和王先謙所考，因爲劉德和劉安時代不相及，淮南詔獄乃係劉澤詔獄，因涉及淮南鴻寶祕書而誤。書之屬淮南，固不得因獄之非淮南而有疑義。因郊祀志因云劉更生獻淮南枕中鴻寶祕之方，不言爲劉澤也。今案御覽九八八引淮南萬畢術中有『朱沙爲澒』之語（澒卽汞，氾勝之書亦有此語，與淮南同時），可證淮南確有丹砂的經驗。

　西漢求仙之術今所知者，僅此而止。列仙傳所稱神仙雖然有服食丹沙之事。但此書決非劉向所作，從宋代陳直齋已經懷疑。其書雖仿列女傳，但語法全和列女傳不類，最顯明的是列女傳贊，不用對偶，而列仙傳贊，多用對偶。商丘子胥條其地名則有後漢的高邑，凡此等類，均可證明其後出，宜其不見於漢志。所以此書雖言服食丹沙，卻不能證明西漢已有其事。

　不但如此，方士鍊藥，雖然爲對付君主和貴族，想出鍊丹沙化黃金的方法；但在一般人心目中，神仙仍然是求的。仙人唐公房碑云：

> 居攝二年，君爲郡吏。……旁有眞人，左右莫察，而君進美瓜，又從而敬禮之。……乃與君神藥。……以藥塗屋柱，飲牛馬六畜。須臾有大風玄雲來迎公房，妻子屋宅，六畜，儵然與之俱去。

學仙本來非捐家室不可的，卽漢武帝尙稱『誠得如黃帝棄妻子如脫屣耳』。此則妻子、屋宅、六畜，『儵然』與之俱去。如此得仙，誠天下之大樂，豈特南面王不易而已哉？然而鍊丹沙的人卻從不敢作此想。抱朴子勸人學仙可謂極辭令之美，但決無一語及於飛昇到屋宅。神仙傳稱劉安雞犬昇天，雖大抵從唐公房事演化而成，但已加以修改，不及屋宇。因爲劉安的藥是『煎泥成金，凝鉛爲銀，水鍊八石』；若可飛昇屋字，則古來之畫棟彫梁，皆以丹青爲飾，阿房長樂，早已蔚爲雲表之大觀，縱在劉安本人恐亦不至相信也。由是可知方士術藝，與流俗傳聞，標準不同，方法亦異。此由方士早已從求仙變爲鍊藥，流俗尙因仍從前之傳說。

大抵在東漢的方士已經注重服食 ， （以前當然也服食，如漢武說差可少病，史記扁鵲倉公傳，齊王侍醫自鍊五石服之，之類，但東漢有專重服食者。導氣之說亦見於莊子呂覽淮南，然固不稱爲內丹也。）論衡道虛篇云：

> 道家或以導氣養性，度世而不死。……道家或以藥物，輕身益氣，延年度世，此又靈也。夫服食藥物，輕身益氣，頗有其驗。若夫延年度世，世無其效。百藥愈病，病愈而氣復，氣復而輕矣。

論衡譏服食而不譏泛海求仙，可知東漢中葉之方士，早已舍棄海上求仙之法。所以求不死之方，則爲導氣或服藥。導氣卽包括後世所謂內丹，服藥卽包括後世所謂外丹。但所稱百藥不純指丹沙耳 （超奇篇『入山見木，長短無所不知；入野見草，大小無所不識。然而不能伐木以作室屋，探草以和方藥』。則所謂方藥仍以百草爲主也。）古詩驅車上東門篇『服食求神仙，多爲藥所誤。』亦未明言丹沙也。

有系統的服食丹沙大約是東漢末年之事，太平經

> 一者眞記諟冥諟憶，二者仙忌詳存無隱 ； 三者探飛根吞日精 ， 四者服開明靈符，……十者服華丹，……二十者作白銀紫金。（一，七。）

華丹當然和丹砂有關，至於周易參同契則全書幾卷爲鍊治丹沙之法。朱子語類一二五周易參同契節雖然說：

> 坎離水火龍虎鉛汞之屬，只是互換其名，其實只是精氣二者而已。精水也，坎也，龍也，汞也；氣火也，離也，虎也，鉛也。其法以神運氣結而爲丹，陽氣在下初成水，以火鍊之，則凝成丹。

參同契朱注也以內丹來解釋，但到了『可入口』、『刀圭』等字，便無法解釋了。

服食丹沙之事至三國更盛，世說言語篇：

> 何平叔云，服五石散，非唯治病，亦覺神明開朗。注云：『秦丞相寒食散之方，雖出漢代而用之者寡，靡有傳焉。魏何晏首獲神效，由是大行於世，服者相尋也。』

秦丞相不知何許人，漢三公無姓秦者。魏曹眞或謂姓秦，然魏人向待以宗室，不溯本
姓。惟魏明帝幸臣秦朗見明紀注引魏略，稱明帝卽位授以內官爲驍騎將軍給事中，四
方以附近至尊，多賂遺之，富均公侯。又曹眞傳引魏略曰：『太祖爲司空時納晏母並
收養晏，其時秦宜祿光阿蘇亦隨母在公家，並見寵如公子，蘇卽朗也』是朗與晏處境
全同，其方當有互傳之機會。丞相侍者曰宜祿，秦丞相之稱或涉其父而誤也。五石散
卽丹砂、雄黃、白礬、曾青、慈石，見抱朴子金丹篇；此與參同契丹方爲異黨，但至
抱朴子已兼收之。晉人甚重視此方，清俞正燮癸巳類稿有專篇言及，近人周樹人亦曾
論及，惜多未詳言出處耳。

漢書田千秋傳云：『上每對羣臣，自歎鄉時愚惑，爲方士所欺，天下豈有仙人卷
妖妄耳；節食服藥，差可少病而已。』蓋武帝時僅欲以丹沙鍊金，所服者當爲其他藥
物，尚非丹沙。故未中毒，因差可少病，年至七十餘。自後晉人服丹沙者鮮不中毒。
至魏道武帝服寒食散以死（見魏書本紀），唐憲宗服金丹以死，穆宗餌金石之藥以死，武
宗服方士藥，竟喜怒失常以死，宣宗季年中風毒（並見唐書本紀），尤昭昭在人耳目者
也。至唐太宗服胡僧藥以死，見舊唐郝處俊傳，然謂爲婆羅門舊方，或與中國術士未
可類及。王銍默記所載玄宗事，則野史謬悠之談，固難置信矣。

方士對於鉛和汞並重，在參同契作者時已開始。其關於鉛的如：

故鉛外黑，內懷金華，被褐懷玉，外爲狂夫。金爲水母，母隱子胎；水者金
子，子藏母胞。眞人至妙，若有若無。彷彿大淵，乍沈乍浮，退而分布，各守
境隅。望之類白，造之則朱。鍊爲表術，白裏貞居，方圓徑寸，混而相拘。

可見對於鉛的神祕觀念，還是由於鉛丹的紅色而起，所謂『望之類白，造之則朱』。
本來鉛白加熱卽可得密陀僧：

$$PbCO_3 \longrightarrow PbO + CO_2$$

密陀僧再加熱卽可變爲鉛丹，而且又是可逆反應：

$$6PbO + O_2 \rightleftharpoons 2Pb_3O_4$$

所以在方士看起來，有變動不居之感。這和丹砂加熱可成水銀，水銀與硫黃同加熱，
又復還爲丹砂，是一樣的神祕，故硫黃有黃芽之稱也。
神仙傳云：

天門子者姓王名綱，尤善補養之要，故其經曰……陰人所以著脂粉者，法金之白也。是以眞人道士，莫不留心注意，精其微妙，審其盛衰。

這似乎透了一點消息， 金丹和婦女的塗飾有關。 在匈奴的烟支未普遍使用到中國以前，婦女的塗澤就是朱和粉。殷虛中還發現盛朱的器具。鉛和汞是金丹家的兩翼，而都在婦女面上尋得， 不能不算奇事。 世說容止篇注引魏略稱何平叔云：『晏性自喜，動靜粉白不去手』或者又有他的特別原因，不僅爲修飾而已。

服食之事以唐爲最盛，宋時已爲餘波，如春渚紀聞所關專章，乃鍊金非服食也。其得大名者，則爲論衡所稱導氣養性一類。宋代得名最大者爲陳希夷，然史稱隱居武當山九室，服氣辟穀，歷二十餘年。其對周世宗則曰：『陛下爲四海之主，然以致治爲念，奈何留意黃白之事乎？』對宋太宗則曰：『搏山野之人，於時無用，亦不知神仙黃白之事，吐納養生之理，非有方術可傳；假令白日昇天，亦何益於世？』（宋史隱逸傳）。朱熹注參同契發明內丹之旨，卽其遺教。至元代丘處機亦以清心寡欲爲長生久視之道（元史釋老傳）。 蓋服食之術其費甚大，不接近帝王貴冑則力不能舉，養生導引爲費甚微，仍可從事隱逸。故後代雖有林靈素陶仲文，亦可有陳希夷、丘長春。前此文成五利固不必論，卽傑出如葛洪猶必爲縣令嶺南，寇謙之亦必依附權貴，賢如李鄴侯仍非仙非俗，爲舊史所譏也。近代以還惟聞鮑春霆罷歸以鍊丹致疾，至一般道士則以北平之白雲觀爲大宗，卽承自丘處機，自不復有鍊丹之事。其支流蕃衍傳播爲過去士夫間，如同善社、悟善社、道德社、紅萬字會等，亦皆以靜坐求長生，不從事於金丹寒食散矣。

附註：關於中國方士的進展，美國 Obed S. Johnson 作有中國鍊丹術攷（商務印書館出版，並有譯本）。 其書許多地方都是正確的， 只前兩章牽入老莊，殊爲強勉， 講後期的發展， 未根據道藏，亦爲美中不足。又 A. Waley 在英國 Bulletin of School of oriental Studies 有補正一篇，前幾段是關於引書的提要，後兩段頗有意見。惟對方士那羅邇娑婆寐事謂新唐書言其死於長安，因不能決其歸國與否。實則新書亦採自酉陽雜俎，惟調停舊唐書及酉陽雜俎曰：『後術不驗，聽還，不能去，死，』非更有所據（其言謊詐之事亦採自段氏，爲舊書所無）。新唐書好擅改，如郝處俊傳之『靈草祕石』，改作『奇花怪石』，有傷原意，無當宏旨，卽其例也。自不如據舊書及會昌一品集之方士論爲得。

又據余季豫先生寒食散考，秦丞相當爲秦承祖之誤，至於將參同契釋作內丹者，按思光弟（勞榮瑋）意，當始於隋蘇元朗之青霞子，今並及之。

淮南地形訓牡土之氏，御于赤天，赤天七百歲生赤丹，赤丹七百歲生赤澒，赤澒七百歲生赤金。註赤丹丹砂也。

淮南子說山訓染者，先靑而後黑則可，先黑而後靑則不可，工人下漆而上丹則可，下丹而上漆則不可。

淮南人間解鉛之於丹，異類殊色而可以爲丹者，得其數也。

江文通有丹沙可學賦。

黃土與中國農業的起源跋

因爲地形構造的特殊，中國的民族發展以及文化發展在舊大陸中也是非常特殊的。過去因爲考古的發現不夠，一般學者只能拿兩河流域，埃及，印度的文化體系來比照，因此就忽略了中國史前及有史時期上古一段的獨特現象。近年考古的材料增多，許多的假設被糾正過來。但是其中一個非常重要的問題，農業發展的問題，還缺少成系統的，精詳的研究。何炳棣教授這一部黃土與中國農業的起源可以被稱做劃時代的巨著。

人類文化發展史上的一元或多元的問題，是一個繚繞不清的論戰。不過無論如何決不能就一掃而光的看法來論定。就人類本身來說，人類只有一個屬(spicies)，不論是那一個人種（race）都可以和別種人互相傳代，不可能是多元的。魏敦瑞 （Franz Weidenreich） 蒙古人種直接到北京原人的理論，已經因爲爪哇原人也有門齒箕形刻文一事，全部動搖。但蒙古人種在東亞形成，卻又顯然是在一種特殊寒冷而乾燥的環境之下，經過了長期自然淘汰的結果。誠然他們也受了外來的影響，但其獨立發展的事實終究不能忽略。

中國的雨量差不多全部受季風的控制。尤其在黃河流域，一年的雨量集中在夏季一季。這種過分集中的雨量，如其當時種植夏種秋收的穀類，是有用的，但若利用泛濫的河水退後的土地，那就天時不合。若從另外一點來說，黃河流域的多春兩季誠然都比較乾旱，卻一般講來，多數時間還是有一些雨量，使得耐旱的植物繁茂起來，還未曾變到沙漠的程度。但這也只是一種邊緣性質的植被，在若干年之中就可能有一年全不降雨，或只降極少的雨，使一些區域完全漠化。這就是中國歷代的地方行政中，備荒一事成爲一件極端重要的工作。

舊大陸的農業起源地帶，不論兩河流域，埃及以至於印度河流域，地形都是簡

單的，這種簡單的地形只有甘肅省內的河西地方可以比擬。至於華北地區從湟河流域
向東直到山東半島，地形都很複雜。依照丁文江中國分省新圖的中國氣候區域圖，
華北地方（除東北及西藏新疆以外）可分爲五種不同的區域，卽⑴西寧及湟水流域屬
於西藏高原區，⑵甘肅、河西地方及一部分綏遠河套地方屬於沙漠草原區，⑶甘肅
的蘭州附近，寧夏，綏遠，察哈爾及熱河地方屬於草原區，⑷甘肅及陝西秦嶺以北地
帶以及山西汾水以西，屬於黃土高原區，⑸淮水以北至長城地帶，包括山西，河北，
河南，山東及江蘇北部屬於大平原區。這個區畫的根據是合理的，但還是相當的概
括，例如關中平原和天水及平涼兩個谷地就和一般的黃土高原有別。而在大平原區之
中更有太行山區，伏牛山區，泰山山區及膠萊山區幾個山地，而且洛陽谷地及燕山太
行麓地又和一般的沖積大平原有別。尤其在史前及上古時期黃河三角洲及淮河三角洲
是相連一個大沼澤區域，更增加地理上的複雜性。

　　複雜的地形（如其在可以全部利用條件之下），就會形成複雜的民族和文化，過
去中央研究院陶雲逵先生調查雲南省境民族分布的情形，就發現民族的分布和海拔的
垂直高低有密切的關係。這因爲高山區域，海拔的高低就區分了不同的生活方式，就
和文化的適應發生了不可分的事實。在史前及上古時期，在部族或部落社會組織之
下，當未形成爲城邦及帝國的時期，在複雜地形之中，當然會因不同的生活狀態而分
布著不同的民族成分。

　　現在專就黃土高原的特殊狀況來說，至少可以形成兩種不同的文化，河谷文化及
草原文化。河谷文化從安特生以來經過石璋如先生、夏作銘先生及晚近的調查已經大
致可以看出其分布。至於草原文化，雖然在考古的發現上不多，但就歷史的記載來
看，高土高原實是最好的游牧地帶，如其農耕的帝國稍稍疏於防守，北方邊塞上的游
牧民族就會大量的湧進來。當河谷文化發展時期，顯然的對高原地帶的草原未曾利
用，那就游牧民族的侵入和佔據將成爲不可避免的事。

　　河谷文化產生在黃河支流的幾個河谷的臺地上，這些臺地因爲甘肅省的造山運動
還未停止，而河流的削刻也正在進行，所有臺地都高出河面甚多，並且還有越是早期
文化的臺地，高出河面越多的現象。但是當這種文化正在進行時，他們利用的地形已
經是臺地，還是顯然的。臺地的功用是一方面取水容易，另一方面對於外敵和野獸也

易於防守。尤其是在一般乾燥地區，谷地比高原上植物容易生長，而在黃土地層中，更有一種特殊之點，卽黃土爲垂直節理，在雨季時水容易滲到地層中成爲地下水，這在較低的河谷之中，植物的根有時還可以和地下水接觸而幫助其生長。

但是河谷文化中的各部落是分散的，難以形成城邦以至於帝國，只有在外力控制各種刺激之下，才容易辦到。和甘肅的黃河支流類似的情形，尙有西康，青海，及西藏各部族。其中的羌族到漢代尙未統一，也未嘗建國，到受到漢族的刺激，才漸次叛變，直到姚氏時才建立國家。其後在青海的吐谷渾還是鮮卑族的建國，直到吐谷渾瓦解以後，吐谷渾控制下的吐蕃民族才從吐谷渾原有的政治建設下建立起來。至於上古時代建立邦國更屬不易，國家的創建，第一靠組織，第二靠交通。這就需要游牧民族戰爭及狩獵的組織更需要從西方輸入戰車的利用上，因此在這個黃土高原上早期活動的民族，不論「華夏」和「戎狄」，最先應當只有兩種區分，「士」和「農」，士是講射御的，農是講耕稼的。士和農也就是世代的君子和小人。（商的相士或周的后稷，只是商周王族把祖先造成的農神，商頌「相士烈烈，海外有截」所以相士實是一個光輝的戰士，生民篇對於后稷的強調，可能是故意洗刷周代祖先的「戎俗」。）到了殷周兩代長期的演變後，士和農的界線也就淡薄起來，才成爲春秋戰國的社會。至於華北平原部分，因爲情況比黃土高原更爲複雜，更不容易把當時較詳的可能性顯示出來。不過黃土高原的文化，根據考古的成績，顯然較華北平原的更早，所以黃土高原的農業經營方式，應當是一個基本的方式，這種基本方式再逐漸適用於華北平原的山麓地帶，然後再推廣平原及沼澤的邊緣。換言之，中華文化還是從彩陶文化發展融會而成，而在稍晚的時期吸收了沿海的黑陶文化。因此黃土高原農業的起源與發展，正代表中國以及東方的農業上的基本問題。

蒙古地區是一塊老的陸地，但從季風吹到華北大量的黃土，卻是第四紀以後的事。這種黃土由於風成的證明，何炳棣先生已在本篇中引證了一件事實。中國的黃土經過了充分而均勻的攪拌，非風不可。並且過去北京大學地質系也做過顯微鏡的檢查，證明這種黃土是有稜角的，只有風成的才有這種現象。黃土的堆積，炳棣先生已經指明雨土的事實，但除去大量雨土以外，凡是華北的城市，尤其是山西，陝西，甘肅一帶地方，每年多春之際常會有一二次「黃風」，漫天漫野的黃土降下來，這種外來的黃土雖然不至於埋沒人畜成災，但長期而不斷的堆積，也自然增加黃土的厚度，然後再由黃土高原沖積到華北平原。渤海的海岸是下降海岸，可是黃土的堆積足可抵償海岸的下降程度而有餘，這就是渤海還是日漸縮小，而華北的沼澤逐漸形成平地的原因。

一般人好以黃河比擬尼羅河，實則對於中國文化來說，是比擬不倫。因為黃河三角洲，所謂古代「九河」所在的地方，完全是沮洳澤地，再因為中國正處於季風帶，夏秋之間大雨，黃河泛濫的時間，正是農作繁忙之際，所以黃河有百害而無一利。只有河套區域，處於沙漠地帶，正可利用黃河灌漑，這就是黃河惟富一套的說法，但是河套區域的灌漑及農作的利用，是漢武帝以後的事，和中國文化的發源不相關涉。

炳棣先生指出中國農業的起源和黃土的關係是十分正確的。這個新穎的見解足可以明白的解釋先史的重要問題。就農業的起源都在農業的邊緣地帶這一個原則來看，中國和兩河流域，和埃及，和印度河流域是相同的。所不同的，就在中國和舊大陸其他地方的適應性不同，這就決定在黃土的性質上。

黃土的特殊性質，是垂直的節理和稀鬆多空易於滲水，除去一部分山谷地帶以外是不能生長樹木的。這一點我們雖不能在化石上得到證明，但還可以從現存的甘肅東部的黃土高原上得到啓示。甘肅東部的黃土高原，雖然還具有高原的特徵，但和美國大峽谷附近的高原一比，就顯明的現出不同的景色。甘肅的黃土高原，並非是一片平坦的，而是經過了雨水的侵蝕，形成了破碎的「山」和「谷」。如其不從數十里方圓整個局勢來看，會分辨不出這是一個高原地形。這就表示著黃土土質的鬆脆，也就表示華北區域夏秋間的雨水，對於土壤的沖刷還是可驚的。這種狀況之下，大河支流的臺地，當為最安全的地區。除去上述臺地防守較易，種植較易，並易於取水以外，防洪水的泛濫，當然也是一個重要因素。

所以在同一原則之下，同是一樣的游牧環境的邊緣地帶，當着需要發展農業生產的時候，在近東和中東最適宜的地區是大河的冲積平原，而在中國史前及上古，卻是最好的選擇是大河支流沙谷中的臺地。因為地形不同，種植時間不同，也就有選種不同的區別。

就森林和草原的分佈情形來看。華北區域無疑的是以草原為主，只有一些河谷以及河谷中臺地區是些森林地帶。這是從現代的華北(包括黃土高原及華北平原)比較而知的。再以美國加利佛尼亞的南部爲例,這是一個半沙漠地帶,一般屬於草原形態,但山谷及窪地仍然是些森林。河谷中的臺地所以能夠發展文化的,也就是原來屬於森林,再轉變爲耕地。依照漢書地理志的敍述到相當於現在甘肅省地區顯然都是草原地帶。但是說到天水和隴西卻說「山多林木民以板爲室屋……故秦詩曰在其板屋」。這所說的山多林木,無寧說「山谷多林木」,本來黃土高原,不可能有森林,但這一帶正是渭河河谷所在,也正是河谷的森林地帶。這是特殊的例子,正可證明華北地方森林的珍貴。再以近代的調查來比較,依照丁文江申報館地圖,每年平均雨量七百五十公厘的線是從青海東南部積石山向東,再到隴南北伸到天水附近,達到六盤山,然後再南縮到秦嶺,到豫西鄭州附近再南縮到淮河沿岸。此外除去東北區域的東部以外,只有山東半島北部,泰沂區域及燕山區域三處不太大的範圍。這三處現在也還是森林地帶,那麼漢書地理志對於天水隴西的特寫,正表示其餘地方不是森林地帶。古今氣候區域差異並不大。如同孟子「牛山之木嘗美矣」一個例子,是向來常舉的森林破壞的例子,這個地區據趙岐注說「齊之東南山也」正在沂山區域,也就是正在每年平均雨量七百五十公厘範圍之內。這種符合的現象決不是偶然的。誠然,中國森林地帶曾經疏於保護,在有史時代以來有些破壞,也是事實,但決不如一般的想象,曾經有非常廣大的森林地帶。

關於氣候問題,炳棣先生提出了黃土高原的氣候一直是乾燥的意見,並且舉出了許多科學研究的證據,這是非常重要的。今後我們可以認爲是一個標準的定論,一點不必懷疑。過去徐中舒先生對於殷人服象問題,有很好的見解,至今仍然有用,可是他卻提出古代華北氣候是煖而濕的結論,後來 Karl Wittfogel 敎授更加強這種古代煖而濕的看法,董作賓敎授根據甲骨也有辯駁。但是兩方的證據都還不算堅強。當時我是同情董先生的說法的,在十年前曾經問過張鏡湖先生,張先生根據花粉的研究,認爲西洋在四五千年來氣候變化不大,可是當時並無人就中國地質上的花粉來做研究。現在炳棣先生已在這一方面找到了近人研究的結論,在我個人的看法,當然認爲是值得採信的。

在研究西周植被時,炳棣先生根據詩經來作爲基本背景來論斷,這是很正確的方法。其中豳風的地理決定，我從前也同意徐中舒先生的看法，不過近來許多年，我卻認爲豳決不可能是魯。豳是周公的采邑，魯卻是周公長子伯禽的封國。周公旦所以稱做周公，就因爲他的采邑永在周代祖先的故居，始終未領有魯國的原故。整個的西周時代，周公旦的另外公子的後人一直承嗣爲周公，與魯公有別。豳風是專屬於周公本人及其部屬的，當然不是魯。所以把豳認爲陝西的一部分，當然合理，似乎不必再追溯其他的證明。

炳棣先生分析山，原和隰之中，樹木分配的百分比是應當可信的，其中引到丁文江先生的看法也是正確的，當然丁先生的話也需要照炳棣先生意見稍加修正。卽東起海濱，西到新疆，在秦嶺大別山以北的區域，除去了若干山谷以外，多屬於半草原（Semisteppe）地帶。但其中乾燥的程度，越東越漸次減低。雖然一直到海，平地沒有森林，沼澤卻一直不少。其中如山東微山湖區一直還是沼澤，這個沼澤區的延伸遠比今日廣大的多；同樣，河北省南部從寧晉，鉅鹿等縣望東，也是一個大沼澤區。這些沼澤區，我想還是舊日低地以及海底的遺跡，黃土的冲積雖快，仍然一時壍不起來。

詩經以外，禹貢當然是一個重要的根據。不過我的看法和幾位師友顧頡剛先生，辛樹幟先生，屈翼鵬先生都不完全一樣。我的看法，禹貢的九州是周禮九州的修正本（雖然周禮是根據周禮著者同時人的論點，並且說禹貢作者一定看到了周禮。）周禮一書應當是戰國早期人的看法，而禹貢一篇就代表戰國中晚期人的看法。周禮的九州大致是代表國家的疆域，而禹貢就專以地區爲主了。周禮的九州是：(1)揚州（代表越），(2)荊州（代表楚），(3)豫州（代表周和韓，其時華山尚未入秦），(4)青州（代表齊），(5)兗州（代表泗上十二諸侯，尚以魯爲主，因宋尚未強大），(6)雍州（代表秦），(7)幽州（代表燕，此時燕已出現爲大國），(8)冀州（代表魏），(9)幷州（代表趙）。孟子所說的「海內之地方千里者九，齊集有其一」，正和此相符。

至於禹貢一篇，其地理知識當然比較秦漢人爲陋，譬如閩廣地理，就全然不知道。但其中也有若干點非春秋時人所能想像的，例如：

(1) 把華陽黑水惟梁州的四川區域特別劃成一州，必當在秦國據有巴蜀以後，還把巴蜀地理形勢有了詳細調查才知道，顯然還在秦惠王取蜀後若干年。

(2) 說到導河積石，至於龍門西河，顯然是在趙武靈王擴展領土到河套區域以後，並且還在秦伐義渠以後。

(3) 禹貢有徐州當在宋都彭城附近繁榮之後。

顧先生認為是紀元前三世紀做成，應無問題。只是顧先生認為是秦人做的就很不一定，因為此篇把冀州列為第一，而且還把冀州畫的特別大，不像秦人的口氣，反而像信陵平原君門客，甚至呂不韋門客的口氣。其中最大的錯誤當然是「黑水」成為不可追溯的名稱。岷山導江尚不算大錯（如同美國人認為 Mississippi 河在 Minnesota 的 Grand Rapid 附近發源一樣，倒也沒有甚麼嚴重），其中江漢不分，和「三江」同入震澤，再行入海，卻成為不容諱言的大錯。足證禹貢作者並非楚人，或者楚國地理對於長江下游根本未曾做好的原故。不過無論如何，決不是作者憑調查或憑傳說所得，其根據圖籍或圖經，是不容懷疑的。炳棣先生比較之下，認為和詩經中反映的大體相符，這是很有意思的，正可證明禹貢所記物產的正確性。

再從周禮職方氏來看，也大致看出差不多的結果：

揚州　其穀宜稻。

荊州　其穀宜稻。

豫州　其穀宜五種（注，黍稷菽麥稻）

青州　其穀宜稻麥。

兗州　其穀宜四種（注，四種黍稷稻麥，但疑仍以作黍稷菽麥為是，因為小青河區域確甚宜稻而滋陽曲阜卻又不是可以種稻的地方。）

雍州　穀宜黍稷。

幽州（河北北部）　穀宜三種（注，三種黍稷稻，似乎應當改作黍稷麥。因為河北境內的雨量比黃土高原要充足些。但北方只有宜麥不宜稻的地方，卻不大可能有宜稻而不宜麥的地方。）

冀州（山西）　其穀宜黍稷。

并州（河北南部）　其穀宜五種。

在以上各州地方，可以分為三個大區域，(1)揚州及荊州為一個區域。(2)豫，青，兗，幽，并為一個區域。(3)雍州和冀州為一個區域。正和現今的長江流域，華北平原及黃土高原三個不同的區域相符。炳棣先生認爲黃土高原種麥是勉強的，證以周禮職方氏更可見西元前四世紀時期的學者，確實有此認識。

詩經中的植物名稱確都是偶然提到的，但就詩經時代的生活來說，恐怕在詩經中所說以外，也決不會太多，照論語中孔子說學詩可以「多識鳥獸草木之名」，所以詩經中包括的植物名稱在古時一般知識之中，應當佔着一個相當大的比例。當然有些極普通的植物也會忽略掉，例如銀杏 (*Ginkgo biloba, L.*) 是中國特有的植物，詩經以及爾雅都未曾提到過。至於其他松柏科植物，那就不僅古人不曾詳細分辨，就是現在的人，除去對於植物分類學做過工作的，也時常說錯。譬如在祁連山區的檜就被人叫做柏樹，而雲杉也就被人叫做松樹。

雙子葉離瓣植物的藜科的藜和錦葵科的多葵，在古代確實是常吃的菜蔬，甚至有時當飯來吃。據法顯的遊記，他從爪哇回到廣州，遇風漂流，到了靑州的長廣縣境，看到栽種的藜藿就知道是中國地方。可見栽種藜藿，直到東晉還是這樣。至於多葵一項更是古人常食，如古詩「靑靑園中葵，朝露待日稀」。又如「采葵莫傷根，傷根葵不生」。到了唐代如王維詩「松下淸齋折露葵」，露葵雖然或來指蓴菜，但王維隱居在終南山下，不在江南，卻不是產蓴菜的地方。所以露葵還應當指多葵 (*Malva Verticillata, L.*) 而言。

多葵一稱多莧菜，雖然李時珍說今不復種。但吳其濬在湖南時就大量種多葵食用。到了現在，除去湖南還經常把多葵當蔬菜，甚至湖南人到過的地方，如同昆明，西安以及臺北，在菜場上都會有多葵出現。多葵的衰落，可能是被菠菜所代替，不過古代的風氣還會在大湖區域保存着。

穀物中最難解決的困難點還是高粱的問題。過去中外學者一直認爲高粱爲外來植物，在漢以前沒有，所以不必計入在五穀或六穀之中。所以我在居延漢簡考證（四十九年臺北排印本六十頁）引用 Dr. Michael J. Hagerty 的看法認爲高粱是外來穀物，稷和稉爲同類。但現在已發現了問題，炳棣先生就引證了晚近的發現，證明高粱爲中國舊有，而不屬於外來植物。那麼高粱爲外來的看法根本不能成立，而高粱的認識就得重新鑒定。

清儒之中自程瑤田以後，王念孫和段玉裁都認爲稷是高粱。但吳其濬植物名實圖考中的「蜀黍卽稷辯」卻提出異議。依照程氏的解釋是以高粱爲稷亦卽秫，而穄卻和粟爲同類。換句話說，程氏認爲所有的黃米，小米都是黍，而造酒的秫是稷。吳氏則根據經籍，辨明粟和穄（亦卽穈亦卽秫）是兩類，粟既不同於穄，則稷應當卽是穄。至於高粱一物是晉以後的蜀黍，不在六穀範圍之內。如再根據西方學者的意見，高粱是外來的，正和吳氏的意思可以相輔而行，倘若不是晚近高粱遺跡的發現，這個問題就可以完全解決了。

當然吳氏粟穄不同的意見是完全正確的，粟卽粱，也就是北方人所指的小米相當於 *Setaria italica*；穄卽黍，也就是北方人所指的糜子，相當於 *Panicum miliaceam*；在這兩種之中各有粘不粘的類別。粘與不粘並非分別的條件，而是糜子（漢人稱爲穈）的穗是直而硬的，中國及西洋都來做掃帚。小米的穗是像貓尾一樣下垂的，絕不能做掃帚。吳氏書中的畫的粱和黍都相當正確。

但是吳氏的結論，卻還不能使人完全折服。他最後決定的三種是粟，黍，穄，也就是粟，黍，稷。所說的穄，實是黍的不黏的一種，在山西就叫做 chi tzǔ。因爲華北沒有入聲，這個名稱可以寫成穄子，也可能寫成稷子。吳氏認爲就是稷，是從聲音上想出來的。

若從古音上來說，那就穄和稷完全不能通轉。穄字段氏表列在十五部，而稷字段氏表列在一部。十五部卽「脂部」，而一部卽「之部」，脂部和之部是不可通轉的。依照 Prof. Bernhard Karlgren 的 *Granmata Serica*，穄字應爲 tsiad，稷字應爲 tsiěk，不在同組，不可相通（董同龢先生上古音韻表，穄爲 tsïäd，稷爲 tsiěk 也差不多的）。所以穄和稷在上古是完全不同的兩個字，也就穄不是稷。吳氏從音讀下手，顯然錯誤。再說，穄在古記載中應和黍爲同類，吳氏所舉出的穄子（或稷子）也是黍類。可是古代黍是黍，稷是稷，稷決不可用黍來替換。漢代只有認粱（卽粟）爲稷的，卻不曾認黍稷爲一物。

程瑤田根據的是鄭玄的看法，鄭玄作月令注，說稷爲首種。他的注于正確性有多大，確屬疑問。譬如蔡邕就認爲首種的是麥，仍然有充足的理由。不過就鄭玄言鄭玄，程瑤田認爲鄭玄指的是高粱，並未曾有多大的錯誤。魏張揖稱高粱爲木稷卽在鄭玄稍後，所以鄭玄知道高粱，並非不合理。吳氏在他辯駁之中，對於鄭玄注不能提出有力的反證，就成爲他立說中的漏洞。

　　當然最大疑問，還是張華賈思勰諸人爲甚麼不知高粱的舊名，只用蜀黍蘆穄等名稱。這卻應當採用吳氏的話來解答。吳氏說：「凡俗之呼穀者……但隨俗呼名，不復識別，正如今人曰小米，曰穀子，其類乃不可究詰，夫豈一種哉？愚夫愚婦思轉相傳，物以音變，音以地殊，凡古物在今不能指名者皆是也」。吳氏這個理論是正確的，所以張華賈思勰不能知道高粱的舊名並不就是高粱沒有舊名，而是他們只採取了俗稱。炳棣先生已經指出，高粱是耐旱的農作物。黃土高原正好種植。但是到西漢中期以後，黃土高原已推行種麥（參見居延漢簡），種麥就不能種高粱，這大約就是高粱種植減少，以致被人忘卻的原因。只有蜀地多山，比較特別宜於高粱，後來農人就把它認爲蜀的特產了。

　　不過高粱雖爲中國本土舊有農作物之一，也並不能說就是稷。程瑤田諸氏認高粱爲稷之說，仍然未必正確。漢儒之中除去鄭玄以外，大都認粟爲稷。自然，稷也是可能爲粟的，因爲⑴稷爲百穀之長，而禾字則爲穀類總名，重要性相同。再就禾字造字的形體來說，甲骨文以次都作岁，上面有一個下垂的穗，正是 *Setaria italica* 的特點。⑵詩經七月「黍稷重穋」是指黍稷生長略有先後，大致同一節令收穫，詩經楚茨：「我黍與與，我稷翼翼」，是黍稷同時生長。不會懸殊到高粱和黍稷的分別。尤其是詩經黍離：「彼黍離離，彼稷之苗」鄭玄箋在此忘了他平時的見解也只有說：「我以黍離離時至，稷則有苗」（下節言「彼黍離離，彼稷之穗」又言「彼黍離離，彼稷之實」所說亦不準確，不過黍稷大略同時生長，則是事實。）與他在月令注中認爲正月種稷之說矛盾。此處的稷，只有認爲粟才合適。⑶在經典中向來是黍稷並稱，稷是非常重要而普遍的品種，不論高粱，或是黍的一支穄子，都不足以當稷。只有粟那樣重要的糧食，才能和黍對立。所以漢人以粟當稷之說，也還有考慮之必要。

　　依照周禮天官鄭玄注：鄭眾對於九穀的意見是黍，稷，秫，稻，麻，大小豆，大小麥九種。鄭玄卻認爲是粱，黍，稷，麻，大小豆，小麥及苽九種。鄭眾所舉有秫無粱，鄭玄所舉有粱無秫。因此鄭眾的前三種是黍（*Panicum miliaceum*），稷（*Setaria italica*），秫（*Andropogan Sorghnm* 即高粱，但說文「秫稷之黏者」，又高粱可稱爲木稷或蘆稷，這是稷字廣泛的應用）。鄭玄的前三種，換成了粱（*Setaria italica*），

黍（*Panicum miliaceum*），稷（*Andropogan sorghum*），依然還是同樣的三種，但
對於舊名的估定卻大不相同。在鄭玄注月令中，也不期而然的採用了他自己的看法。
到了清儒，自程瑤田採用鄭玄說，陳奐，王念孫，段玉裁也都依從程氏的論點。其實
他們的論據並不堅強，決不可以認為定論。只是高粱倘若不是外來的，在「九穀」之
中不論把高粱叫做甚麼，總得給高粱一個位置，這一點卻是不必懷疑的。炳棣先生現
在提出來這個問題，確實十分重要。

　　在近數年之中，對於中國上古史問題的綜合觀察，當以張光直和許倬雲兩先生為
最有貢獻。現在何炳棣先生把這本專著發表，對於許多觀點都有了更新的啟示。這就
使中國上古史的研究更進一步了。

一九六八年十月勞榦跋

關東與關西的李姓和趙姓

　　從唐代的寒山詩中，已經說到了『張、王、李、趙』，就是說，張、王、李、趙四大姓，在唐代的人數中，已經占了一個相當的比例，因而就形成了當時的俗語。在這四大姓之中，王姓不出自一源，戰國時周室和六國王家的後裔，都被稱爲王姓，可以不論。張姓本爲周大夫，後來入晉爲晉國大夫，再後又爲韓國的世卿，這一支族人爲什麼澎漲到這機大，現在沒有確切理由可以解答，也只好存放著不論。只有李趙二姓的淵源流別，尙有可以討論的地方，現在就按這兩性加以論敍。

　　李趙二姓有一個類似的地方，就是這兩姓早已分爲東西兩支、東支在三晉區域，西支在秦。這兩支各自發展，到了唐代還成爲不同的兩系。這種有趣的事實，是值得加以討論的。

　　甲、李氏　　講氏族的書，大致將李氏的來源，認爲和臯陶的官職『理官』有關，並且還溯源於老子，如林寶元和姓纂卷一：(註一)

> 李——帝顓頊高陽之裔，顓頊生大業，大業生女華，女華生咎繇(同臯陶)，爲堯理官。子孫因姓李氏，(註二)云云。裔孫理徵得罪于紂，其子利貞，逃難伊侯之墟，食木子得全，因變姓李氏。利貞十一代孫老君，名耳，字伯陽，居苦縣賴鄉，曲仁里。曾孫曇，生二子，崇，璣。崇子孫居隴西，璣子孫居趙郡。崇五代孫朔生伯考，伯考生尙，尙生李廣也。廣以後生唐高祖李淵。

這是把李氏分爲趙郡和隴西兩支。而這兩支都被認爲老子的後人。以現今的觀察來評斷，這一段的問題很多，難以相信。就中臯陶爲『理官』一事，本來就根據非常薄弱。因爲尙書堯典的臯陶是：『汝作士』，孟子中亦稱：『舜爲天子，臯陶爲士。』不是做

（註一）　元和姓纂多已亡失，遺文散見於永樂大典及秘笈新書，此據係徐洪瑩校補元和姓纂輯本。

（註二）　此節自秘笈新書輯者，『云云』以下爲當時省略文字。

理官。理的本字原爲治玉，引申爲治訟獄，其義不至太早。管子小匡篇：『弦子章爲理：』尹知章注：『獄官也。』這是一部戰國時的書，又禮記月令：(註一)『孟秋之月，……命理瞻傷，視創。』鄭注：『理，治獄官也。有虞氏曰士，夏曰大理，周曰大因寇。』月令的文字也不會比戰國更早。所以理官可能爲六國時的官名，鄭玄的夏曰大理，可能也是一種揣測之辭。皋陶旣然未嘗做理官，那就卽使曾經有一個理姓，也是把皋陶附會上去的，可況還有『改理爲李』的一段曲折。至於說裔孫理徵得罪于紂，其子利貞逃難伊侯之墟，食木子得全，因變姓李氏，更是一個不可信的俗說。古代命氏同音字本可固相假借，漢初尚然，殷商當然更是如此，用不著改同音字。況且『食木子得全』更不成話。姓氏書中此類甚多原不必深究。不過李氏出於皋陶，向來爲人所信，所以還得分辯一下。從來把李氏分爲趙郡及隴西兩支來敍述，這是因爲這兩支在唐代都是望族。並不定是同宗。至於姓氏書中說是老子之後，更是不可信的。因爲老子的後人，在史記中曾特別道及。史記老莊申韓列傳說：

> 老子之子名宗，宗爲魏將，封於段干，宗子注，宮，玄孫假，假仕於漢孝文帝，而假之子解爲膠西王卬太傅，因家於齊焉。

所以老子的後人在齊，而趙郡和隴西的李氏，都不是老子的後人。尤其隴西李氏是不然的，司馬遷在李將軍列傳說：

> 李將軍廣者，隴西成紀人也。其先曰李信，秦時爲將逐得燕太子丹者也。

司馬遷和隴西李氏有私人的交誼，假如他們眞和老子有關，他決無不說之理，反而只說一個普通的將領李信。而且老子後人在齊，不在隴西，所以隴西李氏非老子之後是一個不成問題的事。唐朝封老子爲玄元皇帝是高攀。這一點眞不如明太祖拒臣下提議攀附朱熹，還是英雄的本色。(註二)

理李二字本屬同音字，假如有姓理的，改爲李姓是可能的，如同韓改爲何，豼改

(註一) 呂氏春秋孟秋紀同，淮南子時則篇無此句，又按此段『理』的地位在『有司』之下，可能是『吏』的借字。

(註二) 帝王中如劉裕稱楚元王後，却是可能的，因爲楚元王非帝王嫡系，無繼承權。稱元王後，是彭城劉氏一般習慣，似乎不是出於劉裕始以此自稱。這和唐稱老子之後，利用老子的神秘傳說的是不相同。至於趙宋稱趙廣漢之後，至少亦是唐時舊說（見元和姓纂）非從宋開始。

爲郭，司徒改爲申屠，最改爲晁，轅改爲袁，橋改爲喬，諸如此類，是數不完的。倘若記載上戰國以前有姓理的人，那從理轉爲李未嘗不可能。無奈歷史上從來未曾有過姓理的人（除去明末理安和因爲不願與李自成同姓，改李爲理以外）。當然，理李二字可以通用，但兩漢人敘述李姓祖先，以及漢朝李姓的碑文都不說到其先人爲皋陶，因理官得姓之事。只有唐以來氏族書才說及，可見其說出於唐代李氏族人的附會，不足採信的。(註一)

　　李氏支派衆多，雖然老子的後人只占李氏一小部分，但從老子的姓氏却可以比附其他李氏支屬得氏的淵源。老子的職守是守藏史或是柱下史，也就是史官的一種。按照左傳中的例子，如史蘇，史角之類，凡是做史官的，都只稱史某而不再稱姓氏。也就是這種職務的人都可以史爲氏。所以李耳卽柱下史耳，也自然的可稱爲史耳。又史使，李三字本音義相通。左傳僖公十三年：

　　　　行李之往來，共其乏困，君亦無所害。

杜預注：

　　　　行李，使人。

孔穎達正義：

　　　　襄八年傳云：『一介行李，』杜云：『行李，行人也。』昭十三年傳云：『行理之命，』杜云：『行理，使人。』李理字異，注則同，都不解理字。周禮行理以節逆之，』賈逵曰：『理吏也，小行人也。』孔晁注國語，其本亦作李字，注云，『行李，行人之官也。』然則兩字本通用，本作理，訓之爲吏，故爲行人使人也。

所以使，李，理，吏諸字本可互相通用，而以上諸字又可以與史字通用。元和姓纂卷六史姓：

（註一）　唐張守節史記老子列傳正義說：『玄妙內篇云，李母懷胎八十一載，逍遙李樹下，遂割左腋而生。』又唐司馬貞老子列傳索隱云：『按葛玄云，李氏女所生，因母姓也。又云，生而指李樹，因以爲姓』所以道經中老子是指李樹爲姓，在唐人注史記時尙用此說，還沒有『改理爲李』之說，可見這種說法，較道經之說爲晚出，因此未曾爲史記注家所引用。唐人氏族之書任意附會祖先，如林氏本爲姬姓，世居於齊，而林寶便附會爲比干之後，所以鄭樵譏林寶不知林氏所自出。研究氏族的人尙如此，何況其他。

周太史史佚之後，以女弟爲戾太子良娣，生史皇孫進，進生宣帝，恭子高。
這是不錯的，不過史姓當出於曾爲史官的人，却不會都是周太史史佚之後。
鄧名世古今姓氏書辨語卷九云：

> 便　姓書漢少府便樂成，望出魯國，誤矣。謹按霍光傳：『故長史任宣謂霍禹
> 曰，「使樂成小家子也，得幸大將軍，至九卿封侯。」』師古曰：『使姓也，字
> 或作史，』然則使史通用，而姓書誤其字畫，以使爲便也。

所以姓『史』的可以有時寫成姓『使』，而『使』文和『李』字在古時音義並通，依照
古人的姓，不嚴格的用一定寫法，那就姓使的，姓史的，和姓李可以隨便在用了。所
以『史耳』假如寫作『李耳』，或『李耳』寫作『史耳』都是非常可能的。

因此姓李的祖先以官爲氏，大致是不錯的，不過應當是周代史官或行人官的後
世，若認爲皋陶之後，那就顯然是一種附會。

當然，皋陶爲士，士字和史雖然聲母清濁不同相去遠些，但還可以互相通轉。姓
氏中尚有『士』姓，元和姓纂云：

> 士　帝堯之裔杜伯之子隰叔爲晉士師，至士蒍生伯成缺，缺生會子孫氏焉。後
> 漢未交阯太守士燮。……士燮後生義總，唐戶部郎中。

卽姓氏書並不認爲士姓爲皋陶之後。士姓爲皋陶之後，並非不可能，只是認爲晉士師
之後，時代較近，更爲合理。至理姓爲皋陶之後，却絕對不成理由。現在既不承認士
姓爲皋陶之後，那就從士轉爲理，才成爲李姓的可能，就減到最小了。

因此，李姓爲皋陶之後，是不可能的。只有認爲從一般官氏爲姓。如史，使，或
士等類的音轉，才比較合理。假如是以史，使，士諸官爲姓，那就此類的官，春秋各
國皆有，因而李姓可能還是多元的。除去未耳後人到了齊國以外，趙郡及隴西西兩支
李氏，大致也並非同族。至於出於周時那一些有名的人，或者出於無名的人，那就不
必多爲注意了。

新唐書七十一宗室世系表說：

> 李氏出自嬴姓，帝顓頊高陽氏生大業，大業生女華，女華生皋陶，字庭堅，爲
> 堯大理，生益，(註一)益生恩成，歷虞夏商，世爲大理，以官命族爲理氏。紂之
> 時，理徵字德靈爲翼隸中吳伯，以直通不容於紂，得罪而死，其妻陳國契和與

子利貞，逃難於伊侯之墟，食木子得全，遂改理為李氏。利貞亦娶契和氏女，生昌祖，為陳大夫家於苦縣。生彤德，彤德曾孫碩宗，周康王賜采邑於苦縣，五世孫乾，字元果，為周上御史大夫，娶益壽氏女嬰敷，生耳，字伯陽，一字聃，周平王時為太史。其後有李宗，字尊祖，魏封於段，為干木大夫。生同，為趙大將軍。生兊，為趙相。生躋，趙陽安君。二子曰雲，曰恪，恪生洪，字道弘，秦太子太傅，生與族，字育神，一名汪，秦將軍。生曇，字貴遠，趙柏人侯，入秦，為御史大夫，葬柏人西。生四子，崇，辨，昭，璣。崇為隴西房，璣為趙郡房。

崇字伯祐，隴西守，南鄭公，生二子，長曰平燕。次曰瑤，字內德，南郡守，狄道侯。生信，字有成，大將軍，隴西侯。生超，一名伉，字仁高，漢大將軍，漁陽太守，生二子長曰元曠，侍中次曰仲翔，河東太守，征西將軍，討叛羌於素昌，戰歿，贈太尉，葬隴西狄道東川，因家焉。生伯考，隴西河東二郡太守，生尚，成紀令，因居成紀。弟向，范陽房始祖也。尚生廣，前將軍。二子，(註二)長曰當戶，生陵字，少卿，騎將尉。次曰敢，字幼卿，郎中令，關內侯，生禹，字子通，弟忠，頓丘房始祖也。禹生丞公，字丞公，河南太守。生先，字敬宗，蜀郡北平太守，生長宗，字伯禮，漁陽丞，生君況，字叔干，一字子期，博士議郎。太中大夫，生本，字上明，郎中，侍御史生次公，字仲居，巴郡太守，西夷校尉。弟恬，渤海房始祖也。次公生軌，字文逸，魏臨淮太守，司農卿。弟潛，申公房始祖也。軌生隆，字彥緒，長安令，積弩將軍。生艾，字世績，晉驍騎將軍，魏郡太守。生雍，字儁熙，濟北東莞二郡太守，生二子，長曰倫，丹楊房始祖也。次曰柔，字德遠，北地太守。雍孫蓋，安邑

(註一)　此處是一點也不可信的，皋陶未為大理，其官名為士，正見前考。益與皋陶為同時人，非皋陶子，據堯典，益為虞，調伏鳥獸，更未曾做過大理。又段干為地名，此云封於段，為干木大夫，亦誤。

(註二)　據漢書五十四李廣傳：『廣三子，曰當戶，椒，敢，皆為郎，當戶早死，乃拜椒為代郡太守，皆先廣記……敢男禹，有寵於太子，然好利，亦有勇。當戶有遺腹陵，將兵擊胡，敗降匈奴，後人告禹欲亡從陵，下吏死。』此云二子，與漢書異。此或real出於隴西李氏家藏譜牒。（椒或無後，故不著）不必以其與正史異而懷疑，至於老子及老子以前世系，顯然出於附會，不可以此相比。

房始祖也。柔生弇，字季子，前涼張駿天水太守，武衞將軍。生昶，字仲堅，涼太子侍講。生暠。

(暠)字玄盛，西涼興聖皇帝。十子，譚，歆，讓，愔，恂，翻，豫，宏，眺，亮。愔，鎭遠將軍房始祖也。其曾孫系，平涼房始祖也。翻孫三人，曰丞，姑臧房始祖也。曰茂，燉煌房始祖也。曰冲，僕射房始祖也。曾孫曰成禮，絳郡房始祖也。豫玄孫曰嗣，武陵房始祖也。

歆字士業，西涼後主，八子。勗，紹，重耳，弘之，崇明，崇產，崇塘，崇祐。重耳字景順，以國亡奔宋爲汝南太守。後魏克豫州，以地歸之，拜恆農太守，後爲宋將薛安都所陷。後魏安南將軍豫州刺史。生獻祖宣皇帝熙，字孟良，後魏金門鎭將，生懿祖光皇帝，諱天賜，字德眞。三子。長曰起頭，字安侯，生達摩，後周羽林監，太子洗馬，長安縣伯，其後無聞。次曰太祖（虎，後周柱國大將軍，唐國襄公）。次乞豆，定州刺史房。(註一)

以上所舉的隴西李氏來源，當出於隴西李氏原來譜牒，大致可信。不過據元和郡縣志唐朝的先代，其祖塋實在趙州的昭慶縣。並且再據有河北省隆平縣的唐光業寺碑，都可以證明唐朝的先世累代均葬在此處。據唐人追述唐室的先世，出於隴西，後徙武川，與趙州，趙郡並無淵源，何故葬在毫不相干的趙郡境界。此必李唐先世本爲趙郡人，後徙武川，祖塋仍在趙郡。及周太祖（宇文泰）入關，『諸姓子孫有功者，並令爲其宗長，仍撰譜錄，紀其所承。又以關內諸州爲本望』（隋書三十三經籍志史部譜序篇序）。於是原非關內籍貫的功臣，也改爲關內的郡望，趙郡的李氏，也就自然的換成了隴西李氏(註二)。等到後來隋唐時代，還是保存著舊有的傳統，不會輕易的改囘去，隴西李氏的人雖然知道不是，但世族攀附一事已成南北朝以後的常態，與天子同族，也是很好的。趙郡李氏的人當然不敢輕議國姓，只有沉默。這一點在李吉甫（他就是趙郡李氏中人）的元和郡縣志，排列出來趙郡李氏的宗塋，並參雜唐代帝室祖先的宗塋，未嘗不是故意漏出了一個消息來。

(註一)　册府元龜帝王部帝系門，舊唐書一，高祖紀，新唐書一高祖紀，北史一○○序傳，晉書八七涼武昭王傳並同，但以新唐書宗室世系表所述西涼之世族爲詳。

(註二)　以上的意見採用陳寅恪先生：唐代政治史述論稿。

其次，關於趙郡李氏，新唐書七十二宰相世系表有以下記載：

趙郡李氏出於秦司徒量，次子璣字伯衡，秦太傅。三子，雲，牧，齊。

牧爲趙相，封武安君，始居趙郡。趙納頓弱之間，殺牧。齊爲中山相，亦家焉。卽中山始祖也。牧三子，汨，弘，鮮。汨秦中大夫，詹事。生諒，左車，仲車，左車趙廣武君，生常伯，遐，遐字伯友，漢涿郡守。生岳，德文，班。岳家長卿，諫議大夫，生秉，義。秉字世範，潁川太守，因徙家焉。生翼，協，敏。敏五大夫將軍，生謨，道，朗。謨字道謀臨淮太守，生哆，華，旭。哆字子讓，上黨太守，生護，元。護字鴻猷，酒泉太守，生武，昭，奮。武字昭先，東郡太守，太常卿，生讚，脩，奕，就。脩字伯游，後漢太尉，生諒，叔，訓，季。諒字世益，趙國相，生膺，字元禮，河南尹。生壞，瓚，瑾，瑾字叔瑜，東平相，避亂後居趙，生志，恢，宣。恢字叔與生定，臺，獎，碩。定字文義，魏水衡都尉，漁陽太守，生伯括，機，叔括，季括。機字仲括，太學博士，臨江樂安二郡太守，生羣，瓌，密，楷，越。楷字雄方，晉司農丞，治書侍御史，避趙王倫之難，徙居常山。五子，輯，晃，芬，勁，叡。叡子勗，兄弟居巷東，勁子盛，兄弟居巷西。故叡爲東祖，芬與弟勁共稱西祖。輯與弟晃，共稱南祖。自楷徙居平棘南通，號平棘李氏，輯字護宗，高密太守，子愼，敦，居柏仁，子孫甚微，與晃南徙故壘，故輯晃皆稱南祖。晃字仲黃，鎮南府長史，生羲字敬仲，燕司空長史，生吉，字彥同，東官舍人，生聰，字小時，尚書郎，二子眞，融。——在西祖系中，最知名的有李吉甫李德裕父子，皆爲宰相。

遼東李氏，璣少子齊，趙相，初居中山，十三世孫寶字君長，後漢玄菟都尉，徙襄平，生雄，車騎長史。生亮，字威明，原武令。生敏，河內太守，生信。生胤，字宣伯，晉司徒，廣陸成侯。生固字萬基，散騎侍郎。生志字彥道，陽平太守。嗣廣陸侯。弟沈，沈孫柉。——在此系中有後周太師，隴西公李弼，李弼的後人有唐初的羣雄李密，和唐德宗的宰相李泌。(註一)

(註一)　李弼在後周封隴西公，可見曾一度改爲隴西郡望，到了唐代，才又改回來。新唐書八十四李密傳（舊唐書五十三）李密以兄稱李淵，當亦由於舊譜俱屬隴西的原故。

江夏李氏，漢酒泉太守護，次子昭，昭少子就，後漢會稽太守，亮陽侯，徙居江夏平春。六世孫式，字景則，東晉侍中，生巘，巘生尙，字茂仲，生矩，字茂約，江州刺史，生充，字弘度，中書侍郎，生顥，舉孝廉，七世孫元哲。元哲徙居廣陵。——在此系中著名的有李善李邕父子。

漢中李氏：漢東郡太守太常卿武孫頡，後漢博士，始居漢中南鄭。生郃，字孟節，司徒。生因，字子堅，太尉。生三子，基字憲公，慈字季公，爕字德公安平相，十二世孫德林。——德林子百藥，百藥子安期相高宗。

據以上的引證，李氏除去了一般的庶姓不計在內以外，分爲趙郡和隴西兩大支。趙郡李氏有居關中的(如漢中李氏)隴西李氏也有居關東的(如范陽李氏)，不過大致說來還是東西兩大支別。李濟先生的 The Formation of the Chinese People，曾經對李氏的兩支，列過一個總表，其式如下：

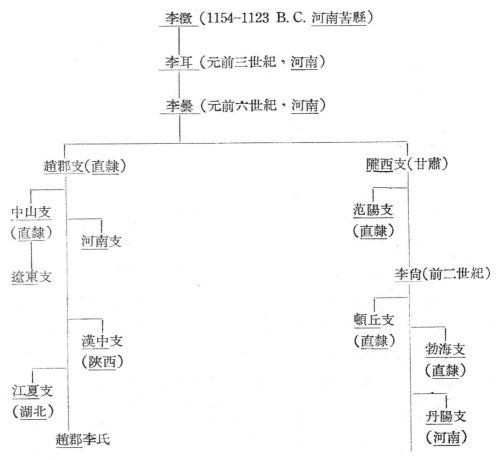

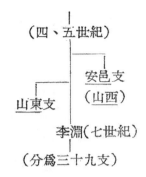

乙、趙氏和李氏相同，也是分爲東西二支。據新唐書七十三下宰相世系表，趙氏：

> 趙氏出自嬴姓，顓頊裔孫伯益，帝舜賜以嬴姓。十三世孫造父，周穆王封於趙
> 城，因以爲氏，其地河東永安縣是也。六世孫奄父，號公仲，生叔帶，去周仕
> 晉文侯，五世孫夙，獻公賜采邑於耿，河東皮氏縣有耿鄉是也。夙生共孟，共
> 孟生衰，字子餘，諡曰成季，成季十八世孫遷，爲秦所滅，趙人立遷兄嘉爲代
> 王，後降於秦，秦使嘉子公輔主西戎，西戎懷之，號曰趙王。世居隴西天水西
> 縣。公輔十二世孫融，字長，後漢右扶風，大鴻臚。融七世孫瑤（後魏河北太
> 守。）

這是以天水趙氏爲主的，不過趙氏在關東諸地的，也還有不少。元和姓纂趙姓下：

> 下邳　漢丞相趙周之後，十二代孫廞，魏廣陵太守，玄孫晉平原太守。
>
> 平原　後漢太守趙憙之後，本南陽宛人，徙平原。
>
> 河間蠡吾縣　本名潁川，亦趙王遷之後。漢京兆尹廣漢之後徙河間，裔孫全
> 穀，唐金部員外郎洪州都督。
>
> 信都　尚書左丞趙涓生博。

其中蠡吾一支，就是趙宋皇室一族所自出，溯源於六國時趙國亡國的昏君趙王遷，未
曾攀附天水。其他下邳，平原，信都，也未攀附天水。並且蠡吾一支，其下說『亦趙
王遷之後』，可見倘有他支稱爲趙王遷之後的，因爲今本元和姓纂不全，無法知道
了。

不過關東趙姓之中攀附天水的，在唐代確實也不少。如：

> 中山　稱本自天水徙中山曲陽，今定州。
>
> 新安　稱自天水徙焉。

南陽穰縣　稱自天水徙焉。

汲郡　本自天水徙焉。

河東　狀云自天水徙焉。

長平　狀云自天水徙澤州。　　　（以上並見元和姓纂）

這是因爲天水趙氏爲唐代趙氏中望族，其他關東諸族，也都以攀附天水爲榮。只有少數的支派未曾攀附天水，趙宋皇室就是其中的一支(註一)。這種情形已經不太多了。

東方的趙氏，無論如何是自成一支的，除去左傳國策，史記，凡晉國及趙國的趙氏，如趙衰，趙盾，趙武，趙奢，趙勝都是東方的趙氏，並且秦漢間亦有不少趙氏的人，如史記一百十三南越尉佗列傳：

南越王尉佗者，眞定人也。姓趙氏。……佗秦時用爲南海龍川令。至二世時，南海尉任囂病且死，召龍川令趙佗……行南海尉事。……自立爲南越武王。……及孝文帝元年，初鎮撫天下，使告諸侯四夷，從代來卽位意，喻盛德焉。乃爲佗親冢在眞定，置守邑，歲時奉祀，召其從昆弟尊官厚賜寵之。

眞定爲故戰國時趙國的領土，和天水不相干，卽趙國亡後，故趙國的趙氏，尚有人在其地，並且還做秦時的邊方官吏。

又如史記十八高祖功臣侯表，深澤侯趙將夜：『以趙將漢王三年降』，趙將而姓趙，當是趙人而非秦人。此外如江邑侯趙堯，『從御史大夫周昌爲趙相而伐陳豨』（又見史記九十六周昌列傳）須昌侯趙衍『後爲河閒守』，俱與趙國地界有關，也可能是趙國境內的人。又漢書十八外戚恩澤侯表：『周陽侯趙兼，以淮南王舅侯，（文帝元年）四月辛未封，六年，有罪免。』趙兼也是一個趙國的人。史記一百十八，淮南衡山濟北王傳：

淮南厲王長者，高祖少子也。其母故趙王張敖美人。高祖八年從東垣過趙，趙王獻之美人，厲王母得幸焉。有身：趙王敖弗敢內宮，爲築外宮而舍之。及貫高等謀反柏人，事發覺，並逮治王，盡收捕王母兄弟美人繫之河內。厲王母亦繫，告吏曰：『得幸上有身。』吏以聞，上方怒趙王未理趙王母。厲王母弟趙

> 竟因辟陽侯言呂后。呂后妬，弗肯白，辟陽侯不彊爭，及厲王巳生厲王，竟，
> 卽自殺，吏奉厲王詣上，上悔，令呂后母之，而葬厲王母眞定。眞定，厲王之
> 母家在焉。父世縣也。(註一)

這是說眞定有姓趙的累世在這個地方住，當然決不是從天水搬去的。

此外趙姓可以確知爲關東諸郡人的，如漢書八十八儒林傳：『（鄭）寬中授東郡趙
玄。』又：『趙子，河內人也。』九十二游俠傳：『南陽趙調之徒』。九十九外戚傳：『孝
武鉤弋趙倢伃，昭帝母也，家在河間。』這都是家在淮水以北，函谷以東的地區。而
尤其著名的，當然是涿郡蠡吾人趙廣漢。趙廣漢雖然不見一定是趙匡胤的嫡系祖先，
不過地域是相同，當不是全無根據的。

關西的趙氏，照姓氏書的傳述，爲趙公子嘉的後人，這是不可信的。誠然，秦滅
六國以後，六國之後，秦始皇仍然保存下來。但大都如同史記九十魏豹傳所說：

> 魏豹者，故魏諸公子也。其兄魏咎，故魏時封爲寧陵君。秦滅魏，遷咎爲家
> 人。

這裏說的很清楚，秦把六國後人，只是遷爲家人，並未曾做進一步的迫害。遷爲家人
就是把他們貶爲平民。他們的生活，就看他們治生能力怎樣。例如戰國策說齊王建後
來被秦『置之松柏之間，餓而死。』正和漢書佞幸傳說鄧通當窮餓而死一樣用法，鄧
通到死時，尚有長公主『令假衣食』，並非餽餒而卒，只是抑鬱而終。齊王建大約亦
屬此類。看來代王嘉被徙於秦，照一般降王世族的結果看來，把他的家徙居天水，作
老百姓，當然可能。不過說秦人重用他的子弟來治西戎，却有些不像。而且趙公子嘉
的後人，從此變成關中彊族，也是可疑的。

案關中的趙姓，實在應當是秦國的宗室，史記五秦本紀論：

太史公曰：『秦之先爲嬴姓。其後分封，以國爲姓。有徐氏，郯氏，莒氏，終
黎氏，運奄氏，菟裘氏，將梁氏，黃氏，江氏，脩魚氏，白冥氏，蜚廉氏，秦
氏。然秦以其先造父封趙城爲趙氏。』

(註一)　索隱：『案漢書作母家縣，謂父祖代居眞定也。』和趙佗家同在一地，眞定是趙氏聚居之處，一直到
　　　三國時蜀大將趙雲也是眞定人。

這裏說的很清楚，秦國的公族並非秦氏，而是沿襲的用趙氏為姓。所以史記云秦始皇本紀說：

> 及生名為政，姓趙氏。

淮南子人間篇說

> 秦王趙政，兼吞天下而亡。

正和此處相應。關於始皇姓趙，司馬貞在史記秦始皇本紀索隱列舉兩說：

> 系本作政，又生於趙，故曰趙政，一曰秦與趙同祖，以趙城為榮，故姓趙氏。

都是不對的，其實司馬貞未注意到秦本紀論，故有錯誤。這裏當然要以史記證史記，用『秦以其先造父封趙城為趙氏』來解釋才可以。有此一句，證據明確，秦公室用趙姓當然毫無爭辯或懷疑的必要了。

史記八十八蒙恬列傳說：

> 趙高者，諸趙疏遠屬也，趙高昆弟數人，皆生隱宮。

這裏所謂『諸趙』，究竟是什麼意思，從來無適當的解釋。當然這兩個字決不會是毫無意義的。漢人用諸字的，例如諸項，諸劉，諸呂，齊諸田等，都是指的包括許多可注意的人組成的彊宗大族。這裏『諸趙』一辭，當然也不會例外。也就是說趙高是非常遠的秦宗室，比趙高近的房分，還有許多人。

在西漢時代，關中的趙氏，如漢書五十五，衞書霍去病傳：『趙食其殺枒人。』漢書九十酷吏傳：『趙禹犛人也。』漢書九十二游俠傳：『槐里趙王孫……雖為俠而恂恂有退讓君子之風。』俱是關中的趙姓。而九十七外戚傳：『李成趙皇后本長安宮人』也應當作為長安籍的宮人來解釋。因為凡外戚傳所記諸后妃，皆有籍貫，獨趙皇后只說『長安宮人』可見長安就是籍貫了。又漢書六十九趙充國辛慶懇傳：『趙充國隴西上邽人也，後徙金城令居。始為騎士，以六郡良家子善騎射補羽林。』也當然是祖籍關中的人。凡此關中的趙姓，其祖先皆為秦時的『諸趙』，也就是當為秦的公族，而非趙的公族。

元和姓纂以為秦姓出於秦國，當然是錯的。鄧名世古今姓氏書辯證原序說：

> 自風俗通以來（如姓苑，百家譜，姓纂）凡有所長，盡用其說，穿鑿訛謬，必

辨駁之。始於國姓，餘分四聲。(註一)……姓纂稍能是正數十條，而齊秦之屬，亦所未暇。(守山叢書閣本據玉海補)

所以他對於秦姓另輯有新的材料，今本卷六十六：

秦氏，出自姬姓，周文公世子伯禽父，受封爲魯侯。裔孫以公族爲魯大夫者，食邑於秦，以邑爲氏。春秋魯莊公三十一年，書築臺於秦卽其地也。莊公大夫曰秦子，乾時之後，代君任患，而身止於齊，其家遂昌阜於魯國。昭公時有大夫曰商，曰遄，又有堇父者，仕孟氏爲孟僖子車右，以力聞諸侯。商孫，西巴，有仁心，嘗放麑與其母，孟孫召爲太子傅而託國焉。漢興，高祖用婁敬策，徙大姓實關中，秦氏始自魯徙居扶風茂陵。西漢有襲與羣從，同時爲二千石者五人。世號萬石秦氏。襲孫彭，字伯平，爲後漢循吏，有傳。自彭而下，顯者代不乏人。

所以秦姓應當是別有來源，不關秦國。戰國時亦只有東方人姓秦的(如燕將秦開)，而秦人卻未聞有姓秦的，若是公族那就不應毫無所聞了。至於日本姓秦的，自稱爲秦始皇之後，也只能認爲雖是中國遷入日本的移民，卻不能認爲秦代的宗室。秦代宗室遺留在關中的，還都是姓趙。

在南方的長江流域還未曾充分開發的時期，中國東西兩方的區分，更比較南北的區分還要重要。這一點傅斯年先生的夷夏東西說曾有詳考。一直到了漢代，關東和關西仍是重要的兩大區分。李氏和趙氏的東西南支，正可作爲代表。西支是代表秦，東支是代表三晉。在李姓中，西支的代表是漢代著名將軍李廣，東支的代表是趙國著名大將李牧。在趙姓中，西支是秦的公族，在漢代可以趙充國爲代表，東支是趙國的氏族，在漢代以趙廣漢爲代表。氏族的整理，在唐代是一個重要時期，因爲建都長安，而關中氏族顯著優越。唐代皇家可能就是由趙郡冒充隴西，但李弼的後人還是把他們歸入到原有遼東一支去。宋代皇家本來就是關東的人，並未冒充天水趙氏，不過後人講氏姓還是以西方的隴西(李氏)和天水(趙氏)爲主。宋以後考試制度用彌封方法，郡

(註一) 今本仍用永樂大典輯佚而成，所闕不少。趙姓在「三十小韻」下，非在卷首，已失舊第。並且趙姓下所敍僅有『漢京兆尹度漢之後居涿郡，代臨年紀，而僖祖皇帝生焉。』一小段，關於宋代國姓的考證，決不止此，今並闕遺。

望世族不太重要。於是凡李皆是隴西，凡趙皆是天水，郡望成了一種氏姓的代稱，不再含有分別支系的意義了。

本工作進行時，承中國東亞學術計劃委員會推薦哈佛燕京學社補助，特此志謝。

古書重印問題

最近在《中央副刊》看到陳祚龍先生有關重印古書的文字，這的確是很值得注意的，因此我也很願意就我的看法來絞說一下：

翻印古書中的問題，當然最重要的是圖書的採訪，讀者的需要，圖書館庋藏上的方便，以及書店的成本，如其忽略了任何一點，這部書的刊行就不算成功。雖然，世界上不會有十全十美的事，只要缺點不十分嚴重也就過得去了。

版本的決定是一件相當困難的事，保存古籍和供給應用有時往往是互相衝突的。譬如《四部叢刊》的五經是無疏的單注，在校勘上自有其地位，可是就應用說來，就遠不如藝文翻阮刻的《十三經注疏》。胡偉克先生的二十五史，其中《史記》用的是南宋印北宋監本，這是現存的一部最早的《史記》印本，卻可惜只有集解，遠不如黃善夫本，甚至殿本，及瀧川《會注》用處大。所以憑什麼標準去選本子，其中大有出入。任何一種有價值的叢刊既然都有它的缺點，看來只有兩種分別刊行的辦法可走：一種是商務《古逸叢書》的辦法，專存古本，不講應用（當然，現在用不著像《古逸叢書》的大字本，有線裝《四部叢刊》那樣也就夠了）；另一種是藝文影印《十三經》《二十五史》那種辦法，以有用為主，版本次之。不過藝文還有改善的餘地。《十三經》還得附一個簡單的索引（至少要一個篇目的索引在每冊後面）。《二十五史》中除去王注兩《漢書》，盧注《三國志》，吳注《晉書》以外，其餘的能不用殿本最好不用殿本，殿本雖刻書在乾隆樸學盛行之時，可是還有妄改的地方（例如〈留侯世家〉角里先生宋本皆作角里，卻偏要改成甪，而不知甪字不合六書）。這些問題在印書時無從預料，只有盼出版家隨時改進。

版本的選擇是一件事，而書籍的選擇又是一件事。按理說來，凡是未曾印過的，或印過而罕見的都值得重印。但如何選擇，又是一個難得決定的事。例如國藏善本叢書是一件十分有價值的工作，卻因戰事而停頓，變成決而不行。

四庫珍本中，雖然終於印出，但有許多罕見則有之，珍卻未必。珍也可指有用而言，其中眞值得讚揚如《武經總要》、《蜀中廣記》等究竟不多（嚴格說來，四庫本並不好，有些書被清代畫家畫的失眞，完全不是那回事了），這又牽涉到當時動手選擇人的興趣問題。不過目前情形和過去稍有不同，現在如故宮博物院院長蔣慰堂先生，中央圖書館館長屈翼鵬先生都是擅長經史的飽學之士，假如經過他們審定之後，大致就不會有所偏頗了。

近來有些書縮印太小，的確不成話。其中像商務的《四部叢刊》、藝文《二十五史》印的還好，不過紙質應當至少用模造紙而不宜用新聞紙。裝釘方面現在台灣是精裝的線太短太細（精裝不可省材料），而平裝的書，面太薄，都不合規格，可能影響國際的銷售，應當注意。

至於線裝或洋裝那種好，一直是爭執不定，這要考慮到圖書館管理人的意見。國外圖書館除去沒有精裝，一定要買精裝的，國內也有這個傾向，因爲只有精裝才便於管理，線裝雖可做一個布函去裝，但是不僅其中次序容易顛倒錯亂，而且還會遺失一二冊，增加管理的麻煩。古籍線裝是一個旣成事實，圖書館管理人無可如何，新印的書如還要線裝，管理人除去暗中咒罵幾句以外，當然還可以抱一個「如能不買就不買」的消極抵制的辦法。

元月十九日寄自美國

《中國古代書史》後序

　　《中國古代書史》是錢存訓教授英文名著《書於竹帛》的中文增訂本。這部書接觸到許多書寫、銘刻、紙張、工具，以及一切有關中國書籍的許多問題，給予世界的學者對中國這個獨特性的文化及其貢獻一些更深切的了解，使得拘虛於西方書籍的發展，而不知天外有天的人們得以廣開聞見。自從這部書出版以來，許多大學的中國文學系及歷史系曾指定作爲參考書；同時一些重要刊物也撰作書評，加以推介。對於促進中國文化在世界上應有的地位是具有非常深切的意義的。只是原本用英文寫定，對於國內的學人仍然不如閱讀中文更爲方便，所以此次中文本的刊行，實在是一件值得慶幸的事。

　　中國古代的書寫方法和書寫工具，因爲記載不夠詳明，一直有許多誤會。此書經存訓先生廣爲搜集證據，澄清了不少問題。首先提示出甲骨中的許多因素，然後再申述銘刻的重要性，給予讀者一些新鮮的意念。譬如書中指出，甲骨文的字彙已經有四千六百多，其中僅小半可以認識，比較金文使用的字彙，並不算少。周代製作金文時期，是可以寫長篇作品的，那麼以商代當時情形來論，應當也可以產生長篇作品，這個意見至爲正確。甲骨文用途特殊，所以辭彙不同，何況就現有的甲骨文來看，發展的程度已經相當的純熟。如其就現有可以認識的字，再加上形聲和假借來拼湊，把《尙書》中的〈盤庚〉中篇用甲骨文來寫，是不生太大的問題的（〈盤庚〉三篇之中，上下兩篇作者性格較爲仁恕，中篇作者性格較爲暴戾，不似出於一人之口，非常可能中篇爲原有記載，上下兩篇爲周代史官補寫的）。如其〈盤庚〉中這一篇文字曾經用甲骨文字體書寫過，再證以甲骨文中的「冊」字，可以證明古代文書必用許多根竹簡來寫，再行用繩索編連。也是意識到現存的龜甲及獸骨是本來用爲占卜，其用於記事，就一般性來說，只是占卜的附屬用途，而正式記事應仍靠用竹簡。

「簡」字是從竹的，金石文字中只能推溯到石鼓文，但文獻中《詩經》已有「簡」字，存訓先生用削竹的方便來推定簡的製作，是一個創獲。簡的質料可以用竹製，也可以用木製。只是竹做成簡卻不能做成牘，木做成牘比做成簡還要方便些。古代的冊籍是用簡而不是用牘，所以簡的原始製作應當是竹製而非木製的。本來《詩經‧衛風》所說的淇澳的綠竹，正在舊日殷商的境內。到了東漢初年，光武帝曾發過「淇園之竹」，唐時劉知幾曾經懷疑過北方是否產竹一事，不過他或者是未十分注意地理環境與特殊物產的事實。就一般情況來說，黃河水域各處是不產竹的。可是幾個特殊地區是以產竹著稱，例如陝西的華縣，河南的淇縣和輝縣都是產竹區。徐世昌因為住在河南輝縣的百泉，當地多竹，所以他自號水竹村人。這種特殊產竹地區的情形，直到現在仍和《詩經》時代一樣，也就意識到殷商時代竹子的來源，不是在遙遠的南方，而是在殷商的畿內。

竹簡以及類似竹簡的竹籤，在中國的使用是非常普遍的。其採用可以推到極遠古的時代。除了做記錄用的竹簡以外，其他如吃飯所用的箸，演算所用的籌，卜筮所用的策（甚至於馬鞭也叫做策，所以古代馬鞭也可能用竹鞭），都是同一類的竹簡或竹籤。直到後代紙已經用的非常普遍，可是神祠的香案上，官吏的公案上，還保持著籤筒以及從簡策演下來的竹籤。直到民國初年，官吏還沿襲舊制。在新式法院成立後，才廢掉籤筒（但在京劇的道具中仍可看到）。至於神祠中的籤筒，那就在今日的台灣或香港，還一直保持著。此外，清代抽籤的方法（這和《後漢書‧劉盆子傳》的「探符」一樣），不僅在部員外放要用掣籤，甚至於決定達賴喇嘛的候選人，也間或用金瓶掣籤的方法。可見籤籌一類的傳統，對於中國文化及習慣的重要性。

對於中國書法的行款問題，在本書第九章中，存訓先生曾經提到中國文字的排列自上而下，自右而左的原因，和右手有關，是十分確切的。如其再找一下書寫和竹簡的關係，就更為明白。因為書寫時是左手拿簡，右手寫字，一般是一根簡一行字，並且為著左手拿簡方便起見，空白的簡是放在左邊的。等到把一根簡寫完，寫過的簡為著和空白的簡不相混，也就左手一根一根的向右邊推去，並且排好。在這種情形下排出的行款，總是寫好的第一根簡在最右，以次從右排到左，更由左手拿著的簡是直立的，而一般人手執細長之物是與手指垂直的；於是中國字的行款，成爲自上而下，自右而左了。

至於中國字體的寫法，橫行時每字的筆總是從左上角開始向右去寫，所以橫行的字自左而右，應當是中國字最合理的排列(這和亞拉伯文自右而左的筆順正好相反)。其所以歷來橫行字的排列自右而左，還是受到古代竹簡排行的影響，事實上寫來是很彆扭的。現在日本、韓國的市招大都改爲橫行自左而右了。台灣和香港目前的市招雖然仍是自右而左，但人類社會總需向方便的路走去，看來也不可能沿襲太久，改成爲自左而右，是可以預見的事。

桑樹本來是野生的喬木，滋生在黃河三角洲，商湯禱雨桑林，〈鄘風〉稱「期我乎桑中」，《莊子・養生主》稱「合乎桑林之舞」，在甲骨文中也屢見桑林巫舞的記錄，顯示著古代桑林瀰漫著一些區域。蠶絲的採取，應當和大量桑林的存在有關。到了現在，中國北部除去還採取野蠶的絲以外，仍然還可以養育家蠶，民國初年山西省就辦過蠶桑傳習所，蠶絲的產品在山西的國貨陳列所展覽過，只是就客觀條件說，華北養蠶的氣候早已不如四川(三國時蜀漢就靠錦的出口)，以後再趕不上長江下游，並且也趕不上珠江下游。更加上宋代以後，草棉逐漸移植中原，對於代替蠶絲的效用來說，比蔴好得太多(江南有黃道婆傳說，陝甘也是產棉區，卻無此傳說，顯示陝甘的棉不是從廣東海道傳來，因爲在新疆高昌早就種草棉了)，所以華北很少有家蠶蠶絲的生產了；但就歷史來說，仍不能忽略養蠶這一個事實。

從長沙馬王堆發現的彩繪來看，這種彩繪的方法，應當可以追溯到春秋或戰國時代的。《尚書・皐陶謨》(〈皐陶謨〉可能暫定爲戰國時代作品，但所記之事應當更早)說到「日、月、星辰、山、龍、華蟲作繪；宗彝、藻、火、粉米、黼、黻、絺繡，以五朵彰施於五色作服。」這裡指明了日、月、星辰、山、龍、華蟲在王的袞服上用繪，而其他比較簡單的圖案等用繡，正和馬王堆彩繪的禪衣可以參證。如其絲織品上可以彩繪，那就也當然可以用筆來寫字了(繪字今本作會，但馬鄭本的眞古文作繪)。若再證以《論語》中的「子夏問曰：『巧笑倩兮，美目盼兮，素以爲絢兮，何也？』子曰：『繪事後素。』」這個「素」字，一般注家都引〈考工記〉「凡畫繢之事，後素功」以爲證。《周禮》鄭玄《注》說「素，白朵也」，並不清楚。《論語》朱《注》說：「謂先以粉地爲質，而後施五朵」，說素功爲施粉，也有失舊義。所以素就是《說文解字》所說的「白緻繪……取其澤也。」「素功」是把繪面打磨光澤，然後才能在上面繪畫。也就是說繪畫時先要做好光面的繪帛。在孔子時，繪帛既然可以繪畫，自然也可以作爲寫字的用途了。

帛書的觀念爲用紙的第一步，存訓先生已經指明，現在再談造紙的開始。紙的發明雖然公認爲蔡倫的功績，但蔡倫仍然可能是一位改良的人，而不一定就是創始的人。其中最重要的證據是 1957 年在西安霸橋西漢墓中發現的許多古紙殘片。這些紙片經化驗以後，證明爲植物性纖維，並黏有蔴的殘存。當然這些紙片是否和後來的紙一樣作爲書寫之用是另一個問題，容以下討論。不過霸橋紙確是紙，而且是公元以前的紙，應當是不生問題的。

倘若比較霸橋紙和我所發現的居延紙，那就可以看出有趣的事實。霸橋紙是沒有文字的，居延紙有文字，而絕對的年代卻不清楚。當我做那篇〈論中國造紙術的原始〉的時候，把時代暫時定到永元十年(公元 98 年)的前後，這只能是那張紙最晚的下限。再晚的可能性不太多，而較早的可能性還存在著。因爲居延一帶發現過的木簡，永元兵物冊是時代最晚的一套編冊。其餘各簡的最下多數都在西漢時代，尤其是昭帝和宣帝的時期。如其討論居延紙的時代，下限可以到永元，上限還是可以溯至昭宣。只是爲了謹慎起見，當寫那篇稿子的時候，覺得寧可估計的晚些，不要估計的早些(在我做〈論漢代的陸運與水運〉的時候，我認爲漢代的商船不越過麻六甲海峽〔Strait Malacca〕，是從來講古代南海交通所有各種論斷之中，一個最保守的論斷，也是爲著謹慎的原故)，所以只說了下限而不說上限。現在西安霸橋既然發現了類似的紙，那麼這片居延紙的年代就不需規定的那麼極端的嚴格了。雖然絕對的年代還不清楚，但從與霸橋紙的相關性看來，霸橋紙應當在某種情形之下可以寫字的。

當時我要把居延紙的時代壓後的原因，是因爲我當時以爲蔡倫造紙不僅是一個技術問題，還要加上質料的問題。蔡倫以前都是以廢絮爲紙，到了蔡倫才開始如《後漢書‧蔡倫傳》所說：「造意用樹膚、蔴頭及敝布、魚網以爲紙。」這是不很正確的，因爲在霸橋紙造成的西漢時代，已經用蔴頭一類的植物纖維了。因而蔡倫造成的紙，不應當屬於質料方面，而是僅僅屬於技術方面。

如其蔡倫的紙屬於技術方面，其所造成的紙，一定比霸橋紙好，也一定比居延紙好。至於好到什麼程度，那是不妨加以推定的。因為不論霸橋紙或居延紙都是民間所有，這些紙都是只能將就算做紙，其實都是厚薄不勻稱，邊緣不規則的。照〈蔡倫傳〉說：「元興元年，奏上之」，那奏上給皇帝的紙，自然必需勻稱和規則。這是起碼的需要，也許就是當時可能的進展。如其真是這樣，這就在造紙的路程上，奠定了一個重要的基石，而開始使紙以書寫為主要的用途。

既然蔡倫以前的紙，是不勻稱、不整齊，那麼雖然可以用做書寫，其原有用途應當不全是為著書寫的，書寫只是附帶的用途，其主要的用途是什麼是需要再討論的。所以就得追溯到植物性紙的前身，動物性纖維的紙，以及所謂「漂絮」那一件事。

關於「漂絮」形成造紙的事，我在〈論中國造紙術的原始〉中，根據《說文》及段《注》的意見先申述過，陳槃先生再根據我的看法重申一次。「漂絮」對於紙的關係是有因果性的，但依照這些年中新材料的發現又得重新加以討論。

首先要問漂絮是漂洗什麼絮？是新絮還是舊絮？其次要問漂絮是做什麼用？為富人用，還是為窮人用？然後才好作進一步的申論。漂絮所漂的絮，依照文獻上材料來看，應當是舊絮不是新絮。新絮是清潔白皙的，用不著再漂。只要直接裝入袍內，便成絲棉袍了。所以要漂的，就是因為穿著了許多年的舊袍，裡面的絲棉從一片一片的便成了破碎的塊，再加上雜質和灰塵，使絲棉變了顏色，尤其是可能還加上氣味，就不能不再加以漂洗。漂洗以後，再撕成一片一片的形狀。雖然新絮的疏鬆潔白，是不可能再恢復的，不過漂洗以後比較黏緊一點的成張舊絮，仍然可以裝成為次等的絲棉袍的。這種成張的舊絮，不如新絮（今稱張棉）的溫煖，但裝多一點，仍然可以有其效用。從另一方面看，這種撕成無定形小張的舊絮，表面上卻比新絮要光滑。在非正式場合之中，也許更好作為書寫之用。

這種漂過的絮既然是用過的舊絮，而且還是用得差不多不堪再用的舊絮，經過漂洗、改造以後，當然是給窮人用而不是為富人用的。《論語》孔子說：「衣敝縕袍，與衣狐貉者立，而不恥者，其由也與？」縕袍指舊絮的袍，舊絮不如新絮煖，所以裝的臃腫，一看就知道。如其縕袍再加破敝，當然更不成樣子了，和裝狐貉之裘的人來比，是十分不成比例的。從這一點來看，漂絮的人當然也就是窮人了。《莊子·逍遙遊》說：「或以封，或不免於洴澼絖(卽漂絮)」，也正是一個貧富的對比。舊絮既然爲窮人裝袍之用，爲了價廉易得，應當有時也用舊絲的代替品上場，這種代替品也就是從舊絲的動物纖維內參用了舊麻破布一類的植物纖維，或甚至全部用了植物纖維，拿來打碎撕破，再用樹皮一類的黏性材料，黏結成一塊一塊無定形的薄片。拿這種代替品裝入袍中，雖然更不如舊絲絮的好，卻也一般可以作爲保煖之用。霸橋漢墓中發現的紙張，其中都是不定形的碎片，卻不曾在上面書寫過一字，我不相信這是作爲寫字用的紙張。最大的可能，還是次等「縕袍」之內所裝的「著」(也可能是〈公孫弘傳〉所說「布被」一類的覆蓋物，其中也有「著」的)。因爲年深日久，袍的裡和面都腐敗化去了(也許裡和面是絲製的，那就更容易腐朽，如其是薄麻製的，也比這種較爲堅緻的「紙」易腐些)，只剩了內部的「著」，這就是所謂霸橋紙，但是這種「紙」卻和居延有字的紙屬於同類的形式和質料，如其把這兩處不同的發現連結起來，正看出西漢一代(或者西漢到東漢)，從「假紙」到「眞紙」的演變。也更可以看出中國紙的演變和埃及的紙草走的是完全不同的道路。更進一步來說，如其我們從 (1) 古代桑林，(2) 育蠶，(3) 用絲棉作著，(4) 漂洗舊絲棉作著，(5) 用碎麻破布作舊絲棉的代用品，(6) 初期紙的作成及書寫，(7) 造紙方法的改進可以供皇帝的御用，就知道「紙」這一種文化上的重要工具，發明的經過，眞是一件不尋常的事。在人類文化史上是值得如何去推崇、去表揚的。

存訓先生這部大著，體大思精，牽涉中國全部書寫及銘刻的起源和演變，十分重要。承他不棄，要我來做跋。我本想就我所知道的一一的來介紹，並且補充一下。不過爲著體裁，應當有相當的斷制。所以我只就其中幾個比較重要的問題，依照我的看法，再來引申一下，因爲這是平常討論所討論不到的。當然對於一個問題，討論越多，也可能錯誤越多，這就希望存訓先生和讀者加以指正了。

出版品概況與集的編印

（一） 歷史語言研究所出版品的概述

在叙述集刊的大致以前，先將出版品的大致叙述一下。

歷史語言研究所因爲刊物的種類比較多，所以分類也比較複雜，爲明瞭起見，大致的系統是：

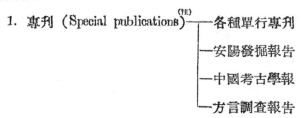

1. 專刊（Special publications）[注]——各種單行專刊
   ——安陽發掘報告
   ——中國考古學報
   ——方言調查報告

2. 單刊（Monographs）——甲種（Series A）——洋紙雙面印者
   ——乙種（Series B）——中國紙單面印者

3. 集刊（Bulletin）——集刊
   ——集刊外編

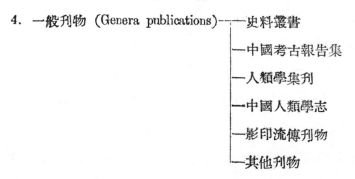

4. 一般刊物（Genera publications）——史料叢書
   ——中國考古報告集
   ——人類學集刊
   ——中國人類學志
   ——影印流傳刊物
   ——其他刊物

其中集刊是定期的論文專集；集刊中的論文倘若篇幅太長，可以刊行單冊的，卽

（注）　各類名稱大致據民國三十七年國立中央研究院歷史語言研究所出版品目錄，但各類之英文譯名，據二十二年國立中央研究院刊物目錄。

列為單刊。各種的專門著作歸入專刊。此外史料叢書，中國考古報告集，人類學集刊因為自成一個條貫，所以不列入專刊之內。安陽發掘報告因為在編次專刊之時即已編號，中國考古學報與安陽發掘報告性質相近，仍然編入專刊。

關於各種刊物的編號：在專刊之中，每種都有一個編號。單刊之中，甲種和乙種各有各的編號。集刊是每年出一本，倘若每季出一冊時，一冊即算作一分，四分合為一本。有時因為特殊的需要或特殊的情況下，再出集刊外編，如蔡孑民先生六十五時，集刊出了兩冊慶祝蔡元培先生六十五歲論文集，在四川李莊時因為印刷不便又出了兩種集刊外編，一為六同別錄，一為史料與史學，但復員南京之後仍然將這兩種編入集刊了。

中國考古報告集，編號為種，在一種之下再分為本，本下再分為冊。人類學集刊一年一卷，卷下再分期。史料叢書不編號，但史料叢書中的明清史料分甲乙丙丁等編，每編分十本。

截至現在，專刊已編號的共計有三十三種（其中有三種尚未印成），單刊甲種共計有二十一種（有一種未印成），單刊乙種共計有五種。集刊已出至第二十二本。一般刊物中史料叢書已出七種，中國考古報告集已出兩種三本，人類學集刊已出兩卷，中國人類學志已出一種，影印流傳書籍已出兩種，其他刊物已出四種。

現存最近的書目，是民國三十七年四月印成，當時由那廉君先生和我編次的。曾經由孟真先生看過。本所刊物的印刷，在民國二十四年以前由本所自行經理印刷。民國十七年出版的集刊第一本由香港商務印書館承印。以後印刷集刊第二本至第四本由上海中國科學儀器公司承印。其他刊物由北平京華印書局承印。至二十四年本所與商務印書館訂約承印本所書籍，並代為經銷。此後均由商務印書館承印。民國三十年香港淪陷以後，本所在李莊石印的有六同別錄，殷歷譜，莫話記略，上古音韻表稿及居延漢簡考釋。在重慶排印的有集刊第十本及史料與史學。

本所印刷事宜抗戰以前由孟真先生自行主持，抗戰時宜交由董彥堂先生主持。復員以後董先生出國，組織了一個出版委員會，因為在這個時期由我暫任集刊的編輯事項，為方便起見，當時所有的出版物，關於集稿，發排及校對，也由我經手再寄到上海去，直至董彥堂先生歸國為止。

關於印刷事務的經理，最先是吳亞農先生和陳驥塵先生，故程雨蒼先生也在北平曾過一個時期，抗戰以後，則由楊時逢先生經手。

（二） 集刊的編排與印刷

本所集刊是民國十七年十月在廣州創刊的。當時集稿的辦法，編排的辦法，和印刷的辦法都有獨特的風格，尤其是集稿的標準把歷史和語言兩種學問的範圍中，表現着新的方向：1. 開闢了現代語言學在中國發展的新園地。2 加強了歷史學和語言學中的密切聯繫。3. 切實闡明了在歷史範圍之內的，不論是歷史學，考古學，校勘學，人類學，民俗學，或者是比較藝術，都不是『經國之大業，不朽之盛事』，而是上天下地，動手動脚去找的材料。這個標準一直遺留下來，成為集刊穩固的基礎與堅定的方向。

集刊在第一和第二本時，由孟真先生自編，三本以後，組織編輯委員會，由孟真先生及陳寅恪、趙元任、李濟之，羅莘田諸先生擔任委員，而由莘田先生任常務，負集稿，付印，校稿等責任。到李莊以後常務一職由董彥堂先生擔任，一直到現在，只是董先生出國時期，由我暫行代為負責。

集刊在印刷方面每版是用着橫三十七字，直二十七行，共計九百九十九字的版心。這種版心有幾種好處，1. 每版比一千字只差一字，容易計算字數。2. 每版印的字比較多些。3. 字與字之間，不必插入鉛塊，易於排版。

封面的形式是從第二本開始決定的。在第一本時，封面只有國立中央研究院歷史語言研究所集刊的標題，和第一本的分數，刊印日期，發售地址。而內封面則有法文集刊標題："Institut National de Chine Bulletin de l'Institut Historique et Philoloque Tome 1: Fascicule 1——Canton 1928" 等字，但到第二本起，便封面前印上中文的目錄，底封面印英文的目錄，和以後集刊的形式完全相同了。集刊是有單行本印贈作者的，第一本刊印時印二十五冊單行本，第二本以後改為五十冊。第五本以後本來仍準備贈作者五十冊的，因為商務印書館為着銷路問題，希望減少，所以改為三十冊。但作者如預先要求加印至五十冊時，還是可以贈送的。

集刊論文排列的次序，完全以收稿的先後為序。只是六同別錄是依照各稿內容涉及的時代為先後的。後來改編為第十三本和第十四本，仍然按照這個次序。依時代為先後的好處是眉面清晰，條理井然；只是編輯時一經編定，便不能再行抽換改動，有些時候不方便罷了。

(三) 集刊文稿書寫格式

在田野考古報告刊行時候，曾經擬定了一個文稿書寫格式，不過只有傳抄，並未印出來。到抗日戰爭結束以後，便大致依照田野考古報告的書寫格式，再參照集刊過去一般習慣，擬定了一個書寫格式，分送給本所同人，以便為書寫時的根據，期望集刊各篇的書寫形式，大致可以歸於一律。當時擬定的格式如下：

今為排印便利，迅速，及免除錯誤起見，擬定下列書寫辦法，請寫稿時注意。

一、凡集刊文稿一律用集刊稿紙橫行書寫。

二、題目用大號字（鉛字頭號）從第三行起佔兩行。著者姓名從第五行寫起，用中號字（鉛字三號）佔一行。論文從第七行寫起。

三、論文之標題，照下列次序標之：

1. 分章標題用四號字，從第四字寫起，以一二三四標之，題佔一行。

2. 分節標題用五號字，從第三字寫起，以 1 2 3 4 標之，題佔一行。

3. 分段標題用五號字，從第二字寫起，以甲乙丙丁標之，題後空一字接寫之。

4. 分小段標題用五號字，從第三字寫起，以子丑寅卯標之，或用 a b c d 標之，題後空一字接寫。

四、每段開始空二字。句點，半句點，逗點，引號，括弧等均佔一字。引用之材料為大段者，各行前均空三字。

五、引號一律用雙引號，卽『 』；內引號用單引號，卽「 」。若中部再有引證，再用 " " 及 ' ' 為符號。

六、標號人名及地名用——，書名號用～～，加於字下。

七、括弧內之字，與括弧外相同，均用五號字排。附注用脚注 (Foot notes) 或注於全文之後一律用六號字排。若不得已而用舊式笺注體裁，請用小字雙行書寫，用六號字排，不加人地書名標號。

　　出版品和集刊都是孟真先生精心注意的成績。而其間董彥堂先生經手努力的地方也特別多。以上只是就我所知道的大略說一點。至於有關考古刊物在本所刊物中尤其佔重要的位置，還是李濟之先生始終其事的，濟之先生將另有文字，所以也不再詳述了。

（四） 集刊目錄的分類

　　集刊出到現在，已經有二十二本了。在二十本上冊以前，都在三十七年的出版品目錄中登載了各期論文的目錄。因為有四百多篇檢查不易，現在先作一個大致的分類，並且將二十本下冊和二十一本二十二本也加入到分類的目錄下面。

　　這一個分類的目錄，完全為便於檢查。所以分類也大致照着歷史語言研究所大致工作的範圍來分類。計為：1. 經籍問題及校勘。2. 歷史（一般性）。3. 哲學史及宗教史。4. 社會史及經濟史。5. 古代民族及古代地理。6. 古代藝術。7. 歷法及自然科學。8. 文學。9. 語言學，中國古音及現代漢語研究。10. 非漢語語文研究。11. 文字及訓詁。12. 考古學。13. 古器物學。14. 體質人類學。15. 文化人類學。這十五類四百四十八篇論文，另外還附有五篇紀念文字，都是傅孟真先生在世時寫成的。其中有許多是傅先生自己的文章，有許多是傅先生指導之下作成的，有許多是傅先生看過，修改過，或者討論過的。有許多是利用傅先生苦心搜集下的材料。現在因為時間有限，篇幅有限，不能一篇一篇的做提要或評論。但我想一想這一個分類的目錄拿來紀念傅先生也許還有若干用處，時間有限恐怕仍然免不了錯處，還請讀者賜教。

1. 經籍問題及校勘

跋唐寫本切韻殘卷　董作賓　第（1）本　　周易爻辭的時代及其作者　余永梁　（1）

周頌說　傅斯年　（1）

戰國文籍中之篇式書體一個短記　傅斯年　（1）

敦煌劫餘錄序　陳寅恪　（1）

論考證中國古書真偽之方法　高本漢著　王靜如譯　（2）

彰所知論與蒙古源流　陳寅恪　（2）　　蒙古源流作者世系考　陳寅恪　（2）

劫灰錄跋　朱希祖　（2）　　　　　　戴東原續方言稿序　羅常培　（2）

學考叙目　丁　山　（3）　　　　　重印朝鮮世寶實錄地理志序　孟　森　（3）

鹽鐵論校記　勞　榦　（5）　　　　　　豳風說　徐中舒　（6）

誰是齊物論的作者　傅斯年　（6）　　　記唐音統籤　兪大綱　（7）

敦煌石室寫經題記序　陳寅恪　（8）

敦煌本心王投陀經及法句經跋尾　陳寅恪　（8）

讀洛陽伽藍記書後　陳寅恪　（8）　　　唐集志疑　岑仲勉　（8）

讀全唐詩札記　岑仲勉　（9）　　　　　跋封氏聞見記　岑仲勉　（9）

跋唐摭言　岑仲勉　（9）　　　　　　　續勞格讀全唐詩札記　岑仲勉　（9）

論白氏長慶源流並評東洋李白集　岑仲勉　（9）

白氏長慶集僞文　岑仲勉　（9）

白集醉吟先生墓志存疑　岑仲勉　（9）　兩京新記卷三殘卷復原　岑仲勉　（9）

古讖緯書錄解題四種　陳　槃　（10）　敦煌唐咸通三備殘卷解題　陳　槃　（10）

居延漢簡考釋序目　勞　榦　（10）　　登科記考訂補　岑仲勉　（11）

補唐代翰林兩記　岑仲勉　（11）　　　讖緯釋名　陳　槃　（11）

讖緯溯原　陳　槃　（11）　　　　　　古讖緯書錄解題　陳　槃　（12）（17）（22）

古讖緯全佚書存目解題　陳　槃　（12）　古詩紀補正叙例　逯欽立　（12）

讀高青邱威愛論　王崇武　（12）

跋歷史語言研究所所藏明末談刻及道光三讓本太平廣記　岑仲勉　（12）

四庫提要古器物銘非金石錄辨　岑仲勉(12)　宣和博古圖撰人　岑仲勉　（12）

從金澤圖錄白集影葉所見　岑仲勉　（12）

文苑英華辨證校白氏詩文附按　岑仲勉　（12）

從文苑英華『中書』『翰林制誥』兩門所收白氏文論白集　岑仲勉　（12）

補白集原流事證數則　岑仲勉　（12）　居延漢簡補正　勞　榦　（14）

王逸集牙籤考證　張政烺　（14）　　　翰林學士壁記補注　岑仲勉　（14）

跋南嶽紀談　岑仲勉　（15）　　　　　茆泮林莊子司馬彪注考逸補正　王叔岷(15)

漢晉遺簡偶述　陳　槃　（16）

古讖緯書錄解題附錄　陳　槃　（17）　說文序引尉律解　張政烺　（17）

唐臨冥報記之復原　岑仲勉　(17)

記明實錄　吳晗　(18)　　　　　後漢書殘本跋　傅斯年　(18)

北宋刊南宋補刊十行史記集解跋　傅斯年　(18)

北宋刊南宋補刊十行史記集解後跋　勞榦　(18)

絳守居園記集解附絳守居園記句解書目提原　岑仲勉　(19)

易林斷歸崔篆的判決書　胡適　(20)　　宋范祖禹書古文孝經石刻校釋　馬衡　(20)

南宋寫本南華眞經校記　王叔岷　(20)　　莊子校釋後記　王叔岷　(21)

讖緯命名及其相關之諸問題　陳槃　(21)　　說文引秘書爲賈逵說辨正　張政烺　(21)

跋日本高山寺舊抄卷子本莊子殘卷　王叔岷　(22)

洛陽伽藍記補注體例辨　徐高阮　(22)

兩宋諸史監本存佚考　趙萬里　(慶祝蔡元培先生六十五歲論文集以下簡稱蔡論集)

元典章校補釋例　陳垣　(蔡論集)

Surun Passage du "Cheng-won ts'ing-Tcheng lou". Paul Pelliot　(蔡論集)

2. 歷　史　(一般性)

建文遜國傳說的演變　胡適　(1)

明季桐城中江社考　朱倓　(1)　　　　吐蕃彝泰贊普名號年代考　陳寅恪　(2)

召穆公傳　丁山　(2)　　　　　論所謂『五等爵』　傅斯年　(2)

鈔本甲乙事案跋　朱希祖　(2)　　　吳三桂周王元年釋疑　朱希祖　(2)

明成祖生母記疑　傅斯年　(2)　　　李唐氏族之推測　陳寅恪　(3)

清始祖布庫雍順之考訂　孟森　(3)　　李唐氏族之推測後記　陳寅恪　(3)

由陳侯因資錞銘黃帝論五帝　丁山　(3)

再述內閣大庫檔案之由來及其整理　徐中舒　(3)

說儒　胡適　(4)　　　　　　　周東封與殷遺民(互見地理類)　傅斯年　(4)

宗法考源　丁山　(4)

戈射與弩之溯及關於此類名物之考釋　徐中舒　(4)

讀姚大榮馬閣老洗冤錄駁議　容肇祖　(5)　　武曌與佛敎　陳寅恪　(5)

李德裕貶死年月及歸葬傳說考辨　陳寅恪　(5)

三論李唐氏族問題　陳寅恪　（5）　　　金史氏族表初稿　陳　述　（5）

蒙古史札記　岑仲勉　（5）　　　　　　明懿文太子生母考　李晉華　（6）

明成祖生母問題彙證　李晉華　（6）　　跋明成祖問題彙證並答朱希祖先生　傅斯年（6）

兩唐書玄宗元獻皇后楊氏傳考異兼論張燕公事蹟　兪大綱　（6）

內閣大庫殘餘檔案內洪承疇報銷冊序　李光濤　（6）

明初建州女眞居地遷徙考　徐中舒　（6）　　三朝北盟會編考　陳樂素　（6）

八旗制度考實　孟　森　（6）　　　　　　五等爵在殷商　董作賓　（6）

李唐武周先世事蹟雜考　陳寅恪　（6）　　東晉南朝之吳語　陳寅恪　（7）

阿保機與李克用盟結兄弟之年及其背盟相攻之推測　陳　述　（7）

殷周之際史蹟之檢討　徐中舒　（7）　　春秋『公矢魚于棠』說　陳槃　（7）

明太祖遣僧使日本考　黎光明　（7）　　府兵前期史料試釋　陳寅恪　（7）

新元史本證　陳叔陶　（7）

南朝境內之各種人及政府對待之政策　周一良　（7）

中國丹沙之應用及其推演　勞　榦　（7）　曳落河考釋及其相關諸問題　陳述　（7）

劉復愚遺文中年月及其不祀祖問題　陳寅恪　（8）

東都事略撰人王賞稱父子　陳　述　（8）　明史德王府世系表訂誤　李晉華　（8）

從漢簡所見的邊郡制度　勞　榦　（8）　　契丹世選考　陳　述　（8）

明初之用兵與堡寨　王崇武　（8）　　　　頭下考　陳　述　（8）

論魏孝文之遷都與華化　勞　榦　（8）　　貞石證史　岑仲勉　（8）

清人入關前求欵之始末　李光濤　（9）　　漢代兵制及漢簡中的兵制　勞　榦　（10）

論明太祖起兵及其策略之轉變王崇武（10）　漢武後元不立年號考　勞　榦　（10）

宋史職官志考正　鄧廣銘　（10）　　　　查繼佐與敬修堂釣業　王崇武　（10）

兩漢刺史制度考　勞　榦　（11）　　　　漢代社祀的源流　勞　榦　（11）

跋高句麗大兄冉牟墓誌兼論高句麗都城之位置　勞　榦　（11）

兩關遺址考　勞　榦　（11）　　　　　　讀明史朝鮮傳　王崇武　（12）

舊唐書逸文辨　岑仲勉　（12）　　　　　回回一詞的語源　岑仲勉　（12）

吐魯番木柱刻文略釋　岑仲勉　（12）　　清太宗求欵始末提要　李光濤　（12）

清入關前的眞象　李光濤　（12）

記奴爾哈赤之倡亂及薩爾滸之戰　李光濤　（12）

論建州與流賊相因亡明　李光濤　（12）

記清太宗皇太極三字稱號由來　李光濤　（12）

記崇禎四年南海島大捷　李光濤　（12）　　清太宗與三國演義　李光濤　（12）

謚法濫觴於殷代論　屈萬里　（13）　　論漢代的內朝與外朝　勞　榦　（13）

劉綎征東考　王崇武　（14）　　宋遼聘使表稿　傅樂煥　（14）

續貞石史　岑仲勉　（15）　　唐方鎮表正補　岑仲勉　（15）

抄明李英征曲先故事並略釋　岑仲勉（15）　　遼金乣軍史料試釋　谷霽光　（15）

秦漢間所謂符應論略　陳　槃　（16）　　論漢代之陸運與水運　勞　榦　（16）

魏晉南朝的兵制　何茲全　（16）　　李如松征東考　王崇武　（16）

遼史復文舉例　傅樂煥　（16）　　戰國秦漢方士考論　陳　槃　（17）

漢代察舉制度考　勞　榦　（17）

論萬歷征東島山之戰及明清薩爾滸之戰　王崇武　（17）

明成祖朝鮮選妃考　王崇武　（17）　　阿保機卽位考辨　楊志玖　（17）

洪承疇背明始末　李光濤　（17）　　魏晉之中軍　何茲全　（17）

北魏尚書制度考　嚴耕望　（18）　　論崇禎二年己巳虜變　李光濤　（18）

北朝地方政府屬佐考　嚴耕望　（19）　　毛文記釀亂東江始末　李光濤　（19）

論中國造紙術之原始　勞　榦　（19）　　釋漢代之亭障與烽燧　勞　榦　（19）

論早期讖緯及其與鄒衍書說之關係　陳　槃　（20）

董文驥與明史記事本末　王崇武　（20）

朝鮮壬辰倭禍中之平壤戰役與南海戰役　李光濤　（20）

釋偘楚　余嘉錫　（20下）　　讀魏書李冲傳論宗主制　余　遜　（20下）

洪武二十年太孫改律及三十年律誥考　黃彰健　（20下）

宋史刑法志考正　鄧廣銘　（20下）　　殷禮的含貝與握貝　高去尋　（20下）

乣軍考釋　陳　述　（20下）　　清末漢陽鐵廠　全漢昇　（21）

古社會田狩與祭祀之關係　陳　槃　（21）　　記明季朝鮮倭禍之中原漢奸　李光濤（21）

明季流寇始末　李光濤　(21)　　　　侯與射侯　陳　槃　(22)

漢代的亭制　勞　榦　(22)　　　　　九族制與爾雅釋親　芮逸夫　(22)

漢代地方官之籍貫限制　嚴耕望　(22)　　朝鮮壬辰倭禍與李如松東征　李光濤(22)

記朝鮮宣廟中興誌　李光濤　(22)

後金汗國姓氏考　朱希祖　(慶祝蔡元培先生六十五歲論文集)

戰國後中國內戰的統計和治亂的週期　李四光　(蔡論集)

　　3. 哲學史及宗敎史

大乘義章書後　陳寅恪　(1)　　　　　南嶽大師立誓願文跋　陳寅恪　(3)

天師道與濱海地域之關係　陳寅恪　(3)　武曌與佛敎　陳寅恪　(5)

楞伽宗考　胡　適　(5)　　　　　　　三百年前的建立孔敎論　陳受頤　(6)

論太平經抄甲部之僞　王　明　(18)　　周易參同契考證　王　明　(19)

浮圖與佛　季羨林　(20)　　　　　　黃庭經考　王　明　(20)

禁不得祠明星出西方諸問題　陳　槃　(21)

支愍度學說考　陳寅恪　(蔡論集)　　　陶宏景的眞誥考　胡　適　(蔡論集)

譯注明成祖遣使召宗喀巴紀事及宗喀巴釋成祖書　于道泉　(蔡論集)

　　4. 社會史及經濟史

耒耜考　徐中舒　(2)　　　　　　　　漢代奴隸制度　勞　榦　(5)

證高力士外傳釋『變造』『和糴』之法　俞大綱　(5)

古代灌漑工程起源考　徐中舒　(5)

南宋杭州的消費與外地商品之輸入　全漢昇　(7)

北宋汴梁的輸出入貿易　全漢昇　(8)　宋代廣州的國內外貿易　全漢昇　(8)

宋代南方的虛市　全漢昇　(9)　　　　中古自然經濟　全漢昇　(10)

宋末通貨膨脹及其對於物價的影響　全漢昇　(10)

南宋稻米的生產與運銷　全漢昇　(10)　漢簡中的河西經濟生活　勞　榦　(11)

唐代物價的變動　全漢昇　(11)

唐宋時代楊州經濟景況的繁與衰落　全漢昇　(11)

北宋物價的變動　全漢昇　(11)　　　　南宋初年物價的大變動　全漢昇　(11)

宋金間的走私貿易　全漢昇　（11）　東晋南朝的錢幣使用與錢幣問題　何玆全　（14）

元代的紙幣　全漢昇　（15）　　　唐宋政府歲入與貨幣經濟的關係　全漢昇（20）

古代灌漑工程發展史之一解　翁文灝（蔡論集）

　　5. 古代民族及古代地理。

周頌說（附論魯南兩地與詩書之來源）　傅斯年　（1）

靈州寧夏楡林三城澤名考　陳寅恪　（1）　殷人服象及象之南遷　徐中舒　（2）

大東小東說　傅斯年　（2）　　　姜原　傅斯年　（2）

殷周文化之蠡測　徐中舒　（2）　　論阻卜與韃靼　王靜如　（2）

獻夷考　丁　山　（2）　　　清史稿中建州衞考辨　孟　森　（3）

重印朝鮮世宗實錄地理志序　孟　森　（3）　周東封與殷遺民　傅斯年　（4）

漢晋閩中建置考　勞　榦　（5）　　兩漢戶籍與地理之關係　勞　榦　（5）

兩漢各郡人口增減數目之推測　勞　榦（5）　說廣陵之曲江　傅斯年　（6）

明初建州女眞居地遷徙考　徐中舒　（6）　漢魏晋北朝東北諸郡沿革表　余　遜　（6）

南朝境內之各種人及政府對待之政策　周一良　（7）

說宇文周之種族　周一良　（7）　　發羌之地望與對音　鄭天挺　（8）

外蒙於都斤山考　岑仲勉　（8）

魏書司馬叡傳江東民族條釋證及推論　陳寅恪　（11）

天山南路元代設驛之今地　岑仲勉　（11）　吐魯番一帶漢回地名對證　岑仲勉　（12）

理番新發見隋會州通道記跋　岑仲勉（12）　元初西北五城之地理考古　岑仲勉　（12）

象郡牂柯與夜郎的關係　勞　榦　（14）　舊唐書地理志舊領縣之表解　岑仲勉（20）

北魏洛陽城圖的復原　勞　榦　（20）　僚爲仡佬試釋　芮逸夫　（20）

兩漢州制考　顧頡剛　（蔡論集）　　夷夏東西說　傅斯年　（蔡論集）

　　6. 古代藝術

調查雲岡造象小記　趙邦彥　（1）　論魯西畫象三種　勞　榦　（8）

漢畫所見游戲考　趙邦彥　（蔡論集）　古代狩獵圖象考　徐中舒　（蔡論集）

　　7. 歷法及其他自然科學

幾何原本滿文譯本跋　陳寅恪　（2）　叢甓甲骨金文中所涵殷歷推證　吳其昌（4）

殷歷中幾個重要問題　董作賓　（4）　　　陽燧取火與方諸取水　唐擘黃　（5）

殷商疑年　董作賓　（7）　　　　　　　　殷歷譜後記　董作賓　（13）

殷代月食考　董作賓　（22）　　　　　　　十二等律發明者朱載堉　劉復　（蔡論集）

　　　8. 文　學

敦煌本維摩詰結文殊師利問疾品演義跋　陳寅恪　（2）

西遊記玄奘弟子故事之演變　陳寅恪（2）　　花月痕的作者魏秀仁傳　容肇祖　（4）

李德裕貶死年月及歸葬傳說考辨　陳寅恪　（5）

說彈詞　李家瑞　（6）　　　　　　　　　敦煌寫本張淮深變文跋　孫楷弟　（7）

由說書變成戲劇的痕跡　李家瑞　（7）　　　讀東城老父傳　陳寅恪　（10）

讀鶯鶯傳　陳寅恪　（10）　　　　　　　　講史與詠史詩　張政烺　（10）

玉溪生年譜會箋平質　岑仲勉　（15）　　　說文筆　逯欽立　（16）

形影神詩及東晉佛道思想　逯欽立　（16）　問答錄與說參請　張政烺　（17）

述酒詩題注釋疑　逯欽立　（18）　　　　　元微之悼亡詩及艷體詩箋證　陳寅恪（20）

陶淵明年譜稿　逯欽立　（20）　　　　　　一枝花語　張政烺　（20下）

敦煌本韓朋賦考　容肇祖　（蔡論集）

　　　9. 語言學，中國古音及現代漢語研究。

聲調之推斷及『聲調推斷尺』之製造與用法　劉　復　（1）

慧琳一切經音義反切聲類考　黃淬伯（1）　耶穌會士在音韻學上的貢獻　羅常培（1）

楊選杞聲韻同然集殘稿跋　羅常培　（1）

上古中國音當中的幾個問題　高本漢著　趙元任譯　（1）

跋高本漢的『上古中國音當中的幾個問題』並論冬蒸兩部　王靜如　（1）

顎音跋　劉文錦　（1）　　　　　　　　　閩音研究　陶燠民　（1）

關於瑽櫛韻的討論　（第一本附錄）　　　支脂之三部古讀考　林語堂　（2）

中國古音（切韻）之系統及其演變　高本漢著　王靜如譯　（2）

聽寫倒英文（英文）趙元任　（2）　　　　反切語八種　趙元任　（2）

用 b d g 當不吐氣清破裂音(英文)　趙元任　（2）

切韻魚虞之音值及其所據方言考　羅常培　（2）

中原音韻聲類考　羅常培　（2）　　　釋重輕　羅常培　（2）

兒音（a）的演變　唐虞　（2）

Dr. Jones, Kwing Tong Woo 共作的 Supplement to the Cantonese Phonetic Reader 的

勘誤　劉學濬　（2）　　　　　切韻 â 的來源　李方桂　（3）

康熙字典字母切韻要法考證　趙蔭棠（3）　知徹澄娘音值考　羅常培　（3）

集韻聲類考　白滌洲　（3）　　　　洪武正韻聲類考　劉文錦　（3）

敦煌寫本守溫學殘卷跋　羅常培　（3）

對於中國古音重訂的貢獻　卓古諾夫著　唐虞譯　（3）

東冬屋沃之上古音(英文)　李方桂　（3）　記咸陽方言　劉文錦(附劉君傳)　（3）

漢字的字調跟語調(英文)　趙元任　（4）　釋內外轉　羅常培　（4）

泰興何石閭韻史稿本跋　羅常培　（4）　乙二聲調推斷尺　劉復　（4）

音位標音法的多能性(英文)　趙元任（4）　關中聲調實驗錄　白滌洲　（4）

論中國上古音的－ i wang,－ i wak,－ i wag（英文）　李方桂　（5）

方言性變態語音三例　趙元任　（5）　　中國方言當中爆發音的種類　趙元任（5）

通志七音略研究　羅常培　（5）　　就元秘史譯文所見之中國人稱代名詞　王靜如(5)

與高本漢先生商榷『自由押韻』說兼論上古楚方音特色　董同龢　（7）

經典釋文和原本玉篇反切的匣于兩紐　羅常培　（8）

喻三入匣再證　葛毅卿　（8）　　　廣韻重紐試釋　董同龢　（13）

廣韻重紐的研究　周法高　（13）　　切韻魚虞之音讀及其流變　周法高　（13）

說平仄　周法高　（13）　　　　楚文 t d 的對音　周法高　（14）

等韻門法通釋　董同龢　（14）　　切韻指掌圖諸問題　董同龢　（17）

上古音韻表稿　董同龢　（18）　　陽華涼水井客家話記音　董同龢　（19）

全本王仁煦刊謬補缺切韻的反切下字　董同龢　（19）

古音中的三等韻　周法高　（19）　　中山方言　趙元任　（20）

唐本說文與說文舊音　周祖謨　（20）　玄應反切考　周法高　（20）

中國語的詞類　周法高　（23）

A Prehininary Study of Enghih Intonation (With American Variants) and its Chinese

Equivalents. 趙元任 (蔡論集)

Some Turkish Transcriptions is the Light of Irregular Aspirates in Mandarin. B. Karlgren (蔡論集)

On a Peking, a St. Petersberg and a Kyoto Reconstruction of a Sanskrit Stanza Transcribed with Chinese Characters under Northern Sung Dynasty. A. von Stael-Holslein (蔡論集)

陳宋淮楚歌寒對轉考 林語堂 (蔡論集)

切韻閉口九韻之古讀及其演變 羅常培 (蔡論集)

關中入聲之變化 白滌洲 (蔡論集)

    10. 非漢語語文研究

記保儸音(英文) 史祿國 (1)　　　廣西凌雲猺語 李方桂 (1)

西夏文漢藏譯音釋略 王靜如 (2)　　　聽寫倒英文(英文) 趙元任 (2)

西文佛母孔雀明王經考釋序 陳寅恪 (2)

中台藏緬數目字及人稱代名詞語源試探 王靜如 (3)

梵文顎音五母之藏漢對音研究 羅常培 (3)

釋定海方氏所藏四體字『至元通寶』錢文 王靜如 (3)

藏文前綴音對於聲母的影響(英文) 李方桂 (4)

遼道宗及定懿皇后契丹國字哀冊初釋 王靜如 (4)

契丹國字再釋 王靜如 (5)　　　廣西太平府屬土州縣司譯語考 聞宥 (6)

Voiced plosives and Affricates in Ancient Tibetan A. Dragunov (7)

The Hypothesis of A Pre-glottalized Series of Consonants in Primitive Tai 李方桂(11)

武鳴土語音義 李方桂 (12)　　　苗傜語聲調問題 張琨 (16)

記栗粟音兼論所謂栗粟文 芮逸夫 (17) 莫話記略 李方桂 (19)

Chipewyan Consonant 李方桂 (蔡論集)

佛母孔雀明王經龍王大仙衆生名號夏梵藏漢合璧校釋 王靜如 (蔡論集)

    11. 文字及訓詁

釋朱 商承祚 (1)　　　　　殷契亡尤說 丁山 (1)

數名古誼 丁 山 （1） 　　　說冀 丁 山 （1）

剡字解 徐中舒 （1） 　　　漢字中之拼音字 林語堂 （2）

金文嘏辭釋例 徐中舒 （6） 　　　骨文例 董作賓 （7）

說滴 葛毅卿 （7） 　　　釋牢 胡厚宣 （8）

卜辭雜例 董作賓 （8） 　　　論雍巳在五期背甲上的位置 董作賓 （8）

釋𢆶用與𢆶御 胡厚宣 （8） 　　　卜辭同文例 胡厚宣 （9）

六書古義 張政烺 （10） 　　　論詩經的何曷胡 丁聲樹 （10）

『何當』解 丁聲樹 （11） 　　　『碚』字音讀答問 丁聲樹 （11）

卜辭記事文字史官簽名例 胡厚宣 （12） 　　　奭字說 張政烺 （13）

說文燕召公名醜解 張政烺 　　　自不跟解 屈萬里 （13）

甲骨文从比二字辨 屈萬里 （13） 　　　甲骨文類比研究例 張京權 （20下）

積微居字說 楊樹達 （20下） 　　　早晚與何當 丁聲樹 （21）

甲骨文斷代研究例 董作賓 （蔡論集） 　　　刑中與中庸 丁 山 （蔡論集）

右文說在訓詁學上之沿革及其推測 沈兼士 （蔡論集）

釋否定詞弗不 丁聲樹 （蔡論集）

12. 考古學

平陵訪古記 吳金鼎 （1） 　　　甲骨年表 董作賓 （2）

昂昂溪史前遺址 梁思永 （4） 　　　譚『譚』 董作賓 （4）

山東滕縣下黃溝村宋代墓葬調查記 潘懋 （11）

河南後岡的殷墓 石璋如 （13） 　　　傳說中周都的實地考察 石璋如 （20下）

小屯龍山與仰韶 梁思永 （蔡論集）

13. 古器物學 （附金文）

匜敦跋 丁 山 （2） 　　　遹敦考釋 徐中舒 （3）

當塗出土晉代遺物考 徐中舒 （3） 　　　陳侯四器考釋 徐中舒 （3）

莽權價值之重新考訂 劉復 （3） 　　　戈戟餘論 郭寶鈞 （5）

說尊彝 徐中舒 （7） 　　　邵王之諹鼎及殷銘考證 張政烺 （8）

四庫提要古器物銘非金石錄辨 岑仲勉 （12）

宣和博古圖撰人　岑仲勉　(12)　　　研究中國古玉問題的新資料　李　濟　(13)

評『漢前古鏡的研究』並論淮式鏡之時代問題　高去尋　(14)

古玉新銓　郭寶鈞　(20下)　　　　豫北出土青銅器史兵分類圖解　李　濟　(22)

小屯殷代成套兵器　石璋如　(22)　　從實驗上窺漢石經之一斑　馬　衡　(蔡論集)

殷盧銅器五種及其相關之問題　李　濟　(蔡論集)

宋代吉金書籍逃評　容　庚　(蔡論集)　　古器釋名　郭寶鈞　(蔡論集)

14. 體質人類學

Evidence of the Asymmetry of the Human skull derived from Contour Measurement.

　吳定良　(蔡論集)

On the Influence of the Observational Error in Measuring Stature, Span and Sitting

　height upon the resulting Indices.　丁文江　(蔡論集)

15. 文化人類學

占卜的源流　容肇祖　(1)　　　　廣東北江傜山雜記　龐新民　(2)

九子母考　趙邦彥　(3)　　　　　粵西傜山調查雜記　龐新民　(4)

記廣東北江傜山荒洞傜人之建醮　姜哲夫　(4)

拜王　姜哲夫等　(4)　　　　　打花鼓　李家瑞　(5)

關於壓夢之名稱分佈與遷移　陶雲逵　(7)

幾個雲南土族的現代地理分佈及其人口之估計　陶雲逵　(7)

伯叔姨舅姑考　芮逸夫　(14)　　　苗語釋親　芮逸夫　(14)

倮文作齋經譯注　馬學良　(14)　　番民圖騰文化之研究　凌純聲　(16)

釋甥舅之稱謂　芮逸夫　(16)

倮文作齋獻藥供牲經譯注　馬學良　(20)

乾隆以來北平兒歌嬗變舉例　李家瑞　(蔡論集)

16. 紀念文字

發刊辭　蔡元培　(1)　　　　歷史語言研究所工作之旨趣　本所籌備處(1)

李晉華君事略　(8)　　　　　　陶雲逵君事略　(17)

撰文人共上蔡元培先生書　(蔡論集)

十一、英文論著

Six-Tusked Elephants on A Han Bas-relief

I wish to express my gratitude to Professor L. S. Yang for valuable discussions and to Dr. Kenneth CH'EN for calling my attention to several importan pictures in Indian art.

The exact date of the introduction of Buddhism into China is not known, nor are traditional stories on the early contact between China and India reliable since they are usually mixed with legend.① The most credible early record is to be found in the biography of Prince Ying of Ch'u 楚王英 in *Hou-Han shu*.② In the reign of Ming-ti 明帝, Prince Ying worshipped Buddha in his princedom, a practice that was approved by the Emperor in a decree issued to the prince in the year 65 A.D. During the one hundred and fifty-seven years from this time to the fall of the Later Han dynasty in 222 A.D., there were few historical records pertaining to Buddhism. The story of the first missionaries, Kāśyapa Mātaṅga and Dharmaraksa, and that of the establishment of the White Horse Monastery are evidently not reliable. Buddhist temples seem to have been built③ and Buddhist art may have been introduced into China during this period. However, no relics from this time have been noted by Oriental and Western scholars, and Buddhist art in China is generally supposed to have begun in the Six Dynasties.

I have found a depiction of six-tusked elephants on a bas-relief from T'eng-hsien 滕縣 (Fig. 1) which apparently is an indication of early Buddhist influence on Chinese art.④ The date of this relief, judging from its technique and style, must be Later Han. I have also seen in the collection of Academia Sinica, now in Taiwan, an ink-rubbing of another T'eng-hsien relief dated Chien-ch'u 建初 (76-83 A.D.) in the reign of Chang-ti 章帝. Presumably the bas-relief depicting six-tusked elephants also dates from about the same era.

T'eng-hsien is situated in the southern part of Shantung, not far from the city of Hsü-chou in Kiangsu which in Later Han times was the capital of the princedom of Ch'u. From the existence of the bas-relief there, it is evident that Buddhist influence in this coastal area was already considerable in the first century A.D.

In Buddhist legend, the six-tusked elephant was one of the innumerable previous incarnations of the Buddha. While he was living as an elephant king in the forests of the Himalayas, his second wife died from jealousy and being reincarnated as a queen of Benares, charged a skilled hunter to kill the elephant king. The latter, being the manifestation of a bodhisattva, was impervious to any evil, but he allowed himself to be killed, offering his tusks to the hunter before he died. The queen, on seeing the tusks, also died, heartbroken.

In an ancient sculpture from Sāñchī (Fig.2)[5] and in an Ajaṇṭā wall paintng (Fig.3)[6] the elephant king with six tusks is shown as the main subject, but in other Indian sculptures, the elephant king is generally represented with two tusks. Alfred Foucher devoted a special chapter to the subject,[7] but he noted only the elephant with one or two tusks and was unaware of the fact that one with six tusks had been depicted. In the original edition of Albert Grünwedel's *Buddhistische Kunst in Indien*[8] neither illustrations nor explanations of the six-tusked elephant are found, but the English version enlarged by James Burgess includes one picture of the six-tusked elephant,[9] and the revised German edition of Ernst

Waldschmidt contains as many as four.[10] In more recent publications, illustrations of the six-tusked elephant are given in René Grousset's *The Civilizations of the East*[11] and in Benjamin Rowland's *The Art and Architecture of India*,[12] but in these works the explanations for the six tusks are not especially detailed.

Buddhist traditions concerning the six-tusked elephant may best be classified into three groups: the previous incarnation of the Buddha,[13] the elephant of Indra, king of the gods,[14] the elephant of Samantabhadra 普賢 Bodhisattva.[15] The representations on most ancient Indian sculptures belong to the first of these groups.

The elephants on the T'eng-hsien bas-relief, however, seem to belong to the second group, because people with weapons are shown riding them. In Indian legend Indra rides a six-tusked elephant into battle against the asuras or warring demons, since this elephant can be changed into many other elephants with six-tusks. It is likely that stories about the six-tusked elephant were imported into China, but its representation in Chinese art was not necessarily copied from an Indian example, for both show a considerable difference in style. For example, in Indian art the tusks are arranged parallelly, three on each side; but in the T'eng-hsien relief only two of the three tusks on a side are parallel.

Examples of Samantabhadra Bodhisattva riding the six-tusked elephant may be seen in the wall paintings of Tun-huang. One of these is reproduced in Aurel Stein's *The Thousand Buddhas*,[16] and four are in Paul Pelliot's *Les grottes de Touen-houang*.[17] These paintings may be assigned to the Sui or T'ang dynasties. In addition, an early Japanese Painting on the same subject has come down from the Heian Period.[18]

FIGURE 1

BAS-RELIEF FROM TENG-HSIEN
(Corpus des pierres sculptées Han)

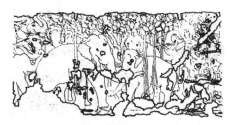

FIGURE 3

AJANTA WALL PAINTING (CAVE X)
(The Art and Architecture of India)

FIGURE 2

SCULPTURE FROM SĀÑCHĪ
(Courtesy of the Musée Guimet)

PLATE I

FIGURE 4

TENG-HSIEN WALL PAINTING
(Photograph by Sun Chang-ju)

PLATE II

1. T'ang Yung-t'ung 湯用彤, *Han Wei Liang-Chin Nan-pei-ch'ao Fo-chiao shih* 漢魏兩晉南北朝佛教史 (Shanghai, 1938) 16-30.

2. *Hou Han shu* (K'ai-ming ed.) 72 (*lieh-chuan* 32) .5b-6a.

3. Henri Maspero, "Le songe et l'ambassade de l'Empereur Ming," *BEFEO* 10 (1910). 95-130; and "Les origines de la communauté bouddhiste de Lo-yang," *JA* 225(1934). 86-107.

4. *Corpus des pierres sculptées Han*, published by Centre d'études sinologiques de Pékin (Peking, 1950), Vol. I, Plate 113.

5. Photograph reproduced by courtesy of the Musée Guimet, Paris.

6. Cf. Benjamin Rowland, *The Art and Architecture of India* (Baltimore, 1953), p. 66, Fig · 5. Reproduced here by permission of the author.

7. *The Beginnings of Buddhist Art* (Paris, 1917), pp. 185-97.

8. Berlin, 1893, 1900.

9. Grünwedel, *Buddhist Art in India*, translated by Agnes C. Gibson, revised and enlarged by James Burgess (London, 1901), p. 157, Pl. 108.

10. Grünwedel, *Buddhistische Kunst in Indien*, revised by Ernst Waldschmidt(Berlin, 1932), p. 55 and Plates 73, 74, 93.

[11] New York, 1931-1941. Cf. Vol. 2, p. 13, Fig. 7.

[12] See note 6.

[13] *Hua-yen ching* 華嚴經 (60 *chüan* version) (*Taishō Tripitaka* [hereafter *TT*] Vol. 9, No. 278) 7.439; *Hua-yen ching* (80 *chüan* version) (*TT* Vol. 10, No.279)15.79;*Ta chuang-yen lun* 大莊嚴論 (*TT* Vol. 4, No. 201)12.33;*Fo pen-hsing chi ching* 佛本行集經 (*TT* Vol. 3, No. 190)56.910.

[14] *Ta chih-tu lun* 大智度論 (*TT* Vol. 25, No. 1509) 56.146; *Ta pao chi ching* 大寶積經 (*TT* Vol. 11, No. 310)66.377; *Ting sheng wang yin-yüan ching* 頂生王因緣經 (*TT* Vol .3, No. 165) 5.402-04.

[15] *Miao-fa lien-hua ching* 妙法蓮華經 (*TT* Vol. 1, No. 62) 28.61.

[16] Aurel Stein, *The Thousand Buddhas* (London, 1921) Pl. 13.

[17] Paul Pelliot, *Les grottes de Touen-houang* (Paris, 1914-1924), 3, Plates CLV, CLXV, CLXIX and 5, Plate CCCXVI. Plate CLV is the same subject as Fig. 4 of this article which is reproduced from a photograph taken by my friend Shih Chang-ju 石璋如.

[19] Cf. the article by Matsushita Ryūshō 松下隆章 in *Bukkyō geijutsu* 佛教藝術 (*Ars Buddhica*) 6 (1950), 39-50. In addition to the six-tusked elephant, there are references to a seven-tusked elephant in *Ta fang-pien Fo pao-en ching* 大方便佛報恩經 3 (*TT ts'e* 3, No. 156), 149 and to a ten-tusked elephant in *Cheng fa nien ching* 正法念經 21 (*TT ts'e* 17, No. 721), 120. These were probably derived from the story of the six-tusked elephant.

本篇轉載自 Harvard Journal of Asiatic Studies.

City Life and The Chinese Civilization

The present age is the age when East and West must integrate. Rudyard Kipling's famous line, "East is East and West is West, and never the twain shall meet," is read today, such an anachronism that it will shortly vanish from the memory of man.

It is generally understood that Western civilization is an urban civilization. No exception can be made of that of the Land of Two Rivers, nor that of Egypt or of the Hellenic World. When we consider Eastern civilization, especially Chinese civilization, we usually assume it to be a rural nature. In other words, Western civilization is thought to be one of activity while that of the East is one of placid inactivity.

There is no evidence to support this hypothesis whatsoever. Studies of Chinese History reveal that the opposite is the case.

Excavations made at the Yin site of Anyang disclosed unequivocally the fact that this ancient capital of the Middle Kingdom was populated by a citizenry completely urbanized. Relics found among the ruins show a marked difference from those found in the former city suburbs. Whereas many bronze vessels were recovered within the city site, only stone tools could be retrieved in the old countryside except in those burying grounds that belonged to the nobility. This conclusively proves that urban culture of the Yin-Shang times had already reached the bronze age, even though rural culture still remained in the stone age.

For the period extending from the Western Chou to the early part of the Eastern Chou (approximately 1000-200 B.C.), we have more records available from old classics. All evidence testify to the fact that city life was more responsible for the development of Chinese civilization. The plan of a city generally included a royal ancestral shrine, an altar dedicated to the state guardian angel, royal palaces and market places. These structures signify that, in ancient China, three elements were dominant in the city states: religion, sovereignty, and commerce. Under the prodding of commerce, handicrafts appeared and flourished.

According to the Book of Kuantze, the common people fell into four categories, the soldier, the farmer, the craftsman, and the merchant. Three of the four inhabited the city, only the farmer lived in the country. Clearly, the urban people were the leading classes supported by the rustics.

Shih Ching, or Book of Odes, a collection of some three hundred ancient poems, was composed of selections of the works of feudal lords, ladies and tenant farmers. The majority of the poems in the collection had been written from the viewpoint of city inhabitants. "The Seventh Moon," a poem that describes the life of the farmers and is well-liked by many a Chinese scholar, contains lines indicating how the farmers were subordinate to the lords.

> "The spring day is slow,
>
> So many artemisia have been gathered.
>
> Sad is the girl,
>
> Who has to go back with the young lord."

and

> "Hunting fox
>
> For the furcoat of the young lord."

> "When grains are harvested,

To the lord's palace they go for processing."

"To the court the farmers repair,

    And, lifting the wine cups,

    Shout: 'Long live the Noble Lord.'"

Lines like these in this ancient pastoral show clearly that the farmer did not stand as high in station as the city inhabitant.

With the further development of the city states in the period of the "Spring and Autumn (770–403 B.C.)," the self sufficient economy of earlier days had given way to commercial activites among the cities. Commerce became increasingly important, especially in the Huang Ho Delta and along the East Sea coast. Big merchants such as Fan Li and Tuan-mu Ts'u were thus enabled to make great fortunes in East China in the fifth century B. C., at a time when the Confucian school of philosophy had barely emerged.

It is uncertain whether this economic prosperity had actually been instrumental in the advent of sages. Still, it must be conceded that such economical development had made possible more widely spread cultural diffusion and exchange of knowledge, which in turn promoted new and more profound schools of thought. The development of philosophical ideas must therefore be traced to the expansion of commerce.

At the time of the Warring States, major cities of the various kingdoms were populated by urban people. Lin-chih, capital of the state of Chi in the western part of the Shantung Peninsula, was inhabited by some seventy thousand families. According to the census statistics of Han some three or four hundred years later, a family was composed of about five persons. The population of a city of seventy thousand families would amount, therefore, to three hundred fifty thousand persons. It was definitely no small figure in ancient times.

Quite a number of ruins representing the culture of the Warring States have been excavated in recent years. The site of Chin-tsun in Loyang is a famous one and that of Changsha is another. Many fine bronzes and lacquerworks are found which have been exhibited in the United States and European museums. These finely wrought relics were made by the hands of craftsmen who were city dwellers, not rustics.

City dwellers also wielded great sway in government matters. They were so obstructive to the centralization of authority in fact that the Legal School of philosophy was prompted to advance a principle of 'looking down on the merchants.' Privileges of the merchants were either restricted or severely curbed by ancient Chinese law. Yet all the Legalists could do was to downgrade the merchants politically, for they could not wipe out merchants as a class. Toward the end of the third century B.C., Emperor Ch'in Shih Huang Ti vanquished all the warring states and China became one unified absolute monarchy. Since the government needed tax money for support, the position of the merchants was somewhat improved and they kept amassing wealth.

From the foregoing, it is now clear that China was unified. Roads were extended into new regions and improved for easier prospered. But provisions for this large metropolis depended upon the Grand Canal, which brought silk and food from the Yangtze Delta.

Amassing of wealth always influences the development of education. During the Sui period, a new examination system was founded. More educated people won government positions through selective competiton, [even when the successful candidate belonged to the lower classes that in the past precluded him from any such positions.] Eminent scholars flocked to the cities either to seek appointments or to gather knowledge, and this was naturally to the advantage of the city inhabitants.

During the Sung dynasty the Yangtze Valley and the Yangtze Delta had been the cradle of geniuses. More people from the southern provinces were candidates in the state examinations. In the Ming and Ch'ing eras, officials came from the cities within the radius of the Tai-hu Lake Basin. This is accounted by the fact that the wealth of all China had been concentrated in the Yangtse Delta because of the Grand Canal and the Yangtze River.

From the Sung dynasty onward, cities in the Yangtze Delta come to be so important and so prosperous that Kaifeng, a business center on the banks of the Grand Canal was made into the new capital of the reunited Chinese Empire, while Sian could no longer hold its former special position. This continued until one and a half centuries later when nomadic peoples migrated from the north and adopted Peking as their capital.

Peking was the connecting point of the culture of the steppes and that of the crowded cities. Since the reign of Kublai Khan of the Mongol Dynasty, a new Grand Canal was lengthened from the old Grand Canal towards Peking. Thus Peking became a sort of satellite city in its economic and cultural position to the cities in the Yangtze Delta.

From very early times, Soochow has been an economic and political center in both the Tai-hu area and the Yangtze Delta. The center shifted many times to Yangchow north of the Yangtze which was more accessible to North China. Actually, Yangchow had been a more important city during the Han, the Sui-Tang, the Sung through the Ch'ing dynasties, the only exception being the Six Dynasties when China was divided control of the sovereign. The betterment of communication facilities proved most favorable to merchants. Further development of helpful economic conditions during the period of the Han dynasty saw Chinese goods crossing the snowy peaks of the Pamir

Plateau into Sogduia and India. It is common knowledge that General Chang Chien was the first Chinese who made a name in Central Asia and that Tang Meng pioneered in the regions of Yunnan and Burma. But it was the Chinese merchants who blazed the trail.

〔In the past a member of the lower class was excluded from such positions.〕

In the Han period, Chinese silk products had been exported to every part of the Old World. A highway that extended from Sian to Rome via Central Asia came into existence and was known as the Silk Route because of the prosperous silk trade. This came to pass through the efforts of urban citizens, the merchants and the craftsmen, not of farmers or soldiers.

More and more booming cities were established, including Sian, Loyang, Chengtu, Hantan, Soochow, Changsha, Lintse and Canton. The most notable fact at this time was that Canton, also known by its former name Panyu, was the center of water transportation between the South China Sea and the Indian Ocean. Here Chinese silk was the main merchandise that could be exchanged for gold pearls and ivory.

From the beginning of the third century to the end of the sixth century A.D., the Yangtse and Sikiang valleys were separrated from China proper and belonged to the states of Wu, Eastern Tsin and the Southern Dynasties. Many refugees migrated into the newly founded kingdoms and made them prosperous. Enlargement of cities and expansion of commerce were common in South China during this period. Great strides were made in handicrafts which found encouragement in the concentration of wealth among the inhabitants of cities.

When China was again unified by the Emperor of the Sui Dynasty, the Grand Canal that became the main waterway connecting the South to the

North was completed. The fabulous capital of Changan or Khumdan was erected to be the cultural and economic center in Eastern Asia. The Celestial Khan became the leader of many countries and his capital into two, with the Huai River serving as demarcation. Whenever China was reunited, Yangchow would immediately be changed into a commercial center of the whole country.

Self-made merchants were the most powerful capitalists in the Ming-Ch'ing period; as their resident city, Yangchow was extravagantly prosperous. Cultural excellences, including high class cooking, splendid handicrafts, poets and writers, printing of books, artists and even singsong girls, were all concentrated here. In the thirty seventh year of the Reign of Chien-Lung, (1772), a historic collection of books known as the "Ssu Ku Chuan Shu (A Complete Collection of Books in Four Stacks)" was issued in seven copies, of which three were respectively housed at the dual cities of Yangchow which continued its position until the cultural center of the Delta was removed to Shanghai.

Shanghai has been the main port of modern China. Not only wealth but every element that makes Chinese civilization has been concentrated in this commercial city. This is not an accident. On the contrary, it is the result of a national tradition which may be traced to the very birth of Chinese culture.

本篇轉載自 Proceedings of the First International Conference of Historians of Asia. (Nov. 25-30, 1950), Manila.

On the Inscription of Che Ling Tsun (矢令尊)

I. A Version into Modern Script

隹八月辰在甲申①。王令周公子明保②

尹三事③四方④，受卿事寮⑤：丁亥。令矢告

于周公宮⑥。公⑦令造同卿事寮，隹十

月月吉。癸未⑧。明公朝至于成周⑨。造令舍⑩

三事。令罘卿事寮。罘諸尹。罘里

君⑪。罘百工⑫。罘諸侯⑬。侯、田、男⑭。舍四方令，旣

咸令⑮。甲申，明公用牲于京宮⑯。乙酉。用

牲于康宮⑰。咸旣。用牲于王⑱。明公歸自

王。明公賜大師⑲鬯金小牛。曰。用祼⑳。賜令㉑鬯

金小牛，曰。用祼，廼令曰。今我唯令女二人大

罘。矢奭㉒眔右㉓于乃寮。以乃有事，作冊。令

敢揚明公尹厥宜。用乍父丁㉔寶尊

彝敢追明公商于父丁。用光父丁。

雋㉕册

II. Notes

1. Chia-shen（甲申）Would be the first day (or the second day) of the Eighth Moon. On the contex below, the day Kuei-wei（癸未）must the first day (or the second day) of the Tenth Moon and there were fifty-nine days from Chia-shen to Jen-wu（壬午）, the yesterday of Kuei-wei. In the formula of the lunar calender fifty-nine days are usually to form two lunar months (moon). Inside of these two lunar months, one longer month with thirty days and one shorter month with twenty-nine days are contained. At a view of Tung Tso-pin's（董作賓）Chung-kuo Nien-li Tsung-pu（中國年曆總譜）there are not so many possibilities from 1111 B.C. to 961 B.C. through 150 years, except 1095 B.C., 1090 B.C., 1064 B.C., 1054 B.C., 1028 B.C., 1007 B.C., 981 B.C., 976 B.C., and 961 B.C. Now, according to the Genealogy of the State Lu（魯世家）in Shih Chi（史記）the inauguration of the third lord was counted as 157 years before the first year of Kung-ho（共和）(841 B.C.) So the last year of the secnd lord Po-ch'in（伯禽）(the son of Chou Kung 周公) must be in 999 B.C. It means, only one possibility, the year 1007, could be adapted to this condition.

   A significant information brought from this inscription is related to the year of Chou Kung's death. Since the appointment of Po-ch'in was due to the status of heir apparent of Chou Kung, he had to turn to the new position after his father's death. This fact is very important of the political and cultural history of ancient China.

2. "Ming-Pao"（明保）was a combination of the honorary title "Ming" (brilliant) and the personal name "Pao" for lord Po-ch'in, Chou Kung's son.

3. "Yin"（尹）means a leader or to be a leader in an office. "San-shih"（三事）means three main parts in the government, namely: ssu-tu the minister (chancellor) of people, ssu-ma the minister (chancellor) of troops, ssu-k'ung the minister (chanceilor) of works.

4. "Ssu-fang"（四方）means the four directions as the areas outside from the king's domain.

5. "Ch'ing-shih-liao"（卿事寮）or（卿士寮）means the office (with staff) of a minister or prime-minister.

6. "Chou Kung Kung" （周公宮） indicates the TEMPLE of Chou Kung impossibly for his residence. Because Po-ch'in was chou Kung's son, a messenger was uselessly sent to his father except sent to his father's temple.

7. This "Kung" refers Chou Kung. The order of Chou Kung should be taken from oracle of the temple. The day "Ting-hai" （丁亥） was considered as a lucky day in the Chou period; thus a lucky day was suitable to do some service in a temple.

8. "Yüeh-chi" （月吉） or "Chu-chi" （初吉） indicates the beginning of lunar month. It might cover three to four days especially for the first day.

9. "Cheng-chou" （成周） indicates Loyang where a new capital had been built by Chou Kung for the purpose to communicate the feudal lords near the eastern coast with connection to the Kuan-chung （關中） valley where the king's residence was situated. The detail of the relation between the king's residence (Hao-ching 鎬京) and Cheng-chou was unclear in the record of history. This inscription reveals a valuable information, that the central administration with the staffs of ministers was in king's residence, and Loyang was for the meeting of lords and people only.

10. "She" （舍） means （予） or （與）, to give.

11. "Chu-ying" （諸尹） means the head officials; "li-chün" （里君） means the heads of local small quarters.

12. "Po-kung" （百工） means varies kinds of handicraftsmen. It shows in the beginning of the Chou Dynasty the situation of the handicraftsmen was so important, comparing with the Topa Wei Dynasty and the Yüan Dyasty.

13. "Chu-hou" （諸侯） indicates the feudal lords.

14. "Hou", "tien" and "nan" （侯，旬，男） indicate the areas of the feudal lords, far and near. The lords in the area of "hou" were the lords of large states but far from the king's capital. The lords in the area of "tien" were the lords of the medium states closed to the king's Domain. The lords in the area of "nan" were the lords of small states inside if the king's domain. In a view of Tso-chuan Chin was originally a state of tien (in the second year of Huan Kung 桓公) and Cheng was a state of nan (in the thirteenth year of Chao Kung 昭公). Of course, Ch'i （齊），

Lu （魯）, Sung （宋） and Wei （衞） should be the states in the area of hou.

15. "Hsien-ling" （咸令） means the order was accomplished.

16. "Ching-kung" （京宮） indicates a palace in Loyang.

17. "K'ang-kung" （康宮） indicates another palace in Loyang. It might be newer and larger than Ching-kung since it is more commenly seen in bronzes.

18. "Wang" （王） indicates the king's residence "Hao-ching".

19. "T'ai-shih" （太師） must be the grand musician in the court.

20. "Jang" 祭 means a sacrifice. This character is composed with two parts, 示 and 乘. The first part "shih" （示） indicates something related to gods or spirits. The second part （乘） is no longer used in the later development of the formation of character but the meaning could be still traced. It shows ears of abundant corps hanging around the grain, therefore it should indicate the good harvest. The character for good harvest in later times is "jang". 穰. In Shuo-wen Chieh-tzu （說文解字） the word "jang" 禳 is explained as a sacrifice for removal of calamity. It is a synonym of "jang" 禳. We can determine these two characters were developed from the same origin which referred a sacrafice both for gratitude of good harvest and for request of the removal of calamity.

21. "Ling" （令） and "Chê" （矢） refer to same person, while Che was his personal name, and ling means "chia-ling" （家令）, a house manager.

22. "Shih" 爽 is a character loan （假借） for "che" （擇）, to select.

23. "Fu-tin" （父丁） was the title in temple of Che's father.

24. "叴右" means "tso-yu" （左右）, the attendents.

25. A combination of a bird and the charater "ping" （丙） was a sign of Che's family.

III. English Translation

In the Eighth Moon at the day Chia-shen （甲申） His Majesty ordered Lord Ming Pao the son of Chou Kung to be the head of the office of three chancellors, of the feudal lords from all directions, and with a staff as (prime-) minister. On the day Ting-hai （丁亥） Che was sent (by His Highness Ming-pao) to Chou-kung's temple to report and (His Highness) was permitted to attend his office with a staff as (prime-) minister.

To the beginning of the Tenth Moon, on the day Kuei-wei (癸未), the Lord Ming (Pao) went to the court in Cheng-chou (成周). He issued his order to the three chancellors, to all of the staff of ministers, to all of the heads of offices, to all of the local chieftains, to all of the handiscraftsmen, to all of the feudal lords (far and near) in all of the areas: hou, tien and nan. This order was given to everywhere.

While the order had been given, the Lord Ming (Pao) sacrificed with cattle in the Ching Palace at the day Chia-shen. (甲申). To the next day Yi-yu (乙酉) (the Lord Ming) sacrificed with cattle in the K'ang Palace. When the sacrifices were all completed, the Lord Ming returns to the king's capital and sacrifices with cattle there. The Lord Ming bestows the grand musician wine, copper and a small cow, ordering to sacrifice for good harvest and for removal of calamity. Then His Highness bestows his ling (house manager) wine, copper and a small cow, ordering to sacrifice for good harvest and for removal of calamity. After all (His Highness) orders "Now I order fwo of you only to (transfer my opinion) to the people." Che then selects his assistants from the staff waiting for service. He makes this inscription. Ling (the house manager) ventures to prsise the Lord Ming as the head of the cabinet. He hereby makes a valuable vessel venturing to transfer the gift trom Lord Ming to his father Ting for the glory of his father Ting.

From Wooden Slip to Paper

I. Wooden and bamboo slips and tablets

According to records and explorations, there is only one kind of slip made of bamboo, but there are many variations of wooden tablets. In the fourth century thousands of ancient bamboo slips[1] were found at the northern part of Honan but the original ones were destroyed very early. The bamboo slips dated from the third century B.C. from the new exploration are those of Wu-li P'ai (五里牌) and Yang-t'ien Hu (仰天湖) at Changsha, Hunan. They would be considered the earliest ones among the slips. The later ones are the wooden slips of the Han Dynasty which were discovered in the area at the western side of the Great Wall, as the titles *Tunhuang Han Chein* (敦煌漢簡) and *Chuyen Han Chien* (居延漢簡) indicate. Beside these Han slips, some wooden slips of the Chin (晉) Dynasty have found at Sinkiang (Chinese Turkestan) and they contained some variations both in size and in calligraphy compared to those of the Han. All of these give us the most ditails for the kinds of manuscripts on wood, showing the writing methods used in the ancient way.

There are many sizes—long or short, broad or narrow—made of wood for many kinds of writing, but the narrow slip may be considered as the fundamental size since it was taken directly from the bamboo slip. The ancient character *chien* (簡) is composed of a pictographic symbol *chu* (竹, bamboo) at the top, which means that the slip must have been made of bamboo in that period. In the following categories there are various kinds of wooden tablets for writing:

A. Chien or slips

This is the narrow and longer size of bamboo and wood, about nine inches in length, half an inch wide and one-eight of an inch thick. In general it was written on with one or two lines. As for a book it was always longer and narrower and written on with one line. When many slips are bound with strings, it becomes a roll and is callde *ts'e* which means a volume of a book.

B. Ts'e or rolls

These are many slips bound together with string into a roll to make a book, which were the origin of many kinds of scrolls. The word *ts'e* was used in many ways, such as "book, plot, law, to examine the scholars," etc. These different meanings may be traced from the original "book" and its uses.

To bind the *chien* into *ts'e,* they must be arranged on a table and bound with strings. According to the volume of Chü-yen the scroll was first bound with two strings, and according to the volume of Wu-wei it was bound with three strings. This shows that the number of strings varies according to the length of the original slips. The roll is made in the same way as the bamboo screen (the screen or drape made of bamboo splints), which means that the method used for the screen was taken from that of the bamboo slips.

When paper was invented and came into popular use the roll of paper and the lines of characters on the paper were adapted from the slips. In the Chinese way one volume may be called one roll. With the invention of wooden blocks to print pages of books the shape of the book was gradually changed from a roll to a volume, yet the old term *chüan* (卷＝捲, roll) is still preserved in chapters of every ancient book.

C. Wooden tablets

The wooden board and wooden tablet were both called *pan* (版) in ancient times and were used for writing. However the wooden tablet also had the name *tu* (牘), used especially for correspondence. As for the board, there were three uses: (1) to paint maps and make notations of records on the maps; (2) to announce an edict or order from the throne or high official at the front of a gate; (3) used as a tablet with writing or inscriptions to show the name of a building or an office. But its use for public and private correspondence was the most important of all its uses.

There were some letters found between the slips of Tunhuang and Chü-yen which were all written on a wooden tablet. From the discovery of Lop Nor some complete letters with wooden covers are seen. The main part of the letter is a broad tablet some six inches in length and two to three inches in width. A cover of the same size was used to write the address. This cover is thicker in order to contain a hole to put a piece of clay to stamp a seal. Then a string was used to tie the cover to the main letter, and the clay piece was sealed on the knot.

D. The edged stick

The stick was called *ku* (觚). It was said that this stick may have contained three or four edges to make the plain faces on which to write. However, among the wooden slips only four-faced sticks are found.

There were two uses for *ku*. One was for schoolboys, used because it was solid and hard and not easily broken. It may be compared to modern books made of cloth and used in the kindergarten. The other was for orders sent to the frontier. In order to show that it was genuine a seal was stamped on the face of the edged stick.

After paper was invented seals were quite easily stamped with ink or colored oil. Compared to using a stamp hole, it is less clumsy. Finally, no stamp hole is found in modern manuscripts, and nobody remarked about the old way until the wooden slips were revealed.

II. Ways of making and writing on slips

The slips used quite a different system from the books since everything was different. We saw the remains of the Han slips from Tunhuang, Chü-yen and Wuwei and the Chu slips[2] of Changsha. From them many facts can be stated as follows:

A. *The material of the slips*

The material of the slips was always made of bamboo or wood. Bamboo was much easier to make into strips than wood, therefore the character *chien* was used with the radical *chu* (bamboo) to signify that the slip was made of bamboo. But the production of bamboo was limited to the damp areas. Thus no bamboo can be found in farmost northern China.[3] Along the border of the Great Wall there is always a desert or semi-desert climate. Only coniterous and other desert trees grew there with the result that wood was used instead of bamboo for slips.

We have not found the tools of the carpenters of Han to enable us to make an exact explanation of the methods of handicrafts of that period. From the well polished surface of the slips, however, we know that the saw and plane must have been used. The slips found from the northwestern frontier proved to be the local wood from that area which are the spruce, willow, poplar, aspen and reeds.

The slips were made and sold by carpenters. On the wooden slip was written: to pay sixty coins to buy two hundred slips.[5] The average wage for a workman at that time was three hundred coins per month, i.e., ten coins per day. Sixty coins would be the wages for six days. Even though the material was not expensive the work to make two hundred slips would probably take five days. Now, roughly speaking the workman could make forty slips per day; if he worked ten hours each day, or four slips per hour. Thus the tools of the carpenter were not very good. Since the slips were expensive, the used slips were always re-planed for re-writing.[ct]

B. The length of the slips

The usual length of the slips was nine inches, which was considered a foot in the Han period. But in special cases it would be longer.

The longest slips of Han measured three feet and were used for law books. The books for classics used slips measuring two feet and four inches. Edicts from the throne determined the length of a foot or an inch during Han. It was the slips for common use which measured one foot. The short ones were used for labels and measured four and one-half inches.

The width of the slips measured one-half inch on the average, but broader ones may have measured from one inch to one and one-quarter inches. Therefore the system of the length of the slips was not standardized.

An average slip contains one or two lines, and each line contains twenty to fifty characters. Thus the number of characters was not strictly limited.

The Han slip of Wu-wei were the longer ones used to write the classics, measuring two feet and four inches, and containing on the average of sixty characters but sometimes as many as 123 characters. These slips were bound with strings to make a roll. Usually two rows of strings were used, but sometimes two, three, four and five rows of strings were used. All of the strings were made of hemp.

C. Marks on the slips

From the Han slips we find many kinds of marks on the slips, especially those of Wu-wei.[6] These marks expressed the way of punctuation, which was called *chang-chü* (chapter and stop), an important point for scholars of the classics. Sometimes a student studied the classics from a famous teacher and the term *chang-chü* was used. So far *chang-chü* would be the most important for the classics. The marks found on the Han slips would be rendered as the original way of *chang-chü*, which had been forgotten for more than one thousand years.

The following give the marks and their explanations:
□ A square, to denote the beginning of a chapter.

• A point, to denote the beginning of a chapter or a paragraph. In common use it shows the beginning of a conclusion.

○ A circle, to denote the beginning of a chapter or a paragraph.

△ A triangle, to denote the beginning of a chapter or a paragraph.

： Double points, to denote the repetition of the preceding character.

▢ Brackets, to show the deletion of a character.

／ A slash at the beginning of the composition.

✓ A hook appeared both in the slips from the frontier (Tunhuang and Chü-yen) and the classics from Wu-wei, to show a stop either in or at the end of a sentence. Its explanation is found in Hsü Shen's *Shuo-wen Chieh-tzu*,[7] where it says a hook marks a stop in a sentence. Tuan Yü Tsai's commentary gives more details in explaining the hook. However, it was not used at every stop, but was sometimes used with ambiguous meaning.

— A horizontal line, to count or record a number.

ㄋ ㄕ 多 1 various kinds of signatures, especially used as a receipt to mark on the record.

D. Making the slips

Fresh bamboo, in order to be used for slips, must be prepared by a special method. It was called "Sai-ching"[8] (reducing the green)—baking the green bamboo over a fire to change it into dry bamboo of a yellow color for the purpose of avoiding harmful insects. After the bamboo is dried,[9] a craftsman splits it open and cuts it into slips. These slips must then be planed to a smooth surface for writing.

There are very few wooden slips, the making of which has been recorded. However, the late professor Tung Tso-pin and I had tried to make a volume of imitation wooden slips as specimens of the Han calendar. It was made by a country carpenter in Szechuan using old fashion tools. First he split the lumber into boards; then he planed the board and separated it into slips. This is the way of a contemporary carpenter, but I believe they were made in a similar way during the Han since iron tools were also used at that time.

E. The writing knife as an eraser on slips

On both bamboo and wooden slips were found mistakes in writing. For correcting these mistakes the knife-eraser was used. This knife was called *hsüeh* or *shu-tao*, according to different periods.[10] Either *hsüeh* or *shu-tao* meant, to scrape the surface of slips to make it smooth for re-writing. Even the shape, size and material were gradually changed from Chou to Han, but the use was the same.

When paper was invented in China and became widely used the slips were forgotten and the knife-eraser was abandoned. People did not know what a knife-eraser was and many misunderstandings occurred. Fortunately shavings with characters on them were discovered at Edsin Gol. They testified to the fact that mistakes were erased from slips by shaving them with a knife.

On the other hand knives inscribed with characters were discovered, which identified the size and material used in the Later Han Dynasty. One was found at Tien-hui Shan, Chengtu, Szechuan, dated 184 A. D., and the other was found by Lo Chen-yü, dated 104 A. D. The former was made of bronze and the latter was made of iron. Due to the special inscriptions, they would be considered luxurious ones. However, the common ones would be similar to them.

The application of the *shu-tao* was not only for erasing but was also for reconstructing the slips. Since slips were too expensive, the used slips would be scraped to make new ones. The sharings from Chü-yen contain not only one or two characters but are also as long as a whole slip. This shows that a new slip was reconstructed from a used one.

III. The development of Chinese characters and its relation to slips

A. *Four categories of Chinese characters*

Chinese characters may be divided into four categories:

(1) *Chuan-shu* or seal characters; (2) *Li-shu* or clerical style; (3) *K'ai-shu* or regular tyle and (4) *Ts'ao-shu* or draft (grass) style. Chuan-shu is the archaic style of the oracle bones and bronzes. *Li-shu* was the legal style in the Han Dynesty, and it was variously called *pei-pei* (northern tablet style) or *Wei-pei* (the style of the Northern Wei Dynasty) in the Six Dynasties, but it was still one kind of *li-shu*. At the beginning of the T'ang Dynasty the real *K'ai-shu* or regular style was formed, although the tendency to use the *K'ai-shu* began in the Western Chin Dynasty. *Ts'ao-shu* was another traditional line parallel to *li-shu*. It was used for writing quickly, especially a draft, thus it took the name *ts'ao-shu*. *Ts'ao* meant "draft" and sometimes "grass." In the Han period the draft style was taken from the

li-shu but a part was also taken from the seal style as a tradition from the Warring States. Since it was quite different from the draft style of the period from Chin to T'ang, a special name, *chang-tsao*, was given to it by the scholars to differentiate it from later ages. "Chang" meant a memorial to the throne because the draft of a memorial was always written in the draft style during the Han Dynasty.

During the Chin period there were two kinds of draft style. One was called *hsing-ts'ao* or just *ts'ao-shu*, which was found from many specimens written by the famous calligrapher Wang Hsi-chih and his followers up to the Ming and Ch'ing Dynasties. The other was called *hsing-shu* or running style, which is a variation of the regular style so that it is more easily recognized than the old draft style. However, the *hsing-shu* is not standardized because the older style is mixed in with it. In this way there is no clear distinction between *hsing-shu* and *ts'ao-shu*.

Han slips were written in two styles: *li-shu* and *chang-ts'ao*. Only a very small proportion was written in the *chuan-shu* style. *Li-shu* was the formal style used in formal letters, *chang-ts'ao* was the common style, thereby being more popular than *li-shu*. However, the difference between *li-shu* and *chang-ts'ao* was not very great. Consequently, these two styles were mixed up in common use and no standard style of *li-shu* or *ts'ao-shu* was formulated.

The following is an outline of the development of Chinese characters:

Pre-Han	Chuan-shu	Oracle bones Bronzes Stone drum inscriptions Various kinds in the Warring States period Small seal style	
Han to Chin	Li-shu	Li-shu Six Dynasties style[11]	Ts'ao-shu { Chang-ts'ao Ts'ao-shu Hsing-shu
T'ang and Later periods	Regular style (K'ai-shu)		

B. The development of Li-shu

At the end of the Warring States period the style of characters was gradually changed from pictographs into straight-stroke characters and from a decorative to a simple style found in the dominant state of Ch'u. Ch'u bronzes from Shou-hsien show that characters were written in a very simple way. Bamboo slips from Changsha show the same tendency, although they are constructed quite differently from the *li-shu* of Han.

Wei Heng,[12] a famous calligrapher of the Chin Dynasty, said that *li-shu* was created by Cheng Miao. He was imprisoned for ten years and devoted himself to reforming characters into a new style. Finally he succeeded and memorialized to the throne. Then he was set free and became a royal secretary. This new style was used widely by the low official class, thereby receiving the name *li-shu* (slavery-writing) or tso-shu (clerical writing.) This meant that *li-shu* was the style used by the low official class, while the legal style (small seal) was rather difficult to write. The *li-shu* style was the easiest to write.

During the reign of the Han dynasty *li-shu* seemed to be more dominant than ever. We do not know which style was used in the beginning of Han for official documents and dispatches, but it is clear that at the time of Emperor Wen, the dictation of the Book of History from the old scholar Fu Sheng was written in the new style (*li-shu*). Therefore, when the pieces of that book in old style characters were found, the difference between the new version and the old version became a serious subject of argument between scholars at the end of the Former Han Dynasty. This evidently shows the significance of *li-shu* in early Han.

After the wooden slips were discovered, the earliest ones of the time of Emperor Wu were revealed. They showed that *li-shu* had become popular and was in common use.

Inscriptions on stone tablets were very common in the Later Han. Almost all of the tablets were inscribed in *li-shu* except for the few in small seal. Nobody considered *li-shu* or *chuan-shu* as art,[13] and all of the stone inscriptions were unsigned, showing that they were made by craftsmen and not by artists, as was the case in the T'ang Dynasty.

The outstanding characteristic of *li-shu* is the duck beak at the end of a horizontal line. In the Chin Dynasty (fourth century) the duck beak was reserved for the oblique strokes only. In the Han Dynasty every character had a pattern of long horizontal lines and short vertical lines. But in the fourth century the pattern became square. These are the great differences between the Han *li-shu* style and that of the Six Dynasties.[14]

C. The development of Ts'ao-shu

Ts'ao-shu, or the grass style was a writing style for fast writing. It was developed from the seal style and modified by the *li-shu*. Therefore its strokes were close to those of *li-shu* and contained something of the functions of the seal style.

Ts'ao-shu may be subdivided into *chang-ts'ao* (or quick writing for drafts), *ts'ao-shu* (specifically called quick writing during the Chin period), *hsin-shu* (a branch of *ts'ao-shu* since it is derived from *li-shu* or *k'ai-shu* for quick writing), and *kuang-ts'ao* (a very free writing of *ts'ao-shu*). Above all the most important style is *chang-ts'ao*, which is the typical quick writing that appeared on the wooden slips.

Because *Chang-ts'ao* was the earliest type of *ts'ao-shu* and did not appear in the bronze and stone inscriptions, very few specimens of it were preserved before the wooden slips were discovered. *chang-ts'ao* was very popular in Han society. Two text books were taught to the school boys of Han: the *Tsang-chieh Pien*, written in *li-shu* and the *Chi-chiu Pien*, written in *chang-ts'ao*. The *Chi-chin Pien* had been lost since the *Chien-tze wen*, which was compiled in the Liang Dynasty and became very popular during the T'ang, was substituted for it. It only preserved a small number of Han wooded slips. Fortunately the *Chi-chin Pien* is well preserved in several re-copied manuscripts from the Sung Dynasty. These manuscripts were transferred to stone inscriptions and reprinted in recent years.[15] The structure of these characters is very useful in comparing them with those from the wooden slips, although the writing has been slightly changed due to the tracings.

According to the Han slips, *li-shu* and *chang-ts'ao* are not two independent types. Many characters may be written in both ways on the same slip. This means many slips have two types of writing styles. Even a typical *li-shu* slip would be written very quickly, something like *chang-ts'ao* in its strokes. Thus the stone inscriptions of the Han Dynasty were only permanent memorials which were not found in common use. Practically, *li-shu* was always used in comparing quick writing styles. This is the origin of *hsing-shu* or the running style.

IV. The invention of paper and paper-making

A. *The origin of paper*

Paper is a Chinese invention. It has no relation to the Egyptian 'papyrus', although it is something resembling papyrus and the word 'paper' is derived from the word 'papyrus'. In Chinese paper is called *chih*[16] which has no relation to the word 'papyrus.'

According to Hsü Shen's *Shuo-wen* and its commentary by Tuan Yü-tsai,[17] the original meaning of *chih* was a piece of worthless silk. This silk was torn, beaten and washed and taken from worthless clothes and made into puffy balls or sheets to be used for stuffing of a wadded coat.

Chuang Chou, a famous Taoist philosopher of the fourth century B.C., told a story[18] of a workman who sold a prescription for chapped hands in cold water for one hundred pieces of gold to a general to help him win a battle in winter. This workman had the drug for many generations, and it was used when washing disgarded silk in cold water. The way to washing was called *p'ing-pi huang*. *p'ing-pi* meant "floating to wash" and *huang* meant "worthless silk". In a commentary[19] on Chuang-tze, *huang* meant *hsü* or worthless silk." This kind of silk was always used for wadded coats.

When the worthless silk was stuck together it appeared in small pieces which became sheets of quasi-paper. The only reliable earlier source was a record of a case in 12 B.C., in which the Empress Chao Fei-yen was involved. She murdered the emperor's concubine, the mother of a baby prince, using a poisonous drug wrapped in *ho-ti*.[20] *Ho-ti* was explained in a commentary as a small piece of *Chih*. Since genuine paper was said to be invented in 105 A.D., this so-called paper would be quasi-paper or pieces of silk stuck together.

The fragments of quasi-paper were discovered in Pa-chio in 1957, and it was said that they were made of vegetable fiber.[21] This fact shows that a long time before the paper inventor Ts'ai Lun, silk fibers had been changed into vegetable fiber. According to professor Shun-sheng Ling, quasi-paper was produced from bark-cloth of the Southern Hsien tribes.[22] It is a very good thesis, but we are earnestly awaiting further proof from the discovery of the Han remains.

Even before Ts'ai Lun, vegetable fiber had been used to make quasi-paper, but this paper was too rough for regular use. From the biography of the famous scholar Chia Kuei in the *Hou Han Shu*,[23] it is said that his *Tso Chuan* study was recognized by the throne which in turn ordered it copied into two sets, one on bamboo slips and the other on paper in 76 A.D.

This record is found only in the *Hou Han Shu*, while it does not appear in the *Hou Han Chi*, an annual history earlier than the *Hou Han Shu*. The *Hou Han Shu* was compiled by Fan yeh (—445) based on seven different versions of the *Hou Han Shu*. Comparing this with the relics of the earlier ones, (quoted from the *Lui Shu* or classified Refernce Book), his work shows

rather more than the original. Since *Chih* may be explained as silk[24] during the third century A.D., Fan yeh's explanation of *Chih* as indicating silk is reasonable. The *Tso Chuan* was a large book which required a large amount of paper to write it. It would have been impossible to find so much genuine paper thirty years before the invention of Ts'ai Lun.

The most important record of the invention of paper is from the Biography of Ts'ai Lun in the *Hou Han Shu*.[25]

Ts'ai Lun (his other name was Ching-chung) was born in Kuei-yang.[26] At he time of Chien-ts'u (76-83 A.D.) he was appointed as hsiao-huang men and promoted to Chung-chang Shih[27] under Emperor Ho. Lun was a learned and devoted man, being careful not to incur the anger of the throne. Later he was appointed as the Shang-fang ling, the director of handicrafts for the palace. In the seventh year of Yün-yüan (97 A.D.) he was ordered to inspect the swords and other utensils, every one of which was refined and used as the standard for later generations.

During the ancient times bamboo slips were tied together to make books, and the pieces of woven silk were given the name *Chih*, used to write on. Both of them were inconvenient since silk was too expensive and slips were too heavy. Ts'ai Lun created the idea of making *Chih* from bark, worthless hemp, rags and fishing nets. He offered the method to the throne in the first year of Yüan-hsing (105 A.D.) and received recognition of his talent. Then paper became broadly used and was called the "paper of Lord Ts'ai."

Another record is one based on the *Tung-kuan Han-chi*, an official history from the court of the Later Han Dynasty:[28]

Ts'ai Lun, *tzu* Ching-chung, a native of Kuei-yang, served [at the court] as Chung-chang-shih. He was a man of talent, warm, loyal and careful. When he was not busy with the duty of his office he usually shut himself up and refused to see visitors, exploring his relation to nature. When he was charged with the office of Shang-fang he initiated the idea of making paper from tree bark, old rags and fishing nets. He submitted the process to the emperor in the first year of Yuan-hsing (A.D. 105) and received praise for his ability. From this time on paper has been in use and it is universally called the "paper of Ts'ai Lun."

Both of these texts agree that paper was offered to the throne in the year 105 A.D.[29] If we connot find further reliable evidence it would be considered a land-mark in the histry of paper making in the world.

Even if paper had been invented in the second century, it was not widely used in society from the biography[30] of the *Hou Han Shu*, when Wu Yu was young his father was planning to write the classics on bamboo slips just some ten years after the invention of paper. The slips should have been more popular than paper. But according to the *Yi-li* remains from the new discovery in Wu-wei, the wooden slips were still widely used at the end to Later Han. Up to the Chin Dynasty (265-420 A.D.) paper was more commonly used. Both Chin slips and Chin paper were discovered in Chinese Turkestan, showing the significance in the increase of paper. The records of population were divided into two categories at the beginning of Eastern Chin (317 A.D.): one was called the yellow record, especially for natives in the Yangtze valley, made of wooden slips; the other was called the white record, especially for the immigrants from the north, made of paper. This fact meant that the use of paper paralleled the use of slips. However, the increase in the use of paper continued for three centuries from the time of its invention.

B. Discoveries of Early Paper Specimens

Early paper specimens are very few since paper is not easily preserved. Except for those found from exploration, no Han paper exists. *Pin-fu Tieh*, written by Lu Chi, is a unique specimen of the earliest paper in the third century. Some manuscripts attributed to Wang Hsi-chih of the fourth century may possibly be specimens of early paper but it is very difficult to say whether they are original or copied. At the end of the nineteenth century Sir Aurel Stein found some pieces of early paper in Sinkiang. These pieces are quite valuable, but the most outstanding manuscript to be found was that of Li Po, a high-ranking Chinese official of Turfan in the fourth century. It was found at the time of the Tajimana Expedition at the beginning of the twentieh century.

Ouasi-paper from Pa-chiao is said to be part of the relics of the Former Han Dynasty (206B.C.-8.A.D.).[31] However, there were no characters on it. The earliest paper with writing still extant would be the piece from the bank of Edsin Gol. This paper was discovered in the autumn of 1942 by me (with Mr. Shih Chang-ju).

Mr. F. Bergman, a member of the Sino-Swedish expedition, had discovered seventy-eight wooden slips in a roll from the very site from which this paper was discovered. This roll was dated between the fifth and tenth years of Yung-yüan (93-98 A.D.). Thus this paper must have been made around that period.

Tsakhortei is a plain in the desert on the eastern bank of the Edsin Gol River, not very far to the south of a hill named Bayan Bogedo. This site was never explored and a hole in it existed very clearly. Looking at the edge of the hole, I found that the old deposits had not cleared off, I then ordered the workmen to dig it. A paper ball had fallen to the bottom of the hole, but it was of no particular consequence since nothing was found to compare with this paper for determining its exact date.

The roll of slips was in the same site with this paper, thereby giving evidence of the date of the paper. The earliest date on the slips was 98 A.D, which was seven years earlier than the invention of paper. However, there is the possibility that this roll was buried some ten years after the invention of paper. In this case we do not have sufficient reason to say that this paper preceded the Ts'ai Lun specimen.

This piece of paper is rather rough and without the bamboo splint pattern as was made in the later period. From the test of professor Yin-ch'an Wu of the Department of Botany at Tung Chi University, this piece was found to be a kind of vegetable fiber, showing that it was made of rotten hemp or used fishing net, without any evidence of silk. According to the paper relics from Pa-chiao vegetable fiber had been used for a long time before Ts'ai Lun. Thus the invention of Ts'ai Lun would be a new method and not the discovery of a new material.

From the biography of Ts'ai Lun in the *Hou Han Shu* it was said that every kind of utensil was made by him in a refined way. Therefore we may consider that genuine paper-making just used the old materials in a refined way to make from the rough, irregular small pieces the large, fine and regalar sheets. Then the paper was more similar to silk. This was the first step in using paper for letters and books in human civilization.

We do not know the size of the original paper in the Han period but according to the paper rolls from the Caves of Tunhuang the paper was always about eight inches in height with vertical black lines which were clearly adapted from the rolls of bound wooden slips. Because the roll of slips was used in the time of Ts'ai Lun we would infer that this size and form was used from the beginning of paper making.

P. S. Thanks are due to Mr. Arthur Switkin, for his help to this article.

FOOT NOTES

1. Chin-shu Chio-chu (Yee Wen ed.) chuan 51, pg 977, Biography of Ch'u Hsi.

2. Wu Wei Han Chien, Peping, 1964.

3. Everywhere South of the Chin-ling Mountain Range and the Huai-ho (River) may produce bamboo. But on the northern side of them the production of bamboo is limited to special areas. The famous areas are Hua-hsin in Shensi and Pai-chuan (Hundred Springs) in the County of Hui in Honan. In the main part of Kansu, northern Shensi, central and northern Shansi, bamboo is impossible to plant. In Hopei, near Peiping, bamboo is planted in some gardens but it has no commercial value. In the T'ang Dynasty a famous historian, Liu Chih-chi, doubted that bamboo was planted in the county of Chi in the period of the Book of Poetry and the beginning of Later Han. Yet he did not know that bamboo was certainly growing at Pai-chuan, bordering the county of Chi.

4. Sir Aurel Stein: On Ancient Central Asian Tracks, Chapter 10, pg. 148, Pantheon Books (1964).

5. Slip No. 55.5, in *Documents of the Han Dynasty on wooden slips from Edsin Gol*, comp. by Kan Lao.

cf. Na Chi-liang: The Ch'i-pi or Battle-ax pi disc. Part I, The National Meseum Bulletin Vol.1, No. 5, 1966 Taipei.

6. *Wu-wei Han Chien*, Peiping, 1964, p. 71. They were discovered at Wu-wei, Kansu, in 1959 and first appeared at Kao Ku 5 in 1960.

7. *Shuo-wen Chieh-tzu*, vol. 12, p. 639. E-wen press.

8. It was also called "han-ching" (sweat the green) because the liquid inside of the bamboo sweats through to the outside after baking.

9. This is the way a modern craftsman makes bamboo chopsticks.

10. See Tsien Tsun-hsun, *Written on Bamboo and Silk*, pp. 174-178. Professor Tsien translated "Shu-tao" as "book-knife", but I prefer to use "writing" instead of "book". In Chinese "Shu" may be used either for "book" or for "to write". Combining the slips into a book was only one part of the process of slip making (The fragment from scraping is called "fei" 柿).

11. The Six Dynasties Period is also referred to as the Epoch of the Division Between North and South. The six dynasties refers to the dynasties of Wu, Chin, Liu-Sung, Ch'i, Liang and Ch'en. Wu was at the same time as Wei (in the Three Kingdoms Period). Therefore the Six Dynasties Period is that period covering the There Kingdoms Period to the end of the Epoch of the Division Between North and South.

12. From the Biography of Wei Kuan in the *Chin Shu*. The name of Cheng Miao was found in Hsu Shen's *Shuo-wen* (preface), but Hsu said he was the creator of the small seal style. Many commentaries on the *Shuo-wen* pointed out that there must be a faulty line on the original slips, since the small seal style was used by The First Emperor of Ch'in in his various inscriptions. It would have been impossible for it to have been created by a person of humble origin.

13. Only manuscripts in grass style were rendered as art. It may be that the manuscripts were written by famous persons themselves, and the lines of grass style were sometimes related to the lines of painting.

14. This style falls between *li-shu* and *k'ai-shu*. Generally it is attributed to *k'ai-shu*. However, we do not find any evidence that scholars of the Six Dynasties considerd their writing style any different from Han *li-shu*. On the other hand, T'ang calligraphers considered the *K'ai-shu* of T'ang as being in a different category from the Han style. Emperor Hsuan-tsung wrote an inscription at T'ai-shan using *li-shu* which was clearly different from the current style of that time. It first occurred when *li-shu* became an archaic style.

15. The recopied *Chi-chin Pien* (originally written by Huang Hsiang) was reprinted in the *Chi-shih-an Tsung-shu* by Lo Chen-yu. The most popular one is recopied *Chi-chiu Pien* by

Chao Tze-ang in the *San-hsi-tang Fa-tieh*. Wang Kuo-wei made a statement on the *Chiao Sung-chiang Pen Chi-chin Pien Hsu* (p. 67, *Kuan-tang Chi-lin*, Yee-Wen ed., 1956). Among the Han slip from Tunhuang there are some pieces of *Chi-chin Pien*, but they were written in *li-shu*.

16. According to Tung T'ung-ho's *Shang-ku yin-yun Piao-kao*, Academia Sinica, Lichuang. 1944, P. 116, the ancient sound of *Chih* would be Kieg.

17. *Shuo-wen Chieh-tzu Chu*, Yee-Wen press, 1955, p. 666.

18. *Chuang-tze Chi Shih*. Shih-chieh Book Co., 1955, p. 19.

19. The main commentary on Chuang-tze was written by Kuo Hsiang in the Chin Dynasty.

20. *Han Shu*, Yee Wen press. p. 1696. The *Han Shu* was written by Pan Ku who died in 92 A.D. before the invention of genuine paper. Besides this source, there was another story from the *Han-wu Ku-shih* about the slandering of a crown prince with the use of paper, but the *Han-wu Ku-shih* has been proven to be a forgery. Therefore it is not quoted.

21. Fragments of quasi-paper of the 1st or 2nd century B.C. were discovered at Pa-chio in Shensi. *Wen-wu ts'an-kao tzu-liao*, No. 7, 1957, pp. 78-79. Also from Kuo Mo-jo's (cf, Ling, Shun-sheng: Bark-cloth, Impressed pottery, and the Inventions of Paper Making, Academia Sinica, Taipei, 1963).

22. Shun-sheng Ling, *Bark-cloth, Impressed Pottery and the Invention of Paper and Printing*, Taipei, 1963, pp. 16-26.

23. *Hou Han Shu*, Yee-wen press, 36/446.

24. Tai-ping Yu-lan (605) quoted Wang Yin's *Chin-shu*: "In the six year of T'ai Ho (232 A.D.), professor of the Royal College Chang Yi presented his new book, *Ku-chin Tzu-ku*, which said that in olden times *chih* was (a roll of) white silk cut into lengths according to the number of words to be written on it.

25. *Hou Han Shu*, vol. 78, Yee-wen press, p. 897.

26. Second rank of eunuch in Later Han.

27. First rank of eunuch.

28. From professor T. H. Tsien's translation in *Written on Bamboo and Silk*, p. 136. The original *Tung-kuan Han-chi* was lost. This issue in the *Chu-chen-pan Ts'ung-shu* was re-collected from the *Yun-lo Ta-tien*. As a chief eunuch, one could not shut himself off from service to the throne. Therefore I doubt whether it is a genuine source. But the part which concurs with the *Hou Han Shu* is reliable.

29. In the *Hou Han Chi* (by Yuan Hung in the fourth century A.D.; Commercial Press in *Ssu-pu Ts'ung-k'an*) it was said that Empress Teng was established as the Emperor's main consort. She then asked the various provinces to contribute *chih* and ink cakes only and that the other presents should be abolished. This was in the year 102 A.D., three years before the invention of paper. There might have been some refined specimens of paper produced at that time but it is unlikely that the use of paper became popular in the various provinces. Since Yuan Hung lived in the fourth century the word *chih* then meant both paper and silk. We do not know the exact meaning of *chih* here to use it for paper.

30. *Hou Han Shu*, 64, Yee-wen press, p. 750.

31. Tien Yeh: Shensi *Sheng Pa-chiao Fa-ksien. Hsi-han-ti-chih. Wen-wu Ts'an-kao Tsu-liao*, vol. 6, 1957. And Kuo Mo-jo's *Hsin Chung-kuo Kao-ku-ti Shuo-ho*, 1962, p. 83.

本篇轉載自 Chinese Culture.

The Division of Time in the Han Dynasty as Seen in The Wooden Slips

In the study of the wooden slips which was published in 1960, I denoted some ideas based on the records of the Han Dynasty and the research on the Han sun-dial by Professor Liu Fu (劉復). Some seven years later I have made a new revision of the edition contained in *Chü-yen Han chien K'ao-cheng*. An article by Mr. Chen Meng-chia (陳夢家) entitled "A Reconstruction of the Han Dynasty Calendar Based on the Han Slips" was published in *K'ao-ku Hsio-pao*, nos. 1–2, 1965. Certainly he has the right of his presentation, particularly, since he worked on the article for such a long time. But his basic thesis is that the Han division of time was divided into eighteen units perday. I find it extremely difficult to agree with his opinion In the following I would like to prove that each day was divided into twelve units.

A. THE DECIMAL DIVISION, THE HUNDRED SECTION AND THE FIVE DIVISIONS OF NIGHT

The oldest way of recording days was the chia-tzu (甲子) system, which consited of a combination of two series of numbers, namely, t'ien-kan (天干)and ti-chih (地支); t'ien-kan was divided into ten units and ti-chih was divided into twelve units. Matching odd with odd and even with even of the two series, they formed sixty different combinations for naming the days. The original hsün (旬) system of the Yin-Shang civilization for naming days was the deceimal system; the division into twelve units may have been borrowed from another civilization. This basis may be used to explain the decimal division of a day and the hundred section for the further division of a day.

In the fifth year of Chao-Kung (Duke Chao of the State of Lu) there was a statement on the recording of time.[1] "The number of suns is ten, therefore oneday contains ten hours, and it is identified as ten ranks (of state). The King ranks first, lords rank second, ministers rank third. As for a day, noon

---

1. "Ch'un-ch'iu Tso-Chuan", *Shih-san Ching Chu-su, Chüan* 43. Yee-wen ed. pp. 743-44

〔日中 jih-chung〕 is the highest, dining time 〔食 shih〕 is second and day-break 〔且 tan〕 is third." During the day two divisions preceded noon. Thus two other divisions must exist after noon. According to this method the divisions of day time must be: (1) day-break (且 tan); (2) early dining time (食 shih); (3) noon (日中 jih-chung); (4) later dining time (餔 pu); (5) dusk (昏 hun). Hun was always the opposite of tan (dawn) according to the chapter Yüeh-ling of *Li Chi*. (禮記) 。

However, there was an explanation in the commentary of Tu Yü in *Tso Chuan*. (左傳杜預注) He said the ten divisions were identified as: (1) jih-chung (日中 noon); (2) shih-shih (食時 early dining time); (3) p'ing-tan (平旦 day-break); (4) chi-ming (雞鳴 cock's cry); (5) yeh-pan (夜半 mid-night); (6) jen-ting (人定 man-settled); (7) huang-hun (黃昏 twilight); (8) jih-ju (日入 sunset); (9) pu-shih (餔時 later dining time); (10) jih-yi (日昳 sun-declined). This explanation seems to be plausible but there is a problem that was not indicates by former scholars, and that is that there were only three divisions in the interval between mid-night and noon, whereas there were five divisions in the interval between noon and mid-nght. There would be no reason for the ancients to use this unequal division.

Thus far Tu Yü's idea is not a feasible one, and it must be changed into the following; (1) jih-chung (noon); (2) shih-shih (early dining time); (3) tan-shih or p'ing-tan (day-break); (4) jih-ch'u (日出 sunrise); (5) chi-ming (cock's cry); (6) yeh-pan (mid-night); (7) jen-ting (man-settled); (8) jih-ju (sunset); (9) hun-shih or huang-hun (twilight); (10) pu-shih (later dining time).

By this arrangement the divisions are dividen either from noon to mid-night or from mid-night to noon. This leaves the problem of a different arrangement from that of the twelve divisions of the Han Dynasty, which had also been mentioned in the commentary of Tu Yü.[1] According to the order given in the *Tso Chuan*, jih-ch'u (sunrise) must precede p'ing-tan (day-break), but from the records of the Han and later periods, p'ing-tan follows jih-ch'u. In a similar way, the order of the ancient huang-hun (twilight) and jih-ju (sunset) would be reversed. Therefore, the order of hours for the Han Dynasty was: (1) yeh-pan; (2) chi-ming; (3) p'ing-tan; (4) jih-ch'u; (5) shih-shih; (6) yü-chung (隅中); (7) jih chung; (8) jih-yih; (9) pu-shih; (10) jih-ju; (11) huang-hun; (12)

---

1. Tu Yü said: "The Yü-chung (隅中) and jih-ch'u (日出) are not included in the order". These two divisions were two extra hours of the Han Dynasty.

jen-ting.

Even though the division of hours was changed in the Han Dynasty, the farther division of hours was retained in the old way. Hence one day was not only divided into twelve hours but it was also divided into one hundred sections, which could not be evenly divided between the twelve hours.

The old system divided the day time into five parts. In a similar way the nighttime should be divided into five parts. Although the record of Ch'un-ch'iu times could not be found, the division of night in Han times followed the same pattern.

The five divisions of night was called Five Nights, namely; (1) chia-yeh (甲夜); (2) yi-yeh (乙夜); (3) ping-yeh (丙夜); (4) ting-yeh (丁夜); (5) wu-yeh (戊夜). The name Five Nights was adopted from the name of t'ien-kan, or the decimal system for the arrangement of days.

These five parts were in turn used for the guards both inside the palace and outside of the frontier. Tsai Chih's *Han Yi* (蔡質漢儀)[1] said:

"In every palace, when the waterclock is finished the guards must start after the drum is beaten and rest after the bell rings. They are in place by the order of their credentials, when chia-yeh is finished they call on yi-yeh and then the five changes."

The five changes in Chinese is wu-keng, which was followed by many dynasties and was preserved in some places under the Chinese Republic.

In the slips[2] the system of five night was also used. An important example is: "A [beacon] fire [was seen] in yi-yeh [second section of night]; a fire in ping-yeh [third section of night]; and a fire in ting-yeh [fourth section of night]." In the *Han Shu* we find the "tiao-tou[3] was beaten to warn each camp at every section of the five nights."[4] It was to show the night guard at the

---

1. "Han Kuan Liu Chung", *Ssŭ-pu pi-yao*, Chung-hua Book Co. Taipei.
2. Slip no. 88 in the Documents.
3. Tiao-tou (刁斗) was a pan made of bronze which was used for cooking by day and for a warning gong at night.
4. It was said by Tu Chin (杜欽) in the Biography of Hsi-yü (西域) in *Han Shu* (pu-chu chüan 96, p. 1678). The commentary of Yen Shih-Ku said: "A night contains five turns (keng 更), hence the pan must be taken in turn". Cheug Hsüan's commentary in the Ssŭ-wu-shih (司寤氏) of *Chou Li* (shih-san-ching chu-su, Chou Li Chuan 36, p. 549) said: "Nignt time means the order of hours at night like the present chia (甲) to wu (戊)". Shuai-Keng (率更) was a Han official according to Yen Shih Ku's commentary in "*Han Shn Pai-kuan Piuo*" (*Han Shu Pu-Chu*, Chüan 19, p. 307). His duty was to attend the waterclock in the palace Shuai means to lead and Keng means the turn. From the meaning of the title, "Keng" at night was quite important, therefore the system of five sections of night was retained in Han and preserved through some two thonsand years.

northern and western borders

We find the materials for the five-nights through the Wei and Chin Dynasties, but by the end of the Northern and Southern Dynasties people knew the five turns only with ignorance of its origin. As Yen Chih-tui's *Yen-shih Chia-hsün* (顏氏家訓)[1] said:

"Someone asks me what is the meaning of five-turns [wu-keng] in one night. I explained in the following way: 'During the Han and Wei periods it included chia-yeh, yi-yeh, ping-yeh, ting-yeh and ping-yeh. Sometimes it was called Ku [鼓 drum], as yi-ku, erh-ku, san-ku,ssu-ku and wu-ku, or sometimes Keng [更 turn], as yi-keng, erh-keng, san-keng, ssu-keng and wu-keng. Every one of these names was divided into five sections [because there are five variations for each of the turns in direction which are pointed out by the tail of the Dipper). Suppose the first moon is to the yin [寅 nee] and the Dipper's tail is pointing to yin [nee] in the evening sky [8 0'clock]. When day breaks [about 4 0'clock], it points to wu [午 south]. From yin to wu there are five turns [yin (寅), nee; mao (卯). cast; chen (辰), see; ssu (巳), sse and wu (午), south]. Even when the night is longer in the winter and shorter in the summer, the directions which the Dipper's tail (斗柄) points out will not be more than six nor less than four. The number of sections is always five. Keng means 'in turn,' therefore the sections of night are called five keng."

Here the explanation of the five keng or five turns is quite clear. However, it was based on a theory of later development-the duo-decimal system of twelve divisions-used to explain the old decimal system of ten divisions.

Under the decimal system, one hundred units (刻 k'e) were divided equally among the ten hours (時 shih), as in *Tso-chuan*. But in Han times, twelve hours were used under the duo-decimal system, indicating a difficulty in distributing the hundred ke equally.

The only method was to attribute to every hour (shih) eight and one-third ke. It was rendered thus:

First hour: beginning on the line and ending $1/3$ the distance from the last line (11 P.M.–1 A.M.)

Second hour: beginning $2/3$ the distance from the-limit and ending $2/3$ the distance from the last line. (1 A.M.–3 A.M.)

---

1. *Yen-shih Chia-hsün,* chüan 17, p. 38. Shih-chieh Book Co.

Third hour: beginning $^1/_3$ the distance from the limit and ending on the line (3 A.M.–5 A.M.).

Fourth hour: beginning on the line (5 A.M.–7 A.M.).

Fifth hour: beginning $^1/_3$ the distance from the limit. (7 A.M.–9 A.M.)

Sixth hour: beginning $^2/_3$ the distance from the limit and ending on the limit line. (9 A.M.–11 A.M.)

Seventh hour: beginning from the limit line. (11 A.M.–1 P.M.)

Eighth hour: beginning from $^1/_3$ the distance to the limit line. (1 P.M.–3 P.M.)

Ninth hour: beginning from $^2/_3$ the distance to the limit line and ending on the limit line. (3 P.M.–5 P.M.)

Tenth hour: beginning from the limit line. (5 P.M.–7 P.M.)

Eleventh hour: beginning from $^1/_3$ the distance to the limit line. (7 P.M.–9 P.M.)

Twelvth hour: beginning from $^2/_3$ the distance to the limit line and ending on the limit line. (9 P.M.–11 P.M.)

In Han times, time was not kept so exactly. K'e was the smallest unit for daily use. Thus the surplus $^1/_3$ at the end of the first hour, the surplus $^1/_3$ at the beginning and the end of the second hour and the surplus of $1^1/_2$ at the beginnnig of the third hour (and the surpluses of the other hours) would be considered as the secondardy k'e to the next k'e. From the record of the Han Slips, the ordinal number for k'e is not more than seventh.[1]

This method of distribution was too complex and impractical, therefoe the scholars attempted to change to the one hundred and twenty k'e to adopt it to the duo-decimal system of hours. This first change was in 5 B. C. and the second was in 9 A.D. The former was ordered by the usurper Wang Mang, but was invalid at the fall of the usurped dynasty fourteen years later. According to "T'ien-wen Chih" (Record of Astronomy) in *Sui shu*(隋書)[2], Emperor Liang Wu-ti (梁武帝) had changed the system from 100 k'e to 96 k'e. Unfortunately it was not used under the unification of the Sui Dynasty.

The system of one hundred sections was described in the *Wu-tai Hui-yao*: "In the fourth year of Tien-fu (天福) of Later Chin (：晉), Ssu-tien Chien (An

---

1. In *Chü-yen Han-chien K'ao-cheng*, p. 68, the pa-feng(eighth feng or eighth ke)was recorded, but from a review of the original photograph of slips numbered 317. 27 and 56. 41 the Character Pa (eight or eighth) is unclear. Therefore there may be no eighth K'e in every hour. However, in the Han time there were no independent k'e, between two hours as that Sung calender did. of. *Chü-yen Han-chien Kao-cheng Pu-cheng* BIHP. vol. 14, pp. 236-237.

2. The records of the institutions in *Sui Shu* refer to the dynasties from Chin to Sui.

official of Astronomy supersision) memorialized to the throne about the Book of the waterclock: 'Every day is divided into one hundred k'e, distributed among twelve shih [hours]. Every hour contains eight and one-third k'e. Every k'e contains eighty-one fen [分 minutes][1]. One hour contains eight k'e and twenty fen.'" This was a later development of the tenth century. There was no change in ·the seconds of the k'e system.

Up until the Catholic fathers reached China at the end of the Ming Dynasty the new system of ninety-six k'e per day was advocated. But it was only during the Ch'ing Dynasty[2] that it was first used. In the ninth year of K'ang-hsi(1671)the western theory was proved by the testimony of Father Ferdinandus Verbiest, and the 96 k'e system became popular. But the one hundred section system had been used intermittently for two thousand years during which time the duo-decimal system appeared.

This new system of 96 k'e is a combination of the old Chinese system and the western system, in which one shih contains eight k'e. In other words a k'e is fifteen minutes or a quarter of an hours. By this way minutes and seconds are easily adapted under the k'e. Even now, in modern Chinese, one hour (formerly hsiuo-shih or small shih) or one shih contains four k'e, which may be traced to its development during Han times.

B. THE DUO-DECIMAL DIVISION OF HOURS IN HAN TIMES

In the previous chapter, the decimal (天干 t'ien-kan) and the duo-decimal divisions (地支 ti-chih) were apparently derived from two different systems. They had been combined for use and traced to the Shang Dynasty, but each one may have been used separately.

This contradiction clearly appeared in the system of timely record. Even though the ten divisions was used in Ch'un-ch'iu times, the tendency towards the use of twelve divisions increased and became dominant in the Han Dynasty. It may have originated in the warring states period. There is no question that the standard measurement during Han was the system of twelve hours in a day.

From the Chü-yen slips come the following examples refering to the division of one day:

1. In Han times fen and k'e were the same thing. This was a new development of the T'ang Dynasty, influenced by the theory of India and indirectly by Greeks.
2. "*Shih-hsien Chih*" (Record of Calendar) in *Ch'ing Shih-Kao.*

(1) yeh-pan [mid-night].[1]

yeh-pan chin-shih [the end of yeh-pan, or the end of the division of yeh-pan].[2]

yeh-ta-pan san-fen [the second part of yeh-pan passed three fen].[3]

yeh-shao-pan [the first part of yeh-pan].[4]

yeh-ta-pan [the second part of yeh-pan].[5]

yeh-hsiao-pan [hsiao = shao, the first part of yeh-pan].[6]

yeh-pan [mid-night].[7]

yeh-shih-shih [night lunch-time]···yeh kuo-pan [night passed half].[8]

yeh-kuo-pan [night passed half].[9]

yeh-shih-shih [night lunch-time].[10]

yeh-shih [night lunch].[11]

(2) Chi-ming [cock's cry]

chi-chien-ming [the beginning of the cock's cry].[12]

chi-ming [cock's cry][13]

chi-fu-ming [cock's second cry].[14]

chi-ming [cock's cry].[15]

chi-ming [cock's cry].[16]

(3) Ping-tan [day-break]

---

1. There are some variations of yeh-pan because on each side of mid-night there were two days referred to. In the slips yeh-hsiao-pan or yeh shao-pan might be related to the first day of the first half of yeh-pan, in which night had not passed half; and yeh-ta-pan might be related to the second day or the second half of yeh-pan, in which night had passed than half. Yeh-shih-shih (night lunch time) was indicated while people ate. Becanse there were only two lunch times in one day, one who watched at night must have a time for lunch and the lunch-time was more suitable at the first halt of yeh-pan, for the interral from the second lunch to yeh-pan. was the same length as that from the first lunch to the second lunch
2. Slip no. 503.5 in *Documents*. H(Chü-yen an-chien K'ao-cheng, pp. 30-33)
3. Slip no. 185.3 in *Ibid.*
4. Slip no. 224.23 in *Ibid.*
5. Slip no. 317.27 in *Ibid.*
6. Slip no. 270.2 in *Ibid.*
7. Slip no. 130.8 in *Ibid.*
8. Slip no. 565.4 in *Ibid.*
9. Slip no. 523.24 in *Ibid.*
10. Slip. no. 184.24 in *Ibid.*
11. Slip no. 188.21 in *Ihid.*
12. Slip no. 503.5 in *Ibid.*
13. Slip no. 161.2 in *Ibid.*
14. Slip no. 193.11 in *Ibid.*
15. Slip no. 82.1 in *Ibid.*
16. Slip no. 157.14 in *Ibid.*

ping-tan [1]

ping-tan [2]

ping-tan [3]

ping-ming [day-light].[4]

(4) jih-ch'u [sunrise]

jih-ch'u [5]

jih-ch'u [6]

jih-ch'u [7]

(5) shih-shih [lunch-time] or tsao-shih[early lunch]

shih [lunch].[8]

tsao-shih [early lunch] and shih-shih [lunch-time].[9]

tsao-shih chin [end of early lunch].[10]

shih [lunch].[11]

tsao-shih [early lunch].[12]

shih-shih [lunch time].[13]

(6) tung-chung [east to noon]

jih-tung-chung [sun rises east to noon].[14]

jih-tung-chung shih [the time of sun-rise east to noon].[15]

(7) jih-chung [noon]

chung-shih [noon time].[16]

jih-kuo-chung-shih [sun passed noon].[17]

jih chung shih [sun at noon].[18]

1. Slip no 522.3 in *Ibid*.
2. Slip no. 185.3 in *Ibid*.
3. Slip no. 143.12 in *Ibid*.
4. Slip no. 127.25 in *Ibid*.
5. Slip no. 502 .1 in *Ibid*.
6. Slip no. 170.4 in *Ibid*.
7. Slip no. 317.1 in *Ibid*.
8. Slip no. 506.6 in *Ibid*
9. Slip no. 506.2 in *Ibid*. Shih-shih was divided into two parts-tsao-shih and shih-shih. It was the same in *Huang-ti Nei-ching Su-wen*. where shih-shih was given as two terms-tsao-shih and yen-shih.
10 Slip no. 170.4 in *Ibid*.
11. Slip no 239.34 in *Ibid*
12. Slip no. 317.27 in *Ibid*.
13. Slip no. 56.37 in *Ibid*.
14. Slip no. 506.6 in *Ibid*.
15 Supplementary Slip no. 16 in *Ibid*.
16. Slip no. 484.18 in *Ibid*.
17.18. Slip no. 523.24 in *Ibid*. jih-kuo-chung shih meant the time just past noon, thus differing, from jih-hsi chung shih, which meant the sun had declined to west of center.

jih chung shih [sun at noon].[1]

(8) jih tieh [sun declines]

jih-hsi chung-shih [sun passed west from noon].[2]

jih-hsi chung-shih [sun passed west from noon].[3]

jih tieh chung shih [sun declines from noon].[4]

jeh tieh [sun declines].[5]

(9) hsia-pu [later lunch]

hsia-pu shih [later lunch time][6].

jih-pu shih [later lunch-time during the day].[7]

hsia-pu [later lunch].[8]

hsia-pu [later lunch].[9]

hsia-pu [later lanch].[10]

hsia-pu [later lunch].[11]

hsia-pu [later lunch].[12]

(10) jih-ju [sunset]

jih-ju shih [sunset time].[13]

jih-ju-shih [sunset time].[14]

jih-ju [sun set].[15]

(11) hun-shih or huang-hun [twilight]

hun-shih [twilight].[16]

jih hun-shih [sun at twilight].[17]

hun-shih [twilight].[18]

1. Slip no. 143.12 in *Ibid*
2. Slip no 187.23 in *Ibid*.
3. Supplementary Slip nos. 126.40 and 332.5 in *Ibid*·
4. Slip no. 132.17 in *Ibid*.
5. Slip no. 56.41 in *Ibid*.
6. Slip nos. 506.16 and506.17 in *Ibid*.
7. Slip no. 288.30 in *Ibid*.
8. Slip no. 212.2 in *Ibid*.
9. Slip no. 132.17 in *Ibid*.
10. Slip no. 229.34 in *Ibid*.
11. Slip no. 157.14 in *Ibid*
12. Slip no. 3.22 in *Ibid*.
13. Slip no. 495.19 in *Ibid*.
14. Slip no. 383.99 in *Ibid*.
15. Slip no. 161.16 in *Ibid*.
16. Slip no. 505.6 in *Ibid*.
17. Slip no. 506.19 in *Ibid*
18. Slip no. 502.3 in *Ibid*.

yeh hun-shih [evening twilight].[1]

hun-shih[twilight].[2]

huang hun-shih [twilight].[3]

(12)　jen-ting [humans settled]

jen-ting shih [humans settled time].[4]

jen-ting [humans settled].[5]

Looking at the above records, there are clearly twelve divisions the same as those applied for the last two thousand years.

From Wang Chung's *Lun-heng*[6], *Huang-ti Nei-ching Su-uen* (黃帝內經素問)[7] and the T'ang Folk songs from *Tun-huvng Chui-so* 敦煌綴瑣[8] the order of time will be arranged as follows:

Han slips	*Lun-heng*	*T'ang Folk songs*
1. yeh-pan (夜半)	yeh-pan (夜半)	yeh·pan tzu (夜半子)
2. chi-ming (雞鳴)	chi-ming (雞鳴)	chi-ming chou (雞鳴丑)
3. ping-tan (平旦)	ping tan yin(平旦寅)	ping-tan yin (平旦寅)
4. jih-ch'u (日出)	jih-ch'u mao(日出卯)	jih-ch'u mao (日出卯)
5. shih-shih (食時)	tsao-shih (早食)	shih-shih chen (食時辰)
6. tung-chung (東中)	yen-shih (宴食)	yü-chung ssu (隅中己)
7. jih-chung (日中)	jih-chung (日中)	cheng-nan wu (正南午)
8. jih-tieh (日昳)	jih-tieh (日昳)	jih-tieh wei (日昳未)
9. hsia-p'u (下餔)	hsia-p'u(yen-pu)(下餔)	p'u-shih shen (晡時申)
10. jih-ju (日入)	jih-ju (日入)	jih-ju yu (日入酉)
11. hun-shih (昏時)	huang-hun (黃昏)	huang-hun hsü (黃昏戌)
12. jen-ting (人定)	jen-ting (人定)	jen-ting hai (人定亥)

The terms from Han to T'ang are the same. The problems are (1) How the terms originated and (2) How the coincidence with ti-chih (i.e., tsu, chou, yin, mao,)began. ?

Turning to the first problem, we find that five of the twelve terms appeared in the *Tso chuan*, which means that the terms had been created when the

---

1. Slip no. 505.22 in *Ibid.*

2. Slip no. 495.28 in *Ibid.*

3. Slip no. 185.25 in *Ibid.*

4. Slip no. 505.19 in *Ibid.*

5. Slip no. 484.18 in *Ibid.*

　　Lun-heng, Chien-shih pien, Shih-Chieh Book Co., Taipei 1955, p. 2 31.

6. *Huang-ti Nei-Ching su-wen*, Chüan 4.22 and 65.

7. Liu Fu. *Tun-hunang Chiw-so*, Chüan 35. Acadimia Sinica, peking.

decimal system was in use. Hence the terms for time were used at the beginning of Han and were recorded in th *Shih chi* (史記) :

"K'ang Hsiang attacked Han from Hsiao in the morning. When he went to Peng Chen he beat down the Han troops at jih-chung."[1]

"The King entertained soldiers and met on the battlefield at tan."[2]

"The later first year, fifth moon, ping-hsü, the earth quaked; at tsao-shih the earthquaked again."[3] 'you, boy, can be taught,' he said. After five days come here at ping-ming. [chang] Liang was astonished, but kneeled and said, 'yes'. Five days later, at p'ing-ming, the old man come before Liang arrived, saying, 'why would [you] ge so late, come earlier in another five days.' On that very day Liang came at chi-ming, but the senier was still there. He Ordered Liang to come earlier in another five days. Liang came there at yeh-pan and the old man succeeded. After a while he gave Liang a bundle of books, saying.' Be a tutor of the real king with them.'[4]

"Han Hsin reached the Chin-hsing pass. He started on his march at yeh-pan. At ping-tan he went from that pass with the banner and drum of the chief general."[5]

In the above, yeh-pan, chi-ming, p'ing-ming (ping-tan) and tsao-shih were the same as that of the slips. Particularly according to the story of Chang Liang,[6] the three divisions—jih-pan, chi-ming, p'ing-ming-were connected, which showed that the divisions were unchanged from the beginning of the Han Dynasty. In other words, the duo-decimal system had existed at the beginning of the second century.

Of course there was the other system in the "T'ien-wen Pien" (天文篇) of *Huai-Nan Tzu* (淮南子)[7] which divided the day into fifteen divisions instead of the popular nine divisions. The fifteen divisions are: chen-ming (jih-ch'u), fei—ming (new), tan—ming (p'ing-tan), tsao-shih, yen-shih (both taken from shih-shih), yü-chung (yü chung or tung-chung), cheng-chung (jih-chung), hsiao-chien (new), pu-shih (pu-shih or hsia-pu), ta-chien, ta-ch'ung, hsia-ch'ung (all three were taken from jih-tieh), hsüan-chü (jih-jn), huang-hun (huang hun or hun-

1. *Shih Chi*, Chüan 7, Yee-wen Book Co., p. 153.
2. *Ibid.*, Chüan 8, p. 169.
3. *Ibid.*, Chüan 11, p. 205.
4. *Shih Chi*, Chüan 55, pp. 812-13.
5. *Ibid.*, Chüan 92, p. 1060.
6. It was perhaps not a trne story, but it was told before the time of Ssu-ma Ch'ien.
7. *Huai-Nan-Tru*, Chüan 3, Shih-chieh Book-Co. Taipei, 1955, p. 44.

hih), ting-hun (new). These divisions were from the *Huai-Nan Tzu* only; they were not used by the Han astronomer. Therefore we do not consider them as belonging to a practical system.

The division of time into twelve units was fixed at the beginning of the Former Han Dynasty. Naturally these were easily attributed to the twelve ti-chih. But at the end of the Former Han, the time was called "chia" (加) (to add) to some of the ti-chih, such as, "jin chia mao" or "jih chia shen", etc., and not "mao shih" or "shen shih". It means a position referring to that day and not the name of a position which was also the name of the time.

A combination of ti-chih and the time division may be traced to the astrologist Yi Feng (翼奉) in his biography in *Han shu*.[1] "In the second year of Ch'u-yüan of Ch'eng-ti [48 B. C.], he was called to court. Then he memorialized to the throne, saying that 'the day Kuei-wei (癸未) of the First Moon[2] [the day plus shen][3] there was a tornado from the south-west……. It indicated that some wicked servants were by the side of the ruler.' One year later, in the third year of Ch'u-yüan of the Fourth moon, on the day yi-wei pai-hao kuan [White Crane Hall] of Wu-ti's tomb was burned. Feng memorialized again, saying, 'the Pai-hao Kuan was burned in the Fourth moon on the day yi-wei, and the time was the day plus mao, your servant had confidence in his theory."

This was the first time that the duo-decimal divisions of the day had been combined with the "plus" of the ti-chih, and it must have been created by Yi Feng, an eminent confucian astrologist. Hence that method may be very easily accepted by other scholars.

"Seventeen years later, in the third year of chien-shih [30 B.C.] in the reign of Ch'eng-ti, on the first day wu-shen of the Twelfth moon, the sun was eclipsed at the time of 'plus wei'." as quoted from the memorial of Tu ch'in.[4] In a similar case, "in the second year of Chien-p'ing under Ai-ti [5 B.C.] the sun was eclipsed on the First day of the Fourth moon. Li ch'in memorialized to the throne, saying that 'the time was day plus ch'en'." Both of these showed that the combination of time with ti-chih had been gradually acepted.

The San-t'ung Li (三統歷 calendar of the Three Dynasties), which was a

---

1. *Han Shu*, Chüan 75, p. 1401-1404.

2. According to the Commentary, Kuei-wei was the twenty-second day, becanse there was no Kuei-wei in the First moon of the first year of Chu-Yüan.

3. In the text it was "jih chia shen", which means the day plus shen. It indicates the ninth time division and is identified as "hsia-pu".

4. *Han Shu*, "wu-hsing chih", Chüan 27, p. 655. Yee Wen edition.

new creation of a systematic calendar by Liu Hsin at the end of the Former Han Dynasty, as quoted by Pan Ku in the "Lu-li chih" (律歷志) of *Han shu*, did not give any significance to the combination of time and ti-chih.[1] This means that Liu's calendar was based on the traditional pattern without the ti-chih combination of hour-divisions. He by nomeans opposod the latter system. In fact he was the designer of the cultural institutions of the usurper Wang Mang, whose ouder of the reform of the calendar was based on the ti-chih combination system.

Nine A. D. was the first year of Shih-chien-kuo of Wang Mang, (王莽) the date in which he changed the Han Calendar system into his own system.[2] He changed the Twelfth moon of the former year into the First moon of the new year (to use the moon of chou as the beginning of the year) and changed chi-ming (the second division of a day) to the chou hour. These reforms showed that Wang considered the "earth-virtue" to be his lucky element, and the ti-chih chou was one representative order of the earth. under that arrangement ch'ou (丑) was not only a "plus-number" to chi-ming but it was also chi-ming itself. It would be the first time that this trend was used-tzu-shih, (子時) ch'ou-shih, (丑時) yin-shih, (寅時) etc. For yeh-pan, chi-ming, ping-tan, etc.

Comparing the "Wu-hsing Chih" (五行志) of *Han Shu* (漢書) and that of *Hou Han Shu*, (後漢書) there is a great difference. In the *Han Shu*,[3] jih-chung, pu-shih and hsia-pu were used for recording time in the reign of Han Wu-ti, whereas in *Hou Han Shu*, shih-jih chia-mao (時日加卯 day time plus mao), which means jih-ch'u (the fourth hour) is used for recording time in the reign of Hou Han Kuang-wu-ti.

Wang Ch'ung's *Lun Hung* (論衡) was completed in the second year of Ch ang Ho (88 A.D.) (the reign title of Chang-ti). It was later than the time of Chien Wu. He said in "Lan-shih pien" (調時篇) 'of his book'.[4]" "One day is

---

1. Chen Meng-chia guoted the beginnings of heaven, earth and man as they were related to the order of ti-chih. He considered they were the time of day, but the evidence is very weak. This is because they were the applications of ti-chih extended from its use for days to months to years, etc., and finally to the universe as a whole, which would not be referring to the divisions of a day.

2. "Biography of Wang Mang", *Han Shu Pu-Chu*, Chüan 99, p. 1728.

3. "Wu-hsing Chih", *Han-Shu Pu-Chu*, Chüan 27, p. 654 gives the first Year of Yüan-Kuang and the fourth Year of Cheng-ho of Han Wu-ti, *Hou Han Shu Chi Chieh*, Chüan 18, "Wu-hsing Chih", p. 1215 Gives the Seventh Year of Chien-wu of Han Kuang-wu-ti in the Commentary quoted in Ku-chin chu.

4. *Lun Heng*, "Chien Shih Pien", p. 231. Shih-Chieh Book Co.

divided into twelve shih 〔hours〕, namely, ping-tan yin, jih-chu mao, etc. Twelve moons are 'set-up' as yin, mao, etc. They are the same as that of the 'hour-plus'." It is clear that the term "plus-hour" had become very popular by the beginning of the Latter Han Dynasty.

To name an hour with ti-chih as chia-shih (加時 plus-hour) was too awkward. Men preferred to use ti-chih for shih directly. Hence in the Chin Dynasty (third century) this direct method was used. In the Chin Slip from Lop Nor the following is recorded:[1] "The meeting will be on the twenty-fourth day of this month at mao-shih. According to the in formation this letter arrived at shen-shih."

Mao shih had been called jih-ch'u and shen-shih had been called hsia-pu in the Han Dynasty. But in that time it was changed for the purpose of simplicity, and it has been followed through more than two thousand years to the present day.

C. SUNDIAL AND WATERCLOCK

The beginning of a day, except when Wang Mang changed from chi-ming for a short time, in the Han period and the following dynesties began at the center of yeh-pan, that is the day always starts from zero o'clock on the twenty-four hour clock.

There was no reliable evidence for the beginning of a day before the calendar reform of Tai ch'u (太初 104 B.C.). During Tai-ch'u, however, it was standardized and continued for many centuries, that is, the day began from the center of mid-night. In the "Li-shu" (歷書) of *Shih Chi*,[2] the first year of Tai-ch'u was said to be a standard year because the winter solstice was at the center of midnight and that day was chia-tzu (甲子 the first day of the sexagenary cycle).

The difference between the Former and Later Han dynasties was that the system of time division was more refined in the Later Han. Accoring to the slips, the "fen" is the smallest unit and is identified as "k'e". But from the

---

1. *Lin Shan Chin-chien*, Chüan 2, Pu-shu No. 29, pg. 8.
2. *Shih Chi*, chüan 26, pg 499, Yee-wen ed, —According to Huan T'an's Hsin Lun (桓譚新論) from Yen K'o-chün (嚴可均): Ch'üan Hou-Han Wen (全後漢文); Chüan 15, pg. 2. Shih-chieh Book Co. ed, Taipei), the beginning of a system of the Calender was always based on the winter selistice in the *mid-night* of the day Chia-txzŭ, In the Lü-li Chih of Ssŭma Piao's Hsü Han Shu (pg. 1108, Yee Wen ed), it is said that the day of a system of calender would be beginning from *yeh-pan tzŭ*. Hence the *mid-night* or *yeh-pan* as the order of ti-chih in tzŭ area is alwaysthe beginning of a day and the beginning of a year and even a system of a calender.

"Lü-li chih" of *Hou Han Shu*,[1] a fen is one-tenth of a "K'e". Thus the term fen has different meanings at different periods in history.

The system of the Former Han was seen in the pieces of Han Chiu-yi,[2] and that of the Later Han was seen in the Lü-li Chih. They may be compared in the following manner:

Time of Year		K'e of Day	K'e of Night
Winter Solstice	F. Han	41	59
	L. Han	45	55
Beginning of Spring	F. Han	46	54
	L. Han	48.6	51.4
Beginning of Summer	F. Han	62	38
	L. Han	62.4	37.6
Summer Solstice	F. Han	65	35
	L. Han	65	35
Beginning of Autumn	F. Han	62	38
	L. Han	62.3	37.7
Beginning of Winter	F. Han	46(?)	54(?)
	L. Han	48.2	51.8

This means that one-tenth of a k'e was seen from the water clock during the Later Han Dynasty.

But this so-called day or night was a standard issued by the government for the purpose of changing water twice a day, of course the Chinese territory of that time was an area between twenty and fifty degrees latitude. Thus it was impossible to use the same standard for day and night uniformly. At any rate, it would have been rather crude to use it in the northern border area.

The water clock of the Han Dynasty cannot be traced through archaeological means. It is only based on pottery bottle with a pottery basin. Under the bottom of the bottle a small hole was drilled for the purpose of allowing water to drip through. Along the wall of the pottery basin marks must be carved to indicate k'e or minutes. However there were the records of the design of the T'ang and the Sung dynasties; they were the sets containing some boxes to make sets of waterclocks. They were probably used in the imperial palace to show the complex decoration in which the significance of the astrologers was seen.

---

1. *Hou Han Shu Chi-chieh*, chüan 3 of Chih, pg. 1108, Yee-wen ed.
2. Han Chin-yi means the old system of the Han Dynasty. *Han-Kuan Liu-Chung*, Ssǔ-pu Pi-yao, Chung-hua Book Co. Han-Chia-yi Pu-yi, Chüan 2, pg. 1.

But for daily use at the frontier, simple and practical ones were required, not complex.

In every offfice, whether at the frontier or inland, there were one set of waterclocks, one for day and one for night. In the wooden slips and in the "Lü-li chih" of *Hou Han Shu* chou-lou (晝漏 day waterclock) and jih-lou (夜漏 night waterclock) were differentiated as one set of time according to the seasons. When day began night ended, and when night began day ended. It means that one set of waterclocks were changed in turn everywhere.

The sun-dials of Han had been discorceed, although no more waterclocks are found. The three dials can be based, for purposes of comparison, on the time units of Han. One was owned by Tuan Fang (端方), as recorded in *T'ao-tsai Ts'ang-shih chi* (匋齋藏石記)[1] (and now is in the Historical Museum of Peking), another was owned by Chou chin (周進), and recorded in *Chü-chen Tsao-t'ang Han-chin Shih-yin* (居貞草堂漢晉石影)[2] and finally, the third is owned by the Toranto Museum of Canada, and was photographed by Liu Fu (劉復) for his article entitled "The Sun-Dials of Western Han" in the *Bulletin of Chinese Studies* of Peking University. [3]

The sun-dial, according to its spaces, may be divided into one hundred degrees. But only Sixty-nine degrees (or k'e) are shown by inscriptions of lines and marked with numbers. That dial may be used in Ai-hun city in Helungchiang in the summer solstice, as described by Professor Liu Fu In many places on the Chinese mainland, many k'e are not required even in the Summer.

The pole in the center of a dial must be adjusted on an angle according to the latitude of the position in question [4], and the main central line must point north. A stick is then erected at its center, the shadow of which shows the time on a given degree around the circle. In the following are the times [5] referring to the numbers of the circle:

1. *T'ao-chai Ts'ang-shih Chi* Chüan 1. pg. 3-8.
2. *Chu-chen Ts'ao-t'ang Han-Chin Shih Yin*, pg. 2.
3. Peking University: Kuo-hsio Chi-K'an. Vol. 3, No. 4 (1932) 573-610, and Joseph Needham: "Science and civilization in China" Vol. 4, pp. 261-298.
4 It might be by the way of adjusting the inclination of the central pole in the sundial. That pole was controled by four ropes at the four corners of the dial.
5. Here it indicated the central time in Chinese way as mao-cheng (卯正) which meant mao had passed a half, and wu-cheng (午正) meant wu had passed a half. Since mao began at 5 A. M. and endded at 7 A. M., the 6 A. M. was called mao-cheng. In similar way the 12 O'clock noon was called wu-cheng.

Time	Number
ping-tan (yin, 4 A.M.)	$1^1/_2$
jih-ch'u (mao, 6 A.M.)	10
tsao-shih (ch'en, 8A.M.)	$18^1/_2$
tun-chung (ssu, 10 A.M.)	$26^1/_2$
jih-chung (wu, 12 noon)	35
jih-yi (wei, 2 P.M)	$43^1/_2$
hsia-pu (sheng, 4 P.M.)	$55^1/_2$
jih-ju (yu' 6 P.M.)	60
huang-hun (hsü, 8 P.M.)	$68^1/_2$

The use of the sun-dial was limited to the day-light hours and good weather. It should be accompanied by the waterclock which was the main recorder of time in the palace, office and watch-tower. The dial was used to adjust the accuracy of the waterclock. Since the waterclock was so fragile, none remain today. The method of recording time must be found from the inscriptions on the dial and compared with the information from books and slips. Howerer it is very clear that there may be some later developments, such as the application of the term "ti-chih" to the name of the time. The main duo-decimal system still remained through the various dynasties.

PS. Many thanks are due to Mr. Walter Switkin for his help in the work of this article.

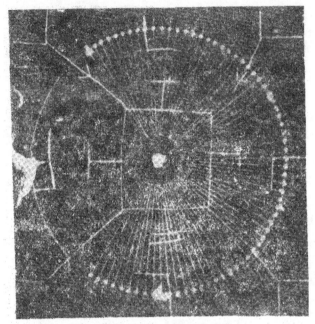

(1) Han Sun-dial from Suiyüan

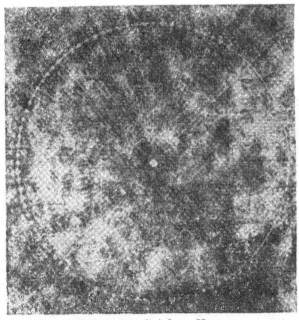

(2) Han Sun-dial from Honan

漢簡中的記時法 （中文提要）

　　中國記時法，商代的制度不詳，可能是只有且夕等名稱卻不是把一日分成一定的時區，不過據左傳上的記載，春秋時已把一日分作十時了，這種十進制的計時法，正是把一日分爲百刻的基本來源。

　　從漢代的材料中，顯然的可以看出來把它從十進制改爲十二進制，這或者和十二方位有關。依照淮南子天文篇，十二支分配到二十八宿，那就在漢初，或者更早至戰國時期，十二方位已經分配定了。日晷的日影和杙上十二支的方位是有關係的，那就一日分十二時比較一日分爲十時，就日晷的關係上說，更爲切實。何況十二的數目，可以用三除盡，可以用四除盡，在工作分配上更有它方便的地方。

　　居延漢簡中所用的記時法是十二進制的。有時一時會分爲前後兩個小單位，但並不妨礙十二時的計算法。淮南子天文篇雖然有一種十五分法的名稱，但這是以白天時爲限的，也就是從卯初至酉末爲七時，加倍爲十四時，再加上入夜的桑楡，總爲十五時。倘若把日夜都加倍，就成爲二十四時，還是十二進制。

　　十二時制和百刻制是不能互相配合的，即每時合 $8\frac{1}{3}$ 刻。西漢沒有刻以下的名稱，但從西漢的日晷來看，卻可能有半刻的算法。那就三分之一刻可能就按半刻去算。東漢以後一刻再分爲十分（依照漢簡，西漢刻就是分），那就三分之一刻就可以三刻半來計算了，這種算法雖然奇零，卻也簡單。不像宋代在每時八刻之外，每隔三時還有一個獨立的刻，作爲『加時』，再每月變更『加時』的位置。這實在太複雜了，直到清初才有一日分爲九十六刻的改革。

　　從漢簡計時法牽涉到的是日晷用法的問題。日晷上的指針不可以直放的，必需有一個傾斜度數，依照當地緯度及季節來調整。漢代的日晷，依照漢栻的構造來比較，大致是平放的。調整的應當專以中心的標桿（表）爲限。這個標桿依照漢代日晷及淮南子中的材料，是用四條繩（四維）繫著的。標桿的傾斜度就由四條繩來調整。

調整時一定要有標準。除去對準當地北極星的方向，還應當把標桿照出日影的長短記到日晷上，然後再按時調整。匋齋藏石記那塊日晷，除去原有刻度以外，後來記上的刻畫十分顯明，這就表示依照各地特殊情形，記到日晷上的事實。日晷上的符號普通被稱做ＴＬＶ（和ＴＬＶ式漢鏡相同），其中Ｖ是代表四維的，Ｔ的橫畫應當表示夏至的日影。Ｌ的橫畫應當表示冬至的日影。只要日晷上有這兩種記錄，標桿應當調整的傾斜度，就容易解決了。

本篇轉載自中央研究院史語集刊

Frescoes of Tunhuang

I. INTRODUCTION:

From very early times, Frescoes have always occupied a predominant position in Chinese painting. From the Han and the Wei Dynasties onward, paintings began to appear on paper and silk, but they were far less important. The advent in China of Buddhism gave an added incentive to this particular branch of fine art. As frescoes in Buddhist temples and monasteries became also objects of worship. It is a matter of great regret that most of the ancient temples have been long razed to the ground and that only the caves at Tunhuang, with its remote location and dry climate, have been able to preserve their paintings.

The Frescoes of Tunhuang are housed in the caves of the Thousand Buddhas, 12 miles southeast of Tunghuang City, Kansu Province. They show a decided influence of the Buddhist Caves at Ajanta in Hyderabal India, so that they are housed not in rooms but on the walls of caves dug in precipitous cliffs. The paintings were first executed in the second year of the reign of Chien Yuan of the Former Ch'in Dynasty (365), and carried on through Northern Wei (386-556), Northern Chou (557-580), Sui (581-618), T'ang (619-906), the Epoch of the Five Dynasties (907-959), down to the 3rd year of Ching Yu in the reign of Emperor Jen Tsung of the Sung Dynesty, when the place fell into the hands of the Tangut Kingdom. (1032-1227) In their turn, the Tanguts continued the work too, but only in a very small way. The caves of Tunhuang had then begun their decline.

The Ming Dynasty did not think much of the place. When the Manchus restablished Tunhuang during the reign of Emperor Yung Cheng (1723-1735), however, Chinese emigrants began to come in great hordes and to develop and explore the place. New Chinese paintings again appeared in the caves there, even, though artistically speaking, these late comers are a far cry from the original ones.

During the Northern Wei and T'ang Dynasties, Tunhuang had been an important juncture in east-west communication. Many a merchant or nobleman, in his desire to please the gods, contributed large sums of money for the erection of Buddhist statues and murals. As almost every cave excavated before or during the T'ang Dynasty has its distinguishing features to set each one apart from the other, It is fairly evident that the objects d'art in the caves were not wrought by local artisans, but by expert craftsman brought from some remote place especially for the purpose. With the exception of those preserved in its Caves of the Thousand Buddhas most of the paintings done prior to the T'ang Dynasty are no longer extent, so that these caves constitute, in a sense, the finest museum of medieval Chinese painting to be found anywhere and offer the most reliable measure for assessing and arranging the latter's chronology.

Apart from those photographs taken by the Chinese themselves these frescoes have been photographed primarily by Sir Aural Stein (as published in *Innermost* Asia and *Ruins of Desert Cathay*), and by Paul Pelliot (as published in *Les Grottes de Touen-houang*). The latter's work is expecially praiseworthy for its richness of material and it is a pity that, owing to technical difficulties obtaining at the time, the pictures have all been executed in monochrome.

On the whole, the frescoes may be divided into four categories: (1) patterns, (2) stories, (3) portraits of Buddhas and (4) portraits of worshippers.

Pattern are of two kinds: (1) *tsao-ching*（藻井）and *t'ien-hua*（天花）, both decorations for the ceiling, the former being designs that revolve around a domical center at the middle of the ceiling and the latter, scattered designs under the sloping roof with no central point; and (2) mariginal adornments along the sides of the frescoes. They all show distinct characteristics identifying them with the period in which they were produced.

Stories generally illustrate the life of Buddha Gautama, the popular version of the Sutra Amitaba, the Sutra of One Hundred Parables, the Sutra Vimalakirti, and such as have been mentioned in other Buddhist scriptures. The store is very rich and to a great extent also portrays the social life of medieval China.

The majority of the Portraits are of Sakyamuni, (Gautama) the others being distributed among Amitabha, the bodhisattvas and devas. In general, portraits done before the Sui Dynasty are chiefly of bodhisattvas in Chinese clothing, while those done during and after T'ang times are dressed like Indians, with devas attending upon them, cither beside the doors or in the four corners near the ceiling.

Donors who gave money to the construction of these caves were painted too, and their portraits with their names written thereon constitute the last category. As these were cxecuted in different ages, their clothing and omaments give us a clear picture of the times and customs they represent. The first period, encompassing the fourth Century through to the seventh, shows the influence off Central Asia, the clothes in the portraits are so tight fitting they may be worn even today. The second period starts with the eighth century, and the clothes of this period are so loose fitting they look like the Japanese kimono. From the Western Hsia (Tangut) Dynasty on, women are dressed in the long gowns worn chiefly by Tangut-Tibetan women.

Landscapes and architectural fcatures are but backdrops in the murals off Tunhuang, yet they have historical significance too. Places of the Northern Wei and T'ang Dynasties are drawn in great detail, showing minutcly the abacuses and the arches of a definitely Chinese order. They can be adopted harmoniously near the entrance of a level-roof or Grecian edifice or in the center of the more modernistic cubic buildings.

As to landscape, painting we know it was quite developed during Tang times but as an art it achieved maturity only in the Epoch of the Five Dynasties. The murals show clearly the evolutions from Northern Wei to Tang. Landscape painting has been considered as representative of the Chinese style of painting, but this medium of artistic expression has not been formed overnight.

In 1943, the National Government of the Republic of China set up an Art Research Institute a the Caves of the Thousand Buddhas charged with the cataloguing of these caves. Of the 427 caves then counted, 309 were bigger ones. They occupy a length of 1612 meters with over 2000 statues. The murals occupy a total area of over 25000 square meters.

Tunhuang murals reproduced in the National Historical Museum of Taipei are based on Kodachrome transparent films taken by Mr. Lo Chimei at the caves, which are projected on white walls, then traced and painted the original color. This work was executed by Mr.K.M.Hu. The most desirable way of reproduction would be facsimiles of some caves in their entirely, but, because of lack of space, we have to be content with reproductions representative of murals of the different dynasties, chronologically arranged.

They are, to be sure, merely a selection, but it is hoped that lovers of Tunhuang art will be enalbed to see in them in something approching the original armosphere.

II. TUNHUAG PAST AND PRESENT

Tunhuang is situated at the westernmost end of the corridor west of the Yellow River, 650 li from Suchow and 240 li from Ansi. If the place is approached from Ansi, it is necessary to leave the Kansu-Sinkiang Highway, travel in the boundless Gobi Desert, and pass one ruined and uninhabited city, and two villages each with only one family as its entire population before reaching the city. On the way, snow-capped mountains are seen far south, together with many beacons, left over from T'ang times, consisting of one big mound and four small ones, which, in times of old, were used for signally purposes by sending up puffs of smoke in the Red Indian fashion.

That Tunhuang could have attained great importance in its day, so far removed from China Proper as it is, can be attributed to its geographical location. It used to be the principal oasis west of the Chiayu Pass, and when one goes farther west from Tunhuang, whether it is to Hami in the north or to Lolan (a ruin near Lake Lobnor) in the west or to Charklik in the southwest, one has to trek the desert for seven or eight days. From very early times Turkestan prescented two menacing hazards for the Chinese traveler, one is the Muztagh Ata, rearing 7-8000 feet above the Pamir Plateau; the other is the Ghost Sand dunes between Tunhuang and Shan-shan, an area uninhabited by man or beast, and where mirages offer endless perils.

It can be then that Tunhuang was in its day a fertile place amid miles upon miles of wasteland, and an important communication center where traders going west had to store their goods and equip themselves for the hard trip ahead. The place also yielded gold dust, and was the meeting place for traders dealing in embroideries, raw medicine, spices, gold, silver and precious stones.

Metescological changes over the last few thousand years have made glaciers recede, wet and cold climates dry and hot. In central Asia, where the armies of Alexander the Great Once marched, it is now extreaching difficult to provide for a caravan of 20 people. Tunhuang was the victim of these fickle changes. It had been the most peaceful region in the land during the Northern and Southern Dynasties, yet it suffered seriously from natural setbacks. The national strength of the Sui and the T'ang Dynasties was hardly equal to that of the Han, and what with the invasions by the Khitan Tartars and the Mongolians, the situation there worsened until the place was abandoned in the Ming Dynasty, and its people ordered removed to inside the Chiayu Pass. In the process, the population here dwindled, cultivated land became desolate through disuse, and the surrounding desert made its inroads. When Emperor Yung Cheng of the Ching resettled the place, it could never return to its pristine state.

The Tunhuang of Han, or, for that matter, of Tang times, was better than the Tunhuang of today, and to a great degree. In volume 420, Tai-Ping Kuang-Chi, it is recorded that, "Northwest of Shachou (Tunhuang), is the Black River, deep enough for boating. It frequently floods so much that houses and fields are ruined. As a result, no crop can be planted there and the inhabitants have to move away."The Black River is now known as the Shuleh River. According to the Records of Turkestan Waterways, when General Yueh Chung-ch'i under Emperor Yung Cheng led his expedition here, only small craft could be managed, and even these had to be sunk when he reached the River of Two Pagodas. At present, the lower valley of the Shuleh River is navigable only for a very short period in the year. the natives, there used to be snow several feet deep in winter, blocking all traffic between Tunhuang and Ansi, but even snow has decreased in volume in recent years.

The decrease of snow accounts partially for the story. The reduction of tillable land can also be attributed to the abusive logging activities on Mountain Chilian. Tunhuang has no coal deposit and its populace of 26,000 has to rely on wood from the mountain for cooking and heating. When the forests on the mountain are more and more reduced, the snowline recedes higher and higher, until the mountain completely loses its power to meditate with the climate. There is now almost no district in Northwest China which is really self-sufficient, and before the main railway is completed, no constructive work can be carried out there.

In size, Tunhuang is comparable to the part of Kiangsu Province south of the Yangtse River, yet its tillage is no bigger than 30 li (15 Kilometers) east-west and 20 li south-north, exclusive of another piece of cultivated land at Nanhu, which is about 5 or 6 li in circumference. The rest of the area is nine tenths desert and one tenth pasturage, which, owing to lack of irrigation, has to be left unused except by some occasional Mogolians who come with their flocks of sheep.

The old city of Tunhuang is situated west of the Tang River, while the new city is on the other bank. The history of this walled city can be guessed conveniently on the basis of the broken pieces of Han pottery and the Yuan pagodas found there.

But, since it was abandoned during the Ming Dynasty and its western half was washed away by the Tang River, all that is left of it now is an area half a Kilometer west-east and one Kilometer south-north, renamed the Lihsien Fang, or Lihsien Section.

At the northwest corner of the new city, built during the reign of Emperor Yung Cheng of the Ch'ing Dynasty, is another walled area called the"Inner City," which occupies one fourth of the whole city. Surrounding this in the east and the south is the "City Gate Zone," which makes up the remaining three-fourths. The west wall of the "City Gate Zone" is actually the east wall of the old city, which, because of the shift of course of the Tang River, is left standing across the waterway. The city government is in the Inner City, as are most of the people living here. The business district if the street outside the East Gate. Export here consists of only cotton, and its imports are cotton cloth and machine-made goods. The place is good for raising cotton because Tunhuang is the lowest in elevation and has the least rainfall among all the cities in the Yellow River corridor. From wooden blocks of the Han Dynasty discovered here it is learned that clothing constituted a major problem in ancient times because silk piece goods had to come from far east. Now that Tunhuang has plenty of cotton, the problem no longer exists. This is one result of east-west communication.

80 li north of Tunhuang lies the north end of the Great Wall of the Han Dynasty. It has been erroneously though that the Great Wall runs east to Shanhaikuan and west (or north) to Blungchi, Actually, however, it ended at Chiayu Pass in the west during the Ming Dynasty, and, what is left of the Han Great wall ends near the Fuchang Beacon, west of the Yumen Pass. Inside the confines of Tunhuang, the Great Wall runs west along the Shuleh River, built with laver upon laver of adobe blocks and of some plant stalk. Salty water was used in mixing mud, which, when aged, became like glue. Along the Wass are many beacons, approximately one in every ten li. The

beacons are built with mud cakes or adobe. It was near here that Sir Aurel Stein found the Han wooden blocks. The Yumen Pass is a walled city 80 80 feet in area, about 250 li from Tunhuang.

The Caves of the Thousand Buddhas are on the U-shaped bluff of a canyon 12 miles southeast of Tunhuang. 30 li east of the canyon is the trident-like Mountain of Three Hazards, and 30 li west of it is the Mountain of Noisy Sands. The caves are on the eroded cliff west of the piece of terrace ground between the two mountains extending, north and south, 2 kilometers. The three-stratum caves command a small brook, and number over 500 of which 330 are fully furnished with frescos and effigies. Among these latter, 70 constructed and furnished during the Northern Wei (House of Toba, 386-501) and Sui Dynasties (581-618), and over 200 were done during Tang and early Sung times. The works in the Wei caves have a strong resemblance to the works at Turfan, Sinkiang, and Ajanta, India, whereas those of T'ang and the Epoch of the Five Dynasties are eminently Chinese. This divergency bespeaks rather eloquently the great significance that attended the conquest of the Chen Dynasty by Emperor Wen Ti of Sui.

Since no paintings of Wei and few of Tand exist today aside from those at Tunhuang, the art treasure of the Caves of the Thousand Buddhas is important and valuable on many counts, the least of which would be that is serves as a museum of medieval Chinese art.

III. THE CAVES OF THE THOUSAND BUDDHAS AND MURAL PAINTINGS OF TUNHUANG

The art of mural painting first began to appear during the New Stone Age. Even today there are colored murals of that age left in some mountain caves in France and Spain. On the walls of tombs of the Yin Dynasty, too, are found patternic decorations. *The Questions to the Heavens* by Chü Yuan were raised when the author saw the pictures of ancient monarchs on the walls in the royal ancestral shrine of the Kingdom of Chu. During the Han Dynasty, walls in the royal courts were also embellished with drawings of former kings and eminent administrators, and the Arcade of Unicorn and the Cloud Terrace were built for housing the portraits of famous officials of the time. These murals are, to be sure, no longer extant, but it is known for certain that, in the Eastern Han Dynasty, many shrines which formed part of some cemeteries had pictures in bas relief after court murals, as some of these are still preserved to this day.

When it was still confined to the reaches of India, Buddhism had already had frescos on cave walls dedicated to the illustration of its teachings. Since the religion was introduced to China, its drawings had been widely adopted in the newly erected temples. Many caves were prepared for the accomodation of this alien art, notably the Cave of the Thousand Buddhas at Tunhuang, which are said to have begun during the Dynasty of Former Chin (beginning 365 A.D.). Many new caves and paintings were added to the old in the subsequent Dynasties of Northern Wei, Sui and T'ang, with each period showing specific characteristics. At the begining of the Sung Dynasty, these caves became a veritable storehouse of Chinese art.

Geography explains the existence of this artistic storehouse. The corridor west of the Yellow River is a narrow but long strip of fertile soil. North of the corridor is a great desert, while south of it the terrain is rugged with high mountain ranges on which snow remains unmelted all the year round. The corridor is therefore the only inhabitable place which, by its location, happened in ancient times to be also the center of communication between East Asia and Central Asia, a position that was significant both politically and culturally.

During the period of the Warring States and the early years of the Han Dynasty, the land had first been occupied by the Yüeh-Chih and Usun tribes, and later by the Huns, the exploited its strategical position to control the whole Turkestan. In 121 A.D., Emperor Wu Ti of Han sent an expeditionary force headed by General Huo Chü-ping and vanquished the Huns. The district was first opened to military colonization and then civil settlement. When the area was sufficiently cultivated, four prefectures were established here; Wuwei, Changyeh, Tsiuchuan and Tunhuang of which the last one was the westernmost.

Oasis though the four prefectures west of the Yellow River all are, they have to depend on water from the southern mountains for all purposes, as there is little rain in the year. Yet, because water from melting snow is more punctual and certain than rain, the district never complains of drought, but is quite fertile and well irrigated.

Tunhuang occupies an especially favorable position in this area in that it strategically guards the gateway to Yang Kuan and Yumen Pass, and that it is the first port of entry in China for any cultural importation from the continental west via Turkestan. With the stationing here of governors of the whole district during both Later Han and T'ang, Tunhuang early achieved a high level of culture which found expression in its Buddhist paintings and its Buddhist paintings and its collection of books.

The Cave of the Thousand Buddhas is a popular name. It was officially called from the T'ang Dynasty to the Yuan as the *Mokao Cavern*. They are 40 li from Tunhuang City, and consist of caves excavated out of a sheer cliff. To the south is a fountainhead which forms a little brook flowing through a canyon and out at the north end to disappear in the desert. On either side of the brook are planted populars. Needless to mention that the cliff is the produce of the endless erosion of the brook.

It is said that during the reign of Former Ch'in, a Baddhist friar from inland China came to dig the first cave. Because of the geographical location of the place and the prevalence of Buddhism at the time, the caves became, in Yuan Dynasty, a veritable honeycob one mile in length.

The murals preserved here have been fortunate in that Tunhuang never became too prosperous or easily accessible, and for quite a time it was not even in Chinese hands, so that they never met the fate of those at Changan or Loyang, which have all been destroyed, but remained as they originally were as late as the Ming Dynasty, with some poor renavation jobs done to them only in the Ch'ing or Manchu Dynasty. On the other hand, they have been unfortunate too, in that they stayed in oblivion until the last years of Tsing.

The first thing from Tunhuang to come to people's notice has not been the murals but the popularied versions of Buddhist scriptures stored in a vault in the Caves of One Thousand Buddhas. In 1900, an itinerant Taoist named Wang came from Hupeh. (It will be noted that, though the west region of Kansu Province were originally Buddhistic, the religion had declined during the last few centuries, and the Caves Of One Thousand Buddhas lodged by lamas had but few monks by them. The prevalent religion at this particular juncture was Taoism, whose priests performed various rites and services for the people and worshiped Buddhist images.) He had made the journey to find a living.

Wang the Taoist obtained one of the caves as his quarters. Everyday be copied Taoist scriptures for his use at the rites. One day he noticed a crack on the wall, and, digging into it, came upon a niche wherein were stored many sacred books. These he used as presents to people who made donations to him.

In March, 1907, Sir Aurel Stein of England then sent on a tour of archaeological research by the government of British India arrived at the Caves of the Thousand Buddhas after he had discovered a sizable amount of wood slips, documents of the Han Dynasty. He bribed the Taoist and took with his some of the more complete sets of Buddhist tales and pictures. Later, the French sinologist, Paul Pelliot, did the same thing. Many of the books stored here are different from those in print. When both Stein and Pelliot photographed and published their find, scholars all over the world came to know the name of the Caves of The Thousand Buddhas and the great treasure of art that miraculously existed there.

There are points one would do better to bear in mind: First, regarding statues, because the rocks here were unsuited for sculpture, clay was used instead. Special attention, there-fore, should be paid to the pigments used on the statues besides postues besides posture. The fact that the statues retain their original color indicates the quality of pigments used. Comparable to these are the statues at the Mechi Hill near Tienshui, Kansu, also of Wei, but less in number and size. As the statues at Tunhuang comprise all periods, comparative work may be carried on between them and other Buddhist sculpture at Yün-Kang, Lung-Men, the Cliff of One Thousand Buddhas (Kuangyuan, Szechuan). Tachu, Mount Tsi-hsia (Nanking) and Mount Tien-lung (Taiyuan, Shansi). Furthermore, as Tunhuang has been the center of communication between China and Turkestan, comparison may also be made between the statues here and those in Indian Central Asia.

Second, the murals, including the patterns of Tsaoching decorations inside of dome and Tienhua, (ceiling patterns) usually the cynosure of all attention, began early and continued long, so that they represented the progress and advancement of Chinese painting from around the 5th Century down to early Ming. This unbroken continuity of nearly 1,000 years in painting cannot be found at any other place in the country, enabling people to revise many of their misconceptions about ancient Painting or painters.

Then, in the repertoire of Chinese art, it will be noted that the original wealth of native patterns of China has been augmented by that of Central Asia. From the Sun Dynasty on, as painting came to be more and more the pastime and medium of expression for scholars, pattern designing has been greatly neglected. This results in the near poverty in China along this line, espeeially from the unilitarian point of view. With the coming to notice of Tunhuang murals, attention has been dirccted also to the patterns. In the rearrangement and cataloging of these patterns are involved not only their design but also coloring, so that a difficulty is posed. When we get around to finishing the job, however, there can be no doubt but that the patterns will offer potentialities for application and enhance the value of this particular part of China's artistic heritage.

Furthermore, though the murals are generally religious in nature, they encompass also landscape, furniture and utensils, plants, wildlife, dances and rituals, and scaled down buildings.

Even the Buddhist stories portrayed here offer fields for exploration, as they varied with the development and the fashion of the different schools and times. Researches on Tunhuang Murals by Eieiche Matsumoto of Japan which investigates into the stories remains the most important reference book in this field, but much leaves still to be desired.

Third, architecturally, the caves, with the murals, are also a great museum of architecture. They show the relationship between the architecture of China and that of India. The most salient feature in the Wei paintings are far as architecture in concerned, is the use of $\wedge$-shape arch, found also in the caves at Lung-Men and Yun-Kang, and the Hohuryu Temple of Nara, Japan, which was built during the Sui Dynasty of China. For T'ang architecture, they very important record is found in the bas reliefs at the Wild Geese Tower, Sian, but here at Tunhuang there are also models.

In conclusion, it is safe to say that the artistic treasure at Tunhuang is comprehensive in subject matter and important for further research. How to make use of all this great legacies of China's culture and civilization remains the concern of all who will have interest in the problem.

IV. PATTERNS AND MURALS OF TUNHUANG
ANALYTICAL SURVEY

1. Periods of the Murals

The Murals at the Caves of The Thousand Buddhas, Tunhuang, are the prize of Chinese art, in periods ranging from the Northern Wei, Northern Chou, Sui, Tang, the Epoch of the Five Short Dynasties and Sung. In this period of several centuries and dynasties, the content is a veritable priceless wealth. Their value is especially enhanced by the fact that few T'ang paintings exist today, let alone those of the Northern Wei. Yet, here in these caves, many productions of Northern Wei, Sui and T'ang are preserved. They are the fountainhead tobe tapped in the compilation of any history of Chinese art, and they offer an accurate measure for chronologieal arrangement of all art works.

And this arrangement for periodic study at the Caves is imperative.

The first thing to go on in this arrangement is the inscriptions, which are found in many of the Caves, some even with dates and years. Based on these inscriptions, further work to be carried on will be an analysis of the composition, pigmentation, style, subject matter and other technique or inspirational touches, wherein will be found some common similarities. These similarities, in turn, will be grouped, and with the groups thus produced, their application can be made to deduct out the relationships between the ears and the murals.

From their style, at least the following of the murals of the Caves are fairly evident as far as their chronology is concerned.

A. The area north of the Nine-Storeyed Tower (the highest building at the Caves, in which is put an erect Buddha of T'ang Dynasty) and the Scripture Vault (the niche in which popularized versions of Buddhist scriptures were found), which consists of the caves on the second and third strata counting from the bottem. They style of the statues here is one of simplicity and vigor It concerns itself not so much with superficial resemblance as with compositional harmony of the entire work. Its coloring is simple, vigorous, lumbersome. If the piements used here, the most important are azurite, ocher, cinnabar and ceruse. The result is a strong contrast, and a vivd impression for the vision. Together with the location of this area and its inscriptions, it is deduced that the Caves of The Thousand Buddhas started from hereabout.

Some of the caves here have the same style as do those at Yun-kang, Shansi, so it is further deduced that they had been created before the Northern Wei removed its capital to Loyang. The cave used as prototype for the work of chrono logization is the No. 83 (according to Mr. Chang Ta-chien's cataloguing), which belongs to the Western Wei. Some in scriptions in it are dated. For instance:

Established: The Fourth Year of Ta-Tung of the Great Dynasty of Wei.

The 28th Day of the Fourth Moon of the Fifth Year of The Great Dynasty of Wei.

From this telltale inscription and a comparison of the style used in the neighboring caves and that of the Wei sculptures of Yun-kang and Lung Men, the relationships will become apparent. With the deductions gained here, it is fairly easy to decide which of the caves hereabout are Wei creations.

Also in the vicinity is a cave of the Sui Dynasty. In coloring, it resembles that of Wei, but in style softer or, to put it another way, more Chinese. The representative inseriptions is in the No. 96 cave:

The First Moon of the Fifth Year of Kai-Huang (the Reign Cylcle of
    Emperor Wen Ti of Sui)

To be sure, the distinction between the caves of Wei and Sui is not so pronounced. By the same token, there is a special style for the transitory years between the Sui and the T'ang Dynasties. Caves of this period could have been produced either during the reign of Emperor of Yang Ti of Sui or of Emperor Kao Tsu of Tang. But, on the whole, caves of this series are definitely different from T'ang makes. The facial expressions, costume creases and general appearance of the statues in these caves are quite comparable in detail to those at Yun-kang and Lung-Men. And the mariginal patterns and nimbuses in them also bear strong resemblance to those at Yun-kang and Lung-Men caves of the Wei-Sui period.

B. The caves on the first stratum south and north of the last-mentioned series of caves (which face east) represent a style that is different. It is later than the last, and there caves, in addition to inscriptions bearing the Cycles of Reign of Emperors T'ai Tsung and Kao Tsung, both of early T'ang, is also what remains of a monument of Empress Wu Tse-t'ien's time. According to a lama at the Upper Temple (the Lei-Yin Temple), this monument was excavated outside the entrance to the No. 134 cave, and later transported to the office of the Tunhuang Art Research Institute at the Center Temple (the Huang-Ch'ing Temple). The site of the excavation is evidently where the porch used to be, and when the porch decayed, the monument was buried underground. The murals in No. 134 cave are typical of the style of this period.

There are other evidences pointing to the period of these caves:

1) The form of Chinese characters belong to early T'ang in the fashion of the famous caligraphers of the time: Yu Shih-nan and Chu Sui-liang, and comparable to the epitaphs on tombstones of the time.

2) The shape and pattern of the nimbuses on the heads of the Buddha statues are typical of early T'ang, comparable to carvings of this period at Lung-Men.

3) For man's wear, the use of the hood-like headgear with soft side a appendages and of narrow-sleeved gowns fashionable in early T'ang. For woman's wear, tight-fitting costumes like those of Northern wei and Sui but different from the looser garments of later T'ang.

Thus, from the incribed date, the written characters, the fresco as well as the patterns, the caves have to belong to the period between the reign of Emperor Tai Tsung and Empress Wu Tse-t'ien. They are of the second category here by labled the Early T'ang.

C. A period that is again later than the last. In inscription there are dates of T'ien-Pao (reign cycle of Emperor Huan Tsung of T'ang). The characteristics of this period are a brighter coloring, more regular and elaborate pattern adornments. The worshipers' portraits are especially at variance with earlier once: what has been light and brisk is now loose and even-tempered, reflecting a period that has enjoyed an unprecedentedly long time of peace. In living habits, quiescence takes the place of industry. Even the faces of women match the loose garments they wear: plump and circular. For convenience, this period will henceforth be referred to as the prosperous T'ang.

D. The years from the aforesaid period, through the reigns of Emperors Su Tsung and Dai Tsung, down to the time of Emperor Te Tsung, when the prosperity of the Emperor Huan Tsung epoch and the rebellion of General An Lu-shan have ail become a thing of the past while some of the modes of living still remains despite the fact that the national strength has much declined. In this era, the cave murals are dedicated primarily to stories arranged parallelly like Chinese screens. The era is the forerunner of late T'ang, even though in style it still follows the last period. This is the mid T'ang.

E. During the time after the reign of Te Tsung and down to Shuan Tsung, Tunhuang was occupied by the Tibetans and some worshipers are found in tibetan dress in some caves. There also Tibetan dynastic inscriptions too, though still in Chinese, but net many in number. Since General Chang I-ch'ao under Emperor Shuan Tsung recovered the place and was appointed governor of the district, his family and relatives notably the Li's and the So's, established many new caves. In the Five Short Dynasties, the House of Tsao succeeded the Chang's to control the area until the early years of Sung Dynasty, and continued to put up new caves. Some of these caves are quite large in size, with dates identfying their period.

During this period, the most important structure is the monument erected by the Li's recording a renovation of the caves. It is at the same time the best preserved and with the lengthiest inscription of all the monuments at Tunhuang. The murals mentioned on the monument tally with those in the cave, a fact that points up to the mutual relationship of the two. Later than this come the inscription by So Hsun, also of late T'ang, and those by several generations of the Tsao family, of the Five Dynasties and the Sung. The incriptions on the caves of the Tsao caves are especially important as historical data on early Sung architecture.

The costumes of this period are generally more or less similar to those of the prosperous T'ang, but more stereotyped, or more bluntly, backneyed. Even though some of these caves are more imposing in size, the murals lack the quality of originality and creativeness. This is perhaps due to the fast that, during the Northern Wei and T'ang, when Tunhuang was an-important juncture on the east-west route, more Turkestan or farther west travelers and Chinese artists came and went this way, who, being more expert at the art showed up with more creations, so that the caves may differ with each other. During the epoch of the prosperous T'ang, there were less artists among the scholars and their job were taken over by artisans, so that conventionality became more and more pronounced. The era of late T'ang saw even less trafficking between the place and Chinese Proper until communication dwindled to almost nothing during the Sung Dynasty, and the paintings came up with little new element. In mid Sung, just before the Western Hsia (Tangut Dynasty) occupied the place, they became so degenerated that no artistic value remained at all.

F. After the occupation of Tanhuang by the Tanguts to the Yuan Dynasty, many caves were set up. The Tangut caves as well as Yuan ones have their characteristics too, and the Tangut pattern designs radically differ with those of early sung. In style, Tangut murals are more like those of

Ming and T'ang techniques are different and that the Tanguts, having adoptedf the Sung technique earlier, when Tunhuang became independent were so shut off they could get no fresh inspirations from China.

For Tangut style, the illustrative instances are:

Hallway in No. 75 cave; with the images of ten monks on the northern wall and one cleaning maid on the southern wall; also the word for "Heaven" in Tangut.

On the lintel of the No. 258 cave, inscription in the reign cycle of a Tangut Dynasty: The Seventh Moon, First Year of Tien Ch'ing.

In No. 270 cave, the woman worshiper still wears Sung costume, but the men worshippers wear Tangut-style gown with large patterns and Tangut hat.

No. 201 cave, with statue of Tangut worshipper, and inscriptions in Uigur on north wall; murals in same style as in No. 75 cave.

The caves of Yuan Dynasty are generally in another area north of here, but some are near the Nine Storeyed Tower that look like Yuan. Some other belong to the reign of Emperor Chien Lung of Tsing, with apparent Tsing distinguishing features and Tsing inscriptions. The latest additions doneby Taoist Want in the last years of the Tsing Dynasty, even cruder than those of the Chien Lung period.

2. The Evolutions in Cave Shapes and Periodic Characteristics

Among the murals of Tunhuang, patterns seem to be more sensitives to the change of period. Almost every era has its distinct patterns. The most important ones are (1)Tsaoching, (2)curtains, (3)nimbuses, and (4)mariginal decorations, each with some special features of its own. These patterns are accurate gauges in analyzing the periods, showing as they do the trend of evolution in each stage of development, For wantof space, explanation will be limited to only the Tsaoching and the draperies.

In the first period of Northern Wei and Sui, the structure of the cave ceilings are of two kinds; in the first half, roll-back Tienhua is used while in the next half the domic design prevails.

For the rool-back Tienhua, the No. 213 cave may be used as an example. The cave is rectangular in shape, and a little farther back from the center is a square column on which is a miniature pagoda adjoining the Tienhua on the ceiilng. The back, left and right sides of the caves all have niches. Back and left and right of the column the ceiling is flat, and front of the column is a roll-back or up-side-down V shaped Tienhua. The arrangement is also found at the caves at Yun Kang.

As to paintings, the space front and back of the roll-back shape are checquer-like squares in which are drawn lotus flowers and fairies on wings.

For the domic Tienhua, No. 83 cave will serve as an illustration. This is the cave with the Ta Tung inscription, with no column in it. The ceiling is level, painted with the Tsao-ching. The sides surrounding the level space droop down to form something like an upturned basin. This form is more akin to those of the Sui and T'ang caves and therefore is surmised as later than the roll-back Tienhua.

Take, again, the No. 96 cave, of Sui, has a Tienhua arrangement that is quite similar to that in the No. 83 cave-another proof that this forms comes later. The construction of this kind of Tienhua and Tsao-ching must be in imitation of some northwest Indian or Central Asiatic temple. The center of the ceiling was originally composed of tier upon tier of square frames placed criss-cross, decreasing in size as the tiers went up, so that viewed from down under a design like is formed.

Belonging to the roll-back variety of ceiling patterns are, to name a few, the Nos. 81, 94, 88, 89 North, 92 North, 94, 95, 97, 100 North, 210, 212, 213, 214, 215, 215 South, 217, 219, 240, 242, 243, 248, 249, 251, and 252 caves.

Belonging to the domic variety of ceiling patterns are, among others the Nos. 75, 82, 83, 83 North, 86, 87, 88, 89, South, 90, 91, 93, 96, 96 South, 101, 218, 218 South, 234, 236, 250, 253, 266, 273, and 274 caves.

From the sequence of the numbers, it can be seen that from No. 81 to No. 100 North, the caves are of one group, while from No. 210 to No. 252 is another series of caves and that both these groups are the earliest at Tunhuang. After these two groups come the caves from No. 75 to No. 218 to No. 274; all of these are later additions. Traces of these increment are found in the periods of the murals and the locations of the caves themselves.

After the caves of Wei and Sui, the most noteworthy are the caves of early T'ang. The best quality about them is that each has a stock of mural paintings with a personality all their own, that a view on seeing them will be left speechless with admiration. These caves all have domic ceiling arrangements. They consist of the Nos. 24, 25, 26, 27, 28, 29, 30, 31, 32, 34, 35, 38, 56, 64, 69, 72, 73, 77, 100, 102, 105, 106, 107, 108, 113, 114, 115, 119, 121, 124, 125, 127, 128, 132, 135, 136, 137, 138, 139, 140, 141, 175, 176, 177, 178, 181, 182, 184, 185, 187, 188, 189, 190, 191, 191 South, 192, 193, 194, 195, 197, 198, 199, 199 North, 199 South, 200, 202, 103, 204, 205, 206, 206 South, 207, 208, 209, 211, 222, 223, 224, 226, 232, 247, 261, 262, 263, 265, 267, 168, 269, South 269, 272, 275, 277, 284, 291, 292, 293, 294, 296, and belong generally to the early T'ang. Some people consider that some of these are actually Sui caves, but since typical Sui caves were though erected during the reign cycle of K'ai-huang and typical T'ang caves were erected during the reign cycle of Cheng-kuan (of Emperor T'ai Tsung), and since all these caves are nearer to Cheng-kuan than to K'ai-huang, it does not seem proper to consider the ones in question as of Sui. Naturally, as during the transition from Sui to T'ang there had not been much change in the condition at this district so that little shift of style would have occured, it is only possible that some of these caves are actually produces of Sui, but then when evidences are sought for, the weighing of factors such as a fixed standard seems only ressonable.

Some of these caves underwent some renovations during late T'ang too, but the early T'ang elements are still recognizable, with the exception of Nos. 109, 134, and 174, which, though with early T'ang murals, are early Wei in architecture. The only difference is that, whereas the square column in Wei caves is surrounded on all sides by niches, in these caves there are riches only out front. They should have been considered Wei, and probably were the earliest ones. but they had no doubt decayed so much during early T'ang that a complete renovation job had to be done to them and did.

The difference between early T'ang and Wei is tremendous, so tremendous, indeed, it seems that an artistic revolution had taken place. Such revolution can happen only on the strength of very extraordinary causes, such as the territorial and therefore influential expansion of the T'ang under Emperor Tai Tsung and the subsequent thriving of the fine arts. If so, what we call Sui caves may well be those erected during the reign of Emperor Kao Tsu, T'ai Tsung and the subsequent thriving of the fine arts. If so, what we call Sui caves may well be those erected during the reign of Emperor Kao Tsu, T'ai Tsung's father. There are at these differences between Sui and early T'ang as follows:

1) The imitation of three-tier square frame arrangement of Weo on top of the ceiling, the ▣ ornament, was set aside in T'ang, and various Tsao Ching patterns were painted instead, allowing more freedom for composition.

2) In the center of all Wei Tsaoching is a lotus flower, with distinct

petals and seeds painted neatly on the center. In T'ang this was replaced sometimes by rose or peony, arranged in rows one behind the other. Lotus petals gave may to big red peony petals too, and the petals in turn were made up with smaller flowers.

3) Colors of Wei are rather simple, while in early T'ang each line was shaded down with layers of different pigments, from vermilion to pinck, verdure, light green, indigo, ronbin's egg blue, lavender, violet, white and black, with special attention paid to harmony; a fact in opposition to the strong contract of Wei.

4) In Wei the flying fairies were on the triangular checkers on the four sides of the Tienhua, used only as decoration not the theme. But in T'ang the flying fairies and the flying dragons were part of the whole scheme, fanciful curves and curlicues were drawn around them to give them an appearance of animation.

This method was retained until the prosperous and the mid T'ang, but less exquisite in color scheme and more bright in tone, and somewhat formalized. But real conventional, regimentation in this art did not come until late T'ang.

The late T'ang art is a follow-up of the former age, but at this time, though a great variety of theme stories is shown in the individual caves, the same can hardly be said of composition and pattern adornment, which are so much alike. For patterns, early T'ang had changed the Wei lotus peony, with the petals formed by sidelong flowers, and, at this time, though the general scheme was the same, it was much simplified and formalized. By the same token, the minute outlining and shading in early T'ang had degenerated to just coloring the whole frame of the petals. Then, though the textture of petals was minutely etched out, the color was the same for the whole flower, whereas now to avoid monotony the adjoining petals had different colors. This change is, to be sure, rather gradual, as is the decrease in attention to detail. The cave that has the Li monument is the best of this lot, while the cave of the Tsao's is very crude.

3. The Tsaoching and the Drapery-like designs

The tsao-ching of the early and the mid T'ang, though different from cave to cave, had, besides the tsao-ching adornments, only simple looking drapery designs. These designs were again a relic of the Wei Dynasty, only in the Wei caves the embelishments have little variety. The drapery ornamentation of early T'ang, though still simple, was predominantly tassle-like in form, coming as it was from a different origin from tha tof Wei. After mid T'ang it became more complex, and in late T'ang it was yet more leaborate. For example:

No. 36 cave (early late-T'ang), has tsao-ching in the shape of four folded petal lotus surrounded by three rows of eight-petal peonies, outside of which are rolled grass, strung beads and triangular tassle designs.

No. 53 cave (early Sung) has tsao-ching in the shape of a green circle, with three white rabbit joining ears. From the inner circle, there are twelve folded petal lotuses, facing inward, farther out are squares and outside them are: (1) sidewise six-petal peonies, (2) slanting rhombuses, (3) strung beads, (4) folding ribbons, (5) strung beads, (6) sidewise six-petal peonies, (7) rolling grass, (8) triangles in the middle of flowers and tassle designs.

The No. 36 cave has the early late T'ang tsao-ching, with fewer outside rows; No. 53 cave is early Sung and has more outside rows. After the early days of Sung, another style was formed. Now to the center of the variegated lotus were added dragon or the diamond club designs, with more fixed rows of tsao-ching ornamentation. For example:

No. 50 cave, green ground, has raised golden dragon with red tinged cloud-like ribbons on black ground around it, and farther out are 24 peonies, alternately painted green and white. Outside that is a big diamond, with four golden dragons on the four corners. At the extreme out is a band formed with strung beads.

In such caves as the No. 62, the design in the center of tsao-ching is a coiled dragon, the No. 116, a pair of dia mond clubs forming a cross, and the No. 87 more or less like the No. 116, while in the designs outside the tsao-ching they are completely in similitude. This probably suggests that there were only a few painters at Tunhuang at this time sothatn ot hing so that nothing original was possible.

As for the caves of Yuan and Ming Cynasties, like the No. 43, the tsao-ching is just adorned with six-petaled lotuses, or the No. 45, the design in the tsao-ching is the Six-word Formula in Sanskrit. All very simple, plain.

An early as the Northern Wei, drapery designs had adorned the four sides around the Tsao-ching. These arrangements have one thing in common: At regular intervals there is a cord for tying up the draperies, and below the draperies themselves are two rows of triangular tassles. The upper row of these tassles is usually green on the edges and blue in the center and the lower, light gray on the edges and white in the center. The upper part of the draperies sometimes has rectangular or lozenge designs, alternately white, black, gray and green in color. On the lozenges, with the exception of the black ones, which show white thread, are strung with black thread, as in the case of the Nos. 90, 91, 12, and 93 caves.

In early T'ang drapery designs were very complicated. The main part of the draperies became especially long, and the tying cord was absent, the triangular tassles smaller, or rectangular in sharpe, with oblique, circular or rhomboid tassles, which, if oblique, would be painted in different colors. Stringing from those tasseles would be green or white beads and pearls. This style is seen at caves Nos. 179 to 211 and Nos. 260 to 299.

Drapery designs of mid and late T'ang retain the fashion of early T'ang, the only difference being that the triangular tassles, which were formed with acute angles, now became right or blunt, with a sidewise flower added to the space between two tassles. Besides the suspending tassles were added pearls, and floating ribbons of assorted sizes. In No. 305 cave, the color of the drapery is red, the tassle red on top and green at bottom, the suspending tassles and beads green, ribbons white with green sides and red flowers.

In mid Sung the drapery was the same as late T'ang, only more stereotyped. On the top part of the drapery is a peony on its side, on red ground, with opposite green and white flowers, and on the bottom are blue green flowers with a alanting flower in the center. The suspending band is white with green sides and alternate green and white up-side-down lotus designs for tassle. After Sung, there are only this design, the variation being only in its length.

The Tangut caves differed from the Sung caves for divergencies in model. For example, the passageway in No. 75 cave conforms to late-T'ang in that it has only the suspending beads and tassles but not the up-down lotus so common in Sung designs. Yet there is a difference between it and that of T'ang: there is more distance between the beads and tassles, and the triangular tassle arrangement is discarded. So the difference is, after all still obvious.

V. PELLIOT'S LES GROTIES DE TOUEN HOUANG

The Caves of the Thousand Buddhas at Tunhuang, started in the Northern Wei Dynasty and stopped in the Yuan Dynasty, at the same time serve as a living history of Chinese fine art complete with specimen, and offer the most reliable measure for the latter's evaluation. Many books, notably those by Stein, have published photographs of the Caves and their contents, but the most systematic comprehensive on the subject is no doubt Pelliot's *Les Grottes de Touen Houang.*

Pelliot went to Tunhuang during the years from 1906 to 1909, and lived at the Caves in 1907. The Caves constitute a total number of three temples: the Lei-in Temple on the upper hand, the Huang-ch'ing in the middle, both sinicized lamaseries, and the San-ch'ing Palace at the lower. This Santsing Palace was where Wang Yuan-lu, a Taoist priest, lived, and where Pelliot parlayed with the former on the purchase of some Buddhist scriptures stored in a niche in the Palace. He spent most of his time on selection of books, and the remainder on taking pictures with his aide. What was done at this time was published in Paris in 1924 under the title of *Les Grottes de Touen Houang.* There are all together 375 photographs in collotype, bound in six volumes. Mr. Ho Ch'ang-chun commented expertly on the work in an article published in the No. 10, Vol, 28 issue of the Tung-fang Magazine (Eastern Magazine of Commercial Press) (1931). As a great scholar on east-west communication, Mr. Ho made many highly original propositions. The present article attempts to elaborate where Mr. Ho's neglected.

Volume I

Figures 1—7: Full view of the Caves of the Thousand Buddhas.

It is to be born in mind that the 5-storeyed edifice in Figure 6 has been rebuilt to have nine storeys while the ballustrade in front of the Sung corridor in Figure 7 is no longer.

Figures 8—11: Murals and statues in No. 1 cave. The murals belong to late-Tang, and some of the added statues were done in the Tsing Dynasty. Figure 10 is a Tsing picture while Figure 11 is one of late-Tang.

Figures 12—14: Murals in No. 6 cave; late-Tang.

Figures 15—32: Murals in No. 8 cave. Paintings on the upper tier belong to the Five Short Dynasties, on the lower, Sung Dynasty. After Figure 25, all pictures were produced during the Five Short Dynasties.

Figure 33—36: Murals in No. 12 cave. They are supposed to belong to late-Tang, but with paintings of Tsing Taoist figures.

Figures 37—40: Murals in No. 14 cave. Figure 37 shows statues of a more recent period. The upper parts of Figures 38 and 39 are late-Tang and the lower, Sung. Figure 40 is a picture of Sung.

Figures 41—42: The Wheels on either side of the entrance to, and murals showing Amoghapasa Budhisattva with thousand-arms in, No. 16 cave.

Figures 43—49: No. 17 cave, late-Tang murals. Figure 43 shows Buddha vanquishing some evil spirit, Figures 44-49 show some lady out on an excursion.

Figures 50—51: Murals in No. 18 cave, belonging to the same period as those of the No. 17 cave.

Figures 52—54: No. 19 cave, with a reclining Buddha of late-Tang. The statues and murals are most exquisite and best preserved.

Volume II

Figure 65: No. 19 cave, showing the Nirvana of Buddha, of late-Tang.

Figures 66—67: No. 31 cave, early-Tang, variations of the Pure Land.

Figures 68—69: The statues of worshipers on either side of the entrance to No. 32 cave. The murals here are early-Tang while the statues are late-Tang.

Figures 70—71: Murals at the left and the extreme right in No. 34 cave.

Figure 72: Mural on left wall in No. 34 cave.

Figures 73—74: Murals in No. 41 cave; mid-Tang, well preserved.

Figure 75: Right wall mural in No. 42 cave showing the 1000-handed Avalokitesvara, early Tang.

Figures 76—77: Left side of No. 44 cave; early-Tang murals and statues.

Figures 78—81: Murals on either side in No. 46 cave, late-Tang.

Figure 82: Statues in far right corner in No. 49 cave, late-Tang.

Figures 83—84: Niche and murals on either side in No. 51 cave; late-Tang.

Figures 85—92: Murals and statues in No. 52 cave; late-Tang.

Figure 93—94: Part of murals on either side of No. 52A and No. 52B caves; late-Tang.

Figures 95—96: No. 53A cave, mixed, but murals done mostly during mid-Tang.

Figures 97—99: Statues on left side and murals on both in No. 45 cave. Paintings are late Tang; effigies are more recent.

Figures 100—103: Murals and statues on the left side of the Gentral altar in No. 58 cave. All belong to early Tang, except the 19 figurines at the back of the statue of Buddha Nirvana, which belong to Tsing.

Figures 104—105: Murals and right-side altar in No. 59 cave, both early Tang, but the former are restoration of earlier ones.

Figure 106: Altar of early Tang and rightside murals of late Tang in No. 61 cave.

Figures 107—108: Sung murals on either side in No. 62 cave, showing Marjusuri and Samantabhadra.

Figures 109—110: Plaque and altar at entrance to No. 63 cave, with inscriptions attesting to its late-Tang origin. Also a late-Tang corridor, one of a few still remaining in the land.

Figures 111-113: Murals and statues in No. 64 cave; work began in early Tang, enlarged in Sung and restored in Tsing.

Figure 114: A full view of Nos. 65—69 caves.

Figures 115-116: Murals and statues in No. 66 cave, with the likeness of a woman worshiper identified as some Uigur princess.

Figure 117: Extreme interior and altar in No. 67 cave; Sui cr early Tang.

Figures 118—125: Murals in No. 70 cave; early Tang.

Figures 126—127: Murals in No. 71 cave, Sui ro early Tang.

Figure 128: Late-Tang murals.

Volume III

Figures 129—131: Late-Tang murals and niche.

Figures 132—149: The Cave of Tsao, believed to be Northern Sung.

Figures 150—153: Murals of arhats by the Tanguts and altar with statues of some recenter period; all in No. 76 cave.

Figures 154—157: Early-Tang murals in No. 77 cave, with the statue of a Taoist guardian god—very out of place.

Figures 158—161: Murals in No. 79 cave; Tangut.

Figure 162: Altar in No. 80 cave, with mid-Tang statues.

Figures 163—168: Murals of late-Tang and niche with Tsing statues in No. 81 cave.

Figures 169—172: Murals in niche in No. 82B cave. Blackened by the Russians in 1924.

Figure 173: Murals in No. 83 cave.

Figures 174—176: Murals and altar in No. 84 cave, started in late Tang, renovated by the Tanguts, with Tsing statues.

Figure 177: Late-Tang altar in No. 96 cave.

Figures 178—179: Murals in Caves No. 99 of late-Tang with Sung additions, and No. 101, Northern Wei.

Figures 180—185: Murals in No. 12 cave, rather unique in style, but may be Tangut judging the patterns.

Figure 186: Wei murals in No. 101 cave.

Figure 187: Late early-Tang murals in No. 104 cave.

Figure 188: Right-side mural in No. 108A cave, of Tang. Darkened with smoke.

Figures 245—247: Late early-Tang statues in No. 120F cave.

Figures 248—250: Murals and niche in No, 120G cave, early and late Tang.

Figures 251—256: Northern Wei Murals and alter in No. 120N cave.

Volume V

Figures 257—268: Murals in No. 120N cave. The figurines in Figures 264 and 266 have long since lost their heads.

Figures 269—270: Murals in No. 120 cave, with statues of ownshipers of early Tang.

Figure 271: No. 121 cave, of Wei, with entrance of Sung.

Figure 272: Murals and niche in No. 122 cave, originally Wei but completely renovated in early Tang with later additions.

Figures 273—274: Head of Buddha in No. 126B cave, of Wei; repaired.

Figure 275: Wei murals in No. 129 cave.

Figures 276—279: No. 130 cave, of Wei, with early-Tang additions and Sung Corridor.

Figures 280—295: Murals and statues in No. 135 cave. Statues of Wei or earlier.

Figures 189-190: Wei murals in No. 110 cave, the best.

Figures 191—192: Wei statues in central niche in No. 110Acave, generally believed to be the oldest in the caves.

IV

Figures 193—194: Three niches in No. 111 cave, all Wei.

Figures 195: Statues of worshiper in No. 112D cave, late Tang, but with inscriptions in Tangut and Uigur.

Figures 196—197: Niche and murals in No. 114 cave, early Tang.

Figures 198—232: Murals in No. 117 cave, executed in Northern Sung but retained late-Tang style. Figures 198-202 show the murals along the sides of the passageway of this cave, by some Tanguts, with inscriptions in both Chinese and Tangut; the rest are Buddhist stories.

Figure 232: The upper part of No. 117 cave, with traces of Wei, Late-Tang and Sung.

Figures 233—243: Murals in the various compartments in No. 118 cave.

Figure 244: Murals of late-Tang in No. 119 cave.

Figure 286: Niche in No. 135F cave, early Tang statues and Sung morals.

Figures 287—292: Murals in No. 135C cave, late early-Tang.

Figure 293: Statue of Deva in No. 136 cave, with Sung alterations on
corridor.

Figures 294—295: Niche in No. 137A cave Northern Wei.

Figure 296: Statue of Wei worshiper in No. 137H cave.

Figures 297—299: Murals of No. 138 cave, Tang or the Five Short Dynastines.

Figure 300: Outside niches of No. 139 cave.

Figure 301: Early-Tang murals in right-hand compartment of No. 139 cave.

Figure 302—304: Early-Tang murals in No. 139A cave.

Figures 305—306: Early-Tang Statues and murals in No. 139B cave.

Figures 307—311: Early Tang murals in No. 140 cave but the statues and
backdrop in Figure 309 are Tsing rather crude.

Figures 312—313: Tangut mural and worshiper in No. 140A cave.

Figure 314: Sung idols and murals in No. 142 cave.

Figures 315—317: Early-Tang murals in No. 144 cave.

Figures 318—320: Murals in No. 416 cave early Tang with plaque in the
reign of Empress Wu Tso-t'ien.

Volume VI

Figures 321—322: Early Tang murals and statues in No. 146 cave.

Figure 323: Sung worshiper in No. 147A cave.

Figures 324—325: Niche and murals in No. 149 cave. The Buddha heads are Tsing renovations.

Figure 326: No. 159 cave, Tsing idols.

Figures 327—328: Early Tang niche Sung murals and Tsing statues in No. 161 cave.

Figures 329—333: Late-Tang murals, Sung Bodhisattvas and Tsing statues, No. 168 cave.

Figure 334: Late-Tang murals and Tsing statues in niche in No. 169 cave.

Figures 335—339: Murals in No. 167 cave, early-Tang but the deva pictures outside are late-Tang.

Figure 340: Late-Tang sketches in No. 167A cave.

Figures 341—343: Murals in No. 171 cave.

Figures 344—346: Murals in No. 181 cave, Yuan Dynasty.

Figures 347—351: Murals in No. 182 cave, also Yuan.

Figures 352—367: Tablets and plaques in the various caves.

The crescent fountain and circular towers in them are destroyed.

Figure 368: Scripture manuscripts in the Scripture Niche.

Figures: 369—370: Monuments of Elders Suo and Yang, with inscriptions front and back, now broken in five.

Figure 371: The Scripture Hall at Lei-in Temple.

Figures 372—376: The Great Buddha Temple of Tunhuang, with T'ang statues and Ch'ing renovations. The temple is now inside the West Gate of the City, but was originally outside the East Gate in Tang Dynasty. This peculiar state of affairs is brought about by a perverse shift of course of the Tang River, which left only the east wall of the old City of Tunhuang. When a new city was built in Ch'ing Dynasty on the east bank of the River, the east wall of the old city was used as the west wall of the new.

VI TUNHUANG MURALS AND CHINESE PAINTING

The Murals of Tunhuang occupy a very important position in the history of Chinese painting. It is the purpose of this article to make a general survey on the subject.

Drawing as an expression of human experience, both physical and emotional, made its advent as early as the New Stone Age. Some of the works by artists living 20000 to 30000 years before the present are still found in mountain caves in southern Europe. Whether this art had evolved from some central areas and then spread out or sprung up in many places simultaneously, it is certain that it was something shared by most of the inbabitants of the world 3000 or even 10000 years ago.

Crude depictions of birds, animals and various patterns have been found on colored earthenware of great antiquity in the Pigmented Pottery Area at the upper Yellow River valley, and in appearance the pictures rather closely resemble those made by the Indians of North America. Excavations made at the Ruins of Yin, Anyang Hsien, Honan, brought to light many more pictures, quite of number of which being patterns.

According to ancient Chinese history, King Wu-Ting of Yin, living about 1300 B.C., was trying to find an able administrator when he dreamed of being given one by the Lord of Heaven. On waking up, he ordered his court artist to make a portrait of the man in his dream, posted it, and actually got him. The legend may not be whole credible, but it is worth remembering that it came in circulation during the Chou Dynasty (1122-255 B.C.), indicating that the art of portrait making was then definitely established.

The earliest drawings preserved to this day, or rather discovered at present, are all on lacquerwork, a Chinese specialty. One is a lacquered box with people on it discovered in Changsha, Hunan, the other is a plank from some ancient king's coffin, with clouds and dragons painted on it, discovered at Shouhsien, Anhuei. Both were executed 200 or 300 years B. C. A later one is a lacquer box found at Pyongyong, Korea, with people on it, made about one century A.D.

Etchings, especially those in has relief, of the Eastern or Later Han Dynasty (25-220 A.D.) fare much better. Important findings are made in Shantung Province. The "Stone Carvings of Northern China," written by the French Sinologist, E. Chavannes, contains many illuminating facsimiles. Besides the Temple of Chu Yu, Hsiao-T'ang Mountain and Wu Liang Shrine that he noted, there are other important objects d'art of the same kind at Liang Cheng Mountain, T'enghsien and Nanyang, and tomb gates and bricks in Szechwan. The earliest of all is the carvings at the Temple of Chu Yu, which demonstrate in minute detail of Han craftsmanship; then came those of T'enghsien, which are more decorative but less artistic.

The lines on the lacquerworks of the Warring States and of the Han Dynasty, and in the bas reliefs of the Temple of Chu Yu, all spoke clearly of the Chinese technique of organization: easy, simple, but brisk, expressing most vividly a given object with just a few well placed lines. The technique with which Ku K'ai-chih (of Chin Dynasty, 4th century A.D.) painted his Model Women (British Museum, London) and the Goddess of the Lo River (Freer Gallery of Art, Washington D.C.) is a direct descendant of that of Han.

When Buddhism was introduced into China during the Eastern Han Dynasty, religious painting came too. From the reign of Emperor Chang Ti

(76-88 A.D.) Buddhist themes began to appear in Chinese carvings. In the Kingdom of Wu (one of the Three Kingdoms, 220-277) Buddhism prospered and, inevitably, exercised some influence on Chinese fine art. For example, Ku Kai-chih painted Buddhist pictures, and his Manjusuri Budisattva and Vimalakirti (a theme widely adopted in many of the Tunhuang frescos, especially those produced during T'ang) has become the model for artists of later ages. In the picture, the Bodhisattva was dressed as an Indian while the hermit was costumed in Chinese, indicative of the change that took place in all Buddhist stories after their introduction to China.

During the disintegration of China that occurred in the 4th Century A.D., when China was divided in two parts, the South retained their Chinese tradition, as in the case of Ku K'ai-chih, while the North admitted more exotic elements, as can be seen from the style and technique embodied in the Northern Wei paintings at Tunhuang.

Tunhuang is situated in the western most part of Kansu, adjoining Sinkiang. Geographically, it is more a part of Sinkiang, but its inhabitants are North Chinese in language and religion. In 353 A.D., when the place was a part of the Former Chin, a monk arrived and dug the first cave on a cannyon bluff 12 miles northeast of Tunhuang. This in time were augmented through the ages down to the Ming Dynasty. In 1941, Mr. Chang Ta-Ch'ien, the renowned artist, catalogued the caves. There are, by his count, 305 main caves, exclusive of minor ones.

One third of these caves belongs to the Northern Dynasties, the statues and fresco paintings being in the same fashion as the carvings at Yun Kang of Tat'ung, Shansi, and Lungmen, Loyang, Honan. In comparison with southern works, the northern paintings exhibit a tone that is more forceful and expansive, and colors that are louder and more vivid; frequently two opposite complementary colors were used for strong contrast. It may be said that this imported style represents strong passion whereas the native style of China is more an expression of cool sagacity.

China was united again when Emperor Wen Ti of Sui Conquered the southern Kingdom of Ch'en in 589. In the caves at Tunhuang, there appeared at the time a pronounced change too. The Sui paintings, while colored in the same way as earlier productions, showed in tone an evident blending of southern element. The gentleness and attention to detail of this new school of painting did not belong to that at Yun Kang, but was similar to the carvings of the Sacred bones Pagoda at Mount Ch'i-hsia, Kiangsu, also of this time. This blending, to be sure, bespeaks the effort of the Sui Dynasty toward reconciliating all existant elements, but, since the Dynasty was founded by Chinese, art traditions of the land found more favor with the ruling class. This is the reason that Sui art is predominantly traditional Chinese tempered with just some foreign elements.

The change that occurred from Sui to Tang had been so gradual no conspicuous trace could be detected. But once the change gecame established, the difference was obvious. The early T'ang, taking the reigna of Emperors Kao Tsu, T'ai Tsung, Chung Tsung and Jui Tsung (cir. 620-700), had one consistent characteristic in its art style: more sinicization. In color, richer and softer in tone, not so strongly contrasting or provocative as of old. Early T'ang murals are still very symmetric, but in the age dubbed Prosperous T'ang (713-755), symmetry was put aside and the color, though still rich and exquisite, becamme less deliberate. During mid-T'ang, murals became larger in size but cruder in craftsmanship. Down to the Sung Dynasty, mural painting fell into a rut and ushered in the decline of Buddhist art, though at the same time Taoist art began to flourish.

The fact that none is a forgery among all the murals at Tunhuang makes them a standard and trustworthy gauge for measuring medieval Chinese painting. Aside from Buddhist stories, the patterns adorning the caves are also valuable in helping determine the period in which they were produced, as every period has its particular patterns that differ from those of any other age. Great variety is found among those of the Early and Prosperous Tang, but even they have significant divergencies.

Buddhist mural painting was very much in vogue during the T'ang Dynasty. At the time, almost all the temples, monasteries and convents in the country could boast some famous works of this category. For example, during the reign of Emperor Kao Tsung (650-683), the Rev. Shan Tao spent his whole life on painting over 300 walls with The Varied Aspects of the Pure Land. Under Emperor Hsuan Tsung, Wu Tao-tse, the greatest Chinese artist of all times, painted over 300 rooms with Buddhist legends in Changan and Loyang. At Tasheng-tsu Temple, Chengtu, Szechuan, 8524 rooms remain intact with murals executed in the different dynasties, starting with The Sung Dynasty (420-453) of the Southern Dynasties (not to be confused with the Sung founded by the House of Chao which existed 960-1276). When Emperor Wu Tsung of Tang outlawed Buddhism in 845, and ordered the destruction of all Buddhist establishments, the murals housed therein were destroyed in toto. Thus, with the exception fe Fa Lung Temple, Nara, Japan, and Boolkook-sa Temple, Kyoungju, Korea, only those at Tunhuang remain of all the murals produced prior to this period. The place was then lost to the Turfans, and not recovered until about ten years after the great man-made calamity, when Wu Tsung's successor reinstated Buddhism.

When China was split in two in the 4th century, scholars at the south were greatly enchanted with the scenic beauties there. Landscape painting began to flourish as a result, and artistic theories evolved too. Tsung Ping and Wang Wi, two cminent lovers of nature living in Sung, advanced some ideas on landscape painting. Hsieh Ho of Southern Tsi Dynasty laid down six rules on painting, which remain to this day as basic requirements for all artistic compositions: (1) vividness, (2) special touch, (3) faithfulness to appearance, (4) faithfulness to color, (5) arrangement and (6) imitation.

This period produced quite a number of great artists, but how they worker is a matter chiefly for speculation. The works of Chang Sheng-yu, for instance, survived only to the T'ang and Sung Dynasties, and only some imitation works done in Sung and Ming Dynasties exist to give us some idea as to the way in which he treated green hills and red trees. It is doubtful, however, that the imitators themselves had seen Chang's original pieces.

Tang fared better on this count. Some original paintings besides religious ones are still preserved. Of these, the earliest are the Portraits of Kings (Boston Museum of Fine Arts) by Yen Li-pen, all done with slender outlines, just as those at Tunhuang of comparable period.

Li Sze-hsun and Li Chao-tao, father and son, commonly known as General Li Sr., and General Li Jr., also left behind some works, but the Summering at Kiucheng Palace, in the father's name, is hardly authentic, and the Evcursion among Spring Hills (both at the Palace Museum) by the son is suspiciously like one produced during late T'ang or the Epoch of the Five Short Dynasties. The one, probably the only, reliable work by the Junior General is another Excursion now stored at the Chinese Central Museum. Its style and the costume of the figures all suggest the authenticity of the picture, even though it was unfortunately labled North Sung by Emperor Chien Lung of the Manchus and there by discredited.

Emperor Ch'ien Lung, though a great patron of fine arts, was hardly a competent connoisseur. He had labled the genuine Junior General as a fake because he had pronounced the faked one as real, in the same way that he confused the two versions of A Lodge in Fu-ch'un Mountain by Huang Kung-wang of Yuan Dynasty. Of landscape painters in early Ch'ing, the more distinguished ones include Wang Shih-min, Wang Chien, Wang Huei, Wang Yuan-Ch'i, Wu Li, Huei Ke, Shih Tao Shih Hsi and Pa Ta Shan Jen.

Reflective of the Chinese belief that man is identifiable with nature, landscape has always been the major theme in painting. As has been mentioned, the art began in the East Chin and the Southern Dynasties and flourished during Tang, but in and before Tang artists were more concerned which etching out the outlines and coloring, and the most fundamental method of shading and creasing for rocks was invented and adopted only during the Five Dynasties. The great masters who employed successfully this method at the time were Ching Hao, Kuan T'ung, Tung Yuan and Chü Jan, but few of their works are extant today.

In the Northern Sung Dynasty (House of Chao), every emperor had an art academy wherein he kept his artists, a fact that explained the more pictures in existence of this period. Tang paintings are all but entirely extinct, while there are at least over one hundred paintings of Northern Sung to be found in the world. Of the masters of this period, among academians were Yen Wen-kuei, Kuo Hsi and Li T'ang; among nobilities, Wang Hsien; and among scholar-artists, Li Ch'eng, Fan K'uan and Mi Fei. Kuo Hsi and Li T'ang are especially worthy of note with their great-size scrolls of landscape.

Chao Po-chiu, of royal blood, followed in the footsteps of the two General Li's, and invented the indigo-green landscape and architecture painting, during the Southern Sung. A new development was under way then too.

Whereas landscapes in Northern Sung were usually gigantic serolls comprising many mountains and rivers, those of now became greatly reduced in size as well as objects portrayed. This school of landscape painting was best represented by Ma Yuan and Hsia Kuei. It has been speculated that they painted smaller pictures to show their lamentation of the fact that their country's territory had been much reduced, but this is not true. When an art has developed along any given line long enough that no more exploration or enhancement is possible, artists simply search for other forms for expression and further development.

Another Artistic feature of Sung is the development of the application of caligraphy to the art of drawing. As the writing of Chinese ideograms and drawing were both done with the same brush and under the same principles, it was just one step further to make the two identical. Drawing bamboos is, therefore, but an extension of caligraphy. Many caligraphers are known to be great painters of the bamboo, the orchid, the plum tree and the chrysanthemum, notably Su Shih and Wen T'ung, both of Sung, who created a fashion that is still followed almost 1000 years later.

I am indebted to Professor Hou Chien for his excellent editorial works.

本篇轉載自中華叢書『敦煌藝術』

The nineteen old poems of the Han Dynasty and some of Their Social Implications

The *Nineteen Old Poems* may be considered as a landmark in the development of Chinese poetry. Roughly speaking, the development of Chinese poetry can be divided into four periods. First was the Shih-Ching① period, from the beginning of Chou to the end of Ch'un-ch'iu.② The second period was the Ch'u Ts'u Period,③ from the end of Ch'un-ch'iu to the end of Western Han. The third period, the Ku Shih (Old Poem) Period, extends from the end of Western Han to the end of the Six Dynasties.④ The fourth period was the Chin-ti Shih (Recent Style Poem) Period, from the end of the Six Dynasties to the reformation of Chinese literature in the twentieth century.⑤ In T'ang-Sung times, this form of poetry was developed into many different patterns so as to be adaptable to different songs. This form in its various types was called *ts'u*. In the Yüan Dynasty, there was another transformation of *ts'u*, which was called *ch'ü* and was frequently employed in the theater.

The situation of Ku-Shih was most important to the development of the later forms. The linkage of Ku-Shih and Chin-t'i Shih was quite close, while the differences between Ku-Shih and the antique forme (such as Shih Ching and Ch'u Ts'u) were evident. This means that the influence of Ku-Shih on the literature of recent times (from T'ang to Ch'ing) was dominant. Ku-Shih arose from folk songs in Han times and was possibly influenced by the importations of Central Asian music which did not have any connection with Shih Ching and Ch'u Ts'u.

The beginning of Ku-Shih might be regarded as the beginning of the five-syllable poem, which, however, has not been decided. Mei Shen (220 B.C. ?-140 B.C.?), a famous writer in the Pre-Wuti time, was said to be the first poet who wrote Ku-Shih, but this theory has proved unreliable. Li Shan's (?-689)⑥ *Commentary on Chao-ming Wen Hsüan* (An Anthology of Literature by the Prince Chao Ming (501-531)⑦ of the Liang Dynasty), says:

> The *Nineteen Old Poems* are in the form of five syllables in a line. The writers were unknown. Some say the writer was Mei Shen. This is quite doubtful. We have found some lines from these poems, such as: "I drive a carriage up to the Eastern Gate" and "I wander about the streets of Wan and Loyang" which had to belong to the Eastern Han Age, and could not be regarded as the writing of Mei Shen at all.

In the anthology of Chao Ming, the Nineteen Poems were considered to be anonymous, and another selection by Hsü Ling (506-583) called *Yü-tao Hsin-yün*, which was done a few years after *Wen Hsüan*, put eight of them under Mei Shen's name. Li Shan agreed to Chao Ming's idea, but many scholars, in the later dynasties, followed the theory of Hsü Ling. Even Ting Fu' Pao, the compiler of the *Complete Poems of the Han, Wei, and the Six Dynasties*, had the same opinion as Hsü, although this book was published in 1916. That Chao Ming and Li Shan's opinion proved to be correct is the result of researches during the last thirty years, and now this has become common knowledge among students of Chinese literature.

Chu Yi-tzun (1628-1709), an eminent scholar at the beginning of the Ching Dynasty, criticized the opinion of Prince Chao Ming and the *Commentary* of Li Shan. He said:

> The original copy of *Chao Ming Wen Hsüan* was composed of one thousand volumes. He cancelled out the clumsy parts and simplified

it into thirty volumes. This may be called a most careful revision, but many pieces in it are also false. The *Nineteen Old Poems* in the *Wen Hsüan* are found to contain eight poems written by Mei Shen. Besides the eight pieces (the poem "I drive a carriage to the Eastern Gate" is also found in the various forms of verse of the *Collection of Songs*) , the other six pieces from the Nineteen Poems are not found in *Yü-Tai Hsin Yün* The fifteenth poem of *Chao Ming Wen Hsüan*, "Man's age hardly approaches a hundred, yet he always worries for a thousand years, Too short is the time of day, too long is the time of night, Journey abroad with candles, why not?"

is the "Old Song" of the Hsi-men Hsing. The original text is, "We do live merrily, to be merry is in order just now, How can we sit in sadness and melancholy, to wait for tomorrow?"

In *Wen Hsüan* it is changed into "Enjoy yourself in the present, Do not wait for something tomorrow."

In the original text, "Greedy for wealth and caring for expense, they would be laughed at by their descendants" was changed into "Only fools care about expense, they would be laughed at by their descendants".

In the original text, it is "Naturally we are not Prince Chiao the immortal, Our life cannot be counted equal"

and it is changed into "Mindful of Prince Chiao the immortal, hardly can we hope to follow him"

To change irregular syllables into five-syllable lines, to change the order of lines, to drop the author's name Mei Shen and others, and to give to different poems a general title as "Old Poem" might be done by the scholars in the Wen-Hsüan Building.

(A writing on *Yü-tai Hsin Yün*, from *Pu-Shu-ting Chi* by Chu Yi-Tzun.)

From the critique of Chu, there are two main points to be mentioned:

(1) the original poems were changed by the compilers of *Wen-Hsüan* in the following ways:

a. From irregular-syllable lines into five-syllable lines,

b. The author's name was dropped to "Anonymous":

(2) the "Old Poem" was based on old songs.

The first point has been proved wrong, because at the end of the Western Han, the style of the five-syllable poem was formed and it was employed in the folk songs. There is no reason to say that the form of the *Nineteen Old Poems* was changed by the compilers of *Wen Hsüan*. Moreover, some pieces said to be the writing of Mei Shen were unreliable, and dropping the author's name was necessary in that case. Only the second point is right, because many of the Old Poems were set to music when they were composed.

There were two kinds of Old Chinese verse, "shih" and "fu". "shih" (the "Old Poem") was specially for songs and "fu" was for reading aloud only. Every piece in the "shih" style in the *Book of Odes* was for singing. But Ch'u Ts'u, which was mixed with "shih"and "fu", might be used in both ways, for example, for singing or reading aloud; *Chiu Ko* (Nine Songs) was in the style of "shih" and *Li-sao* was in the style of "fu".

Pan Ku, a great historian of the Western Han Dynasty, who explained the form of the verse in the "Record of Literature" in the *Han Shu* (The History of the Han Dynasty), said:

> *Fu* is a branch of Old Poem for reading aloud without singing. A man who can compose *fu* while climbing a hill may be qualified to be a great officer.

So ancient Chinese verse was divided into two kinds, "Shih" for the purpose of singing and "fu" for the purpose of reading. Every piece of "shih" in the Han Dynasty always referred to song. Until Chien-an times (196-220) works of Ts'ao Ts'ao (155-220) with his sons and his subjects led a new direction for poetry. The fundamental rule in the specimen of the "five-syllable poem" was established in this time, but every piece of Ts'ao Ts'ao was in the style of *yüe-fu*, composition for songs. Ts'ao Pi and Ts'ao Chih, the sons of Ts'ao Ts'ao, with seven great poets, who were called the Seven Geniuses, had written many new works, including "*yüe-fu*" and "non-yüe-fu". During the Chin Period, the portion of "non-yüe-fu" increased. The meaning of "shih" was changed to refer to poetry to be read without music.

Seventeen of the *Nineteen Old Poems* were translated by Arthur waley. He omitted the eighth one and the eighteenth one, because, he said, of their marked inferiority. For my part, I consider these nineteen pieces, which are the only extant works in the five-syllable style, as the popular songs of the Pre-Chien-an Period. They must be considered as a whole in order to discover the path of development of Chinese poetry and no part should be omitted because of anyone's point of view in literary criticism.

Here is a new translation of the *Nineteen Old Poems*. Some parts of them are adapted from Waley's version, but most of them are based on my own understandings. I beliere it will be more exaet than other translations.

(1)

It is a long way for me to go,

To live a life apart from you.

The distance is in myriads of miles,

We are in different corners of the earth.

Rough and long is the road,

We do not know whether we can meet again.

The Tartar horse depends upon the north wind,

Vietnam birds nestle on the southern branch.

My journey is farther and farther, day by day,

My belt is looser and looser, day by day.

Floating clouds shade the bright sun.

The traveler does not think of returning.

Longing for you makes me old,

The year draws suddenly into cold.

Do forget me for I am cast away,

"Good health to you" are the only words to say.

(2)

Green, green,

The grasses are by the river bank,

Thick, thick,

The willow trees are in the garden.

Fair, fair,

The girl is in the tower,

White white,

She is sitting at the casement window,

Bright, bright,

Her decoration in powder and rouge,

Thin, thin,

She puts out her pale hands.

Once she was a dancing girl,

Now she is a wandering man's wife.

The wandering man went, but did not return.

It is hard alone to keep an empty bed.

(3)

Green, green,

The cypresses are on the mount.

Gross, gross,

The stones are in the stream.

Man's life within this world,

Is like the sojourning of a hurried traveller.

Be glad for a cup of liquor,

And a little friendship is no little matter.

Yoking my carriage I urge my wearied horses,

I wander about Wan and Loyang in the streets.

How fine in Loyang town everything is!

The "hats and belts" go seeking each other out.

Long boulevards are intersected by lanes,

Wherein are the mansions of princes and lords.

Two palaces stare at ench other from afar,

Each with twin towers rising over a hundred feet.

By prolonging the feast let us keep our hearts gay,

And not be anxious with urging thoughts.

(4)

Of today's glorious feast

The pleasures are difficult to describe,

The xylophone player gives lingering sounds

Beautiful new melodies are offered to the Muse,

High morals are expressed in the lofty words,

Those who hear these songs will know the truth.

Although everyone wishes for something in his heart

The thoughts of each are unexpressed:

"A lifetime of human lodging in this world

Passes suddenly as flying dust.

Why do we not drive out with the best horses

To seize the nighway's very pass?

Let us not keep our humiliation and poverty

To be hindered always by toil and difficulty."

(5)

A high building is on the Northwest,

As high as the floating clouds.

Fine silk drapes look from the spare window-sills,

Its hip-roofed towers are built on three steps.

From it are coming songs with strings

The tune sounding Oh! how sad!

who can compose so sad a tune?

Surely it must be Chi Liang's wife.

A clear and shrill atmosphere scatters

The sound as it twinkles in the midst of its progress.

Sighs are heard from the strings

Grief remains from her stimulating emotion.

She does not regret that her song is so sad

But minds that so few can understand the meanings,

Thinking of her wish to be a pair of whooping cranes

Wandering over the open sky with long wings.

(6)

Wading in the river to pluck lotus

I find fragrant herbs plentiful in the orchid swamps.

Which one shall I send?

It is to the further land

I look for my home place.

A long way with no ending opens.

In same will, but in different regions,

We are both sorrowful through ages.

(7)

Bright moon illumines the night prospect.

House cricket chirps at the eastern wall,

The Dipper points the "first moon of winter"⑧:

How clear the stars are!

White dew goes down to the moor-grasses.

The season changes so quickly.

Autumn cicadas cry among the trees,

The swallows are gone for their comfort.

A former schoolmate of mine

Took flight as with six wings,

Never thinking of one who had taken his hand,

He abandons me as foot prints.

Sagitarius is in the south and the Dipper north,

And Aquila does not carry a cart.

Surely, while a friend cannot be stable as stone

Of no profit is one so inconstant.

(8)

A lonely bamboo grows at the Tai-shan⑨ foot,

So firmly planted is its root.

To be a bride for you as I can

Is close as the dodder on the rattan.

The dodder grows in its proper season,

A couple meets for proper reason.

Marriage will be taken through a thousand miles,

A long way is prevented by swamps and hills.

Longing for you makes me old,

Waiting for your sedan till the weather is cold.

Do pity the fragrant orchid,

The petals compressed, shining bright,

As you neglect its glory, left untaken,

It will follow the faded grasses and be rotten.

You are certainly high in your righteousness,

And how will you think a humble wife does?

(9)

A precious tree grows inside the yard

Its green leaves bright and glossy,

I pulled the branch and picked the blooms

Thinking to give them to one I love.

The fragrance full in my sleeve and breast

Is very difficult to send such a long way.

How can this bloom be worthy to send?

I just feel our parting has been too long.

(10)

Far away is the Farmer Star⑨,

In bright white is the River Damsel

Her hands appear so pale and thin,

Impatient to play on spinning looms.

She cannot accomplish her daily task

with tears falling as heavily as rain.

While the River is clear and shallow,

How far is the distance to wade?

Plentiful are rivers with no fords:

Silent is the couple with no words.

(11)

Returning by carriage from far away

I drive along a long way

With no boundary. I look around.

Spring winds shake a hundred kinds of grass,

Everything I meet is newly changed,

Why do not people become aged?

Prorsperity and decline alike are doomed,

Too briefly to raise ourselves we live.

Human beings are no metal and stone,

No one can become immortal,

Suddenly the last day comes.

Only glory and fame will be precious.

(12)

The eastern city wall stands high and long

Its every connected part winding along,

Whirlwinds blow there to shake the vast earth,

Massive and green are the autumn grasses.

Alternation is in the seasons,

End of this year so quickly comes.

"Morning Bird" thinks with bitter heart,

"Cricket" grieves with burdened mind.

Be freed from your feeling,

Do not limit yourself by much restraining.

There are many beauties in the northern states

Elegant ones as fair as jade.

Wearing her silk suit

She sings at the door's outside.

So sad is the song!

High tones show that the pillars close.

Arranging her inner belt with deep feeling,

She staggers and hesitates,

And wishes to be a pair of flying swallows

Carrying mud for a nest in your house.

(13)

I drive a carriage up to the Eastern Gate⑩,

Looking at the domes of the Northern Hills.

The ancient dead are hidden in them.

Even night is a long time.

Eternal sleep is diving under yellow springs,

Never to awake through thousands of years.

Age and life are short as morning dew.

Year after year passes swiftly as the sojourner,

No one can endure as metal and stone.

Thousands of years succeed each other,

Even sages and philosophers cannot stand.

Alchemists seek for immortality,

Most of them are betrayed by drugs.

We had better to drink strong liquors

And to dress in thick bright silks.

(14)

The dead passed far and far,

Their remains lie near and near.

Going through the gates of the city wall

I saw plenty of graves and tombs,

Ancient graves were ploughed into farms,

Pines and cedars were felled for fuel.

Only white poplars blow with sorrowful winds,

whistling sadly into travellers' hearts.

Wishing to come back to the father land

I worry, How can I return with empty hands?

(15)

Man's age hardly approaches a hundred

Yet he worries for thousands of years,

Too short is the time of day,

Too long is the time of night.

Journey abroad with candles, why not?

Enjoy yourself in the present,

Do not wait for something tomorrow.

Only fools care about the expense

They would be laughed at by their descendants.

Mindful of Prince Ch'iao⑪ the immortal,

Hardly can we hope to follow him.

(16)

The year comes to the end with piercing cold

Mole-cricket cries sorrowfully in the evening.

Cold wind grows gradually fierce,

She worries that the traveller has no coat.

Giving brocade sweater to the wandering girl,

The intimate one does not care for her.

Sleeping alone all the long night

She dreamed with longing of a figure.

The husband is still in dreaming pleasant.

Humbly offering her the reins of his carriage,

He wishes to have her seductively smiling,

To take her hands and return with her.

But he stays only a little while,

And he does not enter the double ourtains.

Without the wings of a hawk

How could she fly over the winds!

Gazing around in thought

She stretches her neck to look far away.

Hesitantly, with deep sadness,

A tear follows along the pair of doors.

(17)

The cold air reaches in the first moon of winter,

How chilly is the north wind!

Awaiting the longness of night in much sorrow,

I see the lonely sky arranged with stars.

The moon waxes in the fifteenth of this month

And the frog and rabbit wane in the twentieth.

A guest comes from far away,

He brings a bundle of wooden slips:

It is written, "A long desiring is the start,

And parting so long is the end."

These words I carried in my bosom and sleeves,

They did not vanish during three years.

These are the great feelings

Worrying the neglect from you, my respectfulness.

(18)

A guest comes from a far place,

He delivers me a roll of patterned silk.

We are at a distance of thousands of miles,

Good wishes are heartfelt as this:

Decorated with a colored pair of "Mandarin ducks!"

These are good for use in coverlets,

They may be stuffed in "long thinkings"

And edged in "never loosenings",

As fast as glue mixed with lacquer.

Who can separate these two?

(19)

How fine is the bright moon!

It shines through my thin draperies.

Being sleepless with sadness,

I put on my garments to get up to walk,

Thinking of you, so pleasant in your journey.

But to return early is the best way.

When I go through the door in loneliness,

No one can sympathize with my words of pain.

Stretching my neck to look for you in vain,

I go weeping back to my room, with tears

Down to my coat and skirts.

These nineteen poems may be considered in four groups according to their contents, as follows:

(a) Songs for entertainment

"Green, green, the grass is by the river bank" (2)

"Green, green, the cypresses are on the mount" (3)

"A high building is on the Northwest" (5)

"The eastern city wall stands high and long" (12)

"I drive a carriage up to the Eastern Gate" (13)

"The dead passed far and far" (14)

"Man's age hardly approaches a hundred" (15)

"Of today's glorious feast" (4)

"Returning by carriage from far away" (11)

(b) Love songs

"Wading in the river to pluck lotus" (6)

"Far away is the Farmer Star" (10)

"A lonely bamboo grows at the Taishan foot" (8)

"A precious tree grows inside the yard" (9)

(c) Lyric songs for ladies

"The year comes to the end with piercing cold" (16)

"The cold air reaches in the first moon of winter" (17)

"A guest comes from a far place" (18)

"How fine is the bright moon" (19)

(d) Lyric songs for men

"It is a long way for me to go" (1)

"Bright moon illumines the night prospect" (7)

Now I shall explain these four groups in the following sections. First, the group for entertainment. In the time of the Han Dynasty, the entertainments were always combined with music, for example:

His excellency returned by the way of Pei, furnishing liquors in the Palace of Pei, callinf all his old friends, with their sons and young brothers. Twenty boys in the Pei were taught to sing. When the entertainment was in progress, his excellency played the lute.

(Han Shu I, *The Annuary of Kao-ti*)

Yang Yün, in a letter to Sun Hui-tzung, said:

I have been suffering during the past three years. The farmer's life is one of great toil. On the holy days, we cook sheep and entertain ourselves with a oup of wine. I am a native of Chin, and I am skilled in the songs of Chin. My wife is a girl of Ch'ao and she is skilled at *Se*. The singers are some man-slaves and maid-slaves.

(Han Shu 66, *The Biography of Yang Yün*)

Ma Yung (an aristocrat and a famous scholar of the Later Han time) always gave his guests a reception with liquors and music.

(San-ju Cha-lu, from *The Commentary of Hou Han Shu, 64: Biography of Chao Chi*)

In the text of Han Shu and Hou Han Shu there are many examples of musical amusements for use in entertainment. The three examples above show the role of music in the royal court, in the house of an aristocrat, and in the family of a retired officer.

In the inscriptions of Han paintings, there are many pieces concerning entertainment, such as *Wu-liang Ts'ih*, *Hsiao t'ang Shan*, especially in the *Yi-nan* inscription. According to the record of Tzo-chuan, almost every part of *Fung* and *Ya* in the *Book of Odes* was suitable for the music of entertainment. Every piece of the *Nineteen Old Poems* was usable in entertainments according to traditional usage at the time of the *Book of Odes*. However, there are some pieces written especially for entertainments, such as the poem "Of today's glorious feast and revel" (4) which had been indicated for singing at a party; on the other hand, it is mentioned that what should be performed immediately afterwards was "Beautiful new melodies are offered to the Muse." This shows that the song of this poem would be among the last ones performed and there would be other songs to play prior to it.

The *Nineteen Old Poems* represent only one selection of popular songs from the Later Han Dynasty. A great many of these songs have been lost, but the survival of the *Nineteen Old Poems* shows that they have significance as a specimen of this age. We can find indications to show that there may have existed some poems that can be performed before "Of today's glorious feast and revel."

From the record of Han Shu, we know that the singers were always female ones. Therefore the songs were intended to express the women's feelings, and the poems "Green, green, the grass is by the river side" (2) and "A high building is on the Northwest" (5) are obviously designed to express the sentiments of the singers.

In Han times, music imitated the folk song practice of antiphonal singing and response (chang and ho), and some sections of these poems may have been performed as follows:

A. The setting of "green, green":

Singing–"Green, green, the grass is by the river bank" (sung by girl to show her wishes to the guest)

Response–"Green, green, the cypresses are on the mount" (response by guest to show that his philosophy is "let us keep our hearts gay")

B. The setting of "A high building on the Northwest":

Singing–"A high building on the Northwest" (sung by the girl to indicate her wish)

Response–(1) "The eastern city wall stands high and long" (from a guest, with "eastern city wall" to respond to "Northwest", and with "a pair of flying swallows" to respond to "a pair of whooping cranes")

(2) "I drive a carriage up to the Eastern Gate" from the second guest, to follow the regional indication of the first guest and to prolong the plaintive thought of the dead.

(3) "The dead passed far and far" or "Returning by carriage from far away" from the third guest to emphasize the idea of sorrow.

(4) "Man's age hardly approaches a hundred" (response from singing girl to conclude the meanings.

The remnant of this custom may be found in the system of Japanese geisha.

Because the conclusion is the poem "Man's age hardly approaches a hundred", this became a most important one in this series, and its variation by means of adding song has come down to us.

The original style is:

Sheng$_1$ nien$_2$ pu$_5$ man$_3$ pai$_5$
(life)   (year)   (does not)   (full)   (hundred)

Ch'ang$_2$ huai$_2$ ch'ien$_2$ sui$_4$ yu$_1$
(often)   (think)   (thousand)   (year)   (sorrow)

Chou$_4$ tuan$_3$ k'u$_3$ yeh$_4$ ch'ang$_2$
(day)   (short)   (to worry)   (night)   (long)

Ho$_2$ pu$_5$ ping$_3$ chu$_5$ yu$_2$
(why)   (does not)   (take)   (candle)   (to wander)

Wei$_2$ lo$_5$ tang$_1$ chi$_5$-shih$_3$
(to do)   (pleasant)   (must)   (in time)

Ho$_2$ leng$_2$ tai$_4$ lai$_2$-tzu$_1$
(why)   (can)   (to wait for)   (future)

Yü$_2$-che$_3$ ai$_4$-hsi$_5$ fei$_4$
(fools)   (care of)   (expense)

Tan$_4$ wei$_2$ hou$_4$ shih$_4$ chih$_1$
(only)   (to be)   (following)   (generation)   (laugh)

Hsien$_1$-jen$_2$ Wang$_2$-tz'e$_3$ Ch'iao$_2$
(immortal)   (prince)   (name of the prince)

Nan$_2$ k'o$_3$ yü$_3$ teng$_3$ ch'i$_2$
(difficult)   (capable)   (with)   (equal)   (to expect)

The variation is the *Hsi-men Hsing* from the *Li Yüeh Chih* of Chin Shu; it is called a *Se Tiao Chü* (A Song for the 25-string xylophone):

Chu$_5$ Hsi$_1$ men$_2$
(go out)   (west)   (gate)

pu$_4$ nien$_4$ chih$_1$
(walk)   (to think)   (it)

Chin$_1$-jih$_5$ pu$_5$ lo$_5$
(today)   (not)   (pleasant)

tang$_1$ tai$_4$ ho$_1$ shih$_1$
(must)   (wait)   (what)   (time)

fu$_1$ wei$_2$ lo$_5$ wei$_2$ lo$_5$ tang$_1$ chi$_5$shih$_1$
(that)   (to do)   (pleasant)   (to do)   (pleasant)   (must)   (in time)

ho$_1$ leng$_2$ tzo$_4$ ch'ou$_1$ fu$_5$-yu$_5$
(why)   (can)   (sit)   (sad)   (melancholy)

$tang_1$ (must)　　fu_5 (then)　　tai_4 (wait)　　lai_5–tzu_1 (future)

$Ying_4$ (drink)　　$ch'un_2$ (thick)　　$chiu_3$ (liquor)

$Chih_5$ (fry)　　fei_2 (fat)　　niu_2 (cow)

$Ch'ing_3$ (please)　　hu_2 (call)　　$hsin_1$ (heart)　　$shuo_3$ (who)　　$huan_1$ (like)

$k'o_3$ (can)　　$yüng_4$ (use)　　$chieh_3$ (release)　　$ch'ou_2$–yu_1 (sadness)

jen_2 (man)　　$sheng_1$ (life)　　pu_5 (does not)　　man_3 (full)　　pai_5 (hundred)

$ch'ang_2$ (often)　　$huai_2$ (think)　　$ch'ien_1$ (thousand)　　$suel_3$ (year)　　yu_1 (sadness)

$chou_4$ (day)　　$tuan_3$ (short)　　$k'u_3$ (to worry)　　yeh_4 (night)　　$ch'ang_2$ (long)

ho_2 (why)　　pu_5 (does not)　　$ping_3$ (take)　　chu_5 (candle)　　yu_2 (to wander)

Tzu_4 (self)　　fei_1 (is not)　　$hsien_1$–jen_2 (immortal)　　$Wang_2$–tzu_1 (prince)　　$Chiao_2$ (name of the prince)

Chi_4–$huei_4$ (to count)　　$shou_4$–$ming_4$ (life)　　nan_1 (difficult)　　$yü_3$ (with)　　chi_2 (to expect)

Tzu_4 (self)　　fei_1 (is not)　　$hsien_1$–jen_2 (immortal)　　$Wang_2$–tzu_1 (prince)　　$Chiao_2$ (name of the prince)

chi_4–$huei_4$ (to count)　　$shou_4$–$ming_4$ (life)　　nan_1 (difficult)　　$yü_3$ (with)　　$ch'i_2$ (to expect)

jen_2 (man)　　$shou_4$ (life)　　fei_1 (is not)　　$chin_1$ (metal)　　$shih_5$ (stone)

$nion_2$ (year)　　$ming_4$ (life)　　an_1 (how)　　ko_3 (can)　　$ch'i_2$ (to expect)

$t'an_1$ (to covet)　　$ch'ai_2$ (wealth)　　ai_4–hsi_5 (to care of)　　fei_4 (expense)

$t'an_4$ (only)　　wei_2 (to be)　　hou_4 (following)　　shi_4 (generation)　　$ch'ih_1$ (laugh)

It is very clear that the original is a unit in composition and the variation has broken it into pieces and rearranged the order to serve the musical purpose. This varied form may be considered as having been through a long development in music to form a very different variation which is found in the *Li-yueh-ch'ih* of Chin Shu. We can understand, however, this original piece was very popular in Han society, since it has survived even in a form of very different variation.

The poem "Of today's glorious feast" may be considered as another concluding song for a feast. It shows strongly the feelings of the class of intelligentsia, which contained a surplus of members in political positions. In the Later Han Dynasty, there were too many students studying in the national college in Loyang, and the only way to an occupation for those ftudents was to seek employment in the government. The serious competition sor occupations became a trouble of this age, and consequently the Han Empire was disunited and lacked a stable central government for some three hundred years. It was the melancholy of this age and was clearly expressed in these poems.

So in these two poems, "Man's age" and "Of today's", we see represented the sentiments of two different classes. "Man's age" expresses the longings of an aristocrat for immortality, and "Of today's" the inclination of a member of the intelligentsia to seek for earthly success. Down to the Chin Dynasty, these same feelings were preserved in the aristocratic class, just as the song was preserved in its variation, and the fellings of the intelligentsia were expressed in the new poems which were composed by Tzo Sze (240?-300?), Fu Hsüan (217-278), T'ao Ch'ien (371-427), and others.

Lu Chi (261-303) was one of the intelligentsia, but he was born in a noble and wealthy family. Although his ambitions were thwarted since he

was a native of Southern China, which was the former domain of the Wu
Kingdom taken over by the Chin forces, his family still held a position of
privilege in his own country. Therefore his feeling was quite different from
that of the poor intelligentaia. "Imitation of the Old Poem" written by Lu
Chi was quoted in volume 30 of *Wen Hsüan.* It said:

> To invite my intimate friends for a night of leisure,
>
> I supply wines at the Pavilion of Welcoming Wind.
>
> Ch'i slaves play the song of Liang-fu,
>
> Chin beauties sing the song of Chang-nü.
>
> Greivous sounds echo from the gable,
>
> The remains of the melody rush to the zenith,
>
> All the guests are of one will.
>
> Countless cups are within our reach,
>
> Fine eloquency is our gallant speech
>
> Just like the roay rays in the morning.
>
> A short life in this world is man's portion and estate:
>
> How bitter to think that pleasure begins so late!
>
> Suppose that the birds waiting for daylight
>
> Pour forth their sound before the sun rise?
>
> Do not remain in humiliation and poverty
>
> Always living in gloom and sighs.

In this poem, we can discover the differences between the details of Lu
Chi's expression and that of the other anonymous poets. It is clear that the
former exhibits individual feelings and the latter depiot collective feelings.

As to the love songs, there are only four of them among the nineteen
poems. The proportion of this type is smaller here than it is in the "Kuo
Feng"[12] of the *Book of Odes.* The reason for this might be the increased

power of parents to interfere with the will of their sons and daughters and to control decisions involving marriage. In the ancient Chinese social system, the center of the society was the clan, which developed into the Chinese family system through many centuries. A full description of this system would require many volumes, but it still can be simplified to explain the marriage system. Before the Ch'un-ch'iu (or Spring-Autumn) time, Chinese society was under feudalism, with different customs prevailing in different regions. Loyang, the capital of the royal sovereignty, however, was also the center of civilization and of a movement to formalize and standardize social institutions, which was called "li" and was led by the priest class, the "t'ai shih", "t'ai chu" and "t'ai po". From the record of Kuo-yü and Tzo-chuan, the opinions of these priests were esteemed as a standard of political and social conduct. Their opinions were accumulated through centuries to form the system of "li", the regulations for controlling folk usages. This "li" has become the principal foundation of Chinese social practice for three thousand years. On one hand, it created high moral standards to enlighten Chinese people and other oriental peoples; on the other hand, it was too emphatically patriarchal, and caused the human rights of women to be neglected in each and every philosophical school. The position of women gradually went down, and girls could not express any opinion regarding whom they should marry. This might be the main cause of the reduction in the number of love songs during the Han Dynasty. There were no more wandering princes to sing serenades under the window of a castle in the moonlight.

The lyric songs for ladies were clearly limited to a narrow area of feeling. This was a result of the relation between a housewife and her often absent husband. In Han times, only farmers could live with their wives.

Those men who were students in Loyang, the capital, or merchants who went to the large cities to seek their fortunes, could not take their wives from their native country to live with them. These absent husbands might occasionally meet geishas, but the housewives could not take lovers. "Giving brocade sweater to the wandering girl/The intimate one does not care for her" and "Thinking of you, so pleasant in your journey/But to return carly is the best way" were calls from these ladies' hearts.

In similar circumstances were the absent young men who had delayed their weddings, and whose fiances were in lonely waiting. "As you neglect its glory, left untaken/It will follow the faded grasses and be rotten" was the heartily sorroful cry of these girls.

Finally, there are two pieces only that are lyric songs of men. These show that the competition for positions was very keen, and that appointments in the government had become favors bestowed on individuals by men of higher position. As a result of these conditions, some notable families whose members had taken high positions obtained many subordinate officials. These former subordinate officials were called *Ku-li* and had still to be loyal to their former bosses. This might be one reason for the absolute control of political affairs by high officials for many generations during the Six Dynasties in Chinese history.⑬

(I am indebted to Dr. R. C. Rudolph and to Mrs. Molly Mignon for looking through and editing this article, especially in the translation of the poems.)

¹ *Shih Ching.* (詩經) or the *Book of Odes,* is said to be a selection of songs by Confucius. The fundamental form was characterized by four syllables in each line.

² From 1025 B.C., the beginning of the Chou Dynasty, to 552 B.C., the birth of Confucius:

Shang-sung, the "Odes for shang", might be considered as the works of Duke Hsiang of Sung (宋襄公) State in the Chün-ch'iu period.

3 *Ch'u T*su (楚辭) was a collection of verses attributed to the people of Ch'u, a state in the southern part of China along the Yangtze River. It was compiled in the Han Dynasty, and contains works from the Chu State (notably *Chü Yüan's Li Sas* and other works by Sung Yü) and works written in Chu style by the Han authors after Chu was destroyed.

4 The fundamental form of the Ku Shih (古詩) of Han times is five syllables to the line. Tho origin of this form is an interesting problem in the history of Chinese literature. Hu Shih (胡適) (*Pal-hua Wen-hsüeh Shih*). Cheng Chen-to (鄭振鐸) (*Chung-kuo Wen-hsüed Shih*). and Lu K'an-ju (陸侃如) (*Chung-kuo Shih Shth*) touched on this problem. In recenl yoars, Liu Ta-chieh (劉大杰) (*Chung-kuo Wen-hsüe.i Fa-*chan *Shih*, 1955, Chung-wha Book Co.) has a special chapter (PP. 140-151) dealing with it.

5 *Chin-ti Shih* (近體詩) is always in five or seven syllables for each line. It implies the followlng forms:

(1) *Chüeh-chü* (絕句) with four lines, (2) *Lü Shih* (律詩), with eight lines, and (3) Pai *I*ü (排律), more than eight lines. The number of the lines must be a multiple of four.

6 Li Shan (李善), a scholar in the T'ang Dynasty. His famous work was the *Commentary for Won Hsüan*.

7 Prince Chao Ming (昭明太子): Chao Ming was a posthumous title. His name was Hsiao T'ung (蕭統), and he was the eldest son of Hsiao Yen (蕭衍), founder of the Liang Dynasty. He became the crown prince of Liang. He compiled *Wen Hsüan*, the first issued collection of the anthology of great authors.

8 According to the fifth line, white dew indicates autumn season, but third line shows something eontrast. It meaus in the mid-nighr the handle of Dipper is moved to North. Cf. Kan Lao: *Ku-shih Ming-Yüeh Chiao Yeh-kuang Chieh-hou Chieh*, Wen-Shih Magazine, 1934.

9 It refers to the Consteuation of Aquila.

10 Eastern Gate indieates one of the Jates of Loyang, and Northern tlills indicates Pei-mang. Shan in which many nobles buried.

11 Prince Ch'iao was said to be one son of the King of Chou turned into immortal.

12 國風.

13 More intormations Cf. Kan Lao: *"Ku-shih Shih-chice Shou Yu"Chi Wen-hsio Shang Chih Kuan-hsi*. Shih Hsio, Giant Publisher, Taiwan, 1976.

A Review of Joseph Needham's "Science and Civilization in China"Vol. 4, Part 3.

Joseph Needham, with the collaboration of Wang Ling and Lu Gwei-djen. *Science and Civilization in China*. Volume 4, *Physics and Physical Technology*. Part 3, *Civil Engineering and Nautics*. New York: Cambridge University Press. 1971. pp. lvii, 931. $55.00.

This book by Professor Joseph Needham is surely an outstanding work, one that will bring the author an eminent reputation in the field of the history of sciences. In it the author gives much important information and discusses civill engineering and nautical technology.

The first part of this volume is a description of the roads, walls, buildings, bridges, and canals, together with the systems of irrigation, hydraulic engineering, and water conservation. The second part deals with sailing craft, the technical development of the ship both in time of peace and war, and some information on sea routes of ancient Chinese sailors. The author not only depicts Chinese techniques in the greatest detail ever presented in the Western world, but he also gives more exact identification of Chinese civil engineering with English technical terms, especially for Chinese buildings constructed under systems extremely different from those of the West. The viewpoint of this book goes a long way toward helping Westerners, as well as Chinese students with modern training, to better understand ancient Chinese architecture.

Among the valuable information in this book are several points that impressed me. Since some problems might be solved with further discussion, they are pointed out separately. The design of a house, with its many steps of development, should be traced to the single tent. The reconstruction of the ruin of Hsiao-tun before the tenth century B.C., discussed by Mr. Shih Chang-ju, should be considered as the basic pattern of the Chinese house, which is related to both the *Book of Rites* (*I-li*) and the later development, from the design of the imperial palaces (and Buddhist or Taoist temples) to the typical ground plans of the house of the common people. The steps of the development of the ground plan are: first, a hall with two main front pillars and a left wing; second, a hall with left and right wings; third, for a palace, the wings developed independently into three halls in one line (compare Liu Tun-chen, *Tung-hsi-tang K'ao*), and for a common house, both of the wings led into the side rooms (socalled *Hsiang-fang*); fourth, opposite the hall there might be the main gate with two side rooms, but for a common house it becomes a row of three rooms, and the main gate moves to the right side by the row. This is the typical pattern of *Ssu-ho Yuan* or the compound.

Needham is very enthusiastic in tracing the tradition of the Chinese house system to the classics of rites. It is a rather hard task, however, because very few scientific studies could be found in this field. *San-li-tu* by Nieh Chung-I of the Sung dynasty is simply a collection of constructions. During the Ch'ing dynasty all of the scholars without exception followed Nieh's assumption, including Jen Chi-yun, whose work is mentioned by the author.

The only article with an entirely different method is Kan Lao's "Li-ching Chih-tu Yu Han-tai Kung-shih" ("The System in Classics of Rites and the Relation to the Buildings of the Han Period," in the special issue of *Kuo-hsueh*

Chi K'an, Peking University, 1939), which is based on the actual relics and which has a ground plan that is totally different from the traditional view of N'ieh Chung-I. It is unfortunate that it was not seen by Needham because of the limits on its circulation during the Sino-Japanese War.

Another point that impressed me, which was noted by Needham, is that a town or a city, other than a Chinese village growing from unofficial administration, was established for political purposes. In Chinese history there was no distinction between a castle and a town because the towns or cities were not creations of burghers and never achieved any degree of autonomy with regard to the state. Furthermore the author adopted a typical city plan by E.A. Gutkind, which is a square inside the city wall with crossed streets and a drum tower at the center. All of these are true, but I would like to suggest two points for discussion. Since the development of the Chinese city is very complex, the best way to manage the study is by tracing and analyzing its history.

The historical development before unification, which came during the Ch'in Empire, was a sequence of progress from tribal administration, city-states, and kingdoms to empire. In ancient China the Chou dynasty was not truly feudal, and in the later Chin dynasty (300-420 A.D.), feudalism was incomplete. In the former there were no burghers, and in the latter there were castles (so-called *wu* or *pao*) with burghers, but they were all wiped out by imperial power very soon. In *Han Kuan I* the author Ying Shao of the Later Han period indicated that the assistants of a magistrate might be compared with ministers of a ruler in the ancient state. It means that the *hsien* (district) was transferred from the city-state. Of course the city of a *hsien* was adopted from the mode of a city-state. *Ya-men* was certainly derived from the palace of a former lord. According to *Chou-li* the palace was located at the southern part of the capital. It may be compared with the *Ya-men*, which was always situated at the south of a city. The drum tower could only be traced back to the main beacon tower of the Han dynasty. (According to Han wooden slips, the drum was used in the beacon tower.)

Note A on page 73 is based on the late E.A. Gutkind's work in which he considered that Chinese cities were square or rectangular rather than circular, round, or irregular because in former times Chinese cities were designed with the belief of the ancient "squared earth" theory. I do not think it is a uniform regulation in China. Evidently it is found that the cities to the north of the Ts'inling Mountains and the Huai River are always square or rectangular, while to the south of this line the cities are always round or irregular. In my previous article, "The Cities of Southern Style and Northern Style," I mentioned that northern cities were built planned, but that southern cities were transformed from villages which arose naturally. I think it should be an important supplementary idea to this book.

Needham indicates that a curving roof is a very characteristic and beautiful feature of Chinese buildings. He gives more important information from *Ying-tsao Fa-shih* and research and pictures from *Ying-tsao Hsueh-sheh*. He wonders, however, about the reasons why ancient Chinese buildings were always made of wood instead of stone, which was used in other countries like Greece, India, and Egypt and which allowed many monuments to endure. It cannot be surmised that China had no stone suitable for great buildings similar to those of Europe and Western Asia; in China stone was used only for tomb-construction styles and monuments and for pavements of roads, courts, and paths. Needham points out that perhaps further knowledge of social and economic conditions might illumine the matter of the form of slavery, known in China in different ages but never equivalent to slavery in the Occident, which could dispatch thousands at a time to hard labor in the quarries.

In my opinion this explanation is good, but there are some other elements besides it. On page 262 of this book (in figure 876) Needham explained the illustration showing that the Chinese always had men of genius for the efficient organization of mass manpower. On careful study of Chinese civilization, the dolesmen are found in many parts of China. In the records of oracle bones it was shown that several ancestors of the Shang royal family. such as Shang-chia, Pao-I, Pao-ping, and Pao-ting, were worshiped in the stony shrine. But in later ages the ancestor temples were built of wood. Later a very famous story was recorded about the ancestor temple of Wang Mang that was built from lumber taken from the luxurious palace of Han Wu-ti. In the *Book of Poetry* we find a description of the new palace built fin the beginning of the Chou dynasty—"It is as beautiful as a pheasant ly ing." Thus the invention of the wood curving roof as the trend in the development of Chinese building is due to its magnificent beauty. Since beautiful wooden palaces and temples could be well protected within the longevous power of the rulers, they neglected to consider the importance of monuments.

本篇轉載自 American Historical Review.

The Early Use of Tally in China

Knotting string is said to have brought the dawn on Chinese culture. This method of record keeping is also found used in Ryukyu islands as well as among the Indian tribes in Southern America. In the case of the Indians, the string knotts indicate the number of days of festivals or eclipses. The Indians in British Columbia, instead of using string knotts, are found to have used sticks and hairs to show the number of different animals①. These facts show that strings or sticks were widely used for record keeping among the primitive peoples of the world and the ways they used them could serve as valuable comparison to the ancient custom of the Chinese people.

Both strings and sticks were widely used during the development of Chinese culture. The use of the sticks is particularly significant. Many parts of ancient Chinese culture were related to the use of sticks and its influence is still observable in many Chinese cultural elements.

Firstly, the Chinese numerals may be traced to the notches of sticks. From the relics in Pan-po of Sian City②, the numerals are considered to be the earliest form of Chinese characters. This finding casts doubt on the hypothetic assumption that the hieroglyphics or the pictorial symbols appeared first in the development of Chinese characters. This finding however helps explain the origin of Chinese numerals and the manner in which they were first written down. The notches of sticks can also be compared to the marks on the notched tallies. Through such a comparison we may explain why the ancient Chinese numerals were arranged in that way.

Secondly, the mechanical counting tools in the world should be traced to the stick calculating and the abacus of the Chinese people. Stick calculating is a method which uses sticks instead of writing. The sticks are arranged in different denominations of singles, tens, hundreds, thousands and so forth. When a number is desired, the sticks are placed into position according to their respective denomination. Each given position is limited to five sticks. If the number exceeds five in any given position, then some different forms of arrangement are used. To add is to put more sticks and to subtract is to take away the sticks in the similar manner the beads on abacus are manipulated. In principle, the stick calculating is the same as abacus calculating. The only difference is that abacus has beads instead of sticks. If the abacus is in any way related to the modern computer, we should recognize the fact that the stick calculating in China was the earliest forerunner.

Thirdly, the bamboo was always made into slip-size for the use of writing. Due to this particular feature, early Chinese books were in the form of boundles of slips connected and bonded together by ropes or other strings. This is quite different from the Babylonian bricks or Egyptian papyruses, and this is due to the Chinese special system of the stick using. In the Middle Ages, when paper was widely used in China, paper books were carefully sized and columned in imitation of the old form of slip combination.

Fourthly, the chopsticks belong to the same category of the use of sticks. Chopsticks, like other kinds of Chinese sticks, are usually made of bamboo, occassionally of wood. They are the earliest attempt to use tools instead of hands. Of course, this is the extended usage of sticks with regard to other kinds of stick using such as counting sticks, writing sticks and so on. (The use of sticks in divination as in the case of the Book of changes is another form of stick using.)

Aside from these uses of sticks, the most important and most widely used over the world in many tribes of non-Chinese speaking peoples are the use of sticks as tally. Tally is a kind of two-stick combination with notched cuts as marks or numbers for use as money credit, as an order of purchase, as a passport and as an identification of the status of an aristocrat. Tallies may be made of wood, bamboo, bronze, or even the most expensive jade as found described in ancient records and among artifacts in modern archaeological finds.

Now, I would like to itemize the different forms of Chinese tally.

The earliest known tallies are notched sticks of wood or bamboo. This was recorded by ancient scholars in the classics. In the section of *Hsi-ts'u* or the *Appendix to the Commentary of the Book of Changes*③ it is said that in the remote antiquity, the ancients used the knot of strings in the management of government affairs. It is also said that in later times, the sages changed it into words in the form of notches on sticks for the purpose of managing hundred of officials and for the inspection of thousands of people. This explanation of the origin of the Chinese records is just a hypothesis, but it is a hypothesis full of possibility that we can find no logical ground to reject it.

According to the Classics, the first stage in the evolution of Chinese writing was the formation of Shu-ch'i④. Here shu means to write with brush and chi means to carve with knife. Many scholars are of the opinion that in the ancient time, the characters on wooden or bamboo slips were inscribed. Such opinion is not substantiated by material evidences, In recent archaeological finds, there is no slip that had been carved except the cut marks on the side of slips used as tallies. A close examination of the slips, woodern or bamboo, one will find that to insrcibe characters on the thin pieces of them may be a very clumsy way. That is why it was never in fact done. Thus the early use of Ch'i or carving is limited to the tally only.

Now, let us examine the construction of the ancient character ch'i (契) for a moment. Its meaning and its application will become clear through such an examination. The character "ch'i" 契 is composed of three parts. The bottom part is a character "ta" 大 which is a variation of "mu" 木 which means wood. The upper part is composed of "chieh" 丯 and "tao" 刀. The latter "tao" 刀 is a knife while the former "chieh" 丯 shows intched teeth. Therefore it is clearly a tally. This means that in ancient times, carving is limited to the tally only as we have asserted above. And this is supported by archaeological evidences.

That kind of tally may be considered to be the original form. There are many records from the Chou dynasty through the Han dynasty concerning the uses and forms of the wooden or bamboo tally. Moreover some genuine specimens of tallies are found in the Tun-huang and chü-yen sites the fact of which indicates that tallies were widely used in the ancient Chinese World.

Aside from wood or bamboo, tally could be made of bronze. Both seal and tally were used in ancient China and both could be made of bronze. For identification purposes, they were used in the similar way. In the ruins of Anyang, a seal was found. Some scholars contend that though seals were widely used in the ancient Near East, it is still possible that the ancient Chinese conceived it independently, thus they claim that the seal is of

Chinese origin. However they cannot prove it. Since many things of Western origin such as the Chariot, the spear were also found in the Anyang ruins, it indicates the possibility that the Anyang civilzation was not as homogenous as it was supposed. Thus whether the single seal was of Chinese origin is still difficult to say. However, the use of the seal by the Chinese gradally became common during the Warring States period. During the Ch'in-Han period seal became the legal identification from the emperor down to different ranks of officials in all parts of China. The seal thus replaced the tally for the most part. In the *Yü-fu Chih* (or the Record of Carriage and dress) of the *Hou Han Shu*⑤, it is said that seal was provided for every official in charge of management post. Tally, on the other hand, was only given in special cases. The seal is also used in lieu of signature by private persons. This use may have started during the Warring States period, continued through the Ch'in-Han period down to the present time. It is very common among the modern Chinese as well as Japanese and Korean. But when we trace the early usage we should say that the importance of the use of various kinds of jade was more dominant than seal.

From the discovery of Shang and early Chou sites, jade are found in many sites while seals only in very few ones. This is quite contrary to the findings at the sites later than the Warring States and Ch'in-Han. In the *Book of Chou Li*⑥, chapter T'ien-jui (or the Keeper of Auspicious Materials), it is recorded that the main variety of jade are in five patterns: kuei, pi, chang, huang and tsung (these are called Wu-jui or five auspice in the *Po-Hu T'ung*). According to the terminology of the scholars in the field of Chinese archaeology, kuei (圭) is identified as the jade knife or jade ax, pi (璧) as the jade disc with an aperture in the center, huang (璜) as a half of the pi sometimes used as a main part of a jade pendant, and tsung (琮)

as a jade tube. All these patterns are familiar items in the collections of ancient Chinese jade. But it is very significant that chang (璋) has not found in any site or in any collection.

In the Classics, the term chang is frequently mentioned. For example, in the *Book of Poetry*⑦, chang is used as toy for a new born boy. For a new born girl, the toy is not chang, but pottery. This quotation is always used by the Chinese people in case of child birth. However, nobody knows what is the pattern of chang except that it is an instrument made of jade. Since it is so common and so important, why no chang was found so far? I am of the opinion that no chang is identified so far does not mean that no chang was found or existed. What it means is likely that the scholars have failed to recognize it.

This problem of identifying chang stemmed from the explanation of chang in the *Shuo-wen*⑧ (the first dictionary of Chinese characters). It is said there that the chang is a half of a kuei. Generally speaking, it is always with a hole. If it is separated into two halves, the hole must be on the side of both halves as half of a hole. This explanation is unclear upon close reading. Ever since *Shuo-wen's* time, there has no real half ax or half knife been discovered. If we cling to this definition of chang, the identification will not be possible. A commentator named Hsü Hao of the Ch'ing dynasty said that the object normally considered as "half kuei" should not be considered as such. A kuei, in his opinion, is indeed the half of a whole. Separately, they are called kuei, but when put together, they constitute one chang. In other words, the chang is a set of two kuei which are used as counterparts in one unit. And the unit is called chang. In actual usage, one is to be held in office while the other is given to the messenger as a means of identification. This is a new idea and a very valuable one in the effort of identifying chang from the thousand pieces of ancient Chinese jade.

Unfortunately, scholars in the Ch'ing dynasty did not pay much attention to Hsü's opinion. Everybody still clinged to the obscure *Shou-wen* explanation. This conflict can best be resolved by re-examine the archaeological finds. But the scholars in the field of ancient curiocity did not take hint from archaeology. Consequently a category of jade which can so clearly be identified as chang are given many unsuitable names during the time of the Ch'ing dynasty.

This category of jade occupies a very important position among all types of ancient jade. It is a disc with a cavity in the center and with teeth around the circumference. The teeth are arranged irregularly in size as well as in distance. This jade is identified as hsüan-chi (璇璣), believed to be an astronomical instrument by a famous scholar at the end of the nineteenth century, Wu Ta-chen. Since there was no better explanation, many scholars accepted his idea, including Berthold Laufer in his outstanding work *Jade, A Study in Chinese Archaeology and Religion.* Although Laufer was somewhat doubtful of the explanation, he could not offer a more satisfactory one.

Wu Ta-chen's theory was based on the chapter Yao-tien in the Book of History. It is said there that the ancient king regulated the seven policy (to pray for the regularity of the seven luminaries) with hsüan-chi and yü-heng. What are hsüan-chi and yü-heng? Comparing the explanations given in the earlier half of the Eastern Han (25-146 A.D.) in the *Shuo-wen* with that of the later half (147-220 A.D.) as expressed by Ma Jung, Cheng Hsüan and Ts'ai Yung, we find a significant change between them, The *Shuo-uen* said that both hsüan-chi and yü-heng to be simply jade, but the scholars in the later half of the Eastern Han said that they were astronomical instruments. This difference in explanation shows that to consider hsüan-chi and yü-heng as astronomical instrument was strictly a later invention. It should not be regarded as the original meaning of the hsüan-chi and yü-heng. If this expanation is only a product of the second century, it certainly should not be applied to the Chou dynasty.

Moreover, jade is fragile, it is not suitable to be used as any part of machine except bearing in watch. The assumption of Han scholars that jade was used as certain part of machine was just a fantasy. The explanation of such nature is not reliable. However, since the explanation has formed a tradition of its own, Wu Ta-chen accepted it and used it for the identification of that teethed jade. If the teethed jade was really a part of a machine, it should have been used as a gear. If it is any kind of gear, the teeth would have to be regular, for no gear has irregular teeth. Furthermore, the irregularly arranged teeth on hsüan-chi are very narrow. The only comparable object would be, say, the teethed edge of a key. Taken all these into consideration, such a disc with irregular teeth should not be considered as a gear, and the only possibility is that it is a kind of tally.

According to the *Chou Li*⑨, the only pattern of jade with teeth is chang (the teeth is called she or shot) and one kind of chang which is especially designed to raise troops is called ya-chang or the tusked chang. With a review of the ancient jade remains, we would say that the jade disc with teeth should be identified as chang, the jade disc with three wings and with teeth on the wings should be identified as ya-chang, both of which are generally referred to as hsüan-chi and thus wrongly considered to be astronomical instruments.

Aside from chang, there are other varieties of jade. For example, the tiger shaped jade (it is called hu, a composite character with jade and tiger) was said in the *Shuo-wen* to be an auspicial jade tally designed for raising troops. Such use of hu cannot be found in the *Chou-Li*. Sun Yi-jang, a late ch'ing scholar said that to use hu to raise troops should be the practice of the Warring States period, not of the Chou dynasty, for it is recorded in the *Lü-shih Chün-chiu* only (the particular passage in which this information is given survived in the quotation of the *Tai-ping Yü-lan*[⑩] only and cannot be found in the *Lü-shih Chün-chiu* itself). When we compare hu with the Shang jade tiger (from George Eumofopulos Collection in London), we will find that hu has irregular teeth on the tiger's head and tail. And it is used as tally. Therefore, jade tallies could be in different shapes. The common feature is that all of them have teeth of irregular sizes.

Down to the time of the Warring States, the tally used to raise troops was changed from jade to bronze and was called hu-fu (虎符). The term hu-fu first appeared in the Biography of Lord Hsin-ling in the *Shih Chi*[⑪], in which a very exciting story of the stealing of a hu-fu in order to relieve the State Chao is given. There are bronze tiger tallies in archaeological finds. They are called hu-fu of Yung-ling and Hsiu-ch'i. Both of them are proven in the study conducted by Wang Kuo-wei to be the relies of the Ch'in of the Warring States period. The use of the tiger tally was continued through out the two Han dynasties as evidenced in the *Han Shu* and the *Hou Han Shu*.

Chieh (節) is also used as a kind of identification. In the Record of Hundreds of Official in the *Hou Han Shu*, fu-chieh ling or the director of the Department for Tallies and Tokens, was as his duty to keep both fu and chieh. Chieh was a tasselled staff given to the imperial messenger to show his authorization. Because the pole was made of wood, no real artifact survived the ravage of time. But we can still find them in Han paintings, Chieh can be considered as an extension of tally, The original meaning of

Chieh is joint or knot of wood or bamboo. In that sense, it may be related to the cuts of tallies.

Henri michel in his artiele "Sur Les Jades Astronomiques Chinoise[12]" suggested that this kind of teethed jade might be the astronomical instrument, in so far as every group of its three parts around the dise shows in the same way arranged as the seven points in the Great Dipper. I do not believe this explanation is a truth. To triplicate the points of Dipper around the disc does not make any sense for observation. The meaning to use seven points should be more likely a code in pattern for a tally. This code is just used for a special disc, because other jade discs could not be adapted to this code.

[1] Franr Boas: *General Authrology*, Pg. 271

[2] *Sian Pan-Po* (西安半坡) Pg. 197

[3] *I-ching*, "Hsi-ts'ŭ", Part Ⅱ (易經繫辭) (Yee-wen ed.) Pg. 166

[4] Ting Fu Pao *Shuo-wen Chieh-fs'ŭ Ku-lin*(說文解字詁林) (Commercial Press ed)pp. 1865-1866

[5] *Tung-Kuan Shu* (東觀書) quo ted in the commentary or *Hou Han Shu* (Chi-Chieh 後漢書集解, Chüan 120, Yee-wen ed.) Pg. 1386

[6] Sun I-jang: *Chou-li Cheng-I*, (周禮正義) chüan 39, (Kuo-hsüeh Chi-pen Ts'ung-Shu, commercial Press ed.) pp. 1-13

[7] *Book of Poetry*, "Ssu-Kan" (詩經斯干) in "Ta-ya" (yee-wen ed.) pp. 387-388.

[8] Ting Fu-pao: *Shuo-wen Chieh-tsŭ Ku-lin* (commercial Press) pp. 140-141

[9] Sun I-jang: *Chou-li Cheng-I* (commercial Press ed.) pg. 13

[10] *Tai Ping Yü-lan* (太平御覽) chüan 808 (Hsin-Hsing ed.) pg. 3522

[11] *Shih Chi* (史記) chüan 77, (yee-wen ed.)pg. 958

[12] Melangos Chinois et Bouddhigues, Juillet, 1951, pp. 151-16.

本篇轉載自顧里雅先生（Prof. H.G.Creel）祝壽專號。

The Corruption under the Bureaucratic Administration in Han Times

From the middle part of the Spring and Autumn period to the beginning of the Warring States era was an age of gradual changes, one of the most important being the founding of political organizations in the transition from feudalism to bureaucracy.

As a result of a long period of peace and stability in the Chou dynasty, the middle class gradually emerged between the aristocrats and serfs, and their role in the society appeared to be growing in importance. Moreover, in the Ch'in and Han dynasties, although the former feudal lords no longer maintained their political status, yet the former aristocrats from the different feudal states still preserved their wealth①. They were either landlords or rich merchants. For instance, the five families from the T'ien clan of Ch'i state in modern Shantung② and the three families, Chao, Ch'ü and Ching, from the royal clan of Ch'u state in modern Hupei, maintained their position, their influence, and their money up to the Han period.

During the beginning years of the Han dynasty, the importance of the merchants for the court was very obvious. The Han government actually adopted the theory of the Legalist school, a theory which included oppression of the merchant class; yet the influence of the merchants remained undiminished because of their wealth.

At the beginning of the Spring and Autumn period, the leading merchants had already appeared. The information concerning their activities was mentioned in the *Tso Chuan* on several occasions③. However, the economic power of the merchants was not so dominant until the beginning of the Warring States period, according to the recorded biographies of wealthy people in the *Shih Chi*. In addition, the aristocrats escaped to other feudar states with their followers since their own power was destroyed by other aristocrats. Then they settled down in foreign lands. For instance, warlords Fan and Chung-hang of Ch'in state escaped with their herds of cattle. The original purpose of the cattle was for temple sacrifices, but in their new habitat they had to use the cattle exclusively for farming④.

Thus, during this period the role of the middle class was enhanced as the number of feudal states decreased. Although political power was still in the hands of the hereditary feudal lords who protected their own interests, the wealthy middle class could still manage to find ways and means to struggle for their own survival. Since there was no democratic institution in ancient China to protect the interests of the middle class, they had no other choice except to work to the top of the ladder by means of bribery. A good example is the famous story of Lü Pu-wei⑤, a rich merchant who became the prime minister and a powerful lord of the enlarged Ch'in kingdom because of his wealth and political tactics.

If we study the final victory of Ch'in over the rest of the Middle Kingdom, we find that the Ch'in victory not only depended on its military strength but also on its intelligence and legerdemain. The Ch'in court bribed the high ranking officials of other states with a large quantity of gold before taking any military action against them⑥. The tactics of bribery worked very effectively. For instance, Ch'i state in the east had been next in power only to Ch'in. It enjoyed many years of peace during the reconstruction period, a period filled with turmoil. However, its prime minister,

Hou Sheng, accepted bribes from Ch'in which caused Hou Sheng to lower the defenses of Ch'i⑦. Consequently the Ch'in army was able to take over Ch'i state very easily.

Since the power of the government was always held by the imperial ruler, an individual government official could not exercise undiluted responsibility, and, therefore, tended to be afraid to take responsibility. Thus, the bureaucracy was formed both in the central and local administrations. For lower ranking officials to bribe their superiors was a common thing, because it was the only effective way to keep their positions. Corruption was an inevitable consequence.

The law of the Ch'in and Han dynasties was very strict and clearly stated the punishment for corrupt officials⑧. It said that those involved in corrupt practices should be dismissed from their offices and never be appointed again. However, in the biographies of the *Han Shu* and the *Hou Han Shu,* we find that the high ranking officials were often reappointed even though they had previously been involved in corrupt practices.

We also know on the basis of their biographies that a number of officials were honest. However, it should be said that their purity was limited, because some illegal revenues were collected by local administrators⑨. This practice was unofficially permitted by the ruler. And while evidences of this practice during the Han period were few, this tradition persisted up to the Ch'ing dynasty. For instance, the Yung-cheng Emperor (1678-1735) of the Ch'ing dynasty made this practice official. He said, quite frankly, that any district magistrate was permitted to take ten percent of the levied land taxes. It was only the Yung-cheng Emperor who had the courage to admit to this practice publicly, even though it had been carried on throughout Chinese history.

Corruption was widespread even among the imperial family and eunuchs in the palace. The male members of the imperial family practiced polygamy, especially the emperor himself. The emperor was surrounded by hundreds of concubines, female attendants, and eunuchs. No official was allowed to enter the private chambers of the emperor in the palace. As a result, it was very natural that the close associates of the emperor exercised great influence on him, particularly the eunuchs.

This complicated situation in the palace did not show clearly during the beginning years of a newly established dynasty, However, after a few generations, some naive emperors were strongly influenced and sometimes even controlled by the eunuchs. Cases of corruption occurred constantly under the reign of Yuan-ti in the Former Han and under the reign of Huan-ti and Ling-ti in the Later Han[10]. It was common practice for many eunuchs to be bribed by ministers or governors who had to yield to the eunuchs' wishes in order to keep their positions. And these ministers and governors did the same toward lower ranking officials such as the magistrates. Thus, a chain of bribe givers and bribe takers was formed down to the lowest government officials who received their portion from the pockets of the common or the poor people. This system became one of the main causes of the mass revolts against the imperial government which ultimately caused its collapse. In other words, corruption grew to such proportions that the common people, ordinarily passive, rose up against it.

In the palace, sometimes the emperor, as well as the eunuchs, was involved in bribery. For instance, the Ling-ti Emperor in the Later Han dynasty requested bribes from every candidate for chancellor or minister[11]. The price for the position of chancellor was said to be one thousand pieces of gold. Besides eunuchs, the imperial relatives used to exert influence on the ruler too. Consequently, it was also a common practice for the imperial relatives to take bribes from various officials. We can find many instances of officials bribing prominent imperial relatives in order to obtain higher positions in the government.

According to the information derived from the writings on the wooden slips of the Han dynasty, the salary for a lower ranking government official was too small to support his family. A chief clerk received 600 coins per month in the Former Han[12]. With this amount of coins, he could purchase ten bushels of millet, which is approximately ten hectolitres of millet. An assistant clerk would receive still less than this amount. A magistrate's monthly salary was comparatively more, yet it was not enough to provide for his needs. Tsui Shih, a scholar of the Later Han dynasty, observed this situation and commented[13]:

> The position of a district magistrate is equivalent to that of a lord in ancient time, but the monthly salary he receives is only equivalent to the wage paid to a door keeper in ancient time. The present salary for a magistrate is twenty bushels of millet and two thousand coins. He should at least have a servant who will attend to him. However, he has to pay his servant one thousand coins a month for the latter's service. The quantity of grain he receives is only enough for himself, a servant, and a horse. So there is nothing left to support his family. Under these circumstances, how can an official avoid becoming involved in bribery?

It is clear that an official's monthly salary was not sufficient to support his family during the Han period. The local officials, therefore, had to look for financial resources to solve this problem. The common practice of officials in the local administrations was to collect extra taxes from markets, tax-

collecting stations, and the like. These extra taxes were shared by the
governors and magistrates with their staffs. This kind of practice was
widespread in every province of imperial China. This practice continued
from the Han period down to the nineteenth century. As a result, the income
of a leading local official was much more than that of the officials who
worked in the central government in the capital. There is much evidence
to indicate that the officials in the central government had a strong desire
to be transferred to local administration for better pay. I would like to
mention three such cases.

> The famous alchemist called Ko Hung was appointed by the emperor
> of the Chin Dynasty as the chief clerk of the prime minister, but he
> asked to be transferred to a local region as a district mayor
> instead⑭ .

> The former king of the Former Liang (前涼) was given the title
> of a feudal lord by the Eastern Chin (晉) emperor after his capture
> by the Chin army. Since he was poor, he asked the Chin government
> to appoint him as a governor instead⑮ .

> The famous poet T'ao Ch'ien of the Chin dynasty asked the government
> to appoint him as a magistrate in order to save some money for
> setting up a farm⑯ .

As mentioned above, the local officials' incomes were higher than central
government officials' incomes because the former were permitted to
collect extra taxes A book called *Shen chien* written by Hsün Yüeh in the
Later Han dynasty⑰ explains why this practice became institutionalized and
accepted. The book describes the situation as follows:

> The standard pay scale for government officials of the Han dynasty
> is too low, and the nonquota personnel for public services are too

many. As a result, the financial resources of both the government and the people have suffered enormously in order to support the local officials and the nonquota personnel.

The local administrators had to find ways and means to pay the salaries of hose nonquota personnel by themselves. Collection of extra taxes by the local dministrators was, therefore, permitted by the central government. Obviously, all these problems led to corruption.

In conclusion, a middle class appeared in the Chou dynasty because of its long period of peace and stability. The displaced aristocrats in war torn states preserved their wealth and settled down in foreign lands. They were either landlords or rich merchants. Each government official felt insecure in a bureaucratic government and had to survive by flattering his superiors. the salary of government officials was too low and the government unofficially permitted the low salaried administrators to levy extra taxes to supplement their income. In addition, the eunuchs and the imperial relatives demanded bribes from officials by taking advantage of their close relation to the ruler. All these conditions led to corruption throughout imperial China.

[1] The wealth of such aristocrats was preserved in the powerful families, including the Chao, Chü, and Ching families of Ch'u state and the T'ien family of Chi state. They moved into the Kuan-chung area (around the capital Chang-an) under the reign of Kao-ti and Wu-ti of the Han dynasty.

[2] From the *Huo-chih chuan* ("The Biography of the Wealthy People," *Han shu*, chung 90). It is said the T'ien family in Kuan-chung comprised most of the rich merchants, including T'ien Ch'iang and T'ien Lan.

[3] The most famous story is that a merchant of Cheng named Hsüan Kao first discovered the invasion by Duke Mo of Ch'in and saved his country.

[4] In *Kuo* yü (*Ssu-pu tsung k'an*, chüan 15, p.8), Tou Chun said, "Suppose the Chung-hang and Fan families did not pity the people's suffering and wished to monopolize the power of Chin,

now their descendents are going to Ch'i as farmers and their cattle for sacrifice in the temple are converted to service on the farm."

5 Ssu-ma Ch'ien, *Shih chi*, chüan 85, "The Biography of Lü Pu-wei."

6 *Chan kuo ts'c*, chüan 6, ch'in 4, T'eng Yo was sent as a messenger to the eastern states with ten thousand pieces of gold. (Shang-wu, p. 31).

7 Ssu-ma Ch'ien, *Shih chi*, chüan 47, "Genealogy of the Chi State" Chen Ching-chung, at the end of this chapter.

8 *Hou Han shu*, chüan 45, "Biography of Yuan An". (Yi-wen ed. p. 543).

9 Kan Lao, "A Letter to Prof. Yen Keng-wang", *Ta-lu magazine* vol. 28, no. 4,p. 115.

10 *Han shu*, chüan 93, a powerful eunuch received gifts and bribes of one hundred million coins (Yi-wen ed., p.1590). This case happened under the reign of Yuan-ti, *Hou Han shu*, chüan 78, "The Biography of Eunuchs" (pp. 896-906).

11 *Hou Han shu*, chüan 5, p. 157, and chüan 78, p. 905.

12 Kan Lao, "Some Estimates on the Salary of the Han Dynasty," *Bulletin of the College of Arts at* National *Taiwan University*, no. 3, pp. 11-22.

13 *Ch'üon han han wen*, chüan 46, p.9.

14 *Chin-Shu, Chüeh-chu.* chüan 72, p. 18.

15 Ibid., chüan 86, pp. 45-46.

16 Ibid., chüan 94, pp. 49-51

17 *Shen cheen*, chüan 2, (*Ssu-pu tsung-k'an*, p. 15).

本篇轉載自 Studia Asiatica, 陳受頤先生祝壽專號。

The Capital of Loyang; a Historical Survey

I. A Historical Sketch of Loyang

In Chinese history, many cities became capitals in various dynasties. There is a capital monument in the valley of the Huang Ho (黃河) River, namely the Old City of Loyang (洛陽).

Many people of different races, speaking diverse languages, lived in the ancient Chinese continent. These peoples were gradually unified by the Shang (商) and Chou (周) Empires. In order to concentrate political power, a city was established for the assemblage of the leaders of the city states, This was Loyang. In the beginning of Chou, residence of the royal family was always in Hao (鎬), a town near modern Sian. The regime moved to Loyang about three hundred years later, in 770 B. C. During this time the Chou Dynasty was called Eastern Chou.

After Eastern Chou, many dynasties fixed their capital in Loyang. The Grand Khan Wei Hsiao Wen (魏孝文) of the T'opa (拓拔) Dynasty moved his capital from P'ing-ch'eng (平城) to Loyang and thoroughly changed nomadic customs for Chinese civilization. Loyang was selected neither for its military nor for its economic position, but for its traditional importance. Classics, folklore and even astrology maintained that Loyang was the center of the Celestial Empire

The selection of Loyang as a capital started with the sovereignty of Chou Kung (周公) When he swept away rebellions from the east, the power of the central government was increased more than at any time prior to it.

To control east China, a new colony for the Chou people, and to connect west China, the fatherland of the Chou people, Loyang valley became the connecting route from west to east. Therefore, a city as seen first in Chinese history was built, and nine tripods, the sign of the sovereignty of the traditional Chinese Empire, were moved into it.

From the point of view of Chinese geography, Loyang contains its special nature, as the link of the east and west part of the Huang Ho Valley. There was a marked difference in culture between these two parts. Many aspects show very clearly in the remains from ancient ruins. Roughly speaking, in the east there was a kind of coastal culture and in the west a kind of inland culture. Black pottery (黑陶) is a typical feature representing the east and painted pottery (彩陶) a typical feature representing the west. The original place of the Yin-Shang (殷商) people was unknown, but the heart of the Yin-Shang Kingdom was at the eastern coast. On the other hand, the Chou people came from the northwestern plateau. When Yin-Shang territory was conquered by the Chou force, the technique of management became a serious problem. The east coast was not settled until after the success of the long three-year expedition of Chou Kung. Loyang was a connection of east and west, and it became the most important center in the Chou Regime.

In the Han (漢) Dynasty, Kuan-tung (關東) or East of the Pass and Kuan-hsi (關西) or West of the Pass became two main parts of this empire. Military actions were dominant in Kuan-hsi and economic actons were dominant in Kuan-tung. Generals were always from Kuan-hsi and Ministers were always from Kuan-tung. In Western Han (202 B.C.—7 A.D.), the defense of the northern border was so important that the capital had to be situated in Changan (長安) of Kuan-hsi (Sian in modern times). Loyang (of Kuantung) was a subordinate city to Changan. But all economic resources came from Kuan tung. Loyang was the main deposit station for various kinds of goods to be transported. In Eastern Han, the former enemy Hsiung-nu(匈奴)was divided into many parts, and they surrendered to the Han Regime. Therefore the problem of defense became loose and the capital moved to Loyang because it was close to the economic center.

After the end of the Eastern Han, China was divided into three kingdoms. The largest and most powerful one was Wei (魏). While the royal ruler of the Wei was only a military leader, his stronghold as a chief military city was Yeh (鄴), a ruin in the suburb of modern Anyang. The military leader became King, and the chief city moved to Loyang as being in the suitable Chinese tradition. When China reunified in the Chin (晉) Dynasty, Loyang became a capital of all of China. It was a legal capital to the Chinese people even in the hearts of gentry in the Southern Dynasties period.

China was reunified by the Sui (隋) Emperor, whose power was in a base from western China. By and by, Sian became an international center in the period of the Sui-T'ang (隋唐) Empire(581-907). The Grand Canal was built, and wealth from everypart of this empire was concentrated in Sian by way of it. Many cities became more prosperous along this Canal. The largest one was Loyang.

The function of the Grand Canal was to convey food and goods from the Yangtze Delta to the new capital of Changan (or modern Sian). The waterway of this Canal might be divided into two parts; the better section was from Loyang to the Yangtze Delta and the worse section was from Loyang to Sian. Because the Huang Ho River to the west of Loyang was so muddy and unstable, cargoes and foods were always stored by the suburb of Loyang, waiting a favorable season to be shipped. There was more storage of food in Loyang than Changan, so that in the T'ang emperor with his attendants and officials always came to Loyang for economic purposes in drought years.

Five Dynasties (907–960) were successively established after the collapse of the T'ang. Kaifeng (開封) and Loyang were dual capitals in this age. In 936 A.D., Peking, Tatung (大同) and their subordinate areas were taken by the Khitan Empire, thus breaching the line of national defense. The Hopei Plain situation became most serious and dangerous, and the capital at Kaifeng was enforced with a million soldiers. Under this condition, Kaifeng became very crowded, while Loyang by contrast was rather secluded. There were many offices in Kaifeng and many garrisons in the suburbs, but in Loyang there were instead many fine gardens set up by high officials in retirement. With the fall of the Northern Sung (宋) (1127), Loyang was despoiled.

From the rise of Chou to the fall of Sung, or more than 2,400 years, Loyang was important in Chinese history. During the Empires of the Chin and Yuan, Loyang no longer took a leading role in Chinese politics. The political history of China entered the "Peking Era", and the "Sian–Loyang Era" vanished. However, with the extension of the railway system the importance of Loyang may be restored to some extent.

II. Loyang As A Center of the World in Chinese Legend

For economic reasons, the situation of Loyang is better than Sian (even better than Peking, for Loyang does not have to transport food across the Huang Ho). However, the position of Loyang is not distinguished by economics only. Loyang is a national monument for the Chinese people. Loyang as a capital was determined by Chou Kung, an ancient sage worshipped by the Chinese people, especially the Confucian School. The *Chou Li* (周禮), traditionally said to have been edited by Chou Kung, was a blueprint for a projected kingdom. It is clear that the capital of the celestial kingdom is Loyang.

In the chapter *Ta Szu-t'u* (大司徒), or the Vice-Grand Chancellor and the Minister of Interior, in the *Chou Li* (周禮), it is said:

"To survey the distance① of earth, the t'u-kuei (土圭)② is used to check the sun's shadow and to find the center of the world. Shadow is short at the south where it is hot. Shadow is long at the north where it is cold. Only it is measured in one Ch'ih (尺) and five ts'un (寸) at the center of the world in the winter solstice.

"This is the very point of the meeting of heaven and earth."

In the notes of *Chou Li* by Cheng Hsüan (鄭玄), this point is denoted as Loyang. This explanation was based on the astronomical knowledge of ancient times.

Under the foot of the Sung Shan Hill (嵩山) near Loyang, there is an old temple with an old observatory. It is called "the terrace for surveying the sun's shadow of Chou Kung" (周公測影台). In 1936, Mr. Tung Tso-pin and Mr. Kao Pin-tze of the Academia Sinica did archaeological work on it and published a report. They showed that the astronomy survey was done there for a long time and that many evidences of the Chinese calendar were based on the survey of the variation in seasons of the sun's shadow.

The Chinese people had a kind of religion to worship natural power which contained two features, *yin* and *yang* (陰陽), and five elements, metal, wood, water, fire and soil (五行). The mutual distribution of the two features and five elements made for mobility of nature and human affairs. From the "Yüeh-ling" (月令), monthly changes, in the *Li Chi* (禮記), dress, food, dwelling and everything of the lords had to be changed according to the special type of the elements relating to each month. From the "Wu-hsing

Chih," the Records of the Five Elements in the *Han Shu* (漢書五行志), political affairs were considered related to meteorological phenomena. This Chought was clearly explained in the *Ch'ün-ch'iu Fa ≈ Lu* (春秋繁露) of Tuis thoung-shu (董仲舒). It was the so-called "mutual response of heaven and man" (天人感應). Loyang was thereby considered to be the center of the natural world, and it had to be the capital of the Celestial Empire. If it was neglected, the peace of the dynasty would be unsettled as a consequence.

In ancient Chinese astronomy, there were three schools, *Hsüan-yeh* (宣夜), *Hunt'ien* (渾天) and *Kai-t'ien* (蓋天). The theory of *Hsüan-yeh* has been lost. In the theory of *Hun-t'ien* it was considered that heaven is wrapped up as an egg and that earth is inside in the center as a yolk. The theory of *Kai-t'ien* was more developed by the Mathematic School of Chou P'i (周髀). The main conception of the Chou-p'i School was derived from the survey of the sun's shadow in the winter solstice and the summer sclstice with a standard view in Loyang. Therefore, the students of this sohool thought that the earth is a dish, surrounded by a deep sea and covered with a dome of heaven. In the center of this dish was Loyang. Therefore the position of Loyang in the political arena was supported by "science" in ancient times.

Down to modern times, the foundation for the support of Loyang in so-called "science" has vanished. But as a national monument of the Chinese people, Loyang must be counted first, for it has occupied a ecntral position in traditional Chinese thought for many centuries.

¹ It is said to be the distance from south to north.

² A t'u-kuei or ground dial is for the purpose of measuring the length of the sun's shadow.

本篇轉載自 Journal of China Society.

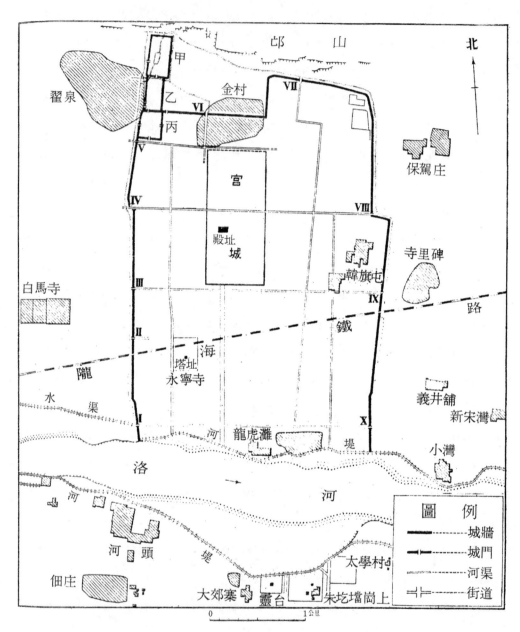

漢魏洛陽地圖

The Periodical Circles in the Chinese History

Any continuing process contains within it a periodic nature. There is no exception for either living or inanimate things, while birth and death vividly illustrate the process of living things, and the four Seasons run their cources. Even in the alternating day and night, lies evidence of the natural law. The whole universe, in fact, embodies this cycle. However it can not all be deduced by human beings.

The history of China is no exception. A view due to the unique geographic situation, the chains of mountains, wide oceans and extensive deserts, constitutes the limits separating other countries of the glove, to cause lacking of regular communication between China and foreign countries before the Opium War. Although there was some evidence that the Chinese were influenced by other cultures. As these influences did not enter into main trend of the key impulsions, the history of China has passed through several similar situations which coincide with periodic changes.

The periodic law is not composed of simple reasons. Furthermore, cycle follows cycle. people still can not solve the problem of searching the ultimate cycles of the universe.

The dynasties in Chinese history themelves are of a periodic nature, which represent periods of prosperity and adversity, and of peace and turmoil. Generally, excluding the short periods in Chinese history, the typical dynasty ran from two hundred to three hundred years.

These cycles are certainly impossible to trace in detail. Generally, however, the following were the more prominent causes:

I. The rise and fall of the imperial family coindide with the dynasty's fate—Not only the imperial family, as a whole, but also all families have their periodic revolutions. On the idea of "no single house and land lasting thousands of years was without the changing of eight hundred landlords" as Chinese proverb said, the inevitable fate of each individual family is usually easier to determine, since most of descendants in the big family led abmormal and half-isolated lives. After the family (having been sustained by the titled relationship between prince and minister) deteriorated until the relationship was no longer in effect, it was time for a new dynasty to begin its cycle.

It is easy to explain that the government under the despotic monarchy is responsible to the monarchy alone. Both of the legislative and of the executive power to a monarch are absolute. Since, in history, a typical Oriental country had never met a contrasting power presented in an organized form, such as a Pope in religion. For the same reason, human beings (even a brilliant man with his potential) are limited by their concentration and amount of interest inclinations or bias. And when thousands of the people affairs depend on the arrangemeut by one single hand, the threat of both by physical conditions and by the judgment of out-of-predicating successor is inevitable. Thus the system constructed at the birth of a dynasty could not be an ideal one efficiently to execute without shortcomings. The national affairs become more complicated; the system becomes weaker. A particular dynasty, reigning over a long period of time, would be very difficult to adapt to the contemporary situation. When it became a serious handicap to the nations progress it was again a time to renew the dynasty.

It is unfortunate that a nation's future was depending upon a single family's fate. As for the family in general, the bigger the family holdings the easier it goes to fall; because the members of a big family mostly lack independent characteristics and could not cope with problems for hemselves. After a few generations these families would naturally go into a decline. Comparing them to the common family, the large wealthy families situation would by far be the more serious, especially the princes and princeses usually had to lead half isolated lives and had very little knowledge in dealing with people. Moreover, most of them were even weak physically to cause they died young.

In Chinese history there were many instances where the royal family lacked successors, such as in the dynasties of the Western Han, Eastern Han, T'ang, Sung, Ming and Ch'ing. The series of royal family portraits gives the clue to their physical weakness. It is very difficult not to imagine how the nation broke loose when its rulers were both mentally and physically approaching the breaking point.

II. The corruptive practices within the political organization and the deminishing or each dynasty. The political situation under the autocratic monarchy is wholly responsible to the rulers, thus this system is also called 'jen-chih' (人治 opposit to the constitutional state). Under this system political orgizations are rather superricial. Because the 'law 'which the political orgnization is based on can not control an emperor. Rather say that the emperor of an empire nolds the legisiatures rights and changes the laws at his own convenience. On the other hand, being a dictator the danger can come from even the emperor's own rollowers. Thererore almost from the very beginning of each dynasty the law and the administration became the victims of the struggies between the emperors and their courtiers. The law was constantly changed and added to by the emperors, and was further attacked by the latter emperors. It is nature that after a certain time the law can not keep the nation in order any more. The following are a fow of the more famous examples:

Before Han Wu Ti, China operated under the prime ministry system which means that most of the politic decisions had to be carried out by the prime ministry who, in some way, bears similarity with the bureaucratic ministry of the western constitutional monarchy. From the inset of his reign, Wu Ti, a brilliant but suspicious ruler, was against this system.

First, he used his mother's half brother T'ien Fen as prime minister instead of his grandmother's nephew Tou Ying. Later he was again very unhappy about Tien's agressiveness. Once he said to Tien: "Have you finished appointing officers? I wish to appoint some too." Thus, through out his reign, he was extremely against power of the prime minister. His endeavours towards these, were:

a. Operating an "inner court" to replace the prime iminister. The so called inner court consisted or advisors and private secretaries. With their help the emperor could manage the excutive affairs, and give orders to carry out, to reduce the political importance of the prime ministry and finally to take away the legisiative power of the prime ministry and to make that office only an excutive department.

b. Breaking the tradition of the prime ministers from aristocracy into the literati from common families. To emphasize the control of the throne the prime ministers were always threatened to be punished. Consequently, the ministers under the air of tear, dared not to express their own ideas, showing themselves as a "meal member of the eourt" only.

As a result of this heavy attack, the emperor weakened the minister's power. Only not the Han emperor used these technics, it actually brought the way of orthodox tradition to the later time.

It developed in two ways. First change the one prime minister system into a numerous ministry system. Secondly, each dynasty began to use close courtiers to take over the power of a minister. When these courtiers became as powerful as the prime ministers. The competitions among the courtiers began, so did the chaos. During the reign of Ming T'ai-tsu, the prime ministry was abolished, and he adapted the system of the six divided sections, mutually governed and operated under the grand scholars of the 'Han-lin Yüan' (The imperial aeademy) and supervised by the chief eunuch from Ssu-li Chien. In the later Ming times, the grand scholars became the actual prime ministers, but the chief-eunuch still held the power of supreme minister. The problems increased and became bigger as every day went on. Untill there was no way to solve them.

Because of the emperors suspicious attitude toward their ministers, the power of a minister was always regulated before it began to expand. In order to balance the power struggle between the emperors and their ministers, the emperors always turned the officials to control and inspected among themselves. In reflecting this policy, the officers maintained a negligent attitude. It seems, that always the one who used the corrupt methods won the fame and the uprignt one suffered punisnment. Under these circumstance a country had been held generation after generation. Naturally it carried the nation into chaos.

Not only the traditional central officials could not carry out the policies to sustain the country, but also it occurred in the local political districts. The prefecture system, though basically very simple, became complicated as time and dynasty changed. Thus, the political moral and the executive effect gradually degenerated.

III. The deminishing of each dynasty was also caused by the problems of the gentry families.

The vioient struggle caused the losers venture.

As dictators, the rulers under the guidance of the Legal School surpressed other important social elements to assure their own throne. The first victims were the merchants. The rulers, century after century, had sucesfully depressed the mercantile social status through policies, that mercnants considered the lowest class had been deeply embeded on the mind of the Chinese people.

The mercnants had been always condidered a depraved class by the legalists. All honours were given out by the emperor as his assurance of power. He carefully guarded his privilege of giving punishment and rewards in every possible way. In fear of having this taken away by the merchants, a class who might promote themselves with money. The Chinese rulers in each dynasty publiciy surpressed the merchants from obtaining their power through possible social and economic ways.

In history, this policy had been carried out suceessfully. The emperors divested the merchants social status. To the intellectuals the emperor was the only one to serve and reward. In other words it meant that becoming an official is the only honourable achievement, and the way to achieve it was to pay homage to the emperor. At the begining of each dynasty, the political situtation was still not very steady. Common people were comparably poor, and mostly busy in making a living. Very few thought of making themselves officials. At later times, when economic progress and the political condition. had become somewhat stable, the amount of people who desired to become officials had naturally increased. The following three periods in Chinese history concerned themselves with the suppression of the merchants.

a. The period under the system of recommendation:

This period included the Former Han and the Later Han dynasties. During the Han dynasties officials could be chosen by the amount of property they owned. This policy indirectly opend the way for people to seek money and glory at the same time. The society in Western Han (Former Han) was considerably peacefull and stable. During the middle of Western Han the amount of college students had increased. Though it indicated evidence of the cultural progress, this great number of college students were all preparing to become officials. The competition among them got keener. Persons who railed from the competitions in order to make a living, mostly became the instrument fo ambitious politicians, sucn as Wang Mang who gathered almost ten million this kind of literaties to support him. This also contributed to the reasons of rogle house fallen.

After the foundation of Eastern Han, education situation became more promising, but it made the university a place for unrest and rioting. Though government made several moves to surpress the gentries for interferring with the politics of the royal court wnich led the great unfortunate event called 'Tang Ku (黨錮) Chih Huo', but later, it was still the gentries divided the kingdom into three. Later Han ended by such a cause. It is not difficult to imagine how much literati suffered from the limited careeres in be Later Han Dynasty. These literati wondered around and could not become farmers because of their weak physical conditions, of business men because of their pride; moreover they could not even become monks, because of the scarcity of temples. Thus it is impossibie to say that the riots at the begining of the Three Kingdoms period nad no relation with the gentry problem.

b. The period of the Powerful Clans' monopoly

The recommendation system still remained in name, when the rulers of Wei and Chin dynasties set up another system called the powerful clans monopoly.' This system was more convenient for the persons who had already high positions in the royal court. Also the members of those clans could be named as hign officials. It had been more offectively practiced during Eastern Chin dynasty and Southern Reigns period. From point of view of chosing officiers this system is not fair, however, in speaking of the political settlement if had the beneficial results: (I) Persons from underprivileged families after having no hope to become high officiers started to change into merchants, for the social security. (2) except the ruler grand families also held considerable political power, thus balanced the power between government and the ruler. On the other hand, the heritary system after being applying for a long time, had brought lazy and corrupt decendents into the aristororactic families. Most of them were not qualified to be assistants to their emperors. Such as at the time of Liang Wu Ti and in the reign of Chen, although the emperor tried to use several new people. It was too late for them to be available to defend their sovereignty aganist the soldiers of Sui which were marching southward.

c. The period of the Examination system.

From Sui Dynasty to the end of Ch'ing Dynasty, the examination had been tracticed for almost thirteen centuries, and had deeply influenced politics and modern society of China. The beneficial point of this system lies on it's fairness of chosing officiers. Under this system, the examiners can choose officials without considering their social background. It was considered the best system among the three. Because even the recommendation system could be controlled by only a few people. As a matter of fact, the system showed the key issue had been controlled by powerful families since the Eastern Han dynasty. But the examination system had been in practice as long as thirteen centuries and had never fallen into any ambitious family's hands. Later even the names on the answering sheets had to be sealed in order to have a more adquate results. The road toward officials for the pour and the underprivilaged families had been widened.

Concerning security of the society, this system, somehow, achieved of that purpose. As for the examination, no matter what requirments the candidates had to face. The evaluation of the answers totally depended upon the personal judgement of the examiner. Bias was inevadable. It is clear why the system failed to reach to the majority. Though it still behold some shortages it was extremely hard to be changed, after all it had been practiced for such a long time. Then the increased population made the problem worse. Society could not be secured by this system, on the contrary, at times in some riot and turmoil, the upheavals in Chinese history such as: Huang Ts'ao, Hung Hsiu-ch'uan, and Niu Chin-hsing (the main assistant of Li Tsu-ch'eng) all had one time at least, failed from the examination. These facts showed how little this system had played on toiling people together. But it was only in the period of Sung, the emperor paid attention to this cricic. Once Sung T'ai Tsung appointed all the candidates in the court in order to release their problem. He also tried to make some other arrangements to settle the gentries problems. However the burdern was so heavy to lead Sung regime into bureaucracy until its collapse by foriegners attack.

IV. The population problem. The population problem is one of the key issue with the fate of each dynasty, but it is not the only one with the fate. China never had population problems till the end of Warring States, the battle before that time still remained in the ancient men to men style. Since then there were city to city battles; the largest one contained with some seventy thousand residents.

After the formation of Han, population seems reduced by some extent. As history recorded that when Han Kao Ti appointed Ch'en P'ing as the earl of Chü-ni the population of the county had been reduced serionsly. It is recorded in Han shu, the population restored later:

> "At the forth, fifth year of the reign of Wen and Ching, the once exiled people had returned, the reregistration of thirty to forty thousands, thesmall district had even duplicated the populations. All the districts had been rich and strong."

At the begining of the Han dynasty, the maximum of population limits in the district under earl's fief was ten thousand households. After the period of Wen and Chin to the reign of Han Wu Ti within six years, the populations of bigger dis districts had been implicated; the small districts had duplicated their residents. Then ano ther one hundred and forty years had gone, at the period of Han P'ing Ti the numbers of households increased to 12230000, and the population increased to 59594978. At that time it was the greatest population in the world.

Since then almost no exception that after each great political changes the population reduced sharply, and extended again after a period of peace. Therefore the population formed a circle by the a chronological increase or deerease. Still a greater population in Chinese history had been ocurred at the Han period. The population of China between Han and Ch'ing is recorded as following:

The second year of Chung-yüan in the reign of Emperor Kuang-wu in the Eastern Han Dynasty (57A.D.)

families 4,279,634　　　persons 21,007,820

The second year in the reign of Yung-shou of Emperor Huan (156A.D.)

families 16,070,906　　　persons 50,066,856

The first year in the reign of T'ai-k'ang of Emperor Wu in the Chin Dynasty (280A.D.)

families 2,450,804　　　persons 6,163,863

Later Chou at the period of Ta-hsiang (579A.D.)

families 3,590,000　　　persons 9,009,604

the population of Ch'en(in same time)

families 500,000　　　persons 2,000,000

total　4,090,000　　　　　11,009,604

Sui, Dynasty the second year of Ta-yeh of Emperor Yang

families 8,907,536　　　persons 46,019,956

T'ang Dynasty, in Chen-kuan period (627-649A.D.) of T'ai-tsung

families 3,000,000

Tang, the fourteenth year of T'ien-pao of Hsuan Tsung (755A.D.)

    families 8,919,309   persons 52,919,309

Sung Dynasty, Kai-pao, the ninth year, T'ai Tsu   (976A.D.)

    families 3,090,504

Sung Dynasty, T'ien-hsi the fifth year, Chen Tsung (1022A.D.)

    families 8,677,577   persons 19,930,320

Sung Dynasty, T'sung-ning the first year, Hui Tsung (1106A.D.)

    families 20,019,050   dersons 43,820,769

Yuan Dynasty, Chih-yuan the twentyseʌenth year, Shih Tsu(1290A.D.)

    families 13,296,206   persons 58,834,771

Ming Dynasty, Hung-wu the fourteenth year, Tai Tsu (1380A.D.)

    families 10,654,362   persons 59,873,305

Ming Dynasty, Chia-ching the first year, Shih Tsung (1512A.D.)

    families 9,721,652   persons 60,861,273

Ch'ing Dynasty, Kang-hsi the fifty year of Sheng Tsu (1662A.D.)

                   persons 277,554,431

Ch'ing Dynasty, Tao-kuang the twentieth year of Hsüan Tsung

                            (1840A.D.)

        persons 462,730,000

Within this period, the great chaos could be dated were: (1) the riot at the end of Wang Mang (Hsin). (2) At the age of Three Kingdoms. (3) the reckless time at the end of the Sui Dynasty. (4) the Five Dynasties (at the end of the T'ang Dynasty). (5) The confusions at the end of the Yuan Dynasty. (6) The disorderly period at the end of the Ming dynasty. On a views of those periods, people lost in wars, lootings, mascares, with disease and famines. Evidence would be too cruel and too sad to be repeated here. Description as following are often written in history book "Every where was ruined within thousand miles."

To draw the conclusion that most of the human disasters were caused by war, and in return the population explosion also trubuted to the cause of war, and in China this problem mostly being created by its ppeculiar social consciousness and peculiar social organizations.

Chinese, as all the other nations, beheld the remains of it's primitive tradition. Nevertheless, this remains still influence Chinese society greatly. Even Chinese do not often keep self conscious about that the Chinese society always involves in the clan orgnization, and clans hold certain degrees of power in society, politics and the economic field. Sometimes clan power is more dominate than guild, and it extended so wide to reach to every aspect of Chinese life.

Clan, however had occupied an important position in human social history, originally. Since the main function progressed from city toward imperial country, the function of the clan eventually lost it's importance, yet China still remain in this tightly organized social form. It may be explained by following reasons: Firstly, gentry class played a great role at keeping the clan's influence to the society, since the basic moral concept of the tradition were rooted to Chou's feudalism. On the surface, the terms as 'ethics', "righteousness", "rites", and "reason" primarily has no inseperable relations with the kindred society. However, the rites in Chinese tradition was originated from the ritual sytem of Chou, again, so as in the principles of various philosophers "keep in good terms with ones relatives" was also the principle of "Chou's Rites" (周禮) which being constructed on the base of the kindred society, although the society was complete different from the society of Chou that imtimated relations in the same imperial families was still the important part of the social morality.

Secondly, according to Chinese original belief, the dead also acquired the same daily needs as living beings, and kept sacrifices as an important rite. Again, according to the Chinese tradition sacrifice could only be performed by relatives of the dead. Hence, persons without descendents became most unfilial virtue to their ancestors. On the other hand, persons obtaining many sons and daughters, became the bcst guarantee. And the nobles who held high position were able to raise their large families certainly endeavored to seek more descendents from concubines. This also was the reason why China was in the big family tradition.

Thirdly, imperial policy stimulated people concentrated. Since kindred families is useful for the government, especially in regent ten canturies, examination system repllced the heritary tradition. Royal court was no longer monopopied by the powerful clans any more. The emperors also did not held the suspisions toward aristrocratic families any more. All of the members in a big tamily with many generations living together frequently got reward from government as "the family of righteousness" (義門) . Officially stimulation helped to increase the dependency within the members of the family and dewelled continuously on their native soil for centuries As most people. centralized in certain area, more serious population problem might be created.

According to the records of Chinese farming fields;

The first year of Yuan-shih reign of emperor P'ing in Western Han dynasty (I.A.D.)

8,275,536 ch'ing (頃)

The first year of yuan-hsing reign of emperor Ho in Eastern Han dynasty (105A.D)

7,320,170 ch'ing

The ninth year of K'ai-huang reign of Emperor Wen of Sui (589A.D)

19,404,267 ch'ing

The period of T'ien-pao of Emperor Tang Hsüan Tsung of T'ang (746A.D.)

14,303,862 ch'ing

The fifth year of T'ien-hsi reign of emperor Chen Tsung of Sung (1021A.D)

5,247,584 ch'ing

the twenty six year of Hung-wu reign of T'ai Tsu of Ming (1393A.D)

8,507,623 ch'ing

The sixth year of Wan-li reign of Shew Tsung of Ming (1578A.D.)

7,103,976 ch'ing

The twentyforth year of K'ang-hsi reign of Sheng Tsu of in Ch'ing (1675A.D.)

6,098,430 ch'ing

the thirty first year of Ch'ien-lung reign of Kao Tsung of Ch'ing (1765A.D.)

7,414,095 ch'ing

under the reign of Kuang-hsü of Ch'ing (1875-1908A.D.)

9,181,038 ch'ing

Since the measuring system of one dynasty was different from another, however from this chart one still would be able to draw the conclusion that soil for plough in China were limited, most of China mainland are covered with mountains and highlands. The agriculture area were concentrated on the area such as the lower division of Huang Ho, Yang-tze River and Hsi River plains. Before the Republic of China founded, Sung-Liao plain was still not fully developed. Besides those plains, the high lands as Szechwan basin had been used, but Yunnan and Kweichow were developed very late.

Geographically the lower division of Huang Ho and Yang-tze River are all in the Monsoon area, the amount of rain for each season is not always perdictable. Same as in India, China often had dry seasons. When the population reach to the point of saturation, famine disaster occured, easily. Refugee in usual steps firstly were driven out from the disaster area. Then secondly started the riot. In Chinese history, the turmoil aroused at the end of Wang Mang, T'ang, Yüan, Ming and Ch'ing each dynasty were the good examples. It is really more correct to call these events "a refugees' turmoil" rather than "the farmers' revolution" as called by the contemporary historians. As mentioned before this turmoil also was responsible for the turning overof each era.

The most serious point lied that the problem always increased gradually by time, while a dynasty draw away from it's early period, the more problems should increase. When the problem became incurable, the throne should be fallen. In general, a dynasty, under the regular conditions runs around three hundred years long. Let we explain Some dynastic units less than three hundred.

1. Wang Mang, the period right after Western Han, in reality, was but the extension of the that time. If Wang Mang, had not made mistakes on economic policy, Western Han might have sustained another hundred year. If Wang Mang had not the ambitions to be a sage but a king, his reign could have last for quite more. As for explaing why Eastern Han was rather short, one of the important reasons was that several emperors died young, then the relation between imperial house and gentry class broke up again.

2. West Chin could have been a long reign. Since from the first year of T'ai-kang of Chin Wu Ti (280 A.D.) till K'ai-huang the eight year of Sui Wen Ti (588 A.D.) were roughly three hundred years. Somehow because the inadequite settlement of emperor Chin Wu Ti to over due the local military power, thus country could not remain in peace. Then, the sucessor right after emperor Wu was imbecile Hui Ti on the throne to bring the disorder of the whole nation.

3. There was no difference between North and Southern Sung, if Northern Sung had kept a better relation with Khitan on the northern border to hinter the rise of Nuchen then probably Capital Pien could be a capital untill the period of the invasion of Monguls.

4. Most of the emperors of Yuan dynasty were not familiar with Chinese culture, and many of them still adapted the nomads traditions, Furthmore, Mongols and Chinese people were treated unequally, and the Chinese middle class never reached to the kernel of management. Then this dynasty did not last long to this period.

Because of the influence of Neo-Confucianism, Chinese people in Ming, Ch'ing throught two dynasties had led peacefull lives. Shortly after the rising of Neo-Contucianism in Sung dynasty, the thought of "loyalty only to one master" had strongly influenced Chinese gentries and kept it's power for a long time. It helped the aristocratic monarchy to set up the order in society. Even while the nation was under the control of the foolish rulers such as; Wu Tsung, and Hsi Tsung of Ming, starting a revolution had never gone through people's thoughts.

Certainly this was not the morality in modern sense. After the fallen of Ch'ing dynasty, the thought of "loyality" became lost it's effection. "May-forth Movement" had given the traditional thought a last blow. But one should also not to neglect the fact that feudalism plays a very important rule on toiling people togheter and remained in peace.

We just discuss the politic circle of the history, it also means the rising and fallen of the dynasty,. Many of the time political changes attributed political reasons, and culture could only became a subordinate cause.

There was an article "To analysis the cycle of rising and fallen in Chinese history"by Ssu Kuang Li, published in the Bulletin of the Institute of History and philology of Academia sinica in celebration of Dr. Ts'ai Yüan -pei's sixty-tive birthday (1933). Dr. Li tried to find the clue from analysing the amount of wars in each year. The same method being used in geographic history. However, it is still not reliable, because war itself lack ofobjective substance. According to Dr. Li's conclusion, the history of China in every cycle can be divided as following:

1. The period of war.
2. The period of construction.
3. The first time of tranquility.
4. The second time of tranquility.

Then history draws time back to the period of war again.

In his opinion the Warring States, Northern and Southern reign, Southern Sung these numeral dynasties were all included in the first period. Chin, Sui and Yuan three dynasties belongs to the second period. (a short but forming period). Western Han, T'ang and Ming were divided as the third period, and the Eastern Han, Northern Sung and Ch'ing were considered as the second period of tranquility. Therologically his method only explaned a part of the historical phenomenon. Most of the time the facts were not identical with the four periods. However the important theory he emphasized is that the rising and fallen of each dynasty is not the rising and fallen of each political idea. His Preliminary work is good, but it requires more modification and more explanation.

Wars are not the causes but the results of the politic confusion. In order to have a full explaination of the history, one should study the causes of the political chaos instead of the results. Thus, by using this method, three periods should be made. Three questions probably would be asked:

1. What are the causes in forming the special type of dynasties such as Chin, Sui and Yüan, and what are the different and similar points among these three dynasties?

2. Does the first dynasty always last shortly?

3. Why after the first dynasty there were always two peaceful periods followed? Is it possible that there would be more than two periods followed? Why always two?

4. Why there is always a great war after the period of tranquility?

Each one of the three periods, Ch'in, Sui and Yüan, began with a powerful government which not only ended the period of chaos, to control the whole nation but also was strong enough to drive away the border enimies. Thus, the rulers were able to concentrate on constructing the new regulations and policies, however, those dynasties also became the victims of their ambitions yet inexperienced rulers. Ch'in sped up to the tragedy ending because of the Ch'in governments unrealistic polices. While Sui and Yüan dynasties had not rendered their people in undisturbed or calm lives. Their policies also condamned their dynasties own fates. Psychologically, the rulers excitement to the new enviroment can also count as an important reason for these three unusual type of dynasties in Chinese history. Since these three periods all followed by a lengthen period of confussion., people were so excited that more frequently were over confident on their abilities to guide the nation. Ch'in Shih Huang, the self titled "above all the highest sage", with his dream of everlasting empire, overdid the legalist's theory; Emperor Yang of Sui over drew the project for the whole nation which was unable to achieve without a thorugh designed process. Chinese culture was belittled by Yüan's rulers. In consiquence, it brought the great impact on the politic practice.

On account of this human behaviors, the first dynasties after each period of chaos are inveritalble short. The overdo on the exercise of politics is the main reason to shorten the period of each dynasty. On the other hand, if the rulers was not so enthusiastic to change everything rapidly, their throne, would be lasted longer than the others. Such as Yuan in comaparrison to the other two had done it's achievement.

There were numeral overlaped periods in Chinese history, such as Eastern and Western Han dynasties. Sung and T'ang dynasty; Ch'ing and Ming Dynasties. There were no serious or revolutionary changs among the cutural, social or political system except imperial house. It means if the hereditary rulers could be good ones, generation by generation, the dynasty would be survived longer than regular period, but it is impossible, except a constitutional government.

It might be oceured a third one following those some sets of du-overlaped dynasties to ensure peace. A view of Chinese history shows, the Wei, the Chin, and even Fu Chien of the Former Ch'in were qualified to form a new-stable and longer dynasty as a peaceful successor of the Two-Han Dynasties. But every one of them failed. It might be by occational cause and it might be by historical destinies. Because under a period followed a long time with du-dynastic stability, many facts in culture were going rotten. corruption had been infiltrated deeply into every part of the society, Furthermore the explosion of population formed more problems of that age. After all, the tragedy of those dynasties was inevadible. Ang leader involved to that type of age should be the victim of historical trend, without difference with refonmation or non-refor mation, revotution or non-rerolution, revotution or non-rerolution.

In China it always a new power either came from outside or had some connections with the alien influence after each era ended by the collaps of the old aritocratic monochy. As for the surviving of the new power it was uncertain totally depending on how it adapted itself to the historical trend which was always ignored wholly or partially from every ruler's conscience.

This theory has not evidence to predict the future of modern China. If China becomes a real demorcratic nation as the nations in western Europe and in northern America, then the history would be total different. China, obviously is in steps toward industry and democracy. No matter how hard the road would be and no one can prevent this approach. China is also developing toward more internationized way. The "isolated and self sufficient concept" will be broken by history. Though as a big nation, the transition is rather slow, the future history of China is still towards another different chapter. One the other hand, however, if the Chinese historical trend still keeps in the traditional limit, the second period of the fourth cycle is just stepping on the way up to date.

Thanks with Mrs. Sheau-mann Hsieh for her assistance of this article.

A View of History and Culture of China

Ancient History

China's topographic features have produced a profound impact on her history. A look at the map will show that China constitutes a distinctive region in East Asia. This region is bounded by mountain ranges and plateaus in the north, the west, and the southwest, but faces the seas on the east and southeast. The plateaus and mountain ranges which cut China off from the surrounding areas have, to a certain extent, endowed Chinese culture with a degree of isolation. At the same time, because this large region is in the temperate zone, its inhabitants have assimilated other cultures in addition to having developed their own creative resources. Even ancient Chinese culture vaguely showed certain elements resulting from indirect outside contacts. Relations with alien cultures became more intimate as time went on.

In the ancient dynasties ethnological components in the China region were highly complex. The principal stock was Mongolian, mixed with Caucasian strains and with the South Pacific islanders. The language of the early-day inhabitants in the China region can only be described as the Hua-Hsia (華夏) language. Linguistically, the present-day Chinese, however, belong to the Sino-Tibetan family. The Hua-Hsia culture made rapid progress, and in due course through the extension of the Hua Hsia civilization, the Chinese language has come to be spoken by the majority of the people in China.

The discovery of the Peking Man, the Upper Cave Man, and other fossils in China proves that there were human inhabitants in China in very early days. Though thus far there is no evidence to link these early dwellers definitely with the Hua Hsia group, nevertheless one may assume that the growth of the Hua Hsia group was closely connected with the Yellow River or its tributaries. Today, due to large-scale deforestation and soil erosion in the Wei and Fen River valleys over the past centuries, the Yellow River (of which these two streams are tributaries) is muddy and largely unnavigable. In ancient days, however, the Yellow River valley was an ideal cradle for a superior culture. On its upper reaches, along branches in Kansu and other tributaries in Shensi, there are today many tracts of terraced land still preserved in remarkably good condition. Relics of pre-historic ceramics in color have been discovered. On its lower reaches the Yellow River flows through the provinces of Shantung, Hopei and Honan, where in early days there were interlinked streams and canals as well as many areas of marshland, which, after artificial drainage, were turned into fertile arable land. This factor must have hastened the development of the lower reaches of the Yellow River.

The Chinese are "children of the yellow earth." The fertile loess helped develop China's agricultural civilization. Down the centuries, the yellow sands have been blowing from the Mongolian plateau into North China and all the way south to the Ch'in Range and the area north of the Hwai River. The building of drainage ditches in the loesscovered areas to prepare the land for cultivation has been traditionally an important public works project of the Chinese Government. sze-k'ung, the "keeper of workers, " one of three ranking officials in ancient China, was actually the minister of water conservancy. According to legend, Hsia Yū, founder of the Hsia Dynasty, first distinguished himself as a successful engineer in water control.

Shang And Chou Dynasties

From the excavations at Chentseyen (城子崖)[1], we have learned that there were at least two different types of culture in ancient China. Besides the early Colored Pottery Culture in western China, there were the Black Pottery Culture of eastern China and the Grey Pottery Culture of the Shang Dynasty.

Around 1400 B.C., King Pan Keng (盤庚) of the Shang Dynasty moved his capital from the vicinity of Shangchiu in southern Honan Province to Anyang in northern Honan. The earliest relics discovered by Chinese archaeologists came from this period, from which subsequently they date antiques with a relative degree of accuracy. Bronze ware may have been made in an even earlier period, but existing pieces came from the Shang Dynasty.

The earliest form of the Chinese language known to us, namely, the writings on oracle bones, also date from this period. It is these bone writings which have made possible a more detailed understanding of early Chinese culture.

At this time, the Shang Dynasty had already taken shape as an empire. Its power extended to Shantung in the east, Hopei in the north, Anhwei in the south, and Shensi in the west. It controlled numerous city states. Furthermore, through the feudal system, it assigned some cities and towns to nobility as "pension districts. " War, ceremonial sacrifices, and hunting were the main activities in the life of a Shang king, who lived in a palace of wood. People of the Shang Dynasty had already progressed from nomadic life to agriculture. They knew that the winter solstice came annually, that each full moon marked a month, that an extra month added every three years adjusted the calendar and celestial differentials. They used vehicles for war and transport, and their combat vehicles in many respects resembled those of the Egyptians.

About 1100 B.C., King Wu of Chou (further to the west) conquered the Shangs. The Chous were a nomadic tribe in the upper Wei River valley, though they had learned primitive agriculture. After conquering the Shangs, they absorbed much of the Shang culture. Due to the outstanding political talents ao the Duke of Chou (周公), one of King Wu's younger brothers, the Chous were fble to unify the country, thereby initiating a more glorious period in Chinese history. After King Wu's death, while King Cheng was a minor, the Duke of Chou was the regent. It was he who extended the Chous' territorial control to the Yangtze valley and who had rites instituted and music written for various ceremonial occasions. He also adopted royal primogeniture (passing the throne to the eldest son), and instituted feudalism which prevailed during the Chou Dynasty.

More relics have been found of the West Chou Dynasty than of the Shangs. Besides bronze ware, there are writings helpful in historical research. For instance, the *Book of Ancient Records*, the *Book of Odes*, the *History of Warring States*, and the *Historical Records* by Szu-ma Chien, provide much recorded material. The year 841 B.C., marking the joint administration of the Duke of Chou Ting (周定公) and the Duke of Shao Mu, (召穆公) has become a definitely confirmed date from the standpoint of the chronologists.

Because of the constant threat of barbarian tribes to the north and the rebellions of feudal princes, the West Chous moved their capital from presentday Sian to Loyang in the east. The period thus begun was known as the East Chou, which was divided for convenience into two periods: the Era of the *Chun Chiu*② and the Era of the Warring States. The former, because of the wealth of material in *Tso's History* (Tso Chuan 左傳), is a most rewarding period for students delving into China's ancient history. Moreover, on the basis of items unearthed to date, we know that this was a period of great change. It was during this period that several of the feudal princes, through gradually expanding their territory, set up virtually independent states.

Toward the end of this period, people began to use oxen and tools made of iron in farming. This practically revolutionized agriculture and resulted in an increase in population, expansion of cities and towns, and rise in importance of commerce. The increase in population in turn resulted in bigger wars and changes in military tactics. In social structure, the breakup of the feudal system was followed by the formation of bureaucracy. Toward the end of the *Chun Chiu*, politics became the business of "family stewards", subsequently paving the way for ordinary civilians to rise even to the premiership. This development created an objective need for learning, and stimulated the growth of scholarship.

Early Philosophies

By the time of the Chou Dynasty, China's philosophical thinking was fast approaching maturity. The most important discovery was human value. From the *Book of Odes* and the *Book of Ancient Records*, we know that moral concepts were already firmly established during the period of West

Chou. Confucius (551–479 B.C.) gave greater substance to the already existing moral concepts by moving from *chung* (faithfulness) and *shu* (tolerance) to the highest ideal of human life, i.e., "everything in its proper place". Confucius may have implied the idea that "human beings are born naturally good" but he certainly did not elaborate on it. This is something which was left for Mencius to expound.

Confucius showed great respect for culture. Consequently, his disciples and their successors became the custodians of China's ancient culture. Such things as *li* (rites), *yueh* (music), *shih* (poems), and *shu* (history) were all propagated by scholars of the Confucian school. But the Confucianists were not without their difficulties. Take the question of "human beings born naturally good", Mencius agreed and gave more development. The Confucianists were opposed to government by despotic rulers, and yet at the same time they sought to maintain the original social order. Whenever these two branches of Confucian thought could not agree, they started a serious controversy among themselves.

Of the various schools of Chinese thought, the Confucian school was the most comprehensive, and as a result, also the most complicated. By comparison, the Taoists occupied a secondary place in Chinese philosophy, though the principal tenet of Laotze on "do nothing" later had a tremendous influence on Chinese thinking.

Many Chinese today are so called image worshippers. However, ancient classics such as the *Book of Odes* and the *Book of Ancient Records* did mention a supreme deity *Ti*. Aside from ancestors, the deities worshipped by the Confucianists were extremely simple. But the fact remains that the Chinese did not worship images in the early days. Even today most Confucian temples are devoid of images. The Chinese learned idol-making from the images of

Buddhist temples of Ganchara, a state in northwest India, in a tradition far away from the art of Greeks. As for Taoism, its origin was not religious. It was evolved by ancient alchemists who mixed witchcraft with Buddhist rituals in evolving something which has had very little in common with China's primitive religions.

The introduction of Buddhism in the first century was an event of major importance in the history of China's religions. But Buddhism borrowed many of its deities from Brahmanism. This is especially clear in the case of Buddhism's esoteric school. Buddhism produced extremely complicated repercussions in China. On the one hand it gave rise to many puritanic individuals; on the other, it led to the inclusion of Buddha among the deities for worship. In religious doctrine, the Chinese people, aside from engaging in scholastic work, developed free-thinking *Zen*, and also influenced the growth of Confucianism during the Sung Dynasty (960-1279). Neo-Confucianism, otherwise known as the "Philosophy of Reason in Confucianism," which flourished both during and following the Sung Dynasty, whether expounded by one scholar or another, more or less bears evidence of the influence of *Zen*.

The Chin-Han Period And Origin of Chinese Institutions

A knowledge of China's political institutions, legal system, and the division of the country into administrative districts is essential to the understanding of its history. All three were passed on from the Chin and assumed definite forms during the Han Dynasty (206 B.C.-A.D.219). All subsequent dynasties took their legal and political institutions from the Chin and Han dynasties.

Emperor Shih (秦始皇), founder of the Chin Dynasty, completed his conquest of the six kingdoms⑨ in 221 B.C., thereby unifying China. He adopted the political doctrines set forth by Han Fei, China's Machiavelli, and became a mysterious, despotic and totalitarian emperor. He ordered many books burned and many scholars buried alive, so that there would be only Legal School of thought within the confines of his empire. He failed in his attempted purge. Shortly after his death, revolts toppled his empire. But many of the institutions he started were retained and liberalized during the Han Dynasty.

The central government during the Han Dynasty was in the hands of the Grand Chancellor and the Chief Superintendent. The latter served as Deputy Grand Chancellor. Under the Grand Chancellor there were nine Ministers in charge of public finance, justice, reception of visitors, and the household affairs of the emperor. By the time of Emperor Wu (140-88 B.C.,) *Shang Shu Ling* (尙書令), the chief confidential secretary, rose in importance and, from the 3rd century on, became the *de facto* Grand Chancellor or premier. Dynsties later, other secretaries to the emperor became ministers.

As for the legal system, Hsiao Ho, a Grand Chancellor in the Han Dynasty, rewrote the Ch'in laws into the *Nine-Chapter Code*. This code included laws on robbery, forgery, court sentences, arrest of fugitives, judicial procedure, marriage, unauthorized public construction, maintenance of stables and public treasuries. Though the *Nine-Chapter Code* was primarily a criminal code, it also contained certain provisions on civil cases and judicial procedure. Though its various articles were revised during subsequent centuries, the criminal, civil and procedural codes of the Tang Dynasty were handed down to the Manchus, and became the blueprint for the legal systems of Japan, Korea and Vietnam.

Not until the end of the Manchu Dynasty did China begin to evolve new codes in conformity with the European system. The Chinese legal system revolving about the family was meant to promote morality, and as compared with other systems, the Chinese legal system is very well organized, and as important as the Roman and Moslem Codes.

Population Movements and Social Changes

The Six Dynasties (220-589) covered the Wei, the Tsin (Chin), and the Southern and the Northern Dynasties. It was a period of many changes. with many civil wars, and large-scale migrations of nomadic tribespeople from outlying regions into the interior. These resulted in great cultural changes, especially following the introduction of numerous Buddhist sects. Also due to the impact of Buddhist art, Chinese art underwent a renascence and blossomed forth in many new fields. The great mural Paintings and carvings found in the Tunhuang, Yungkang. Lungmen and Tienlungshan caves were all products of this period. Buddhist. influence on Chinese philosophy and thought also developed from this period on.

China's racial composition, of course, has never been a pure one. For instance, during the Chou Dynasty there were repeated inroads of nomadic tribes from the northwest. Only later were these barbarian immigrants absorbed by the Chinese. During the Era of the Warring States, these tribes moved eastward and westward across the steppes. Some of the bronze ware of this period clearly shows Scythian designs.

Besides the nomads of the Chou Dynasty other frontier tribespeople moved into China during the 300 years from the first century B.C. to the second century A.D. Many were prisoners taken in frontier wars, or warriors who had surrendered to the Chinese, while others came to China of their own accord as peaceful immigrants. Among these were Mongolians and Mediterranean peoples who were still in the nomadic and primitive agricultural stages. Some were of a similar culture while others retained their tribal mores. Some moved into China's interior, while others stayed north of the Great Wall. Toward the end of the West Tsin Dynasty (296-316), when China suffered from bad government and civil wars, these various tribes declared themselves as independent states. Finally they came to control the entire Yellow River valley. This was known in Chinese history as the period of "Five Barbarian Trlbes Causing Chaos in China." Chinese in the Yellow River valley withdrew to Nanking, where they set up a new government. This marked the beginning of the East Tsin Dynasty, which was followed by the Southern Dynasties.

Chinese influence, which crossed the Yangtze River at the time of Emperor Shih of Chin, subsequently reached the Wu Range (five mountain ranges in South China) extending down to the Indo-China peninsula. In this vast region lived aborigines, such as the Miao, the Yao, the Tai, the Mon-Khmer and Indonesian tribes. Chinese governments during the Ch'in and Han dynasties pursued a positive policy in developing this region with the result that most of the original inhabitants accepted Chinese culture. During this long historical period, there was continuous turmoil in the Yellow River valley, and millions of refugees fleeing from war and chaos left North China for the Yangtze River valley and the Pearl River area in the south. As a result of this mass migration, the culture south of the Yangtze River became more Chinese, and the immigrants developed the areas south of the Yangtze until eventually they surpassed the Yellow River valley. Furthermore, the opening of the coastal areas of southeast China put the Chinese in a position to trade with India, Persia and the Arab countries, and in due course some merchants from these countries settled down in China.

For many years the Yellow River valley was under the control of non-Chinese tribes who constituted the new ruling classes. As in the case of the Germanic invasion of Rome, the coming into power of non-Chinese tribes made a profound and permanent effect on the political and social conditions of the area. However, problems between the "barbarians" and the Chinese continued to crop up, and the political situation continued to change. For 80 years, there was a succession of dynasties dominated by Chinese barbarians or barbarian-like Chinese, until the rise of two families of the latter, namely, the Yangs and Lis, who founded the Sui and T'ang dynasties respectively.

Sui and Tang Dynasties

Achievements during the period of the Six Dynasties, not only symbolized a rebirth of China's own culture but also stimulated new cultural developments in other oriental countries, especially Japan.

The cultural foundation of the Sui Dynasty was laid by the mixed ruling class composed of Barbarians (the Hu) and the Chinese of the Northern Dynasties. After conquering the Southern Dynasties. the northerners transplanted the cultural accomplishments from South China to the north. Representative of the artistic styles of the time were the wall murals and clay images in the Tunhuang caves. The art of the Northern Wei Dynasty was endowed with rich foreign elements while the art of the Sui Dynasty was obviously developed from what the Northern Wei had to offer in addition to a certain original Chinese content which in turn was evidently obtained from the Southern Dynasties. Among the emperors of the Sui and T'ang dynasties, Emperor Yang of the former was most fond of the art and manners of the Southern Dynasties. He even preferred to live in Yangchow (a preference which eventually led to the downfall of his dynasty). Emperor T'ai Tsung of the T'ang Dynasty took this lesson to heart and was cautious of what the southerners had to offer, yet his love of literature and calligraphy indicates that he was also inclined toward the Southern Dynasties. As a matter of fact, this was already the vogue of the time and not the peculiar taste of a few individuals. This is the reason why Tang paintings show a predominance of southern Chinese styles.

Beginning with Emperor Wen of the Sui Dynasty, Changan④ became China's capital and was entirely rebuilt according to city planning, with straight wide streets, magnificent palaces and government offices, official residences, civilian dwellings, and markets. During the T'ang Dynasty, owing to China's rise in national strength, Changan became a city of international importance. Countries to the east, such as Japan and Korea, all sent envoys and students to Changan. Monks and merchants from the "lands in the west," or countries in central Asia, came to Changan in groups aud many of them settled down there. Religions also played an important part. Besides Buddhism, Zoroastrianism, Manes and Nestorian Christianity all had their own monasteries or churches in Changan. The stone table discovered in Sian, on which is inscribed the story of Nestorian Christianity in China during that period, is still a most important documentary proof.

Subsequently, T'ang artists adopted many more new touches from foreign art including music, dances and games from Central Asia. Yuchih Yitseng, a famous T'ang painter, was a native of a kingdom in present-day southern Sinkiang. The shadow technique which Wu Tao-tze, a leading T'ang painter, created and which has remained the base for Chinese landscape painting, can also be traced to influence from countries bordering China's west boundaries.

Li Yen-nien, a famous Chinese musician during the Han Dynasty, was the first one to adopt Central Asian music. During the T'ang Dynasty, Samarkand, Bokhara, Kabdana, and Brahmin music flourished. All these, and the instruments used, though Chinese in some respects, still clearly show Indian and Central Asian influences.

On the other hand, Chinese arts and skills spread to the western lands. For example, Persian paintings and designs indicate Chinese influences. As to the art of making paper and satin, Chinese influence on the western countries was particularly great. In national wealth and in military strength, China had no equals anywhere during that period.

T'ang culture was many-splendored and variegated. From the Chou Dynasty to the Han Dynasty, the Chinese Were partial in art to the Peach blossom. From the T'ang Dynasty on, they utilized the peony in painting and pottery. Lotus was the only flower used for decorative purposes in Buddhism before the Tang Dynasty, but since then Buddhist decorations began to use peony as well.

Many T'ang relics are in existence today. The poetry, painting, and calligraphy of the period marked the beginning of new techniques, many of which are still in use. The three-color T'ang pottery was the forerunner of exquisite Chinese porcelains in subsequent centuries. The T'ang Code, still intact, was a comprehensive legal system. The practice of holding competitive examinations for official posts, perfected during the T'ang Dynasty, was a contribution of major importance to the civil-service system. The Buddha Light Monastery on Mt. Wutai, still very well-preserved, is a large wooden edifice built during the T'ang Dynasty. In the Tunhuang caves many colored images and mural paintings are still remarkably well-preserved (unless destroyed by the Communists). The portrait of Emperor T'ai Tsung of the

T'ang Dynasty, now in the Central Museum in Taiwan is the earliest relatively reliable likeness of a Chinese emperor.

From the sung Dynasty to the Nineteenth Century

The Sung Dynasy (960-1276) was a militarily weak dynasty, and finally the Sungs were conquered by the Mongols. Nevertheless, it was during this dynasty that gunpowder was invented, the compass put to practical use, paper currency introduced, and the art of printing popularized. It was the dynasty that broke all previous records in trade with Persia and the Arab countries. Sung handicraft and art, in silk-making and porcelain-making, holds an unusually high position in the world's art. In the field of philosohy, the Philosophy of Reason as propounded by Confucian scholars of the Sung Dynasty, was a new development in Confucian thinking.

The Northern Sung (960-1126) had its capital in Kaifeng, while the Southern Sung had its capital in Hangchow. Both Kaifeng and Hangchow were conveniently located from the standpoint of communications. This shows that the Sung rulers picked their capitals more for economic reasons than for reasons of strategy. Kaifeng owed its prosperity to the canals. The completion of the old Grand Canal under Emperor Yang of the Sui Dynasty assured Changan, then the capital, of the economic support of the Yangtze delta.

The Grand Canal, a man-made northsouth waterway, constituted acomplete transportation system by itself. It had three sections with Loyang in the center. The first from Yangchow to Kaifeng was the principal route whereby the material resources, food and cloth, of the south were moved to the north. The shallow waters of the Wei River formed the second section of the canal system. To bolster the border defence in the north, food and other supplies were moved northeastward on water from Loyang, and this was the third section of the old Grand Canal. Of the three, the first was the most important from the standpoint of transportation capacity and commerce. That was why Kaifeng became prosperous, and at the time of the Sung Dynasty came to be chosen as the national capital.

The peaceful life, however, through more than one and half century, was ended by the fallen of the beautiful capital, Kaifeng, to the hands of Nuchen Tartars, while the Sung government was collapsed from the mismanagement of a vicious prime minister on his post of twenty years.

From the beginning of the Twelveth Century to the seventh decade of the Thirteenth Century China was separated into two kingdoms, Southern Sung and Kin (Nuchen). After another one and half century the Mongul Empire unified them and the famous Khublai Khan became the leader of the largest territory in his time.

Peking (or Peiping) had been enlarged as one of the great cities in the world. Marco Polo the son of a Venetian merchant returned from China to release the most colorful memories in his Travels in which the attractive stories enchanted Christopher Columbus to start his fruitful expedition. With eighty-eight years, the throne of the Mongul Empire was then turned down and transferred to a chief of the rvolutionary army to build the house of the Ming Dynasty.

Peiping, China's later capital, was the meeting point of agricultural cul ture, steppe culture and foreign culture by sea. Following the completion of the new Grand Canal, Yangchow retained much of its earlier prosperity, while Tientsin gained new importance. During the Ming Dynasty, Shanghai, being closer to the seacoast, already showed a tendency to supplant Yang-chow, and after its formal opening as a treaty port in 1842, it quickly became China's economic center.

China's culture during the long period from the 10th century to the 19th century, though not completely devoid of progress, was largely at a standstill. There was little development in the field of thought. Chinese society continued to be dominated by imperial examinations, bureaucrats, small landowners, and gentry. Nor was there much change in the material aspect of living between the Sung Dynasty and the Manchu Dynasty.

Of some importance was the introduction to China of Western learning and thoughtby the Jesuit fathers, and of corn and potatoes indirectly by way of America, during the last years of the Ming Dynasty. The former was instrumental in the Chinese calendar revision and the national land survey during the reign of Emperor Kang-hsi of the Manchu Dynasty, but otherwise did not have much influence on Chinese academic pursuit. The latter, however, proved to be an immense boon in that the hilly regions in China's southwest came to be cultivated to spearhead a new economic development in such provinces as Yunnan and Kweichow. Unfortunately, the Chinese people failed to appreciate the importance of Western learning during this period. Yet Chinese thought left a deep impression on European philosophers, economists, and even artists during the 18th century.

The Manchu Dynasty's major contribution in the field of learning was in verifying and editing ancient classics. Many important works were produced from the beginning of the dynasty till the reigns of Emperor Chien-lung and Emperor Chia-ching. It is a matter of regret, however, that no advance was made in natural sciences. Outstanding scholars were interested in mathematics but their influence on Chinese scholarship in general was limited.

The main purpose of Chinese scholars during the Manchu Dynasty was to "penetrate" the classics and to "put them in use," or simply to elaborate on ancient teachings. They did not seek to understand nature, nor proceed on the basis of scholarship for scholarship's sake. Therefore, it may be said that Chinese efforts in the academic field during this period resulted in an incomplete cultural renascence, which was not accompanied by an industrial revolution.

China Since the Nineteenth Century

The 19th century marked the beginning of the Manchu Dynasty's decline.

Both the political power and economic wealth of the Manchu Dynasty reached their zenith during the reign of Emperor Chien-lung (1736-1795). Though an able sovereign, Emperor Chien-lung showed signs of senility in his old age and his favorite courtier Ho Shen virtually held the reins. As a result the administration began to deteriorate. High officials, both in Peking and in the provinces, had very meager knowledge of what was going on elsewhere in the world. When Sir George Macartney, the British envoy, arrived Peking in 1793, no one in the government from Emperor Chien-lung on down appreciated the importance of international trade.

Malad ministration gradually led to domestic unrest. Beginning in 1796, the country was rocked by a series of uprisings. First, there were the disturbances caused by bandits in Szechwan and Hupeh Provinces. These were followed by practical raids on the coast south of the Yangtze. Though all these were soon put down, a more extensive uprising broke out in 1850. This was the Taiping Rebellion, which resulted in the devastation of many erstwhile prosperous provinces. The rebellion had a side eflect, through the large influx of refugces, in fostering the growth of Shanghai from an ordinary coastal town into China's leading metropolis, a development which subsequently influenced to a great extent China's economic conditions.

From the end of the reign of Emperor Chien-lung till the twentieth year of the reign of Emperor Tao-kuang (1840), the Chinese Government showed little or no interest in international trade. On the other hand, Britain was vigorously pushing her trade with the Orient. This irreconcilable conflict, especially that of the trade in opium, was the cause of the Opium War, during which the weakness of the Manchu Dynasty was completely bared. In the Treaty of Nanking, it was stipulated that China should open five port cities to foreign trade. This represented China's first step to emerge from self-imposed isolation to the field of international trade. There are similarities between the circumstances under which the Treaty of Nanking was concluded and those under which Commodore Matthew C. Perry forced Japan to open her ports to foreign trade in 1854. Unfortunately, however, because of her extremely heavy historical and traditional burden, China did not find it as easy to move into the new world as Japan did. Most of China's problems during the past century have had their origin in China's inability to adjust herself to the impact of Western influence on Asia.

Tseng Kuo-fan's success in suppressing the Taiping Rebellion in 1864 saved the Manchu Dynasty from an impending collapse, but it also caused some new developments. The first of these was the rise in power of the Han people (the majority ethnic group of the Chinese nation) both in military affairs and in local government, which in turn paved the way for the Revolution of 1911. The second was the growing jealousy of the Manchus, who controlled the court in Peking, and put obstacles in the way of numerous reform measures, thereby causing a delay in China's progress. Thirdly, such Han military leaders as Li Hung-chang and Tso Tsung-t'ang, who cooperated with Tseng Kuo-fan in putting down the Taiping Rebellion, gradually came to realize the importance of Western learning and technical skills, and this realization hastened China's trend toward modernization.

During the three decades from 1864 to 1894, there was enough determination on the part of Chinese leaders, at least among the better informed and far-seeing ones, to make progress in China. But in this respect China differed from Japan. Whereas in Japan from Emperor Meiji on down, efforts at modernization received nationwide support, in China similar efforts met with strong opposition. Thus, whatever Li Hung-chang and his contemporaries succeeded in accomplishing developed from grim struggles.

China's gains in modernization during this period, therefore, were neither solid nor adequate. At the time of the first Sino-Japanese War in 1894, the Chinese navy was superior in tonnage, but inferior in the number and caliber of its guns and the training of its officers. The Chinese army was also inferior in equipment, in training, and in logistic capability. China's defeat was, therefore, a foregone conclusion. Under the Treaty of Shimonoseki, China was forced to cede Taiwan to recognize Korea as being within Japan's sphere of influence, and to pay huge indemnities. China's international position fell considerably and her financial resources greatly dwindled. She had less and less capital available for reconstruction.

In 1898, despite the Empress Dowager's opposition, Emperor Kuang-hsu took the scholars, Kang Yu-wei and Liang Ch'i-chao, into the government and launched a reform movement, which in both scope and method was patterned after that previously enforced in Japan. Unfortunately, the reform movement lasted only 100 days. It was overthrown by the Manchu nobility who worked through the Empress Dowager, and Emperor Kuang-hsu himself became a captive in the palace.

The same Manchu nobility who obstructed the reform movement, later resorted to medieval witchcraft as personified by the Boxers in an attempt to drive all foreigners from China. This attempt, known as the Boxer Uprising, came to a dismal end in 1900 when the Empress Dowager vainly tried to pit North China troops against the allied forces. By the Protocol of 1901, China had to pay large indemnities. Though Emperor Kuang-hsu remained powerless, the Empress Dowager was no longer as strongly opposed to reforms as before. Consequently, China's modernization during this period proceeded at a relatively quickened pace.

Because of the Boxer Uprising, the Manchu Dynasty lost prestige in the eyes of the Chinese people until it finally fo rfeited its leadership entirely. The revolutionary forces, on the other hand, gained in momentum, and before long Dr. Sun Yat-sen became the focus of the Chinese people's hopes and aspirations. Shortly after the outbreak of the Revolution of 1911 at Wuchang, the Manchu Dynasty came to an end.

The Republic of China was founded in 1912. Though a republican form of government was established, actual power and control of the armed forces were in the hands of the military commanders, whose leader was none other than Yuan Shih-k'ai. while Dr. Sun had no control over these military commanders.

Later, even after Yuan's death, the country was divided into semi-autonomous regions, each lorded over by a military commander. The hope of China's progress into an era of constitutional government grew dim. Finally, Dr. Sun had to set up an opposition government in Canton in order to continue his revolutionary efforts.

Though Dr. Sun died in 1925, the revolutionary forces he had founded subsequently unified the country in1927-1928. Under the leadership of General

Chiang Kai-shek the Northern Expedition to wrest China from the warlords was completed. China acquired a new purpose and a new direction in her political, economic, and cultural activities. The Chinese people began to look toward the future with new confidence. The unexpected Japanese invasion of the Northeastern Provinces (Manchuria) in 1931 halted this rapid progress.

There were Chinese troops in the Northeastern Provinces at the time of the invasion, but there were also a large number of Japanse troops known as the "Kwantung Army" who had been in occupation of the South Manchurian Railway zone since the Russo-Japanese War of 1904-5. From the occupation of China's Northeastern Provinces, more or less through a coup, the Japanese, with their appetite thus whetted, moved on, trying to occupy the whole of China and the entire Southeast Asia and to turn the region into a so-called Great East Asia Co-prosperity Sphere. Japan went down in defeat in World War Second. The long war had the following bad effects on China:

1. It interrupted and delayed the Chinese Government's reconstruction plan.

2. It caused a general dislocation in social conventions and economic institutions, thus giving the Communists the chance to drive a wedge in.

3. While the government forces sustained losses during the Sino-Japanese War, the Communists took advantage of the situation to expand their territory with the result that the harder the Government was pressed by the Japanese, the greater became the Communists' military strength.

4. War-weariness.

5. Inflation.

China fought Japan for eight years from 1937 till 1945, and for six years more, if one goes back to the loss of Manchuria. Japan was organized along mcdern economic lines, while China, with the exception of a small area in and around Shanghai, was still largely undeveloped. This means that China had to fight under extremely difficult conditions. Yet, inspired by President Chiang's leadership, the Chinese people fought long and hard, and together with the allies, defeated Japan. But China was exhausted, and her cities and countryside were in ruins.

Owing to the Manchus' erroneous policies during the last days of their dynasty and the ambitions of rival warlords in the early years of the Republic, China had a late start in modernization. The national government strove hard to build China up industrially, but, because of the Japanese invasion, did not have full opportunity. Although the government tried its best to develop the southwestern provinces during the Sino-Japanese War, its accomplishments left much to be desired. This gave the Communists a chance to raise on their military power and furious propaganda against the Central Government. The propaganda labelled the Chinese Reds "agrarian reformers" and not real Communists. Under dissembling occations some allies turned to help the Communists to bring pressure on the government. Caught between internal and external pressures, the Central Government, being Seriously injured from the Second Sino-Japanese war, finally withdrew from mainland.

The Chinese Covernment moved to Taiwan in 1949. Here, during the past ten years, it has chalked up a remarkable record of reconstruction. The per capita income of all Taiwan inhabitants has been considerably increased as compared with days under Japanese control. It has been able to implement policies, such as the land reform, in Taiwan which it never had opportunity to carry out on the Chinese mainland. Politically, the election of local officials by popular suffrage is one such instance. In education, illiteracy has been largely eliminated. The main purpose for Taiwan today is going to build a standard of political democracy and economical freedom, with a confident hope to bring this excellent wish to share with all of Chinese people in future.

1 In Lihchen Hsien, Shantung Province. *See* Chentseyen, published by Academia Sinica, 1933.

2 *Chun Chiu* is actually the name of the *History of the State of Lu*, generally attributed to Confucius.

3 The six kingdoms were Chu, Tsi, Yen, Han, Wei, and Chao.

4 Changan is near present-day Sian (in Shensi Province).

本篇轉載自1959 China Year Book.

On the Chinese Ancient Characters

A

I. The Chinese Language and its Lexicons

China, as is well known, is one of the largest nations is Asia and in the world. However, due to its geographic environment--mountainous areas with towering mountain ranges, deserts, and oceans--for a long period China remained veiled and isolated form the Western world.

This relative isolation resulted in one of the distinctive features of this culture; namely, its monosyllabic language and hieroglyphic characters. The origins of this monosyllabic language has yet to be determined with any certainty, mainly due to the fact that it is seemingly a unique phenomenon. A comparison, however, with related languages may indicate that this language is a variant form of a distinctive type. Compared to Egyptian and American Indian scripts, the hieroglyphic Chinese characters may be independent creations that evolved sometime around the Shang Dynasty.

The Chinese people trace their origins to the Hsia people, a feudal state covering Southern Shansi and Western Honan. Those who lived across and beyond their frontiers were the so-called "barbarians". These barbarians employed a different type of language. However, as Chinese culture gradually extended outward, these barbarians naturally came into contact with its language and people. It is our conjecture that originally the Shang people were not Chinese; however, that over an extended period of time, they adapted the culture and language of the Hsia people. Naturally, therefore, the Shang people should be considered as being a branch of the Chinese.

From Shang to Chou, more than one thousand years elapsed, and during that time, tribes evolved into city-states and city-states in turn developed into kingdoms. In 221 B. C., Ch'in Shih-huang successfully unified the Seven Kingdoms to form an empire and for the first time, China became a political unit. Before this time, the people of the Seven Kingdoms used hieroglyphic Chinese Characters but these hieroglyphs differed in form as compared to the scripts inscribed on the various relics discovered at various ruin sites in the different regions of the Chinese mainland.

The standard script of the Ch'in Dynasty was called "hsiao-chuan" or "small turned lines", generally translated "small seal". This particular script was made the standard form of writing by the Prime Minister Li Ssu in his text book *Ts'ang-chieh Pien*. A variant form of the "small seal" script called the "li-shu" or "clerk script" was also in use. This latter script was not for formal usage but being relatively easy to write, it was employed mainly for practical, everyday writing. Approximately one hundred years from the beginning of and up to the end of the Han Wu-ti Dynasty, the li-shu or clerk-script was used extensively in the records of the Northern frontier.

After a period of time, both the chuan-shu and the li-shu were established as standard forms of writing. In the twelfth year of the Yung-yuan (100 A. D.) and eminent scholar Hsü Shen undertook his great work, the *Shuo-wen Chieh-tzu*, the first dictionary of Chinese characters. This work exhibits several notable features. For example, this dictionary was the first to introduce the use of radicals and contained 9353 characters. Moreover, this was the first dictionary of Chinese etymology with explanations the used the li-shu in order to explain the chuan-shu. Therefore, it was to become the original source and the key to ancient Chinese characters; that is, the basic Chinese etymological dictionary.

Above all the *Shuo-wen* was the first work to arrange characters with etymological explanations of the characters. The *Ts'ang-chieh Pien* and the other works that followed and supplemented it were considered to be wordbooks or glossaries but they provided no explanations. Similarly, works such as the *Erh-ya*, *Fang-yen*, *Kuang-ya* and *Shih-ming* contained numerous characters and even some verses of the poetic genre known as "fu" and were used as glossaries but they too originally were without explanations or notes. According to the "Yi-wen Chih" or "The Record of Classics and Literature", of the *Han-shu*, there existed two types of commentaries to the *Erh-ya*; one by the "wen hsüeh" of Chien-wei Province and the other by Liu Hsin, but none of these were compiled by the original author as in the case of the *Shuo-wen*.

The *Yü Pien* by ku Yeh-wang in the Liang Dynasty (502-566), followed the *Shuo-wen* as the second dictionary of its kind. Following the same sys-tem as the *Shuo-wen*, the characters were classified under 542 radicals, two more than in the *Shuo-wen*. However, the *Yü Pien* contained a greater number of characters and additions were later made in the T'ang and Sung periods.

In 1031-1039 of the Sung period another new dictionary listing still more characters was compiled; this was the *Lui Pien*. It was produced from the rhyme books. The first one of the rhyme books is *Chieh-yün*.

In the Sui period (601), a systematic rhyming dictionary, the *Chieh-yün*, made its appearance; it shared many common features with the etymological dictionaries which preceded it. Through the Sui, T'ang, Five Dynasties, and the beginning of the Sung, the rhyming dictionary went through a process of change and enlargement. Specifically beginning with the *Chieh-yün* and through the succeeding works, *T'ang-yün*, *Kuang-yün* and finally, the *Chi-yün* which is the largest rhyming dictionary ever compiled. On the other hand, the *Lui Pien* integrated all the characters listed in the *Chi-yün* and thereby, became the largest etymological dictionary of its kind.

With the appearance of the *Tzu Hui* in the Ming Dynasty, a major change in the system used in the dictionary was introduced. In contrast to the *Shuo-wen*, the *Tzŭ-Hui* employed a system of counting the number of strokes, beginning with the radical of the first character. The "stroke system" simplified the task of locating characters, as contrasted with the system in the *Shuo-wen*; however, the accurate recognition of a radical within a character was not without its difficulties. Therefore, this system, which was later adopted by the *Kang-hsi Tzŭ-tien* and most modern Chinese and Japanese dictionaries, was employed mainly for its simplicity and convenience and not necessarily for its scholastic value.

II. *Shuo-wen* as the Basic Source in the Identification of Ancient Characters

In the *Shuo-wen* there are three types of characters; namely, the "small seal", the "clerk script" and the so-called "ku-wen" or "ancient character". The small seal and clerk script were legal scripts in the Han period but the "ancient character" originates from a different source. It is derived from the inscriptions on ancient bronzes, mostly from the ancient ruins of the Chou Dynasty in which the archaic scripts were found, most of which belong to the period of the Warring States. The bronze inscriptions as recorded in the *Han-shu* were limited in number and therefore, were not arranged in a systematic manner as they were in the Sung Dynasty. In the *Shuo-wen* there are a few characters identified with those of Chou bronze. The scripts of the Warring States period were categorized into many types for the sake of identification. The most famous ones were the *Ku-wen Shang-shu* or the "Book of History in Ancient Script", *Chou-li*, and *Tso-chuan*; the studies conducted on these works gave rise to a new school at the end of the Former Han Dynasty. This school was called "Ku-wen Hsioh-p'ai" and it exerted lasting influence on the scholastic trends of the Later Han Dynasty. The script as contained in the *Shuo-wen*, however, has passed through many hands and differed from the real, archaic inscription. Thus, not only was the 'Ku-wen" or "ancient script" from the *Shuo-wen* not perfectly reliable but the stone inscriptions as contained in the *San-ti Shih-ching* or "Classics in Three Styles" of the Wei Dynasty were also not perfectly reliable. This shows that only the small seal and the clerk script which were the legal scripts of the time are the only available scripts that can be approached with assurance and certainty.

Because there were only very few scholars who had actually seen bronze inscriptions for themselves, a quasi-ancient style of script called the "K'o-tou wen" or "tadpole character" was used among scholars. The so-called "ancient script" was first included in the *San-ti Shih-ching* and subsequently in the "Pi-lo-pei" of the T'ang period, the *Han-chien* by Kuo Chung-Shu and the *Ku-wen Ssǔ-sheng Yün* by Hsia Su in the Sung period. Hsüeh Shang-kung's *Chung-ting kuan-chih* or "Inscriptions for Bells and Tripods" makes faithful transcription from bronze vessels; this can be seen in those pages that remain today, printed from ink-squeezed plates; that is, the stone tablets with the original inscriptions. However, the reprints from wooden blocks have been changed into the "tadpole style" as in the case of former scholars. Until Yüan Yüan of the Ch'ing Dynasty issued his *Chi-ku-chai Chung-ting Kuan-chih*, the exact form was those that appeared in a book from wooden blocks.

III. A Historical Sketch of the Development of Characters

Chinese characters developed from hieroglyphs and reaching further back, they may be traced to the simple picture-drawings of primitive times. The depiction of animal figures can be found on painted pottery but no relationship has been established, linking them with hieroglyphs. Some Signs on the pottery vessels from panp'o of Sian may be considered as the earlier origin of the characters and the characters inscribed on the oracle bones of the Yin-Shang period may be rendered as the earliest extant real characters.

The "Introduction" of the *Shuo-wen* notes that knotted strings and the eight trigrams were used in keeping records prior to the use of characters. There is, however, a great deal of controversy regarding the truth of this statement. It is true that the method of knotted strings has been referred to by the Greek historian Herodotus who mentions that King Darius sent knotted strings to Ionia. Furthermore, they have appeared in the Ryukyu Islands, the South Pacific, and on the African continent, furnishing strong evidence that it existed in ancient China.

However, the so-called eight trigrams are much too simple to be used as a means of keeping records.

The eight trigrams are found in the *Book of Changes* and constitutes its nucleus. Recent scholars have suggested that the *Book of Changes* was compiled in the Tenth or eleventh Century B.C., at the beginning of the Chou Dynasty. Without doubt, certain ideas with philosophical implications of a Chinese nature are found in this work; however, the principal use of the *Book of Changes* was limited to purposes of divination.

The terms "yin" (--) and "yang" (—) and the eight trigrams for heaven (☰), earth(☷), water(☵), fire(☲), thunder(☳), mountain(☶), wind(☴), and swamp (☱) were used mainly for divinatory purposes and by no means were they intended to deal with every aspect of the primitive world. As we learn in the "Shuo-kua-chuan" or "Discussion of the Diagrams", appended as supplementary material to the *Book of Changes*, each diagram covers a wide range of things and can be applied without any logical explanations. This indicates that the contents of this book are suited to the practice of divination but are too obscure for everyday use. Although ancient China was divided into separate nations, in none of these nations was the eight trigrams ever used in the place of words.

The only possible conclusion is that the knotted strings were in use in diverse regions but that the original pictographs came into being in a limited area. From its use within that limited area, these pictographs gradually extended outward. And thus, the first step in the development of the Chinese character took place.

"Chia-ku" or oracle bones are considered the earliest writings of China except the signs of Panp'o and their discovery has been limited to the area of Yin-Hsu; that is, the Anyang County of Ho-nan Province. The fact that the Cheng-chow site, which does not antedate Anyang by too many years, did not yield any relics with scripts has never been explained. This indicates, perhaps, that the use of hieroglyphs on oracle bones was a rather new development in the period of Hsiao-tun (or Yin-Hsü) (circa 1300 B.C.)

Oracle bones are made up of bones of cattle or tortoise shells on which inscriptions have been made. A study of the inscriptions reveals that the king practiced divination whenever beset with doubts regarding some matter and the diviner had faithfully recorded the questions posed by the king.

The basic formative principles of Chinese writing had appeared in the oracle bone inscriptions; they may be classified as follows: (1)Pictograms to depict human bodies, animals, insects, plants, natural and artificial objects. (2)Ideograms indicating abstract ideas or the position and the measurement of things. (3)Phonograms which included the borrowing of sound and the combination of pictogram and sound. (4)Combination of two or characters to express a single meaning. All of these principles are still in operation as the bases for the written character.

Oracle bones were first discovered toward the end of the Nineteenth Century and due to the fact that the bases of paleographic research had been established ever since the Chienlung-chiaching period, the identification of the inscribed scripts was accomplished with relative ease.

When the oracle bones were first discovered, although in small and limited numbers, those scholars with long experience in the study of bronzes and the classics showed great interest in them and in fact were the most suited to undertake the study of these bones.

Sun Yi-jang, an eminent scholar, was one of the first to take up the study of these oracle bones. He had done outstanding work on the *Chou-li* and on bronzes. Though he had few sources available to him, he opened up this area of research for later scholars such a Lo Chen-yü and Wang Kuo-wei.

The scientific explorations at Anyang by the Academica Sinica between 1930 and 1937 was the most productive period in the course of oracle bones research. Thousands of pieces of bones and shells were unearthed. The sets of transcribed ink-squeezed plates, *Hisiao-tun*, still comprise one of the most important sources for this field of study.

Bronze inscriptions were used by the royal family and the feudal lords from the Shang Dynasty through Western and Eastern Chou up to the time of the

Warring States. Many changes occurred but the traditional line can still be traced. In the Han Dynasty the ancient inscribed bronzes appears to have influenced some scholars toward a trend of study called the "ku-wen-hsüeh" or "study of ancient forms of writing". Hsü Shen, the compiler of the "*Shuo-wen*", was the most important among these.

But for a long time, as long as ten centuries, no new developments were made in this field of study. However, at the beginning of the Sung Dynasty, two brothers of the Hsü family, Hsü Hsüan and Hsü Kai studied the *Shuo-wen* from the standpoint of textual criticism and introduced a new era in the history of paleographic studies. In the Middle Age of Northern Sung (early Eleventh Century), a famous poet and prose writer, Ou-yang Hsiou, compiled his famous *Chi-ku Lu* or "Collection of Ancient Inscriptions".

Following the appearance of the *Chi-ku Lu*, a number of major works in the field of ancient inscriptions were brought forth. Among these the following are extant: *k'ao-ku T'u* by Lü Ta-lin (compiled in 1092), *Hsüan-ho Po-ku T'u*, a compilation undertaken at the orders of the emperor (1107), *Chung-ting Yi-chi Kuan-chih* by Hsüeh Shang-kung (1144), *Hsiao-tang Chi-ku* by Wang Chiu (1176). In all of these works, the original inscriptions were deciphered and identified with modern characters. The identification of characters was based on a careful and meticulous comparison of the original inscription with the small seal characters of the "*Shuo-wen*".

The identification of characters constituted a new field of study for the Sung Scholars and therefore, their studies contained many errors, which were subsequently criticized by the scholars of the Ch'ing period. For example, Wang Kuo-wei (1877-1927) writes: "After the Chienlung-chiaching periods of the Imperial Dynasty, there was a renaissance in ancient studies. Scholars looked down upon the books of the Sung Dynasty and did not desire to quote from them. With regard to my personal opinion, the *k'ao-ku T'u* and the *Po-ku T'u* were well written. Their work on the depiction of figures and their discussion of the ancient systems of writing reveal many achievements...With respect to the identification of characters, the Sung scholars have achieved an original accomplishment. Great scholars such as Juan Yuan and Wu Ta-ch'eng are unable to go beyond these sources. Without doubt, many errors are found in their works; however, this was not entirely avoidable by these eminent scholars of the Imperial Dynasty. "This passage indicates that the studies made by the Sung scholars formed the basis for the investigative efforts of the later Ch'ing and Min-Kuo scholars.

Through the Yüan and Ming Periods, archaeological studies were generally dormant. At the beginning of the Ch'ing Dynasty Ku Yen-wu and Chu Yi-tsun emerged as precursors in a movement, which emphasized the systematic study of ancient classics and characters, setting a basis for a fresh approach to the study of ancient sources. The Emperor Ch'ien-lung was strongly influenced by the method of the "Han school". He issued orders to the scholars in the Imperial Academy to compile the works *Hsi-ch'ing Ku-chien* and *Ning-shou Chien-ku*, with the *Hsüan-ho Po-ku T'u* serving as the model. Private publications on the inscriptions of bronzes, which were to be compiled in a similar style were also emerged. The most famous ones are Juan Yüan's *Chi-ku-chai Chung-ting K'uan-chih* and Wu Shih-fen's *Chün-ku Lu Chin-wen*. The former work comprised one of the earliest examples of a careful and detailed study in the Ch'ing Dynasty while the latter was one of the most complete of that period.

Along with the study of inscription, in the Ch'ing period great weight and value was placed on philological studies. Following Ku-yen-wu, Chiang Yung, Tai Chen and Ch'ien Ta-hsin were the preeminent figures of this particular field of study. However, Tuan Yü-ts'ai's commentary to the *Shuo-wen* was regarded as the most valuable work with respect to the study of characters. Tai Chen who had devoted his energies to the classics, philology and mathematics was the mentor of Tuan. Influenced by his teacher, Tuan developed his studies in a more logical manner as compared to other contemporary scholars. During the period Tuan was active as a scholar, the study of bronze had achieved relatively high standards. Although Tuan did not use bronze studies as evidence in his research, he did produce very useful explanations for bronze study. Numerous scholars of later years criticized Tuan for the uncritical confidence that he placed on his approach; however, there is little doubt that his considerable achievements outweigh faults his studies may contain.

In the early part of this century, there was increased activity with respect to both the study of bronzes and oracle bones, both on the part of oriental--Chinese and Japanese--as well as Western scholars. Their efforts resulted in the publication of many new findings, research papers, and also new dictionaries. All of the combined to exert great influence on the study of the *Shuo-wen*. The *Shuo-wen Chieh-tzŭ Ku-lin* by Ting Fu-pao, published in 1937, brought together all the available studies on the *Shuo-wen* and the characters included therein and also included the researches that had been done on bronzes and oracle bones. (A reprint of this work, without revisions, was issued in Taiwan in 1960.)

A number of specialized dictionaries for bronzes and oracle bones have been published, all arranged according to the system used in the *Shuo-wen*. For oracle bones, the first dictionary to appear was Lo-cheng-yü's *Yin-hsü Wen-tzŭ Lui-pien*; this was followed by the *Chia-ku Wen-pien* prepared by Sun Hai-po. And more recently, we have Chin Hsiang-heng's *Hsü Chia-ku Wen-pien* and Li Hsiao-ting's *Chia Ku Wen-tzŭ Chi-shih*. As Far as dictionaries of bronze inscriptions age concerned, the *Shuo-wen Ku-chou Pu* of Wu Ta-cheng is the earliest one, followed by the *Chin-wen Pien* of Young Ken. The latter work has been revised but has not incorporated the more recent findings in this field.

IV. The Development of the Li-shu Style

The li-shu is a variation of the small seal and is not related to the characters of the Kingdoms of the Warring States, with the exception of the Ch'in Kingdom. According to Wang Kuo-wei's *Shih-chou-pien Su-cheng Hsü* and *Chan-kuo Shih Ch'in Yung Chou-wen Liu-Kuo Yung Chou Wen Sho*, only the Ch'in state followed the old style of chou, and it was used to write *Shih-Chou Pien* specially. This old style was termed "chou-shu"; it was more complex with respect to strokes and closer to the bronze inscriptions as preserved in the *Shuo-wen*. In the Ch'in

Dynasty, there were eight different styles with regard to characters. "Chou-wen" is basically the same as ta-chuan (large seal) in contrast to the hsiao-chuan(small seal).

This conservatism of the state of Ch'in is derived from the fact that the "Ch'in" empire occupied an area that had formerly been of Chou and on which the capital Fung-Hao had been situated. This particular area had been the centre of Chou culture from the beginning of Chou to the year 771 B.C., a period spanning more than two hundred years and perhaps up to three hundred years. Since the area had been occupied by barbarian tribes, in the process of recovering this area by the state of Ch'in, numerous buildings were lost in the conflagrations and many books were lost. However, those traditions such as script styles remained and were accepted by the ruling family. In the middle period of the Spring and Autumn, the script underwent a slight change and became more complex in form as evidenced by such styles as the chou-wen and the ta-ch'uan. But such styles of writing proved to be impractical and necessitated a process of simplification which resulted in the hsiao-chuan or small seal. This hsiao-chuan was adopted as the formal or legal script of the Ch'in Dynasty.

As shown in the *Shuo-wen*, and shown in the script used in engraving edicts on weighing stones or on measuring vessels was the small seal. However, the script style of both the large and small seals was very cumbersome and impractical in terms of simple, everyday use, whether for formal or private, personal purposes. From the Chu bronzes excavated at Shou-hsien or the silk and bamboo slips from Ch'ang-sha, the scripts were improved into a style with rapidly executed strokes. Similar evolution of styles occurred in the Ch'in state and gave rise to the li-shu and the ts'ao-shu. The preface to the *Shuo-wen* mentions that the li-shu was an invention of Ch'eng Miao. A passage by Wei Heng, quoted in his biography contained in the "Chin-shu", states that Ch'eng Miao was a clerk in the offices of Yün-yang County. During the period of imprisonment which lasted for ten years, Ch'eng Miao compared and arranged the strokes of the seal style in order to create a new and simpler script. Due to the ease of this newly developed script, it was widely adopted for official usage. Ch'eng Miao was, as a result, released from prison and promoted to the post of Imperial Secretary by the Emperor Ch'in Shih-huang. In the history of the development of the script during the Warring States, it would not be entirely correct to call the li-shu a wholly original creation. However, there is no doubt that the systematic arrangement of strokes of the li-shu was accomplished by Ch'eng Miao, resulting in a script highly practical for official use and far simpler and more economical in terms of effort. Since the li-shu had been arranged on the basis of the small seal characters, the latter was easily identifiable as component parts. This brought about in the Ch'in-Han periods a remarkable standardization of the li-shu for everyday use. A study of the Han wooden slips shows that from the time of Emperor Han Wu-ti (the latter half of the Second Century B.C.) every type of official document employed the li-shu. This sweeping change indicates that the adoption of the li-shu had been in process for a long period of time and that it must have been an important script ever since the time of Emperor Ch'in Shih-huang.

Toward the end of the Former Han Dynasty, a serious controversy developed between two schools, the "Chin-wen" and the "Ku-wen" schools. Chin-wen or "modern text" points to the classics that were transcribed from oral transmissions or from newly compiled commentaries. On the other hand, Ku-wen or "ancient text" referred to the archaic style which was preserved in the books that escaped burning such as the *Chou-li* the *Tso-chuan* of the Chun-chiu or those which were newly discovered in the walls of dwellings inhabited by the descendants of Confucius; for example, the *Ku-wen Shang-shu*. Chin-wen was written in li-shu and the Ku-wen in the style of chuan-shu. The association of li-shu with Chin-wen, the "modern text" school, indicates that the li-shu had become the predominant contemporary style of writing during the Former Han Dynasty.

Up to the Later Han Dynasty, a large number of inscriptions were made on stone tablets. Excepting a few scripts such as the small seal which was used in the Yüan An and Yüan Ch'ang tablets, these inscriptions were done in the li-shu. This fact clearly suggests that the small seal had, by this time, become an outdated script and had become obsolete as far as practical use was concerned.

During the more than four hundred and fifty years that span the beginning of Han to the beginning of Chin, the script style underwent a gradual transformation. For example, the horizontal lines ere drawn with a definite stop at the end of the stroke instead of using a rush-like stroke at the end. This was the initial step which was to eventually result in the development of the k'ai-shu from the li-shu.

Between the k'ai-shu, which is a variant form of the li-shu, and the li-shu itself, there is no clear and definitive distinction, since the transition from the latter to the former was a gradual one. This much is, however, clear; in the Former and Later Han Dynasties, the characters inscribed on wooden slips or on stone tablets are all in a rectangular form but in the Wei Dynasty of the Three Kingdoms they were altered and took a square form. This change to the square form was also one of the changes which resulted in the k'ai-shu. In the case of these squarely formed characters, the brush stroke ending of the horizontal lines were greatly de-emphasized. This again was in accordance with the transition toward the k'ai shu.

A comparison of the Pi-yung Pei of Western chin and the Tsuan Pao-tzŭ tablet of Eastern Chin shows that the basic writing style was similar but that there is greater evidence of the k'ai-shu influence found in the latter. The calligraphers, therefore, considered the former to be in the style of li-shu while the latter was considered to be k'ai-shu. However the model, representative k'ai-shu style is to be found in the tablet inscriptions of the T'ang Dynasty; for example, the inscriptions since the time of the calligraphers Yü Shin-nan, Ou-yang Hsün, and Ch'u Sui-liang.

During the approximately four hundred years that lapsed from the period of Wei-Chin to the T'ang, the k'ai-shu passed through several changes. Therefore, in order to distinguish these, recent calligraphers have labeled those inscriptions coming before the T'ang as Wei-pei or Pei-pei (Northern tablet). The appellation, Wei-pei or Pei-pei, was used due to the fact that this style was generally used in the age of the Northern Dynasties and especially in Northern Wei. This Wei-pei script constitutes one variant form of the k'ai-shu.

At the end of the Ming Dynasty, one further evolution of the k'ai-shu took place. This was called the Sung style for wood block printing. In the Sung Dynasty the wooden blocks always followed the style of Ou-yang Hsün but were arranged in a more regular style. Up to the first half of the Ming, the wooden blocks used the current style of the Ming script. Until the Chia-ching times (1522-1566) many of the book printings were based on the Sung edition with some aspects arranged in a more regular style. This resulted in the formation of a new style which was to subsequently exert influence on the modern Chinese an Japanese styles of stereotyping.

V. Ts'ao-shu and Hsing-shu

The ts'ao-shu or the "grass script" had already been inexistence before the appearance of the li-shu of the Ch'in. The bamboo slips from Changsha of the Chu state show that the ts'ao-shu style of writing was being used with great skill in that period. The *Shin Chi* also notes that the great poet Chü Yüan had drafted a memorial using the ts'ao-shu.

The *Shuo-wen* states that the ts'ao-shu originated in the Han period. This may be implying that the chang-ts'ao (the ts'ao-shu peculiar to the Han Dynasty), was created in the Han period but that this rapid swift style of writing had been in existence for a long period of time. As the characters evolved away from simple picture drawings, there was no need to draw the strokes slowly, with care and exactness. This is the reason that the term "ts'ao-shu" might have been coined in the Chun-chiu or Warring States and the term "chang-ts'ao" in the Han although this style of rapid writing must have been in existence at a much earlier period.

However, the style of the ts'ao-shu simply followed popular usage and there was no set standard text for it. The *Chi-chiu Pien* compiled by Shih Yü at the end of the First Century B.C. was purported to be a standard text for chang-ts'ao. According to the Tunhuang wooden slips, the Han version of it was in the li-shu style, suggesting that "chi-chiu" simple meant "quick or rapid" and by no means referred to chang-ts'ao. This work was a summary of the *Tsang-chieh Pien* and contained important characters and naturally it became a standard text for the ts'ao-shu. This *Chi-chiu Pien* in standardized chang-ts'ao was allegedly written by the calligraphers from Han to Chin, calligraphers such as So Chin, Chung Yu, Huang Hsiang, Madam Wei and Wang Hsi-chih. The only extant copy is the one by Huang Hsiang of the Wu state in the period of the Three Kingdoms; furthermore, this particular text has been copied by Chao Meng-fu of the Yüan Dynasty and Sung Chung-wen of the Ming Dynasty.

When compared with the script used on the wooden slips, the chang ts'ao script in the *Chi-Chiu Pien* is definitely similar to that of those of the Former Han period. However, the *Chi-chiu Pien* was made into a standard work and original Han writing was not. This reveals that the ts'ao-shu, or chang ts'ao, in the Han Dynasty was not as strictly defined as it was to be by the scholars of later dynasties. The situation was quite similar to that of k'ai-shu and hsing-shu; there existed no definitive standards separating the various styles. There existed a style with extremely differing strokes and composition which was called ts'ao-shu but between this extreme ts'ao-shu and the formal li-shu, there existed numerous vitiations which precluded the determination of two definitive categories of styles. Therefore, scholars of the Ch'ing period coined the term "ts'ao-li" and Chou An compiled a work for stone inscriptions using this style of writing titled *Ts'ao-li Tsun*.

Although the main features of the chang-ts'ao differed with the li-shu, certain elements in its construction were still derived from the conventional style of the Warring States. For this reason the identification of the chang-ts'ao was never an easy task. As the li-shu evolved into k'ai-shu, a natural process of simplification took place with respect to the old fashioned chang ts'ao. This change took two forms. First, the development of the k'uang-ts'ao style ("unrestrained style") which was an extremely free form of writing in which no single character was separable in a given line. Naturally the style became increasingly difficult to identify. Second, there was the development of a modernized ts'ao-shu, from the ancient to a modern, current style. This style was called the "hsing-shu" or "running style".

With respect to the hsing-shu, the changes have come from the k'ai-shu directly and without regard to the traditional structure. Thus, the ku'ang-ts'ao is more difficult to identify than the chang-ts'ao but in contrast, the hsing-shu is more easily discerned than the chang ts'ao. Both of these styles are found in the reproductions of the stone-carvings; that is, the traced manuscripts of Wang Hsi-chih in various types of collections of ink-squeezed writings called "tieh" in Chinese or "chö" in Japanese. This does not mean to imply that these two styles were the creations of Wang Hsi-chih but that rather that his manuscripts had remained extant in contrast to the lost works of other scholars. This may have been largely due to the fact that Wang Hsi-chih's manuscripts were held in high esteem by T'ang T'ai-tsung and were gathered together from the various regions of his domain and preserved by inscribing them into stone. The new style employed by Wang was taken over by the public on a large scale and subsequently became the new and standard model of handwriting in the T'ang Dynasty; furthermore, it continued to exert influence in the ensuing periods.

Besides ts'ao-shu and hsing-shu, there exists another character of relatively simplified style called the "chien-tzu", that is, literally "simplified character". The "chien-tzu" may be related to the origination of the hsiao-chuan because hsiao-chuan simply means "simplified seal style". Moreover, in the stone inscriptions of found in Northern China, and in the scrolls of manuscripts from Tunhuang Coves as the Buddhist sutras and the fictional works many of these simplified characters are found. During the Sung Dynasty the wood block printing resulted in the publication of increased numbers of fictional works; which, in turn, saw an increased use of simplified characters. However, it is only in the past fifty years that scholars have considered this style with any esteem. Subsequently, it came to be adopted in China and in Japan. Regarding its practicality, however, some problems still remain.

These simplified characters may be the result of a process of adaptation of former, archaic, styles or may be entirely new creations. Adaptation is characterized by the following aspects: a) The adaptation of ancient characters.

b) The adaptation of non-classical common characters. c) Adaptations from the ts'ao-shu style.　d) Adaptations through borrowing characters from the classics. e) Adaptations through borrowing characters of common usage. The process of creating new characters--in contrast to adaptation--is marked by the following aspects: a) The creation of new characters with sound or phonetics as the basic consideration. b) The creation of new characters with meaning or ideography as the basic consideration. c) The creation of simplified characters by the deletion of certain strokes.

VI. An overview of Chinese Calligraphy

The Chinese character is drawn with the same implement as used in painting, the writing brush. Therefore, calligraphy has always been considered as a form of fine art, sharing equal status with the art of painting.

Art, however, is essentially based on the expression of an artist's individual character. For this reason, calligraphy as an art form was suited only to the styles of li-shu, k'ai-shu, and ts'ao-shu, and the styles coming before the Han Dynasty, the variant forms of the seal style, could not be considered as constituting fine art. For example, the seal forms were employed as decorative designs and were always in the same form, evidencing little of the writer's individual character. In this regard, they are similar to the letters of the Western alphabet, which have many different forms but are never considered to be works of art.

When the li-shu was in usage in the Han Dynasty, the control of the brush for the sake of artistic writing was quite difficult. This was the cause of the great variance that exists in the different manuscripts which were written by different calligraphists. Some scripts were written with elegance; others with awkwardness. This revealed that the same script could be written differently in accordance with the difference of the individual character of the calligraphist. This was the bases for the emergence of famed calligraphers.

From the latter half of the First Century B. C., the term "shih-shu" or "expert writing" appeared in the *han-shu*. However, inferring from statements contained in the biographies, the term "shih-shu" seems to refer not necessarily to writing as art but to mundane writing which happened to be elegantly executed. However, this concept underwent a gradual change. At the end of the Former Han, at the beginning of the First Century A. D., a leader of society named Ch'en Tsen had the reputation for great skill in brush writing. Those who received letters from Ch'en Tsen preserved them and regarded them as valuable possessions. This stemmed from two factors: first, the artistic elegance of the writing and second, the social status of the writer.

Toward the end of the Later Han Dynasty, in the first year of Kuang Ho (178 A.D.) the Emperor Ling-ti appointed those calligraphers who exhibited outstanding ability to the Imperial College of Hung-tu Gate. (Where the picture of Confucius and his disciples were painted to indicate the emperor's reverence.) Some of these students were to be promoted to the post of Governor. Consequently, the art of calligraphy enjoyed the favour of the emperor and as a result, this influenced the rapid improvement of this particular art in later years.

During this period the most famous of the calligraphers emerged. The period of Eastern Chin (317-420 A.D.) was considered the golden age of Chinese calligraphy with Wang Hsi-chih and his son Wng Hsien-chih as the preeminent figures. The writing of these two calligraphers were reproduced in stone inscriptions as "t'ieh" during the T'ang and Sung Dynasties and exerted a great influence on the calligraphers of following periods.

Wang Hsi-chih's influence on the art of writing in the T'ang gave birth to a new and revolutionary trend. Thus, two categories of k'ai-shu came into existence, the "pei' and the "t'ieh". The "pei" includes the stone inscriptions from the Ch'in Dynasty to the Sui Dynasty, particularly the so-called "pei-wei" or Northern Wei style. The "t'ieh" includes the reproductions from the writing art of the Three Kingdoms through Ch'in and down to the Ming and Ching works, including the stone inscriptions from the beginning of the T'ang Dynasty.

Due to official custom and the influence of the examination system, the method of writing belonging to the "t'ieh" category predominated. This category of writing was the standard form until recent times. However, ever since the Nineteenth Century the scholars, influenced by archaeological findings and studies, revived the writing style of the Northern Wei and began to employ it for their personal use. Still, for the most part, pragmatic writing, so to speak, involving official drafts, letters, books and so forth were in the "t'ieh" style.

"Shu-hua-t'ung-yüan" or literally translated "writing-art-identical-origin" is a well-known phrase among Chinese calligraphers and painters. The phrase points to the fact that many calligraphers painters and many of the painters were at the same time calligraphers. This is due to the fact that in Chinese painting pictures are drawn with lines and in calligraphy, characters are drawn with strokes. Both lines and strokes are executed in a similar manner and moreover, the instrument used, the brush, is also quite similar in its physical construction.

When the tip of the brush touches the paper, the calligrapher as well as the painter must control the brush with respect to its pressure and swiftness of stroke. Through pressure and stroke, the individual character of the calligrapher or artist is revealed. They manifest time, space, skill and inclination, and the different variations achieved the bases for the evaluation of a particular work of writing or painting, in terms of their artistic merit.

The principle of "shu-hua-t'ung-yüan" exerted marked influence on both writing and painting in several different areas. With respect to practical writing, scholars came to place great emphasis on writing as an art and thus, spent a great deal of time and energy on acquiring its proper technique. In time this high esteem for the art of calligraphy lead to its being included in the requirements of the "palace-examinations" for the scholars of the Imperial Academy. (These scholars constituted a pool of potential candidates for official positions within the court.) Furthermore, memorials form ministers and governors were required to be written with acceptable calligraphic skill. This development occurred mainly in the Ch'ing Dynasty.

With respect to painting, the artist limited himself to the use of the brush and water in drawing lines. This technique proved to be delimiting. There is no question that great paintings were produced in China, Japan, and Korea, but due to the definite limitations of both technique and implements, their works never manifested the wide diversity evident in Western art. However, within the confines of such limitations, numerous painters produced outstanding creations, often expressing their personal viewpoint with a single stroke of the brush.

B

I. A Discussion of the Six Categories of Chinese Characters

To express a complex idea, the picture-drawing is inadequate to serve as parts of speech in the grammatical construction of a sentence. By the time of the oracle bones, the Chinese character had advanced to the stage where it could be used in the composing of sentences. The characters were used, moreover, not only for the depiction of various figures but also for the representation of sound. Thus, the necessity of dividing the characters into different categories arose. Liu-shu or fully translated "the six categories of characters" was first mentioned in the *Chou-li*; however, the bases for it had been in existence for more than one thousand years.

According to available evidences, the *Chou-li* was compiled in the middle period of the Warring States. At that time, the Chinese character had already been fully developed. However, there is no detailed explanation of the liu-shu in that work. At the end of the First Century, in the Later Han Dynasty, Cheng Chung for the first time labeled the six categories of the liu-shu. Later in the *Han-shu* Pan Ku designated these same categories in the "Yi-wen Chih"; finally, Hsü Shen dwelled on them in detail in his *Shuo-wen Chieh-tsŭ*.

However, the arrangement of the six categories as determined by these three scholars show a variance. The differing order shows the development in the relationship among these categories and indicates which ones were of an earlier date and which ones were of a later period. Views regarding such problems became a topic for extended controversy among the scholars from the Sung to the Ch'ing.

The arrangements of the six categories by Cheng Chung, pan Ku, and Hsü Shen respectively are presented below:

Cheng Chung: Hsiang-hsing (pictograms)

Hui-Yi (logical combination)

Chuan chu (synonyms)

Ch'u-shih (symbolic indication)

Chia chieh (phonetic loan)

Hsieh-sheng (phonetic combination)

Pan Ku: Hsiang-hsing (pictograms)

Hsiang-shih (symbolic indication)

Hsiang-yi (logical combination)

Hsiang-sheng (phonetic combination)

Chuan chu (synonyms)

Chia-chieh (phonetic loan)

Hsü Shen: Chih-shih (symbolic indication)

Hsiang-hsing (pictograms)

Hsing-sheng (phonetic combination)

Hui-yi (logical combination)

Chuan chu (synonyms)

Chia-chieh (phonetic loan)

Most scholars of the Ch'ing Dynasty borrowed the terms employed by Hsü Shen but adopted the arrangement as fixed by Pan Ku. This was due to the fact that most scholars leaned toward the explanations presented in the *Shuo-wen* of Hsü Shen but did not agree with his judgment of "symbolic indication" (chih-shih) as being the primary category in the order of classification.

Logically the six categories of characters should not be considered to be of a like class. The four categories of hsiang-hsing, chih-shih, hui-yi, and hsing-sheng describe the nature of a character; whereas, the final two categories of chuan-chu and chia-chieh describe the relationship between characters. Therefore, Tai Ch'en and Tuan Yü-ts'ai considered the former four to be "substantive" and the latter two to be "functional" in nature. This is a scientific and revolutionary concept in the explanation of the liu-shu. However, numerous scholars in studying the *Shuo-wen* were not in agreement with this concept which departs from conventional views. These scholars continued to consider all of these categories to be of equal status or class with respect to the origins of the method of creating characters, as noted by the ancients.

More recently scholars have introduced new methods of classification in contrast to the liu-shu system. For example in his work *Ku Wen-tzŭ-hsüeh Tao-lun*, T'ang Lan sets forth the following arrangement:

1. Hsiang-hsing (pictogram)

2. Hsiang-yi (ideogram)

3. Hsiang-yü (word representation)

4. Hsiang-sheng (sound representation)

5. Hsing-sheng (form and sound)

On the other hand, T'ang Lan made the following outline to illustrate the categories in his system of classification:

1. Fen-hua (separation)

    a. From hsiang-hsing to hsiang-yi

    b. From one hsiang-yi to a second hsiang-yi

    c. From one hsing-sheng to a second hsing-sheng

2. Yin-shen (extension)

    a. From hsiang-hsing to hsiang-yü

    b. From hsiang-yi to hsiang-yü

    c. From one hsing-sheng to a second hsing-sheng

3. Chia-chieh (borrowing)

    a. From hsaing-hsing to hsiang-sheng

    b. From hsiang-yi to hsing-sheng

    c. From one hsing-sheng to a second hsing-sheng

4. Chuan-chu (here it means transferring,

    a. From hsiang-sheng to hsing-sheng

5. Kuei-na (induction)

    a. From hsiang-yi to hsing-sheng

6. Tseng-yi (increase)

    a. From hsiang-yü to hsing-sheng

With reference to the terminologies used by Tai Ch'en, "substantive" (t'i) and "functional" (yung), the first five belong to the class termed "substantive" and the sixth to the "functional". This classification is more complex and less practical than the old method of categorization and therefore, by virtue of their clarity and practicality, the present writer adheres to the systems of Tai and Tuan.

Relatively clear definitions as to the meaning of the six categories of the liu-shu have been set forth by Hsü-shen and a synopsis of these are presented below. It may be noted that the explanations regarding the chuan-chu category is the least satisfactory with respect to clarity of meaning.

1. Hsiang-hsing (pictogram) refers to the category of characters which are written in the manner of pictures, using curved lines to depict the form of various objects.

2. Chih-shih (symbolic indication) refers to the category of characters which depicts a certain position or meaning, which can be comprehended by viewing the symbolic arrangement of the character itself.

3. Hui-yi (logical combination) refers to the category of characters which combines two characters to form an entirely new character with a new meaning.

4. Hsing-sheng (phonetic combination) refers of the category of characters which combines characters of form and sound.

5. Chuan-chu (synonyms) refers to the category of characters which retains a certain element while altering the construction of other parts and creating words of similar meaning.

6. Chia-chieh (phonetic loan) refers to the category of characters which borrows other characters of like sound since it has no character of its own.

All the explanation rendered above are clear excepting that which concerns "chuan-chu", which is ambiguous. Tai Ch'en asserted that "synonyms" offered the clearest explanation for chuan-chu. The present writer feels that it is quite useless, for the purpose of furthering the understanding of ancient Chinese characters, to offer awkward explanations on the relation between combination of strokes or on the mutual influence of sound between characters.

The other problem relates to the category of "yin-shen" or "extension". Generally, the Ch'ing scholars considered this to be a sub-type of chia-chieh while others included it under the classification of chuan-chu. According to Tai Ch'en, the former view is the correct one, for the chuan-chu is limited to synonyms. However, this controversy is limited to the liu-shu classification system; without the added category of "yin-shen" (extension), this problem would not exist.

This problem stems form the definition of chuan-chu as stated by Hsü Shen. He writes: "To construct a type from a common beginning, with the same meaning being mutually accepted; like 'k'ao' and 'lao'; this is called chuan-chu."

Here, Hsü Shen's definition is unclear. First, what is mean by "type" and what is meant by "beginning". Both words possess diverse meanings. Second, his examples of "k'ao" and "lao" have the same meaning, a similar construction, similar sound and identical origin. Thus, on the bases of his definition and his example numerous variations become possible. If one should consider every one of the liu-shu to constitute an equally fundamental rule a satisfactory explanation cannot be achieved.

Aside from Tai Ch'en's definition of chuan-chu as a synonym, other scholars offered other explanations; they affirmed that chuan-chu refers to:

1. Same characters which had changed their forms. For example, "lao" has one part turned to the right while in the character "k'ao" the same part faces the left.

2. The relation between every character and the first character in a group. Thus, from the group the chuan-chu may be divided into many branches but attributed to the leading one.

3. Two or more characters under the same radical, (that is, from one beginning and with the same meaning.)

4. Two or more characters with the same meaning and with similar sound.

5. The third, fourth and fifth tones all with the same meaning as the first tone are called chuan-chu.

6. The extension of meaning in the same character; this is called Yin-shen.

The above explanations, including the explanation of Tai Ch'en, add up to seven different explanations. This diversity is a result of the original ambiguity in the definition and example put forth by Hsü Shen. Practically speaking, the first four categories alone are sufficient and the explanations of the chuan-chu are superfluous. Among all the explanations, only Tai Ch'en's is relatively clear and the present writer, for the sake of expediency, accepts his explanations as a working definition.

This does not mean that the explanations of chuan-chu in the area of sound is incorrect or that the comments on extension are useless; however, any explanation of sound is useless for the explanation of the construction of characters and any comments on extension strays far from the original definition and example as given by Hsü Shen. Tai Ch'en's explanations are to be appreciated for their simplicity.

According to Tai Chen, the category of extension cannot be related in any way to chuan-chu. It can, however, be classified as one of the two branches of chia-chieh or it may be either considered as an independent category outside of the liu-shu or as a sub-category of liu-shu.

Regardless, the liu-shu must be considered the standard and the fundamental system of classification; on the other hand, it must not be regarded as perfect and beyond any further emendation.

II. The Pictogram

Pictograms most likely developed and evolved from picture-drawings, which might have been very much like the pre-historic sketches found in caves or the pictures used for communication by the American Indians. On the Chinese continent there exists a type of picture-correspondence among the Moso people, the Tibeto-Burmese speaking tribes living on the Northern borders of Yünnan Province. It is somewhat akin to the pictures of the American Indians but the picture-drawings of the Moso have been improved upon so that every unit of a picture has been assigned a particular meaning and is drawn in a fixed manner. A series of pictures cannot express a given sentence since it can be interpreted in different ways. The later development of the Moso pictures tended toward the possibility of sentence construction. Words, besides picture-nouns, were used as loan words from nouns with the same sound. The combination of pictograms and loan words made the construction of sentences possible. This is the process through which a written language begins to come into being.

Compared with the Moso pictograms, the development of the Chinese script indicates a high degree of specialization. The former moved from picture to sound but in the latter case, the development was from picture to both sound and meaning. Thus, the Chinese character developed in an increasingly complex manner. Even though the number of phonogram-combinations among Chinese characters is great, Chinese characters cannot be considered in a simple phonetic way.

This is the reason for the complexity with respect to the categorization of Chinese characters, which were classified into six categories or into four categories with two sub-categories. This caused a wide divergence between the written Chinese and the spoken language; that is, the formation of a way of expression independent of the spoken language and of the times. The Chinese character is in this sense a symbol which expresses meaning and is not an expression of the spoken language.

For these reasons, compositions in Chinese characters have retained a similar style for thousands of years; that is, the style prevalent in the Spring and Autumn and the Warring States periods are still used among some scholars of the present time. Moreover, it has spread widely into all areas of China despite the existence of differing dialects or into other cultures which do not speak Chinese at all.

This characteristic of unchanging continuity over a long period of time and of spreading into a vast area, marked by different cultures, reveal a special characteristic in comparison with other written languages. On the other hand, the symbolic nature of the Chinese character, especially in the wen-yen style, resulted in a simplicity of language which did not render itself easily to analytical expression and therefore to ideological development. Naturally, mathematical and philosophical statements can be translated into the wen-yen style, but the resulting translation is always rough and difficult to comprehend. Should one translate freely, the translated version would be far from precise. Moreover, the Chinese characters are definitely limited in regard to certain syllables. This prevents the Chinese language from functioning effectively in the field of science; most particularly in the fields of biology, chemistry, an medicine. In recent times, in concurrence with the Literary Revolution and the use of the "pai hua", the wen-yen style was adopted and adapted for use in scientific writing.

However, the problem of terminology remains a hindrance to scientific progress among Chinese scholars. A set of standard scientific terms have been created by the Chinese government but they are quite in-adequate and are useful n the compilation of simple materials only: high school text books, simple scientific reports, etc.

The only alternative open to Chinese scholars in the field of science is to either write in a foreign language or to write in the "pai-hua" style, interspersing Latinized terms and other borrowed word. This would be considered as falling in the category of "chia-chieh" as far as the traditional liu-shu classification is concerned.

However this may be, in other fields, the Chinese character has been used with great creativity and meaning. It has prevailed for millennia and has attracted countless number of creative artists and thinkers to it as a means to compose delicate sentences of wit and of philosophical meaning. From ancient times the Chinese character has been used to express profound and significant ideas with only a few syllables in extremely simple constructions. Although even now the wen-yen style is quite inadequate for scientific expression it holds great promise and potential in the field of literary expression.

The origins of the Chinese character, as mentioned previously, can be sought in the pictogram. Furthermore, these pictograms can be divided into different groupings: a) natural objects, b) animals and insects, c) plants, d) the human body, e) manufactured objects.

Some of the objects, for example, included under these headings are as follows:

a. Natural Objects

the sun	日	日
the moon	月	月
the rain	雨	雨
the snow	雪	雪

b. Animals and Insects Etc.

fish	魚	魚
swallow	燕	燕
scorpion	萬	萬 (a loan word for "ten-thousand")

c. Plants

wood	木	木
grass	草	草

d. Human Body

man	人	人
child	子	子

e. Manufactured Objects

clothing	衣	衣
vehicle	車	車
tripod	鼎	鼎
door	門	門

Further illustrative comments on the following:

b) Animals and Insects Etc.

Animals such as ____ (hsiang; elephant) in oracle bone; ____ in small seal; 象 in conventional style. ____ (ma; horse) in oracle bone; ____ in small seal; 馬 in conventional style. ____ (pao; leopard) in oracle bone; ____ in small seal; 豹 in conventional style.

Birds such as ____ (niao; bird) in oracle bone; ____ in small seal; 鳥 in conventional style. ____ (yen; swallow) in oracle bone; ____ in small seal; 燕 in conventional style.

Fish such as ____ (yu; fish) in oracle bone; ____ in small seal; 魚 in conventional style.

Snake (sheh) ____ in oracle bone; ____ in small seal; 蛇 in conventional style.

Wan ____ (man meaning originally "scorpion") in oracle bone; ____ in small seal; 萬 in conventional style, as a loan word for "wan" meaning "ten thousand".

Legendary creatures such as ____ (feng; phoenix) in oracle bone; ____ in small seal; 鳳 in conventional style. Possesses an extended meaning "wind" because the ancients believed that the phoenix was the largest bird to fly in the wind. (In later Chinese called p'eng 鵬). ____ (lung; dragon) in oracle bone; ____ in small seal; 龍 in conventional style. ____ (hung; rainbow) in oracle bone; ____ in small seal; 虹 in conventional style. This character for rainbow depicts a two-headed dragon fround on carved jades and from the bas-reliefs of the Han Dynasty.

c) Plants

____ (mai; barley) in oracle bone; ____ in small seal; 麥 in conventional style. ____ (sang; mulberry tree) in oracle bone; ____ in small seal; 桑 in conventional style. ____ (mu; tree or wood) in oracle bone; ____ in small seal; 木 in conventional style. ____ (ts'ao; grass) in oracle bone; ____ in small seal; 草 in conventional style.

d) Human Body

_人_ (jen; man) in oracle bone; _ㇵ_ in small seal; _人_ in conventional style. _妻_ (nü; woman dressed in ancient mode) in oracle bone; _ㇻ_ in small seal; _女_ in conventional style. _手_ (shou; hand) in bronze inscriptions; _ㇷ_ in small seal; _手_ in conventional style. _齒_ (chih; teeth) in oracle bone; _齒_ in small seal; _齒_ in conventional style.

e) Manufactured Objects

Shelters: _郭_ (kuo; suburbs) in oracle bone; _郭_ in small seal; _郭_ in conventional style. _門_ (men; door) in oracle bone; _門_ in small seal; _門_ in conventional style. _户_ (hu; a single door) in oracle bone; _户_ in small seal; _户_ in conventional style.

Means of Transport: _車_ (chu; vehicle) in oracle bone; _車_ in small seal; _車_ in conventional style. _舟_ (chou; boat) in oracle bone; _舟_ in small seal; _舟_ in conventional style.

Vessels: _爵_ (chüeh; goblet) in oracle bone; _爵_ in small seal; _爵_ in conventional style. _鼎_ (ting; tripod) in oracle bone; _鼎_ in small seal; _鼎_ in conventional style.

In the examples set forth above every character forms a single pictogram which in turn represents a single object. However, besides the single pictogram, there are other pictograms which are formed through combination, thus forming another separate category of pictograms.

Among the pictograms formed by means of combining other pictograms, there are two classifications. First, those characters which are composed of two or more parts of which one part represents the main idea of the character while the other part(s) enlarges upon that idea or meaning. Second, those pictograms which have undergone slight alterations in some form or another in order to express a change in meaning. Chinese scholars have termed the former category "combined pictogram" and the latter, "altered pictogram".

Regarding the "combined pictogram" the examples below may provide some indications as to its nature.

_果_ (kuo; fruit) in small seal; _果_ in conventional style. This pictogram combines two parts; ⊕ represents the picture of a fruit and 米 is the character for "mu" or tree. The combination is intended to show fruit on a tree. However, in the oracle bone style, it is written 米 which is a single pictogram and not a combination.

米 (mi; ground millet or rice) in small seal; 米 in conventional style. Former scholars determined this to be a combination of pictograms. However, according to the oracle bones, it is drawn 米 ; in which the points represent the grains and the line is not a character; therefore, this is a single, uncombined pictogram.

巢 (ts'ao; nest) was first found only in this small seal style; 巢 in conventional style. This pictogram consists of three different parts; 巛 depicts a bird; 臼 depicts the parts of a nest; 木 depicts the tree in which the nest is to be found. This character therefore must be classified as logical combination and not a pictogram.

彗 (hui; broom). In oracle bone 彗 or 彗 showing the broom and the dust or hand. 彗 in conventional style. Therefore, this must be considered as an ideogram and not a pictogram.

眉 (mei; eyebrow) in small seal. In oracle bone it is drawn 眉 or 眉 showing the eye with eyebrows. 眉 in conventional style. This is also an ideogram and not a pictogram.

The class labeled "altered pictogram" is illustrated below:

矢 (chieh) in small seal and 矢 in oracle bone depicts the slanting of a head. 矢 or 側 in conventional style. This is also an ideogram and not a pictogram.

屮 (kuai) in small seal; 乖 in conventional style. This represents the horns of a goat and therefore, is a pictogram.

未 (wei; taste) 未 in conventional style. This is the same as 味 . In conventional style 味 and 味 in oracle bone style. It indicates a relation to wood, such as the spices that come from wood. Hence it is an ideogram and not a pictogram.

The systematic classification of Chinese characters, above all, requires a methodology that is scientific and simple. Complex, ambiguous categorizations can serve no useful purpose. The present writer therefore prefers to consider only the single, uncombined pictogram to be classified as a pictogram and suggests that other pictograms, made up of any manner of combinations be placed in other, different categories.

III. Ideogram

Ideograms or "chih-shih" refers to those characters that represent a thing or an idea and is a further development and modification of the pictogram. Ideograms are more complex than pictograms; not so much in the case of basic ideograms which may be comparatively simple but in the case of ideograms made up of different combinations. These combinations may consist of a sign combined with a sign, a pictogram combined with a sign, a specially constructed picture combined with a sign or a pictogram which may have one element within itself altered.

The basic or primary ideograms are based on very simple signs. The simplest illustration of this is the series of characters used to represent numbers.

一 一 represents one.

二 二 represents two.

三 三 represents three.

亖 四 represents four.

㐅 五 represents five, depicted by two lines forming an "X".

∩ 六 represents six, depicting a forked branch with two strings.

十 七 represents seven, depicting a long string with a short stick.

)(八 represents eight and depicts two curved lines, back to back.

九 九 represents nine and depicts a string with a hook.

丨 十 represents ten and depicts a string with a knot.

百 百 represents one hundred and depicts two circles held under a string.

　　千　represents one thousand and depicts a figure of a puppet on a string.

It can be assumed that the above series originated from an identical series of signs. Moreover, these signs have been attributed to the knotted ropes which Hsü Shen has pointed to as being the origins of written characters. However, Hsü Shen did not specifically state that these numeral characters were derived from the knotted ropes.

The reason for this reluctance can be trace perhaps to the fact that the Han scholars were always deeply influenced by the philosophy of "yin" and "yang" and the "five elements" and therefore, had a natural inclination to explain things in these terms, especially in order to provide a respectable scholastic bases. To explain matters by tracing the origins of characters to knotted ropes was overly simple for these scholars. In these ancient times research and conclusions based on ethnology etc. were not considered scholastically respectable.

In the section below the highly philosophical or metaphysical explanations of Hsü Shen are given and illustrates the approach of the Han scholars in general.

　一　"One" traces its origin to the tao, the great beginning: the "tao" was based on the One, which in turn created, through separation, heaven and earth and transformed itself into all manifestation.

　二　"Two"; two is the number of the earth because it makes a pair with heaven.

　三　"Three" three is the way of heaven, earth and man.

　四　"Four"; four is a "yin" number and shows a square being divided.

　五　"Five"; five refers to the five elements, with two lines intersecting, depicting the involvement of yin and yang within heaven and earth.

　六　"Six"; from the number six in the "Book of Changes". Yin is transformed into the number six; its original form is eight. Therefore six is a combination of ⌒ (to enter) and ＞＜ (eight).

　七　"Seven"; seven points to the correct position of yang which is shown by a horizontal line and a curved line which shows the light yin.

⊃⊂   "Eight" eight shows two lines curving in opposite directions.

ㄐ乙   "Nine"; nine is a variation of yang, revealing a curved form.

In the above, Hsü Shen showed each character to be related to and derived from the "Yin-yang" philosophy. However, this philosophy must have been the product of a civilization much more advanced than what is generally labeled the "primitive world". As far as the oracle bones are concerned, they provide no indication whatsoever that there existed any relationship between these characters and the philosophy of "Yin-yang". The seminal principles of this theory might have originated as early as the Yin-Shang; however, its systematization was achieved in the *Book of Changes* of the early Chou Dynasty. There is no doubt that characters which symbolize numerical figures are apt to be used simply for practical purposes without any necessary connection to metaphysical thought such as the "Yin-yang". From this standpoint the explanations of Hsü Shen must be considered as being of little value in the study of the origins of this category of characters.

Aside from the characters symbolizing numbers, there are other ideograms of simple form; for example:

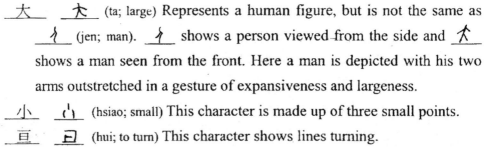

大   大 (ta; large) Represents a human figure, but is not the same as 彳 (jen; man). 彳 shows a person viewed from the side and 大 shows a man seen from the front. Here a man is depicted with his two arms outstretched in a gesture of expansiveness and largeness.

小   ⺌ (hsiao; small) This character is made up of three small points.

亘   曰 (hui; to turn) This character shows lines turning.

亇 (ch'ang, as 長 in conventional style; means "long") depicts a person with long hair.

入   入 (ju, 入 in conventional style; means "to enter") This character shows or points toward the direction of an entrance.

Moreover, there are ideograms that are constructed of two main parts: a line or in some cases, another symbol as the basic part and a second symbol which indicates the main meaning by its relation to the basic part.

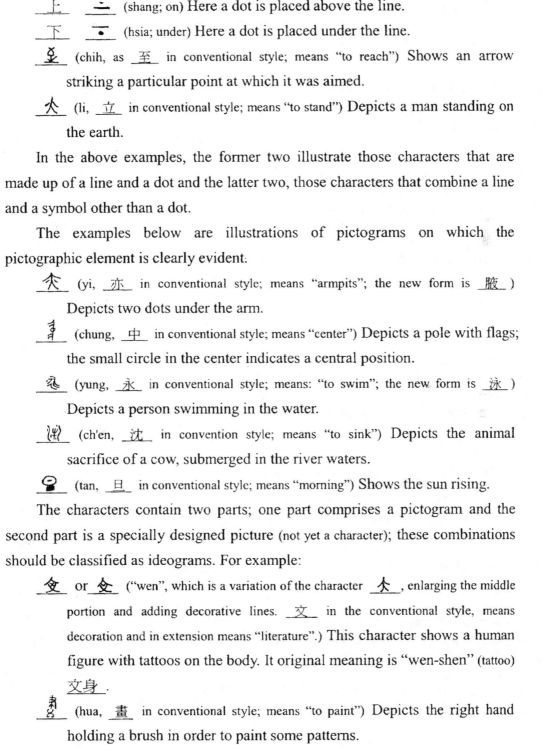

上　⸺　(shang; on) Here a dot is placed above the line.

下　⸺　(hsia; under) Here a dot is placed under the line.

(chih, as 至 in conventional style; means "to reach") Shows an arrow striking a particular point at which it was aimed.

(li, 立 in conventional style; means "to stand") Depicts a man standing on the earth.

In the above examples, the former two illustrate those characters that are made up of a line and a dot and the latter two, those characters that combine a line and a symbol other than a dot.

The examples below are illustrations of pictograms on which the pictographic element is clearly evident.

(yi, 亦 in conventional style; means "armpits"; the new form is 腋) Depicts two dots under the arm.

(chung, 中 in conventional style; means "center") Depicts a pole with flags; the small circle in the center indicates a central position.

(yung, 永 in conventional style; means: "to swim"; the new form is 泳) Depicts a person swimming in the water.

(ch'en, 沈 in convention style; means "to sink") Depicts the animal sacrifice of a cow, submerged in the river waters.

(tan, 旦 in conventional style; means "morning") Shows the sun rising.

The characters contain two parts; one part comprises a pictogram and the second part is a specially designed picture (not yet a character); these combinations should be classified as ideograms. For example:

or ("wen", which is a variation of the character , enlarging the middle portion and adding decorative lines. 文 in the conventional style, means decoration and in extension means "literature".) This character shows a human figure with tattoos on the body. It original meaning is "wen-shen" (tattoo) 文身 .

(hua, 畫 in conventional style; means "to paint") Depicts the right hand holding a brush in order to paint some patterns.

尹 (yin, 尹 in conventional style; means "secretary".)

史 (shih, 𢼸 and 𤓰 in small seal style; 史 and 事 in conventional style; because these two characters were identical in ancient times.) This character means "service" especially with respect to some divine being. It shows a drill consisting of a bow or string with a special top being held by hand. (This type of bow-drill is still in use in China and was used among American Indian tribes.) Drilling holes into bones or shells was a method of causing cracks through heating; these cracks were later read for divine omens. The oracles were gradually transformed into historians and the character "shih" took on the meaning "history".

宮 (kung, 宮 in conventional style; means "palace") Shows the roof covering the palace sites.

正 (cheng, 正 in small seal style and 正 in conventional style; means "correct" or "regular") Shows a foot placed behind a square as a standard.

方 (fang, 方 in conventional style; means "square" but its original meaning might have been "side") Shows a plow with two sides which could be grasped by two men. The ancient Chinese plough was guided by two men on either side.

IV. The Changes in the Pictogram

There are some pictogram characters which have been transformed into ideograms through the changing of one part of the character or of one or more strokes within the character. This modification converts a pictogram into an ideogram, as illustrated in the examples provided below.

夨 (tsê, 矢 in conventional style) This character is derived from "ta" (大) and shows a person slanting his head.

烏 (wu, in small seal and 烏 in conventional style; means "crow") Depicts the crow as being totally black, obscuring even the eyes.

交 (chiao, 交 in conventional style; means "mutual") Shows a person with crossed legs. (This is under a traditional explanation showing incorrect new explanation based on the analysis of bones and bronzes says wu 武 showing a man on march with weapon and hsin 信 to be a phonetic combination.)

V. Logical Combinations

Logical Combinations may be considered a complex ideogram. The ideogram is a variation of a simple picture or pictogram with added symbols, modifications, or changes. The logical combination, on the other hand, is a combination of two or more given characters, often joined together with the addition of certain modifications.

The original Chinese term for "logical combination" is "hui-yi". ("hui" means "to meet, assemble, come together"; "yi" means "meaning".) In the definition given in the *Shuo-wen* it is stated that the "hui-yi" is a category of characters which combine characters from similar categories to indicate a new meaning, as "wu" 武 (brave) and "hsin" 信 (sincerity).

The character "wu" is comprised of two characters "chih" 止 and "ko" 戈 . "Chih" means "to stop" and "ko" means "weapon". This particular combination means "to stop the use of weapons for the sake of peace; this is the way of bravery". With respect to the character "hsin", two characters "jen" 人 and "yen" 言 are brought together in juxtaposition. A combination of "jen" (man) and "yen" (word) expresses the idea that a man must keep his promise or word and that this is the way of sincerity.

Hsü Shen divided characters into two categories: "wen" 文 and "tsŭ" 字 . "Wen" refers to simple symbols or figures and "tsŭ" refers to compounds. According to this classification, the two primary categories of pictogram and ideogram are to be classified as simple symbols and the later two categories of logical compound and phonetic compound are to be classified as compounds. Such categories as synonyms and phonetic loans, which are not original in the creation of characters, may be placed under either category, single or compound, in the structure of the strokes and characters.

Any logical compound must be made up of two or more original characters.

These original characters, which form the basic parts of the logical compound, may be both pictogram or both ideogram; or they may be made up of one or more pictograms and one or more ideograms. Moreover, other elements such as a diagram, a symbol, or a picture-like drawing may be included within these characters.

Therefore, the characters of the logical combination category may be formed according to several different arrangements. These possible arrangements are as follows:

1. The meaning being indicated from the order of the arrangement, from top to bottom, from left to right.

2. The character of the combination being of equal importance.

3. One character in the combination indicating the main meaning while the others serve in a subordinate role.

4. The same character being used twice in order to express the original meaning, extending the original meaning, or changing the original meaning.

5. A logical combination containing a picture-like drawing or symbol.

Naturally the number of phonetic combinations is greater than that of logical combinations. However, during the process of phonetic changes which took place over a period of thousands of years, most of the phonetic combinations altered their original pronunciation from that of the phonetic symbols. Some have considered phonetic symbols to be phonetic combinations and to explain them in terms of their meaning; that is, to consider them to be logical combinations.

Here is a well-known story concerning the great reformer and prime minister, Wang An-shin (1021-1086) of the Sung Dynasty. Su Tung-p'o, hearing that Wang An-shih, the Duke of Ching, had finished his book of terminology (*Tsŭ-shuo*), went to jest with him. He said, "you suggest that the character "tu" 篤 (sincerity) means to 'whip a horse'; I wonder what is humorous about whipping a dog?" (Because the parts that make up the character "hsiao" 笑 [laugh] have the meanings "bamboo" and "dog".) At another occasion, he showed the character for his name

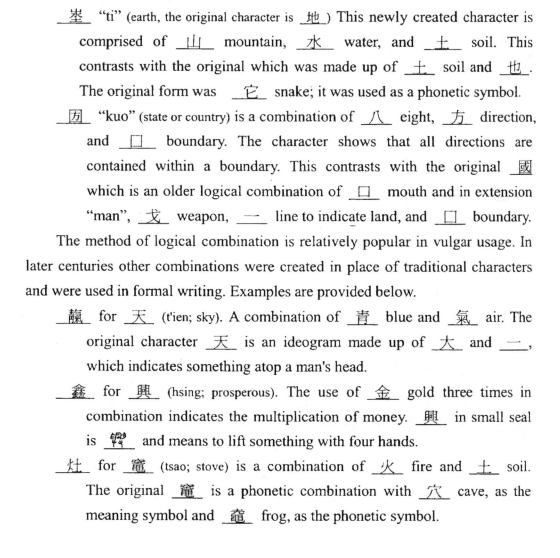

"p'o" 坡 and asked Wang its meanings. Wang replied that it meant "the skin of the earth". ("p'o" means "slope") Thereupon Su retorted, "Then 'hua' 滑 (smooth) must mean 'the bone of the water'!" While both 坡 and 滑 are just phonetic combinations, without any logical arrangement under each of them.

The major official change of other character categories into the category of logical combination concerned the new characters that were ordered by the Empress Wu Tse-t'ien (Reign: 684-704 A.D.) in 690 A.D. These seventeen newly created characters were in use for twenty years in place of the older characters. In the following are examples of these new characters.

坔 "ti" (earth, the original character is 地) This newly created character is comprised of 山 mountain, 水 water, and 土 soil. This contrasts with the original which was made up of 土 soil and 也. The original form was 它 snake; it was used as a phonetic symbol.

囷 "kuo" (state or country) is a combination of 八 eight, 方 direction, and 囗 boundary. The character shows that all directions are contained within a boundary. This contrasts with the original 國 which is an older logical combination of 口 mouth and in extension "man", 戈 weapon, 一 line to indicate land, and 囗 boundary.

The method of logical combination is relatively popular in vulgar usage. In later centuries other combinations were created in place of traditional characters and were used in formal writing. Examples are provided below.

靝 for 天 (t'ien; sky). A combination of 青 blue and 氣 air. The original character 天 is an ideogram made up of 大 and 一, which indicates something atop a man's head.

鑫 for 興 (hsing; prosperous). The use of 金 gold three times in combination indicates the multiplication of money. 興 in small seal is 𦥔 and means to lift something with four hands.

灶 for 竈 (tsao; stove) is a combination of 火 fire and 土 soil. The original 竈 is a phonetic combination with 穴 cave, as the meaning symbol and 黽 frog, as the phonetic symbol.

To see forth other examples of logical combinations, four different types are given below. In each case the character is listed first in conventional style (hereafter, abbreviated as "c. s.").

c. s. 為 [glyph] "wei" In oracle bones it means "to do". A combination of [glyph] (yu; hand) and [glyph] (hsiang: elephant), meaning to "to tame the elephant; to do".

明 [glyph] "ming" bright. (c. s. 明) Combination of [glyph] (kuang; window) and [glyph] (yueh; moon). In the oracle bones, it is written either as [glyph], showing the moon on the window or [glyph] which is a combination of the sun and the moon to show light or brightness.

Secondly, there are characters which are comprised of two parts, of which one part is a single character and the other part is comprised of one character being used two times and at times, up to four times.

受 [glyph] shou; to receive. Shows the hands of different persons delivering a boat which is omitted. In the oracle bones and bronzes, it appears in a more complex form, with the boat represented as [glyph], showing two hands holding onto a boat. [glyph] chou (c. s. 舟) means boat and [glyph] is a variation of [glyph] yu (c. s. 又 and 右) which means hand.

雀 [glyph] chui; short-tailed bird. [glyph] chi, in small seal, meaning "gathering", but it in bones and bronzes are more simple with one bird only. This is a combination of "mu" (木 wood) with three birds perched atop it.

野 [glyph] "ye", in the oracle bones and [glyph] in the bronzes. In the small seal [glyph] and in c. s. 野. A combination of 土 tu; soil and two trees 木 "mu" and depicts a piece of land among trees. In the small seal it is a combination of 田 t'ien, field; 土 tu, soil; and a variation of 邑 yi, village or town.

莫 [glyph] mo. In small seal [glyph]; in c. s. 莫, changed to 暮. A combination of 日 jih; sun and four [glyph] ts'ao or two [glyph] ts'ao and indicates that the sun sets under the grasses.

Thirdly, there are characters which are formed by using the same character twice and thereby, changing its meaning.

珏 玨 chio, in samll seal; 羊 in oracle bone; means "strings of jade". ("yü" 羊 in bones; 王 in small seal; 玉 in c. s.)

友 ⺕ yu, in small seal; and similarity in oracle bone; � in bronze. A combination of two hands (yu, 又 ⺕). The depiction of hand and hand indicates "friendship".

林 林 lin, in oracle bones; and 林 in small seal. A combination of two trees (mu, 木 木) indicates "forest".

劦 劦 hsieh, in small seal; as 力力 in bronze. The c. s. has been changed to 協 . The character means to co-operate. It shows a combination of three 力 li; strength which depicts the form of human muscles.

麤 鹿鹿 chu, showing two deer in oracle bones; and three deer in small seal. The c. s. was converted to 粗 . The original meaning was to leap a great distance and later, was changed to mean "rough". It combines two and later, three deer.

Fourthly, there are those characters which combine more than two characters to express a relatively complex meaning.

福 福 fu; happiness; from the oracle bones. It shows 干 shih; "table for a temple" (示 in c. s.) and 尊 tsun. In c. s. 尊 ; a combination of 酉 (c. s. 酉 yu) and two hands. "Yu" indicates "wine" and "tsun" depicts a large cup of wine for the spirits. The implication is that happiness will be bestowed by the spirits. In small seal and c. s. they have been changed to 福 and 福 respectively.

衞 衛 or 衛 wei, in the bones, and 衞 in the bronzes. A combination of 行 hsing; to show going four ways and 方 (or 方) fang; square, with two or more feet to show guards defending an area. The simplified form, a square 口 and two feet, written 韋 is also used as a loan word meaning leather.

The Transition form Ideograms to Logical Combinations

In its explanation regarding characters presented in the *Shuo-wen* the proportion of characters of the logical combination category was relatively large although much less than those of the phonetic combination category. However, upon tracing the development of those logical combinations backward through the bronzes back to the bones, it became apparent that these logical combinations were not in fact combinations but were rather single ideograms. This fact reveals that the characters of the logical combination category was a later development stemming from the ideograms and moreover, that these ideograms were modifications and derivations of the original pictograms.

Here are several examples to illustrate this development, from the bones through the bronzes and up to the stage of the small seal style.

　　祭 chi; to sacrifice. In c. s. 祭 .The *Shuo-wen* stated that this character is a combination of 示 shih; sacrificial table; 右 yu; hand; and 肉 jou; meat. The meaning is indicated by a hand which takes a piece of meat to the sacrificial table. This is clearly a logical combination. In the bronzes, it is similar to the small seal. However, in the bones it is written 祭 , 祭 ; or 祭 with many variations and always in an abbreviated form. Inside the character, the dots showing the drops of wine are always emphasized. These dots are symbols and not characters, just as the symbol for the piece of meat is also not a character. Therefore, this character is not a logical combination but an ideogram.

　　祝 chu; a priest who specializes in prayer. In c. s. 祝 . In the *Shuo-wen* it shows a man 人 jen, with a mouth (口 kou) on the top, placed besides a sacrificial table, 示 shih. The mouth points to someone who speaks. In the oracle bones, however, the character appeared as 祝 , showing a sorcerer offering wine or as 祝 which showed a sorcerer with a large mouth near a table and as 祝 , depicting a sorcerer with a large mouth in the act of dancing.

chieh; intermediary or armor. In c. s. 介 . The *Shuo-wen* shows a combination of 人 jen; man; and 八 pa; eight or to divide. The character indicates that all men are in a state of separation of alienation and require an intermediary. However, in the oracle bones, it is written . As Shang Cheng-tso stated, quoting Lo Chen-yü, the character shows a man wearing armour, the long stripe showing the leather straps.

chou; secret, density, circle, name of a state. In c. s. 周 . The *Shuo-wen* states that this is a combination of 甩 yung; to use and 口 kou; mouth; and depicts a person skillful with his mouth; that is, skilled in the art of speaking. However, the formation of this character is different in the bones and bronzes. There, the character did not include "yung" in the combination. In the bronzes it was written 嚳 or 囲 and in the bones 囲 , indicating a land with dense crops.

she; to wade. In c. s. 涉 . In the *Shuo-wen* 步 is shown and depicting two feet which means to walk. 水 shui; water or river. In the oracle bones, however, it was always written , which shows two feet with a line in the middle to indicate river. This line is not a character but a symbol.

shi; year of Jupiter. In c. s. 歲 . In the *Shuo-wen* it was classified as a phonetic combination, with 步 pu as the meaning and 戌 hsu; a number symbol for time. But in the commentary of Tuan Yü-ts'ai it is also classified as a logical combination. In the opinion of the *Shuo-wen* "sui" should be considered to mean Jupiter. Since the orbit of Jupiter takes twelve years, starting from the point NNE. The twelve year cycle is a fixed cycle in ancient Chinese methods of calculating time.

However, in the oracle bones, the character for "sui" is written 戌 to depict a weapon which may be a sickle with two points. These two points may be based on two possibilities. First, they may be depictions of the footprints after the harvesting of crops or second, they may point to the two holes in the stone knives which were used for cutting the crops. The harvest was an annual event and therefore, one reaping or cutting meant one year.

　　茻　tsou; to run. in c. s. 走 . In the *Shuo-wen* it is explained as being a combination of "yao" 夭 which means "to bend" and "chih" 止 which means "to on foot". It appears in similiar from in the bronzes. There does exist a question in that "yao" is depicted with two arms down while the top part of the character for "tsou" is drawn with one arm up. This character simply did not exist in the small seal. It appeared in the oracle bones only. While the character 走 did not exist in the bones. Therefore, this character 夭 is used only for the character "tsou" in the bones and it is an ideogram.

　　益　Yi; to increase or overflow. In c. s. 溢 . The original form 益 used to mean "benefit". In the *Shuo-wen*, it is shown as being a combination of 水 shui; water and 皿 min; basin. But in the oracle bones it is written 益 , showing the water filling the basin.

　　阱　ching; trap. In c. s. 阱 . The *Shuo-wen* explains this as being a combination of 阜 fu; a mount and 井 ching; well. It depicts a well on some mountain for the purposes of trapping animals. In the oracle bones, it is written 阱 , showing a deer caught in a trap.

　　射　sheh; to shoot (an arrow). In c. s. 射 . The *Shuo-wen* explains it as being a combination of 身 shen; body or person and 寸 shih; arrow, placing it in the category of logical combination. However, in the bones it is drawn simply 射 and in the bronzes 射 , to show the action of the bow in the act of shooting. These original characters changed to form the character "shen."

　　望　wang; to look or the full moon. In c. s. 望 . The *Shuo-wen* explains this as being a combination of 臣 chen; subjects, 月 yüeh; moon, 壬 jen, which is a simplified sound for 庭 meaning court, a combination which means to go to court under a full moon. However, in the bones, it is 望 which shows a man with his eye emphasized and in looking; in the bronzes, it is 卂 a man standing on earth and gazing at the moon.

恆 heng; constant. In c. s. 恆 . The *Shuo-wen* explains that this is a combination of 二 erh; two, 心 hsin; heart and 舟 chou; boat. The implication is that the heart of the ruler and the hearts of his subjects are constantly in oneness as is the direction of a boat. On the other hand, Hsü-shen states that the ancient character of "heng" was comprised of "yüeh" (moon), implying that the moon is full and then wanes with unwavering constancy. In the bones, "heng" is written 𠄎 to depict the moon.

旬 hsün; a cycle of ten days. In c. s. 旬 . The *Shuo-wen* explains that it is composed of 包 pao; to wrap or include and 日 jih; sun. This combination shows the days being encircled. However, in the bones it appears like this 𠃊 or 𠃑 and shows only the encircling lines.

A study of the above variations show that the development of the ancient character proceeded from the original ideograms to the later logical combinations. Similarly, there was an evolution from the pictogram and ideogram toward phonetic combinations. This latter change will be dealt with in the following chapter on phonetic combinations.

勞榦教授著作目錄

任長正　編輯

前　言

　　勞榦（貞一）教授，湖南長沙人。生於 1907 年 1 月 13 日。中央研究院院士。曾任台灣大學教授，美國洛杉磯加利佛尼亞大學教授。勞先生是海內外知名的秦漢史魏晉南北朝史權威，文學家及教育家。學問淵博，著作等身。這個目錄就是爲慶祝他九十華誕而編輯的。目錄共收集三百三十八項，計專書 19 本，論文 196 篇，雜文等 123 篇。內容分五大類。爲 (1) 專書，(2) 論文，(3) 雜文，(4) 書評及序跋，(5) 英文日文韓文著作。這個目錄較十年前爲貞一師八秩榮慶所編輯的增加了許多，尤其在分類排列方面改良了不少。目錄仍以出版年代的先後次序排列。時值圖書資訊網路系統 (Internet) 發達的今日，線上書目 (Online Bibliography) 的儲備，線上檢索 (Online Search) 的諮詢，以及全文影像光碟 CD-ROM 的儲存，具有著驚人的進展與成果。這對中外學者在尋找資料及運用操作方面，既迅速又完整。而吾師的輝煌著作，更將繼續流傳廣遠及雋永。

（一）專著

1.《曬藍本漢簡釋文》，手稿 (1936 年)。[1]

2.《居延漢簡考釋》(譯文)，《中央研究院歷史語言研究所專刊》之 21(台北：1943 年)。[2]

1　《曬藍本漢簡釋文》是勞榦教授在 1934-1936 年與余遜先生合作研究的成果。當時是將釋文手抄在西北科學團稿紙上，然後予以曬藍而成。共計 304 頁，3055 簡，分別為卷上卷下。原係勞先生保存，後捐給中央研究院歷史語言研究所傅斯年紀念圖書館，是一孤本，也就是現今所稱的「曬藍本」。

2　《居延漢簡》在李莊的手寫本，原分為釋文及考證兩部分，釋文 4 冊，考釋 2 冊。到南京後，又重新整理釋文 (未附考證) 交上海商務印書館出版，這是第二次印本。到台灣後，在台北共印兩種，一為居延漢簡圖版之部 (此項圖版以前未印)，一為居延漢簡考釋之部，附考證在內。圖版之部 1957 年初版，1977 年再版。考釋之部附考證，

3.《居延漢簡考釋》(考證)，《中央研究院歷史語言研究所專刊》之 21(台北：1944 年)。

4.《居延漢簡考釋》，附《敦煌漢簡》校文、《居延漢簡》考釋簡號索引 (上海商務印書館，1949 年)。

5.《秦漢史》(現代國民基本知識叢書第一輯)(台北：中華文化出版事業委員會，1952 年)。[3]

6.《魏晉南北朝史》(現代國民基本知識叢書第二輯)(台北：中華文化出版事業委員會，1954 年)。[4]

7.《初中歷史》(台北：臺灣省政府教育廳，1955 年)。[5]

8.《中國史綱》(台北：勝利出版社，1955 年)。

9.《居延漢簡》(圖版之部)，《中央研究院歷史語言研究所專刊》之 21(台北：1957 年初版，1977 年再版)。

10.《敦煌藝術》(歷史文物叢刊第一輯)(台北：中華叢書委員會，1958 年)。[6]

11.《居延漢簡》(考釋之部) 附考證，《中央研究院歷史語言研究所專刊》之 40 (台北：1960 年初版，1986 年再版)。

12.《史記今註》(中華叢書)(台北：中華叢書委員會，1963 年)。[7]

13.《中國的社會與文學》(文星叢刊 40)(台北：文星書店，1964 年)。

14.《從士大夫到小市民》(雲天文庫)(台北：雲天出版社，1970 年)。

15.《勞榦學術論文集甲編》(台北：藝文印書館，1976 年)。[8]

1960 年出版，這是第三次印本，1986 年再版，係經過整理後第四次印出。

[3] 此書 1952 年初版，1964 年四版，1980 年、1985 年、1986 年陸續再版。

[4] 此書 1954 年初版，1959 年、1970 年、1985 年陸續再版。

[5] 此書中國史部分完全由勞生生寫，只外國史部分由夏德儀先生寫。此外在教育廳初中歷史出版之前，有勝利出版公司及中華書局兩種初中歷史，其中勝利所出者，中國史為勞先生所寫，而中華所出者，中外歷史皆為勞先生所寫。教育廳本即以勝利出版者為藍本。

[6] 此書有英文版，見本文第 301 條。中文版者 58 頁，英文版者 52 頁。兩者合訂在一起，但也有單行本。

[7] 此書是與屈萬里先生分擔校註，每篇有作者署名。

[8] 此論文集分上下兩冊，共有 1591 頁。內中收有 79 篇論文，66 篇為中文者，13 篇為英文者。這些論文大都是轉載《中央研究院歷史語言研究所專刊》及其他刊物在 1976 年以前出版的文章。書內的第 69 篇，有兩種情形發生：如果是 "Miao and Chinese Kin Logic"，那就不是勞先生的文章，不知怎的錯排了進去，沒有來得及更正，而書已付

16.《漢代政治論文集》(台北：藝文印書館，1976 年)。[9]

17.《成廬詩稿》(台北：正中書局，1979 年)。

18.《漢晉西陲木簡新考》(台北：中央研究院歷史語言研究所，1985 年)。

19.《古代中國的歷史與文化》(台北：聯經出版事業公司，2006 年)。

(二) 論文

1.〈由九丘推論古代東西二民族〉,《禹貢》第 1 卷第 6 期 (1934 年 5 月)，頁 28-30。

2.〈禹治水故事之出發點及其他〉,《禹貢》第 1 卷第 6 期 (1934 年 5 月)，頁 30-32。

3.〈釋士及民爵〉,《史學年報》第 2 卷第 1 期 (1934 年 9 月)，頁 241-245。

4.〈論狄 (方庭)〉,《禹貢》第 2 卷第 6 期 (1934 年 11 月)，頁 9-11。

5.〈堯典著作時代問題之討論〉,《禹貢》第 2 卷第 9 期 (1935 年 1 月)，頁 30-31。

6.〈再論堯典著作時代〉,《禹貢》第 2 卷第 10 期 (1935 年 1 月)，頁 43-44。

7.〈漢代奴隸制度輯略〉,《中央研究院歷史語言研究所集刊》第 5 本第 1 分 (1935 年 10 月)，頁 1-11。[10]

8.〈鹽鐵論校記〉,《史語所集刊》第 5 本第 1 分 (1935 年 10 月)，頁 13-52。

9.〈漢晉閩中建置考〉,《史語所集刊》第 5 本第 1 分 (1935 年 10 月)，頁 53-63。

10.〈兩漢戶籍與地理之關係〉,《史語所集刊》第 5 本第 2 分 (1935 年 12 月)，頁 179-214。[11]

11.〈兩漢各郡人口增減數目之推測〉,《史語所集刊》第 5 本第 2 分 (1935 年 12 月)，頁 215-240。

印並賣出了若干冊，這是第一種情形；第二種情形是如果第 69 篇所登出來的是 "On the Inscrikfion of Che Ling Tsun(矢令尊)" ，那就是勞先生的文章，用來代替錯排進去者。

9　此書係從勞榦學術論文集摘出 11 篇，另行刊印。其書末附有勞榦學術論文集甲編目錄，第 69 篇標題是 "Miao and Chinese Kin Logic" ，正是前條註釋中的第一種情形。

10　《中央研究院歷史語言研究所集刊》，以下簡稱《史語所集刊》。

11　孫任以都教授將此篇譯成英文，登載在 *Chinese Social History Translations of Selected Studies*, by E-tu Sun and John De Francis, American Council of Learned Societies, Washington, D. C., 1956, pp. 83-102.

12.〈中國丹砂之應用及其推演〉,《史語所集刊》第 7 本第 4 分 (1938 年 5 月),頁 519-531。

13.〈論魯西畫像三石〉,《史語所集刊》第 8 本第 1 分 (1939 年),頁 93-127。

14.〈從漢簡所見之邊郡制度〉,《史語所集刊》第 8 本第 2 分 (1939 年),頁 159-180。

15.〈論魏孝文之遷都與華化〉,《史語所集刊》第 8 本第 4 分 (1939 年 12 月),頁 485-494。

16.〈禮經制度與漢代宮室〉,《國學季刊》第 6 卷第 3 期,《北大四十週年論文集》(1939 年 12 月),頁 124-145。

17.〈伯希和敦煌圖錄解說〉,《說文》第 3 卷第 10 期 (1943 年 5 月),頁 101-105。

18.〈漢代兵制及漢簡中的兵制〉,《史語所集刊》第 10 本 (1943 年 5 月),頁 23-25。

19.〈漢武後元不立年號考〉,《史語所集刊》第 10 本 (1943 年 5 月),頁 189-191。

20.〈居延漢簡考釋序目〉,《史語所集刊》第 10 本 (1943 年 5 月),頁 647-658。

21.〈古詩明月皎夜光節候解〉,《文史雜誌》第 3 卷第 11-12 期 (1944 年 6 月)。

22.〈漢簡中的武帝詔〉,《圖書季刊》新第 5 卷第 2-3 期 (1944 年 6 月),頁 16-18。

23.〈漢故郎中趙羣殘碑跋〉,《史學集刊》第 4 本 (1944 年 8 月),頁 84-86。

24.〈兩漢刺史制度考〉,《史語所集刊》第 11 本 (1944 年 9 月),頁 27-48。

25.〈漢代社祀的源流〉,《史語所集刊》第 11 本 (1944 年 9 月),頁 49-60。

26.〈漢簡中的河西經濟生活〉,《史語所集刊》第 11 本 (1944 年 9 月),頁 61-75。

27.〈跋高句麗大兄冉牟墓誌兼論高句麗都城之位置〉《史語所集刊》第 11 本 (1944 年 9 月),頁 77-86。

28.〈兩關遺址考〉,《史語所集刊》第 11 本 (1944 年 9 月),頁 287-296。

29.〈漢代邊塞的概況〉,《邊政公論》第 3 卷第 1 期 (1944 年 12 月),頁 48-50。

30.〈陽關遺址的過去與現在〉,《邊政公論》第 4 卷第 9-12 期 (1945 年 12 月),頁 28-32。

31.〈論漢代的內朝與外朝〉,《史語所集刊》第 13 本 (1948 年),頁 227-267;又見於《中央研究院集刊外編》第 3 種《六同別錄 (中)》(1945 年 12 月)。

32.〈象郡牂柯與夜郎的關係〉,《史語所集刊》第 14 本 (1949 年),頁 213-228;又見於《中央研究院集刊外編》第 3 種《六同別錄 (下)》(1946 年 1 月)。

33.〈居延漢簡考證補正〉,《史語所集刊》第 14 本 (1949 年),頁 229-242;又見於《中央研究院集刊外編》第 3 種《六同別錄 (下)》(1946 年 1 月)。

34.〈秦漢帝國的領域及其邊界〉,《現代學報》第 1 卷第 4-5 期 (1947 年 5 月)。

35.〈論漢代之陸運與水運〉,《史語所集刊》第 16 本 (1948 年 1 月),頁 61-91。

36.〈唐五代沙州張曹兩姓政權交替之史料〉,《申報》(1948 年 1 月 17 日)。

37.〈中國古代思想與宗教的一個方向〉,《學原》第 1 卷第 10 期 (1948 年 2 月)。

38.〈漢代察舉制度考〉,《史語所集刊》第 17 本 (1948 年 4 月),頁 79-129。

39.〈北宋刊南宋補刊十行本史記集解後跋〉,《史語所集刊》第 18 本 (1948 年),頁 497-502。

40.〈論中國造紙術之原始〉,《史語所集刊》第 19 本 (1948 年 10 月),頁 489-498。

41.〈釋漢代之亭障與烽燧〉,《史語所集刊》第 19 本 (1948 年 10 月),頁 501-522。

42.〈古詩「羽林郎」篇雜考〉,《文史雜誌》第 6 卷第 3 期 (1948 年 10 月),頁 41-45。

43.〈北魏洛陽城圖的復原〉,《史語所集刊》第 20 本 (1948 年),頁 299-312。

44.〈論漢代的游俠〉,《文史哲學報》第 1 期 (1950 年 6 月),頁 237-252。

45.〈「侯」與「射侯」後記〉,《史語所集刊》第 22 本 (1950 年 7 月),頁 126-128。

46.〈漢代的亭制〉,《史語所集刊》第 22 本 (1950 年 7 月),頁 129-138。

47.〈關於張騫墓〉,《大陸雜誌》第 1 卷第 1 期 (1950 年 7 月),頁 13。

48.〈敦煌及敦煌的新史料〉,《大陸雜誌》第 1 卷第 3 期 (1950 年 7 月),頁 6-9。

49.〈龍岡雜記——床與席〉,《大陸雜誌》第 1 卷第 5 期 (1950 年 8 月),頁 21。

50.〈本國史教科書的若干問題〉,《大陸雜誌》第 1 卷第 7 期 (1950 年 10 月),頁 4-6。

51.〈龍岡雜記——大石與小石〉,《大陸雜誌》第 1 卷第 11 期 (1950 年 12 月),頁 21。

52.〈傅孟眞先生與近二十年中國歷史學的發展〉,《大陸雜誌》第 2 卷第 1 期 (1951 年 1 月),頁 7-9。

53.〈漢晉時期的帷帳〉,《文史哲學報》第 2 期 (1951 年 2 月),頁 67-80。

54.〈出版品概況與集刊的編印〉，《史語所傅所長紀念特刊》(1951 年 3 月)，頁 45-60。

55.〈戰國秦漢的土地問題及其對策〉，《大陸雜誌》第 2 卷第 5 期 (1951 年 3 月)，頁 9-12。

56.〈論東漢時代的世族〉，《學原》第 3 卷第 3-4 期 (1951 年 4 月)，頁 54-58。

57.〈敦煌壁畫中的「未生怨」故事〉，《大陸雜誌》第 2 卷第 7 期 (1951 年 4 月)，頁 17。

58.〈從歷史和地理看過去的新疆〉，《大陸雜誌》第 2 卷第 8 期 (1951 年 4 月)，頁 11-15。

59.〈關於漢代官俸的幾個推測〉，《文史哲學報》第 3 期 (1951 年 12 月)，頁 11-22。

60.〈漢代的雇傭制度〉，《史語所集刊》第 23 本上冊，《傅斯年先生紀念論文集》(1951 年 12 月)，頁 77-87。

61.〈秦漢時代的中國文化〉，《大陸雜誌》第 4 卷第 3 期 (1952 年 2 月)，頁 91-98。

62.〈資中城塹〉，《大陸雜誌》第 4 卷第 5 期 (1952 年 3 月)，頁 16。

63.〈秦郡的建置及其與漢郡之比較〉，《大陸雜誌特刊》第 1 輯下冊 (1952 年 7 月)，頁 423-432。

64.〈漢代的吏員與察舉〉，《考銓月刊》第 11 期 (1952 年 8 月)。

65.〈簡牘中所見的布帛〉，《學術季刊》第 1 卷第 1 期 (1952 年 9 月)，頁 152-155。

66.〈漢代的郡制及其對於簡牘的參證〉，《傅故校長斯年先生紀念論文集》，第 1 輯 (1952 年 12 月)，頁 29-62。

67.〈從士大夫到小市民〉，《民主評論》第 4 卷第 9 期 (1953 年 5 月)，頁 236-239。

68.〈南北朝至唐代的藝術〉，《大陸雜誌》第 6 卷第 9 期 (1953 年 5 月)，頁 28-31。

69.〈漢代常服述略〉，《史語所集刊》第 24 本 (1953 年 6 月)，頁 144-183。

70.〈漢代知識分子的特質〉，《民主評論》第 4 卷第 17 期 (1953 年 9 月)，頁 10-12。

71.〈漢朝的縣制〉，《國立中央研究院院刊》第 1 輯 (1954 年 6 月)，頁 69-81。

72.〈戰國時期的歷史地理〉，《中國歷史地理 (一)》(國民基本知識叢書)(1954 年 8 月)。

73.〈秦漢時期戰史〉，《中國戰史論集 (一)》(1954 年 8 月)。

74.〈中國的石質雕刻〉，《中國文化論集 (二)》(1954 年 12 月)，頁 492-503。

75.〈漢代的政制〉，《中國政治思想與制度史論集 (三)》(1955 年 4 月)。

76.〈中韓關係論略〉,《中韓文化論集 (二)》(1955 年 11 月)。

77.〈玉佩與剛卯〉,《史語所集刊》第 27 本 (1956 年 4 月),頁 183-196。

78.〈二千年來的中越關係〉,《中越文化論集 (一)》(1956 年 4 月)。

79.〈論宗教的發展與中國的宗教〉,《民主評論》第 7 卷第 10 期 (1956 年 5 月)。

80.〈中國古代的青銅器物〉,《大學生活》第 2 卷第 2 期 (1956 年 6 月),頁 26-30。

81.〈李商隱燕臺詩評述〉,《文學雜誌》第 1 卷第 1 期 (1956 年 9 月)。

82.〈陶淵明行年雜考〉,《自由學人》第 1 卷第 3 期 (1956 年 10 月),頁 34-36。

83.〈千佛洞壁畫圖案的分析〉,《中國學術史論集 (二)》(1956 年 10 月)。

84.〈正史 (龍岡雜記)〉,《大陸雜誌》第 13 卷第 9 期 (1956 年 11 月),頁 4-10。

85.〈漢代的西域都護與戊巳校尉〉,《史語所集刊》第 28 本上冊,《慶祝胡適先生六十五歲論文集》(1956 年 12 月),頁 485-496。

86.〈雲南境內的漢代縣治〉,《國立中央研究院院刊》第 3 輯 (1956 年 12 月),頁 187-197。

87.〈論文章傳統的道路與現在的方向〉,《文學雜誌》第 1 卷第 4 期 (1956 年 12 月),頁 14-17。

88.〈歷史的考訂與歷史的解釋〉,《學人》,《中央日報文史叢刊 (一)》(1957 年),頁 13-19。

89.〈論中國國故學上的分工〉,《學人》,《中央日報文史叢刊 (一)》(1957 年),頁 62-68。

90.〈史字的結構及史官的原始職務〉,《大陸雜誌》第 14 卷第 3 期 (1957 年 2 月),頁 1-4。

91.〈高適籍里 (龍岡雜記)〉,《大陸雜誌》第 14 卷第 6 期 (1957 年 3 月),頁 5。

92.〈對於白話文與新詩的一個預想〉,《文學雜誌》第 2 卷第 2 期 (1957 年 4 月)。

93.〈中國的社會與文學〉,《文學雜誌》第 2 卷第 6 期 (1957 年 8 月)。

94.〈論漢代的衛尉與中尉兼論南北軍制度〉,《史語所集刊》第 29 本下冊,《慶祝趙元任先生六十五歲論文集》(1957 年 11 月),頁 445-459。

95.〈秦漢九卿考〉,《大陸雜誌》第 15 卷第 11 期 (1957 年 12 月),頁 1-3。

96.〈敦煌千佛洞〉,《學術季刊》第 6 卷第 12 期 (1957 年 12 月),頁 129-131。

97.〈歷史學〉,《中華民國科學誌續編》(現代國民基本知識叢書第五輯) 第 1 冊 (台北:
　　中華文化出版事業委員會,1958 年),頁 95-102。

98.〈說王國維的浣谿紗詞〉,《文學雜誌》第 3 卷第 5 期 (1958 年 1 月)。

99.〈枚乘〉,《中國文學史論集 (一)》(1958 年 4 月)。

100.〈中國歷史上的治亂週期〉,《大陸雜誌》第 17 卷第 1 期 (1958 年 7 月),頁 31-34。

101.〈鹽鐵論所表現的儒家及法家思想之一斑〉,《中國哲學史論集 (一)》(1958 年 9 月)。

102.〈說簡牘〉,《幼師學報》第 1 卷第 1 期 (1958 年 10 月),頁 1-8。

103.〈「李商隱評論」所引起的問題〉,《文學雜誌》第 5 卷第 6 期 (1959 年 2 月)。

104.〈李商隱詩之淵源及其發展〉,《幼獅學報》第 1 卷第 2 期 (1959 年 4 月),頁 1-10。

105.〈居延漢簡考證〉,《史語所集刊》第 30 本上冊,《三十週年紀念專號》(1959 年 10 月),
　　頁 311-491。

106.〈史記項羽本紀中「學書」和「學劍」的解釋〉,《史語所集刊》第 30 本下冊,《三十周年
　　紀念專號》(1959 年 10 月),頁 499-510。

107.〈國立歷史博物館漢唐文物特展的介紹〉,《教育與文化》第 223 輯 (1959 年 11 月)。

108.〈論漢代玉門關的遷徙問題〉,《清華學報》新第 2 卷第 1 期 (1960 年 5 月),頁 40-
　　52。

109.〈論神韻說與境界說〉,《文學雜誌》第 8 卷第 4 期 (1960 年 6 月)。

110.〈北魏後期的重要都邑與北魏政治的關係〉,《中央研究院歷史語言研究所集刊外編》
　　第 4 種,《慶祝董作賓先生六十五歲論文集》上冊 (1960 年 7 月),頁 229-269。

111.〈漢代的「史書」與「尺牘」〉,《大陸雜誌》第 21 卷第 1-2 期 (1960 年 7 月)。

112.〈三老餘義〉,《大陸雜誌》第 21 卷第 9 期 (1960 年 11 月),頁 16-17。

113.〈關東與關西的李姓和趙姓〉,《史語所集刊》第 31 本 (1960 年 12 月),頁 47-60。

114.〈論北朝的都邑〉,《大陸雜誌》第 22 卷第 3 期 (1961 年 2 月),頁 1-5。

115.〈北魏州郡志略〉,《史語所集刊》第 32 本 (1961 年 7 月),頁 181-238。

116.〈說類書〉,《新時代》第 1 卷第 7 期 (1961 年 7 月)。

117.〈論西京雜記之作者及成書時代〉,《史語所集刊》第 33 本 (1962 年 1 月),頁 19-34。

118.〈北魏地理研究〉,《中國學術年報》第 1 期 (1962 年 5 月),頁 437。

119.〈孔廟百石卒史碑考〉,《史語所集刊》第 34 本上冊,《故院長胡適先生紀念論文集》(1962 年 12 月),頁 99-114。

120.〈蔡琰悲憤詩出於偽託考〉,《大陸雜誌》第 26 卷第 5 期 (1963 年 3 月),頁 1-2。

121.〈重印「新疆建置志」跋〉,《大陸雜誌》第 26 卷第 9 期 (1963 年 5 月),頁 1-2。

122.〈秦代史論〉,《思想與時代》第 108 期 (1963 年 7 月)。

123.〈秦郡問題的討論〉,《大陸雜誌》第 27 卷第 10 期 (1963 年 11 月),頁 1-6。

124.〈與嚴歸田教授論秦漢郡吏制度書〉,《大陸雜誌》第 28 卷第 4 期 (1964 年 2 月),頁 115。

125.〈兩漢政府在西域的經營〉,《新疆研究》(1964 年 6 月),頁 7-20。

126.〈中國歷史的週期與中國歷史分期問題〉,《大陸雜誌》第 29 卷第 5 期 (1964 年 9 月),頁 1-8。

127.〈六博及博局的演變〉,《史語所集刊》第 35 本,《故院長朱家驊先生紀念論文集》(1964 年 9 月),頁 15-50。

128.〈敦煌長史武斑碑校釋〉,《香港大學五十周年紀念集》(1964 年),頁 315-319。

129.〈漢代的豪彊及其政治上的關係〉,《慶祝李濟先生七十歲論文集》上冊,頁 31-51 ;《清華學報》(1965 年)。

130.〈古社會田狩及祭祀之關係 (重訂篇)〉,《史語所集刊》第 36 本上冊 (1965 年)。

131.〈戰國時代的戰爭〉,《史語所集刊》第 36 本下冊,《紀念董作賓董同龢先生論文集》(1966 年 6 月),頁 801-828。

132.〈釋莊子天下篇惠施及辯者之言〉,《華崗學報》第 3 期 (1966 年 12 月),頁 309-317。

133.〈戰國時代的戰爭方法〉,《史語所集刊》第 37 本上冊 (1967 年 3 月),頁 47-63。

134.〈漢畫〉,《故宮季刊》,第 2 卷第 1 期 (1967 年 7 月),頁 1-8。

135.〈從木簡到紙的應用〉,《國立中央圖書館館刊》新第 1 卷第 1 期 (1967 年 7 月),頁

3-12。[12]

136.〈幾種古史上不成問題的問題〉,《大陸雜誌》第 35 卷第 4 期 (1967 年 8 月),頁 101-103。

137.〈大學出於孟學說〉,《史語所集刊》第 38 本 (1968 年 1 月),頁 277-284。

138.〈十干試釋〉,《大陸雜誌》第 36 卷第 11 期 (1968 年 6 月),頁 16。

139.〈古文字試釋〉,《史語所集刊》第 40 本上冊,《恭祝總統蔣公八秩晉二華誕暨本所成立四十周年紀念專號》(1968 年 10 月),頁 37-51。

140.〈六書轉注試釋〉,《中國語文》第 23 卷第 4 期 (1968 年 10 月)。

141.〈漢簡中的記時法〉(中文提要),《史語所集刊》第 39 本 (1969 年 1 月)。

142.〈釋築〉,《慶祝蔣復璁先生七十歲專號》(故宮博物院,1969 年 2 月),頁 35-39。

143.〈上巳考〉,《中央研究院民族學研究所集刊》第 29 本,《慶祝凌純聲先生七十歲論文集》(1970 年),頁 243-261。

144.〈漢代政治組織的特質及其功能〉,《清華學報》第 8 卷第 2 期 (1970 年 8 月),頁 228-247。

145.〈論儒道兩家對於科學發展的關係〉,《文藝復興》第 23 期 (1971 年 11 月),頁 5-8。

146.〈漢代黃金及銅錢的使用問題〉,《史語所集刊》第 42 本第 3 分,《慶祝王世杰先生八十歲論文集》(1971 年 6 月),頁 341-390。

147.〈六書條例中的幾個問題〉,《史語所集刊》第 43 本第 3 分,《中華民國建國六十年紀念專書 (三)》(1971 年 11 月),頁 319-333。

148.〈與李樹桐教授論史事書〉,《食貨月刊》第 2 卷第 7 期 (1972 年 10 月)。

149.〈近六十年之秦漢史研究〉,《華學月刊》第 10 期 (1972 年 10 月)。

150.〈中國文字之特質及其發展〉,《東方雜誌》第 6 卷第 10 期 (1973 年 4 月)。

151.〈和千家詩七絕四十首〉,《文藝復興》第 46 期 (1973 年 10 月)。

152.〈敦煌壁畫與中國繪畫〉,《雄獅美術》第 43 期 (1974 年 9 月)。

153.〈周初年代問題與月相問題的新看法〉,《香港中文大學中國文化研究所學報》第 7 卷第 1 期 (1974 年 12 月),頁 1-26。

12　勞榦著 (用英文寫),喬衍琯譯成中文。

154.〈漢代文化概述〉,《總統蔣公逝世周年紀念論文集》(1976 年 4 月)。

155.〈古詩十九首與其對於文學史的關係〉《詩學》第 2 輯 (巨人出版社,1976 年),頁 1-16。

156.〈六十年來的中國史學〉,《香港中文大學中國文化研究所學報》第 9 期 (1976 年)。

157.〈從儒家地位看漢代政治〉,《中華文化復興月刊》第 10 卷第 2 期 (1977 年 2 月),頁 52-55。

158.〈近代中國史學述評〉,《史學論集》(1977 年 4 月)。

159.〈秦的統一與覆亡〉,《史語所集刊》第 48 本第 2 分,《慶祝錢院長思亮七十壽辰論文集》(1977 年 6 月),頁 289-308。

160.〈戰國七雄及其他小國〉,《史語所集刊》第 48 本第 4 分 (1977 年 12 月),頁 619-667。

161.〈釋狄與築〉,《董作賓先生逝世十四週年紀念刊》(1978 年 3 月),頁 41-44。

162.〈釋武王征商簋與大豐簋〉,《屈萬里先生七秩榮慶論文集》(1978 年 10 月),頁 337-341。

163.〈論周初年代和召誥洛誥的新證明〉,《史語所集刊》第 50 本第 1 分,《慶祝歷史語言研究所成立五十週年紀念論文集》(1979 年),頁 29-45。

164.〈粘蟬神祠碑的研究〉,《東方學志》第 23-24 期 (1980 年 2 月),頁 319-321。

165.〈漢代尚書的職任及其和內朝的關係〉,《史語所集刊》第 51 本第 1 分,《紀念李濟屈萬里兩先生論文集》(1980 年 3 月),頁 33-51。

166.〈早期中國符契的使用〉,《簡牘學報》第 7 期 (1980 年),頁 334-339。[13]

167.〈殷曆譜的重計問題〉,《新亞學報》(1981 年)。

168.〈「陳勝吳廣」「呂梁山」「范增」「吳回」「吳山」「吳俊卿」「吳昌碩」「吳大澂」〉,《中華百科全書》(中國文化大學出版,1981 年)。

169.〈商周年代的新估計〉,《中央研究院國際漢學會論文集 · 歷史考古組》上冊,《慶祝中華民國建國七十周年》(1981 年),頁 279-302。

170.〈中國建築之周廬與全部設計之關係〉《國立歷史博物館刊》第 12 輯 (1981 年 12 月),頁 4-6。

---

13 勞榦著,鄭志民譯。

171.〈再論漢代亭制〉，《史語所集刊》第 53 本第 1 分，《趙元任先生紀念專號》(1982 年)。

172.〈從漢簡論「使君」之稱及東西堂之制〉，《大陸雜誌》第 66 卷第 1 期　(1983 年 1 月)，頁 1-5。

173.〈傳統文化與現代衝擊的適應問題〉，《中國文化月刊》第 40 期 (1983 年 2 月)，頁 22-31。

174.〈關於「關東」及「關西」的討論〉，《食貨復刊》第 13、14 期合刊　(1983 年 7 月)。

175.〈從漢簡中的嗇夫、令史、候史及士吏論漢代郡縣吏的職務及地位〉，《史語所集刊》第 55 本第 1 分 (1984 年 3 月)。

176.〈修正殷曆譜的新觀念及新設計〉，《香港新亞學報》第 14 卷 (1984 年 8 月 15 日)，頁 1-65。

177.〈論齊國的始封和遷徙及其相關問題〉，《食貨月刊》第 14 期 7、8 月合刊 (1984 年 11 月)，頁 294-300。

178.〈長安今昔談〉，《傳記文學》第 46 卷第 6 期 (1985 年 6 月)，頁 55-58。

179.〈漢代的軍用車騎和非軍用車騎〉，《簡牘學報》第 11 期 (1985 年 9 月)，頁 1-12。

180.〈未來世界最適應的宗教：佛教〉，《慧炬》第 257 期 (1985 年 11 月)，頁 10-13。

181.〈對於「巫蠱之禍的政治意義」的看法〉，《史語所集刊》第 57 本第 3 分，《吳院長大猷先生八十壽辰論文集》(1986 年 9 月)，頁 539-552。

182.〈五四新文學的洗禮〉，《聯合文學》第 2 卷第 2 期 (1986 年 10 月)，頁 206-209。

183.〈從文化傳統及文化將來討論大乘教在中國及世界的前途〉，《慧炬》第 270 期 (1986 年 12 月)，頁 19-20。

184.〈釋漢簡中的「烽」〉，《中國文字》新 12 期，《嚴一萍先生逝世周年紀念特刊》(1988 年 7 月)。

185.〈從制度方面討論中國文化的展望〉，《歷史月刊》第 9 期 (1988 年 10 月)，頁 14-17。

186.〈道教中外丹與內丹的發展〉，《史語所集刊》第 59 本第 4 分，《李方桂先生紀念論文集》(1988 年 12 月)，頁 977-993。

187.〈漢代的「塞」和後方的重點〉，《史語所集刊》第 60 本第 3 分，《歷史語言研究所成立六十周年紀念專號》(1989 年 9 月)，頁 507-526。

188.〈論鍊丹術中用鉛的開始〉，《大陸雜誌》第 80 卷第 3 期 (1990 年 3 月)，頁 1-2。

189.〈試論光武帝用人政策之若干問題〉，廖伯源畢業論文，勞貞一教授審查 (見附錄第 25-27 頁)，《史語所集刊》第 61 卷第 1 期 (1990 年 3 月)，頁 1-27。

190.〈歷史學的研究和應用〉，《歷史月刊》第 31 期 (1990 年 8 月)，頁 118-121。

191.〈胡適之先生不朽〉，《胡適之先生百歲冥誕紀念特輯》，《傳記文學》第 57 卷 343 期 (1990 年 12 月)，頁 40-42。

192.〈佛教的異化與佛教前途〉，《慧炬》第 334 期 (1992 年 4 月)，頁 30-32。

193.〈從漢簡資料討論歷史走向和社會走向〉，《歷史月刊》第 58 期 (1992 年 11 月)，頁 26-32。

194.〈從甲午月食討論殷周年代的關鍵問題〉，《史語所集刊》第 64 本第 3 分，《芮逸夫高去尋兩先生紀念論文集》(1993 年 12 月)，頁 627-638。

195.〈歷史與考古相互整合的一個方向〉，《聯經公司二十週年紀念冊》(台北：1994 年)，頁 55-57。

196.〈殷周年代的問題——長期求證的結果及其處理的方法〉，《史語所集刊》第 67 卷第 2 期 (1996 年 6 月)，頁 239-262。

(三) 雜文

197.〈建設首都一件最重要的事——市區擴張與江北工業區的建立〉，《中央日報》(1946 年 7 月 27 日)。

198.〈錦瑟詩解〉，《中央日報》(1974 年 5 月 26 日)。

199.〈西漢的藏賄事件〉，《中央日報》(1947 年 9 月 3 日)。

200.〈對於南京市的幾點認識〉，《學原》第 2 卷第 9 期 (1949 年 2 月)。

201.〈漢代剛卯的制度〉，《公論報》(1949 年 11 月 9 日)。

202.〈周秦兩漢的「關」〉，《公論報》(1950 年 1 月 25 日)。

203.〈紀念傅孟眞先生〉，《傅故校長哀輓錄》，原載《臺大校刊》第 101 期 (1951 年 12 月)，頁 72。

204.〈儒道與眞常〉，《中國一周》第 101 期 (1952 年 3 月)。

205.〈論今後的國史〉,《民主評論》第 3 卷第 14 期 (1952 年 7 月)。

206.〈一個對於讀經問題的意見〉,《反攻》第 65 期 (1952 年 8 月)。

207.〈中國書籍形式的進展〉,《今日世界》第 10 期 (1952 年 8 月)。

208.〈河西走廊〉,《今日世界》第 13 期 (1952 年 9 月)。

209.〈關於民俗改善〉,《台灣風物》第 2 卷第 7 期 (1952 年 10 月)。

210.〈論興辦一個中國文學專科學校〉,《民主評論》第 4 卷第 4 期 (1953 年 2 月)。

211.〈談讀書〉,《中國一周》第 146 期 (1953 年 2 月)。

212.〈談古舞問題〉,《中國一周》第 176 期 (1953 年 9 月)。

213.〈中國偉人小傳 (三) 玄奘〉(華國出版社,1953 年 12 月)。

214.〈略論在美國的華僑〉,《中國一周》第 251 期 (1955 年 2 月)。

215.〈儒家正統司馬光〉,《中國一周》第 278 期 (1955 年 8 月)。

216.〈中學國文教材之補充與分配〉,《主義與國策》第 62 期 (1955 年 11 月)。

217.〈美國的人種與華僑〉,《中國一周》第 293 期 (1955 年 12 月)。

218.〈美國的交通〉,《中國一周》第 293 期 (1956 年 1 月)。

219.〈一年來的歷史學〉,《教育與文化》第 10 卷第 11 期 (1956 年 2 月),頁 4-6。

220.〈敦煌壁畫的藝術〉,《中央日報》(1956 年 8 月 15 日)。

221.〈對於李濟先生的簡單敍述〉,《政論周刊》第 105 期 (1957 年 1 月)。

222.〈敦煌藝術的一個介紹〉,《大學生活》第 2 卷第 9 期 (1957 年 1 月)。

223.〈李濟教授的學術地位〉,《教育與文化》第 16 卷第 2 期 (1957 年 4 月)。

224.〈南方型的城市與北方型的城市〉,《中央日報》(1957 年 5 月 28 日)。

225.〈敦煌壁畫的臨摹與歷史博物館的壁畫〉,《新生報》(1958 年 3 月 23 日)。

226.〈從「五四」四十周年紀念談治學〉,《新生報》(1959 年 9 月 15 日)。

227.〈論治學的態度並論「格物」〉,《中央日報》(1960 年 8 月 7 日)。

228.〈鄭成功與中國海外的關係〉,《中華日報》(1961 年 4 月 21 日)。[14]

14　又見於《鄭成功復臺三百周年紀念專輯》。

229.〈舊詩和舊詩上的啓示〉,《文星》第 7 卷第 4 期 (1961 年 11 月)。

230.〈惡性補習問題〉,《文星》第 13 卷第 6 期 (1964 年 4 月)。

231.〈敦煌壁畫的裝飾〉,《中國的社會與文學》(勞榦著)(1964 年),頁 93-106。

232.〈中國歷史中的政治問題〉,《中國的社會與文學》(勞榦著)(1964 年),頁 143-148。

233.〈論國都的建置及唐代以前的都邑設計〉,《中國的社會與文學》(勞榦著)(1964 年),頁 173-197。

234.〈到民主的路〉,《中國的社會與文學》(勞榦著)(1964 年),頁 217-224。

235.〈干支與紀年〉,《中國的社會與文學》(勞榦著)(1964 年),頁 225-228。

236.〈歡迎胡適之先生並談語言運動〉,《中國的社會與文學》(勞榦著)(1964 年),頁 245-247。

237.〈追悼胡適之先生並論「全盤西化」問題〉,《中國的社會與文學》(勞榦著)(1964 年),頁 235-244。

238.〈悼濟安〉,《傳記文學》第 6 卷第 6 期 (1964 年 6 月)。

239.〈董彥堂先生逝世三周年的懷念〉,《董作賓先生逝世三周年紀念集》(1966 年 11 月)。

240.〈古書重印問題〉,《中央日報》(1967 年 1 月 26 日)。

241.〈勞榦先生來函〉,《中央日報》(1967 年 11 月 14 日)。

242.〈記袁守和先生〉,《中外雜誌》第 4 卷第 2 期 (1968 年 8 月)。

243.〈大學時期以前的回憶錄〉,《中外雜誌》第 4 卷第 5-6 期 (1968 年 11、12 月)。

244.〈關中雜憶 (一)〉,《中外雜誌》第 5 卷第 1 期 (1969 年 1 月)。

245.〈關中雜憶 (二)〉,《中外雜誌》第 5 卷第 3 期 (1969 年 3 月)。

246.〈「零與一」只是常識問題〉,《中央日報》(1969 年 4 月 1 日)。

247.〈二度陝北行 (關中雜憶之三)〉,《中外雜誌》第 5 卷第 5 期 (1969 年 5 月)。

248.〈學成之前十年憂患 (關中雜憶之四)〉,《中外雜誌》第 5 卷第 6 期 (1969 年 6 月)。

249.〈暫遊萬里少別千年 (關中雜憶之五)〉,《中外雜誌》第 6 卷第 2 期 (1969 年 8 月)。

250.〈寧羌舊事 (關中雜憶之六)〉,《中外雜誌》第 6 卷第 4 期 (1969 年 10 月)

251.〈桃花源記偶記〉(上、下),《中央日報》(1969 年 11 月 13、14 日)。

252.〈對於中國文字改革的意見〉,《新時代》第 9 卷第 2 期 (1969 年 12 月)。

253.〈憶陳寅恪先生〉,《傳記文學》第 17 卷第 3 期 (1970 年 9 月),頁 31-33。

254.〈中國歷史與民族精神教育〉,《從士大夫到小市民》(勞榦著)(1970 年),頁 1-3。

255.〈中韓的歷史關係〉,《從士大夫到小市民》(勞榦著)(1970 年),頁 95-98。

256.〈詩的欣賞與選讀〉,《從士大夫到小市民》(勞榦著)(1970 年),頁 130-131。

257.〈「渺」「眇」及其他通用字寫法與讀法〉,《從士大夫到小市民》(勞榦著)(1970 年),
     頁 198-199。

258.〈丁未新春從電視見芝加哥紐約大雪數尺慨然有作〉,《從士大夫到小市民》(勞榦著)
     (1970 年),頁 205。

259.〈對於觀光事業的幾個意見〉,《中華文化復興月刊》第 4 卷第 1 期 (1971 年 1 月)。

260.〈記朱家驊先生〉,《浙江月刊》第 3 卷第 4 期 (1971 年 4 月)。

261.〈勞榦教授來信〉,《食貨月刊》第 3 卷第 1 期 (1973 年 4 月)。

262.〈秦漢時代的長城〉,《勞榦學術論文集甲編》(1976 年),頁 1083-1084。

263.〈詩的感受〉,《中華聯誼會通訊》第 22 期 (1976 年 9 月)。

264.〈記張君勱先生並述科學與人生觀論戰的影響〉,《傳記文學》第 29 卷第 3 期 (1976
     年 9 月),頁 82-84。

265.〈華北名城與名泉〉,《中外雜誌》第 21 卷第 2 期 (1977 年 8 月)。

266.〈勞榦教授的自述〉,《湖南文獻》第 6 卷第 4 期 (1978 年 10 月),頁 53-58。

267.〈佛與菩薩的「姓」的問題〉,《中央日報》(1980 年 4 月 27 日)。[15]

268.〈五四的反省〉(一) (二),《中國時報》(1980 年 5 月 4、5 日)。

269.〈中國人的飲料的問題〉,《中央日報》(1980 年 11 月 20 日)。[16]

270.〈關於中文直行書寫〉,《中央日報》(1981 年 11 月 12 日)。

271.〈從民族文化精神看一神教信仰〉,《美國洛杉磯世界日報》(1994 年 4 月 13 日)。

272.〈陳寅恪與俞大綱偉佚詩〉,《慶祝中華益壯會創立二十周年特刊》,《美國加州益壯

15　用「成厂居士」筆名發表。

16　用「成厂居士」筆名發表。

會會刊》第 28 期 (1994 年)。

273.〈修憲最重要問題——明確總統否決權〉，美國洛杉磯北美南加州華人寫作協會，《文苑》第 11 期 (1996 年 5 月 26 日)，頁 8-9。

(四) 書評及序跋

274.〈評曾資生著「兩漢文官制度」〉，《社會經濟集刊》第 7 卷第 1 期 (1944 年 6 月)，頁 142-143。

275.〈孫毓棠著「中國古代社會經濟論叢」〉，《社會經濟集刊》第 7 卷第 2 期 (1944 年 12 月)，頁 154-160。

276.〈胡煥庸著「縮小省區轄境命名之商榷」〉《社會經濟集刊》第 7 卷第 2 期 (1944 年 12 月)，頁 173-174。

277.〈評史岩著「敦煌石室畫像題識」〉，《社會經濟集刊》第 8 卷第 1 期 (1949 年 1 月)，頁 157-163。

278.〈評方豪的「中西交通史」第一冊〉，《三民主義半月刊》第 3 期 (1953 年 6 月)。

279.〈跋陳槃「春秋大事表列國爵姓及存滅表譔異 (中)」〉，《史語所集刊》第 27 本 (1956 年 4 月)，頁 183-197。

280.〈評雷夏「圓仁入唐求法巡禮記」及「圓仁入唐事跡」〉，《清華學報》新第 1 卷第 2 期 (1957 年 4 月)，頁 262-265。

281.〈孟森著「明代史」〉，《學術季刊》第 6 卷第 4 期 (1958 年 6 月)，頁 133-134。

282.〈蔣夢麟「西潮」評介〉，《新生報》(1960 年 2 月 12 日)。

283.〈蘇瑩輝著「敦煌學概論」序〉(1961 年 7 月)。

284.〈李樹桐著「唐史考辨」序〉(1963 年 12 月)。

285.〈何炳棣著「黃土與中國農業的起源」跋〉(香港：中文大學，1969 年)。

286.〈評唐蘭「古文字學導論」〉，《香港中文大學中國文化研究所學報》第 3 卷第 1 期 (1970 年 9 月)。

287.〈錢存訓著「中國古代書史」後序〉(香港：中文大學，1975 年)。

288.〈馬先醒著「漢簡與漢代城市」序〉(簡牘學會，1976 年)。

289.〈勞榦著「勞榦學術論文集甲編」自序〉(台北：藝文印書館，1976 年)。

290.〈勞榦著「居延漢簡圖版之部」再版序〉(台北：中央研究院歷史語言研究所，1977 年)。

291.〈評余英時「論戴震與章學誠」〉，《香港中文大學中國文化研究所學報》第 10 卷第 1 期 (1979 年)，頁 219-225。

292.〈馬先醒著「簡牘學要義」序〉(簡牘學會，1980 年)。

293.〈馬先醒著「居延漢簡新編」序〉(簡牘學會，1981 年)。

294.〈「周士心畫集」序〉(簡牘學會，1981 年)。

295.〈張其昀著「中華五千年史　秦漢史」序〉(台北：文化大學，1981 年)。

296.〈蘇瑩輝著「瓜沙史事叢考」序〉(商務，1983 年)。

297.〈金惠著「創造歷史的漢武帝」序〉(商務，1984 年)。

298.〈彭雙松「徐福研究」序〉(富蕙圖書出版社，1984 年)。

299.〈「周士心陸馨如金婚畫集」序〉(自印，1995 年)。

(五) 英文及日文著作

300. "Six-tusked Elephants on a Han Bas-relief", *Harvard Journal of Asiatic Studies*, Vol. 17 (1954), pp. 366-369.

301. "Frescoes of Tunhuang", *Collected Paper on History and Arts of China*, Taipei (National Historical Museum, 1958). [17]

302. "*A View of History and Culture of China*", *China Year Book 1959-60* (Taipei: China Publishing Co., 1959), pp.11-31.

303. Review of six articles:

(一)Ho Ch'ang-ch'un, "Ch'in-mo nung min ch'i i ti yuan yin chi ch'i li shih tso yung". 賀昌群：〈秦末農民起義的原因及其歷史作用〉。

(二)Ch'en P'an, "Han chien sheng i". 陳槃：〈漢簡賸義〉。

(三)Ch'en P'an, "Han chien sheng i chih hsu". 陳槃：〈漢簡賸義之續〉。

17　此書有中文版，見本目錄第 10 條《敦煌藝術》。

(四)Ch'ien Ts'un-hsun, "Han tai shu tao k'ao". 錢存訓：〈漢代書刀考〉。

(五)Chang Ping-chuan, "Lun ch'eng tao pu tz'u". 張秉權：〈論成套卜辭〉。

(六)Tai Chun-jen, "Pu fen tai ch'uan t'i ti hsiang hsing". 戴君仁：〈部分代全
體的象形〉。

Revue Bibliographique de Sinologie, No. 7 (Paris, 1961) , pp. 62, 63, 64, 200,
221, 232.

304. "The Capital of Loyang: A Historical Survey", *Journal of China Society*, Vol.
1 (Taipei, 1961), pp. 36-39.

305. "City Life and the Chinese Civilization", *Proceedings of the First International Conference of Historians of Asia*, Nov. 25-30, 1960 (Manila, 1962),
pp.326-331.

306. "From Wooden Slip to Paper", *Chinese Culture*, Vol. 8, No. 4 (Taipei, 1967),
pp. 80-94.

307. "Fu Ssu-nien", *Biographical Dictionary of Republic of China* (ed. by Howard L. Boorman and Richard C. Howard; Columbia University Press, 1968),
Vol. 2, pp.43-46.

308. "The Division of Time in the Han Dynasty as Seen in the Wooden Slips",
Bulletin of the Institute of History and Philology, Academia Sinica (Taipei,
1969) . Vol. 39, pp. 351-368.

309. "A Review of Joseph Needham's *Science and Civilization in China*, Vol. 4,
Part 3", *American Historical Review* (1975), Vol. 80, No. 2, pp. 459-461.

310. "The Corruption under the Bureaucratic Administration in Han Times",
*Studia Asiatica: Essays in Asian Studies in Felicitation of Seventy-fifth An-
niversary of Professor Ch'en Shou-yi* (ed. by Laurence G. Thompson; San
Francisco: Chinese Materials Center, 1975), pp. 67-76.

311. "The Early Use of Tally in China", *Ancient China: Studies in Early Civilization* (ed. by David F. Roy and Tsuen-hsuin Tsien; Hong Kong: The Chinese
University Press, 1978), pp.91-98.

312. "On the Inscription of Che Ling Tsun(矢令尊)",《勞榦學術論文集》(台北：藝文

印書館 , 1976), pp.1405-1410.

313. "The nineteen old Poems of the Han Dynasty and some of their Social Implications",《勞榦學術論文集》(台北 : 藝文印書館 , 1976), pp. 1491-1516.

314. "The Periodical Circles in the Chinese History",《勞榦學術論文集》(台北 : 藝文印書館 , 1976), pp.1547-1567.

315. The History of the Han Dynasty, Vol. 1, Character text selections by Kan Lao, Vol. 2, selections with preface by Kan Lao, *Research Manual Series* (ed. by Ta-tuan Ch'en and Frederick W. Mote; Chinese Linguistics Project, Princeton University, 1983-).[18]

316.〈漢簡しこついて〉,《東方學》第 11 期 (1955)。

317.〈儒道兩家の科學發展に對する關係〉,《問題と研究》第 1 卷第 11 號 (1972),頁 1-13。

318.〈訪勞貞一院士談高句麗好太王碑作者 : 高明士〉,《韓國學報》第 3 期 (1983 年 12 月),頁 61-65。

319. "Chü yen Han chien", Written by Kan Lao, edited by Norma Farquhar,《居延漢簡》(台北 : 中央研究院歷史語言研究所 , 1986), revised edition. pp.1- 145. [19]

18　Vol.1 是中文,是將所選的資料影印訂成一本,81 頁。Vol.2 是註釋,前面有一篇序,說明為什麼選這些資料。註釋是用英文寫,336頁。此書如果要寫成中文書目,可用「中國文史資料導讀──漢史部分。普林斯頓大學中國語言學研究組出版」。

19　《居延漢簡》(見本目錄專書第 11 條) 在 1986 年再版時,附有一個很長的英文說明書,是勞榦教授寫成,再由 Mrs. Norma Farquhar 校訂過。

後　記

　　2016 年底金發根兄來信給我，說臺北蘭臺出版社有意出版父親的學術著作文集，要我和蘭臺的盧瑞琴社長連絡，商量詳情。這是這部選集的開始。

　　父親部分的著作已經出版過兩部文集，一部是 1976 年藝文印書舘印行的《勞榦學術論文集甲編》上，下兩冊，另一部是 2006 年聯經出版公司印行的《古代中國的歷史與文化》。我們(家兄延煊，舍妹延靜，及舍弟延炳) 曾經希望把能夠搜集到所有父親的著作，再印一部完整的全集。這個計劃是習史的家兄主持，他在 2012 年已開始著手，但因有不少的困難，進行的不夠理想。直到 2015 年間，家兄身體不適，我才開始協助他。之後不幸家兄辭世，對一個學工而文史外行的我來講，深感這個計劃太大，沒有能力完成這樣的重任。因此決定縮小範圍，先從較耗時的方案開始，搜集沒有納入前二文集中的父親著作，出版一部新文集。前二文集雖有重新編排再印的必要，但可以暫緩進行。自 2016 年中開始，我終於搜集到一百餘篇分散在各處刊物的父親論著，已委託福建教育出版社編排印行一部《勞榦先生著作集》。

　　當我接到發根兄來信的時候，非常欣慰，覺得正合我最初另一部分的計劃，重印兩部舊的文集。很快的我們就和盧社長達成共識，蘭臺同意把兩部舊文集的論文合在一起，出版這部《勞榦先生學術著作選集》。盧社長同時也和藝文及聯經連絡，證實沒有原二文集版權上的問題。

　　這兩部舊文集出版相距日期長達三十年之久，但大部分的內容相隔不到二十年。在整理這些論文時，我覺查到父親最初曾經有個構想，那就是將第二部論文集收入原來係屬直排及其他《甲編》漏列的論文，再加上《甲編》出版之後十餘年間的著作，名爲《乙編》。但在 1990 年初籌劃出版聯經的文集時，父親就把這個構想放棄了。在內容方面，聯經的文集做了分類的工作，但藝文的文集並沒有什麼重要的編排順序。由於此選集的一個目的是供給學者翻查的便利，而父親也提過，多篇論文是彼此相關的，集合起來才可以互相補充和互相

比較。爲此，在和蘭臺討論編排這部選集時，適當的分類就一直是我誠守的原
則。幸得蘭臺請到了考古、簡牘著名學者何雙全先生，參與及引領分類編排的
工作，方使此選集達到極高的標準，固此謹向何先生致最深的謝意。盧社長自
始自終大力的支持，她的貢獻和辛勞，實在是功不可沒！在這其間，蘭臺出版
社盡力克服了很多困難，同時也得到楊容容編輯的鼎力合作，在此一併致謝！

勞延炯 謹識二〇二〇年 五月 四日

國家圖書館出版品預行編目資料

勞榦先生學術著作選集（四）／勞榦
--初版-- 臺北市：蘭臺出版社：2020.9
 ISBN：978-986-99137-0-6(全套：精裝)
1.中國史 2.學術研究 3.文集

617　　　　　　　109006855

勞榦學術研究叢書1

勞榦先生學術著作選集（四）

作　　者：勞　榦
總 編 審：何雙全
編　　纂：盧瑞琴
主　　編：盧瑞容
封面設計：塗宇樵
出 版 者：蘭臺出版社
發　　行：蘭臺出版社
地　　址：台北市中正區重慶南路1段121號8樓之14
電　　話：(02)2331-1675或(02)2331-1691
傳　　真：(02)2382-6225
E —MAIL：books5w@gmail.com或books5w@yahoo.com.tw
網路書店：http://5w.com.tw/
　　　　　https://www.pcstore.com.tw/yesbooks/
　　　　　博客來網路書店、博客思網路書店
　　　　　三民書局、金石堂書店
經　　銷：聯合發行股份有限公司
電　　話：(02) 2917-8022　傳 真：(02) 2915-7212
劃撥戶名：蘭臺出版社　帳號：18995335
香港代理：香港聯合零售有限公司
電　　話：(852)2150-2100　傳真：(852)2356-0735
出版日期：2020年9月　初版
定　　價：新臺幣一套18000元整（精裝不分售）
ISBN：978-986-99137-0-6

蘭臺出版社

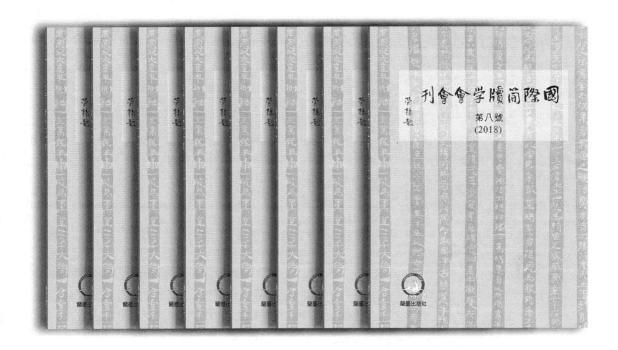

國際簡牘學會會刊

國際簡牘學會會刊以簡牘研究為主，是由台北大學研究簡牘研究專家馬先醒教授和甘肅省文物保護研究所所長，甘肅省簡牘博物館副館長何雙全教授在1991年甘肅國際簡牘學大會後共同成立，組成國際簡牘學會會刊編委會，編輯簡牘論文，由台灣蘭臺出版社出版。國際簡牘學會會刊每期收錄來自兩岸三地之簡牘學著名學者、專家所發表論文，如何雙全、楊劍虹、吳昌廉、陳松梅、周建、謝曉燕、黃輝陽、許道勝、南玉泉、王子今、盧瑞琴等，是研究簡牘學不可錯過之重要學術期刊。

書名	ISBN	出版日期	頁數	定價
際簡牘學會會刊第一號		1974/6/1	324	$1,800
簡牘學會會刊第二號	957-9154-10-4	1978/8/1	314	$1,800
簡牘學會會刊第三號	957-9154-66-X	1977/7/1	496	$2,500
簡牘學會會刊第四號	978-957-9154-80-2	2002/5/1	404	$1,500
簡牘學會會刊第五號	978-986-7626-75-2	2008/11/1	178	$1,500
簡牘學會會刊第六號	ISSN 2220-2498	2011/8/1	445	$1,500
簡牘學會會刊第七號	ISSN 2220-2498	2013/4/1	180	$1,500
簡牘學會會刊第八號	ISSN 2220-2498	2017/12/1	104	$880

簡牘學報

蘭臺出版社

台北大學史學系馬先醒教授師承勞榦先生潛研「簡牘學」多年，並於民國63年初（1974）自創組「簡牘社」。馬教授更結合中外同道，以互相交流為宗旨，籌組「台北市簡牘學會」，期以研究簡牘為主，在簡牘相關新史料、簡牘時代史中廣搜各專題研究成果，將論文彙集成《簡牘學報》，強化簡牘學研究的深度與廣度，是為台灣研究簡牘第一人。

《簡牘學報》於民國63年（1974）6月發行創刊號，現任主編陳鴻琦教授、副主編吳昌廉教授，簡牘學報編委會編製，迄今已發行二十二期。除收錄著名學者、專家之研究成果外，更包含勞貞一先生、張曉峰先生、黎東方先生等論文集專號，以及居延漢簡出土五十年之專號，為簡牘學研究重要學術期刊。

書名	ISBN	出版日期	頁數	定價
簡牘學報第一卷（一、二、三期合訂本）		1974/6/1	324	$1,800
簡牘學報第二卷（四、六期合訂本）		1978/10/1	314	$1,800
簡牘學報第三卷（第五期，勞貞一先生七秩榮慶論文集）		1978/10/1	314	$1,800
簡牘學報第四卷（第七期）		1992/12/1	442	$1,800
簡牘學報第五卷（第八期，張曉峰先生八秩榮慶論文集）		1993/12/1	390	$1,800
簡牘學報第六卷（第九期，居延漢簡出土五十年專號）		1997/12/1	616	$1,800
簡牘學報第七卷（第十期）		1997/12/1	616	$1,500
簡牘學報第十一期		1999/12/1	388	$1,800
簡牘學報第十二期（黎東方先生八秩榮慶論文集）		2002/12/1	388	$1,800
簡牘學報第十三期		2006/11/1	629	$1,800
簡牘學報第十四期		2008/12/1	410	$1,800
簡牘學報第十五期		2011/12/1	352	$1,800
簡牘學報第十六期（精）（勞貞一先生九秩榮慶論文集）	959-915-414-7	1997/1/1	616	$2,500
簡牘學報第十六期（平）（勞貞一先生九秩榮慶論文集）	957-915-415-5	1997/1/1	616	$2,500
簡牘學報第十七期		1999/1/1	388	$1,800
簡牘學報第十八期	986-80347-01	2002/1/1	389	$1,800
簡牘學報第十九期		2006/11/1	630	$2,000
簡牘學報第二十期	977-2074-003	2008/12/1	408	$2,000
簡牘學報第二十一期	ISSN 2074-0743	2013/12/1	616	$2,000
簡牘學報第二十二期	ISSN 2074-0743	2018/6/1	312	$2,000